Imagery and Related Mnemonic Processes

Imagery and
Related Mnemonic Processes

Theories, Individual Differences, and Applications

Edited by
Mark A. McDaniel
Michael Pressley

With 23 Illustrations

Springer-Verlag
New York Berlin Heidelberg
London Paris Tokyo

Mark A. McDaniel
Department of Psychology
University of Notre Dame
Notre Dame, Indiana 46556, USA

Michael Pressley
Department of Psychology
University of Western Ontario
London, Ontario
Canada N6A 5C2

Library of Congress Cataloging in Publication Data
Imagery and related mnemonic processes.
  Includes bibliographies and index.
  1. Mnemonics. 2. Imagery (Psychology). 3. Individu-
ality. I. McDaniel, Mark A. II. Pressley, Michael.
BF385.I42 1987   153.1′4   86-20432

Typeset by Publishers Service, Bozeman, Montana.
Printed and bound by R.R. Donnelley & Sons, Harrisonburg, Virginia.
Printed in the United States of America.

9 8 7 6 5 4 3 2 1

ISBN 0-387-96427-4 Springer-Verlag New York Berlin Heidelberg
ISBN 3-540-96427-4 Springer-Verlag Berlin Heidelberg New York

Preface

Scientific work on mnemonics and imagery conducted in the 1960s and early 1970s was directed at testing enthusiastic claims of the efficacy of memory techniques developed by the ancient Greeks and further refined in the popular literature by "professional" mnemonists. The early research on imagery and mnemonics confirmed many of these claims and also illuminated the limitations of some techniques (e.g., bizarre imagery). As such, these seminal studies clearly were valuable in providing a solid data base and, perhaps as important, making imagery and mnemonics acceptable research areas for experimental psychologists and educators. After this initial surge of work, however, it seemed that subsequent contributions met with the attitude that "mnemonic techniques and imagery help memory, what else is new?" This attitude was not completely justified, however, given the theoretical insights from the work of such imagery and mnemonics pioneers as Gorden Bower, Allan Paivio, and William Rohwer. In the 1980s this claim is completely unjustified. Research on mnemonics and imagery has grown in exciting ways.

Researchers are tapping the area's *theoretical potential*, both in terms of extending basic memory theories to account for the robust effects produced by mnemonic techniques and in terms of using explanations of mnemonic effects to understand basic memory processes. *Individual differences* in the use of imagery and mnemonic encoding activities are also being explored. This research has provided valuable information for basic memory theories (e.g., research on imagery in the blind has important implications for dual coding theory and issues of representation in general) and has offered fresh perspectives on deficiencies and possible interventions for many different populations (e.g., certain cultural, socioeconomic, and learning-disabled groups). *Applications* for mnemonics in the classroom and for people with memory deficits have been designed and evaluated. This work includes extending mnemonics use to prose material and to the acquisition of mathematical procedures and scientific formulas, training students in school to use particular mnemonic devices, and teaching brain-injured patients to use mnemonic techniques to overcome amnesia.

There is much new work of potential interest to a wide variety of specialists: experimental psychologists, educational psychologists, clinicians, and educators.

Because of the diverse appeal of imagery and mnemonics research, however, this work is dispersed among different types of journals, books, and convention presentations. Therefore, it seemed timely and appropriate to assemble some of this "new-look" work in mnemonics and imagery into one volume.

Consistent with the organization of research as outlined above, we divided the volume into three parts. The first section emphasizes theoretical perspectives, the second focuses on individual differences, and the third considers applications. Nonetheless, the boundaries established by this segmentation are not always clear-cut, and consequently most contributions overlap with themes developed in other sections.

Ultimately, we hope that this volume will contribute to the understanding of imagery and mnemonics by providing an accessible information base for the diverse array of interested scholars and by stimulating further research. It is also our hope that this volume makes obvious that imagery and mnemonics theorists and researchers are making a great contribution to the understanding of human cognition.

Our editing of the book was facilitated by the help provided by the Springer-Verlag staff. The people at Springer provided a great deal of assistance and enthusiastic encouragement. Mark McDaniel's contribution was supported in part by the Institute for Scholarship in the Liberal Arts, University of Notre Dame. Michael Pressley's participation was possible through a grant from the Natural Sciences and Engineering Research Council of Canada.

Mark A. McDaniel
Michael Pressley

Contents

Part III   Applications

Contributors

Ian Begg
Department of Psychology, McMaster University, Hamilton, Ontario, Canada L85 4K1

Francis S. Bellezza
Department of Psychology, Porter Hall, Ohio University, Athens, Ohio 45701, USA

Trisha Beuhring
University Personnel Department, University of Minnesota, St. Paul, Minnesota 55104, USA

Susan P. Blackford
Boston Veterans Administration Medical Center, Boston, Massachusetts 02130, USA

John G. Borkowski
Department of Psychology, University of Notre Dame, Notre Dame, Indiana 46556, USA

Laird S. Cermak
Boston Veterans Administration Medical Center, Boston, Massachusetts 02130, USA

James M. Clark
Department of Psychology, University of Western Ontario, London, Ontario, Canada N6A 5C2

Michel Denis
Centre D'Etudes de Psychologie Cognitive, Université de Paris-Sud, Centre Scientifique d'Orsay, 91405 Orsay Cedex, Paris, France

Alain Desrochers
School of Psychology, University of Ottawa, Ottawa, Ontario, Canada K1N 6N5

Gilles O. Einstein
Department of Psychology, Furman University, Greenville, South Carolina 29613, USA

Carole H. Ernest
Department of Psychology, Trent University, Peterborough, Ontario, Canada K9J 7B8

Kenneth L. Higbee
Department of Psychology, Brigham Young University, Provo, Utah 84602, USA

R. Reed Hunt
Department of Psychology, University of North Carolina at Greensboro, Greensboro, North Carolina 27412, USA

Carla J. Johnson
Department of Psychology, University of Western Ontario, London, Ontario, Canada N6A 5C2

Albert N. Katz
Department of Psychology, University of Western Ontario, London, Ontario, Canada N6A 5C2

Daniel W. Kee
Department of Psychology, California State University at Fullerton, Fullerton, California 92634, USA

John F. Lane
Department of Educational Psychology, University of Minnesota, Minneapolis, Minnesota 55455, USA

Joel R. Levin
Department of Educational Psychology, University of Wisconsin, Madison, Wisconsin 53706, USA

Christine B. McCormick
Department of Educational Psychology, University of South Carolina, Columbia, South Carolina 29208, USA

Mark A. McDaniel
Department of Psychology, University of Notre Dame, Notre Dame, Indiana 46556, USA

Matthew G. Margres
Department of Psychology, Washington State University, Pullman, Washington 99164, USA

Marc Marschark
Department of Psychology, University of North Carolina at Greensboro, Greensboro, North Carolina 27412, USA

Margo A. Mastropieri
SCCE, Special Education, Purdue University, West Lafayette, Indiana 47907, USA

Margaret O'Connor
Boston University, School of Medicine, Boston, Massachusetts 02215, USA

Allan Paivio
Department of Psychology, University of Western Ontario, London, Ontario, Canada N6A 5C2

Michael Pressley
Department of Psychology, University of Western Ontario, London, Ontario, Canada N6A 5C2

John T. E. Richardson
Department of Human Sciences, Brunel University, Uxbridge, Middlesex, United Kingdom UB8 3PH

Henry L. Roediger III
Department of Psychological Sciences, Purdue University, West Lafayette, Indiana 47907, USA

William D. Rohwer, Jr.
Department of Education, University of California at Berkeley, Berkeley, California 94720, USA

Thomas E. Scruggs
SCCE, Special Education, Purdue University, West Lafayette, Indiana 47907, USA

Susan Nakayama Siaw
Department of Behavioral Science, California State Polytechnic University at Pomona, Pomona, California 91768, USA

Jack Snowman
Department of Educational Psychology, Southern Illinois University, Carbondale, Illinois 62901, USA

John W. Thomas
Far West Laboratory for Educational Research and Development, San Francisco, California 94103, USA

James E. Turnure
  Department of Educational Psychology, University of Minnesota, Minneapolis, Minnesota 55455, USA

Mary Susan Weldon
  Department of Psychological Sciences, Purdue University, West Lafayette,
  Indiana 47907, USA

Keith A. Wollen
  Department of Psychology, Washington State University, Pullman, Washington
  99164, USA

PART I

Theoretical Perspectives

Given the nominal practical orientation of mnemonics research and imagery-related mnemonics, many might assume that the area is exclusively concerned with the identification of techniques that enhance performance. Although much of the foundation work in the area has focused on functional relationships between mnemonic/imagery techniques and a variety of outcome measures, attention has increasingly been directed at theoretical explanations of mnemonic and imagery effects and at theoretical insights regarding basic processes that emanate from a deeper understanding of mnemonics and imagery. Indeed, as Bellezza (Chapter 2) argues, "the study of mnemonic devices is fundamental to our understanding of human learning and the operation of human memory." (See as well Higbee's Chapter 19, Part III, for reiteration of this theme.) Accordingly, the first part of this volume is devoted to the exciting theoretical contributions deriving from research in imagery and mnemonics.

The first two chapters explore the relationship between mnemonic operations and fundamental theories in contemporary memory research. Clark and Paivio (Chapter 1) review the dual coding model, a systematic theory about the complex encoding operations that transform stimuli so that information is learned and retained. The authors then describe six types of mnemonic encoding operations that implicate various components of the model. Bellezza (Chapter 2) further reinforces the conclusion that mnemonic devices do not represent a form of "unnatural learning," as some have suggested. Bellezza presents a detailed and informed analysis of the relation between mnemonic devices and memory schemas. These chapters, as well as Hunt and Marschark's chapter, described below, underscore the considerable overlap between mnemonic processes (generic as well as specific techniques) and basic cognitive and memorial functioning.

In contrast to Clark and Paivio, who focus on encoding processes, Roediger and Weldon (Chapter 7) explore how retrieval demands influence the mnemonic value of pictorial presentation of material. Roediger and Weldon describe an innovative program of research in which they demonstrate that the picture superiority effect (pictorial presentation of stimuli producing better memory performance than verbal presentation) can be reversed or eliminated by requiring performance on certain "implicit" memory tasks (note that previous reversals of the picture superiority effect have manipulated the encoding stage). Generalizing from their research, Roediger and Weldon note that the retrieval environment must be considered when evaluating the mnemonic efficacy of any mnemonic technique.

Desrochers and Begg (Chapter 3) are concerned with a theoretical account of the keyword mnemonic technique. In their chapter, they develop a memory-theoretic perspective to explain how the keyword method helps people learn items from foreign vocabularies. They adopt a basic theory of how pairs of words are remembered, the organization–redintegration hypothesis, and use it to provide a comprehensive theoretical analysis of why the keyword method is an effective learning device.

Einstein and McDaniel's (Chapter 4) and Wollen and Margres' contributions (Chapter 5) explore the intriguing puzzle of bizarre imagery. Mnemonists have long advocated the use of bizarre imagery for committing material to memory. Consistent with this recommendation, learners predict that they will recall material better after forming bizarre images than after forming common images (Kroll, Schepeler, & Angin, 1986). Many laboratory-controlled studies, however, have failed to report any mnemonic advantage for bizarre images, spurring some researchers to conclude that bizarre images are no better as memory aids than common ones. Einstein and McDaniel reanalyze the literature to find that bizarre imagery does seem to be mnemonically effective in certain prescribed contexts. This insight is corroborated with recent studies in their laboratories and motivates discussion of the theoretical implications for such findings. They offer the view that bizarreness enhances memory through distinctiveness mechanisms. Wollen and Margres continue the discussion on bizarre imagery by noting methodological problems with some studies reporting bizarre imagery effects and by noting that the theoretical base motivating bizarre imagery research has been weak. Wollen and Margres argue that the few theoretical accounts available, including distinctiveness, are too limited to account for the complicated data base. They conclude by proposing a provocative model that attempts to account for the data.

Hunt and Marschark's contribution (Chapter 6) concerns the locus of the mnemonic effects of imagery in general. They suggest a theoretical perspective that emphasizes the roles of shared (or relational) and distinctive information in memory. Their view is that imagery enhances the processing of distinctive item information but not of shared information. This framework is cleverly applied to a number of different paradigms ranging from prose memory to memory for paired associates.

In summary, it is obvious from these chapters that understanding the complex patterns of data produced in imagery/mnemonics research requires complex theories. Contemporary workers are rising to the challenge.

References

Kroll, N. E. A., Schepeler, E. M., & Angin, K. T. (1986). Bizarre imagery: The mis-remembered mnemonic. *Journal of Experimental Psychology: Learning, Memory and Cognition, 12*, 42–53.

CHAPTER 1

A Dual Coding Perspective on Encoding Processes

James M. Clark and Allan Paivio

Dual coding theory emerged several decades ago when a systematic research program was undertaken to examine the role of imagery in human cognition and, if warranted, to restore imagery to its "rightful place" alongside the language processes that then dominated the interests of cognitive psychologists. Early research efforts at the University of Western Ontario demonstrated the contribution of nonverbal processes to human cognitive behavior, even when that behavior involved language (e.g., Paivio, 1963, 1965, 1966; Paivio & Yarmey, 1965; Paivio & Yuille, 1966). We still find useful this work and that of other early investigators, summarized in Paivio (1971/1979), despite the considerable developments that have occurred in the intervening years as more and more scholars have applied their scientific skills to the study of imagery. Paivio (1986) provides a dual coding perspective on some of this recent work. These earlier sources give a more complete description of dual coding theory, which provides for us a useful organization of many cognitive phenomena.

In this chapter we first outline a few basic features of the dual coding model and then we apply those features specifically to an understanding of the diverse operations known collectively as encoding processes. We particularly try to correct the erroneous view that dual coding theory is a theory only about or even primarily about imagery, rather than about the role of both verbal and nonverbal processes in cognitive behavior. Thus, we give equal space to the several distinct processes proposed in dual coding theory, including those that concern imagery. A second objective is to demonstrate the empirical continuities that we see in the work of experimental psychologists over the last century. This goal is motivated by our conviction that progress in understanding human cognition will come only through the accumulation and systematic treatment of masses of conceptually related findings, a view of science captured in the constructive empiricism and convergent operationism on which dual coding theory is based (Paivio, 1971/1979, 1975, 1986a). Given this view, cognitive psychologists should not be too ready to ignore valuable observations from earlier generations of imaginative researchers.

Our major thesis is that dual coding theory (Paivio, 1971/1979, 1986a) provides a systematic and informative perspective on the complex encoding operations that transform and elaborate stimuli which come in contact with the cognitive system. Encoding processes are major determinants of how well new information is learned and remembered, as shown by demonstrations that incidental and intentional learning are equivalent under effective encoding instructions, and that memory performance varies both with instructions to encode information in particular ways and with the amenability of materials to different types of encoding. Moreover, many mnemonic and imaginal strategies benefit learning primarily because they stimulate effective encoding operations.

Dual Coding Theory

A basic premise of dual coding theory is that mental representations retain some of the concrete qualities of the external experiences from which they are derived, in particular qualities associated with distinct linguistic and nonlinguistic events (Paivio, 1971/1979, 1986a). The unique features of these two domains are accommodated in dual coding theory by separate verbal and nonverbal symbolic systems that operate in fundamentally different ways (see Figure 1.1). In essence, dual coding theory postulates verbal and imaginal representations that encode word and object information, respectively, as well as connections that exist between (a) sensory events and the symbolic representations, (b) verbal and imaginal representations, and (c) representations within the two symbolic systems.

Verbal representations or *logogens* (cf. Morton, 1969, 1979) are wordlike entities comprised of visual and phonemic features, with the latter perhaps having priority in human cognition. Logogens demonstrate certain distinct properties characteristic of language. In particular, language consists of discrete, categorical, and separate units that can be isolated from one another and even combined to produce new units. Discrete letters or phonemes (e.g., n, o, s, e) are combined into discrete morphemes or words (e.g., "nose") that can be combined further into phrases (e.g., "bloody nose") and sentences. A second property of language is that it is sequentially constrained with meaning determined by the temporal and serial order of the elements. For example, "nose" is different from "eons" and "John hit" from "hit John." Sequential constraints are further demonstrated by our inability to verbalize more than one sound or word at a time. Thus, we cannot contemplate as words "bloody" and "nose" simultaneously. Finally, words such as "nose" are usually arbitrary patterns that bear little resemblance to the things for which they stand, and such inventions have little meaning except through their mental connections with other events.

Imaginal representations or *imagens* encode modality-specific information about nonverbal, perceptual, and sensory-motor experiences, conscious imagery being one way that imagens manifest themselves. According to dual coding theory, visual–spatial imagens demonstrate the distinctive properties of the nonverbal system better than motor imagens, which are organized both sequentially (as is language) and synchronously. In particular, objects are stored as integrated,

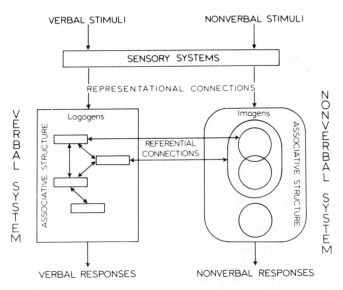

FIGURE 1.1. Schematic depiction of the structure of verbal and nonverbal symbolic systems. From *Mental representations: A dual coding approach* by A. Paivio, 1986, New York: Oxford University Press. Copyright © 1986 by Oxford University Press. Reprinted by permission.

continuous, analogue, or holistic representations that cannot easily be partitioned into discrete elements comparable to letters. Imagens may have identifiable parts (often associated with names) but these parts can be conceptualized as a hierarchical collection of imagens nested within other imagens and are only rarely isolated to be recombined as different objects. Thus, an imagen for "nose" is nested along with other parts in an imagen for "face" and parts themselves can often be broken into finer segments (e.g., "nostrils"). The continuous, analogue nature of imagens is further demonstrated by the observation that presentation of part of an image usually redintegrates the whole and by their amenability to smooth and continuous spatial transformations. For example, we recognize people from partial views (perhaps of a nose) and can imagine translations and other spatial changes of our conscious images. Imagens also demonstrate a synchronous or parallel quality that is absent in language. For this reason, a single imagen can represent simultaneously even complex thoughts that require many words or propositions to describe. A single image for the two-word phrase "bloody nose" provides a simple example of the richness of imaginal representations. Finally, imagens for such objects as "nose" are not arbitrary because they retain some of the object's perceptual properties and are therefore isomorphic with or analogous to the things for which they stand.

The dual coding description of these relatively concrete mental representations, logogens and imagens, is still incomplete, but research on the perceptual representation of words and objects is providing a more elaborate account of these codes. One fundamental question is whether word and object codes are multiple traces of highly specific, concrete, episodic events (i.e., exemplars) or more generic, abstract, prototypical codes in which single representations stand for each word and object (i.e., types). Dual coding theory does not include a level of representation that is any more abstract than logogens and imagens (e.g., a "nose" concept that accommodates both images and words, including synonyms and translations), primarily because present findings can be explained without the hypothesis of single type nodes corresponding directly to concepts or ideas. Thus, the abstract representations of common coding or propositional theories (e.g., Rosenberg & Simon, 1977; Vanderwart, 1984) are superfluous.

According to dual coding theory, logogens and imagens are implicated in three different levels or kinds of processing. *Representational processes* operate whenever logogens or imagens are activated, but they are perhaps most purely seen when mental representations are stimulated relatively directly by suitable words or objects external to the organism. Representational processes include low-level, stimulus-driven aspects of perceptual recognition or identification and are governed largely by the physical characteristics of and experience with the words or objects themselves. Thus, familiarity is the major psychological correlate of representational processes. Word and picture identification tasks are relatively pure measures of this level of processing, which generally operates quite rapidly and automatically. However, more effortful representational processes also contribute to the identification of nonsense materials, either words or objects. For example, someone for whom "nos" and " < " are meaningless patterns may encode them as the word "nose" or as an image of a nose, respectively. The basis of the encoding in both cases is the perceptual similarity of the stimulus to logogens or imagens for "nose" and the contribution of representational processes to the encoding of novel stimuli has a long history in psychology (Bartlett, 1932; Gibson, 1929; Woodworth, 1938; Wulff, 1922, cited in Gibson, 1929) that extends to the present time (Bregman, 1977).

Referential processes operate when imagens and logogens activate representations in the other symbolic system using connections that develop between verbal and imaginal representations as a consequence of increasingly complex experiences with objects and their names. The multiple connections between imagens and logogens provide only potential pathways between the symbolic systems because referential processes are probabilistic. Given appropriate circumstances, however, between-system connections allow the verbal and nonverbal systems to process information together, sometimes in a coordinated and complementary fashion. The actual operation of these referential processes is most purely reflected in such tasks as imaging to words and naming pictures. Thus, referential connections permit the word "nose" to activate various imagens and appropriately shaped objects to activate various logogens (e.g., "nose," "smell," "nez").

Associative processes operate when logogens activate other logogens and imagens activate other imagens. These processes use within-system connections among imagens in the nonverbal system and among logogens in the verbal system, including connections among verbal representations of abstract words that do not refer to concrete things. Such associative networks store knowledge about our verbal and nonverbal worlds. For example, the logogen for "nose" is associatively connected to other logogens (e.g., "smell," "part of body," "face," "red") and imagens for "nose" are associatively related to other imagens (e.g., "face," "eye," "person," "room"), including those within which it is nested. Pure measures of verbal and imaginal associative processes are rare because of between-system referential connections. Nevertheless, verbal associative networks are major determinants of performance on such tasks as word association, whereas imaginal associations are more salient in such complex imaginal tasks as cognitive mapping and (perhaps) memory for concrete schemas or scripts.

Human memory is rooted in these basic mental units and relations. In essence, our reactions to words and objects (e.g., "nose") are composite or aggregate patterns that result from the collective activation of verbal and imaginal representations through a combination of direct external stimulation and spreading activation along internal associative (e.g., "part of body") and referential (e.g., image of "boxer with bloody nose") pathways. Spreading activation occurs simultaneously along multiple paths at each of several successive stages. The sophistication and complexity of human thought arises because the networks are complex and elaborate with multiple connections both within and between the verbal and imaginal systems. Moreover, the networks are dynamic and variable rather than static, with the momentary strengths of connections being especially sensitive to the verbal and nonverbal context. For example, the context of "bloody" produces different imaginal (e.g., "boxer in ring") and verbal (e.g., "fight") reactions to "nose" than would some other context. Dual coding theory maintains that these basic associative and referential structures are sufficiently powerful to explain more complex networks, including those used in metacognitive processing. For example, instructions "to image" provide a verbal context that increases the probability of imaginal reactions relative to instructions "to associate."

In the remainder of this chapter, we describe mnemonic encoding operations that implicate representational, referential, and associative levels of processing for both verbal and nonverbal materials. Examples of the six types of encoding revealed by this dual coding analysis are presented in Table 1.1. Each type has an extensive literature and we focus on the actual encoding operations, mentioning only briefly their mnemonic consequences or other stages of memory. We specifically emphasize tasks that show the encoding operations in as pure a form as possible within the limitations imposed by interactions among the different levels of processing and the assumption that common mental representations may be involved. Such tasks permit us to observe, albeit indirectly, encoding ease as measured by latencies, ratings, self-reports, and other indicators, as well as the subject, item, and situational factors that influence encoding operations.

TABLE 1.1. Symbolic modalities, processing levels, and sample operations.

Modality	Level	Operations
Verbal	Representational	Reading
		Natural language mediation
		Mnemonic keywords
	Referential	Imaging
		Mental comparisons
	Associative	Free association
		Category production
		Free-recall clustering
		Associative priming
Nonverbal	Representational	Perceptual identification
		Assimilation to known object
	Referential	Picture naming
		Object-word comparisons
	Associative	Integration by compound imagery
		Method of loci and cognitive maps
		Concrete scripts and schemas

Encoding Processes for Verbal Stimuli

Memory traces for language result from a combination of representational, referential, and associative encoding processes. These levels of encoding depend partly on one another in that a verbal stimulus can only engage imaginal and verbal associative encoding processes after prior activation of a logogen. However, representational encoding does not guarantee referential or associative processing, which are in turn relatively independent of one another.

Representational Encoding of Unfamiliar Verbal Stimuli

According to dual coding theory, novel verbal stimuli (e.g., the Finnish word "norsu" and the nonsense syllable "cit") are made more memorable by being encoded as familiar words or phrases (e.g., as "nurse" or "city"). Much of the relevant research on representational access has used nonsense syllables, which were recognized even by Ebbinghaus as varying in both memorability and meaningfulness (Jenkins, 1985). The latency to think of a word provides one direct indicator of the ease with which nonsense syllables activate words or phrases (Schaub & Lindley, 1964). Mediators can be produced quickly, as demonstrated by Prytulak (1971) who found that mediators (mostly single words) occurred 96% of the time at a 4-sec rate of presentation. Stark and Calfee (1970) found that the time to transform nonwords (from one to five letters in length) to single words was less than the time to think of sentence mediators and the difference between the two increased as the number of letters increased.

Other indicators of encoding ease have been based on production measures or ratings, including reports of natural language mediation (Montague, Adams, &

Kiess, 1966), pronounceability ratings (Heim, 1973; Underwood & Schulz, 1960), association value (Archer, 1960; Paivio & Madigan, 1968), and meaningfulness (Krueger, 1934). These variables have been shown to correlate with one another (Prytulak, 1971) suggesting that a common mechanism contributes to them all. In particular, the latency for word associates to nonwords is correlated with other measures of ease of encoding (e.g., Johnson, 1964; Ley & Locascio, 1970). For example, Johnson (1964) obtained a correlation of $-.70$ between association value and the latency to say a word. Schaub and Lindley (1964) reported that the median latency was 2.22 sec for high association value syllables, but 8.22 sec for low association value syllables. The authors also found that mediators for high association value syllables were more likely to be single words, to retain the order of the letters, and to be shared with other subjects (i.e., to have higher commonality or dominance) than were mediators for low association value syllables.

The spontaneous reported use of natural language mediators during learning provides information about the stimulus, subject, and situational factors that influence the encoding of nonwords as words. Kiess (1968) observed that the percentage of subjects reporting a mediator increased from 32 to 61 to 87% for low, medium, and high association value syllables, respectively. At the same time, the mean latency of mediators decreased from 2.09 to 1.91 to 1.77 sec. Kiess and Montague (1965) found that all subjects reported mediators for some items, but that the number of mediators reported on the last trial varied widely across subjects from two to eight (out of a possible eight). Verbal reports also showed that some subjects deliberately attempted to form such mediators, indicating a possible role for strategic factors. Kiess and Montague (1965) demonstrated that the number of mediators increased across trials and Kiess (1968) that the percentage of mediators for low association value stimuli increased from 32% at a 2-sec rate of presentation to 47% at a 4-sec rate. In the latter study, the average latency of mediators also increased with presentation time, suggesting that the extra time made it possible for subjects to access more remote mediators.

Several researchers have successfully analyzed nonword encoding operations in terms of the similarity of nonsense syllables to familiar words, an approach consistent with the dual coding position that this recoding involves perceptual features at the representational level. Johnson (1962) had subjects rate whether or not consonant-vowel-consonant trigrams (CVCs) occurred as syllables in the English language and found that easy to pronounce CVCs (Underwood & Schulz, 1960) were more likely to occur as syllables than difficult to pronounce CVCs. In a second study, subjects generated English words that contained the CVCs and the number of generated words predicted ease of learning of the trigrams. More specifically, Greenberg and Jenkins (1964; Jenkins, 1966, 1985) found that the number of phonetic and orthographic substitutions necessary to create words from nonsense syllables (trigrams in one study and four-letter units in another) predicted rated association value and meaningfulness. A similar analysis by Prytulak (1971) showed that such transformations as suffixing were simple and easily decoded (e.g., "cit" transformed to "city"), whereas others, such as substitution of letters and then suffixing, were more complex and difficult to decode (e.g., "zyt" transformed to "city"). A transformational hierarchy predicted ease of learning and pronounceability of the nonsense syllables as well as the latency, probability, and uncertainty of mediator production.

These studies demonstrate that nonsense syllables are often encoded as words, that perceptual similarity is the basis for the encoding, and that memory is largely determined by the ease with which such correspondences are effected. The vocabulary-learning literature supports this characterization. Learning benefits from strategies that explicitly use familiar representations to encode the new words, for example, the systematic use of root words or morphemes (e.g., Pressley, Levin, & McDaniel, in press) and the keyword method (e.g., Atkinson & Raugh, 1975; Desrochers & Begg, Chapter 3, this volume; Pressley, Levin, & Delaney, 1982), which relates an unknown vocabulary word to a familiar concrete keyword or phrase that sounds like the new term (e.g., "couteau" encoded as "cut toe").

Even uninstructed subjects report spontaneous keyword-like mediation and these reports are correlated with learning. For example, in a recent vocabulary learning study with Alain Desrochers and Michael Pressley, we questioned 21 control subjects about the strategies that they used in earlier learning phases of the study. Subjects reported using English words that sounded like the foreign word for an average of 35% of the pairs and the reported use of this technique was very stable as shown by the correlation of .90 between reported use for practice and target lists. The mnemonic relevance of these mediators was demonstrated by correlations of .50 or so between several measures of learning and the reported use of similar sounding English mediators on the target items.

This research with nonsense syllables and foreign words has shown the importance of encoding unfamiliar verbal stimuli in terms of familiar logogens and also some idea of the mechanisms involved. One benefit of such encoding is that internal connections between logogens and other cognitive units permit additional encoding processes, such as imagery, to occur.

Imaging to Words

Dual coding theory postulates that referential connections between logogens and imagens permit indirect activation of images by words, as in imagery production tasks. Moore (1915) found an average reaction time of 1.41 sec for imaging to words versus .56 sec for getting "an auditory-kinaesthetic verbal image of the word itself" (p. 208) or, in dual coding terms, activating a logogen. The difference between these latencies provides a measure of referential processing time, somewhat less than 1 sec for the concrete items used by Moore. This estimate agrees reasonably well with the estimate of ½ to 1 sec arrived at by Paivio (1971/1979) for concrete words. Paivio (1966, 1968) found that imagery latencies were slower for abstract words than for concrete words and Paivio, Yuille, and Madigan (1968) provided extensive imagery and concreteness ratings that were shown to correlate highly with latency (Janssen, 1976; Paivio, 1975). Such ratings provide a convergent measure of the ease or availability of imagery.

Similar investigations have been made of compound imagery with two or more words, although associative processes undoubtedly contribute to this more complex operation. Yuille and Paivio (1967) and Yuille (1973) obtained imagery latencies of approximately 8 sec for concrete pairs and 12 sec for abstract pairs, but faster times have been reported by others for concrete words (Segal, 1976), even for children (Pressley & Levin, 1977), and for meaningful words or phrases (Giannandrea, 1971; Paivio & Begg, 1971). The rated ease of compound imagery correlates with imagery latency and Pressley and Levin (1977) found that faster reaction times were associated with common images about which there was normative agreement, another measure of ease of compound imagery.

Measures based on imagery production and ratings are complemented by subject reports that provide data about imagery encoding under noninstructed conditions. Bugelski (1970) found imagery to be a ubiquitous response to both concrete and abstract words. When subjects described their first thought upon hearing single common words, 85% of the descriptions included an imaginal component. Retrospective reports of naturally occurring imagery, as obtained on such measures as the Individual Differences Questionnaire (Paivio & Harshman, 1983), produce somewhat lower estimates for the probability of imagery. In particular, only 42% of subjects endorsed the item: "I can form mental pictures to almost any word," although more subjects endorsed items about the use of imagery to remember (85%), reminisce (93%), read descriptions (87%), and think (76%).

Reports of spontaneous compound imagery in memory tasks vary with rate of presentation, as one might predict given the latency data. At a 3-sec rate, Paivio and Yuille (1969) found that control subjects reported imagery for only 18% of concrete word pairs and 6% of abstract pairs after one trial. However, with a 10 second rate, Richardson (1978) obtained reports of imagery for 62% of concrete pairs and 26% of abstract pairs. Instructions to image and additional trials increased the reported imagery in the Paivio and Yuille (1969) study, but even after three trials, reports were still below the level found by Richardson.

The ease of imaginal encoding varies with subject, situational, and item factors. For example, imagery latencies correlate with individual differences in imagery ability (Ernest & Paivio, 1971) and compound imagery latencies decrease with grade (Pressley & Levin, 1977). Several potent situational variables have been mentioned already, notably rate of presentation and instructions. The rated ease of compound imagery increases not only with such item attributes as imagery value and concreteness, but also with the associative relatedness of the items (Day & Bellezza, 1983). At a more molecular level, Kosslyn and his colleagues (Farah & Kosslyn, 1981; Kosslyn, 1980) found that image latency increased with object complexity, although latency was not correlated with number of features in a study by Hoffman, Denis, and Ziessler (1983). Interpretation of these findings is further complicated by the fact that complexity has perceptual effects (Long & Wurst, 1984) and is correlated with such other variables as familiarity (e.g., Snodgrass & Vanderwart, 1980) and even imagery ratings (Yuille, 1973). In the latter study, drawing images for abstract pairs took longer and involved more objects and features per object than did drawings for concrete pairs.

Observations about imagery encoding explain a number of imagery effects in both standard memory tasks (for reviews see Paivio, 1971/1979, 1986a; Richardson, 1980) and such learning strategies as the keyword method, which uses imagery to integrate the meaning of each unknown word and its keyword. The beneficial mnemonic effects of both item concreteness (Paivio & Csapo, 1969) and imagery instructions increase with additional study time, presumably because of the time required for images to be activated. In particular, imagery instructions have optimal benefits only with slow rates of presentation (Bugelski, Kidd, & Segmen, 1968; Gruber, Kulkin, & Schwartz, 1965; Wood, 1967), a conclusion that received further support in a study by Bugelski (1968), which showed that mnemonic subjects adopted a slow rate of presentation (8 sec per item) when learning was subject paced. These studies disagree somewhat as to the rate of presentation at which imagery effects first emerge, perhaps because of such uncontrolled factors as the time required for nonreferential processing (e.g., retrieval of rhyme pegwords).

Studies of image generation and studies of memory stimulate additional questions of mutual interest. For example, Pressley and Levin (1978) found that interactive imagery instructions did not facilitate recall by grade 2 children when separate words were presented but did improve recall when separate pictures were presented. These results provide indirect evidence for separate generate and integrate stages to compound imagery, an hypothesis amenable to more direct investigation by imagery production measures. The effects of complexity on imaging may also have mnemonic implications, especially since Yuille (1973) found a substantial 5-sec difference between drawing times for concrete and abstract pairs. Other research shows that subjective imagery is not inevitably associated with good memory performance (e.g., Day & Bellezza, 1983), indicating a need for further investigation of retrieval processes (e.g., Yuille, 1973) as well as the encoding operations emphasized here.

To conclude our discussion of imagery, the findings indicate that the probability and ease of imagery encoding is related to a variety of factors that also influence memory performance in predictable ways. Imagery is only one "deeper" form of encoding for language materials and we now turn our attention to associative encoding processes for verbal stimuli.

Associative Encoding of Words

According to dual coding theory, activation spreads not only to imagens but also to other logogens, as demonstrated by free associations or such restricted associates as opposites (Hollingworth, 1915), properties (Underwood & Richardson, 1956a), instances of categories (Battig & Montague, 1969), and activities

(Bower, Black, & Turner, 1979). The latency of such associates provides one measure of their ease or strength. Cattell (1889) found that free association latencies averaged 1 or 2 sec for well-practiced faculty members. The average latencies for undergraduates were 3 sec for concrete words and 4 sec for abstract words, similar to values obtained by Paivio, (1966). By subtractive procedures, Cattell (1889) concluded that the actual association time was approximately half a second for his two practiced subjects.

Ease of association has also been measured by commonality or dominance of associates, retest stability, order and number of responses in continuous association, number of different words given for each stimulus, judgments of general associability (Kamman, 1968; Murray, 1982), and ratings of such specific relations as typicality (Katz, 1983; Uyeda & Mandler, 1980), similarity (Flavell & Johnson, 1961), and synonymity (Whitten, Suter, & Frank, 1979; Wilding & Mohindra, 1981). For a given type of relation, correlations among the various measures suggest a common underlying mechanism. In particular, associative reaction time decreases with stability (Hull & Lugoff, 1921) and with commonality as shown by Schlosberg and Heineman (1950), who found a correlation of −.80 between log association time and commonality (see Murray, 1978 for a brief history of Marbe's Law). Commonality also correlates with the order and stability of associates (Fox, 1970; Howell, 1970) which are themselves related (Szalay & Deese, 1978).

Associative processes also contribute to priming tasks in which related words facilitate identification (Rouse & Verinis, 1962), lexical decisions (Meyer & Schvaneveldt, 1971), and naming (Warren, 1977) for target items and interfere with such responses as color naming that compete with the primed response (Warren, 1972). Sentence verification (Collins & Quillian, 1969), category judgment (Schaeffer & Wallace, 1969), and other semantic decision tasks invoke similar processes. Related words have been selected for these priming tasks primarily from association norms, thus demonstrating the general equivalence of the two paradigms. Moreover, priming sometimes varies specifically as a function of associative strength (e.g., Rouse & Verinis, 1962; Warren, 1974), but not always (e.g., Warren, 1977).

Many variables influence verbal associative reactions. During childhood, age is associated with decreases in associative latencies (Anderson, 1917) as well as changes in the nature of associations (Nelson, 1977). Specific experiences have selective effects on associations. For example, Foley and MacMillan (1943) found that ambiguous words elicited more "legal" associations from law students and more "medical" associations from medical students. Hollingworth (1915) showed that practice increased the speed of opposite generation, but that association time was still longer than reading time, even after 100 repetitions. One important situational determinant of associative encoding is verbal context, including words that indirectly prime common or shared responses. Convergent association is sometimes slow and difficult, as shown by Yuille and Paivio (1967) who obtained an average latency of 8.5 sec for unrelated word pairs (see also

Colman & Paivio, 1970; Yuille & Paivio, 1968). At the other extreme, category names can be generated in only 1.6 sec with multiple instances from memorized categories (Smith & Magee, 1980, Exp. 4).

The effects of context vary with a host of factors, including the number of shared similarities and rated similarity or cooccurrence of the words (Flavell & Johnson, 1961), the strength of the common responses in the separate associative hierarchies (Coleman, 1964), the number and proximity of context words (Howes & Osgood, 1954; Judson, Cofer, & Gelfand, 1956), the strength of competing responses (Underwood, 1957), and instructions (Reed, 1946; Underwood & Richardson, 1956b). Similar processes explain how instructions to associate with particular types of responses (e.g., synonyms or properties) bias the spread of activation to relevant pathways (e.g., Cattell, 1887). Such self-instructions can also be produced indirectly, as when massing opposite-evoking words early in a free association list increases the number of opposites to later words (Wynne, Gerjuoy, & Schiffman, 1965). The early words presumably activate the logogen for "opposite."

Verbal associative mechanisms contribute to elaboration and organization effects in memory. Elaboration refers here to encoding processes that activate information stored about the word in the verbal system and is related to the idea of depth or levels of processing (Craik & Lockhart, 1972). For example, Paivio (1986b) summarized several studies of elaboration processes with semantic equivalents. One study by Paivio and Lambert demonstrated that generation of synonyms or translations produced better recall for the presented words than did copying them. A second pilot study showed that incidental memory for stimulus words increased as the normative difficulty of synonym generation increased, perhaps because more associative activation occurred when synonym generation was difficult.

Organizational processes operate when presented words are related to one another either directly or indirectly. Direct associations between presented words benefit free recall (Deese, 1959; Jenkins & Russell, 1952), interfere with recognition memory (Underwood, 1965), and either benefit (Murray, 1982) or interfere with (Underwood & Ekstrand, 1968) such associative tasks as paired-associate learning. Convergent associations in which presented words share a common associate contribute to such memory phenomena as clustering in free recall (Borges & Mandler, 1972; Bousfield, 1953; Hudson, 1968), mediational effects in paired-associate learning (Bellezza & Poplawsky, 1974; Miller, 1970), intrusion errors in recognition memory (Rubin, 1983; Underwood, 1965), instantiation effects in sentence memory (Anderson & Ortony, 1975; Gumenik, 1979; Marschark & Paivio, 1977), memory for schemas or scripts (Bower et al., 1979; Kahn, 1985), and the effects of schematic learning strategies (Buzan, 1974; Dansereau, Collins, McDonald, Holley, Garland, Diekhoff, & Evans, 1979; Holley & Dansereau, 1984; Novak & Gowin, 1984). Our approach to the more complex tasks can be illustrated for instantiation effects. In essence, close cues (e.g., "basket") are convergent associates of the words in the sentences (e.g., "The *container* held the *apple*"), whereas distant cues (e.g., "bottle") are not.

Association and memory tasks demonstrate some precise correspondences. To illustrate, Coleman (1963) found that the latency (or order) of individual word associations predicted paired-associate intrusion errors, and Miller (1970) found a correlation of .71 between the strength of primary convergent associations and paired-associate learning by a different group of subjects. We conclude from this and other research that relatively direct indicators of verbal associative processes demonstrate effects having parallels in memory and learning tasks. Verbal associative encoding is the last of the three encoding processes for words and we describe next research on encoding processes for nonverbal materials.

Encoding Processes for Nonverbal Stimuli

Dual coding theory characterizes the encoding of nonverbal stimuli in terms of representational, referential, and associative processes analogous to those that we have discussed for language. Objects are encoded representationally when they activate familiar imagens, which in turn can activate logogens and other imagens by referential and associative processes.

Representational Encoding of Novel Objects

Unfamiliar figures access familiar imaginal representations by processes based on perceptual similarity and transformation. The operation of these processes is demonstrated when subjects draw novel shapes from memory. Gibson (1929) found changes in 43% of reproductions of various nonsense figures and classified 32% of those changes as object assimilations, that is, as reproductions that resembled familiar objects more than did the original stimuli. Verbal reports confirmed that the nonsense figures aroused impressions of objects and that some subjects used assimilation as a deliberate strategy. Even instructions to remember literal impressions of the stimuli did not inhibit meaningful images based on perceptual similarities between the nonsense forms and familiar objects.

Verbal responses have also been used to indicate meaningful encoding of random shapes and nonsense forms (e.g., Danks, 1972; Vanderplas & Garvin, 1959) as well as such nonrandom figures as Blissymbols (Yovetich, 1985). In the Vanderplas and Garvin study, an average of 40% of subjects gave labels for the figures or said that they were reminded of some object. None of the figures was completely meaningless, the lowest association value being 20%. Ellis, Muller, and Tosti (1966) mentioned two other measures of encoding ease, the number of responses in a continuous production task (i.e., frequency or meaningfulness) and the proportion of subjects giving the primary response (i.e., dominance or consistency). Yovetich (1985) measured the proportion of subjects guessing the appropriate concept for Blissymbols and also had subjects rate their representativeness using pictorial appropriateness as one criterion.

No one appears to have used latencies (or stability) to measure the ease of encoding nonsense figures, although such encoding occurs quickly even with brief presentations (Smith, 1914) and appears to be a compelling form of encoding. Gibson (1929) found that it was difficult to suppress meaningful perceptual encoding and the spontaneity of visual encoding has been used to explain the greater Stroop effect observed with Chinese ideographs than with English words (Biederman & Tsao, 1979). Rivera (1959) showed that even subjects learning shared arbitrary labels for different nonsense forms still used distinct perceptual encodings of the individual stimuli to mediate learning. Thus, unique representational codes of the sort discussed here occur even when not required by the task.

Few researchers have investigated relations among the various measures to determine their convergent validity. Yovetich (1985) found a positive relationship between ratings of representativeness and a production measure of guessability. Ellis et al. (1966) varied consistency, by, frequency, and association value independently of one another. Results from paired-associate learning suggested that association value was the most potent variable of the three and that the effects of ease of encoding were stronger for complex figures than for simple ones. However, Ellis et al. (1966) did not report statistical analyses or the correlations among the various measures.

Despite the use of verbal responses in these measures, several findings indicate that the responses reflect largely the degree to which nonsense shapes resemble concrete objects (Paivio, 1971/1979, p. 191). In particular, the interpretation of nonsense figures can be controlled by manipulating visual attention to different parts of the figure (Freeman, 1929) and the representativeness and guessability of Blissymbols are related to concreteness and imagery ratings (Yovetich, 1985). The visual nature of the encoding processes is also obvious in nonsense figures that elicit consistent associations (e.g., over 80% of subjects labeled one of Danks's figures a "rabbit"). This evidence is still limited, however, and some verbal report measures (e.g., meaningfulness) are undoubtedly contaminated by referential and associative processes.

Several variables affect the likelihood of perceptual encoding. Ellis and Homan (1968) found indirect evidence from recognition memory that prior paired-associate learning of irrelevant materials increased the tendency to identify nonsense forms with familiar imagens that had names and facilitated recognition almost as much as prior learning of relevant responses. The paired-associate learning had no effect when subjects were explicitly given meaningful encodings for the figures, presumably because perceptual encoding was already maximized. Other research has shown that appropriate verbal labels can prime specific interpretations of nonsense figures (Carmichael, Hogan, & Walter, 1932; Ellis, 1968; Pfafflin, 1960) suggesting that the effect of label relevance in Ellis and Homan may have been stronger with less time between tasks or with instructions about response relevance.

A number of studies have shown the importance of representational encoding for memory. For example, the number of object assimilations in Gibson (1929) varied widely across subjects and correlated with amount recalled ($r = .71$). Ellis and Muller (1964) explicitly asked what shapes "looked like" and subsequently found that learning the modal responses facilitated subsequent learning of new responses for the stimuli and, under certain conditions, even recognition relative to similar distractors. Yovetich (1985) showed that the representatives of Bliss-symbols predicted performance on several memory tasks, even with concreteness and imagery value controlled.

Research on shape mnemonics (e.g., see visual alphabets in Yates, 1966) has also demonstrated the importance of representational access for memory. The letter learning component of the Laubach method involves images that look like the corresponding letters and begin with the same sound (Laubach, Kirk, & Laubach, 1971). To illustrate, image an "f" as a flower with leaves at the crossbar and a blossom at the top. Laubach et al. (1971) described the ease with which nonreading adults acquire the system and apply it to reading text. Using a similar technique, Isgur (1975) obtained 100% success at letter identification with reading-disabled children after only 5 to 10 min of practice per letter. Isgur also found that even commonly reversed letters were easily learned (e.g., "b" and "d"). Similar strategies or instructions to think of objects that "look like" the patterns to be learned ought to facilitate the many learning tasks that involve novel shapes (e.g., sign language, pictographic languages, foreign scripts such as the Greek letters used in statistics, identification of countries in geography or microscopic organisms in biology, fingerprints).

Activation of familiar imagens by unfamiliar patterns can be studied relatively directly and contributes to our understanding of the processes by which such patterns are learned and remembered. One of the ways that representational encoding facilitates memory is by enabling the learner to invoke higher level processes, including referential encoding (i.e., naming), to which we now turn.

Naming Objects

Mental connections between imagens and logogens permit referential encoding of nonverbal stimuli, an operation that is invoked whenever we name pictures or objects. Although rapid, naming colors and pictures takes longer than reading words (Cattell, 1886a,b). Moore (1915) found that the average time to think of names was 821 msec for pictures versus 562 msec for words. The difference (259 msec) provides one estimate of referential processing time and agrees well with the 260-msec estimate that Potter and Faulconer (1975) obtained by subtracting word-naming latencies from picture-naming latencies. The relative slowness of naming is probably not a result of differential ease of identification, because pictures and words have similar perceptual or identification thresholds (Cattell, 1886a, b; Fraisse, 1968; Moore, 1915), and pictures are categorized even faster than words (Potter & Faulconer, 1975). The difference between identification and naming times for pictures, 227 msec in Moore and 314 msec in Fraisse, provides another estimate of referential processing time.

With respect to other indicators of naming ease, Lachman (1973) reported a positive relation between naming latency and uncertainty or codability as measured by the number and proportion of different labels given for each picture (i.e., commonality). Uncertainty decreases with the number of subjects giving the dominant response (Snodgrass & Vanderwart, 1980) and with the percentage of repetitions (i.e., stability) when pictures are named on two occasions (Butterfield & Butterfield, 1977). Butterfield and Butterfield (1977) also showed that agreement with adult names decreased with uncertainty, especially for young children (4 year olds).

A variety of variables influence the ease of naming. Naming latency decreases with word frequency (Oldfield & Wingfield, 1964, 1965) and increases with age of acquisition (Carroll & White, 1973), although Lachman (1973) reported individual variation in which of these was the better predictor. Frequency has only modest effects on picture identification (Wingfield, 1968), making early perceptual processes an unlikely locus for the effect. However, some of the familiarity effect may result from response production factors (e.g., number of syllables and pronounceability) rather than referential processes. Frequency or practice has also been studied experimentally. Practice benefits picture naming more than reading but never erases the reading superiority (Fraisse, 1960, 1968). For example, color naming still requires an extra 121 msec even after 12 days of practice (Brown, 1915). Oldfield and Wingfield (1964, 1965) reported that unfamiliar pictures benefitted more from practice than familiar objects, but Bartram (1974) concluded that the differential practice effect for familiar and unfamiliar materials was less for photographs than for line drawings.

Familiarity and practice effects implicate age as a central factor in naming. Picture naming develops early, perhaps without specific training (Hochberg & Brooks, 1962), and is as fast as object naming for even 2-year-old children (Zaft & Daehler, 1979), although Nelson (1972) showed that the ability of very young children to name pictures depends on familiarity, visual ambiguity, and amount of detail in the depiction. Despite developmental advantages, Ligon (1932) reported that color naming was slower than reading by a relatively constant amount from grade 1 to adulthood, but when Stroop (1935) transformed the latencies to speeds, the difference between reading and naming increased substantially from grade 1 to grade 9. Lund (1927) even reported faster color naming than reading for young children as did Stanovich (1981), who also found picture naming to be faster than reading. Such global effects ignore the individual differences that characterize the difference between color naming and reading even among adults (Broverman, 1960; Bucci, 1984).

These relatively direct observations about referential processes contribute to our understanding of memory because naming has a positive effect on memory for pictures (Kurtz & Hovland, 1953; Paivio & Csapo, 1973; Robinson, 1970), including the ability to discriminate target pictures from same-name alternatives (Warren & Horn, 1982). Picture naming occurs more readily than imaging to words, which might help to explain why pictures are remembered better than words. That is, pictures will be more likely than words to activate both verbal and imaginal codes, and the two codes have additive effects on recall (Paivio, 1971/1979; Snodgrass & McClure, 1975). In addition, the picture superiority effect disappears when pictures and words are presented at a rate that precludes naming (Paivio & Csapo, 1969). Subjects confuse studied pictures with their names on a recognition test also indicating that names are generated spontaneously during study of pictures (Snodgrass, Wasser, Finkelstein, & Goldberg, 1974).

Picture labeling research has shown that naming develops early, but memory studies suggest that naming is an optional encoding behavior that becomes relatively automatic only later in development. For example, Conrad (1971) found that confusible names had no effect on picture memory in young children (3 to 5 years) but an increasingly disruptive effect beyond 5 years. Yarmey (1974) specifically studied the effects on learning of the normative latency of picture names. Pictures were superior to words as stimuli in paired-associate learning except when both the stimulus and response items involved long naming latencies. Presumably, the study time was insufficient to permit naming of two long latency items.

Several direct measures of naming, especially latency, have been shown to elucidate basic referential mechanisms that may help us to understand parallel effects in memory tasks involving pictures or objects. Naming is only one of two "deeper" levels of processing available for nonverbal materials and we examine next tasks and operations that reflect associative connections among imaginal mental representations.

Imaginal Associative Processing

Dual coding theory describes complex imagens as nested sets of more elementary units spatially organized into continuous, perceptual hierarchies that lack sequential constraints (Paivio, 1971/1979). Imaginal associations have been studied with such tasks as the scanning paradigm, which is analogous to verbal associative tasks and provides a latency measure of imaginal associative processes. Kosslyn (1973) had subjects focus on an imaged or described (i.e., verbal) locus of objects and measured reaction time to verify that the object contained a subsequently named part. Latencies under imagery conditions were faster and less affected by proximity to the focal point than under verbal conditions, and also varied with physical distance rather than sequential order as was the case for descriptions. Studies of cognitive maps have confirmed the effects of distance on scanning time (Kosslyn, Ball, & Reiser, 1978), although instructions influence the strength of such effects (e.g., Goldston, Hinrichs, & Richman, 1985).

The role of imagery in script production has not yet been determined directly (Rabinowitz & Mandler, 1983), but our own phenomenal imagery is strong when we think of such scripts as grocery shopping. Imaginal associations are also implicated by latency data from Barsalou and Sewell (1985), who found that scripts were produced at a constant rate, as though subjects were describing a continuous stream of perceptual events. This pattern contrasts with the bursts and pauses characteristic of production from taxonomic (i.e., verbal associative) categories. In addition, production was slower in the reverse order than in the forward order, consistent with our own script imagery and with other evidence that scenes can be (but need not be) ordered (e.g., relations among the loci in the method of loci).

The potential freedom of imaginal associations from sequential constraints has been demonstrated with a memory probe task in which subjects judge whether items belong to a previously memorized set. Reaction times to judge items as old or new (i.e., scanning times) generally increase with set size, but not if the set has been memorized as an interactive image (Bersted, 1983; Seamon, 1972). This effect occurs unless subjects have described their images verbally (Bersted, 1983; Rothstein & Atkinson, 1975) and is consistent with the hypothesis that associations between images provide access to members in a parallel or a nonordered fashion, a capacity that verbal associative structures do not provide.

Other indicators of imaginal associations have been exploited less fully but are analogous to meaningfulness and related measures. For example, Milgram and Jodelet (1976) gave Parisians place names in Paris with instructions to think of that place and then "wander with the mind's eye to the next specific element" in their mental images. The percentage of association failures for each place (a variable that correlates negatively with dominance and positively with uncertainty) predicted the probability that the place appeared on cognitive maps drawn by the subjects, suggesting that imaginal associative processes mediate map production. That cognitive maps are imaginal is also supported by the ability of people to make precise judgments of distance, orientation, proximity, and other spatial relations (Allen & Kirasic, 1985; Curtis, Siegel, & Furlong, 1981; Hirtle & Jonides, 1985), although Cattell (1895) found considerable variability among subjects in their estimates of distance and walking times as well as in their drawings of cognitive maps.

Several observations directly support our suggestion that these and related effects should be attributed to imaginal processes. With respect to cognitive maps, Moar and Bower (1983) found that all of their subjects reported images of either scenes (in a task that involved relations among locations in a city) or maps (in a task that involved relations among cities). Thorndyke and Stasz (1980) observed that visualization ability was correlated with map learning and interacted with instructions to use effective imagery strategies. A final argument for an imagery explanation (or at least against verbal processes) is the fact that non-human species (e.g., Olton, 1979) and young children have accurate mental maps. For example, Ratner and Myers (1981) found that children as young as 2 years of age accurately verified the contents of different rooms of a house.

Imaginal explanations appear to be challenged by research showing that knowledge about cognitive maps, objects, and scripts is at least sometimes discrete and nonveridical (Allen & Kirasic, 1985; Bower et al., 1979; Kahl, Herman, & Klein, 1984; McNamara, Ratcliff, & McKoon, 1984; Tversky & Hemenway, 1983, 1984). However, these findings are not problematic from the dual coding perspective (see Paivio, 1986a, Chapter 9). Segmentation (i.e., the tendency to divide complex spatial units into parts) and related effects may result from imaginal processes associated with nested imagens (Paivio, 1971/

1979; Palmer, 1977) or from verbal processes. Mandler and Murphy (1983) demonstrated directly that the consistency with which scripts were segmented decreased when verbal cues to segments were removed. Verbal cues (in particular, discrete names for places) may contribute to similar findings with cognitive maps.

Imaginal associative structures, as revealed in these various paradigms, have important implications for understanding memory. The enhancement of cued recall by compound imagery shows that complex images are easily redintegrated from partial cues, perhaps because images are by nature integrated and holistic (e.g., Begg, 1973). Some of the memory benefits of scripts and schemas may occur because words that are related to some episode (e.g., grocery shopping) activate complex mental scenes derived from past experiences. With respect to mnemonic and learning strategies, the method of loci uses an imaginal associative network of familiar locations and spatial learning strategies (e.g., Holley & Dansereau, 1984) represent verbal knowledge as visual networks, much as cognitive maps represent relations among discrete places.

Spatial relations appear to play an important role in both imaginal associative and memory tasks. For example, Snodgrass, Burns, and Pirone (1978) confirmed the dual coding prediction that, relative to verbal processing, imagery would enhance memory for spatial order but not memory for temporal order. Thorndyke and Stasz (1980) showed that good map learners were more likely than poor learners to encode spatial relations among places and that instructions to use such imagery strategies improved map learning, especially for high visualization ability subjects. Mandler and Parker (1976) observed that scene organization had little effect on memory for descriptive information about objects but did influence spatial information.

This concludes our examination of imaginal associative processes and of encoding operations for nonverbal materials. Pictures and objects have been shown to involve representational, referential, and associative encoding processes analogous to those used in encoding verbal stimuli and the results from direct investigations of these processes shed some light on their contribution to memory for nonverbal materials.

Conclusions

We have shown how the encoding of both verbal and nonverbal materials can be conceptualized in terms of the representational, referential, and associative processes proposed by dual coding theory. These encoding processes are amenable to direct investigation by methods that have produced findings relevant to the understanding of memory phenomena, including the effectiveness of different learning strategies. The evidence comes from studies using latency and other convergent indicators of the ease of different encoding operations to investigate how these measures are related to one another and to subject, item, and situational variables under both instructed and spontaneous encoding conditions.

A complete dual coding explanation of memory encoding would describe how metamemory knowledge controls and influences such basic encoding operations as imaging (Flavell & Wellman, 1977; Pressley, Borkowski, & O'Sullivan, 1985). The representational and processing assumptions that we have already described are in fact adequate to explain metacognitive knowledge. In essence, dual coding theory proposes that (a) reflexive knowledge of memory is represented in the same verbal and nonverbal symbolic systems as other knowledge; (b) its acquisition depends upon relevant experiences, including the reflexive application of the learning strategies themselves to strategy acquisition; (c) environmental stimuli activate relevant metacognitive knowledge, either directly (e.g., instructions to "image") or through associative and referential connections (e.g., such learning-related words and events as "remember" and classroom settings); and (d) metacognitive logogens and imagens exert control over the encoding of stimuli by priming general classes of associative or referential reactions (e.g., "image car" versus "synonym car"). Each of these aspects of metacognitive knowledge can be investigated directly. For example, Katz (Chapter 8, this volume) found reliable differences in the tendencies of instructions from various cognitive tasks to elicit verbal and imaginal modes of processing.

Many questions about cognition remain unanswered and new questions emerge every day, but experimental psychologists have learned much since Cattell's pioneering work over 100 years ago. Our fundamental knowledge about cognition is primarily empirical in nature and dual coding theory, conceived several decades ago as a general model of cognition, is a useful framework within which to conceptualize the accumulated research findings that provide an increasingly precise understanding of the memory encoding processes available in the verbal and imaginal symbolic systems.

Acknowledgments. Preparation of this chapter was supported by grant A0087 to A. Paivio from the Natural Sciences and Engineering Research Council of Canada. We thank Michael Pressley and Albert Katz for helpful comments on earlier drafts of the paper.

References

Allen, G. L., & Kirasic, K. C. (1985). Effects of the cognitive organization of route knowledge on judgments of macrospatial distance. *Memory & Cognition, 13,* 218–227.

Anderson, M. A. (1917). An investigation into the rate of mental association. *The Journal of Educational Psychology, 8,* 97–102.

Anderson, R. C., & Ortony, A. (1975). On putting apples into bottles—a problem in polysemy. *Cognitive Psychology, 7,* 167–180.

Archer, E. J. (1960). A re-evaluation of the meaningfulness of all possible CVC trigrams. *Psychological Monographs, 74*(10, Whole No. 497).

Atkinson, R. C., & Raugh, M. R. (1975). An application of the mnemonic keyword method to the acquisition of a Russian vocabulary. *Journal of Experimental Psychology: Human Learning and Memory, 104,* 126–133.

Barsalou, L. W., & Sewell, D. R. (1985). Contrasting the representation of scripts and categories. *Journal of Memory and Language, 24,* 646–665.

Bartlett, F. C. (1932). *Remembering: A study in experimental and social psychology.* Cambridge, England: Cambridge University Press.

Bartram, D. J. (1974). The role of visual and semantic codes in object naming. *Cognitive Psychology, 6,* 325–356.

Battig, W. F., & Montague, W. E. (1969). Category norms for verbal items in 56 categories: A replication and extension of the Connecticut category norms. *Journal of Experimental Psychology Monograph, 80,* 1–46.

Begg, I. (1973). Imagery and integration in the recall of words. *Canadian Journal of Psychology, 27,* 159–167.

Bellezza, F. S., & Poplawsky, A. J. (1974). The function of one-word mediators in the recall of word pairs. *Memory & Cognition, 2,* 447–452.

Bersted, C. T. (1983). Memory scanning of described images and undescribed images: Hemispheric differences. *Memory & Cognition, 11,* 129–136.

Biederman, I., & Tsao, Y. (1979). On processing Chinese ideographs and English words: Some implications from Stroop-test results. *Cognitive Psychology, 11,* 125–132.

Borges, M. A., & Mandler, G. (1972). Effect of within-category spacing on free recall. *Journal of Experimental Psychology, 92,* 207–214.

Bousfield, W. A. (1953). The occurrence of clustering in recall of randomly arranged associates. *Journal of General Psychology, 49,* 229–240.

Bower, G. H., Black, J. B., & Turner, T. J. (1979). Scripts in memory for text. *Cognitive Psychology, 11,* 177–220.

Bregman, A. S. (1977). Perception and behavior as compositions of ideals. *Cognitive Psychology, 9,* 250–292.

Broverman, D. M. (1960). Cognitive style and intra-individual variation in abilities. *Journal of Personality, 28,* 240–256.

Brown, W. (1915). Practice in associating color-names with colors. *Psychological Review, 22,* 45–55.

Bucci, W. (1984). Linking words and things: Basic processes and individual variation. *Cognition, 17,* 137–153.

Bugelski, B. R. (1968). Images as mediators in one-trial paired-associate learning. *Journal of Experimental Psychology, 77,* 328–334.

Bugelski, B. R. (1970). Words and things and images. *American Psychologist, 25,* 1002–1012.

Bugelski, B. R., Kidd, E., & Segman, J. (1968). Image as a mediator in one-trial paired-associate learning. *Journal of Experimental Psychology, 76,* 69–73.

Butterfield, G. B., & Butterfield, E. C. (1977). Lexical codability and age. *Journal of Verbal Learning and Verbal Behavior, 16,* 113–118.

Buzan, T. (1974). *Use your head.* London: BBC Publications.

Carmichael, L., Hogan, H. P., & Walter, A. A. (1932). An experimental study of the effect of language on the reproduction of visually perceived form. *Journal of Experimental Psychology, 15,* 73–86.

Carroll, J. B., & White, M. N. (1973). Word frequency and age of acquisition as determiners of picture-naming latency. *Quarterly Journal of Experimental Psychology, 25,* 85–95.

Cattell, J. M. (1886a). The time it takes to see and name objects. *Mind, 11,* 63–65.

Cattell, J. M. (1886b). The time taken up by cerebral operations. *Mind, 11,* 220–242, 377–392, 524–538.

Cattell, J. M. (1887). Experiments on the association of ideas. *Mind, 12,* 68–74.

Cattell, J. M. (1889). Mental association investigated by experiment. *Mind, 14,* 230–250.

Cattell, J. M. (1895). Measurements on the accuracy of recollection. *Science, 2,* 761–766.

Coleman, E. B. (1963). The association hierarchy as an indicator of extraexperimental interference. *Journal of Verbal Learning and Verbal Behavior, 2,* 417–421.

Coleman, E. B. (1964). Verbal concept learning as a function of instructions and dominance level. *Journal of Experimental Psychology, 68,* 213–214.

Collins, A. M., & Quillian, M. R. (1969). Retrieval time from semantic memory. *Journal of Verbal Learning and Verbal Behavior, 8,* 240–247.

Colman, F., & Paivio, A. (1970). Pupillary dilation and mediation processes during paired-associate learning. *Canadian Journal of Psychology, 24,* 261–270.

Conrad, R. (1971). The chronology of the development of covert speech in children. *Developmental Psychology, 5,* 398–405.

Craik, F. I. M., & Lockhart, R. S. (1972). Levels of processing: A framework for memory research. *Journal of Verbal Learning and Verbal Behavior, 11,* 671–684.

Curtis, L. E., Siegel, A. W., & Furlong, N. E. (1981). Developmental differences in cognitive mapping: Configurational knowledge of familiar large-scale environments. *Journal of Experimental Child Psychology, 31,* 456–469.

Danks, J. H. (1972). Associative responses to novel figures. *Psychonomic Monograph Supplements, 4,* 319–325.

Dansereau, D. F., Collins, K. W., McDonald, B. A., Holley, C. D., Garland, J., Diekhoff, G., & Evans, S. H. (1979). Development and evaluation of a learning strategy training program. *Journal of Educational Psychology, 71,* 64–73.

Day, J. C., & Bellezza, F. S. (1983). The relation between visual imagery mediators and recall. *Memory & Cognition, 11,* 251–257.

Deese, J. (1959). Influence of inter-item associative strength upon immediate free recall. *Psychological Reports, 5,* 305–312.

Ellis, H. C. (1968). Transfer of stimulus predifferentiation to shape recognition and identification learning: Role of properties of verbal labels. *Journal of Experimental Psychology, 78,* 401–409.

Ellis, H. C., & Homan, L. E. (1968). Implicit verbal responses and the transfer of stimulus predifferentiation. *Journal of Experimental Psychology, 76,* 486–489.

Ellis, H. C., & Muller, D. G. (1964). Transfer in perceptual learning following stimulus predifferentiation. *Journal of Experimental Psychology, 68,* 388–395.

Ellis, H. C., Muller, D. G., & Tosti, D. T. (1966). Stimulus meaning and complexity as factors in the transfer of stimulus predifferentiation. *Journal of Experimental Psychology, 71,* 629–633.

Ernest, C. H., & Paivio, A. (1971). Imagery and verbal associative latencies as a function of imagery ability. *Canadian Journal of Psychology, 25,* 83–90.

Farah, M. J., & Kosslyn, S. M. (1981). Structure and strategy in image generation. *Cognitive Science, 4,* 371–383.

Flavell, J. H., & Johnson, B. A. (1961). Meaning and meaning similarity: III. Latency and number of similarities as predictors of judged similarity in meaning. *The Journal of General Psychology, 64,* 337–348.

Flavell, J. H., & Wellman, H. M. (1977). Metamemory. In R. V. Kail & J. W. Hagen (Eds.), *Perspectives on the development of memory and cognition* (pp. 3–33). Hillsdale, NJ: Erlbaum Associates.

Foley, J. P., & MacMillan, Z. L. (1943). Mediated generalization and the interpretation of verbal behavior: V. "Free association" as related to differences in professional training. *Journal of Experimental Psychology, 32,* 299–310.

Fox, P. W. (1970). Patterns of stability and change in behaviors of free association. *Journal of Verbal Learning and Verbal Behavior, 9,* 30–36.

Fraisse, P. (1960). Recognition time measured by verbal reaction to figures and words. *Perceptual and Motor Skills, 11,* 204.

Fraisse, P. (1968). Motor and verbal reaction times to words and drawings. *Psychonomic Science, 12,* 235–236.

Freeman, G. L. (1929). An experimental study of the perception of objects. *Journal of Experimental Psychology, 12,* 341–358.

Giannadrea, V. (1971). Latency of imagery to word stimuli as a function of concreteness and abstractness and increasing phrase length. Unpublished undergraduate paper, University of Western Ontario, London, Canada.

Gibson, J. J. (1929). The reproduction of visually perceived forms. *Journal of Experimental Psychology, 12,* 1–39.

Goldston, D. B., Hinrichs, J. V., & Richman, C. L. (1985). Subjects' expectations, individual variability, and the scanning of mental images. *Memory & Cognition, 13,* 365–370.

Greenberg, J. H., & Jenkins, J. J. (1964). Studies in the psychological correlates of the sound system of American English. *Word, 20,* 157–177.

Gruber, H. E., Kulkin, A., & Schwartz, P. (1965, April). The effect of exposure time on mnemonic processing in paired associate learning. Paper presented at the Eastern Psychological Association meeting, Atlantic City.

Gumenik, W. E. (1979). The advantage of specific terms over general terms as cues for sentence recall: Instantiation or retrieval? *Memory & Cognition, 7,* 240–244.

Heim, J. (1973). A comment on R. C. Johnson: "Reanalysis of 'Meaningfulness and verbal learning.'" *Psychological Review, 80,* 235–236.

Hirtle, S. C., & Jonides, J. (1985). Evidence of hierarchies in cognitive maps. *Memory & Cognition, 13,* 208–217.

Hochberg, J., & Brooks, V. (1962). Pictorial recognition as an unlearned ability: A study of one child's performance. *American Journal of Psychology, 75,* 624–628.

Hoffman, J., Denis, M., & Ziessler, M. (1983). Figurative features and the construction of visual images. *Psychological Research, 45,* 39–54.

Holley, C. D., & Dansereau, D. F. (Eds.). (1984). *Spatial learning strategies: Techniques, applications, and related issues.* New York: Academic Press.

Hollingworth, H. L. (1915). Articulation and association. *The Journal of Educational Psychology, 6,* 99–105.

Howell, D. C. (1970). Free association reliability as a function of response strength. *Journal of Experimental Psychology, 85,* 431–433.

Howes, D., & Osgood, C. E. (1954). On the combination of associative probabilities in linguistic contexts. *American Journal of Psychology, 67,* 241–258.

Hudson, R. L. (1968). Category clustering as a function of level of information and number of stimulus presentations. *Journal of Verbal Learning and Verbal Behavior, 7,* 1106–1108.

Hull, C. L., & Lugoff, L. S. (1921). Complex signs in diagnostic free association. *Journal of Experimental Psychology, 4,* 111–136.

Isgur, J. (1975). Establishing letter-sound associations by an object-imaging-projection method. *Journal of Learning Disabilities, 8,* 16–20.

Janssen, W. (1976). *On the nature of the mental image*. Soesterberg, The Netherlands: Institute for Perception.

Jenkins, J. J. (1966). Meaningfulness and concepts; concepts and meaningfulness. In H. J. Klausmeir & C. W. Harris (Eds.), *Analysis of concept learning* (pp. 65-79). New York: Academic Press.

Jenkins, J. J. (1985). Nonsense syllables: Comprehending the "almost incomprehensible variation." *Journal of Experimental Psychology: Learning, Memory, and Cognition, 11*, 455-460.

Jenkins, J. J., & Russell, W. A. (1952). Associative clustering during recall. *Journal of Abnormal and Social Psychology, 47*, 818-821.

Johnson, R. C. (1962). Reanalysis of "Meaningfulness and verbal learning." *Psychological Review, 69*, 233-238.

Johnson, R. C. (1964). Latency and association value as predictors of rate of verbal learning. *Journal of Verbal Learning and Verbal Behavior, 3*, 77-78.

Judson, A. J., Cofer, C. N., & Gelfand, S. (1956). Reasoning as an associative process: II. "Direction" in problem solving as a function of prior reinforcement of relevant responses. *Psychological Reports, 2*, 501-507.

Kahl, H. B., Herman, J. F., & Klein, C. A. (1984). Distance distortions in children's cognitive maps: An examination of the information storage model. *Journal of Experimental Child Psychology, 38*, 134-146.

Kahn, M. (1985). *An alternative theoretical vocabulary for schema research*. Unpublished master's thesis, University of Western Ontario, London, Canada.

Kammann, R. (1968). Associability: A study of the properties of associative ratings and the role of association in word-word learning. *Journal of Experimental Psychology Monograph, 78*, 1-16.

Katz, A. N. (1983). Dominance and typicality norms for properties: Convergent and discriminant validity. *Behavior Research Methods and Instrumentation, 15*, 29-38.

Kiess, H. O. (1968). Effects of natural language mediators on short-term memory. *Journal of Experimental Psychology, 77*, 7-13.

Kiess, H. O., & Montague, W. E. (1965). Natural language mediators in paired associate learning. *Psychonomic Science, 3*, 549-550.

Kosslyn, S. M. (1973). Scanning visual images: Some structural implications. *Perception & Psychophysics, 14*, 90-94.

Kosslyn, S. M. (1980). *Image and mind*. Cambridge, MA: Harvard University Press.

Kosslyn, S. M., Ball, T. M., & Reiser, B. J. (1978). Visual images preserve metric spatial information: Evidence from studies of image scanning. *Journal of Experimental Psychology: Human Perception and Performance, 4*, 47-60.

Krueger, W. F. C. (1934). The relative difficulty of nonsense syllables. *Journal of Experimental Psychology, 17*, 145-153.

Kurtz, K. H., & Hovland, C. I. (1953). The effect of verbalization during observation of stimulus objects upon accuracy of recognition and recall. *Journal of Experimental Psychology, 45*, 157-164.

Lachman, R. (1973). Uncertainty effects on time to access the internal lexicon. *Journal of Experimental Psychology, 99*, 199-208.

Laubach, F. C., Kirk, E. M., & Laubach, R. S. (1971). *The new streamlined English series: Teacher's manual*. Syracuse, NY: New Readers Press.

Ley, R., & Locascio, D. (1970). Associative reaction time and meaningfulness of CVCVC response terms in paired-associate learning. *Journal of Experimental Psychology, 83*, 445-450.

Ligon, E. M. (1932). A genetic study of color naming and word reading. *American Journal of Psychology*, *44*, 103–122.

Long, G. M., & Wurst, S. A. (1984). Complexity effects on reaction-time measures of visual persistence: Evidence for peripheral and central contributions. *American Journal of Psychology*, *97*, 537–561.

Lund, F. H. (1927). The role of practice in speed of association. *Journal of Experimental Psychology*, *10*, 424–433.

Mandler, J. M., & Murphy, C. M. (1983). Subjective judgments of script structure. *Journal of Experimental Psychology: Learning, Memory, and Cognition*, *9*, 534–543.

Mandler, J. M., & Parker, R. E. (1976). Memory for descriptive and spatial information in complex pictures. *Journal of Experimental Psychology*, *2*, 38–48.

Marschark, M., & Paivio, A. (1977). Integrative processing of concrete and abstract sentences. *Journal of Verbal Learning and Verbal Behavior*, *16*, 217–231.

McNamara, T. P., Ratcliff, R., & McKoon, G. (1984). The mental representation of knowledge acquired from maps. *Journal of Experimental Psychology: Learning, Memory, and Cognition*, *10*, 723–732.

Meyer, D. E., & Schvaneveldt, R. W. (1971). Facilitation in recognizing pairs of words: Evidence of a dependence between retrieval operations. *Journal of Experimental Psychology*, *90*, 227–234.

Milgram, S., & Jodelet, D. (1976). Psychological maps of Paris. In H. M. Proshansky, W. H. Ittelson, & L. G. Rivlin (Eds.), *Environmental psychology: People and their physical settings* (2nd ed.) (pp. 104–124). New York: Holt, Rinehart, & Winston.

Miller, S. (1970). Prediction of mediated paired-associate learning. *Journal of Experimental Psychology*, *86*, 131–132.

Moar, I., & Bower, G. H. (1983). Inconsistency in spatial knowledge. *Memory & Cognition*, *11*, 107–113.

Montague, W. E., Adams, J. A., & Kiess, H. O. (1966). Forgetting and natural language mediation. *Journal of Experimental Psychology*, *72*, 829–833.

Moore, T. V. (1915). The temporal relations of meaning and imagery. *Psychological Review*, *22*, 177–225.

Morton, J. (1969). Interaction of information in word recognition. *Psychological Review*, *76*, 165–178.

Morton, J. (1979). Facilitation in word recognition: Experiments causing change in the logogen model. In P. A. Kolers, M. Wrolstead, & H. Bouma (Eds.), *Processing of visible language* (Vol. I) (pp. 259–268). New York: Plenum Press.

Murray, D. J. (1978). *Introduction to Albert Thumb and Karl Marbe: Experimentell untersuchungen uber die psychologischen grundlagen der sprachlichen analogiebildung* (new ed.) (pp. xi–lxiii). Amsterdam: John Benjamins.

Murray, D. J. (1982). Rated associability and episodic memory. *Canadian Journal of Psychology*, *36*, 420–434.

Nelson, K. (1972). The relation of form recognition to concept development. *Child Development*, *43*, 67–74.

Nelson, K. (1977). The syntagmatic-paradigmatic shift revisited: A review of research and theory. *Psychological Bulletin*, *84*, 93–116.

Novak, J. D., & Gowin, D. B. (1984). *Learning how to learn*. Cambridge, England: Cambridge University Press.

Oldfield, R. C., & Wingfield, A. (1964). The time it takes to name an object. *Nature* (London), *202*, 1031–1032.

Oldfield, R. C., & Wingfield, A. (1965). Response latencies in naming objects. *The Quarterly Journal of Experimental Psychology, 17,* 273–281.

Olton, D. S. (1979). Mazes, maps, and memory. *American Psychologist, 34,* 583–596.

Paivio, A. (1963). Learning of adjective-noun paired-associates as a function of adjective-noun order and noun concreteness. *Canadian Journal of Psychology, 17,* 370–379.

Paivio, A. (1965). Abstractness, imagery, and meaningfulness in paired-associate learning. *Journal of Verbal Learning and Verbal Behavior, 4,* 32–38.

Paivio, A. (1966). Latency of verbal associations and imagery to noun stimuli as a function of abstractness and generality. *Canadian Journal of Psychology, 20,* 378–387.

Paivio, A. (1968). A factor-analytic study of word attributes and verbal learning. *Journal of Verbal Learning and Verbal Behavior, 7,* 41–49.

Paivio, A. (1975). Neomentalism. *Canadian Journal of Psychology, 29,* 263–291.

Paivio, A. (1971/1979). *Imagery and verbal processes.* Hillsdale, NJ: Erlbaum Associates. (Originally published 1971).

Paivio, A. (1986a). *Mental representations: A dual-coding approach.* New York: Oxford University Press.

Paivio A. (1986b). Dual coding and episodic memory: Subjective and objective sources of memory trace components. In F. Klix (Ed.), *Memory and cognitive capabilities: Symposium in memoriam of Hermann Ebbinghaus* (pp. 225–236). Amsterdam: North Holland.

Paivio, A., & Begg, I. (1971). Imagery and comprehension latencies as a function of sentence concreteness and structure. *Perception & Psychophysics, 10,* 408–412.

Paivio, A., & Csapo, K. (1969). Concrete image and verbal memory codes. *Journal of Experimental Psychology, 80,* 279–285.

Paivio, A., & Csapo, K. (1973). Picture superiority in free recall: imagery or dual coding? *Cognitive Psychology, 5,* 176–206.

Paivio, A., & Harshman, R. A. (1983). Factor analysis of a questionnaire on imagery and verbal habits and skills. *Canadian Journal of Psychology, 37,* 461–483.

Paivio, A., & Madigan, S. A. (1968). Imagery and association value in paired-associate learning. *Journal of Experimental Psychology, 76,* 35–39.

Paivio, A., & Yarmey, A. D. (1965). Abstractness of the common element in mediated learning. *Psychonomic Science, 2,* 231–232.

Paivio, A., & Yuille, J. C. (1966). Word abstractness and meaningfulness, and paired-associate learning in children. *Journal of Experimental Child Psychology, 4,* 81–89.

Paivio, A., & Yuille, J. C. (1969). Changes in associative strategies and paired-associate learning trials as a function of word imagery and type of learning set. *Journal of Experimental Psychology, 79,* 458–463.

Paivio, A., Yuille, J. C., & Madigan, S. (1968). Concreteness, imagery, and meaningfulness values for 925 nouns. *Journal of Experimental Psychology Monograph Supplement, 76*(1, Pt. 2), 1–25.

Palmer, S. E. (1977). Hierarchical structure in perceptual representation. *Cognitive Psychology, 9,* 441–474.

Pfafflin, S. M. (1960). Stimulus meaning in stimulus predifferentiation. *Journal of Experimental Psychology, 59,* 269–274.

Potter, M. C., & Faulconer, B. A. (1975). Time to understand pictures and words. *Nature* (London), *253,* 437–438.

Pressley, M., Borkowski, J. G., & O'Sullivan, J. (1985). Children's metamemory and the teaching of memory strategies. In D. L. Forrest-Pressley, G. E. MacKinnon, & T. G.

Waller (Eds.), *Metacognition, cognition, and human performance* (pp. 111-153). New York: Academic Press.

Pressley, M., & Levin, J. R. (1977). Task parameters affecting the efficacy of a visual imagery learning strategy in younger and older children. *Journal of Experimental Child Psychology, 24*, 53-59.

Pressley, M., & Levin, J. R. (1978). Developmental constraints associated with children's use of the keyword method of foreign language vocabulary learning. *Journal of Experimental Child Psychology, 26*, 359-372.

Pressley, M., Levin, J. R., & Delaney, H. D. (1982). The mnemonic keyword method. *Review of Educational Research, 52*, 61-92.

Pressley, M., Levin, J. R., & McDaniel, M. A. (in press). Remembering versus inferring what a word means: Mnemonic and contextual approaches. In M. G. McKeown & M. E. Curtis (Eds.), *The nature of vocabulary acquisition*. Hillsdale, NJ: Erlbaum Associates.

Prytulak, L. S. (1971). Natural language mediation. *Cognitive Psychology, 2*, 1-56.

Rabinowitz, M., & Mandler, J. M. (1983). Organization and information retrieval. *Journal of Experimental Psychology: Learning, Memory, and Cognition, 9*, 430-439.

Ratner, H. H., & Myers, N. A. (1981). Long-term memory and retrieval at ages 2, 3, 4. *Journal of Experimental Child Psychology, 31*, 365-386.

Reed, H. B. (1946). Factors influencing the learning and retention of concepts. I. The influence of set. *Journal of Experimental Psychology, 36*, 71-87.

Richardson, J. T. E. (1978). Reported mediators and individual differences in mental imagery. *Memory & Cognition, 6*, 376-378.

Richardson, J. T. E. (1980). *Mental imagery and human memory*. London: Macmillan.

Rivera, J. de (1959). Some conditions governing the use of the cue-producing response as an explanatory device. *Journal of Experimental Psychology, 57*, 299-304.

Robinson, J. P. (1970). Effects of verbal and imaginal learning on recognition, free recall, and aided recall tests. *Journal of Experimental Psychology, 86*, 115-117.

Rosenberg, S., & Simon, H. A. (1977). Modelling semantic memory: Effects of presenting semantic information in different modalities. *Cognitive Psychology, 9*, 293-325.

Rothstein, L. D., & Atkinson, R. C. (1975). Memory scanning for words in visual images. *Memory & Cognition, 3*, 541-544.

Rouse, R. O., & Verinis, J. S. (1962). The effect of associative connections on the recognition of flashed words. *Journal of Verbal Learning and Verbal Behavior, 1*, 300-303.

Rubin, D. C. (1983). Associative asymmetry, availability, and retrieval. *Memory & Cognition, 11*, 83-92.

Schaeffer, B., & Wallace, R. (1969). Semantic similarity and the comparison of word meanings. *Journal of Experimental Psychology, 82*, 343-346.

Schaub, G. R., & Lindley, R. H. (1964). Effects of subject-generated recoding cues on short-term memory. *Journal of Experimental Psychology, 68*, 171-175.

Schlosberg, H., & Heineman, C. (1950). The relationship between two measures of response strength. *Journal of Experimental Psychology, 40*, 235-247.

Seamon, J. G. (1972). Imagery codes and human information retrieval. *Journal of Experimental Psychology, 96*, 468-470.

Segal, A. U. (1976). *Verbal and nonverbal encoding and retrieval differences*. Unpublished doctoral dissertation, University of Western Ontario, London, Ontario, Canada.

Smith, F. (1914). An experimental investigation of perception. *British Journal of Psychology, 6*, 321-362.

Smith, M. C., & Magee, L. E. (1980). Tracing the time course of picture-word processing. *Journal of Experimental Psychology: General, 109,* 373–392.

Snodgrass, J. G., Burns, P. M., & Pirone, G. V. (1978). Pictures and words and space and time: In search of the elusive interaction. *Journal of Experimental Psychology: General, 2,* 206–230.

Snodgrass, J. G., & McClure, P. (1975). Storage and retrieval properties of dual codes for pictures and words in recognition memory. *Journal of Experimental Psychology: Human Learning and Memory, 1,* 521–529.

Snodgrass, J. G., & Vanderwart, M. (1980). A standardized set of 260 pictures: Norms for name agreement, image agreement, familiarity, and visual complexity. *Journal of Experimental Psychology: Human Learning and Memory, 6,* 174–215.

Snodgrass, J. G., Wasser, B., Finkelstein, M., & Goldberg, L. B. (1974). On the fate of visual and verbal memory codes for pictures and words: evidence for a dual coding mechanism in recognition memory. *Journal of Verbal Learning and Verbal Behavior, 13,* 27–37.

Stanovich, K. E. (1981). Relations between word decoding speed, general name-retrieval ability, and reading progress in first-grade children. *Journal of Educational Psychology, 73,* 809–815.

Stark, K., & Calfee, R. C. (1970). Recoding strategies in short-term memory. *Journal of Experimental Psychology, 85,* 36–39.

Stroop, J. R. (1935). The basis of Ligon's theory. *American Journal of Psychology, 47,* 499–504.

Szalay, L. B., & Deese, J. (1978). *Subjective meaning and culture: An assessment through word associations.* Hillsdale, NJ: Erlbaum Associates.

Thorndyke, P. W., & Stasz, C. (1980). Individual differences in procedures for knowledge acquisition from maps. *Cognitive Psychology, 12,* 137–175.

Tversky, B., & Hemenway, K. (1983). Categories of environmental scenes. *Cognitive Psychology, 15,* 121–149.

Tversky, B., & Hemenway, K. (1984). Objects, parts, and categories. *Journal of Experimental Psychology: General, 113,* 169–193.

Underwood, B. J. (1957). Studies of distributed practice: XV. Verbal concept learning as a function of intralist interference. *Journal of Experimental Psychology, 54,* 33–40.

Underwood, B. J. (1965). False recognition produced by implicit verbal responses. *Journal of Experimental Psychology, 1,* 122–129.

Underwood, B. J., & Ekstrand, B. R. (1968). Linguistic associations and retention. *Journal of Verbal Learning and Verbal Behavior, 7,* 162–171.

Underwood, B. J., & Richardson, J. (1956a). Some verbal materials for the study of concept formation. *Psychological Bulletin, 53,* 84–95.

Underwood, B. J., & Richardson, J. (1956b). Verbal concept learning as a function of instructions and dominance level. *Journal of Experimental Psychology, 51,* 229–238.

Underwood, B. J., & Schulz, R. W. (1960). *Meaningfulness and verbal learning.* Chicago: Lippincott.

Uyeda, K. M., & Mandler, G. (1980). Prototypicality norms for 28 semantic categories. *Behavior Research Methods & Instrumentation, 12,* 587–595.

Vanderplas, J. M., & Garvin, E. A. (1959). The association value of random shapes. *Journal of Experimental Psychology, 57,* 147–154.

Vanderwart, M. (1984). Priming by pictures in lexical decision. *Journal of Verbal Learning and Verbal Behavior, 23,* 67–83.

Warren, L. R., & Horn, J. W. (1982). What does naming a picture do? Effects of prior picture naming on recognition of identical and same-name alternatives. *Memory & Cognition, 10,* 167–175.

Warren, R. E. (1972). Stimulus encoding and memory. *Journal of Experimental Psychology, 94,* 90–100.

Warren, R. E. (1974). Association, directionality, and stimulus encoding. *Journal of Experimental Psychology, 102,* 151–158.

Warren, R. E. (1977). Time and the spread of activation in memory. *Journal of Experimental Psychology: Human Learning and Memory, 3,* 458–466.

Whitten, W. B., Suter, H. W. N., & Frank, M. L. (1979). Bidirectional synonym ratings of 464 noun pairs. *Journal of Verbal Learning and Verbal Behavior, 18,* 109–127.

Wilding, J., & Mohindra, N. (1981). Ratings of the degree of synonymity of 279 noun pairs. *British Journal of Psychology, 72,* 231–240.

Wingfield, A. (1968). Effects of frequency on identification and naming of objects. *American Journal of Psychology, 81,* 226–234.

Wood, G. (1967). Mnemonic systems in recall. *Journal of Educational Psychology Monographs, 58*(6, Pt. 2).

Woodworth, R. S. (1938). *Experimental psychology.* New York: Holt.

Wynne, R. D., Gerjuoy, H., & Schiffman, H. (1965). Association test antonym-response set. *Journal of Verbal Learning and Verbal Behavior, 4,* 354–359.

Yarmey, A. D. (1974). Effect of labelling-latency of pictures in associative learning of pictorial representations and their word labels. *Canadian Journal of Psychology, 28,* 15–23.

Yates, F. A. (1966). *The art of memory.* London: Routledge & Kegan Paul.

Yovetich, W. S. (1985). *Cognitive processing of Blissymbols by normal adults.* Unpublished doctoral dissertation, University of Western Ontario, London, Ontario, Canada.

Yuille, J. C. (1973). A detailed examination of mediation in PA learning. *Memory & Cognition, 1,* 333–342.

Yuille, J. C., & Paivio, A. (1967). Latency of imaginal and verbal mediators as a function of stimulus and response concreteness-imagery. *Journal of Experimental Psychology, 75,* 540–544.

Yuille, J. C., & Paivio, A. (1968). Imagery and verbal mediation instructions in paired-associate learning. *Journal of Experimental Psychology, 78,* 436–441.

Zaft, A., & Daehler, M. W. (1979). Naming response times to objects and pictures in very young children. *Perceptual and Motor Skills, 49,* 162.

CHAPTER 2

Mnemonic Devices and Memory Schemas

Francis S. Bellezza

Mnemonic devices have been considered by some psychologists to represent a form of "unnatural learning" (Jenkins, 1971, 1974; Neisser, 1976, pp. 141–142). In response to these objections, it will be argued here that the study of mnemonic devices is fundamental to our understanding of human learning and the operation of human memory. In fact, the notion of mental cues, so pervasive in the implementation of mnemonic techniques, plays an important role in the operation of memory schemas. The value of comparing mnemonic devices and memory schemas has been mentioned before (Battig & Bellezza, 1979; Bellezza, 1983a, 1986a) but has not been discussed in detail. The purpose of this chapter is to demonstrate the similarities between these two knowledge structures and also to note some of their differences. In fact, instead of considering a mnemonic device as an unnatural and complicated form of learning, the proposal is made that a mnemonic device operates much like a memory schema. Many contemporary theories of memory consider memory schemas as important memory structures that automatically support natural learning. It is proposed here that mnemonic devices are simpler than memory schemas but seem complicated because the learner is very much aware of their operation.

In recent years it has become apparent that a variety of different types of organized memory structures exist. Each of these types of memory structures influences what information is processed and retained in memory, although the effects of these different types of structures on recall are not always the same. For example, Jean Mandler (1979, 1984) has contributed to our awareness of these distinctions by her discussion of the differences between categorical and schematic organization in memory. However, before proceeding further it may be well to review briefly the characteristics of mnemonic devices and memory schemas.

What Are Mnemonic Devices?

Mnemonic devices are techniques for memorizing that through experience over the centuries have been shown to be effective. Considering their reputed effectiveness, one may question why mnemonic devices are not in greater use today. There are a number of reasons for this (Bellezza, 1981), but the main two are the following:

1. Most people in contemporary Western cultures are literate, and information important in the culture can be found in books. A few hundred years ago it was necessary for much information to be stored in memory. Even if one were literate, there was no paper for taking notes on lectures, speeches, sermons, or other events. Also, before the invention of the moveable-type printing press, books were rare and highly valued. Some books were so esteemed that scholars memorized their contents. This was especially true of religious books (Yates, 1966).
2. A good deal of practice is necessary to use mnemonic procedures effectively when a large variety of information must be memorized. However, mnemonic devices still have important uses in classroom learning (Pressley, Levin, & Delaney, 1982).

Organizational and Encoding Mnemonics

Mnemonic devices are of two main types: organizational mnemonics and encoding mnemonics. These two types of mnemonic devices reflect the two main activities of human memory; unitizing and symbolizing (Miller, 1956). Organizational mnemonics organize and interrelate new information in memory so that it can be later recalled. Examples of organizational mnemonics are the method of loci, the pegword mnemonic, the story mnemonic, and the link mnemonic (Bellezza, 1982a). The use of an encoding mnemonic is sometimes necessary before an organizational mnemonic can be used. Encoding mnemonics are used to transform low-imagery, abstract material into more memorable form before an organizational mnemonic is used to store the information in memory. For example, an encoding mnemonic can be used to transform abstract words into high-imagery substitutes so that they can be stored more easily in memory. An abstract word, such as "fiscal," may be replaced by some semantic association, such as "money" or by words similar in pronunciation such as "fish tail." It turns out that for most people the words "money" and "fish tail" are easier to process in memory because these words are familiar and high in imagery. So one of these is used instead of "fiscal." Later, when the substitute word "money" or "fish tail" is remembered, it acts as a cue for the related word "fiscal," and this latter word is recognized as the word that was to be memorized (Bellezza, Day, & Reddy, 1983).

An encoding mnemonic is also available for memorizing numbers. Because words are easier to remember than are numbers, the digit–consonant mnemonic (Bellezza, 1982a, Chapter 5) provides a way of transforming numbers into words, which are then committed to memory. For example, using this system a telephone number such as 473–3904 can be transformed into the words *rock–mummy–bus–arrow*, which can then be memorized using an organizational mnemonic such as the link mnemonic. Later, after the sequence *rock–mummy–bus–arrow* is recalled, it can be decoded into 473–3904.

Both organizational mnemonics and encoding mnemonics make use of mental cues. The role of mental cues is easy to understand in the case of organizational mnemonics. A pegword mnemonic, such as the rhyme "One is a bun, two is a shoe, three is a tree, four is a door, five is a hive, six is a stick, seven is heaven, eight is a gate, nine is a line, and ten is a hen," does nothing more than provide ten easily remembered and imaged mental cues to which can be associated new information. A similar argument can be made for other organizational mnemonics, such as the method of loci, the story mnemonic, and the link mnemonic.

Encoding mnemonics also involve mental cuing, although the operation of mental cues is less apparent in encoding mnemonics than in organizational mnemonics. Whenever a substitute word is created for an abstract expression or for a number, this substitute word becomes a mental cue for the original item. When using the word "money" for the word "fiscal," a visual image is often formed for the word "money." At recall, the visual image of money must first be remembered and from this image the word "fiscal" must be recalled. The mental cue here is a visual image of money. In summary, encoding mnemonics insure that a mental symbol exists for the items of information being memorized, and organizational mnemonics organize these representative symbols in memory. Furthermore, when these symbols are later recalled, they act as mental cues for the items to be remembered.

Important Properties of Mental Cues

Bellezza (1981) suggested four properties important for the proper functioning of mental cues in mnemonic devices. These properties are described briefly below.

Constructibility

If mental cues connected with an organizational mnemonic are to be effective, then they must be generated easily and reliably both during learning (to become associated with new information) and at recall (to be used to cue the new information previously associated with them). Therefore, mental cues that are constructible are easily retrievable from memory during the two critical times in the learning process; during study of the material and during its recall.

A mnemonic device, such as the method of loci, is not effective unless its component locations are well memorized. If a locus is forgotten during recall, then the new information associated with it will also be forgotten. The principle of constructibility of mental cues is related to the principle of encoding specificity (Tulving & Thomson, 1973). For a specific event in memory to be recalled, the context and mental environment connected with the learning of that event must first be activated before the event itself can be recalled. Mental cues can be considered as that part of the learning context stored in memory that must be activated before new information can be recalled.

Bellezza and Reddy (1978) demonstrated the importance of the constructibility of mnemonic cues in an experiment utilizing the story mnemonic (Bower & Clark, 1969). Half of their subjects each fabricated and described a story made up from list words as those words were presented. The other half of the subjects each vocalized elaborations and associations elicited by the presented words. Although the subjects did not expect a test of free recall, those in the story condition recalled .75 of the list words, whereas those in the elaboration condition recalled only .46. The reason for this difference is that subjects in the story condition could construct the story they used during learning, and this story provided a rich set of mental cues. Subjects in the elaboration condition could not utilize constructible cues, because the elaborations had no organization and could not be again constructed in the absence of the list words.

The notion of encoding specificity emphasizes that the cues effective during recall must be the same as those encoded by the subject during learning. Reddy and Bellezza (1983) provided some subjects in the story condition with another subject's story (with the list words removed) as a set of recall cues. These subjects recalled only .27 of the list words, which was significantly worse than the other two conditions mentioned above. Hence, constructible mental cues are necessary for recall, because they have to be constructed in the same manner at two different times, during learning and during recall.

Associability

Not only must mental cues be constructible to be effective, they also must be easily associated with the information the learner wants to retain. Research over the last two decades has shown that the formation of vivid composite images involving both the mental cue and a representation of the information to be remembered is an effective means of retaining the desired information in memory (Bower, 1972; Paivio, 1971). For example, Delprato and Baker (1974) found that the rhyming pegword mnemonic is more effective when easily imaged pegwords are used, such as "one is a bun, two is a shoe, three is a tree," and so on, than when pegwords are used for which it is difficult to form images, such as "one is fun, two is true," and so on.

However, visual imagery is not the only factor that can affect associability. If a mental cue is used that is already related to the information to be associated with it, then the cue and the target information will be easily linked in memory. For example, when using the method of loci, the learner uses familiar images as mental cues. These may be images of his or her own home and its surrounding area. If one of the loci is "garage" and the list word to be remembered is "car," it is easy to form an association between "garage" and "car." The ease of relearning previously associated terms is a well-known finding and was reported in the earliest experiments on memory (Ebbinghaus, 1885/1964).

Discriminability

Mental cues, like physical cues, must not be confused with one another. The ancient Greek textbook of rhetoric, *Ad Herennium*, suggests that locations used in the method of loci not to be too much alike and be at least 30 ft apart, so that the user of the mnemonic does not get the loci confused (Yates, 1966). Bellezza

(1983b, 1986b) has demonstrated that lists of words presented on different and distinct visual patterns are better recalled than those same lists of words all presented on the same visual pattern. It seems that the visual background of the list words becomes part of the mental cue for each list. Hence, the lists with more discriminable mental cues are better recalled than the lists with less discriminable cues.

Invertibility

Invertibility means the existence of a bidirectional association (Ekstrand, 1966) between a mental cue and the new information associated with it. Invertibility is an important property of the mental cues created when using an encoding mnemonic. In the example discussed above, the abstract word "fiscal" could be transformed into the substitute word "money." So the direction of association during learning is "fiscal" → "money." During recall, however, the learner will recall either the word "money" or a visual image of money. In either event, the mental cue "money" must be transformed back into the word "fiscal," so the direction of association at recall is "money" → "fiscal." Paivio (1971, Chapter 8) proposes that associations involving visual imagery are symmetrical in strength, that is, invertible, whereas associations that involve primarily a sequence of verbal representations are asymmetric in strength, that is, not invertible.

What Are Memory Schemas?

Knowledge structures called memory schemas have become very important in theories of human learning and thinking. It is not possible to review here the literature concerned with memory schemas and their development, but reviews and discussion can be found in Alba and Hasher (1983), R. C. Anderson (1978), Rumelhart (1980), Rumelhart and Ortony (1977), and others. Schemas are organized knowledge structures in memory that can be thought of as generic concepts representing objects, persons, situations, events, sequences of events, actions, or sequences of actions. A memory schema is activated when information similar to its content is processed by the cognitive system. Once activated, the schema influences the processing of the new information and provides a mental context for it. If the information is similar enough to the content of the schema, then it is judged an instance of what the schema represents. The schema is thus *instantiated* by the new information (Rumelhart, 1980). For example, if a person sees only an eye and a nose in a picture, with other facial features in a shadow and not visible, the person may infer on the basis of this partial information that he or she should look for a face. This assumes, of course, that the eye and nose have the correct orientation and the correct relative position (Palmer, 1975).

There is a special type of schema called a script that not only aids in comprehending and remembering information but also helps guide behavior (Schank & Abelson, 1977). For example, when eating in a restaurant, the restaurant script activated in memory enables the person not only to expect certain events (such as being shown a table and being approached by a waiter) but also initiates behavior (such as ordering and paying).

The Role of Memory Schemas in Remembering

If a person reading a passage comes upon the sentence "John was hungry, so he entered a restaurant," the restaurant script is activated in memory. The advantage of having this active script available to the reader is that it provides general information about restaurants. However, specific information about this particular restaurant event must be selected from the passage as an instance of the script. If the next sentence is "John sat down near the door and gave his order to Paul," then the generic script allows the reader to infer that John sat down at a table in a particular location and gave his order to someone named Paul who was a waiter. This process is called *slot-filling* because information specific to the restaurant event being read is stored in memory as values for the particular actions, roles, and props involved in the restaurant script (Schank & Abelson, 1977). The script is being instantiated. The table involved is one near the restaurant door, and the waiter involved is Paul. Other information not explicitly mentioned in the passage can be inferred on the basis of what is stored in the generic script. For example, the reader may infer that the restaurant gave John a napkin to use and that the color of the napkin was white.

If the reader later tries to remember the information she read, the restaurant script is again activated and enables the restaurant event described in the passage to be remembered. The slots of the schema contain the information placed there during its most recent activation, although this information is not retained perfectly. Some forgetting may occur. Other types of recall errors can also occur. Because many inferences are made during schema-based comprehension, some information may be recalled that was never presented. These inferences often cannot be discriminated by the learner from the information presented (Bower, Black, & Turner, 1979).

Schemas exist for types of people as well as for events and objects. Recall of information about a person may not be based on information actually remembered but on inferences based on the remembered stereotype of the person (Bellezza & Bower, 1981a; Clark & Woll, 1981).

What is emphasized in the discussion below is not simply the capacity of memory schemas to generate default information when detailed information about an event cannot be retrieved from memory (Alba & Hasher, 1983). Instead, the argument is made that an important role of memory schemas is to retain in memory the particulars of an experienced event by the association of event information to the mental cues provided by the schema.

Memory Schemas as Mental Cues

Bellezza and Reddy (1978) have argued that natural learning and learning using mnemonic devices have a good deal in common. They suggested that events of a typical day are later remembered because the events become associated with the mental cues provided by a "daily-routine" schema. When the components of the daily-routine schema are mentally reviewed, they act as mental cues for any new information recently associated with them. The thought of going to lunch may act as a cue for the fact that a new acquaintance named Wilma was met at lunch. Hence, memory schemas, like mnemonic devices, may be considered as organized sets of mental cues stored in memory.

A good example of a memory structure that can be called either a schema, a cognitive map, or a mnemonic device, depending on the circumstances of its use, is knowledge of one's house. Knowledge of one's house is a schema because it has the necessary characteristics of a schema. For example, it contains some variables that must be instantiated. That is, the conditions and objects in each room of one's house may change from day to day. Also, there are other schemas embedded within one's house schema, such as a schema for the kitchen, and embedded in that, a schema for the refrigerator. Other properties of schemas are also satisfied by one's house schema (Rumelhart, 1980). Knowledge of one's own house is a subschema of the more general house schema.

Knowledge of one's house also comprises a cognitive map (Neisser, 1976), for it enables one to navigate through the house and to know how to get to the bathroom when in the basement and how to get to the kitchen from the front door. Finally, one can use the knowledge of one's house as a set of loci. It is not difficult to use 100 different locations in one's house to recall 100 new items in the same order they were presented (Bellezza, 1982a, Chapter 3). Because knowledge of one's own house is reliably retrieved, it is possible to create loci that provide constructible mental cues.

Memory Schemas and the Four Properties of Mental Cues

If schemas do act as a set of mental cues in a manner similar to mnemonic devices, then effective schematic cues should exhibit the properties of constructibility, associability, discriminability, and invertibility, as do mnemonic cues. My hypothesis is that any organized memory structure of which a person is aware during learning functions as a set of mental cues (Bellezza, 1986a). These mental cues must have the properties of constructibility, associability, discriminability, and invertibility if they are to be effective as recall cues. The argument has already been made that these four properties are important for the successful functioning of a mnemonic device. The argument is now made that these properties are also important if memory schemas are to retain in memory particular information about an experienced event.

Constructibility

By constructibility we mean the reliability by which mental events experienced during learning can be reconstructed at recall to act as mental cues for the new information previously experienced with them. In the Bellezza and Reddy (1978) experiment subjects were able to remember successfully new information by associating it with mental images of the neighborhood in which they lived, that is, with a cognitive map of their neighborhood. However, when they had to associate new information with locations with which they were not familiar, their recall performance was impaired. Bellezza and Reddy showed that it was the constructibility of the neighborhood locations that was critical for recall. The subjects were able to reconstruct their own neighborhood locations more easily than unfamiliar locations and use them as mental cues. When a list of the unfamiliar locations was provided at recall, however, the property of constructibility of mental cues was no longer a factor and recall performance in both conditions was the same.

Bellezza (1986a) presented subjects with a list of randomly selected nouns representing concrete objects. For each noun the subject had to perform one of four tasks. These were (a) give a word or phrase that sounds like the presented word, (b) give a definition of the presented word, (c) give a personal experience involving the presented word, or (d) think of some place in one's house where the named object might be placed. It was predicted that the House task would result in the best free-recall performance, because the House task utilized a cognitive map representing a constructible set of mental cues. Using two different retention intervals, it was found that subjects recalled from 50 to 100% more words in the House task than in any other condition. Other research has also indicated that neither personal experiences (Groninger & Groninger, 1984) nor definitions (Bellezza, Cheesman, & Reddy, 1977) act as constructible mental cues.

There have been few studies that have tried to assess directly the constructibility of memory schemas. Bellezza (1984a) had subjects try to associate words either to personal experiences or to parts of their bodies. Subjects then had to recall both the words presented and the personal experiences or body parts to which they associated the words. Many more body parts were recalled than were personal experiences. From this result it may be concluded that the body schema provides a more constructible set of mental representations than does a schema made up of personal experiences.

In another experiment (Bellezza, 1984b) subjects had to describe common objects such as a car, a cat, a hammer, a chair, and so on. One week later they performed the same task. Only about 55% of the attributes of an object mentioned one week were mentioned the other week. Hence, the constructibility of common object schemas may be somewhat lower than one expects.

Factors Influencing Constructibility

To better understand the notion of constructible cues, it may help to discuss some factors that can influence the constructibility of schematic cues. One such factor is whether a schema is *rule based*. If one accepts the set of natural numbers as comprising a memory schema, then the constructibility of numbers as cues is perfect, because the same numbers, starting with 1, can always be generated in the same order.

A second factor affecting the constructibility of schema-based cues is how often the schema is used. This is a *practice* or *frequency* effect. The letters of the alphabet can be thought of as forming a memory schema, and the constructibility of the letters as cues is very high for literate people. Each time the alphabet is recalled, it can be recited perfectly. Because of their constructibility, natural numbers and letters of the alphabet form the basis of many organizational mnemonics (Bellezza, 1982a, Chapters 3 and 5).

A third factor that can moderate the practice or frequency factor is *schema variability*. All people in our culture have a memory schema for a house. This schema is formed over many years as a result of experience with one's own house but also with many other houses. The house schema may be used often, but it is based on many different houses. And if one is asked to list the components of a house on two different occasions, the two descriptions may be somewhat different. The memory schema for a castle is not used as often as the schema for a house, so the constructibility of cues characteristic of a castle may be greater. If a person is not familiar with a wide variety of castles, the castle schema may represent a stereotype.

A fourth factor, which is related to the three discussed so far, is the *amount of information* in the schema. Some schemas have much more information in them than others because they represent more complicated objects or events. For example, the schema for an automobile may be more constructible than the schema for a house simply because there is less information in it. Although there does not seem to be empirical data connecting the constructibility of schema components with the amount of data in the schema, Bellezza (1984c) showed that the larger a common category, the less constructible was its contents. Subjects were asked to name as many instances as they could of categories, such as fruits, vehicles, and musical instruments. One week later, the subjects repeated this task. Of all the category instances mentioned, a mean of .69 were mentioned both weeks. Furthermore, there was a $-.39$ correlation between the number of instances mentioned for a category and how likely the same instances would be to be mentioned on both tests.

In discussions of the constructibility of mental cues, we assume that the cues are retrieved from memory with a minimum of environmental stimuli. Otherwise, the cues might be considered environmental cues rather than mental cues. Nevertheless, we should include a fifth factor of *environmental context* as possibly affecting the constructibility of schematic cues. In the Bellezza (1984a) experiment, subjects could easily recall body parts because their bodies were physically present. However, environmental context may also have an indirect effect on constructibility. For example, a person may describe a script for an event, such as a birthday party, and do this on two separate occasions. If a person is tested in the same location, then her two descriptions may be more similar than if she were tested at two different locations (Smith, Glenberg, & Bjork, 1978). This may occur even if no birthday party is observable on either occasion.

Associability

The degree of associability of a set of mental cues indicates how easily they become associated to new information. In the course of research on learning it has been found that symbols representing meaningful objects and events are most easily associated in memory (Underwood & Schulz, 1960). More recent research has indicated that mental cues are associable if they involve mental images (Paivio, 1971) or involve schematic representations of real-world objects (Day & Bellezza, 1983). The property of associability is easily distinguished from constructibility. Constructibility indicates how reliably a mental cue or set of mental cues can be generated, and associability refers to how easily new information can be associated to these mental cues once they have been generated. For example, natural numbers are constructible, but not very associable (Bellezza, 1982a, Chapter 5).

In the experiments reported by Bellezza, the House task resulted in better free-recall performance than did the Sound, Definition, or personal Experience tasks. This superiority was attributed to the greater constructibility of the mental cues generated by the House task. In these experiments verbal protocols were collected consisting of what each subject was thinking while performing the various tasks. To some extent, the verbal reports indicated the nature of the mental cues associated with the presented words. After a 3-day retention interval some subjects were presented their own verbal protocols as explicit recall cues. The cued-recall results showed a much different pattern than did the free-recall results. In cued recall the Definition and personal Experience tasks resulted in the best performance. The reason for this was that the mental cues generated in the Definition and personal Experience tasks were the more strongly associated to the presented words that elicited them compared to the mental cues of the House task or the Sound task. Once the subjects were given their verbal descriptions of the mental events, the problem of constructing these mental cues was circumvented.

Other experiments have also demonstrated the difference between the constructibility and the associability of schematic cues. Bellezza (1984a) found that subjects could recall more reliably parts of the body that they had generated earlier than they could recall personal experiences generated earlier. However, a recalled body part was less likely to cue its associated list word than was a recalled personal experience. Although the body part labels were more constructible mental cues, they were less associable than were the personal experiences.

Bandwidth

Mental cues created by mnemonic devices are used to store a wide variety of information. On the other hand, mental cues created by memory schemas are usually used to store information restricted in its meaning. For example, the schema for a chair has cues (slots) used to store information about the components of a particular chair. However, the chair schema cannot be used to store information about a particular automobile. The semantic range of information that can be stored by a set of mental cues has been referred to as the *bandwidth* of those cues (Bellezza & Bower, 1982).

In an experiment reported by Bellezza and Bower (1982, Exp. 2) subjects were asked to learn lists of words using either a set of mnemonic pegwords as cues or using a restaurant script as a framework for the presented words. There were two types of words presented; either randomly selected high-imagery nouns or a set of nouns that fit the restaurant script. Therefore, there were four conditions: two types of cues crossed with the two types of presented words. The best recall occurred when the script cues were used to recall the script nouns. The worst recall occurred when the script cues were used to learn and recall the randomly selected nouns. The random nouns did not fit the script, and subjects had difficulty associating the random nouns with the script framework. Intermediate between these two levels of recall were recall of the random nouns using the mnemonic pegwords and recall of the script nouns using mnemonic pegwords. In fact, recall was approximately the same for these two conditions. These results were interpreted as demonstrating the narrow bandwidth of a schematic set of mental cues compared to a mnemonic set of mental cues. Only script nouns could be stored using the script cues, but the mnemonic cues could be used to remember either script nouns or random nouns.

The bandwidth of a schema plays some role whenever the schema is activated. Information that does not fit the schema may not be attended to (R. C. Anderson, 1978). A number of experiments have shown that information typical of a schema is recalled better than information less typical of the schema (Anderson, Spiro, & Anderson, 1978; Brewer & Treyens, 1981; Graesser, Woll, Kowalski, & Smith, 1980). Smith and Graesser (1981), however, demonstrate that some of the recall of typical events results from successful inferences made from the schema rather than actual recall of the episode. In experiments in which typical and atypical events are recalled equally well, subjects seem to spend more time processing the atypical information during learning (Bellezza, 1983c; Bellezza & Bower, 1981b). Hence, when a set of mental cues and a set of presented information are not easily associated, then extra processing effort may be required by the learner if the information is to be remembered as part of the schematic event.

Discriminability

For a set of mental cues to be effective, they must be discriminable. That is, the learner must not confuse one with another either during the storage phase of learning or during the retrieval stage. There are a number of dimensions upon which cues can differ. For example, mental cues can be similar in meaning, and this can cause a decrease in their effectiveness. Bower et al. (1979, Exp. 3) presented subjects with script-based stories in which some of the scripts underlying the stories were very similar (visit to a dentist, visit to a doctor, and visit to a chiropractor). They found that recall of the script-based stories decreased as the number of similar scripts increased. The similar scripts entailed similar mental cues (waiting rooms, medical instruments, receptionists, nurses, and so on), and the lack of discriminability among the sets of cues resulted in poor recall performance. These results may be interpreted as demonstrating a failure in mental cuing, although it is not clear whether the failure has occurred when new information has been associated with the mental cues or during retrieval using the script.

Mental cues may not be discriminable because of their similarity on episodic dimensions as well as on semantic dimensions. That is, the same schematic cue, like the same mnemonic cue, may become associated with different information at different times. The learner must then discriminate among the various occurrences of the cue in memory on the basis of temporal–contextual factors rather than semantic ones (Bellezza, 1982b).

Thorndyke and Hayes-Roth (1979) demonstrated the importance of discriminability among mental cues used in different episodes. The presented subjects with up to eight passages each made up of the same underlying predicates but with different specific details within each predicate. Each passage was made up of 12 similar sentences always in the same serial position. They found that the predicates in each passage were recalled better as the number of repetitions increased, but the recall of the differing details in the predicates decreased. Their results can be interpreted as showing that subjects were learning a set of mental cues based on the predicates making up the passages. However, repetitions of the cues with differing details in each passage made the different instances of each cue difficult to discriminate in episodic memory. The subjects could not remember what detail was associated with a particular passage because the mental cues from one passage to the next were so similar.

In a second experiment Thorndyke and Hayes-Roth presented a final passage 24 h after presenting passages similar to it. The recall of details from the final passage was significantly better than when the final passage was presented immediately after the earlier passages. Because of the imposed time interval, the final passage was discriminable for those preceding it. In terms of mental cuing, the episodic discriminability of a set of mental cues increased as the time increased from the previous use of the cues.

Invertibility

There is little empirical evidence regarding the bidirectionality of association between schematic cues and information instantiated by a memory schema. However, the invertibility of schematic cues appears to be necessary for components of a memory schema to function as cues during recall. New information is often processed before a relevant schema is activated. During recall, however, schematic cues may be constructed and used to retrieve information that had formerly preceded these cues into conscious memory. Hence, during learning the order of events may have been *new information* → *schematic information*, whereas during recall the order of events must be *schematic information* → *new information*. The bidirectionality of association between schematic cues and new information is a necessary property for recall.

In the experiments reported by Bellezza (1986a), verbal reports of mental events were collected during four types of tasks of which each subject had to report for each list word either a word with a similar sound, a definition, a personal experience, or a place where the referent of the word might be found in his or her house. Three days later subjects were cued with some of the list words and again had to describe the mental events occurring during the first presentation. Also, subjects were presented with a written transcription of some of their verbal reports and had to recall the word that elicited the report. One of the questions addressed in this experiment was whether the verbal reports would elicit the presented words as well as the presented list words would again elicit the same verbal reports. Hence, the invertibility of the mental cues under the four different tasks was tested. For all four tasks, including the schematic House and Experience tasks, it was found that subjects could recall list words from their verbal-report cues about as easily as they could recall their verbal reports from the re-presented list words. This result demonstrates that the mental cues used in this experiment were invertible. Further research, however, is necessary to determine whether invertibility always occurs in schematic learning.

A Comparison of Mnemonic Devices and Memory Schemas

If mnemonic devices and memory schemas are each organized sets of mental cues, then is it necessary to distinguish between the two? The answer is yes, because there are important differences between these two types of memory structures. The purpose of this section is to summarize some similarities of mnemonic devices and memory schemas and also to discuss some of their differences. A summary of the similarities and differences proposed here is shown in Table 2.1.

The Similarities Between Mnemonic Devices and Memory Schemas

Four Properties of Mental Cues

The four properties of constructibility, associability, discriminability, and invertibility, as discussed above, are necessary for both mnemonic cues and schematic cues to be effective in learning. I have already discussed why mental cues generated from mnemonic devices or memory schemas must have these four properties. Mnemonic devices have evolved over the centuries, and the mental cues incorporated into mnemonic devices seem to have the desired properties. The mental cues that are components of mental schemas, however, do not appear to be as constructible as those of mnemonic devices. Memory schemas develop as the result of repeated experiences that are similar but not identical. Variety of experience is reflected in the variable content of memory schemas. Retrieval tests of the components of common object schemas on widely separated occasions have demonstrated this variability (Bellezza, 1984b).

Schematic cues may also be less associable than mnemonic cues, because these cues often can be associated to only a narrow range of semantic information. That is, memory schemas have narrower bandwidths than do mnemonic devices. However, there is no empirical data available to indicate that mnemonic and schematic cues differ with regard to the properties of discriminability and invertibility.

Dual-Purpose Structures

Memory structures, called cognitive maps, can function either as memory schemas or as mnemonic devices. A cognitive map contains information about

TABLE 2.1. Similarities and differences between mnemonic devices and memory schemas.

Similarities	
Four properties of mental cues	The mental cues utilized by both mnemonic and memory schemas must have the properties of constructibility, associability, discriminability, and invertibility.
Dual-purpose structures	The cognitive map of a neighborhood is both a memory schema and the set of loci for a mnemonic device.
Acquisition	Mnemonic devices and memory schemas develop relatively slowly by means of the interassociation of a large number of components in memory.
Single activation	During information processing only one memory structure at a time can be active in conscious memory.
Nesting and embedding	Memory schemas are organized hierarchically. Also, encoding mnemonics can be embedded in organizational mnemonics.
Differences	
Strategic versus automatic activation	Mnemonic devices tend to be activated by strategic decisions. Memory schemas tend to be activated automatically by sensory information.
Guides for behavior	A mnemonic device is not a guide for motor or social behavior, whereas a memory schema often is.
Levels of abstraction	Mnemonic devices include pictorial representations of physical objects and locations. The contents of memory schemas can be abstract.
Bandwidth	Mnemonic devices have broad bandwidths, whereas most memory schemas process a semantically restricted range of information.
Inference	Mnemonic devices cannot be used to infer the nature of missing information, but this is typically done when using a memory schema.
Cooccurrence restraints	Information processed by a mnemonic device is not judged for consistency. Inconsistent information can be detected by memory schemas.

the spatial relations of objects in one's environment and results from experience with these objects. For example, knowledge of the positions of familiar objects and buildings in one's neighborhood forms a cognitive map. Without this cognitive map a person could not move efficiently from one familiar place to another. We think of cognitive maps as being made up of arrangements of symbols just like physical maps.

A cognitive map is considered to be a type of memory schema, for it has many of the properties of memory schemas (Neisser, 1976, Chapter 6). However, a cognitive map, such as knowledge of one's neighborhood, can also provide a set of mental cues needed in the method of loci (Bellezza & Reddy, 1978). Visual images of familiar objects and locations can function as mental cues. They typically (but not necessarily) have the properties of constructibility, associability, discriminability, and invertibility. Of course, the person using a cognitive map as a mnemonic device must know how to associate new information systematically to the mental cues and how to retrieve it later.

Another information structure that can function both as a memory schema and a mnemonic device is knowledge of the structure of the human body. Highly organized knowledge of body parts, such as the face, is certainly a kind of schema (Palmer, 1975). However, parts of the body have also long been used in mnemonic procedures such as the method of loci (Bellezza, 1984a; Hunter, 1956).

Acquisition

Complex organizational mnemonics, such as the 100-pegword mnemonic, must be studied and practiced a good deal before they can be used as effective mnemonic procedures (Bellezza, 1982a, Chapter 3). Sometimes the amount of effort in this preliminary learning can be reduced by utilizing familiar information, as in the method of loci, or by using rhyming, such as in the rhyming pegword mnemonic, "One is a bun, two is a shoe, three is a tree," and so on. The mental cues comprising a mnemonic device must be interassociated in permanent memory in a stable and durable manner before these cues can be used to store additional information.

The development of a memory schema also occurs gradually and depends on those same principles of association by which mnemonic devices are developed. The components of memory schemas become so strongly interassociated over time that forgetting parts of the schema is unlikely (Hayes-Roth, 1977). Both mnemonic devices and memory schemas appear to be associative networks (J. R. Anderson, 1980; Norman, 1982).

The question may be raised as to why information associated with mnemonic or schematic cues does not become part of the permanent memory structure after it is successfully associated with it. Stated somewhat differently, one may ask how the permanent content of a schema can be distinguished from information about a particular event stored in memory by means of schematic cues. Of course, if the same information is repeatedly stored using the same set of mental cues, then that information will become part of the memory structure. However, when learning new information presented only once, the learner is able to distinguish between the associations formed among the mental cues of the memory structure and those formed between the mental cues and the new information. This discrimination seems to be the result of a memory tagging process utilizing temporal–contextual tags (Anderson & Bower, 1972; Bellezza, 1982b; Shiffrin, 1976). Furthermore, the learner is often able to remember whether information has been generated internally by the cognitive system or has originated in the environment (Johnson & Raye, 1981).

Single Activation

It appears that only one mnemonic device or memory schema can be active in memory at any given time. This results from the limited capacity of conscious memory (Mandler, 1975). To demonstrate the difficulty of using two different memory structures at the same time, Reddy and Bellezza (1986) had subjects try to memorize a list of randomly selected nouns or a list of nouns from the same taxonomic categories. Furthermore, some subjects simply studied the nouns, whereas other subjects used the pegword mnemonic to memorize the words. Subjects who simply studied the words recalled .49 of the randomly selected words but .80 of the category words. This was no surprise, because the category words could be organized in memory by their category labels (Bousfield, 1953). However, the subjects using the pegword mnemonic recalled .83 of the randomly selected nouns but only .63 of the category nouns. Why was performance poor when using a mnemonic on the category nouns? Subjects reported that they tried to apply the pegword mnemonic to the category words, but the taxonomic relations among the list words kept intruding into their thoughts and disrupting the use of the mnemonic.

Nesting and Embedding

One of the characteristic features of memory schemas is that they often are embedded in one another (Minsky, 1975; Rumelhart, 1980). For example, a schema for a face has variables such as type of eyes, type of ears, type of nose, type of mouth, and so on. However, each of these components itself represents an organized set of knowledge in memory and has variables to be instantiated. Eyes have color, shape, type of eyelashes, and so on (Palmer, 1975). Another type of embedding can be seen in scripts, such as the restaurant script. The main events of the restaurant script involve entering the restaurant, ordering the meal, eating the meal, paying, and so on. However, embedded in these acts are others, such as deftly using silverware, conversing with the waiter, computing the bill and tip, and so on (Schank & Abelson, 1977).

Embedding also occurs in mnemonic devices, but on a more modest scale. Organizational mnemonics, such as the pegword mnemonic and the method of loci, have been discussed extensively here because these mnemonics represent organized sets of mental cues similar to those of memory schemas. Encoding mnemonics, however, are also important because they generate substitute mental symbols for information difficult to encode into memory, such as abstract words, numbers, and unfamiliar proper nouns (Bellezza et al., 1983). An encoding mnemonic procedure is often embedded in an organizational mnemonic procedure. When material must be memorized that is difficult to represent in memory, an encoding procedure is used first to transform the material. The transformed material is then associated with a mental cue provided by an organizational mnemonic. A more detailed discussion of this procedure can be found in Bellezza (1981).

Differences Between Mnemonic Devices and Memory Schemas

There are a number of important similarities between mnemonic devices and memory schemas, and these have been outlined to support the notion that both mnemonic-based learning and schema-based learning are dependent on mental cuing. However, there are also some important differences between mnemonic devices and memory schemas, and these are discussed below.

Strategic Versus Automatic Activation

A knowledge structure can be activated in two different ways. After information is sensed, it may activate a schematic structure in memory because the sensed information is in some way similar to the schematic information. This automatic activation is known as data-driven or bottom-up activation. Alternatively, a knowledge structure may be activated by the expectations or strategic decisions of the learner accompanied by only a minimal amount of sensory input. This is concept-driven or top-down processing (Norman & Bobrow, 1976). The activation and use of mnemonic devices in remembering is much more a strategic process than is the activation and use of memory schemas. A mnemonic structure is usually not activated by sensory data but instead results from a conscious decision by the learner to utilize some mnemonic technique, which he or she then begins to implement and continues to implement for an entire set of information (Pressley, Borkowski, & Schneider, in press).

On the other hand, the memory schemas activated in visual perception and language comprehension are triggered by sensory input. This sensory input may be minimal and signal in advance the arrival of a greater amount of information to instantiate the schema. For example, the sentence "Joan was hungry, so she entered McDonald's" activates the restaurant script, so that subsequent information regarding the forthcoming events in the restaurant can be comprehended and remembered.

Guide for Behavior

Memory schemas can guide behavior in certain situations. The restaurant script, the dentist script, and the airline script not only provide information as to what to expect in these various situations but also guide behavior in these situations. A mnemonic device is not a guide for behavior.

Levels of Abstraction

There are schemas at many levels of abstraction (Rumelhart, 1980; Rumelhart & Ortony, 1977; Schank & Abelson, 1977). For example, the public-transportation script provides for such variables as type of vehicle, amount of fare, route, schedule, number of attendants and operators, reservationists, and so on. The public-transportation script might have embedded in it more specific scripts, such as the taxi script, the airline script, the train script, the bus script, and so on. The taxi script has variables for patron, amount of fare, place of origin, destination, and so on. In a similar manner the schema for chair is more specific than the schema for furniture but less specific than the schema for a dentist's chair.

Mnemonic devices do not exist on various levels of abstraction. In order for mnemonic cues to be associable, they must represent easily imaged and familiar objects or locations (Paivio, 1971). In fact, even in schema-based comprehension, there is a tendency for the learner to particularize abstract terms. Anderson and Ortony (1975) have reported that when presented sentences such as "The container held the apples," subjects seem to represent in memory the general term "container" by a more specific label such as "basket." This substitution on the part of the learner may be an automatic attempt to increase the associability of the schematic cues by utilizing memory representations familiar and high in visual imagery.

Bandwidth

The bandwidth of a mnemonic device is broader than that of a memory schema. Because of their design, multiple-use mnemonic devices can be used to store information with a wide range of meanings. However, the information that can be associated to the components of a memory schema is restricted to information that more or less "fits" the schema (Bellezza & Bower, 1982). The narrow bandwidth of a memory schema means that some information may be processed less than other information, depending on how well the information fits the schema. There is evidence to show that this is true (Bellezza, 1983c; Bellezza & Bower, 1981b; Friedman, 1979). Hence, the bandwidth of a schema affects what information is attended to and how it is processed.

When information is processed that "fits" a particular schema, this is a signal to activate the schema if it is currently inactive. So the notion of bandwidth is related to the both schematic processing of information and schema activation.

Inference

Inferences cannot be made when using mnemonic devices. This is because organizational mnemonics are sets of mental cues to which can be associated a broad range of information. If information previously associated to a mnemonic cue is unavailable during recall, then no accurate guess can be made as to what that information may be. The bandwidth of a mnemonic device is broad, and the lack of constraints on what information can be stored with a mnemonic device means that no inferences can be made about missing information.

Although inferences cannot be made using mnemonic devices, an important role of memory schemas is to aid in the making of inferences. One of the capabilities of an activated schema is to provide default information when information regarding some aspect of the schema is not presented. A script such as the grocery-store script (Anderson et al., 1978) may be instantiated by information about someone entering a grocery store to buy groceries. Though nothing may be stated about how the groceries are paid for, the inference can be made from the grocery-store schema that payment is either in cash or personal check but probably not by credit card. Because the schema provides a prototype made up of variable values most commonly instantiated in the past, information not provided in a new instantiation of the schema can be inferred. The capacity for inference in a schema is the result of its narrow bandwidth. The fact that only a narrow range of values can occur for any of the components of a schema means that it is easy to make a guess as to what component is likely to occur.

Cooccurrence Constraints

When a mnemonic device is used, the particular information associated with one mental cue usually is not related to the new information associated with another mental cue in the mnemonic structure. Separate pegwords or loci are associated with new information independently of one another. A novice instructed in the use of a mnemonic device is instructed to form a separate visual image for each mnemonic cue and independent of the other mental cues (Bellezza, 1982a).

The situation is different with regard to memory schemas. Presented with a sentence such as "Joan was hungry, so she went into McDonald's and ordered clam chowder," most people would immediately note that McDonald's does not serve clam chowder. "McDonald's" is acceptable as a restaurant name, and "clam chowder" is acceptable as a restaurant food, but the two cannot occur in the same restaurant script. Another example utilizing the chair schema is "Joan sat down at the diningroom table and raised her chair." The problem here is that the dining-room chairs typically are not adjustable. A person can certainly understand and remember these anomolous sentences but is immediately aware of the inconsistencies in the variable values for the instantiated schema (Bellezza, 1983c). Hence, the schema is affecting memory processing in a subtle way. Not only is the permanent structure of the schema affecting processing but also it is sensitive to the consistency of the instantiated values.

To deal with these problems of consistency among schema values, Schank and Abelson (1977) have proposed that scripts have *tracks*. For the restaurant script there may be a fancy-restaurant track, a fast-food track, a cafeteria track, and so on. However, these separate tracks do not deal completely with cooccurrence restraints. For example, within the fast-food track the sentence "Joan went into Burger King and ate a Big Mac" seems odd because Big Macs are bought at McDonald's. Of course, there may be a Burger King track and a McDonald's track within the fast-food track. However, the whole purpose of schemas is to reduce the storage of redundant information in memory. Creating a large hierarchy of tracks within each script or schema defeats the purpose of a schema. Just how schemas detect and process inconsistent information is not clear.

Conclusion

Mnemonic devices and memory schemas have many characteristics in common, such as their reliance on memory cuing, but there are some important differences between them. Nevertheless, mnemonic devices should not be criticized as representing unnatural learning. A case can be made that a mnemonic device is a kind of simple memory schema, and that learning using a mnemonic device is a somewhat simpler process than learning using a memory schema. Research designed to explore further the similarities and differences between mnemonic devices and memory schemas should result in better understanding of human learning and its relation to the memory system.

References

Alba, J. W., & Hasher, L. (1983). Is memory schematic? *Psychological Bulletin, 93*, 203–231.

Anderson, J. R. (1980). Concepts, propositions, and schemata: What are the cognitive units? In H. E. Howe, Jr. & J. H. Flowers (Eds.), *Nebraska Symposium on Motivation* (Vol. 28, pp. 121–162). Lincoln, NE: University of Nebraska Press.

Anderson, J. R., & Bower, G. H. (1972). Recognition and retrieval processes in free recall. *Psychological Review, 79*, 97–123.

Anderson, R. C. (1978). Schema-directed processes in language comprehension. In A. Lesgold, J. Pellegrino, S. Fokkema, & R. Glaser (Eds.), *Cognitive psychology and instruction*. New York: Plenum Press.

Anderson, R. C., & Ortony, A. (1975). On putting apples into bottles – a problem of polysemy. *Cognitive Psychology, 7*, 167–180.

Anderson, R. C., Spiro, R. J., & Anderson, M. C. (1978). Schemata as scaffolding for the representation of information in connected discourse. *American Educational Research Journal, 15*, 433–440.

Battig, W. F., & Bellezza, F. S. (1979). Organization and levels of processing. In C. R. Puff (Ed.), *Memory organization and structure* (pp. 321–346). New York: Academic Press.

Bellezza, F. S. (1981). Mnemonic devices: Classification, characteristics, and criteria. *Review of Educational Research, 51*, 247–275.

Bellezza, F. S. (1982a). *Improve your memory skills.* Englewood Cliffs, NJ: Prentice-Hall.

Bellezza, F. S. (1982b). Updating memory using mnemonic devices. *Cognitive Psychology, 14*, 301–327.

Bellezza, F. S. (1983a). Mnemonic-device instruction with adults. In M. Pressley & J. R. Levin (Eds.), *Cognitive strategy research: Psychological foundations* (pp. 51–73). New York: Springer-Verlag.

Bellezza, F. S. (1983b). The spatial-arrangement mnemonic. *Journal of Educational Psychology, 75*, 830–837.

Bellezza, F. S. (1983c). Recalling script-based text: The role of selective processing and schematic cues. *Bulletin of the Psychonomic Society, 21*, 267–270.

Bellezza, F. S. (1984a). The self as a mnemonic device: The role of internal cues. *Journal of Personality and Social Psychology, 47*, 506–516.

Bellezza, F. S. (1984b). Reliability of retrieval from semantic memory: Noun meanings. *Bulletin of the Psychonomic Society, 22*, 377–380.

Bellezza, F. S. (1984c). Reliability of retrieval from semantic memory: Common categories. *Bulletin of the Psychonomic Society, 22*, 324–326.

Bellezza, F. S. (1986a). Mental cues and verbal reports in learning. In G. H. Bower (Ed.), *The psychology of learning and motivation* (Vol. 20, pp. 237–273). New York: Academic Press.

Bellezza, F. S. (1986b). A mnemonic based on arranging words on visual patterns. *Journal of Educational Psychology, 78*, 217–224.

Bellezza, F. S., & Bower, G. H. (1981a). Person stereotypes and memory for people. *Journal of Personality and Social Psychology, 41*, 856–865.

Bellezza, F. S., & Bower, G. H. (1981b). The representational and processing characteristics of scripts. *Bulletin of the Psychonomic Society, 18,* 1–4.

Bellezza, F. S., & Bower, G. H. (1982). Remembering script-based text. *Poetics, 11,* 1–23.

Bellezza, F. S., & Reddy, B. G. (1978). Mnemonic devices and natural memory. *Bulletin of the Psychonomic Society, 11,* 277–280.

Bellezza, F. S., Cheesman, F. L., & Reddy, B. G. (1977). Organization and semantic elaboration in free recall. *Journal of Experimental Psychology: Human Learning and Memory, 3,* 539–550.

Bellezza, F. S., Day, J. C., & Reddy, K. R. (1983). A comparison of phonetic and semantic encoding mnemonics. *Human Learning, 2,* 49–60.

Bousefield, W. A. (1953). The occurrence of clustering in the recall of randomly arranged associates. *Journal of General Psychology, 49,* 229–240.

Bower, G. H. (1972). Mental imagery and associative learning. In L. Gregg (Ed.), *Cognition in learning and memory* (pp. 51–87). New York: Wiley.

Bower, G. H., & Clark, M. C. (1969). Narrative stories as mediators for serial learning. *Psychonomic Science, 14,* 181–182.

Bower, G. H., Black, J. B., & Turner, T. J. (1979). Scripts in memory for text. *Cognitive Psychology, 11,* 177–220.

Brewer, W. F., & Treyens, J. C. (1981). Role of schemata in memory for places. *Cognitive Psychology, 13,* 207–230.

Clark, L. F., & Woll, S. B. (1981). Stereotype biases: A reconstructive analysis of their role in reconstructive memory. *Journal of Personality and Social Psychology, 41,* 1064–1072.

Day, J. C., & Bellezza, F. S. (1983). The relation between visual-imagery mediators and recall. *Memory & Cognition, 11,* 251–257.

Delprato, D. J., & Baker, E. J. (1974). Concreteness of pegwords in two mnemonic systems. *Journal of Experimental Psychology, 102,* 521–522.

Ebbinghaus, E. (1964). *Memory: A contribution to experimental psychology* (H. A. Ruger & C. E. Bussenius, Trans.). New York: Dover Books. (Original work published 1885.)

Ekstrand, B. (1966). Backward (R-S) associations. *Psychological Bulletin, 65,* 50–64.

Friedman, A. (1979). Framing pictures: The role of knowledge in automatized encoding and memory for gist. *Journal of Experimental Psychology: General, 108,* 316–355.

Graesser, A. C., Woll, S. B., Kowalski, D. J., & Smith, D. A. (1980). Memory for typical and atypical actions in scripted activities. *Journal of Experimental Psychology: Human Learning and Memory, 6,* 503–515.

Groninger, L. D., & Groninger, L. K. (1984). Autobiographical memories: Their relation to images, definitions, and word recognition. *Journal of Experimental Psychology: Learning, Memory, and Cognition, 10,* 745–755.

Hayes-Roth, B. (1977). Evaluation of cognitive structures and processes. *Psychological Review, 84,* 260–278.

Hunter, I. M. L. (1956). Mnemonic systems and devices. *Science News, 39,* 75–97.

Jenkins, J. J. (1971). Second discussant's comments: What's left to say? *Human Development, 14,* 279–286.

Jenkins, J. J. (1974). Can we have a theory of meaningful memory? In R. L. Solso (Ed.), *Theories of cognitive psychology* (pp. 1–20). Potomac, MD: Erlbaum.

Johnson, M. K., & Raye, C. L. (1981). Reality monitoring. *Psychological Review, 88,* 67–85.

Mandler, G. (1975). Memory storage and retrieval: Some limits on the reach of attention and consciousness. In P. M. A. Rabbit & S. Dornic (Eds.), *Attention and performance* (Vol. 5, pp. 499–516). New York: Academic Press.

Mandler, J. M. (1979). Categorical and schematic organization in memory. In C. R. Puff (Ed.), *Memory organization and structure* (pp. 259–299). New York: Academic Press.

Mandler, J. M. (1984). *Stories, scripts, and scenes: Aspects of schema theory.* Hillsdale, NJ: Erlbaum Associates.

Miller, G. A. (1956). Information and memory. *Scientific American, 195*(2), 42–46.

Minsky, M. (1975). A framework for representing knowledge. In P. H. Winston (Ed.), *The psychology of computer vision* (pp. 211–277). New York: McGraw-Hill.

Neisser, U. (1976). *Cognition and reality.* San Francisco: W. H. Freeman.

Norman, D. A. (1982). *Learning and memory.* San Francisco: W. H. Freeman.

Norman, D. A., & Bobrow, D. G. (1976). On the role of active memory processes in perception and cognition. In C. N. Cofer (Ed.), *The structure of human memory* (pp. 114–132). San Francisco: Freeman.

Paivio, A. (1971). *Imagery and verbal processes.* New York: Holt.

Palmer, S. E. (1975). Visual perception and world knowledge: Notes on a model of sensory-cognitive interaction. In D. A. Norman, D. E. Rumelhart, & the LNR Research Group (Eds.), *Explorations in cognition* (pp. 279–307). San Francisco: Freeman.

Pressley, M., Borkowski, J. G., & Schneider, W. (in press). Cognitive strategies: Good strategy users coordinate metacognition and knowledge. In R. Vasta & G. Whitehurst (Eds.), *Annals of Child Development* (Vol. 4). Greenwich, CT: JAI Press.

Pressley, M., Levin, J. R., & Delaney, H. D. (1982). The mnemonic keyword method. *Review of Educational Research, 52,* 61–91.

Reddy, B. G., & Bellezza, F. S. (1983). Encoding specificity in free recall. *Journal of Experimental Psychology: Learning, Memory, and Cognition, 9,* 167–174.

Reddy, B. G., & Bellezza, F. S. (1986). Interference between mnemonic and categorical organization in memory. *Bulletin of the Psychonomic Society, 24,* 169–171.

Rumelhart, D. E. (1980). Schemata: The building blocks of cognition. In R. Spiro, B. Bruce, & W. Brewer (Eds.), *Theoretical issues in reading comprehension* (pp. 33–58). Hillsdale, NJ: Erlbaum Associates.

Rumelhart, D. E., & Ortony, A. (1977). The representation of knowledge in memory. In R. C. Anderson, R. J. Spiro, & W. E. Montague (Eds.), *Schooling and the acquisition of knowledge* (pp. 99–135). Hillsdale, NJ: Erlbaum Associates.

Schank, R., & Abelson, R. (1977). *Scripts, plans, goals, and understanding.* Hillsdale, NJ: Erlbaum Associates.

Shiffrin, R. M. (1976). Capacity limitations in information processing, attention, and memory. In W. K. Estes (Ed.), *Handbook of learning and cognitive processes* (Vol. 4, pp. 177–236). Hillsdale, NJ: Erlbaum Associates.

Smith, D. A., & Graesser, A. C. (1981). Memory for actions in scripted activities as a function of typicality, retention interval, and retrieval task. *Memory & Cognition, 9,* 550–559.

Smith, S. M., Glenberg, A. M., & Bjork, R. A. (1978). Environmental context and human memory. *Memory & Cognition, 6,* 342–353.

Thorndyke, P. W., & Hayes-Roth, B. (1979). The use of schemata in the acquisition and transfer of knowledge. *Cognitive Psychology, 11,* 82–106.

Tulving, E., & Thomson, D. M. (1973). Encoding specificity and retrieval processes in episodic memory. *Psychological Review, 80,* 352–373.

Underwood, B. J., & Schulz, R. W. (1960). *Meaningfulness and verbal learning.* Philadelphia: Lippincott.

Yates, F. A. (1966). *The art of memory.* London: Routledge & Kegan Paul.

CHAPTER 3

A Theoretical Account of Encoding and Retrieval Processes in the Use of Imagery-Based Mnemonic Techniques: The Special Case of the Keyword Method

Alain Desrochers and Ian Begg

Introduction

The keyword method is a study technique devised to help people remember unfamiliar vocabulary items. The basic principle underlying this technique consists of associating the unfamiliar word with a familiar word that is physically similar to it. In this first section, we briefly examine the historical origin of the mnemonic keyword method. We have some reasons to expect this study technique to have been invented some time between the epoch of the first celebrated modern mnemonist, Raimond Lullé (1236–1315), and the end of the 19th century. Lullé and later famous mnemonists, such as Lambert Schenkel (1547–1630), were excellent public performers who strongly believed that mnemonic systems could be of practical value in the study of academic subjects. The modern history of mnemotechnics has also been guided by a concern for educational relevance, leading to successive improvements of many techniques. Indeed, many variants of the classical *method of loci* (see Lieury, 1980; Yates, 1966) were developed to facilitate the study of arithmetic, astronomy, anatomy, botany, geography, history, music, and physics.

The function of the keyword method, however, differs somewhat from that of the method of loci and its many variants, which were contrived for helping people remember the order in which relatively familiar ideas were to be recalled. Instead, the keyword method was intended to fix unfamiliar words in memory, regardless of their order in any given list. Therefore, it is primarily in the area of foreign language learning that we expected to find the first explicit description of the keyword method. In the following quote, the Rev. J. H. Bacon, then at the St. Bees College at Cumberland, England, describes the application of what he calls the *phonetic link method* to the study of French vocabulary:

I want to connect in my mind *arbre* with *tree* in such a way that when one is mentioned the other will immediately spring up. *Arbre* is an unfamiliar idea, it is a mere sound to me beyond which I know nothing about it; and it is to be associated with the familiar idea *tree*, about which I know many things. I must then distinctly give utterance to the *sound*, which is the only thing I know about it; and I must ask myself is there any English word with which I am familiar suggested by this sound? O yes; there is the word *arbour* that is a familiar idea to me, very familiar indeed; it is at the end of our garden. It is shaded by an overspreading *tree*. Here, then, I have changed an unfamiliar idea into a familiar one, which is to be associated with *tree*. The mental process, then, is (Arbre) *arbour-tree*, which are to be placed simultaneously before the mind (1862, Part I, pp. 47–48).*

Compare this description with that provided by Richard C. Atkinson some 113 years later:

By a keyword we mean an English word that sounds like some part of the foreign word. In general, the keyword has no relationship to the foreign word except for the fact that it is similar in sound. The keyword method divides vocabulary learning into two stages. The first stage requires the subject to associate the spoken foreign word with the keyword, an association that is formed quickly because of acoustic similarity. The second stage requires the subject to form a mental image of the keyword "interacting" with the English translation; this stage is comparable to a paired-associate procedure involving the learning of unrelated English words. (1975, p. 821)

Despite stylistic differences, the two descriptions emphasize the same two basic cognitive operations: (a) the formation of an acoustic link between the sound characteristics of the foreign word and those of a familiar word, and (b) the formation of a semantic link between the referent of the foreign word and that of the familiar word. It is clear, therefore, that the current keyword method is nothing but Bacon's phonetic link method with a new identity.

The keyword method is, apparently, a newer development than the method of loci, which originated in antiquity. Admittedly, we do not know the exact origin of the keyword method because many relevant documents that predate the 19th century are no longer readily available for scrutiny. However, in Fenaigle's (1813) *New Art of Memory*, probably the most complete account of previous mnemonic systems, a whole chapter (Chapter V) is devoted to the learning of foreign languages without a single description of the keyword method. This chapter focuses almost exclusively on the use of familiar cognates for memorizing new foreign words. For instance, it is shown how familiarity with Latin words and some basic transformational rules can facilitate the acquisition of French words (e.g., L. *frater* → Fr. frère "brother"). One central ingredient of the method described by Bacon and Atkinson is the association of an unfamiliar word form with a familiar one. This principle is well described and documented in Fenaigle's comprehensive account. What remains uncertain is when and by whom the second ingredient of the keyword method, the semantic link between the two concepts, was introduced.

---

*Although the word *arbour* is related to the Latin *arbor* "tree," it is used here in the sense of bower or shady retreat closed in or overarched with branches, shrubs, or other plants; thus it is intended to represent a distinct concept, not a mere cognate. Equally explicit descriptions of the keyword method can also be found in more recent books on mnemonic techniques such as Sayer's (1877, p. 9) and Yule's (1886, pp. 66–67).

The febrile activities of the many promoters of mnemonic systems have, of course, caught the attention of psychologists (cf. Burnham, 1888; Julliot, 1919) and critics (for an informative consumer's report on 19th century mnemonics, see Middleton, 1887). However, the fate of the keyword method and other systems in the early 20th century was quite similar to that of mental images; they were both regarded as very marginal areas of interest. There was occasional reference to the usefulness of the keyword method (e.g., Estabrooks, 1927) but it was not until the 1970s that psychologists began to show a genuine interest in studying it experimentally. The first experimental assessment of the method's effectiveness was reported by Ott, Butler, Blake, and Ball (1973), soon to be followed by the influential studies of Atkinson and Raugh (1975; Raugh & Atkinson, 1975; Raugh, Schupbach, & Atkinson, 1977). The diversity of empirical studies bearing on aspects of the keyword method is now quite remarkable (for reviews, see Levin & Pressley, 1985; Paivio & Desrochers, 1981; Pressley, Levin, & Delaney, 1982; Pressley, Levin, & McDaniel, in press).

Recent interest in mnemonic techniques has been part of the more general growth of cognitive psychology, following the appearance of such influential works as Miller, Galanter, and Pribram's *Plans and the Structure of Behavior* (1960) and Neisser's *Cognitive Psychology* (1967), as well as the more specific interest in mental imagery as championed by Paivio (1971). Our plan in this chapter is to develop a memory-theoretic perspective from which to understand how the keyword method helps people learn items from foreign vocabularies. The perspective we have chosen is the *organization–redintegration hypothesis*, an account that has successfully been applied to memory for pairs of words (cf. Begg, 1972, 1973, 1978a, 1978b, 1982; Begg & Sikich, 1984; Begg & White, 1985; Begg & Young, 1977; Desrochers, 1982, 1983).

We now outline the hypothesis in general terms, leaving some details for later sections. Like most other accounts, the organization–redintegration hypothesis focuses on (a) the content of the memory system after some material has been studied, and (b) the way that content is recovered and used in different retrieval environments. The content of the memory system is assumed to be some number of units or traces (cf. Mandler, 1967; Tulving, 1968, 1983). Each unit is a set of information that pertains to one or more studied items. The number of units and the number of items each represents depend on how the items were studied. If, for example, pairs of items are studied in meaningful interaction, each trace will refer to two items. Thus the content of the memory system is the memorial record of how events were interpreted in the course of initial processing (cf. Craik & Lockhart, 1972).

Memory performance requires that the remembered traces be recovered and used in some task environment. The process of retrieval is a sequence of stages (cf. Martin, 1967; Einstein & Hunt, 1980). The two major stages are access and use. A particular trace is accessed if information in the retrieval environment adequately discriminates that trace; because each trace is assumed to be unitary, access is *redintegrative*, meaning that access with any part of a trace makes the entire informational content of the trace available for use. The trace can be used to meet the requirements of the test only if the accessed information is appropriate for the test (cf. Begg, 1976; McDaniel & Kearney, 1984; Morris, Bransford, & Franks, 1977; Tversky, 1973).

By this account, therefore, memorial success occurs if the retrieval environment makes access with a trace and if the discriminations allowed by the trace meet the requirements of the task at hand. Although the traces cannot be used if they are not accessed, the factors that govern access are independent of the factors that govern usefulness. Access depends on the degree of distinctive similarity (Begg, 1978a) between the test cue and the appropriate trace; the extent to which that trace specifically refers to a particular item is referred to as item-specific information. Redintegration of information beyond the item-specific information that has enabled access depends on how the item has been organized initially with other information; the quality of the organizational bond between items is referred to as relational information. The assumption that item-specific information and relational information are independent (Begg, 1982; Einstein & Hunt, 1980; Humphreys, 1978; Hunt & Einstein, 1981) means that, for example, a railroad imagined alone is no more or less adequately represented than it would be if it was imagined in interaction with a horse—a railroad is a railroad is a railroad.

Thus the theoretical account directs us to contrast initial interpretive processes that separately influence the distinctive item-specific information that governs access with remembered traces, and the organizational processes that relate items so that later access with one also provides access with associated information. The account further directs us to consider the factors in retrieval that govern whether or not existing traces can be recovered and used effectively. With these foci in mind, we present the remainder of the chapter in five major parts. We first consider some reasons that make it difficult to learn foreign vocabulary. Second, we elaborate the concept of a memorial trace. The next two sections respectively elaborate the encoding processes and retrieval processes by which unfamiliar meanings and word forms are learned. Finally, we apply the theoretical account to the question of what makes keywords effective.

Sources of Difficulty in Learning Foreign Vocabulary

Acquiring a large vocabulary, either in one's mother tongue or in other languages, is a most challenging memory exercise. It is difficult because we must remember a large number of linguistic units to be able to understand a language and to speak it. It is also difficult because there are many categories (e.g., relative to syntax, semantics, or social register) to which a linguistic unit can belong. That linguistic units are dual in nature is not a new idea. Saussure (1916) aptly captured it in the distinction he made between the terms *sound pattern* (image acoustique) and *concept*. The sound pattern is an abstraction of actual speech sounds. For example, different speakers pronounce "dog" in somewhat different ways, but we treat these physical occurrences as if they were equivalent. Similarly, the concept is an abstraction of actual objects denoted by a given sound signal. People may indeed mean slightly different things by the word "dog," but there is some aspect of that meaning that makes it distinguishable from other meanings. According to Saussure, it is from the linkage between a sound pattern and a concept that a linguistic sign emerges.

In learning a foreign vocabulary, the study of each of these two components may cause problems of different sorts. All methods of vocabulary acquisition, such as the keyword method, are intended to overcome at least some of them. We shall first discuss various sources of difficulty in learning the meanings of foreign words, and some of the procedures that have been used to measure semantic knowledge in keyword studies. We shall then turn to the factors that affect the learning of foreign word sound patterns and related orthographic representations.

How can we best capture the meaning of a foreign word? The most common answer is to find a translation equivalent in one's native language (e.g., Atkinson & Raugh, 1975; Delaney, 1978; Pressley, Levin, Hall, Miller, & Berry, 1980). In the second stage of the keyword method, as described by Atkinson, learners form an interactive image relating the referent of the familiar translation equivalent and the referent of the keyword. Although the construction of this sort of composite mental structure is hard for young children (see Levin, 1976; Pressley, 1977a; Rohwer, 1973), the difficulty can be overcome. In an ingenious adaptation of the keyword method, Pressley (1977b) and Pressley and Levin (1978) used line drawings of separate referents or of interacting referents to convey the meaning of the vocabulary items.

In some ways, rare words in our own language are foreign to us, and they too need familiar definitions. An example used by Pressley, Levin, and Miller (1981a) is the English word *dogger* which is defined as a "fishing boat" and accompanied by the keyword "dog." The point in each of these various ways of conveying unfamiliar word meanings is that it is not the target meaning that is unfamiliar but only the new word form. The tacit message delivered to the learners is that the meaning of the unfamiliar term is identical to that of its familiar translation equivalent, its picture, or its verbal definition. Strictly speaking, exact equivalents are rare, if they can be found at all. The assumption of semantic equivalence can result in many naming errors in real-life communication. Consider the following example. The class of spherical referents labeled "ball" in English is divided into two distinct categories in French; the spherical objects that can easily be caught with one hand (e.g., baseball) are labeled *balle*, whereas those ordinarily caught with two hands (e.g., basketball) are called *ballon*. If students were to associate the French word *balle* with the English "ball," they would in effect be linking the French word with an English meaning. In order to claim that a study technique is successful at conveying the meaning of unfamiliar words one should be able to demonstrate that learners can identify successfully the objects referred to by the vocabulary item, not just the translation equivalent. This is admittedly a tall order, and probably an unrealistic one. Our intent is not to criticize the keyword method, but to point out the limitations of translation equivalents, definitions, or pictures as means to capture the meaning of an unfamiliar word. The correct use of a particular word in a foreign language is clearly not a simple exercise, and it represents a serious challenge for *all* methods of vocabulary learning. These media, however imperfect they may be, remain the most commonly available and practical means of delineating the approximate signification of a foreign word, even though the semantic fine tuning may be possible only through extensive use in the relevant language community (for a discussion of this issue, see d'Anglejan, 1978).

Let us agree that an understanding of approximate signification is already a large step toward the mastery of a vocabulary item. The next step is to consolidate the link between the new word form and its assigned meaning. This link, as Saussure points out, is arbitrary in the sense that it is not motivated by any natural connection in reality. Nevertheless, language students must learn to respond meaningfully to the new vocabulary item.

The most common method of assessing whether the meanings of unfamiliar words have been learned is to measure the recall of their translation equivalents or of their dictionary-like definitions. However, some recent and innovative attempts to examine other aspects of meaning acquisition must be noted. For instance, Pressley et al. (1981a) had English-speaking university students learn the meaning of rare English words (e.g., hamate, ramekin) and then presented them with sentences in which the vocabulary items were used either correctly or incorrectly. The respondents were to decide whether or not the sentences made sense. In other experiments, subjects were asked to place the studied items in the blanks in a provided text, or to construct a list of novel sentences that contained the studied items. We must welcome the increasing diversity of these measures because they direct us to investigate new and more relevant aspects of semantic knowledge.

In contrast, however, very few methods have been investigated for assessing the learners' knowledge of foreign word forms. In previous research, the foreign word response had to be either pronounced (e.g., Pressley, Levin, Hall, Miller, & Berry, 1980) or written (e.g., Pressley & Levin, 1981). In these applications it would be incorrect to assume that every aspect of the responses was equally unfamiliar to the learners. The smallest phonological unit that is relevant here is the feature, which roughly maps onto the independent gestures of the articulators. Extant data suggest that there are no more than three or four dozen of these features that play distinctive roles in human speech (cf. Wang, 1971). A difficulty for a language learner is presented by features that are not exploited in the native speech system. For example, the contrast between /u/ and /y/ allows French speakers to differentiate between utterances of *au-dessous* "below" and *au-dessus* "above." However, because this contrast is not exploited in English, students of French as a second language must (a) engage in a subtle form of perceptual learning before they can identify the unfamiliar features, and (b) engage in a subtle form of motor learning before they can reproduce the unfamiliar features they now can detect. Because the keyword method is designed to use familiar features that are found both in the foreign words and the familiar words, no one will dispute that the method in and of itself may be insufficient to memorize a vocabulary item that contains unfamiliar articulatory features. It remains, however, that many languages share many features and that the keyword method is intended to take advantage of these commonalities.

A similar argument can be made about the acquisition of written forms. In all the studies reported by Atkinson, Pressley, Levin, and their collaborators, the foreign words were selected from languages that used the Roman alphabet in their scripts. The basic orthographic units or frames were, therefore, quite familiar to the learners. Subjects were never confronted with a foreign script that contained symbols of a syllabary, or logographs. The difficulty would have been especially great if the foreign scripts contained frames that moved within rows from right to left or vertically in columns. Thus, it is not so much at this level that the foreign word forms used in previous research were unfamiliar to the learners; the difficulty the learners faced arises from the ways different languages combine generally familiar articulatory features or orthographic frames.

These sources of difficulty are compounded with another one of at least equal magnitude, namely, the introduction of new rules of correspondence between familiar orthographic frames and phonemes. All scripts based on an alphabetic writing system, unlike those based on a purely logographic system, are intended to reflect the pronunciation of language units. Each language that use the Roman alphabet in its script, for example, can be characterized by a more or less parsimonious set of rules of correspondence between graphemes and phonemes. Because the correspondence rules may differ between the familiar language and a foreign language that share the same writing system, language students may also have to learn how a new utterance is to be represented in writing and how a new occurrence of a written word is to be pronounced.

The Units of Memory

The central concept of the organization–redintegration hypothesis is the memory trace. In later sections we consider the encoding processes that determine the traces, and retrieval processes that govern the use of traces. In the present section we shall characterize the units of memory as being memory traces, each of which is a set of information pertinent to one or more studied items. Traces may themselves be organized in higher order units or chunks (e.g., Mandler, 1967; Miller, 1956), but our interest here is in the properties of traces themselves. The information that comprises a trace may be of many different sorts, including mental images, verbal associations, and affective reactions, depending on how the studied material has been processed. Each piece of information, regardless of its sort, enables some degree of discrimination of the trace and permits some degree of expression, perhaps in speech, drawing, or imagination.

Put most simply, a trace is the result of interpreting an item. More precisely, the interpretive process makes some physical event, in some cognitive context, a unique cognitive event; that event can be called a percept, a meaning, or a memory trace, depending on our interests. Thus the trace is whatever set of evidence regarding a prior occurrence exists in the cognitive system. The important question, however, is not what a trace is, but what it does. The value of a trace, like the value of any set of information, is defined by the discriminations it enables. If the end use can be met by the information, the information has actual value; otherwise it does not. In sum, the contents of memory traces are entirely dependent upon initial processing, and the potential value of a trace is entirely determined by its contents; actual value depends on whether the task for the trace is within the scope of its potential value.

The information in memory traces serves two primary functions, namely, to identify items and to relate items within traces. Item-specific information is the information that identifies specific items; at the extreme, an item could be discriminated in any possible context if the item-specific information is detailed enough. Relational information is the information that binds items together; at the extreme, access with one item guarantees access with other items from the same trace. Others have made the same distinction (e.g., Einstein & Hunt, 1980; Humphreys, 1978; Hunt & Einstein, 1981). The important point to keep in mind about the present conception is that information is a discriminative value (cf. Miller, 1953), not a positive entity; information cannot be seen as pieces of knowledge, but rather as results of discriminations. "Alcoholic beverage" does not discriminate "beer" from "wine" but distinguishes either from any nonbeverage, or any nonalcoholic beverage. Thus a focus on information *is* a focus on function, that is, what the traces can let us do.

Learning Unfamiliar Word Meanings

In the typical application of the keyword method the learner is presented with sets of three items. Each set contains a foreign word, its translation equivalent in the familiar language, and a keyword that sounds like or looks like the foreign word. These three words may be presented on an index card, a slide, or a video monitor. Consider the following hypothetical display:

HÖCKER (BUMP)

/HOCKEY/

In this example, the English word "bump" is the translation equivalent of the German word *Höcker* and "hockey" as a keyword for the new vocabulary item. The keyword in this display is positioned so as to emphasize its physical similarity with the foreign item, and selected so as to permit the construction of a meaningful and coherent interactive mental image (e.g., "A hockey player with a bump on his head"). In a typical experiment, a list of 10 to 40 such sets may be presented at a rate of 10 to 20 sec per set in a single session. The unfamiliar vocabulary word may then be used as a cue for the recall of the translation equivalent in the familiar language, or as a response to be produced by the learner when cued by the familiar translation equivalent. We now consider the use of the foreign term as a cue, and return to its use as a response in a later section.

The keyword method has been found to be an effective way to learn to recall the familiar translation equivalent when subjects are cued by the foreign item. This result has been obtained with learners of different age groups and of different levels of aptitude for language learning. The advantage of the keyword method has appeared in comparison with various control conditions (e.g., when subjects were left to their own devices) and with other study methods. The parametric variations that have been investigated are so numerous that we cannot possibly describe them here (for reviews, see Levin & Pressley, 1985; Paivio & Desrochers, 1981; Pressley et al., 1982, in press).

Encoding

The use of the keyword methods includes two broad procedural steps. The learners first must note the physical similarity between the foreign word and the selected keyword. They then are required to form a mental image in which the referent of the keyword and that of the foreign word (as conveyed by the native language translation) are engaged in some sort of meaningful interaction. These cognitive operations have similar consequences for the encoding process, even though they result in the formation of two distinguishable memory traces.

By the present account, the perception of the physical similarity between the foreign word and the keyword increases the probability that these two items will form a unitary memory trace. This interpretive process then serves to increase the size of the memory trace in the sense that the average trace represents more studied events. The construction of a composite structure by mental imagery also increases the probability that the cognitive representation of the keyword referent and that of the foreign word referent will form a unitary memory trace. The assumption that each of these two procedural steps results in the formation of distinct memory traces is supported by the fact that learning the physical link between the foreign word and the keyword is necessary but not sufficient for the formation of a semantic link between the keyword and the familiar translation equivalent (e.g., Pressley, 1977b; Sweeney & Bellezza, 1982). Nevertheless, the primary function of each step is to reduce the number of memory traces to be formed, and to relate items within those traces. The extent to which each trace can be discriminated from other traces hinges on the quality of item-specific information, and the amount of additional information that becomes available upon contact hinges on the quality of relational information within the contacted traces.

The organization–redintegration hypothesis predicts that relational information encoded by judging physical similarity and by interactive imagery will benefit memory performance that depends on interitem association. The effects of relational information encoded by these two kinds of interpretive processes, however, have received more attention in the general context of memory research than in keyword studies. The role of similarity judgments has been investigated, at least indirectly, in relation to the redintegrative power of word fragments in recall tasks. In several experiments (e.g., Horowitz, Chilian, & Dunnigan, 1969;

Horowitz, White, & Atwood, 1968; Loess & Brown, 1969), subjects were presented with lists of items and then cued for their recall by a fragment of the original items. The main finding was that recall varied according to the position of the fragment within the word; recall was significantly better if the fragments overlapped with the very first syllable or cluster of the item than with the middle or last parts.

The role of relational information has been investigated in numerous studies that compared the effect of interactive and separate imagery on associative memory. The typical finding is that cued recall is far better after interactive imagery than separate imagery instructions (e.g., Begg, 1973, 1978b, 1979, 1983; Begg & Anderson, 1976; Begg & Young, 1977; Bower, 1970; Dempster & Rohwer, 1974; Winograd & Lynn, 1979). Similar results have also been reported in a recent keyword study in which subjects were required to recall two pieces of information but were told how to link only one of them to the keyword referent in the composite image; recall of the nonincluded piece of information was similar to that of control subjects left to their own devices, whereas the recall of included items greatly benefited from keyword instructions (Wieland & Desrochers, 1985). In each of these experiments, interactive imagery instructions are assumed to have resulted in the formation of fewer but larger memory traces.

The organization–redintegration hypothesis also assumes that relational information is independent of information that enables item discrimination. The mere fact that items are encoded interactively does not provide any information about the likelihood that those traces will be successfully accessed. In the memory literature, the general finding is that, despite some discrepancies, interactive imagery and separate imagery do not differ in the number of words recalled in free recall (Begg, 1973, 1978b; Begg & Anderson, 1976; Hasher, Riebman, & Wren, 1976; Janssen, 1976), nor in the likelihood of word recognition (Begg, 1978b; Bower, 1970). However, interactive imagery facilitates recognition relative to a rote rehearsal control procedure (Dempster & Rohwer, 1974), which suggests that imagery enhances the distinctiveness of memory traces. In keyword studies, the advantage of interactive imagery over nonassociative and nonimagery control conditions (e.g., Pressley, Levin, Kuiper, Bryant, & Michener, 1982; Pressley, Levin, & Miller, 1982) also reflects the contributions of both enhanced relational and item information in the memory trace.

Retrieval

According to the organization–redintegration hypothesis, retrieval is a staged process. The first stage, *trace contact*, entails discrimination of a trace. The second stage, *trace use*, entails redintegration of the compound trace, making its informational content available. Finally, the third stage, *trace decoding*, consists of translating mental information into overt responses.

In the use of the keyword method for the recall of a foreign word's meaning, these three stages are applied recursively. When the foreign word is presented as a retrieval cue for the recall of the keyword, the learner must identify the relevant fragment in the foreign word that maps onto the keyword. Once this identification is completed, the keyword may be redintegrated with some probability and decoded from the trace content. Let us emphasize here that the effectiveness of the foreign word for the recall of the keyword is a crucial variable in the success of this study technique. Sweeney and Bellezza (1982) have clearly shown that the probability of recalling the meaning of an unfamiliar item is very small (less than .10) if the keyword has not previously been redintegrated and decoded. We shall return to the variables that may influence the linkage between the foreign word and the keyword in a later section.

The keyword serves in the discrimination of a particular interpretation of its meaning, which may be followed by the redintegration of the appropriate composite image. The learner then faces the problem of discriminating the target item from the composite structure. By the present account, the functional value of relational and item information in target identification is determined by the specificity of the initial interpretation. This specificity of interpretation could entail the consideration of particular aspects of the target that would make it the focal point of the relational set represented in the memory trace (cf. Miller & Geiselman, 1979). The result of this interpretive process would be to enhance the convergence toward the target from any discriminative cue in the trace. Once the target is determined, an overt response may occur.

Learning Unfamiliar Word Forms

We now turn to a more challenging application of the mnemonic keyword method. This method has often been found to help recall of the familiar translation equivalent if the foreign term is used as a cue. However, is the same finding obtained if the familiar translation equivalent is used as a cue for the recall of the unfamiliar foreign word? The latter task is evidently more difficult than the former one, because the learner now faces the challenge of having to learn to produce a new overt response. Although the problem of learning unfamiliar responses received a great deal of attention in studies of verbal learning (e.g., Horowitz & Gordon, 1972; Prytulak, 1971; Underwood & Erlebacher, 1965; Underwood & Schulz, 1960), Pressley, Levin, Hall, Miller, and Berry (1980) were the first researchers to investigate it systematically in the context of the keyword method. Because their experiments are particularly informative we shall describe them in some detail.

In their first experiment, subjects given different encoding instructions were asked to study a list of French and Spanish words. They were then provided with the English translation equivalents and asked to try to recall the foreign terms. The recall protocols were scored in various ways so as to localize more precisely the effect of keyword instructions. When the scoring criterion was perfect recall of the whole word or perfect recall except for one letter, the performance of keyword subjects was quite low (an average of 12%) and it did not differ significantly from that of subjects left to their own devices. However, when the protocols were scored for correct recall of the *keyword fragments*, keyword subjects outperformed the subjects in the control groups. In a second experiment, the keyword condition was compared with a no-strategy control condition on an associative recognition test. This test consisted of presenting subjects with the familiar translation equivalents and having them choose the foreign equivalents from a list that contained each original foreign word paired with a foreign word distractor that shared the same keyword fragment. Once again, the recognition level of keyword subjects did not differ significantly from that of the subjects left to their own devices. However, the keyword subjects selected more pair-mate distractors than the control subjects (19.4% vs. 6.4%, respectively). In a subsequent experiment, keyword subjects and no–strategy control subjects were given four study–test trials in which foreign words had to be produced in response to their English equivalents. By the fourth test trial, a recall difference in favor of the keyword condition began to appear, suggesting that the keyword method may indeed facilitate the acquisition of unfamiliar word forms if there is sufficient opportunity for study.

Pressley and Levin (1981) examined the possibility that the difficulty in learning new word forms could be attributed to the unfamiliar orthographic rules that characterized the foreign words in previous experiments. They reasoned that "if this were the primary source of the problem then if subjects learned unfamiliar English words, with their more predictable morphological constraints, their backward recall might be enhanced by keyword instructions, even though the method was ineffective with respect to backward recall of the foreign words (pp. 72–73)." In their first experiment, keyword subjects and no–strategy control subjects studied a list of very rare English words (e.g., *carlin* "old woman"; *poteen* "Irish whiskey") and were cued with the definition for the recall of the unfamiliar word forms. With a criterion of perfect recall of the whole word or perfect recall except for one letter, the performance of the two groups did not differ significantly. Recall of the keyword fragments, however, was better in the keyword condition than in the control condition. These results closely replicate those obtained with items selected from foreign languages. In another experiment, subjects were taught the form of the unfamiliar English nouns before they were taught their meaning. In the first phase, they learned to recall each word perfectly when cued with the first syllable. In the second phase, keyword and control subjects were instructed to learn the definitions in exactly the same way as in the first experiment. This time, recall of the whole word or of the whole word except for one letter was clearly superior in the keyword condition than in the no–strategy control condition. Thus, it appears that the keyword method permits the formation of effective links from the familiar translation or definition to the keyword but mere access with the keyword fragment is insufficient for the reproduction of the whole unfamiliar item, unless it has been learned previously. We now turn to the difficult problem of encoding an unfamiliar word form.

Encoding

The encoding of an unfamiliar word form again is an interpretive process. We are not concerned here with the perceptual end of the process. Once an iconic or echoic representation is formed, the cognitive system is assumed to attempt to interpret the whole word. This interpretation is possible if the whole word permits the discrimination of a permanent trace in long-term memory. If no such trace is found, as would be the case with an unfamiliar word form, the learners will attempt to render the novel event more meaningful. One way, and perhaps the most important one, of achieving this goal is to transform the representation of the stimulus so as to increase its physical similarity with an event that is already very familiar, such as another word. This general strategy has been dubbed *natural language mediation* in the memory literature (cf. Montague, Adams, & Kiess, 1966; Paivio, 1971; Prytulak, 1971). The cognitive transformations allow the learner to relate the unfamiliar form to a well-integrated unit in memory. The cognitive record of this similarity judgment may then help the learner bind the individual letters or phonemes of the foreign word and preserve their order. The function of the keyword is precisely to induce a more meaningful interpretation of the unfamiliar word form by relating it to a familiar and unitized word form. Thus, by the present account, a whole unfamiliar word form cannot be encoded readily as a unitary trace unless its constituent units are integrated. Subsequent recall of the whole word should be determined by the degree of unitization achieved during the encoding process.

The ideal keyword is obviously one that requires the minimum number of transformations of the foreign word to permit its reconstruction. In practice, however, the range of possible keywords is necessarily limited by the lexical stock of the familiar language. Thus, even the best keyword for a particular vocabulary item may be quite far from ideal. Actual keywords usually overlap only with some adjacent letters (as *bet* or *rug* in the German *Betrug*) or only with some nonadjacent letters in the foreign word (as *duchess* in the German *Durchmesser*); they may also contain phonological or orthographic elements that are not present in the foreign word (as *bowl* for the German *Bohle*). The quality of the overlap may vary greatly among the keywords selected for a vocabulary list. Moreover, this variation may influence the degree of unitization attributable to the mediating keywords. Because of the partial mapping between the keyword and the foreign word, the unitization of the foreign word is unlikely to be immediate and complete. How learners compensate for this insufficient unitization is still poorly understood. It seems reasonable to assume, however, that good learners try to minimize the number of units to hold in memory by optimizing the unitization of the materials to be learned.

The mediational role of the keyword may involve, at least in the short run, a cost-effectiveness tradeoff for the foreign vocabulary learners. On the positive side, the keyword may provide a very efficient means to bind some parts of the foreign word, which would result in storage economy in the sense that fewer traces would be necessary to represent the whole vocabulary item. On the negative side, the information that relates the unfamiliar word form to a native language word may interfere with the correct pronunciation or spelling of the foreign word. The degree of interference is expected to increase inversely with the similarity of the phonological and orthographic characteristics between the two languages. This hypothesis derives from the assumption that the physical shape of the foreign word now provides access to a memory trace that permits the discrimination of its keyword and the use of its related phonological and orthographic information. Although this problem has not received much attention there is some empirical evidence that imperfect orthographic mapping between the keyword fragment and the foreign word can increase the number of spelling errors in the reproduction of the foreign item (see Pressley, Levin, Nakamura, Hope, Bispo, & Toye, 1980). It must be remembered, however, that all studied foreign words will become cognitively related with other foreign words as the speaker progressively reaches new levels of fluency. Consequently, the potential detrimental effects of the mediational keyword likely are quite transitory.

Retrieval

The three stages of trace contact, trace use, and trace decoding again are applied recursively until an overt response is expressed or until one operation fails. When a translation equivalent, a definition, or a pictorial representation is provided as a retrieval cue for the recall of an unfamiliar word form, the learner must first remember the earlier interpretation of its meaning. The discrimination of this particular interpretation may be followed by the redintegration of the appropriate composite image, which likely contains more information than just a representation of the foreign word referent and of the keyword referent. The part of the image that represents the keyword must then be identified, and this process is assumed to depend on how specifically the keyword was interpreted in the encoding context. Once the target is identified, it may be decoded into the correct keyword.

The learner then must identify the relevant fragment of the keyword structure that can serve as a cue for the recall of the unfamiliar word form. This operation is assumed to depend on item-specific information, whereas the redintegration of a part of or the whole foreign word depends on relational information. The memorial consequences of the partial unitization attributable to the mediational keyword are shown in the superior recall of the foreign word fragment that maps onto the keyword (see Pressley, Levin, Hall, Miller, & Berry, 1980; Pressley & Levin, 1981).

What Are the Ingredients of an Effective Keyword?

It has been shown on several occasions that some keywords are more effective than others in the recall of familiar translation equivalents (cf. Atkinson & Raugh, 1975; Raugh & Atkinson, 1975). These observations led Atkinson (1975) to conclude that:

From a practical viewpoint, the important remark is that keywords should be selected using empirical criteria. When there is not enough time to make empirical determinations, a committee of individuals familiar with the language should select the keywords rather than having one person make the decisions. Experience indicates that individual experimenters can come up with some pretty bizarre keywords that work for them but for no one else. A committee approach seems to protect against this problem. (p. 826)

Desrochers, Wieland, and Butler (1984) also suggested that the selection be done in two phases. First, one should list as many candidates as possible; this operation can be done by one or two individuals equipped with a good dictionary and a great deal of patience. In the second phase, a committee may assess each candidate according to criteria that are known to affect learning. The problem encountered in the second phase is, of course, the identification of these criteria. We now consider and speculate on what might be the key ingredients of an effective keyword. The discussion will be guided largely by the theoretical perspective presented in earlier sections of this chapter. Two classes of ingredients are considered, namely, characteristics that pertain to the physical form of the keyword and characteristics that pertain to its meaning.

Physical Characteristics of Keywords

We shall discuss two physical characteristics of the keyword and indicate why they may be important in determining its effectiveness; we shall also examine some of the factors that may restrict the choices of optimal keywords. The first variable is the extent to which the keyword resembles the foreign word. Intuitively, it seems that the link between the German noun *Blüte* with the English "brute" would be easier than with the English "blood." The extent of overlap between a keyword and an unfamiliar word form refers to the number and kinds of cognitive transformations of the keyword that are necessary to reconstruct the foreign form. The better keywords are those that require simpler and fewer transformations. Although this problem has not received a great deal of attention, Prytulak (1971) offers a preliminary classification of possible transformations which could provide some initial direction for future investigations.

The second variable is the position of the overlapping fragment in the keyword and in the foreign word. Extant data indicate that redintegration is best if the word fragment overlaps with the very first part or cluster of the item to be recalled (cf. Horowitz et al., 1968, 1969; Loess & Brown, 1969). If this factor also matters in the application of the keyword method, the keyword "boots" would be expected to be recalled with a greater probability than the keyword "shaft" from the German *Botschafter*. To our knowledge, the redintegrative power of word fragments has not been investigated in the context of the keyword method even though it appears to be a central feature of effective keywords, as a cue for the recall of the foreign word or as a response to the foreign word cue.

Identifying the optimal physical ingredients of keywords is one thing, but dealing with the factors that depress the upper bound of desired optimality is quite another. For many common foreign words it may be difficult to find a keyword that will overlap closely with the first cluster. Judge for yourself and try to find an acceptable keyword for following German nouns: *Abhilfe, Bleiarbeiter, Durchschlag*, and *Geschluchze*. If you try hard enough you may find some potentially useful keywords for these foreign terms. But you will readily appreciate how much easier it is to find English keywords for this second set of German nouns: *Blech*, *Böttcher*, *Decke*, *Flitter*, *Gardine*, and *Hammelfleisch*. The way the combinatorics of phonological features or graphic frames is exploited in a particular foreign language may impose severe constraints on the set of potentially effective keywords that can be generated. It is, therefore, possible that no single effective keyword can be found for many members of a foreign vocabulary. This limitation would be quite serious if we expected the keyword method to solve all vocabulary problems, but we do not. Language learning is a multifaceted exercise, and it would be quite naive to expect a single method to be comprehensive.

Another set of constraints may come from the semantic characteristics of the keyword in interaction with the meaning of the foreign word. In some extreme cases, a choice may have to be made between a keyword that provides a superior overlap with the foreign word and a keyword that permits the construction of a more meaningful interactive image. For example, the German *Querbalken*, meaning "crossbar," may be easier to link conceptually to the keyword "balcony" than to "quebracho," "queen," "quercetin," or "query." We shall now discuss the problem of semantic factors in more detail.

Semantic Characteristics of Effective Keywords

Two semantic factors that may influence the effectiveness of a keyword are its imagery value and the extent to which it permits the construction of a coherent mental structure. It has often been shown that high-imagery items are more effective retrieval cues and are more easily recalled responses in associative learning (cf. Bower, 1972; Denis, 1979; Paivio, 1965); similar effects have also been reported in second-language vocabulary learning (cf. Delaney, 1978; Paivio & Desrochers, 1979; Pressley, Levin, & Miller, 1981b). In the application of the keyword method, whether an unfamiliar word form is used as a retrieval cue or is expected to be produced as a response, the keyword's meaning plays an important mediational role that rests largely on the relational information that links it to other meanings. By the present account, high-imagery keywords are characterized by their effect on the learner and, more specifically, by their capacity to evoke a wide range of context-specific interpretations. This versatility allows the individual to represent the keyword referent and the foreign word referent in a composite image that uniquely specifies their interrelations.

Another factor is the extent to which the studied items permit the construction of a coherent interactive image. Throughout this chapter, we have treated mental images as composite structures of cognitive units. This composite structure is based on coherence relations among its constituent units, and any particular set of coherence relations necessarily implies a particular interpretation of the meaning of each one of the represented events. Because learners' interpretations of a word's meaning are influenced by their knowledge and their beliefs, large individual differences are expected in their ability to construct coherence relations between the meaning of a foreign word and that of its selected keyword. For example, it is quite possible that some individuals will find it easy to construct an interactive image of the pair ANCHOR–DONUT, but others will find it nearly impossible. Note that bizarre images need not be incoherent. Bizarre images are composite structures that include an infrequent or a restricted set of relations. A relational set may be unusual because it departs from daily experiences (e.g., An insurance salesman who also sells vegetables); it may also be restricted because some "real-world" constraints are removed from the thematic coherence of the structure (e.g., A chimpanzee who drives a bus in the Nation's capital). The importance of world knowledge has been addressed in the context of conceptual development (cf. Murphy & Medin, 1985) and language comprehension (cf. Rumelhart, 1980). Insofar as it can determine the success of the construction of interactive images and, thereby, keyword effectiveness, learners' knowledge of the world also deserves special attention. The effects of item imagery value and of potential coherence relations are undoubtedly linked to the frequency of specific experiences with various events. Several measures that are sensitive to the frequency of these events may also be related to keyword effectiveness. The most obvious examples are the frequency of use and familiarity of keywords in the familiar language (for a discussion of these factors, see Gernsbacher, 1983, 1984).

Summary and Conclusion

Our primary purpose in this chapter was to develop a theoretical framework from which to explain how and in what circumstances the keyword method helps people learn items from foreign vocabularies. This account, which derives from the organization–redintegration hypothesis, provides many heuristic concepts for discussing the effectiveness of the keyword method as well as other imagery-based study techniques. Special attention is paid to (a) the content of the memory system after some material has been studied, and (b) the way that content is recovered and used in different retrieval environments. The content of the memory system is assumed to be traces, each of which results from the interpretation of a physical event in a cognitive context. The information in the traces identifies specific items and relates items within traces. The process of retrieval is a sequence of three stages that can be applied recursively: trace access, trace use, and trace decoding. Actual access with a trace depends on the specificity of encoded item information and on the capacity of some cue in the retrieval environment to discriminate that particular trace. This stage may be followed by the redintegration of the compound trace, making its entire informational content available for further use. Finally, trace decoding refers to the process of converting mental information into an overt response through an expressive medium.

The use of the keyword method entails the formation of two basic links, one between the *physical form* of the foreign word and that of the keyword, and another between the *referent* of the foreign word and that of the keyword. By the present account, relational information encoded by physical similarity judgments and by interactive imagery benefits memory performance that depends on interitem association. Productive recall of either the foreign word or its translation equivalent, however, is determined by the interplay of many factors, such as the potential value of the trace, the discriminations allowed by a particular retrieval cue, and the information that is redintegrated after trace access. The central functions of the keyword are to unitize at least some of the constituent parts of the foreign word form and to relate this physical form to a meaning. We have discussed the limitations and the memorial consequences of the keyword method. It appears that advocates of this study technique have some valid justifications for promoting its use in the acquisition of foreign vocabularies. However, scientists must continue to try to delineate its field of potential applications, to identify its limitations and their remedies, and to establish more firmly the relations between theoretical and applied issues.

Acknowledgments. Preparation of this chapter was supported by operating grants from the Natural Science and Engineering Research Council of Canada to the authors. We are grateful to Linda Wieland and Collette Gélinas for their assistance with the library search. We also thank Joel Levin, Mark McDaniel, and Michael Pressley for helpful comments on an earlier draft of this chapter.

References

Atkinson, R. C. (1975). Mnemotechnics in second-language learning. *American Psychologist, 30,* 821–828.

Atkinson, R. C., & Raugh, M. R. (1975). An application of the mnemonic keyword method to the acquisition of a Russian vocabulary. *Journal of Experimental Psychology: Human Learning and Memory, 104,* 126–133.

Bacon, J. H. (1862). *The science of memory.* London: Simpkin & Co.

Begg, I. (1971). Recognition memory for sentence meaning and wording. *Journal of Verbal Learning and Verbal Behavior, 10,* 176–181.

Begg, I. (1972). Recall of meaningful phrases. *Journal of Verbal Learning and Verbal Behavior, 11,* 431–439.

Begg, I. (1973). Imagery and integration in the recall of words. *Canadian Journal of Psychology, 27,* 159–167.

Begg, I. (1976). Acquisition and transfer of meaningful function by meaningless sounds. *Canadian Journal of Psychology, 30,* 178–186.

Begg, I. (1978a). Similarity and contrast in memory for relations. *Memory & Cognition, 6,* 509–517.

Begg, I. (1978b). Imagery and organization in memory: Instructional effects. *Memory & Cognition, 6,* 174–183.

Begg, I. (1979). Trace loss and the recognition failure of unrecalled words. *Memory & Cognition, 7,* 113–123.

Begg, I. (1982). Imagery, organization, and discriminative processes. *Canadian Journal of Psychology, 36,* 273–290.

Begg, I. (1983). Imagery instructions and the organization of memory. In J. C. Yuille (Ed.), *Imagery, memory, and cognition: Essays in honor of Allan Paivio* (pp. 91–115). Hillsdale, NJ: Erlbaum Associates.

Begg, I., & Anderson, M. C. (1976). Imagery and associative memory in children. *Journal of Experimental Child Psychology, 21,* 480–489.

Begg, I., & Sikich, D. (1984). Imagery and contextual organization. *Memory & Cognition, 12,* 52–59.

Begg, I., & White, P. (1985). Encoding specificity in interpersonal communication. *Canadian Journal of Psychology, 39,* 70–87.

Begg, I., & Young, B. J. (1977). An organizational analysis of the form class effect. *Journal of Experimental Child Psychology, 23,* 503–519.

Bower, G. H. (1970). Imagery as a relational organizer in associative learning. *Journal of Verbal Learning and Verbal Behavior, 9,* 529–533.

Bower, G. H. (1972). Mental imagery and associative learning. In L. W. Gregg (Ed.), *Cognition in learning and memory* (pp. 51–88). New York: Wiley.

Burnham, W. H. (1888). Memory, historically and experimentally considered: I. An historical sketch of the older conceptions of memory. *American Journal of Psychology, 2,* 39–90.

Craik, F. I. M., & Lockhart, R. S. (1972). Levels of processing: A framework for memory research. *Journal of Verbal Learning and Verbal Behavior, 11,* 671–684.

d'Anglejan, A. (1978). Language learning in and out of classroom. In J. Richards (Ed.), *Understanding second and foreign language learning* (pp. 218–237). Rowley, MA: Newbury House.

Delaney, H. D. (1978). Interaction of individual differences with visual and verbal elaboration instructions. *Journal of Educational Psychology, 70,* 306–318.

Dempster, R. N., & Rohwer, W. D. (1974). Component analysis of the elaborative encoding effect in children's learning. *Journal of Experimental Psychology, 103,* 400–408.

Denis, M. (1979). *Les images mentales.* Paris: Presses Universitaires de France.

Desrochers, A. (1982). Imagery elaboration and the recall of French article-noun pairs. *Canadian Journal of Psychology, 36,* 641–654.

Desrochers, A. (1983). Effects of instructions and retrieval cues on the recall of French article-noun pairs. *Human Learning, 2,* 295–311.

Desrochers, A., Wieland, L., & Butler, S. (1984). *Lexical materials for experimental applications of the keyword method: English keywords for a German vocabulary.* Research report No. 13, Cognitive Psychology Laboratory, School of Psychology, University of Ottawa, Ottawa, Canada.

Einstein, G. O., & Hunt, R. R. (1980). Additive effects of individual-item and relational processing. *Journal of Experimental Psychology: Human Learning and Memory, 6,* 588–598.

Estabrooks, G. H. (1927). A handy memory trick. *Journal of Genetic Psychology, 34,* 615–619.

Fenaigle, G. von. (1813). *The new art of memory.* London: Sherwood, Neely, & Jones.

Gernsbacher, M. A. (1983). *The experiential familiarity norms and their psychological validity.* Paper presented at the 29th Annual Meeting of the Southwestern Psychological Association, San Antonio, Texas.

Gernsbacher, M. A. (1984). Resolving 20 years of inconsistent interactions between lexical familiarity and orthography, concreteness, and polysemy. *Journal Experimental Psychology: General, 113,* 256–281.

Hasher, L., Reibman, B., & Wren, F. (1976). Imagery and the retention of free-recall learning. *Journal of Experimental Psychology: Human Learning and Memory, 2,* 172–181.

Horowitz, L. M., & Gordon, A. M. (1972). Associative symmetry and second-language learning. *Journal of Educational Psychology, 63,* 287–294.

Horowitz, L. M., Chilian, P. C., & Dunnigan, K. P. (1969). Word fragments and their redintegrative powers. *Journal of Experimental Psychology, 80,* 392–394.

Horowitz, L. M., White, M. A., & Atwood, D. W. (1968). Word fragments as aids to recall: The organization of a word. *Journal of Experimental Psychology, 76,* 219–226.

Humphreys, M. S. (1978). Item and relational information: A case for context independent retrieval. *Journal of Verbal Learning and Verbal Behavior, 17,* 175–187.

Hunt, R. R., & Einstein, G. O. (1981). Relational and item-specific information in memory. *Journal of Verbal Learning and Verbal Behavior, 20,* 497–514.

Janssen, W. (1976). *In the nature of the mental image.* Soesterberg, The Netherlands: Institute for Perception TNO.

Julliot, Ch.-L. (1919). *L'éducation de la mémoire.* Paris: Flammarion.

Levin, J. R. (1976). What have we learned about maximizing what children learn? In J. R. Levin & V. L. Allen (Eds.), *Cognitive learning in children: Theories and strategies* (pp. 105–134). New York: Academic Press.

Levin, J. R., & Pressley, M. (1985). Mnemonic vocabulary instruction: What's fact, what's fiction. In R. F. Dillon (Ed.), *Individual differences in cognition* (Vol. 2, pp. 145–172). Orlando, FL: Academic Press.

Lieury, A. (1980). *Les procédés mnémotechniques.* Bruxelles: Mardaga.

Loess, H., & Brown, A. (1969). Word fragments as aids to recall a whole word. *Journal of Experimental Psychology, 80,* 384–386.

Mandler, G. (1967). Organization and memory. In K. W. Spence & J. T. Spence (Eds.), *The psychology of learning and motivation: Advances in research and theory* (Vol. 1, pp. 327–372). New York: Academic Press.

Martin, E. (1967). Relation between stimulus recognition and paired-associative learning. *Journal of Experimental Psychology, 74,* 500–505.

McDaniel, M. A., & Kearney, E. M. (1984). Optimal learning strategies and their spontaneous use: The importance of task-appropriate processing. *Memory & Cognition, 12,* 361–373.

Middleton, A. E. (1887). *All about mnemonics.* London: Simpkin, Marshall, & Co.

Miller, G. A. (1953). What is information measurement? *American Psychologist, 8,* 3–11.

Miller, G. A. (1956). The magical number seven, plus or minus two: Some limits on our capacity for processing information. *Psychological Review, 63,* 81–97.

Miller, G. A., Galanter, E., & Pribram, K. H. (1960). *Plans and the structure of behavior.* New York: Holt.

Miller, J. R., & Geiselman, R. E. (1979). Extracting target information from composite mental structures. *Journal of Experimental Psychology: Human Learning and Memory, 5,* 555–566.

Montague, W. E., Adams, J. A., & Kiess, H. O. (1966). Forgetting and natural language mediation. *Journal of Experimental Psychology, 72,* 829–833.

Morris, C. D., Bransford, J. D., & Franks, J. J. (1977). Levels of processing versus transfer appropriate processing. *Journal of Verbal Learning and Verbal Behavior, 16,* 519–534.

Murphy, G. L., & Medin, D. L. (1985). The role of theories in conceptual coherence. *Psychological Review, 92,* 289–316.

Neisser, U. (1967). *Cognitive psychology.* New York: Appleton-Century-Crofts.

Ott, C. E., Butler, D. C., Blake, R. S., & Ball, J. P. (1973). The effect of interactive-image elaboration on the acquisition of foreign language vocabulary. *Language Learning, 2,* 197–206.

Paivio, A. (1965). Abstractness, imagery, and meaningfulness in paired-associate learning. *Journal of Verbal Learning and Verbal Behavior, 4,* 32–38.

Paivio, A. (1971). *Imagery and verbal processes.* New York: Holt.

Paivio, A., & Desrochers, A. (1979). Effects of an imagery mnemonic on second language recall and comprehension. *Canadian Journal of Psychology, 33,* 17–28.

Paivio, A., & Desrochers, A. (1981). Mnemonic techniques in second-language learning. *Journal of Educational Psychology, 73,* 780–795.

Pressley, M. (1977a). Imagery and children's learning: Putting the picture in developmental perspective. *Review of Educational Research, 47,* 585–622.

Pressley, M. (1977b). Children's use of the keyword method to learn simple Spanish vocabulary words. *Journal of Educational Psychology, 69,* 465–472.

Pressley, M., & Levin, J. R. (1978). Developmental constraints associated with children's use of the keyword method of foreign language vocabulary learning. *Journal of Experimental Child Psychology, 26,* 359–372.

Pressley, M., & Levin, J. R. (1981). The keyword method and recall of vocabulary words from definitions. *Journal of Experimental Psychology: Human Learning and Memory, 7,* 72–76.

Pressley, M., Levin, J. R., & Delaney, H. D. (1982). The mnemonic keyword method. *Review of Educational Research, 52,* 61–92.

Pressley, M., Levin, J. R., Hall, J. W., Miller, G. E., & Berry, J. K. (1980). The keyword method and foreign word acquisition. *Journal of Experimental Psychology: Human Learning and Memory, 5,* 22–29.

Pressley, M., Levin, J. R., Kuiper, N. A., Bryant, S. L., & Michener, S. (1982). Mnemonic versus nonmnemonic vocabulary-learning strategies: Additional comparisons. *Journal of Educational Psychology, 74,* 693–707.

Pressley, M., Levin, J. R., & McDaniel, M. A. (in press). Remembering versus inferring what a word means: Mnemonic and contextual approaches. In M. G. McKeown & M. E. Curtis (Eds.), *The nature of vocabulary acquisition.* Hillsdale, NJ: Erlbaum Associates.

Pressley, M., Levin, J. R., & Miller, G. E. (1981a). How does the keyword method affect vocabulary comprehension and usage? *Reading Reading Quarterly, 16,* 213–226.

Pressley, M., Levin, J. R., & Miller, G. E. (1981b). The keyword method and children's learning of foreign vocabulary with abstract meanings. *Canadian Journal of Psychology, 35,* 283–287.

Pressley, M., Levin, J. R., & Miller, G. E. (1982). The keyword method compared to alternative vocabulary learning strategies. *Contemporary Educational Psychology, 7,* 50–60.

Pressley, M., Levin, J. R., Nakamura, G. V., Hope, D. J., Bispo, J. G., & Toye, A. R. (1980). The keyword method of foreign vocabulary learning: A investigation of its generalizability. *Journal of Applied Psychology, 65,* 635–642.

Prytulak, L. S. (1971). Natural language mediation. *Cognitive Psychology, 2,* 1–56.

Raugh, M. R., & Atkinson, R. C. (1975). A mnemonic method for learning a second-language vocabulary. *Journal of Educational Psychology, 67,* 1–16.

Raugh, M. R., Schupbach, R. D., & Atkinson, R. C. (1977). Teaching a large Russian vocabulary by the mnemonic keyword method. *Instructional Science, 6,* 199–221.

Rohwer, W. D. (1973). Elaboration and learning in childhood and adolescence. In H. W. Reese (Ed.), *Advances in child development and behavior* (Vol. 8, pp. 2–57). New York: Academic Press.

Rumelhart, D. E. (1980). Schemata: The building blocks of cognition. In R. J. Spiro, B. C. Bruce, & W. F. Brewer (Eds.), *Theoretical issues in reading comprehension* (pp. 33–58). Hillsdale, NJ: Erlbaum Associates.

Saussure, F. de (1916). *Cours de linguistique générale.* Paris: Payot.

Sayer, T. A. (1877). *Aids to memory*. London: Daldy, Isbister & Co.

Sweeney, C. A., Bellezza, F. S. (1982). Use of the keyword mnemonic for learning English vocabulary. *Human Learning, 1,* 155–163.

Tulving, E. (1968). Theoretical issues in free recall. In T. R. Dixon & D. L. Horton (Eds.), *Verbal behavior and general behavior theory* (pp. 2–36). Englewood Cliffs, NJ: Prentice-Hall.

Tulving, E. (1983). *Elements of episodic memory*. New York: Oxford University Press.

Tversky, B. (1973). Encoding processes in recognition and recall. *Cognitive Psychology, 5,* 275–287.

Underwood, B. J., & Erlebacher, A. H. (1965). Studies of coding in verbal learning. *Psychological Monographs: General and Applied, 79* (Whole No. 606).

Underwood, B. J., & Schulz, R. W. (1960). *Meaningfulness and verbal learning*. Philadelphia: Lippincott.

Wang, W. S.-Y. (1971). The basis of speech. In C. E. Reed (Ed.), *The learning of language*. New York: Appleton-Century-Crofts.

Wieland, L., & Desrochers, A. (1985). An application of the mnemonic keyword method to the acquisition of German nouns and their grammatical gender. Paper presented at the 46th Annual Convention of Canadian Psychological Association, June 7, Halifax, Nova Scotia.

Winograd, E., & Lynn, D. A. (1979). Role of contextual imagery in associative recall. *Memory & Cognition, 7,* 29–34.

Yates, F. A. (1966). *The art of memory*. Chicago: The University of Chicago Press.

Yule, G. (1886). *Memory manual* (3rd ed.). St. Louis: G. Yule.

CHAPTER 4

Distinctiveness and the Mnemonic Benefits of Bizarre Imagery

Gilles O. Einstein and Mark A. McDaniel

Imagery mnemonics have been advocated as effective memory devices for at least 2000 years (Yates, 1966). It is only within the past 20 years, however, that controlled laboratory studies have clearly established the memorial benefits of imagery mnemonics. More recently, the practical applications of imagery mnemonics have been explored and these techniques have been shown to be useful for learning prose materials as well as lists (cf. Bellezza, 1981; see Denis, Chapter 9, this volume, for more information on imagery and prose retention), to be effective in educational settings (cf. Bellezza, 1981; Pressley, Levin, & Delaney, 1982) and to enhance memory in special populations (Mastropieri, Scruggs, & Levin, Chapter 16, this volume; Pressley, Johnson, & Symons, in press). These populations include children as young as 3 years old (cf. Pressley et al., 1982), some types of amnesic patients (Baddeley & Warrington, 1973; Jones, 1974; see also Richardson, Cermak, Blackford, & O'Connor, Chapter 14, this volume for a review of this literature), the elderly (Robertson-Tchabo, Hausman, & Arenberg, 1976), and the mentally retarded (see Bender & Levin, 1978). Given the great potential of mnemonic techniques for improving memory in a wide variety of situations, it is important to identify those components of mnemonic techniques that actually have positive effects on memory. Research on these components may also yield useful information on theoretical conceptualizations within the general memory literature. For example, research on bizarre imagery may enhance our understanding of recent theoretical analyses based on distinctiveness (Eysenck, 1979; Hunt & Elliott, 1980; Nelson, 1979).

Two components of imagery-based mnemonics often stressed by professional mnemonists are that the images should be both interactive in nature and bizarre rather than common (Lorayne & Lucas, 1974). (For an interesting review of early and popular views on the benefits of bizarre imagery, see Yarmey, 1984.) Whereas there is complete agreement on the mnemonic benefits of interactive imagery (Bower, 1970a; Wollen, Weber, & Lowry, 1972), the literature on the effects of bizarre imagery is more complicated. In this chapter, we first review the literature on bizarre imagery and identify the conditions under which memory is enhanced through bizarre imagery. We then evaluate several frameworks for integrating the results that have emerged over the past 20 years.

Finally, we suggest some explanatory mechanisms that may be useful for understanding the effects of bizarre imagery.

The early research on bizarre imagery tended to show either that bizarre imagery led to lower recall than common imagery (Collyer, Jonides, & Bevan, 1972; Emmerich & Ackerman, 1979) or that bizarre imagery had no effect on retention (Hauck, Walsh, & Kroll, 1976; Nappe & Wollen, 1973; Wollen et al., 1972; Wood, 1967). In fact, the consistent failure to find positive memorial effects of bizarre imagery led Postman (1975) to conclude, "It is also possible to report that despite popular misconceptions, bizarre images and pictures are no better as memory aids than common ones" (p. 322). Similarly, Bower (1970b) reported that "The evidence for the prescription to use odd, bizarre imagery is, to date, entirely negative" (p. 501). In more recent work, however, the bizarreness effect has been obtained under certain experimental conditions (Andreoff & Yarmey, 1976; Marshall, Nau, & Chandler, 1980; McDaniel & Einstein, 1985, 1986; Merry, 1980, 1982; Merry & Graham, 1978; O'Brien & Wolford, 1983; Pra Baldi, de Beni, Cornoldi, & Cavedon, 1985; Webber & Marshall, 1978; Wollen & Cox, 1981a, b). Although a superficial examination of experiments on bizarre imagery yields a confusing array of contradictory results, the findings of these studies are quite consistent and predictable when several variables are considered. The factors that seem to affect whether or not bizarre imagery influences memory include the type of design (mixed versus unmixed lists), the nature of the criterial task, the nature of the processing task, the presence or absence of interfering material, and the length of the retention interval. Research bearing on each of these factors is discussed in turn. As will be seen, these factors interact and are not necessarily independent. For clarity of presentation, we discuss each of these variables in separate sections. After outlining some methodological problems, we first review studies that have examined the effects of bizarre imagery on immediate retention. Subsequently, we review experiments that have measured recall after long retention intervals and/or those that have included interference between study and test.

Methodological Considerations

It should be noted that despite our focus on the variables listed above, there is still considerable variability among bizarre imagery studies. In other words, a variety of methods has been used to explore the bizarreness effect and so there are many potentially important differences among the studies that we review. One such difference involves whether the specific relationships among the items to be remembered are generated by the subject or by the experimenter. In some studies, subjects are presented with word pairs and instructed to generate their own bizarre or common interactions. In other experiments, the relationships between the items are specified precisely by the experimenter (via sentence frames or interacting pictures). Whereas subject-generated mediators typically lead to higher recall than experimenter-provided mediators (Bobrow & Bower,

1969; Bower & Winzenz, 1970), it is not clear if this factor influences the relative recall of bizarre and common images. Another factor that varies across experiments is that subjects are presented with interacting pictures in some studies and in others, subjects are presented with verbal stimuli describing either common or bizarre interactions and they must generate their own images from these verbal descriptions. Generally, experiments on bizarre imagery have been performed to demonstrate the effectiveness or ineffectiveness of bizarre imagery. As a result, there has been little systematic research directly contrasting the different methods used in bizarre imagery experiments. In the absence of any convincing evidence that one method is superior to another, and in an effort to provide a comprehensive review, we chose not to exercise any particular bias and have included almost all the studies of which we are aware. A few frequently cited studies that have obvious methodological problems were not included (see Wollen & Margres, Chapter 5, this volume, for criticisms of these studies). Where conflicting results arise, we point out methodological factors that may account for the disparate results.

The Effects of Bizarre Imagery on Immediate Recall

In this section, we first review the major variables that seem to influence the bizarreness effect at short retention intervals. For present purposes, short retention intervals are operationally defined as those shorter than 5 min in duration and those that do not include imagery interference within the interval.

Mixed Versus Unmixed Lists

Starting with Wood's (1967) classic research, most of the early experiments on bizarre imagery tested the effects of bizarre imagery in unmixed list designs. That is, some subjects were asked to form bizarre images while other subjects formed common images. This type of design consistently failed to produce the bizarreness effect, regardless of the type of memory test (Bergfeld, Choate, & Kroll, 1982; Collyer et al., 1972; Cox & Wollen, 1981; Emmerich & Ackerman, 1979; McDaniel & Einstein, 1985, 1986; Senter & Hoffman, 1976; Wollen & Cox, 1981a; Wollen et al., 1972; Wood, 1967). In all of these studies, memory for common images was equal to or superior to memory for bizarre images. The regularity of such results, along with the finding that bizarre images take longer to form (Nappe & Wollen, 1973), led researchers to believe that bizarre imagery was both ineffective and inefficient. Later, investigators started using mixed list designs, in which subjects were required to form both bizarre and common images. The bizarreness effect consistently emerged under these conditions (Merry, 1980, 1982; Merry & Graham, 1978; Pra Baldi et al., 1985), thereby indicating that list type is a critical variable. As will be described in the next section, list type must be considered in conjunction with the type of criterial task. The bizarreness effect does occur with mixed lists, but only when the memory task requires subjects to access the images (i.e., free recall). For now, we limit our review to studies that have used mixed lists and free-recall measures of memory. We contrast free and cued recall criterial tasks in the next section.

To this point, the literature is consistent with the suggestion that bizarre imagery is effective in mixed but not unmixed lists. This conclusion, however, involves comparisons among different experiments. Given the variety of materials and procedures used in different studies, this conclusion is not compelling. McDaniel and Einstein (1986) set out to compare directly mixed and unmixed list manipulations of the bizarreness variable. In their experiment, all subjects were presented with 10 noun triplets that appeared as underlined words in sentences. Different groups of subjects were presented with 10 bizarre sentences, 10 common sentences, or five bizarre and five common sentences. All subjects were asked to form images of the sentences and to rate the vividness of the images. After rating the sentences, subjects were asked to free recall the nouns. As shown in Figure 4.1, design type interacted with type of imagery. Bizarre imagery produced higher recall than common imagery with a mixed list but not with an unmixed list. This effect with mixed lists was replicated in four separate experiments. Thus, the results of this experiment confirm the trend present in the literature—that bizarre imagery enhances free recall when common sentences are present in the learning context.

One cautionary note about the McDaniel and Einstein (1986) experiment is that their results should not be interpreted to mean that mixed lists produce higher overall levels of recall. The proportion of total words recalled (from all of the sentences in the learning list) was roughly equal for all three groups. Hence, mixed lists affect the relative recall of bizarre and common materials and not overall recall levels.

The Criterial Task

As mentioned earlier, for mixed-list designs and immediate testing, bizarre imagery facilitates access to the images and not access to the components within the images. In mixed-list designs, the bizarreness effect is consistently obtained with free recall (McDaniel & Einstein, 1985, 1986; Merry, 1980, 1982; Merry & Graham, 1978; Pra Baldi et al., 1985; Wollen & Cox, 1981a, 1981b) but not with cued recall (Andreoff & Yarmey, 1976; Hauck et al., 1976; Kroll, Schepeler, & Angin, 1986; Nappe & Wollen, 1973; O'Brien & Wolford, 1982; Pra Baldi et al., 1985; Webber & Marshall, 1978; Wollen & Cox, 1981a, 1981b) or recognition (Emmerich & Ackerman, 1979; McDaniel & Einstein, 1986). This pattern is evident when making comparisons across experiments and also when evaluating studies that have included both free- and cued-recall tests (Pra Baldi et al., 1985; Wollen & Cox, 1981a, 1981b). Further, when a componential analysis of free recall is performed, bizarre imagery affects the proportion of sentences or images accessed (i.e., the number of sentences for which at least one word has been recalled) and not the proportion of items recovered from the accessed sentences (McDaniel & Einstein, 1986). Thus, bizarre imagery effects appear to be limited to free-recall situations and to be mediated by processes involved in

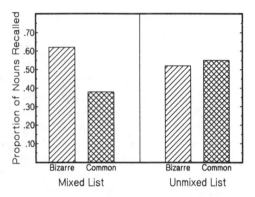

FIGURE 4.1. Mean proportion of bizarre and common items recalled from mixed and unmixed lists.

initial access to the images. Wollen and Margres (Chapter 5, this volume) have reached the identical conclusion in their discussion of the "vertical effects" of bizarre imagery.

Processing Task

The procedures of all experiments that have demonstrated the bizarreness effect and used mixed lists and free recall are remarkably similar. In these experiments, subjects were presented with bizarre and common sentences (and sometimes also abstract sentences) and asked to image the sentences or to image the sentences and then to rate either the vividness of the images or the bizarreness of the sentences. To date, no one has explored the bizarreness effect with pictorial materials (under mixed-list, free-recall, and immediate testing conditions). Thus, it is possible that imagery instructions do not force subjects to form images during learning and that the observed bizarreness effect with mixed lists and free recall has very little to do with imagery. McDaniel and Einstein (1986, Exp. 2) tested this argument by having subjects perform either semantic or imaginal processing on a mixed list of bizarre and common sentences. Imaginal processing was induced by asking subjects to image each sentence and then rate the vividness of each image. Subjects using semantic processing were not instructed to image the sentences but were asked simply to rate the bizarreness of each sentence. The results revealed that semantic and imagery orienting activities produced different effects. The bizarreness effect was observed with imagery instructions but not with semantic instructions. In fact, with a semantic orienting task, subjects recovered more words from the common sentences than from the bizarre sentences, suggesting that bizarre sentences are difficult to integrate semantically. In any case, it appears that imagery instructions encourage subjects to form representations that are imaginal in nature or at least representations that are different from those created under semantic processing instructions. Also, it seems that imagery instructions are essential for obtaining the bizarreness effect.

Summary of Immediate Retention Studies

In summary, the results of the studies reviewed so far reveal a reliable, although complex, pattern. The results indicate that the mnemonic effects of bizarre imagery depend on (a) the design used to manipulate bizarreness (mixed versus unmixed lists), (b) the type of memory task (free versus cued recall), and (c) the type of orienting task (imagery versus semantic). This analysis is quite useful for organizing and understanding the research in the field. In Table 4.1 we have sorted previous studies into four major categories defined on the basis of the design of the learning list and type of recall test. To give the reader some appreciation of the different methodologies among experiments, we have also included cursory descriptions of the materials and instructions used in each study. As shown in Table 4.1, the bizarreness effect has *never* been found in studies using unmixed lists or in studies using mixed lists and cued recall. By contrast, eight of ten studies using mixed lists and free recall have shown superior recall for bizarre imagery relative to common imagery. McDaniel and Einstein's (1986, Exp. 2) failure to conform to this pattern is understandable if the type of processing task is considered. They did not find the bizarreness effect with semantic processing instructions but consistently produced the effect with imagery instructions. Thus, 28 of 29 entries in Table 4.1 conform to the framework that *the bizarreness effect occurs only with mixed lists, free recall*, and *imagery instructions*.

The lone exception to this pattern is the research by Kroll et al. (1986). As can be seen in Table 4.1, Kroll et al. used a mixed-list design and tested subjects for free recall. Despite these similarities to studies that have found positive effects of bizarre imagery, there appear to be three potentially important methodological differences. First, Kroll et al. presented subjects with long lists of sentences (16 bizarre sentences in a list of 56 sentences), whereas shorter sentence lists (five or six bizarre sentences in lists containing 10–18 sentences) were used in the other studies. Perhaps, the bizarreness effect emerges only when a relatively small set of bizarre sentences is present in the learning list. Though possible, the results of a study from our laboratory with longer lists argue against this interpretation (McDaniel & Anderson, 1986, Exp. 2). Second, Kroll et al.'s subjects were asked to form an image for each sentence and then to perform three orienting tasks on each sentence. They initially rated the image for vividness, then rated the sentence for bizarreness, and, finally, rated the degree of interaction among the nouns in the sentence. In the other studies (reviewed in the previous section), subjects were asked simply to image the sentences and rate them either for vividness or bizarreness. The additional processing tasks used by Kroll et al. may have encouraged subjects to focus on the semantic properties of the sentences and not

TABLE 4.1. Summary of experiments comparing the effects of bizarre (Biz) and common (Com) imagery after short retention intervals.

Experiment	Materials	Instructions	Results
Unmixed lists, cued recall			
Bergfeld, Choate, & Kroll (1982)	Line drawings of pairs of objects appearing side by side	Form bizarre or common images	Com = Biz
Emmerich & Ackerman (1979)	Line drawings of pairs of objects along with common or bizarre sentences	Remember which objects were presented together	Com > Biz
Senter & Hoffman (1976)	Bizarre and common line drawings of objects	Use the pictures to associate the objects	Com = Biz
Wollen, Weber, & Lowry (1972)	Bizarre and common line drawings of word pairs	Associate the two words within each pair	Com > Biz
Wood (1967)	Word pairs	Form bizarre or common images	Com = Biz
Unmixed lists, free recall			
Collyer, Jonides, & Bevan (1972)	Word triplets suggesting bizarre or common interactions	Remember which objects were presented together	Com > Biz
Cox & Wollen (1981)	Bizarre and common sentences	Image and rate for bizarreness	Com = Biz
McDaniel & Einstein (1985)	Bizarre and common sentences	Image and rate for vividness	Com = Biz
McDaniel & Einstein (1986)	Bizarre and common sentences	Image and rate for vividness	Com = Biz
Wollen & Cox (1981a)	Bizarre and common sentences	Image and rate for bizarreness	Com = Biz
Mixed lists, cued recall			
Andreoff & Yarmey (1976)	Word pairs	Form bizarre or common images	Com = Biz
Hauck, Walsh, & Kroll (1976)	Word pairs	Form bizarre or common images	Com = Biz
Kroll, Schepeler, & Angin (1986)	Bizarre and common sentences	Image and rate for bizarreness, vividness, and/or interaction	Com = Biz
Nappe & Wollen (1973)	Word pairs	Form bizarre or common images	Com = Biz
Pra Baldi, de Beni, Cornoldi, & Cavedon (1985)	Bizarre and common sentences	Image and rate for bizarreness	Com > Biz
O'Brien & Wolford (1982)	Bizarre and common line drawings of word pairs	Rate picture for bizarreness	Com = Biz
Webber & Marshall (1978)	Bizarre and common line drawings of word pairs	Nonsemantic, semantic, rate bizarreness, or intentional	Com = Biz
Wollen & Cox (1981a)	Bizarre and common sentences	Image and rate for bizarreness	Com > Biz

TABLE 4.1. *Continued*

Experiment	Materials	Instructions	Results
Wollen & Cox (1981b)	Bizarre and common sentences	Image the sentences	Com > Biz
Mixed lists, free recall			
Kroll, Schepeler, & Angin (1986)	Bizarre and common sentences	Image and rate for bizarreness, vividness, and/or interaction	Com = Biz
McDaniel & Einstein (1985)	Bizarre and common sentences	Image and rate for vividness	Biz > Com
McDaniel & Einstein (1986)	Bizarre and common sentences	Image and rate for vividness	Biz > Com
	Bizarre and common sentences	Rate sentences for bizarreness	Com = Biz
Merry (1980)	Bizarre and common sentences	Image and rate for bizarreness	Biz > Com
Merry (1982)	Bizarre and common sentences	Image and rate for bizarreness	Biz > Com
Merry & Graham (1978)	Bizarre and common sentences	Image and rate for bizarreness	Biz > Com
Pra Baldi, de Beni, Cornoldi, & Cavedon (1985)	Bizarre and common sentences	Image and rate for bizarreness	Biz > Com
Wollen & Cox (1981a)	Bizarre and common sentences	Image and rate for bizarreness	Biz > Com
Wollen & Cox (1981b)	Bizarre and common sentences	Image the sentences	Biz > Com

the images. Another possible interpretation is based on the view that distinctiveness underlies the bizarreness effect. According to Klein and Saltz (1976), classifying an item along several different dimensions results in an encoding that is more distinctively specified in the cognitive semantic space. If this is so, then rating sentences on three separate dimensions may obscure any advantages (in terms of distinctiveness) of bizarre sentences. By virtue of sharing fewer features with other ideas in memory, bizarre sentences are inherently more distinctive than common sentences. Thus, the distinctiveness that accrues from performing three separate orienting tasks should enhance the uniqueness mainly of common sentences.

A final source of difference between the Kroll et al. (1986) study and those studies that have found a positive effect of bizarreness concerns the definition of bizarreness. There are many possible ways to define bizarreness and Kroll et al.'s distinctions between bizarre and common materials may be different from those used in the other studies. Nonbizarre and common materials sometimes differ on the dimension of commonness, sometimes on plausibility, and sometimes on both. Although, bizarre and common materials are typically verified by subjects ratings on scales, such ratings are greatly influenced by the nature of the materials in the rating context. Thus, what is common in one study may be bizarre in another and vice versa. For instance, Kroll et al.'s examples of non-bizarre and bizarre sentences are, "A large black ANT crawls in and out of the teeth of a plastic COMB" and "A large black ANT carefully fixes its hair with a plastic COMB," respectively. Whereas neither of these sentences is common, the former is clearly plausible or possible and the latter is not. By contrast, Merry (1982) and McDaniel and Einstein (1986) used common sentences such as "The MAN smoked a CIGAR" and "The DOG chased the BICYCLE down the STREET." Bizarre versions of these sentences were "The HEN smoked a CIGAR" and "The DOG rode the BICYCLE down the STREET." In these cases, the non-bizarre sentences were both common and plausible and the bizarre sentences were uncommon and implausible. By this analysis, there is a greater degree of difference between the bizarre and common materials in the Merry (1982) and the McDaniel and Einstein (1986) experiments than in the Kroll et al. experiments, and this may be important for obtaining the bizarreness effect.

Our intent here is not to promote one method over another but to suggest that these variables may influence the effects of bizarre imagery on memory. Because most of the research in the bizarre imagery literature has been performed in the spirit of demonstrating the bizarreness effect, little systematic research exists on methodological variables that influence the effect. Research of this sort would be quite useful in further specifying the limits of the bizarreness effect and in suggesting theoretical interpretations of the effect.

The Effects of Bizarre Imagery on Delayed Recall and/or Recall After Imagery Interference

It seems that initial failures to find effects of bizarre imagery on immediate recall prompted researchers to test the effects after longer retention intervals. The belief was that long-term tests would be especially sensitive to the effects of bizarre imagery. On the assumption that bizarre images are more distinctive than common images, the argument was that bizarre images should be less susceptible to extraexperimental interference (which by definition is common in nature). Such predictions were supported as researchers found superior delayed memory for bizarre images under a wide variety of conditions—with both mixed and unmixed lists and both free and cued recall. In this section, we review these studies and also point out some inconsistencies in the long-term memory literature. Because of their conceptual similarities with studies using long-term tests, studies that have presented interference between study and test are also reviewed in this section.

The results of 15 studies that have measured retention after long intervals (1 day or more) and/or after interference are listed in Table 4.2. As can be seen in the table, the conflicting results within the four categories make these experiments difficult to summarize. Obviously, there are some important methodological differences that are not captured by the variables of design type and type of

TABLE 4.2. Summary of experiments comparing the effects of bizarre and common imagery at long retention intervals and/or retention intervals that include imagery interference.

Experiment	Materials	Instructions	Interval	Result
Unmixed lists, cued recall				
Bergfeld, Choate, & Kroll (1982)	Line drawings of pairs of objects appearing side by side	Form bizarre or common images	1 day	Com > Biz
Marshall, Nau, & Chandler (1980)	Word pairs	Form bizarre or common images	1 week	Biz > Com
Unmixed lists, free recall				
McDaniel & Einstein (1986)	Bizarre and common sentences	Image and rate for vividness	5 min – intervening list of common images	Biz > Com
	Bizarre and common sentences	Image and rate for vividness	5 min – intervening list of bizarre images	Com = Biz
McDaniel & Einstein (1985)	Bizarre and common sentences	Image and rate for vividness	10 min – intervening list of semantically related words	Com = Biz
Mixed lists, cued recall				
Andreoff & Yarmey (1976)	Word pairs	Form bizarre or common images	1 day	Biz > Com
Hauck, Walsh, & Kroll (1976)	Word pairs	Form bizarre or common images	1–4 days	Com = Biz
Kroll, Schepeler, & Angin (1986)	Bizarre and common sentences	Image, and rate for bizarreness, vividness, and/or interaction	7 days	Com = Biz
O'Brien & Wolford (1982)	Bizarre and common line drawings of word pairs	Rate pictures for bizarreness	1–3 days	Com = Biz
	Bizarre and common line drawings of word pairs	Rate pictures for bizarreness	5–7 days	Biz > Com
Webber & Marshall (1978)	Bizarre and common line drawings of word pairs	Non-semantic, semantic, rate bizarreness, or intentional	7 days	Biz > Com

TABLE 4.2. *Continued*

Experiment	Materials	Instructions	Interval	Result
Mixed lists, free recall				
Kroll, Schepeler, & Angin (1986)	Bizarre and common sentences	Image, rate for bizarreness, vividness, and/or interaction	7 days	Com = Biz
Merry (1980)	Bizarre and common sentences	Image and rate for bizarreness	7 days	Biz > Com
Merry (1982)	Bizarre and common sentences	Image and rate for bizarreness	14 days	Biz > Com
Merry & Graham (1978)	Bizarre and common sentences	Image and rate for bizarreness	7 days	Biz > Com

test. Another problem in systematizing these studies is that many of them have been criticized for containing methodological flaws (cf. Kroll et al., 1986; O'Brien & Wolford, 1982). To avoid making generalizations from less than rigorously controlled experiments, we restrict our review to those studies that do not contain any of the following control problems:

1. Failure to control adequately the types of images that subjects formed (i.e., experiments in which subjects were presented with word pairs or drawings of separate objects and asked to form their own bizarre or common images).
2. Intersentence cuing bias in which the bizarre materials were generated by rearranging words from the common materials. This method of list construction confers a cuing bias in favor of bizarre materials (cf. Wollen & Cox, 1981a).
3. Intrasentence cuing bias in which highly associated target materials were used for common but not for bizarre materials.

Kroll et al. (1986) point out an additional control problem and that is the failure to measure the degree of interaction among the components of bizarre and common images. Given that degree of interaction has rarely been measured in the bizarre imagery studies, we have not excluded studies that have not controlled for degree of interaction. Later, we discuss the importance of this variable.

Unmixed Lists—Cued Recall

As shown in Table 4.2, two experiments have tested the effects of bizarre imagery using unmixed lists and cued-recall procedures and every possible result has been obtained. Neither of these studies, however, is free of the control problems listed earlier and consequently we do not review them.

Unmixed Lists – Free Recall

To our knowledge, no experiments have tested the bizarreness effect after delays with unmixed lists and free recall. McDaniel and Einstein (1985, 1986), however, have performed several experiments in which various types of interference have been presented between study and test. In one experiment (McDaniel & Einstein, 1986), subjects were presented with noun triplets embedded in either bizarre or common sentences. Subjects were required to image these sentences and to rate the vividness of the images. They were then asked to learn an additional set of materials. After recalling the intervening material, subjects were given a free recall test on the initial list. Recall was higher for bizarre images, but only when the intervening learning consisted of common images. When subjects learned either bizarre images or numeric information during the intervening task, bizarre imagery did not facilitate recall relative to common imagery. In another experiment (McDaniel & Einstein, 1985) the intervening task consisted of learning a list of words that was related semantically to the target items in the initial list of bizarre and common sentences. This type of interference did not affect the recall of bizarre and common images differentially.

Taken together, these studies indicate that interpolated activity involving common imagery produces a free-recall advantage for bizarre images (in an unmixed-list design). Further, it appears that this interpolated activity must be similar in format to the target material and be encoded imaginally. Although extra-experimental learning is likely to involve common imagery, it remains to be seen whether or not long delays per se have similar effects on the relative recall of bizarre and common images.

Mixed Lists – Cued Recall

O'Brien and Wolford (1983) have presented what is perhaps the clearest demonstration of an effect of differential forgetting of bizarre and common images. In their experiments, subjects were presented with a mixed list of pictures containing two objects interacting in either a bizarre or common fashion. Subjects were asked to determine whether the pictures contained plausible or bizarre scenes and later were given a cued-recall test. In the first experiment, subjects were tested either immediately or after a delay of 7 days. In the second experiment, testing occurred immediately or after delays of 1, 3, 5, or 7 days. Consistent with the immediate recall literature described earlier, O'Brien and Wolford found equivalent levels of cued recall for bizarre and common materials at immediate testing. With long delays (5–7 days), however, cued recall was significantly higher for bizarre sentences. These results are further supported by Webber and Marshall's (1978) research demonstrating a cued-recall advantage for bizarre materials after a 7-day delay but not at immediate testing. It should be noted that Kroll et al. (1986), using mixed lists and cued recall, have not found an interaction between delay and type of imagery. Also, in explaining the contradictory results, Kroll et al. criticize the above studies for failure to control the degree of interaction in common and bizarre materials.

In summary, the results of these studies suggest the interesting possibility that time differentially affects the memorability of bizarre and common images. The conflicting results indicate, however, that further research is necessary before strong conclusions can be made.

Mixed Lists – Free Recall

Again, there are conflicting results among the studies that fall within this category. Merry (1982) demonstrated a free-recall advantage for bizarre images at both immediate and 7-day delays. Kroll et al. (1986), on the other hand, show no effects of bizarre imagery at either retention interval. Resolutions to these conflicts can be resolved only by systematically studying the methodological differences.

Summary of Long-Term Retention Experiments

As noted earlier, no clear trends emerge when the results of all of the long-term retention experiments are considered. The conflicting results within each category in Table 4.2 preclude consensus on the conditions that produce the bizarreness effect. The results, however, do suggest the interesting possibility that after long retention intervals, the bizarreness effect emerges under a wider set of conditions. When memory has been measured after long delay intervals or after common imagery interference, the bizarreness effect has been found with unmixed as well as mixed lists and with both free and cued recall. These results are in striking contrast to those from immediate retention experiments, wherein the bizarreness effect is limited to mixed-list, free-recall situations.

What is needed is more well-controlled, systematic research to determine the delay and methodological conditions necessary for producing the bizarreness effect. There are several issues that should be considered in this research. One of these concerns the optimal delay interval for obtaining the bizarreness effect. Some researchers have found the bizarreness effect after a 1-day delay (Andreoff & Yarmey, 1976) and others have found the effect only after 5- to 7-day intervals (O'Brien & Wolford, 1982). Another issue revolves around whether the effects of common imagery interference are functionally equivalent to the effects of long delays (or extraexperimental interference). Finally, it would be informative to investigate whether (or under what conditions) delays enhance the bizarreness effect (i.e., produce differential forgetting of bizarre and common materials) or preserve memory differences that exist after original learning.

Existing Explanatory Concepts

To review, the results to be explained are that at immediate retention, the bizarreness effect occurs only with mixed lists and free recall. At delayed retention, the data are less clear but they appear to show that bizarre images are better recalled than common images with both mixed and unmixed lists and with cued recall as well as free recall. In this section, we critically review the theoretical arguments that have been proposed to explain the bizarreness effect. It will be noticed that some of these perspectives assume that the bizarreness effect is a real phenomenon in the sense that bizarreness per se has some effect on encoding, storage, and/or retrieval. Other perspectives, however, assume that bizarreness has little to do with memory and that the bizarreness effect is the product of uncontrolled variables. Another point that should be kept in mind is that different theoretical conceptualizations may be required to explain the short-term and long-term retention results.

Intersentence Cuing

Wollen and Cox (1981a) developed the intersentence cuing explanation to interpret Merry (1980), and Merry and Graham's (1978) initial demonstrations of the bizarreness effect in mixed lists. To understand the intersentence cuing view, the methods of these experiments need to be described. In Merry and Graham's studies, subjects were presented with underlined noun pairs and the bizarreness of the images was controlled by varying the nature of the sentence frames. The bizarre sentences were created by interchanging the nouns that appeared in the common sentences. For example, the common sentences "The MAN smoked the CIGAR" and "The HEN pecked the WORM" were rearranged to form the bizarre sentences "The MAN pecked the WORM" and "The HEN smoked the CIGAR." In examining this procedure, Wollen and Cox (1981a) suggested the possibility of an intersentence cuing bias that favors recall of the bizarre materials. That is, recall of the bizarre sentence "The HEN smoked the CIGAR" suggests associates that appear in other bizarre sentences such as "pecked," "worm," or "man." Wollen and Cox pointed out that this cuing bias among sentences was less probable with common sentences. For instance, recall of the sentence "The HEN pecked the WORM" is not likely to cue items from other sentences such as "man," "smoked," or "cigar."* Thus, Wollen and Cox essentially argue that Merry (1980) and Merry and Graham's (1978) demonstrations of the bizarreness effect are artifacts of the list constructions. Wollen and Cox (1981a) tried to support this argument by demonstrating the bizarreness effect in a situation in which intersentence cuing existed (Experiment 1, using a mixed list) and failing to demonstrate the effect in a situation in which intersentence cuing bias was eliminated (Experiment 2, using an unmixed list). The problem with their experiments is that the presence of intersentence cuing was confounded with design type. Thus, another way of interpreting their results is that the bizarreness effect occurs in a mixed-list design but not in an unmixed-list design.

---

*It should be noted that Wollen and Cox's analysis also confers a decided cued recall (intrasentence cuing) advantage on common sentences. That is, given recall of the word hen, subjects are more likely to generate the words from the common sentence (pecked or worm) than from the bizarre sentence (smoked or cigar).

Despite the logical appeal of the Wollen and Cox argument, several recent studies (McDaniel & Einstein, 1986; Merry, 1982; Pra Baldi et al., 1986) have demonstrated the superiority of bizarre imagery in mixed-list designs when using procedures that avoid the possibility of intersentence cuing confounding. McDaniel and Einstein, for example, used the same noun triplets for the bizarre and the common materials, thereby creating a constant level of intersentence cuing across both sets of materials. Another problem with the intersentence cuing idea is that it does not explain why the effects of bizarreness occur in mixed lists but not in unmixed lists (McDaniel & Einstein, 1986). If intersentence cuing does benefit recall of the bizarre sentence, then this should be the case for unmixed as well as mixed lists.

Degree of Interaction

Kroll et al. (1986) make the case that researchers in the area have ignored and failed to measure a variable that has potent effects on memory—degree of interaction (Bower, 1970a). They propose that bizarreness does not affect memory and that previous demonstrations of the bizarreness effect result from failures to control the degree of interaction across bizarre and common images. They assume that bizarreness has been confounded with interaction in these studies, resulting in situations where the bizarre images are more interactive than common images. Kroll et al. provide support for their position by showing no effects of bizarreness at immediate or long-term retention when degree of interaction was controlled. In summarizing their results, Kroll et al. (1986) state, "The present results demonstrated once again that the bizarreness of the image does not improve memory accuracy once the degree of interaction is controlled. This was true at both short and long retention intervals, with both free- and cued-recall, and at several levels of memory performance" (pp. 49–50).

In our opinion, Kroll et al. (1986) present an important methodological point. Degree of interaction has not been measured or controlled for in the great majority of studies. This has been the case for studies that have failed to find the bizarreness effect as well as those that have obtained it. Hence, in future experiments, investigators would be well advised to ensure that their bizarre and common materials are equally interactive.

Despite the well-documented importance of interactive imagery for memory, there are several problems with using the degree of interaction hypothesis to explain the bizarreness effect. First, Kroll's et al. (1986) failure to find the bizarreness effect may not have resulted from their control of interaction, but from any of a number of other methodological factors. As discussed earlier, there were simply too many methodological differences between Kroll's et al. experiments and those experiments that have found an effect of bizarreness (McDaniel & Einstein, 1986; Merry, 1980, 1982; Merry & Graham, 1978; Pra Baldi et al., 1985) to conclude that degree of interaction accounts for the different results. Further, if degree of interaction is the cause of the bizarreness effect and if this variable is rarely controlled for, then one would expect this variable to operate randomly in the literature. One would certainly not expect to find the systematic pattern of results present in Table 4.1, where the bizarreness effect has only been found with mixed lists and free recall. Another problem with the degree of interaction hypothesis is that interaction has been shown primarily to affect cued recall (Kroll et al., 1986; Wollen et al. 1972). As indicated previously, however, bizarreness mainly affects free recall and access to the images. Kroll et al.'s view also does not explain McDaniel and Einstein's (1986) finding that bizarreness is an effective variable in mixed lists but not unmixed lists. Given that McDaniel and Einstein used the same material in their mixed and unmixed lists, it is difficult to imagine how degree of interaction could be used to explain their results. Finally, it is difficult to reconcile the degree of interaction view with O'Brien and Wolford's (1982) long-term retention results. O'Brien and Wolford demonstrated differential forgetting of bizarre and common materials over a 1-week retention interval. By contrast, Kroll et al. did not find differential forgetting for high and low interactive images. Hence, the effects of these variables do not appear to be parallel.

In sum, whereas we concur with the point that researchers should control the degree of interaction in their materials, Kroll et al.'s interaction hypothesis has difficulty explaining the pattern of results that has emerged in the bizarreness literature. It is premature at this point to conclude that bizarreness has no effect on memory.

Attentional Hypothesis

According to the attentional hypothesis (Merry, 1980; Wollen and Cox, 1981a), unusual or distinctive information attracts interest and attention, resulting in extra processing for the novel events. Within this view, bizarre materials are not inherently more memorable in the sense that they enjoy special status in memory. Instead, the memorial benefits are presumed to arise from additional processing time. The attentional view can account for the finding that the bizarreness effect occurs in mixed lists and not unmixed lists by assuming that a context of common images is necessary to focus attention on the novel or bizarre.

Several results are consistent with this hypothesis. For one, processing times are almost always longer for bizarre images (Nappe & Wollen, 1973). This has been the case for both mixed (Nappe & Wollen, 1973) and unmixed lists (McDaniel & Einstein, 1986). A necessary prediction of the attentional explanation, however, is that subjects should spend proportionally more time forming (and processing) bizarre images in mixed lists as compared to unmixed lists. To date, no one has demonstrated this effect. Another result that supports the attentional view is that in mixed lists, recall of bizarre images comes at the expense of common images. Relative to unmixed list manipulations of bizarre imagery, subjects recall a greater percentage of bizarre images but a lower percentage of common images (see Figure 4.1). This result is compatible with a simple time-sharing explanation of the bizarreness effect, where the bizarre images draw attention away from the common images.

Although some results are in accord with the attentional explanation, others are not. One limitation of the attentional view is that it does not have much predictive power. The literature is replete with experiments that report greater processing time for bizarre images, yet no mnemonic benefits for these types of images (Kroll et al., 1986; Nappe & Wollen, 1973). At the very least, these results suggest that factors other than extra attention are also important. Another problem is that additional attention to the bizarre materials does not appear to be a necessary condition for obtaining the bizarreness effect. McDaniel and Einstein (1986) forced subjects to spend an equal amount of time on bizarre and common images by using fixed presentation rates. In two experiments, using relatively rapid presentation rates (7 and 8.5 sec), the bizarreness effect was still obtained. These results are difficult to reconcile with the attentional theory, which predicts higher recall for bizarre materials only when they receive extra processing. Further, McDaniel and Einstein specifically compared the effects of bizarre imagery with the effects of additional processing time. This was done by presenting subjects with a mixed list of bizarre and common sentences and using short (7 sec) and long (14 sec) presentation rates. Whereas increased processing time enhanced both access to the images and access to the components within the images, the effects of bizarreness were limited to the former measure. Hence, bizarreness and extra attention have different effects on memory.

To date, all of the studies seeking to support or disprove the attentional theory of bizarre imagery have used processing time as their measure of attention. Wollen and Margres (Chapter 5, this volume) point out that a resource allocation or cognitive effort view of attention may prove more fruitful for understanding the bizarre imagery effects. Within this view, more cognitive capacity (as measured by performance on a secondary task) is allocated to the encoding of bizarre images than to the encoding of common images, even though both types of images may require the same amount of total processing time. According to Wollen and Margres (Chapter 5, this volume), this discrepancy in resource allocation should be especially pronounced in mixed lists because subjects view bizarre images as more important or more interesting in mixed lists. This effort or resource allocation view holds some promise for understanding bizarre imagery effects and further research using a secondary task technique is necessary to fully evaluate it. Despite the potential of this effort view for explaining the bizarre imagery results, it is still not clear why differential allocation of resources and/or time should only affect certain measures of retention. For example, why should increased effort to bizarre images only affect access to images and not recovery of items within the image?

One final problem for the attentional theory is that it is difficult to understand the long-term retention results within the attentional perspective. It is not clear how the attentional view can be used to explain the differential forgetting of common and bizarre images. It should be noted that this criticism does not necessarily refute the attentional view. Rather, it suggests that if there is any value to the attentional theory, it is in understanding the immediate, and not the long-term, retention results. In general, though, the data indicate that extra attention is neither a necessary nor a sufficient condition for producing the bizarreness effect.

Distinctiveness Hypothesis

Another view that has been used to explain the bizarre imagery results is based on the concept of distinctiveness (O'Brien & Wolford, 1983; Webber & Marshall, 1978). The distinctiveness framework has enjoyed a good deal of popularity in recent years (Eysenck, 1979; Hunt & Elliott, 1980; Lockhart, Craik, & Jacoby, 1976; Nelson, 1979), in part because it accounts for some results in the memory literature that are difficult to incorporate within the levels of processing framework (cf. Hunt & Elliott, 1980; Stein, 1978). The distinctiveness framework also appears useful for describing the pattern of bizarre imagery results.

According to Nelson (1979), the distinctiveness of an event is inversely related to the number of features shared by that event and other information. Given that bizarre images typically contain exaggerated, distorted, or unusual relationships among component objects, they are by definition, more distinctive than common images. In addition to characterizing the distinctiveness of events in terms of their relationship to other information in memory, distinctiveness is usually defined in a relative manner, in which the uniqueness of an event is also determined by the relationship of that event to other items in the learning context (Jacoby & Craik, 1979). Jacoby and Craik (1979) state that "Distinctiveness requires change against some background of commonality" (p. 3), arguing that rare events are not functionally distinctive unless there are some common elements in the learning context.* If it is assumed that distinctive items are well remembered and that bizarre images are distinctive, then the predictions of the distinctiveness framework are that bizarre imagery should enhance memory whenever common images exist in the learning context. This view would nicely describe the results presented in this chapter: namely, the bizarreness effect occurs in mixed list designs and not in unmixed list designs.

Additionally, if the learning context is broadly defined as including encodings that occur between study and test, then this view can also explain the occurrence of the bizarreness effect with unmixed lists after long retention intervals or after common imagery interference. Intra- and extraexperimental experiences with common images (presumably, we form common images during our normal interactions in the world) may provide the contrastive context necessary to make bizarre images distinctive.

The distinctiveness view seems to be the most promising for integrating the existing results. The distinctiveness framework described so far, however, is purely descriptive. It does not explicate the processes underlying the bizarreness

---

*Notions of both absolute and relative distinctiveness are necessary here. If distinctiveness was defined solely in terms of the list context then common images would be as distinctive as bizarre images in lists that contain an equal number of bizarre and common images.

effect. For example, distinctive memory traces may be more easily activated at recall (Lockhart et al., 1976), they may be less susceptible to the effects of interference (Eysenck, 1979), and/or they may be more precisely reconstructed from the information available at retrieval (Hunt & Einstein, 1981; Hunt & Elliott, 1980; Nelson, 1979). We speculate on these processes in the following section.

Possible Mechanisms Underlying the Bizarreness Effect

The mechanisms usually invoked to explain distinctiveness effects are varied and not easily applied to the bizarreness effect. For example, some researchers (Einstein & Hunt, 1980; Hunt & Einstein, 1981; Hunt & Elliott, 1980; Nelson, 1979) have emphasized the discriminative function of unique or distinctive information. The argument has been that distinctive cues are much more useful than nondistinctive cues in reconstructing the original event and/or in selecting the original event from a set of similar alternatives. They have supported this claim by demonstrating positive effects of distinctiveness with criterial tasks that involve discrimination—such as recognition and cued recall and, to a lesser extent, free recall (Eysenck, 1979). By contrast, the bizarreness effect seems to be mediated by processes that primarily affect initial access to the images. At immediate retention with mixed lists, the bizarreness effect emerges only with free recall and not with cued recall or recognition. Below we speculate on processes that may underlie the bizarreness effect. In evaluating these views, the reader should realize that different mechanisms or a combination of mechanisms may be necessary to explain the entire pattern of bizarre imagery results. Few data have been collected that pertain directly to the theoretical accounts described below. At this point, therefore, there is little basis for supporting one position over another. Instead, we think that these perspectives have heuristic value and may provide profitable directions for future research.

The Organization–Redintegration Hypothesis

The memory pattern outlined earlier is most consistent with Desrochers' and Begg's (Chapter 3, this volume) organization–redintegration hypothesis. (It should be noted that this theory has many components in common with the model presented by Wollen and Margres in Chapter 5, this volume.) The organization–redintegration hypothesis assumes that the distinctiveness of an encoding influences the access of a trace and that recovery of the individual items within the trace (redintegration) is dependent on the organizational or relational bond among the items in a trace. Assuming that bizarreness (in the appropriate context) affects the distinctiveness of the image but not necessarily the integration or interactiveness of the image, then the organization–redintegration perspective predicts that bizarreness should affect trace access but not recovery of items within the trace. As described in this chapter, this is exactly what is found— bizarre imagery enhances free recall and sentence (image) access but not cued recall, recognition, or the number of items per sentence (image) recalled.

The organization–redintegration perspective, however, "explains" only in general terms how distinctiveness enhances access to images. The assertion is that distinctiveness allows the image (trace) to be discriminated from other traces, with trace discriminability being the key for trace identification or contact. By the organization–redintegration view, trace contact or access is the first stage of the retrieval process. The organization–redintegration hypothesis also does not explain why the bizarreness effect is observed only in certain contexts (e.g., mixed lists). One idea is that bizarre images are encoded distinctively only in certain contexts (although without measures of distinctiveness other than memory performance, this account becomes unsatisfyingly circular). This possibility is examined in more detail in the next section.

Encoding Distinctiveness

One approach to understanding the mixed-list versus unmixed-list effects of bizarre imagery is to suppose that bizarre images are encoded differently in these two contexts. In describing the positive effects of distinctive orthography in mixed lists but not unmixed lists, Hunt and Elliott (1980) propose that distinctive orthography is encoded only when orthographically common words are present in the learning context. When all items in a list are orthographically distinct, Hunt and Elliott propose that unique letter patterns are not perceived. They support this argument with ratings of orthographic distinctiveness showing that orthographically distinctive and orthographically common words are rated differently only in mixed lists. Analogously, it may be that the bizarre or distinctive qualities of bizarre images are only noticed (and hence, useful) in mixed lists. To explore this possibility, we recently tabulated data from an unpublished study performed in our laboratories in which subjects rated the bizarreness of bizarre and common images in mixed and unmixed lists. Subjects rated these images on a five-point scale (with 1 indicating common and 5 indicating bizarre) and the mean ratings for bizarre and common images were 3.9 and 1.8 in mixed lists and 3.3 and 2.0 in unmixed lists. Although there was a marginally significant interaction between list type and image type, bizarre images were rated as significantly more unusual than common images in both types of lists. Therefore, it seems that the unusual characteristics of bizarre images are at least perceived, and probably encoded, regardless of whether or not a common context is present. Even so, perhaps more distinctive features of bizarre images are noticed when common features are present in the learning context. Further research is necessary to explore this possibility fully.

Organization and Cue Overload

Bruce and Gaines (1976) have proposed a theory that combines organizational factors with Watkins and Watkins (1975) cue overload hypothesis. This theory was developed to account for the isolation (von Restorff) effect and has recently been used to interpret the high recall of conceptually distinctive events (Schmidt,

1985). According to this view, distinctive items are organized into a separate category and recall is inversely related to the size of the category. Whereas this hypothesis nicely explains the higher probability of recalling bizarre images in mixed lists relative to unmixed lists, this view does not explain why bizarre images are better recalled than common images in mixed-list designs. In most experiments demonstrating a bizarreness effect in mixed-list designs, subjects were presented with an equal number of bizarre and common images. Given that both bizarre and common categories are equal in size, the theory provides no mechanism for explaining the superior recall of bizarre images. Another problem with this view is that clustering of the bizarre images would be expected in recall. Analyses of our data, however, have revealed no clustering by type of image. Although subjects recalled the objects within each image together, there was no tendency to recall the bizarre or the common images together.

Interference

Interference theory has had a long and successful history in explaining many phenomena related to memory. Because similarity is a potent factor in interference, distinctive or bizarre images should be less susceptible to interference from other encodings—encodings that occur prior to, during, or after learning. As applied to the effects of bizarre imagery on immediate recall, the interference theory has difficulty explaining why the bizarreness effect occurs in mixed, but not unmixed, lists. If bizarre images are less susceptible to competition from other encodings, this should be the case for unmixed lists, as well as mixed lists. The finding that bizarreness effects are generally limited to mixed lists is therefore problematic for interference theory, unless it is assumed that there is some "similarity" among bizarre images so that bizarre images are highly interfered with by other bizarre images. It is also not clear why common images are better recalled in unmixed lists relative to mixed lists. According to interference theory, the reverse should occur. Another difficulty for interference theory is that the relative recall of bizarre and common images seems to be unaffected by proactive interference (either intra- or extraexperimental). To date, no one has shown that an initial list of common images enhances the bizarreness effect on subsequent lists (Hauck et al., 1976; McDaniel & Einstein, 1986, Exp. 5).

On the other hand, the interference view appears quite useful for understanding the results of the long-term retention studies and those studies that have included common imagery interference between study and test. As discussed earlier, the bizarreness effect tends to occur under these conditions. According to the interference view, extraexperimental experiences are likely to be common in nature. Bizarre images, therefore, should receive less interference than common images.

Retrieval Inhibition

Retrieval inhibition refers to situations in which retrieval or presentation of a subset of items from a list inhibits retrieval of the remaining items in the list (cf. Nickerson, 1984; Roediger & Neely, 1982). This phenomenon is quite general and occurs with both categorized and uncategorized lists. Another way to describe this effect is that strong items block access to weak items (Roediger & Neely, 1982).

In applying the idea of retrieval inhibition to the bizarre imagery results, it is necessary to assume that bizarre or distinctive images have "stronger" representations in memory than common images. Within this view, the superior recall of bizarre images in mixed lists is because the bizarre images block the common images. In an unmixed list of bizarre images, however, the stronger bizarre images block the weaker bizarre images. Similarly, with an unmixed list of common images, competition occurs among common images. Whereas retrieval inhibition should occur in all three types of lists described above, it is only in a mixed list that this type of blocking confers a recall advantage upon bizarre images. This view also explains the relative levels of recall of bizarre and common images in mixed and unmixed lists. Compared to unmixed lists, mixed lists produce higher recall of bizarre images and lower recall of common images. Retrieval inhibition may also be used to explain the mnemonic effects of bizarre imagery after long delays and after common imagery interference. To do so, however, requires the additional assumption that retrieval inhibition occurs among all images that have been encoded between study and test.

One implication of the retrieval inhibition view is that the output order of the items should correspond to the strength of the items. That is the "strong" or bizarre items should appear earliest in the output. Analyses of data from our laboratories, however, indicate that subjects show no tendency to recall bizarre images prior to common images.

Summary and Conclusions

There is strong evidence that bizarre imagery facilitates performance in mixed lists when immediate retention is tested with free recall. The direct demonstration of an interaction between design type (mixed versus unmixed lists) and imagery type (McDaniel & Einstein, 1986) rules out some artifactual explanations (e.g., increased intersentence cuing or increased interactiveness of bizarre sentences) of this mnemonic effect of bizarre imagery. There is also suggestive evidence, albeit less conclusive, that the bizarreness effect is obtained after long retention delays or after common imagery interference. Although it is clear that bizarre imagery can improve memory performance, it is also clear that there are boundary conditions to this enhancement. More systematic research is needed to specify precisely these boundaries. It seems, though, that neither the often stated recommendations of professional mnemonists nor the negative appraisals of memory researchers (regarding the effectiveness of bizarre imagery) are entirely correct.

The view that bizarre images are remembered better only when they are used in a context that accentuates the distinctiveness of the bizarre images seems to offer the greatest potential for understanding the pattern of bizarre imagery results. At present, however, there appears to be no clearly articulated mechanism that satisfactorily explains how different encoding contexts affect the distinctiveness of bizarre images or how distinctiveness increases memory for bizarre images. Whereas the distinctiveness framework may not ultimately yield a complete understanding of bizarreness effects, it may provide directions for future research and, in so doing, revitalize efforts to understand the mnemonic effects of bizarre imagery.

Acknowledgments. Order of authorship was determined arbitrarily, reflecting the equal contribution of each author. Preparation of the chapter was supported in part by grants to Gilles Einstein from the Research and Professional Growth Committee, Furman University and to Mark McDaniel from the Institute for the Advancement of Liberal Arts, University of Notre Dame. We gratefully acknowledge the assistance of a number of students who contributed to the research and thinking that went into this chapter. They include Jack Cosgrove, Kevin Dunay, Brian Grall, Jennifer Muhlhausen, Gail Ritter, Lydia Roper, Emily Sheets, Andrew Shull, and Melanie Weeks.

References

Andreoff, G. R., & Yarmey, A. D. (1976). Bizarre imagery and associative learning: A confirmation. *Perceptual and Motor Skills, 43,* 143–148.

Baddeley, A. D., & Warrington, E. K. (1973). Memory coding and amnesia. *Neuropsychologia, 11,* 159–165.

Bellezza, F. S. (1981). Mnemonic devices: Classification, characteristics, and criteria. *Review of Educational Research, 51,* 247–275.

Bender, B. G., & Levin, J. R. (1978). Pictures, imagery, and retarded childrens's prose learning. *Journal of Educational Psychology, 70,* 583–588.

Bergfeld, V. A., Choate, L. S., & Kroll, N. E. (1982). The effect of bizarre imagery on memory as a function of delay: Reconfirmation of interaction effect. *Journal of Mental Imagery, 6,* 141–158.

Bobrow, S. A., & Bower, G. H. (1969). Comprehension and recall of sentences. *Journal of Experimental Psychology, 80,* 455–461.

Bower, G. H. (1970a). Imagery as a relational organizer in associative learning. *Journal of Verbal Learning and Verbal Behavior, 9,* 529–533.

Bower, G. H. (1970b). Analysis of a mnemonic device. *American Scientist, 58,* 496–510.

Bower, G. H., & Winzenz, D. (1970). Comparison of associative learning strategies. *Psychonomic Science, 20,* 119–120.

Bruce, D., & Gaines, M. T. (1976). Tests of an organizational hypothesis of isolation effects in free recall. *Journal of Verbal Learning and Verbal Behavior, 15,* 59–72.

Collyer, S. C., Jonides, J., & Bevan, W. (1972). Images as memory aids: Is bizarreness helpful? *American Journal of Psychology, 85,* 31–38.

Cox, S. D., & Wollen, K. A. (1981). Bizarreness and recall. *Bulletin of the Psychonomic Society, 18,* 244–245.

Einstein, G. O., & Hunt, R. R. (1980). Levels of processing and organization: Additive effects of individual-item and relational processing. *Journal of Experimental Psychology: Human Learning and Memory, 6,* 588–598.

Emmerich, H., & Ackerman, B. (1979). A test of bizarre interaction as a factor in children's memory. *The Journal of Genetic Psychology, 134,* 225–232.

Eysenck, M. W. (1979). Depth, elaboration and distinctiveness. In L. S. Cermak & F. I.
M. Craik (Eds.), *Levels of processing in human memory* (pp. 89–118). Hillsdale, NJ:
Erlbaum Associates.

Hauck, P., Walsh, C., & Kroll, N. (1976). Visual imagery mnemonics: Common versus
bizarre mental images. *Bulletin of the Psychonomic Society, 7,* 160–162.

Hunt, R. R., & Einstein, G. O. (1981). Relational and item-specific information in
memory. *Journal of Verbal Learning and Verbal Behavior, 20,* 497–514.

Hunt, R. R., & Elliott, J. M. (1980). The role of nonsemantic information in memory:
Orthographic distinctiveness effects upon retention. *Journal of Experimental Psychology: General, 109,* 49–74.

Jacoby, L. L., & Craik, F. I. M. (1979). Effects of elaboration of processing at encoding
and retrieval: Trace distinctiveness and recovery of initial context. In L. S. Cermak &
F. I. M. Craik (Eds.), *Levels of processing in human memory.* Hillsdale, NJ: Erlbaum
Associates.

Jones, M. K. (1974). Imagery as a mnemonic aid after left temporal lobectomy: Contrast
between material-specific and generalized memory disorders. *Neuropsychologia, 12,*
21–30.

Klein, K., & Saltz, E. (1976). *Journal of Experimental Psychology: Human Learning and
Memory, 2,* 671–679.

Kroll, N. E., Schepler, E. M., & Angin, K. T. (1986). Bizarre imagery: The misremembered mnemonic. *Journal of Experimental Psychology: Learning, Memory, and Cognition, 12,* 42–54.

Lockhart, R. S., Craik, F. I. M., & Jacoby, L. L. (1976). Depth of processing, recognition
and recall. In J. Brown (Ed.), *Recognition and recall.* London: Wiley.

Lorayne, H., & Lucas, J. (1974). *The memory book.* New York: Stein & Day.

Marshall, P. H., Nau, K., & Chandler, C. K. (1980). A functional analysis of common and
bizarre visual mediators. *Bulletin of the Psychonomic Society, 15,* 373–377.

McDaniel, M. A., & Anderson, D. C. (1986). Modulation of environmental reinstate-
ment effects through imaginal and non-imaginal encoding. Unpublished manuscript,
University of Notre Dame, Notre Dame, IN.

McDaniel, M. A., & Einstein, G. O. (1985). Toward an understanding of the bizarre
imagery mnemonic: Effects of design type, intervening learning, and type of test.
Unpublished manuscript, University of Notre Dame, Notre Dame, IN.

McDaniel, M. A., & Einstein, G. O. (1986). Bizarre imagery as an effective memory aid:
The importance of distinctiveness. *Journal of Experimental Psychology: Learning,
Memory, and Cognition, 12,* 54–65.

Merry, R. (1980). Image bizarreness in incidental learning. *Psychological Reports, 46,*
427–430.

Merry, R. (1982). Cues, bizarreness and the recall of images. Unpublished manuscript,
University of Leicester, Leicester, England.

Merry, R., & Graham, N. C. (1978). Imagery bizarreness in children's recall of sentences.
British Journal of Psychology, 69, 315–321.

Nappe, G. W., & Wollen, K. A. (1973). Effects of instruction to form common and bizarre
mental images on retention. *Journal of Experimental Psychology, 100,* 6–8.

Nelson, D. L. (1979). Remembering pictures and words: Appearance, significance, and
name. In L. S. Cermak & F. I. M. Craik (Eds.), *Levels of processing in human memory*
(pp. 45–76). Hillsdale, NJ: Erlbaum Associates.

Nickerson, R. S. (1984). Retrieval inhibition from part-set cuing: A persistent enigma in memory research. *Memory and Cognition, 12,* 531–552.

O'Brien, E. J., & Wolford, C. R. (1982). Effect of delay in testing on retention of plausible versus bizarre mental images. *Journal of Experimental Psychology: Learning, Memory, and Cognition, 8,* 148–152.

Postman, L. (1975). Verbal learning and memory. *Annual Review of Psychology, 26,* 291–335.

Pra Baldi, A., de Beni, R., Cornoldi, C., & Cavedon, A. (1985). Some conditions for the occurrence of the bizarreness effect in free recall. *British Journal of Psychology, 76,* 427–436.

Pressley, M., Johnson, C. J., & Symons, S. (in press). Elaborating to learn and learning to elaborate. *Journal of Learning Disabilities.*

Pressley, M., Levin, J. R., & Delaney, H. D. (1982). The mnemonic keyword method. *Review of Educational Research, 52,* 61–91.

Robertson-Tchabo, E. A., Hausman, C. P., & Arenberg, D. (1976). A classical mnemonic for older learners: A trip that works. *Educational Gerontology, 1,* 215–226.

Roediger, H. L., III, & Neely, J. H. (1982). Retrieval blocks in episodic and semantic memory. *Canadian Journal of Psychology, 36,* 213–242.

Schmidt, S. R. (1985). Encoding and retrieval processes in the memory for conceptually distinctive events. *Journal of Experimental Psychology: Learning, Memory, and Cognition, 11,* 565–578.

Senter, R. J., & Hoffman, R. R. (1976). Bizarreness as a nonessential variable in mnemonic imagery: A confirmation. *Bulletin of the Psychonomic Society, 7,* 163–164.

Stein, B. S. (1978). Depth of processing reexamined: The effects of the precision of encoding and test appropriateness. *Journal of Verbal Learning and Verbal Behavior, 17,* 165–174.

Watkins, O. C., & Watkins, M. J. (1975). Buildup of proactive inhibition as a cue-overload effect. *Journal of Experimental Psychology: Human Learning and Memory, 104,* 442–452.

Webber, S. M., & Marshall, P. H. (1978). Bizarreness effects in imagery as a function of processing level and delay. *Journal of Mental Imagery, 2,* 291–300.

Wollen, K. A., & Cox, S. (1981a). Sentence cuing and the effectiveness of bizarre imagery. *Journal of Experimental Psychology: Human Learning & Memory, 7,* 386–392.

Wollen, K. A., & Cox, S. (1981b). The bizarreness effect in a multitrial intentional learning task. *Bulletin of the Psychonomic Society, 18,* 296–298.

Wollen, K. A., Weber, A., & Lowry, D. H. (1972). Bizarreness versus interaction of mental images as determinants of learning. *Cognitive Psychology, 3,* 518–523.

Wood, G. (1967). Mnemonic systems in recall. *Journal of Educational Psychology Monographs, 58*(6, Whole No. 645).

Yarmey, A. D. (1984). Bizarreness effects in mental imagery. In A. A. Sheikh (Ed.), *International review of mental imagery* (Vol. 1, pp. 57–76). New York: Human Sciences Press.

Yates, F. A. (1966). *The art of memory.* London: Routledge & Kegan Paul.

CHAPTER 5

Bizarreness and the Imagery Multiprocess Model

Keith A. Wollen and Matthew G. Margres

In this chapter, we first outline the historical reasons for interest in the use of bizarre imagery. Next, we review and evaluate critically data that appear to support the mnemonic value of bizarre imagery. We then identify four key phenomena that any theory of bizarre imagery must accommodate. Finally we summarize existing theories and propose a new multiprocess model to account for the data.

Historical Basis for Research on Bizarre Imagery

The use of bizarre imagery to aid recall is a tradition as old as the art of memory itself. Beginning with the *Ad Herennium*, a series of scrolls over 3000 years old, scholars throughout history have recommended the use of active, unusual images to help store information in memory (Yates, 1966). According to the *Ad Herennium*, images should be "active...as striking as possible." Striking was later described as "ridiculous, unusual, rare, emotional, or beautiful" (III, xxii). The purpose of these striking images was to draw and hold one's attention, thereby enhancing recall of the image.

The idea that a striking image would hold one's attention, and therefore be well remembered, was the basis of much of medieval religious art (Yates, 1966). Paintings typically had particular themes and were designed to represent laws, morals, and rules for people to follow. Because literacy was uncommon, laws were recorded in pictures. To insure the public did not forget their laws, the pictures were designed to be as striking as possible. This was often done with depictions of the supernatural that included angels, demons, and other uncanny (bizarre) things.

Today's mnemonists do not stray far from ancient tradition. Imagery is still recommended as a memory aid, and it is argued that images should be both active and bizarre (e.g., Cermak, 1975; Lorayne & Lucas, 1974; Roth, 1961). The advice of these experts is often used as justification for research on bizarre imagery, which makes it important to know exactly what their recommendations are.

Although a great deal of mnemonists' advice has been given through examples and general instructions, a fairly concise consensus can be gleaned from their writings.

1. The image should be interactive and well integrated. The image should not only be active, but the component parts of the image should all be engaged with one another.
2. The image should be striking or bizarre. There are two ways to make an image bizarre—by manipulating the characters of the image, or by manipulating the interaction between the characters. Characters are made bizarre through various types of distortion, whereas interactions are made bizarre by having the characters interact in unusual ways.

A common thread throughout the history of bizarre imagery has been that an image should catch and hold one's attention.

To test these recommendations, careful attention should be paid to the above two points. Often, however, such has not been the case. Researchers frequently fail to control for degree of interaction or to insure that bizarre and common images are equally well integrated. The definition of bizarreness, or lack thereof, has also been a problem. Some researchers have not defined bizarreness other than by instructions to subjects to form unusual, distinctive, striking, bizarre, etc., images. Another approach has been to use experimenters' judgments of the bizarreness of materials, such as sentences or pictures, upon which subjects are to base their images. In other cases, subjects have been asked to rate their own images in terms of bizarreness, thereby opening the door to multiple and changing criteria. The most ambitious attempt to objectify bizarreness has been that of Marshall, Nau, and Chandler (1979), who had subjects describe images they had formed; these descriptions were then catalogued according to the type of "transformations" that were used. The notion that subjects make different types of transformations is a step in the right direction. However, Marshall et al. really just described what subjects did and did not offer a definition that would lend itself to theoretical interpretation.

Research on bizarre imagery has been troubled with contradictory and confusing results. Part of the problem is that researchers have not really paid sufficient attention to what mnemonists have said about insuring image integration, interaction, and bizarreness. The other part of the problem is that the advice of mnemonists does not readily lend itself to the rigors of scientific methodology. Operational definitions of interaction and bizarreness are very difficult. Also, mnemonists often emphasize that bizarre images should be idiosyncratic. Indeed, Lorayne and Lucas (1974) warned that using the example bizarre images supplied in their book might not help memory for that information at all. In trying to maintain experimental control, researchers have frequently contradicted the mnemonists' advice by supplying subjects with pictures or descriptions of the images to be formed. Leaving subjects to form their own images, however, would mean surrendering experimental control over the type of images formed. The net result has been a frustrating methodological and theoretical quagmire.

Data Used as Evidence of a Bizarreness Effect

The current status of the effects of bizarre imagery has been reviewed recently by Yarmey (1984). His review focused almost entirely on problems with experiments that failed to find bizarreness effects. There were virtually no detailed criticisms of experiments used as support for the effect. Because the burden of proof of a phenomenon always lies with those who argue for its existence, we shall take the opposite approach and critically examine data used in support of the effectiveness of bizarre imagery. From this analysis, we shall tease out several key findings that serve as an empirical base for theoretical formulations.

Empirical Demonstrations

Early Studies

Research by Delin has often been cited as support for the bizarreness effect, but the relevance of his data to this issue is in question. In one investigation (Delin, 1968), students were told at the beginning of a class period to form bizarre images for only three pairs of words. Descriptions of the images were rated for degree of bizarreness, and a correlation was found between bizarreness and recall. Because these data are correlational in nature, and because there were no control subjects instructed to form common images, the results are not convincing evidence for the effectiveness of bizarre images.

A second report by Delin (1969a) used relearning of a serial list as the main dependent variable. Subjects first learned a serial list to a criterion of one perfect trial and then relearned either the same list in the reversed order or a completely new list. Half of the subjects were instructed to use bizarre imagery, whereas the other half were left to their own devices. Although subjects who received bizarre-image instructions experienced a greater savings in relearning, the data are not relevant to the question of whether bizarre imagery is superior to common because there is no comparison group given common-image instructions. Moreover, transfer to the reversed serial order is a complex task, as anyone knows who has tried to recite the alphabet backwards. In any task that involves relearning in the reversed order, there is a confounding of the formation of the "new" associations with the increased episodic memory of the response terms.

The third Delin study (1969b) also examined relearning of a serial list, but relearning was in the same order as original learning. This experiment did have a somewhat direct test of common vs. bizarre imagery. Some subjects were told to use vivid, active images using as many sensory modalities as possible. If it can be assumed that these subjects used common images, a comparison is possible with another condition in which subjects were told to form vivid, active, bizarre images using as many sensory modalities as possible. The instructions were extremely complex, and Delin reported that many subjects experienced difficulty in following them, especially in the bizarre-imagery condition; in fact, only 10 of 42 subjects described images that Delin classified "as being in any way bizarre" (p. 88). These facts suggest that the instructions were not very effective in manipulating imagery. The major finding of interest was a greater number of errors for subjects with bizarre imagery. This finding led Delin to conclude that "bizarreness, if it has any effect, reduces the effectiveness of imagery mnemonics" (p. 88). A similar conclusion was reached by Wood (1967). It is interesting that the other Delin studies, which have no appropriate comparison condition, have often been cited as evidence that bizarre imagery is effective, whereas the 1969b study has been ignored.

Random Assignment of Words to Pairs

Some data are of questionable relevance to the study of bizarre imagery because care has not been taken to insure that both common and bizarre images were equally easy to form (e.g., Collyer, Jonides, & Bevan, 1972; Wood, 1967). This is a particular problem when subjects are presented only with pairs of words and are asked to form images using those words, and when words are randomly assigned to pairs. Random assignment is likely to result in unusual combinations of nouns (such as "skillet"–"zebra") which would generally make it easier to form bizarre images than common images. In such cases, the presence of superior recall for bizarre images might better be interpreted in terms of greater ease of forming those images. Andreoff and Yarmey (1976) used random assignment of words to pairs but argued that this was not a problem because of a preliminary study in which eight subjects "indicated that they could evoke the appropriate image for each word pair" (p. 144). It is not clear how the subjects indicated this, or what the means were. However, even if images were evoked, it may have been that bizarre images were formed more quickly and thus rehearsed more than common ones.

Another potential problem with the Andreoff and Yarmey study was raised by Bergfeld, Choate, and Kroll (1982), who pointed out that the imagery used with bizarre pairs may have been more interactive than that used with common ones. Because interaction is known to be a powerful variable (Bergfeld et al., 1982; Kroll, Schepeler, & Angin, 1986; Senter & Hoffman, 1976; Wollen, Weber, & Lowry, 1972), degree of interaction should be controlled.

Delayed Recall

One way to get around the problem of some images being easier to form than others is to present subjects with drawings that depict a bizarre or common inter-action. Such was the approach used by Webber and Marshall (1978). Using a mixed-list design (half bizarre and half common) and cued recall, bizarre interaction was found to facilitate recall at a 1-week interval but not in an immediate test. However, the effect was very small (29% for bizarre vs. 19% for common), quite in contrast to the large effect alluded to by mnemonists. Moreover, the use of a mixed-list design opens the door for subjects to attend more to bizarre images (this issue will be discussed later in the section on attention theory).

An even smaller effect was reported by O'Brien and Wolford (1982), who also presented drawings in a mixed-list design. They found no effect of bizarreness on tests given immediately or after 1 or 3 days. However, bizarre drawings led to significantly greater recall at 5- and 7-day intervals. A problem arises in the interpretation of these data because a bizarreness effect was obtained only when the level of recall was extremely low. In the delayed tests that produced significant differences, the mean number correct (24 possible) was between 0.6 and 0.9 for common images, and between 1.6 and 2.4 for bizarre. With such low means, many subjects would have recalled nothing and would have had zero variance. Even with the arc sine transformations that were used, the variability would have been artifactually low, thereby increasing the probability of finding significant differences. Moreover, the mean number correct at shorter retention intervals was much higher, suggesting the possibility of heterogeneous forms and variances that would also tend to increase the likelihood of finding significant differences. Finally, it should be emphasized that the significant differences in delayed recall were actually smaller than the nonsignificant differences found at the shorter retention intervals.

Vertical Versus Horizontal Bizarreness Effects

Bizarreness could conceivably affect two different types of retrieval, vertical and horizontal. To explain these, imagine a list of 10 sentences arranged vertically on a page such that there is one sentence per line. Imagine also that each sentence has three key words in it, all of which appear on the same horizontal line. In the free recall of such a list, a subject would first of all have to access each sentence, which involves the task of getting from one sentence to another — this we refer to as vertical retrieval. Once a sentence or sentence fragment has been accessed, the subject must attempt to retrieve the keywords in that sentence — this constitutes horizontal retrieval. Thus, vertical retrieval depends upon interconnections among sentences, whereas horizontal retrieval depends upon interconnections within sentences. Cued recall or recognition differ from free recall in that the recall cue or recognition stimulus essentially bypass vertical retrieval. Hence, cued recall and recognition would consist primarily of horizontal retrieval.

The data indicate that bizarreness facilitates vertical retrieval but either hinders or has no effect on horizontal retrieval. Early research virtually always used cues and therefore emphasized horizontal retrieval rather than vertical. Such research usually has found either no difference between bizarre and common images or a superiority for common (e.g., Cox & Wollen, 1981; Emmerich & Ackerman, 1979; Nappe & Wollen, 1973; Senter & Hoffman, 1976; Wollen & Cox, 1981a; Wollen et al., 1972).

Quite different results have been obtained in experiments that involved free recall and, therefore, vertical retrieval. Merry (1980; Merry & Graham, 1978) used such sentences as "The HEN pecked the WORM," and "The MAN pecked the WORM." The subject's task was to form images, rate those images with respect to vividness, and later recall the sentences (only the two nouns were scored). In two experiments, bizarre sentences produced greater recall than common for both immediate and 1-week delayed tests, and for both incidental and intentional tasks.

Wollen and Cox (1981a) replicated and extended Merry's findings by demonstrating that superior recall for subjects with bizarre sentences is obtained only in a free-recall situation. In a cued task that used the first two words of each sentence as retrieval cues (e.g., The HEN, The MAN), common sentences produced better performance.

McDaniel and Einstein (1986) provided a clear empirical separation of vertical and horizontal retrieval. They found that superior recall of bizarre images was based on increased "sentence access" (recall of at least one target word from a sentence) rather than on the number of words recalled within a sentence. In a mixed-list condition subjects had greater sentence access, but if one word was recalled the probability that the other words in the same sentence would be recalled was the same for bizarre and common conditions. Thus, bizarreness enhanced vertical retrieval but not horizontal. When horizontal effects have been found, common images have generally produced greater recall than bizarre (e.g., Pra Baldi, De Beni, Cornoldi, & Cavedon, 1985; Wollen & Cox, 1981a).

The finding that bizarre images do not facilitate horizontal retrieval is contrary to predictions of mnemonists who, for centuries, have argued that bizarreness strengthens associations of the to-be-remembered target word with some cue word (as in the method of loci). Bizarreness does, indeed, facilitate retrieval in the sense of getting from one image to another, but not in the sense of one item in the image cueing other items from that image. Free-recall data, therefore, cannot be used as evidence in support of the advice of mnemonists (see also Merry, 1980; Merry & Graham, 1978; Wollen & Cox, 1981a).

Theoretically Oriented Research

Distinctiveness

The research that provides the most convincing evidence for a bizarreness effect, and is most theoretically grounded, is that conducted by McDaniel and Einstein (1986; see also Chapter 4, this volume). Their research involved the learning of noun triads embedded in common sentences (e.g., "The DOG chased the BICYCLE down the STREET") or in bizarre sentences (e.g., "The DOG rode the BICYCLE down the STREET"). An incidental learning task was used in which subjects were asked to form an image of the described event and to rate that image for vividness. In one experiment, superior free recall of the target nouns (shown in capital letters) was obtained only when a mixed list, half bizarre and half common, was used. When subjects had all bizarre or all common sentences, no bizarreness effect was found.

These data were interpreted in the context of distinctiveness theory; bizarre images should be more distinctive than common images and therefore should be better recalled. The authors did not indicate the specific mechanism by which this result was effected. Although the data appear consistent with a distinctiveness theory, several questions do arise. Why do bizarre images fail to be effective in unmixed-list comparisons? In this same vein, in a mixed-list condition, why are the common images not set apart from the bizarre and, therefore, distinctive? In other words, the common images may well be considered distinctive when contrasted with the bizarre, just as the bizarre are distinctive compared with the common. Finally, why have some mixed-list experiments failed to produce a bizarreness effect (e.g., Nappe & Wollen, 1973)?

One datum that must be accounted for by any theory is McDaniel's and Einstein's finding that bizarre images are rated as being less vivid than common ones. This is difficult for a simple distinctiveness theory to handle because one is put in the peculiar position of arguing that the less vivid bizarre images have more mnemonic value and are more effective than the more vivid common ones. Common images were also better in the sense of requiring less formation time.

A study by O'Brien and Wolford (1982) provides a related example of the lack of a correlation between characteristics of the image and bizarreness effects. One might expect the bizarreness effect to be more prominent in subjects with high imagery ability because such subjects should be more skillful at thinking up effective bizarre images. In fact, however, they found no relationship between imagery ability and the bizarreness effect.

Priority of Recall

In free-recall experiments, it may be that subjects recall more of the bizarre materials because they give priority to recalling them first; recall of the bizarre images may then interfere with recall of common ones. This would not be a problem in between-list conditions because all items would be bizarre or all common. The possibility of priority effects should be checked in all free-recall experiments. Unfortunately, no one has reported data relevant to priority, although McDaniel and Einstein (personal communication) indicated that they did not find such effects in their research.

Image Formation Time and Attention

Many experimenters have reported that subjects spend longer forming bizarre images than common ones. This finding applies when differential ease of forming images is not a problem, such as when care is exercised to insure both common and bizarre images can be made (Nappe & Wollen, 1973), or when the image is suggested by a sentence (e.g., McDaniel & Einstein, 1986). If subjects spend more time on bizarre images, it may be that the bizarreness effect is simply an artifact of more rehearsal for bizarre images than for common. McDaniel and Einstein recognized this problem and conducted an experiment to obviate it. They equated image formation time between bizarre and common images by forcing all subjects to form each image within 7 sec. Even with image formation time equated, bizarre imagery resulted in greater free recall. The experimenters argued that this result was inconsistent with the notion that subjects attended more to the bizarre pairs. However, an attention hypothesis has no particular difficulty with such a finding because it is possible to devote more attention (effort) to bizarre images without spending more time on them (this idea is developed in the section on attention to follow).

Between-List Designs

In their last experiment, McDaniel and Einstein (1986) obtained data they inter-preted as showing that bizarre imagery is effective in a between-lists design. They followed bizarre or common target lists with interpolated activities consisting of intentional learning of either bizarre or common lists. They argued that the inter-polated learning provided a contrast from the target lists. A bizarre target list fol-lowed by a common interpolated list produced greater recall of the target items than having both lists common or having the original list common and the inter-polated list bizarre. Unfortunately, the interpretation of these data is unclear because the interaction was not statistically significant at the .05 level.

Other questions can be raised. If bizarre items are made distinctive when fol-lowed by common interpolated learning, why is not distinctiveness also increased when common items are followed by bizarre? Another question is why the con-trasting properties of the common list do not appear when the "context" is the first list and the recall is of the interpolated, bizarre list (rather than the original list). In answering these questions, an important consideration is the potential role of retroactive interference. A bizarre interpolated list would be more difficult than a common one. If greater task difficulty is associated with greater retroactive interference, there would be greater interference when a common list is followed by a bizarre one than when the order is reversed. Therefore, it is possible that interference, and not a contrast effect, accounted for McDaniel and Einstein's (1986) data.

Another experiment found a bizarreness effect using a between-subjects design (Marshall, Nau, & Chandler, 1980). Subjects were given 60 sec per pair to gener-ate an image and write a description of it. Subjects were told to use bizarre imagery recalled more than subjects told to use common, but the difference was very small (6.8 vs. 4.52 out of 48). Also, the possibility of floor effects renders questionable the statistical assumptions of normality and equality of variances, and consequently the outcome of the analysis may be in doubt.

Image Integration and the Bizarreness Effect

Wollen and Cox (1981a) suggested that common images are better integrated than bizarre. Pra Baldi et al. (1985) found support for this notion. Using the free-recall procedure of Merry and Graham (1978), Pra Baldi et al. found that the probability of recalling all of a sentence given recall of a part was higher for com-mon images. They also found a vertical effect because bizarre images produced higher overall recall. However, the generality of the vertical effect is question-able because it disappeared on replication with a different set of sentences. This latter result emphasizes the necessity of closer examination of the materials.

Delayed Recall

Some researchers have argued that bizarreness effects appear primarily in delayed rather than in immediate tests (e.g., Andreoff & Yarmey, 1976; O'Brien & Wolford, 1982; Webber & Marshall, 1978). However, the strength of such an argument is weakened by the previously mentioned criticisms of these studies and by several failures to find a bizarreness effect when delayed recall was used (e.g., Bergfeld et al., 1982; Delin, 1969b; Hauck, Walsh, & Kroll, 1976; Kroll et al., 1986; Wortman & Sparling, 1974). Moreover, if bizarre images are indeed more distinctive, why do not bizarreness effects appear on immediate recall as well as on delayed? There has been no adequate answer to this question.

Data a Theory Must Incorporate

Several findings can be identified as especially important in theory construction:

1. Any theory must account for the fact that, in free recall, bizarreness increases the probability of getting from one image to another (vertical retrieval) but either has no effect on or decreases recall within each image (horizontal retrieval). Also to be accounted for are the data from cued recall and recognition in which common images tend to produce better performance.
2. A theory must also account for the fact that higher recall for bizarre images is a mixed-list phenomenon. With but two exceptions (Marshall et al., 1980; McDaniel & Einstein, 1986) that are open to other interpretations, no one has found a bizarreness effect using a between-subjects' design. However, experiments using a mixed-list design have frequently produced the effect.
3. Subjects take longer to form bizarre images. If unpaced, why do subjects spend more time forming bizarre images? This result has been obtained repeatedly and is very robust. Any theory of bizarre imagery effects must be able to accommodate such a finding.
4. Bizarre images are consistently rated as being less vivid than common images (e.g., McDaniel & Einstein, 1986). A theory must explain why a nonvivid, "inferior," bizarre image would prove more effective than a vivid common one.

Theoretical Interpretations

Intersentence Cueing

Many different notions have been advanced in attempts to explain results of research on the bizarreness effect. One notion, intersentence cueing (Wollen & Cox, 1981a), was put forth as a potential problem in Merry and Graham's (1978) research. In that experiment, the possibility existed that recall of one bizarre sentence (e.g., "The HEN smoked the CIGAR") could cue other related sentences (e.g., "The MAN smoked the CIGAR"); no such cueing would have been present in common sentences (e.g., "The HEN pecked the WORM" would not cue "The MAN smoked the CIGAR"). Although the initial data were consistent with this interpretation (Wollen & Cox, 1981a), convincing arguments have been raised against it (see Einstein and McDaniel, Chapter 4, this volume). Consequently, no further discussion of this view is warranted.

Image Integration

Another possibility, also advanced by Wollen and Cox (1981a), is that common images enjoy the benefit of greater integration. According to this view, items within the image are "tied together" better such that one item is more likely to call to mind the other item(s). In a related vein, Rohwer (1973) has argued that a verb is an effective connective to the extent that it makes reference to both subject and object nouns. Cox and Wollen (1981) also argue that the verb and two nouns are "more associatively related in nonbizarre than in bizarre sentences" (p. 245).

The most convincing evidence for the integration hypothesis is the finding that common images produce better horizontal recall than bizarre images. For example, common images have been found to produce a higher probability of recalling an entire image given recall of any part (Pra Baldi et al., 1985). Also, Cox and Wollen (1981) found that subjects were more likely to free recall the entire image when the image was common than when it was bizarre. Finally, when part of an image is provided as a retrieval cue, recall of the remaining part of the image has often been found to be higher for common than for bizarre (e.g., Emmerich & Ackerman, 1979; Wollen & Cox, 1981a, b). Common and bizarre images have produced equal cued recall in some instances (see Einstein & McDaniel, Chapter 4, this volume), but no study has found bizarre images to be recalled more completely.

The concept of integration can account for the shorter image formation time for common images, and for the finding that common images are more likely to facilitate horizontal recall. However, the integration notion has difficulty handling situations in which bizarreness has enhanced vertical recall. Also, the integration notion says nothing about why a bizarreness effect is more likely in a mixed-list design.

Elaboration

We view elaboration in a sense similar to that of Craik and Tulving (1975). When presented with a pair of words, such as "dog"–"bicycle," a subject could elaborate by forming an image of a particular dog with particular features that is riding a particular type of bicycle that itself has specific features. Elaboration might also be used to distort the dog so that its legs would reach the pedals, and so that its paws could grasp the handlebars. Other features, such as a hat on the dog, a street, trees, etc., also could be used. All of these added "features" constitute elaboration of the original schematic images evoked by the word pair.

Elaboration has largely been ignored by researchers studying the bizarreness effect, although Yarmey (1984) suggested its use. Emmerich and Ackerman (1979) also used the term, but primarily in a descriptive sense, although they did suggest that "normal" elaboration resulted in a deeper level of processing than bizarre elaboration.

The concept of elaboration offers considerable promise. Subjects who form bizarre images obviously must change their usual images in some way in order to make them bizarre; such changes constitute elaboration. Because common images would require fewer such changes, less elaboration would be involved. Whether or not elaboration produces a bizarreness effect probably depends upon the nature of the elaboration.

Several studies not involving bizarre imagery have demonstrated that the nature of the elaboration is important (e.g., Stein & Bransford, 1979; Stein, Littlefield, Bransford, & Persampieri, 1984). In the latter paper, researchers compared elaboration that integrated sentences (e.g., "The funny man bought the ring that squirted water") with elaboration that did not (e.g., "The funny man bought the ring and told a joke"). The elaboration "that squirted water" integrates the various parts of that sentence and explains the relationship between "funny" and "bought the ring." The elaboration "and told a joke" provides no such integration. Using "The ____ man bought the ring" as a recall cue, integration produced greater recall of the missing word "funny" than did nonintegration. In both cases, the elaborations are sensible and should have increased distinctiveness. Hence, the authors concluded that "elaborations that increase distinctiveness do not always facilitate retention of concepts involved in semantic relationships" (p. 528).

Other evidence that elaboration must relate to the integration of an image to result in facilitation is available in a study by Kulhavy and Heinen (1974). These investigators used sentences rather than imagery, but the procedure is otherwise quite similar. Bizarre sentences were created from common ones by adding unusual adjectives, such as "The *elephant-trunked* tank crushed the *mastachioed* bottle." This type of elaboration was no more effective than simply having the same sentences without the adjectives. Such an outcome is to be expected, for the elaboration would not have helped to integrate the sentence—on the contrary, it could have made integration more difficult.

Data more specific to imagery have been reported by Begg and Sikich (1984). In their Experiment 2, the probability of correctly recalling B given A was .49 when A and B were imaged interactively, but only .35 when an additional "context word" (C) was incorporated into the image along with A and B. Hence, elaboration in the form of the context word reduced recall, leading the authors to conclude that "the value of an interactive image decreases as more items are incorporated" (p. 58). Interpretation of these data for the present purposes is made difficult because subjects were free to form their own images, and no data were provided regarding the content of those images. Thus, we do not know exactly how the context word related to the interaction between A and B, or even if it had any relationship at all. Any given image might have contained just one interaction, or three (A–B, B–C, and A–C). Moreover, it is difficult to speculate about what subjects might have done because the experimenters did not indicate what specific target words were used.

It is reasonable to expect subjects to use more elaboration with bizarre imagery than with common. Even when the image has been "prescribed" by presenting subjects with a sentence (as in McDaniel & Einstein, 1986), the subject would be forced to use elaborative distortions of schematic images; such distortions would be much less necessary for common images.

Evidence for greater elaboration for bizarre images has been provided by Marshall et al. (1979, 1980). For example, the 1980 study showed that the mean number of transformations (such as adding an object) was greater for subjects given bizarre imagery instructions than for subjects given common-imagery instructions. Given the Begg and Sikich (1984) data, it seems reasonable to expect many transformations (elaborations) subjects use either to detract from or have no effect on the integration of one's image. Indeed, the Marshall et al. (1980) study showed that the probability of correct recall was higher for a simple interacting image (e.g., "The canary landed on the buckle") than for one involving the addition of an object (e.g., "The boy watched the canary land on the buckle"); this finding was obtained for both common and bizarre images.

At this juncture, more research is needed that exerts control over the content of the image—especially the elaboration of that image and the type of bizarreness used. It is probably the case that most extant experiments involved some types of images expected to produce facilitation and others expected to produce no facilitation or even interference. The net effect would then depend upon the relative contributions of these two factors.

If it were the case that certain types of bizarre elaboration were effective and others not, there would be a potential explanation for the fact that bizarre imagery is effective for mnemonists but not for most experimental subjects; mnemonists may simply be more adept at using bizarreness in a way that integrates the image. Such a view was suggested by Nappe and Wollen (1973) but remains to be tested experimentally.

The elaboration hypothesis readily explains why subjects given bizarre imagery instructions take longer to form their images. Bizarre imagery leads to greater elaboration and elaboration takes time. It is also reasonable to expect bizarre images to be less vivid because they involve changes from familiar objects and interactions. Moreover, because bizarre images are more complex, subjects may spend less time forming any one part of the image, thereby making them seem less vivid.

The largest problem for the elaboration viewpoint is to account for the vertical nature of the bizarreness effect. It may be that anything, such as bizarre imagery, that reduces horizontal effects increases other possibilities—in this case, a vertical effect. However, this interpretation is speculative at best and not very convincing in any event. Another problem for elaboration is why the bizarreness effect is predominantly a mixed-list phenomenon.

Distinctiveness

The term "distinctiveness" will be used here in the general sense described in several sources (e.g., Hunt & Elliott, 1980; Jacoby & Craik, 1979). According to such views, input involves encoding of distinctive stimulus features. These features differentiate stimuli at input and can be used later as retrieval cues. The more distinctive the encoded features, the more effective they will be in cueing retrieval. Nondistinctive traces would share many features with other items in memory and would, as a result, be more difficult to differentiate and retrieve.

Distinctiveness has been mentioned as a potentially important variable by several researchers. Lesgold and Goldman (1973) used a single cue in the same way in several images or uniquely in each of several images. They suggested that because they found uniqueness to be important, it might be that bizarreness was effective because it also entailed uniqueness. Thus, they espoused a type of distinctiveness theory of bizarreness but provided no empirical tests. The main proponents of the distinctiveness view of bizarre imagery have been McDaniel and Einstein (1986; see also Einstein & McDaniel, Chapter 4, this volume).

Distinctiveness works well in accounting for the vertical effect. By itself, however, it offers no account of why the bizarreness effect is primarily a mixed-list phenomenon, or why it shows up only as a vertical effect. Even in mixed lists, it is not clear why the common images are not so distinct as the bizarre. Why subjects take longer to form bizarre images may be handled by assuming that distinctive images require longer to form, although it is not clear why this should be the case unless the concept of elaboration is also invoked. Finally, a distinctiveness notion, by itself, does not explain why bizarre images are more distinctive and yet are described as less vivid.

It makes intuitive sense for vividness and recall to be related, and several researchers have so concluded (e.g., Anderson & Hidde, 1971; Ernest, 1977; Marks, 1972, 1983; Sheehan, 1966). Given that some research has failed to produce a vividness effect, it may be tempting to dismiss the importance of the fact that nonvivid bizarre images produce better recall than the more vivid common ones. However, a theoretical dilemma would remain. It would still be necessary for whatever theory one proposed to explain how subjects could make effective use of the distinctive features of bizarre images when those images were unclear. At the very least, such a theory would be forced to deal with the fact that the benefit derived from the increased distinctiveness of bizarre images is greater than the liability of their decreased vividness. Incidentally, it is very possible that some of the failures to find a relationship between vividness and recall stems from the scoring method used. Synonyms (such as recalling "doctor" rather than "physician") have generally been scored as errors, but more such decoding errors would be expected with vivid imagery. With nonvivid imagery, subjects would be more likely to rely upon verbal coding and, therefore, make fewer such decoding errors.

Attention

The term "attention" has been used in a number of ways, including selection of one stimulus over another, arousal or alertness, and as differential allocation of a pool of resources (e.g., Moray, 1970; Schneider, Dumais, & Shiffrin, 1984). The focus here is on the notion of resource allocation. Such a notion was presented by Knowles (1963) and elaborated upon by many others (e.g., Kahneman, 1973; Wickens, 1984). According to the resource allocation view, humans have a limited pool of attentional resources that can be concentrated on a single task or divided among two or more tasks. The extent to which division can occur depends upon such factors as the difficulty of the tasks and their modalities.

Attention has been mentioned as a possible interpretation of previous findings (e.g., Wollen & Cox, 1981a). Attention provides a promising interpretation of some data, particularly the puzzle of why the bizarreness effect is especially prominent in mixed-list designs. If subjects are presented with both bizarre and common sentences to image, or if they are instructed to form both types of images, subjects may well find bizarre images more fascinating and therefore devote more attention to them. Subjects may also think that the experimenter's main interest is in the bizarre images and focus more attention on them and less on the common. If all images were bizarre, or if all were common, selective attention to one type of image would not be possible. In the McDaniel and Einstein (1986) experiments, it might have been that subjects devoted more cognitive effort to bizarre sentences than to common ones, and that this increased effort (rather then some characteristic of bizarre imagery) accounted for the greater free recall.

Evidence that subjects do emphasize bizarre images more in a mixed-list design is provided by Marshall et al. (1979, 1980). These experimenters found that subjects used more "transformations" in making bizarre images (i.e., elaborations, such as the addition of an object, change in the size of an object, etc.) when given a mixed list than when the list was unmixed. Other evidence that subjects emphasized bizarre images was provided by McDaniel and Einstein (1986), who found that a mixed list resulted in greater recall of bizarre images but *less* recall of common than was the case in unmixed-list conditions. In all of these instances, a mixed list shifted emphasis toward the bizarre and away from the common. McDaniel and Einstein argued that attention could not account for the presence of a bizarreness effect in their research because the effect was obtained in an experiment that equated the time allowed for image formation. However, attention is not ruled out when image-formation time is equated because subjects may have allocated more attentional resources to bizarre images than to common ones.

One method that has been used to study resource allocation is the secondary-task technique. In this method, subjects are to divide their resources between a primary task (such as pattern recognition or reading) and a secondary task (such as pushing a switch as quickly as possible after the onset of a tone). The more the resources required by the primary task, the less that will be left over to perform the secondary task, thereby resulting in longer reaction times.

The secondary-task technique has been used in a variety of situations (e.g., Posner & Boies, 1971; Reynolds & Anderson, 1982) and has shown that time and effort can be independent. For example, Reynolds and Anderson found that reaction time to a tone increased (thereby indicating greater cognitive effort) even though time on the primary task decreased. To determine whether subjects devote more resources to bizarre images, cognitive effort used to form common or bizarre images could be measured by periodically obtaining reaction times to a probe stimulus (such as a tone) while the images are being formed.

The resource allocation notion provides an interpretation of why mixed-list designs are more likely to produce bizarreness effects. When subjects have mixed lists, they may view bizarre images as more interesting or important and consequently devote more resources to their formation even when image formation time is held constant. If all images were of one kind, there would be no obvious reason to emphasize some of the images at the expense of others, and so there would be no bizarreness effect. In this connection, it is important to remember that the bizarreness effect found by McDaniel and Einstein (1986) involved better recall of part of a list (bizarre items) but poorer recall of the rest (common items). If image-formation time were unlimited, subjects could simply spend longer creating bizarre images.

Attention, by itself, is not a complete model because it cannot handle some types of findings. For example, an attention model would have difficulty explaining why subjects rated bizarre images as less vivid than common ones, or why the bizarreness effects were vertical rather than horizontal.

It appears that theories of integration, elaboration, attention, and distinctiveness all have promising characteristics, but that the phenomena associated with bizarreness research are too complex for any one approach. Consequently, we propose a multiprocess model to account for the data and to provide a basis for future research.

Imagery Multiprocess Model

The proposed model is called the Imagery Multiprocess model, hereafter referred to as IMP. The major components of IMP are outlined in Figure 5.1. Our discussion of the model is divided into two main sections, image formation and image retrieval.

Image Formation

Processes Involved

The "stimulus" in Figure 5.1 consists of whatever information is provided to subjects as a basis for their images, such as a pair of words, a picture, or a sentence. This stimulus prompts a search of memory for appropriate image schemas that can be used in image formation. We assume that the retrieved images are prototypical in nature and are based upon many experiences with the items in question. These schematic images are similar to what have been called generic images (Reese, 1977) or scene schemas (Mandler, 1984).

Once schematic images have been selected, the next step is to modify them such that the two objects interact in some way. When the stimulus consists of items that commonly occur together, such as cup–saucer, the search is brief and

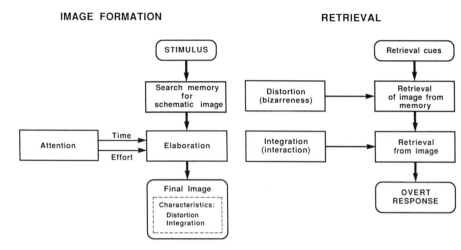

FIGURE 5.1. Processes that occur during image formation and retrieval. Copyright February 1986 by Keith A. Wollen, reprinted by permission.

a schematic image can be used as the final one. In many instances, however, the subject would have no completely preformed schema that could be used. This would be especially true when subjects are told to form bizarre images, such as a dog riding a bicycle. Most of us have never seen a dog riding a bicycle and must elaborate upon the schematic image of dog, the schematic image of bicycle, or both, to form the final image.

Attention is assumed to be indexed by the amount of time and/or effort (allocation of resources) that is expended on elaboration and encoding of features. These features serve to distinguish one image from another and to cue retrieval from memory. The encoding–elaboration process produces images that have varying amounts of distortion and integration.

By definition, schematic images are not bizarre. Consequently, schematic images used as the basis for bizarre images must be modified by elaboration, and the elaboration must be unusual or the resulting images would not be bizarre. For example, if subjects are instructed to form an image of a dog riding a bicycle, they must first choose a schematic image of a dog and another of a bicycle. Then they must elaborate upon the dog (perhaps by elongating its legs so they reach the pedals, giving it paws that can grasp the handlebars, etc.), upon the bicycle (creating a bicycle that would "fit" the dog better), or upon both. The fact that the elaboration results in an unusual image means that bizarre images are more distinctive from (i.e., share fewer features with) schematic images in memory than is the case with common images.

Several types of elaboration can be used, and these will be described by considering a situation in which a subject is given two nouns (N1 and N2) and asked to form an image involving them. If the subject encodes N1 and N2 by using only a connective (C) commonly used to join N1 and N2, a common, relatively unelaborated image results. Elaboration is assumed to consist of (a) an unusual interaction or connective between N1 and N2; (b) depictions of adjectival or adverbial modifiers (M) of N1, N2, or C; (c) depictions of added nouns or connectives; and (d) distortions of any of the above. Distortions of nouns can be of size, shape, animation, etc. Distortions of connectives consist of uncommon relationships between two or more nouns. Finally, distortions of modifiers consist of uncommon adjectival descriptions, such as green dog. In all cases, distortions represent deviations from a subject's schematic images, and elaboration is the process by which images are made bizarre.

An operational definition of bizarreness can be based on the number and nature of distortions used in a subject-generated image, or in the picture or sentence if the experimenter provides these as the "basis" for an image. The most desirable approach would be to determine the degree of each distortion and develop a composite index that incorporated both the degree and the number of distortions. Ideally, bizarreness would be determined idiosyncratically; for example, a "car on top of a pole" could be bizarre for one person but common to another who lived across the street from a used-car lot that advertized itself by a car mounted on a pole. However, idiosyncratic determination would be extremely difficult to accomplish.

Interpretations of Data

Several findings can be accommodated by the portions of IMP discussed so far. In mixed-list designs, subjects typically take longer to form bizarre images than to form common ones. One interpretation is that subjects spend greater time or effort on bizarre items because they find bizarre items more interesting or they believe that bizarre pairs are somehow more important. A second possibility is that subjects need more time to elaborate on common schematic images, or need more effort in order to be able to elaborate within a fixed time period. These alternatives may in fact be interdependent because it is reasonable to expect subjects to attribute greater importance to difficult tasks than to easy ones, and forming bizarre images requires more elaboration and is, therefore, more difficult. Finally, a third interpretation is that forming bizarre images requires subjects to conduct a longer memory search to find schematic images that lend themselves to distortion.

The IMP model also provides a ready interpretation of the often reported finding that subjects rate bizarre images as being less vivid. In forming bizarre images, subjects engage in greater elaboration in the form of more distortion and a greater number of elements, each of which requires image-formation time. By virtue of greater complexity and less time available to any one part of the total image, bizarre images could be regarded as less vivid. Also, it is reasonable to expect distortions, involving things never before seen, to be less vivid than common scenes. With common images, subjects can more readily rely on preexperimental schematic images (e.g., we may already have a schema for "a book sitting on a desk" but not for "a book shaking hands with a desk"). Such preexisting schemas would decrease image-formation time and increase the time available for image "rehearsal." The more schematic an image or the more it is rehearsed, the more vivid it will be.

Retrieval

The IMP model distinguishes between retrieval *of* images and retrieval *from* images. These processes are similar to what Begg has called access of a trace and use of that trace (Begg, 1983; see also Desrochers & Begg, Chapter 3, this volume). Distortion (bizarreness) is assumed to affect retrieval of images whereas integration (interaction) affects retrieval from images. Each of these processes will be considered in turn.

Retrieval of Images: Effects of Distortion

In order to retrieve an image from memory, that image must be distinguished from other images in memory—particularly from other schematic images. Distinctiveness is determined by elaboration, but the effect of elaboration on retrieval depends on the nature of the elaboration used at input. Elaboration can produce varying degrees of distinctiveness and varying degrees of image integration. The relative contributions of these two factors are illustrated in Figure 5.2.

The overall probabilities of free recall shown in Figure 5.2 are based upon data obtained by McDaniel and Einstein (1986). As shown, an unmixed bizarre list has been found to produce approximately the same level of recall as an unmixed

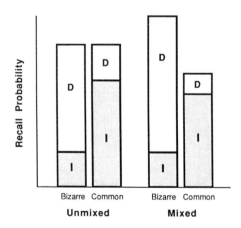

FIGURE 5.2. Relative contributions of image integration (shaded and designated by I) and image distinctiveness (unshaded and designated by D) to the free recall of bizarre or common images in mixed and unmixed lists. The contributions of I and D to recall probability represent speculations and are intended only for relative comparisons. The overall recall probabilities (I + D) are based approximately on data from McDaniel and Einstein (1986). Copyright February 1986 by Keith A. Wollen, reprinted by permission.

common list. However, the relative contributions of distortion and integration are assumed to be quite different. A common unmixed list would produce well-integrated images with little distortion; both of these effects would come about because subjects could rely heavily upon schematic images that were, by definition, well integrated and distortion free. A bizarre unmixed list, on the other hand, would produce poorly integrated images that involve considerable distortion and hence considerable distinctiveness. To create bizarre images, subjects must engage in elaborative distortion, and that distortion has the effect of increasing distinctiveness and, in most cases, decreasing integration; integration would be decreased relative to common schematic images because any interactions formed would, by definition, be unusual and thereby less integrated than common ones. The net result is very little difference in free recall between the two types of lists.

The situation with mixed lists is more complex and speculative. As in unmixed lists, we will assume that common images are better integrated than bizarre ones, but that bizarre images enjoy greater distortion and hence greater distinctiveness. However, the relative magnitudes of these effects is further assumed to be mediated by a contrast effect stemming from the mixture of image types. As a working hypothesis, we will assume that the contrast effect results in differential attention at input. The combination of bizarre and common images could lead subjects to focus on this distinction and not on other, subjective categories (as would have to be used in unmixed lists). Possibly because of greater interest in bizarre images or because of the demand characteristics of the task, attention (time and/or effort) might be increased to bizarre images but decreased to common ones. The increased attention could then result in the encoding of more distinctive features for bizarre images and fewer for common than would be the case in the corresponding unmixed lists. By virtue of having less attention, common images would also probably be less well integrated in mixed lists than in unmixed lists.

The contrast effect in mixed lists may also involve organizational mechanisms. This view is based on the notion advanced by Bruce and Gaines (1976) and extended by others (e.g., Schmidt, 1985) that distinctive items are placed into a separate group or category. Bruce and Gaines assumed an inverse relationship between the number of items in a category and retrievability from that category. This view is essentially the cue overload hypothesis of Watkins and Watkins (1975), although no reference was made to them. As applied to mixed lists of bizarre and common images, it would be assumed that there were two categories (bizarre and common) rather than just one. Furthermore, the number of items within each category would be cut in half in a mixed list because half of the items would be bizarre and the other half common. The smaller category size could then result in higher recall probabilities than would be the case in unmixed lists, where all images would be of the same type.

Unmixed lists would probably also have organization, but it would involve subjective categories rather than ones provided by the experimenter. The features that a subject used to determine each group or category would have to be common to all members of that group and would have to be absent in nongroup members. Each subjective group would then have features that distinguished it from other groups. Such organization could be equally available in both bizarre unmixed and common unmixed lists, but the basis of the organization would probably differ. Subjective categories in bizarre lists might include such features as animation of objects, human-like movements of animals, distortions of size, and so on. Subjective categories in common lists could involve groupings based on human–animal interactions, animal–object interactions, indoor vs. outdoor actions, or whatever. In both bizarre and common lists, the subjective groupings would be based on features common to all group members. At retrieval, these features could be used to cue the redintegration of the images from that group. If the subjective groupings were equally available in bizarre and common lists, recall would be expected to be equal also.

The organizational mechanism might affect mixed lists somewhat differently. In mixed lists, there is a distinct, salient "built-in" basis for organization – namely, bizarre vs. common images. Consequently, subjects would be highly likely to attend to this difference at input. Bizarre images could be distinguished from common images by the presence of bizarre elaborations (distortions). Indeed, such elaborations are required to form bizarre images. The bizarre features could then be used as retrieval cues at output. The common items, on the other hand, might be grouped together on the absence of bizarre elaborations. During retrieval, having a category based on the absence of bizarre elaborations would not be of much benefit, because the same could be said of all schematic images. The absence of bizarre features should provide fewer distinctive retrieval cues than the presence of bizarre features. Moreover, there would not be many retrieval cues based on subjective categories because the presence of such obvious experimenter-provided categories (bizarre vs. nonbizarre) would have resulted in their use to the exclusion of subjective ones. If true, then bizarre images would be better recalled in mixed lists.

Einstein and McDaniel (Chapter 4, this volume) have raised a potential problem with the organizational point of view. If images are organized into categories, one may well expect output clustering by categories. There have been no data reported on this issue, although Einstein and McDaniel have stated that no clustering occurred in their various experiments. However, no details of these tests have been provided, and until we know how clustering has been analyzed, it is premature to rule out its presence. Furthermore, it may be that bizarreness produces effects similar to the orthographic features manipulated by Hunt and Mitchell (1982). In that study, orthographic features were found to aid distinctiveness but there was no clustering based on these features. Clustering was found for semantic (taxonomic) features, however. There is no reason that every organizational feature would have to produce clustering at output.

An interesting corollary of the distinctiveness point of view is that bizarre images should lose their distinctiveness over time and become more and more similar to schematic images. Such a point has been made by Reese (1977; see also Smith & Graesser, 1981, for related arguments stemming from memory for actions) and results in the counterintuitive prediction that bizarreness will become relatively less effective as retention intervals increase. As pointed out earlier, most researchers have argued that bizarre imagery is more, not less, effective at long intervals. However, we also pointed out several problems with these experiments and several failures to replicate the finding. Moreover, there are data showing that in various situations traces do become more generic over time (e.g., Reese, 1977).

Retrieval From Images: Effects of Integration

Once an image has been accessed, the contents of that image must be searched for the target elements. The other image characteristic, integration, facilitates this process. The better an image is integrated, the greater the probability that all of its target elements will be retrieved. The effect of bizarreness on integration depends not on the amount of elaboration but on the nature of that elaboration. In general, bizarre images are less well integrated, thereby accounting for the typical finding of better horizontal retrieval for common images.

Elaboration is an important key to integration, especially in bizarre images. In common images, elaboration would not be necessary if subjects already had a schematic image that could be used (e.g., "The SHADE is on the LAMP"). However, in many cases elaboration would also be necessary for common images. For example, most subjects probably would have schematic images for teacher and street, but it is doubtful that subjects would have a schematic image of a teacher walking down a street; such an image would have to be constructed using elaboration. Elaboration can either tie together the target elements of an image (e.g., "The funny MAN bought the RING that squirted WATER") or not (e.g., "The old MAN threw the RING and jumped into the WATER"). To date, no one studying bizarre imagery has examined the relationship between degree of image integration and retrieval from the image.

The manner in which integration is assumed to work can be explained by means of the following example. Suppose subjects form a relatively unelaborated image of a car hitting a pole. Recall of this image may be no better than recall based on an elaboration making the car green in color. Because the word "green" does not help integrate the image or, perhaps more critically, elaborate upon the interaction of hitting, it is not expected to produce facilitation. If, on the other hand, the elaboration were of a "speeding car," the fact that the car was speeding might explain why it hit the pole and how much damage would have resulted. Extending our examples, suppose a subject told to use bizarre imagery formed a scene in which an animated car stood up on its rear tires and hit the pole with its right front tire in the manner of a boxer. Facilitation might be expected here too because the animation might be relevant to the interaction with the pole. However, if a subject introduced bizarreness by imagining a bizarrely shaped car that ran into a pole, little facilitation would be expected because an oddly shaped car would not in any way tie the elements of the image together. In general, interaction between objects is the key determinant of integration, and so elaboration would be expected to produce facilitation only when it involved such interaction. As was pointed out previously, there are ample data demonstrating the importance of integration.

Vertical Versus Horizontal Retrieval

It should be noted that distinctiveness exerts its effect upon retrieval of images and, as such, facilitates vertical retrieval but not horizontal. In contrast, integration affects retrieval from images and, therefore, facilitates horizontal retrieval but not vertical. By making common images more distinctive or bizarre images more integrated, it should be possible to change, or even reverse, the typical finding of superior free recall for bizarre images.

It should also be noted that the effect of vividness would be on horizontal retrieval rather than vertical. If an image is vivid, the subject should retrieve its elements easily. The individual elements of weak images, on the other hand, would be less likely to be retrieved. Vividness would not be expected to benefit vertical retrieval because vivid images are usually common, and we have many other vivid schematic images. Vertical retrieval would depend on the subject's ability to pick the appropriate image from others, and this process would be facilitated by distinctiveness—not vividness. There currently are no data that separate the effects of vividness on horizontal as opposed to vertical retrieval.

It may be that bizarre images are rated as less vivid because they are more complex than common ones. Research has shown that complex patterns are given lower vividness ratings than simple patterns (e.g., Marks, 1972). The elaboration used to create bizarre images would tend to produce images with greater complexity.

Cued Retrieval

The discussion so far has centered around free recall. However, IMP also works well when cued recall or recognition are used. In such situations, retrieval of the image would not be so much of a problem because part of the image is in effect provided to the subject in the form of a retrieval cue or a recognition stimulus. Consequently, the importance of previously encoded distinctive retrieval features would be reduced thereby reducing the benefit derived from bizarreness. However, subjects would still have to retrieve the missing elements *from* their images, and so integration would remain an important determinant of performance. Because common images are generally better integrated, cued recall and recognition should be higher for common images than for bizarre ones. Furthermore, such a result would be expected for both mixed and unmixed lists.

Conclusions

Mnemonists have, for centuries, argued that horizontal retrieval is greatly facilitated by the use of bizarre images. There has been no empirical support for this claim. Bizarre imagery has facilitated vertical retrieval in highly specific situations, but never horizontal. It makes no sense to continue using an erroneous argument to justify research on bizarre imagery. Such research is legitimate in its own right.

Research on bizarre imagery has suffered from a weak theoretical base. The few theories that have been advanced have been far too limited to account for the existing data. If research on bizarre imagery is to advance beyond its current state, it is necessary (a) to develop operational definitions of bizarreness, and (b) to develop theories that integrate existing data and suggest new experiments. It is in this spirit that the IMP model is offered.

References

Anderson, R. C., & Hidde, J. L. (1971). Imagery and sentence learning. *Journal of Educational Psychology, 62,* 526–530.

Andreoff, G. R., & Yarmey, A. D. (1976). Bizarre imagery and associative learning: A confirmation. *Perceptual and Motor Skills, 43,* 143–148.

Begg, I. (1983). Imagery instructions and the organization of memory. In J. C. Yuille (Ed.), *Imagery, memory and cognition* (pp. 91–115). Hillsdale, NJ: Erlbaum Associates.

Begg, I., & Sikich, D. (1984). Imagery and contextual organization. *Memory and Cognition, 12,* 52–59.

Bergfeld, V. A., Choate, L. S., & Kroll, N. E. A. (1982). The effect of bizarre imagery on memory as a function of delay: Reconfirmation of interaction effect. *Journal of Mental Imagery, 6,* 141–158.

Bruce, D., & Gaines, M. T., IV. (1976). Tests of an organizational hypothesis of isolation effects in free recall. *Journal of Verbal Learning and Verbal Behavior, 15,* 59–72.

Cermak, L. S. (1975). *Improving your memory.* New York: McGraw-Hill.

Collyer, S. C., Jonides, J., & Bevan, W. (1972). Images as memory aids: Is bizarreness helpful. *American Journal of Psychology, 85,* 31–38.

Cox, S. D., & Wollen, K. A. (1981). Bizarreness and recall. *Bulletin of the Psychonomic Society, 18,* 244–245.

Craik, F. I. M., & Tulving, E. (1975). Depth of processing and the retention of words in episodic memory. *Journal of Experimental Psychology: General, 104,* 268–294.

Delin, P. S. (1968). The effects of high and low meaningfulness and interitem association upon the level of difficulty of a serial task. *Psychonomic Society, 76,* 69–73.

Delin, P. S. (1969a). Learning and retention of English words with successive approximations to a complex mnemonic instruction. *Psychonomic Science, 17,* 87–88.

Delin, P. S. (1969b). The learning to criterion of a serial list with and without mnemonic instructions. *Psychonomic Science, 16,* 169–170.

Emmerich, H. J., & Ackerman, B. P. (1979). A test of bizarre interactions as a factor in children's memory. *The Journal of Genetic Psychology, 134,* 225–232.

Ernest, C. H. (1977). Imagery ability and cognition: A critical review. *Journal of Mental Imagery, 2,* 181–216.

Hauck, P. D., Walsh, C. C., & Kroll, N. E. A. (1976). Visual imagery mnemonics: Common vs. bizarre mental images. *Bulletin of the Psychonomic Society, 7,* 160–162.

Hunt, R. R., & Elliott, J. M. (1980). The role of nonsemantic information in memory: Orthographic distinctiveness effects on retention. *Journal of Experimental Psychology: General, 109,* 49–74.

Hunt, R. R., & Mitchell, D. B. (1982). Independent effects of semantic and nonsemantic distinctiveness. *Journal of Experimental Psychology: Learning, Memory, and Cognition, 8,* 81–87.

Jacoby, L. L., & Craik, F. I. M. (1979). Effects of elaboration of processing at encoding and retrieval: Trace distinctiveness and recovery of initial context. In L. S. Cermak & F. I. M. Craik (Eds.), *Levels of processing in human memory* (pp. 1–21). Hillsdale, NJ: Erlbaum Associates.

Kahneman, D. (1973). *Attention and effort.* Englewood Cliffs, NJ: Prentice-Hall.

Knowles, W. B. (1963). Operator loading tasks. *Human Factors, 5,* 151–161.

Kroll, N. E. A., Schepeler, E. M., & Angin, K. T. (1986). Bizarre imagery: The misremembered mnemonic. *Journal of Experimental Psychology: Learning, Memory, and Cognition, 12,* 42–53.

Kulhavy, R. W., & Heinen, J. (1974). Imaginal attributes in learning sentence-embedded noun pairs. *Psychological Reports, 34,* 487.

Lesgold, A. M., & Goldman, S. R. (1973). Encoding uniqueness and the imagery mnemonic in associative learning. *Journal of Verbal Learning and Verbal Behavior, 12,* 193–202.

Lorayne, H., & Lucas, J. (1974). *The memory book.* New York: Ballantine.

Mandler, J. M. (1984). *Stories, scripts, and scenes: Aspects of schema theory.* Hillsdale, NJ: Erlbaum Associates.

Marks, D. F. (1972). Individual differences in the vividness of visual imagery and their effect on function. In P. W. Sheehan (Ed.), *The function and nature of imagery* (pp. 83–108). New York: Academic Press.

Marks, D. F. (1983). Mental imagery and consciousness: A theoretical review. In A. A. Sheikh (Ed.), *Imagery: Current theory, research, and application* (pp. 96–130). New York: Wiley.

Marshall, P. H., Nau, K. L., & Chandler, C. K. (1979). A structural analysis of common and bizarre visual mediators. *Bulletin of the Psychonomic Society, 14,* 103–105.

Marshall, P. H., Nau, K. L., & Chandler, C. K. (1980). A functional analysis of common and bizarre visual mediators. *Bulletin of the Psychonomic Society, 15,* 375–377.

McDaniel, M. A., & Einstein, G. O. (1986). Bizarre imagery as an effective aid: The importance of distinctiveness. *Journal of Experimental Psychology: Learning, Memory, and Cognition, 12,* 54–65.

Merry, R. (1980). Image bizarreness in incidental learning. *Psychological Reports, 46,* 427–430.

Merry, R., & Graham, N. C. (1978). Imagery bizarreness in children's recall of sentences. *British Journal of Psychology, 69,* 315–321.

Moray, N. (1970). *Listening and attention.* London: Penguin.

Nappe, G. W., & Wollen, K. A. (1973). Effects of instructions to form common and bizarre mental images on retention. *Journal of Experimental Psychology, 100,* 6–8.

O'Brien, E. J., & Wolford, C. R. (1982). Effect of delay in testing on retention of plausible versus bizarre mental images. *Journal of Experimental Psychology: Learning, Memory, and Cognition, 8,* 148–152.

Posner, M. I., & Boies, S. J. (1971). Components of attention. *Psychological Review, 78,* 391–408.

Pra Baldi, A., De Beni, R., Cornoldi, C., & Cavedon, A. (1985). Some conditions for the occurrence of the bizarreness effect in free recall. *British Journal of Psychology, 76,* 427–436.

Reese, H. W. (1977). Toward a cognitive theory of mnemonic imagery. *Journal of Mental Imagery, 2,* 229–244.

Reynolds, R. E., & Anderson, R. C. (1982). Influence of questions on the allocation of attention during reading. *Journal of Educational Psychology, 74,* 623–632.

Rohwer, W. D., Jr. (1973). Elaboration and learning in childhood and adolescence. In H. W. Reese (Ed.), *Advances in child development and behavior* (Vol. 8). New York: Academic Press.

Roth, D. M. (1961). *Roth memory course.* Hackensack, NJ: Wehman.

Schmidt, S. R. (1985). Encoding and retrieval processes in the memory for conceptually distinctive events. *Journal of Experimental Psychology: Learning, Memory, and Cognition, 11,* 565–578.

Schneider, W., Dumais, S. T., & Shiffrin, R. M. (1984). Automatic and control processing and attention. In R. Parasuraman & D. R. Davies (Eds.), *Varieties of attention* (pp. 1–27). New York: Academic Press.

Senter, R. J., & Hoffman, R. R. (1976). Bizarreness as a nonessential variable in mnemonic imagery: A confirmation. *Bulletin of the Psychonomic Society, 7,* 163–164.

Sheehan, P. W. (1966). Functional similarity of imaging to perceiving: Individual differences in vividness of imagery. *Perceptual and Motor Skills, 23*(Monograph Supplement 6-V23), 1011–1033.

Smith, D. A., & Graesser, A. C. (1981). Memory for actions in scripted activities as a function of typicality, retention interval, and retrieval task. *Memory and Cognition, 9,* 550–559.

Stein, B. S., & Bransford, J. D. (1979). Constraints on effective elaboration: Effects of precision and subject generation. *Journal of Verbal Learning and Verbal Behavior, 18,* 769–777.

Stein, B. S., Littlefield, J., Bransford, J. D., & Persampieri, M. (1984). Elaboration and knowledge acquisition. *Memory and Cognition, 12,* 522–529.

Watkins, O. C., & Watkins, M. J. (1975). Buildup of proactive inhibition as a cue-overload effect. *Journal of Experimental Psychology: Human Learning and Memory, 1,* 442–452.

Webber, S. M., & Marshall, P. H. (1978). Bizarreness effects in imagery as a function of processing level and delay. *Journal of Mental Imagery, 2,* 291–300.

Wickens, C. D. (1984). Processing Resources in Attention. In R. Parasuraman & D. R. Davies (Eds.), *Varieties of attention* (pp. 63–102). New York: Academic Press.

Wollen, K. A., & Cox, S. D. (1981a). Sentence cuing and the effectiveness of bizarre imagery. *Journal of Experimental Psychology: Human Learning and Memory, 7,* 386–392.

Wollen, K. A., & Cox, S. D. (1981b). The bizarreness effect in a multitrial intentional learning task. *Bulletin of the Psychonomic Society, 18,* 296–298.

Wollen, K. A., Weber, A., & Lowry, D. H. (1972). Bizarreness versus interaction of mental images as determinants of learning. *Cognitive Psychology, 3,* 518–523.

Wood, G. (1967). Mnemonic systems in recall. *Journal of Educational Psychology, 58,* 1–27.

Wortman, P. M., & Sparling, P. B. (1974). Acquisition and retention of mnemonic information in long-term memory. *Journal of Experimental Psychology, 102,* 22–26.

Yarmey, A. D. (1984). Bizarreness effects in mental imagery. In A. A. Sheikh (Ed.), *International review of mental imagery* (Vol. 1, pp. 57–76). New York: Human Sciences Press.

Yates, F. A. (1966). *The art of memory.* Chicago: University of Chicago Press.

CHAPTER 6

Yet Another Picture of Imagery: The Roles of Shared and Distinctive Information in Memory

R. Reed Hunt and Marc Marschark

Consider memory for a round of golf. The event itself consists of 18 holes, but each hole is also an event consisting of different shots; on the other hand, each shot also is an event comprised by different demands. Rarely does a golfer intend to remember the events of a particular round. If, however, golfers are asked about a round, most can give appropriate accounts understandable to whomever is asking the question. For example, if asked by a colleague who has no interest in the game, one simply replies that he played golf. If asked by someone who is interested in the game, a more detailed account can be given. If asked by a suitably fanatical golfer, most golfers can give a stroke by stroke account of the previous experience. Exactly what does a golfer remember?

The Problem of Units of Analysis

For the memory theorist, this question turns on bothersome issues concerning the psychological unit of the golfer's memory. What is the golfer encoding, storing, and later retrieving that allows the varieties of memory performance just described? To what extent are these events stored in some analogue form(s), preserving the sights, smells, and kinesthetic aspects of each? Are the phenomenal images involved in describing a round of golf reconstructed at recall or retrieved wholistically? Are these distinctions theoretically useful or empirically discernable?

The recent history of these questions within cognitive psychology has been dominated by disputes over the qualitative nature of the representation; in particular, the "analogue versus propositional debate" (Anderson, 1978; Marschark, Richman, Yuille, & Hunt, in press; Paivio, 1983; Pylyshyn, 1973; Yuille & Marschark, 1982). At the same time, however, other equally notorious dimensions of the problem have continued to be at issue. In this chapter we shall focus on one such dimension, wholistic versus analytic aspects of memory (see also, empirical considerations by Anderson & Bower, 1973; Anderson & Ortony, 1975; Foss & Harwood, 1975).

The example of the golfer's memory was selected to illustrate the contrast, if not the contradiction, between wholistic and analytic views of memory. For the wholistic memory theory, the real psychological unit of memory is the entire event. Encoding is a matter of grouping discrete elements into an integrated unit, a unit that is different from the sum of its parts (Koffka, 1935; see also Anderson & Ortony, 1975; Marschark & Paivio, 1977). That is, the meaning of the parts is determined by the whole in which they are embedded. For example, the golfer's recall of a putt from yesterday's round is memory for a particular putt defined by a particular hole on a particular golf course with a particular set of playing partners. All of these elements, both perceptual and nonperceptual, constitute the event of a round of golf; to understand memory for a part, one must understand the whole event.

An analytical approach to the golfer's memory begins with elemental units from which the higher order units are constructed. Recall of a putt from yesterday's round is analyzed (and retained) in terms of elements or parts of the event. Recall of the entire round is interpreted as memory for the parts of the round from which the whole has been abstracted. In sum, the whole event, whatever it is, is to be understood by understanding the parts (Anderson & Bower, 1973).

The golf course example, again, illustrates the well-documented, antithetical nature of wholistic and analytic modes of thought. Applied to an understanding of memory, this problem is exacerbated by the theoretician's tendency to frame questions of representation as ontological questions, "What is the *real* psychological unit of memory?" Asked in this fashion, the question begs an answer describing the absolute qualities of the memory trace which, as a theoretical statement, must have generality. At this turn, we are in danger of going out of bounds.

Theoretical formulations of memory representations are guided by empirical observations of memory performance. One obvious point from our golfer example is that people are extremely flexible in reporting past experience; on some occasions memory (or at least retrieval) may appear to be wholistic but on other occasions quite analytic. Further, the "occasions" are established by demands of the memory test. From the observed responses to these demands, the theorist infers encoding and storage processes. However, under different demands, a different response concerning the same event will be given. There should be little wonder, then, that theoretical descriptions of representation tend to suffer from lack of generality.

The attempt to provide an ontologically secure description of the memory representation, a description which ties the theoretical representation to the actual event, requires some definition of "event." Although all might agree that an "event" is some spatiotemporally bounded occurrence, this general definition is not much help when asking what is *really* the psychological unit of memory. Identification of the event on the wholistic–analytic dimension is crucial to deciding what needs to be understood. Clearly, however, any "event" can be conceptually analyzed into parts, each of which is an event. To the extent that the memory system seems capable of identifying "events" under various contextual constraints of retrieval, inferences concerning the "event" at encoding are problematic.

If inferences concerning the psychological unit of memory are in principle lacking generality, how are we to deal with the analysis of memory? For all of the historical railing against structuralism, we do not see the solution in abandoning structural concepts. Processes must operate on something. However, we believe that it may be useful to focus theoretically upon relationships among units rather than the units related (see also Marschark et al., in press). In many cases, the relationships, not the units, are the theoretical (and apparently functional) principles of memory, and the focus upon representational units distracts attention from these principles. Relationships, of course, entail things to be related, but a theory of memory may capture important principles thereof without specifying the absolute qualitative or quantitative characteristics of the units. That is, the *theoretical* unit of analysis may be content free and serve useful theoretical functions while the relationships become the focus of theoretical concern. Let us briefly illustrate and clarify this point by describing two current theoretical perspectives on memory, organization theory and levels of processing, that represent wholistic and analytic views, respectively.

Organization and Distinctiveness

Organization theory, with its roots in Gestalt wholism, emphasizes the importance for memory of encoding and storing an integrated, wholistic unit. Tulving (1974) succeeded in resucitating the principles of organization theory by adding an important retrieval component to the Gestalt emphasis upon grouping. Namely, organization facilitates memory because access to the whole allows access to each of the parts. In memory for a categorized list, for example, organization of the words facilitates recall because access to the category at retrieval allows access to each of the list words from the category. In the case of memory for a visual scene, organization within an image (however it is construed) analogous to the original event facilitates recall of its components through its amenability to phenomenal "scanning."

Although the organized whole is the theoretical unit of analysis in organization theory, the functional principle of memory specified by organization really is a relationship. In particular, organization requires the detection of shared properties among the elements of the eventual whole. In effect, the important principle of organization is similarity. The principles of organization are not tied to particular theoretical units; indeed, the principles have been applied to features, words, propositions, sentences, and so forth. What is important is that the elements, whatever they may be, are psychologically similar on some dimension. Although the details of how this relationship is used to access the individual members has never been adequately specified by organizational theorists, it is this similarity relationship that is the fundamental principle of memory.

On the other hand, the more analytical heritage of levels of processing (e.g., Craik & Lockhart, 1972) will lead to a different set of conclusions. The levels of processing approach has focused upon the encoding of subsets of an event's total set of attributes and has been used to describe the reason memory for an event varies as a function of the particular subset of encoded attributes. The most direct progenitor of levels of processing is stimulus sampling theory (Estes, 1950), the analytic emphasis of which is in stark contrast to Gestalt wholism. Again, in the prototypical laboratory case of memory for a list of words, the levels of processing approach focuses upon single words rather than the relationship among the words, and the units of theoretical analysis are the more atomistic attributes comprising the event.

Memory research from the levels of processing framework has converged on the concept of distinctiveness (e.g., Hunt & Mitchell, 1978; Lockhart, Craik, & Jacoby, 1976), insofar as memory for an event will be an inverse function of the amount of overlap among the encoded features of the event and those of other events. That is, a distinctive encoding is one that does not share attributes with other events. The functional principle embedded in this description of the memory trace is a relationship. Unlike organization theory, however, the relationship prescribed by distinctiveness is difference rather than similarity. The less similar in attribute overlap a particular encoded representation is to other representations, the better will be memory for it. Moreover, the principle of distinctiveness appears to operate regardless of the qualitative nature of the distinctive attributes (Hunt & Elliott, 1980; Hunt & Mitchell, 1982).

This examination of organization theory and levels of processing emphasizes the importance of relationships among elements rather than the particular elements as the operative principles of memory. In the course of such an examination, we indeed see a fundamental difference between wholistic and analytic approaches to memory, a difference which appears paradoxical. On the one hand is the suggestion that similarity among elements of an event is the important principle of memory; on the other hand, that difference among elements of the event is the important principle of memory. Such a conflict between two successful research frameworks begs for resolution.

The Importance and Function of Similarity and Difference

The apparent paradox between organization and distinctiveness basically results from the conclusion that both similarity and difference benefit memory, which in turn seems to require that the two operate independently. Usually, however, similarity and difference are assumed to be inversely related, thus precluding independence. Are both similarity and difference really beneficial to memory? In the few experiments that have manipulated the relationships directly the answer seems to be yes. For example, Begg (1978) and Epstein, Phillips, and Johnson (1975) reported that highly related materials (e.g., beer–wine) are better remembered if attention is drawn to their differences, and unrelated materials (e.g., beer–dog) are better remembered if attention is drawn to their similarities. These data can be understood if we assume that both relationships between the words and the orienting task in which they are encountered influence encoding. In this case, memory is best when the two influences on encoding are not redundant but when one draws attention to similarity and the other to difference.

With these empirical demonstrations of the joint importance of similarity and difference along with the theoretical prescriptions from organization and levels of processing, a theoretical description of how these relationships exert their independent effect seems compelled. Such a description might begin by considering the function of similarity and difference in retrieval. Assuming that retrieval is a process of progressive differentiation of information in memory, the process begins with the delineation of some class from which the target event is to be drawn. This delineation is determined by the cue information, which specifies a class with some degree of precision (e.g., "What did you do yesterday?" versus "What did you do at 11:30 yesterday?"). The function of the shared information in memory, therefore, is class delineation. All members of any class share some information, and the activation of this shared information in retrieval potentiates memory for each class member.

If the memory requirement is for something more precise than the class information itself, however, additional information specific to particular class members must be available. It is this function which is served by distinctive information. That is, distinctive information further differentiates specific events.

In this fashion, the similarity and difference among various events function independently to determine memory performance. Both functions are necessary, although particular retrieval environments may weight the functions differentially. Nevertheless, both organization and distinctiveness are important in service of the progressive delineation of specific event information at retrieval, and, therefore, the shared and nonshared information among events operate to specify a given event.

Resolving the Paradox

However, now we must return to the paradox concerning the independence of similarity and difference. How can the similarity between two events be encoded independently of the difference between the two events? To answer this question, we must adopt a theory of similarity. That is, the solution to the paradox begins by abandoning similarity as an explanation of memory phenomena and realizing that similarity itself must be explained. The trick is then to extend the theory of similarity to memory.

To this goal, we have found Tversky's (1977) set theory model of similarity very helpful. Basically, Tversky's idea is that events can be modeled as sets of elements, and the relationship among events is described as overlap of elements. In particular, similarity is presumed to be the weighted sum of the encoded overlapping elements minus the encoded nonoverlapping elements of two events. The weighting of the sum is to include the psychological process of attention in similarity judgment. That is, regardless of the absolute overlap between two sets, circumstances in which events are experienced may direct attention exclusively to overlapping elements or to nonoverlapping elements, and it is only the attended elements that will affect the similarity judgment.

For the memory theorist, the set theoretical model is one of the major advantages of Tversky's idea. Set theory provides a calculus for describing relationships independent of the particular theoretical description of the elements. Although Tversky identifies the elements as features, the advantage of set theory is that the qualitative description of the elements does not influence the theoretical description of the relationship. For example, under different circumstances one may wish to identify the elements as features, images, propositions, or something else. With set theory, one can avoid the ontological question concerning the real quality of the memory trace, the troublesome question raised in the introduction: the whole event is a set of elements for which other events are subsets and so forth. For any particular circumstances, the theorist can describe the elements of the sets in a fashion appropriate to those circumstances. Memory for words might be described as features; memory for discourse as propositions. The theorist obtains a flexibility as powerful as the flexibility of the memory system to define the content of elements. Most importantly, relationships can be described in a contextually sensitive fashion, and as we saw with organization and distinctiveness, it is these relationships, not the things related, that are the functional principles of memory.

Encoding and Retrieval of Similarity and Difference

The extension of Tversky's idea to memory is fairly straightforward. In accord with Craik and Lockhart's (1972) assumption, we assume that memory is a byproduct of perceptual analysis. This assumption acknowledges that encoding of experiences is in service of establishing meaning: rarely do people intend to remember day to day events. Following Tversky, we assume that the encoded meaning of events can be represented as sets of elements. The particular encoding of a given event is influenced by a variety of contextual factors including the person's intentions, goals, and knowledge of the events. In a given situation, some elements of an event will overlap with those of other events, but some elements also will be different. The contextual influences on encoding in conjunction with the a priori knowledge of the events will determine the relative overlap.

In this view, the encoding of events is represented as shared and distinctive information. Note, however, that it is impossible to describe the shared and distinctive element of a single event in isolation. Shared and distinctive element encoding describes a relationship. These relationships are among the various events constituting the experience, but the relative nature of the theoretical description also refers to the retrieval environment. Indeed, the shared–distinctive information dichotomy is determined primarily at retrieval.

Memory always is initiated by a retrieval cue. Comprehension of this cue is represented as the activation of a set of elements, and this activated set represents the class from which the target event is to be drawn. The cue may be sufficiently specific that the class is very small or even identical to the set representing the target event. More likely, the class specified by the cue will contain a number of members, each of which shares the elements of the cue-specified class. Note that we are not making claims about the necessity and sufficiency of shared elements to define concepts but only that shared elements delineate a particular search set.

If the cue delineates a class from which a particular member must be drawn, information more precise than that provided by shared elements is required. To discriminate among the class members, information specific to a particular event must be available. This discriminative function is served by the nonshared or distinctive elements of meaning activated at encoding. These distinctive elements allow discrimination among various events of the initial experience that share elements of the cue.

Thus, the meaning of an event established at the time of the experience later serves the process of progressive delineation of specific information for memory. Shared meaning activated at retrieval includes the event as a member of the search set. Distinctive aspects of meaning allow precise identification of the event. Thus, both similarity and difference among events are important because they serve different functions in memory.

Implications

Two fundamental implications for memory emerge from this description of the roles of shared and distinctive information in memory. First, recall should be optimal when both shared and distinctive information are available, and, second, aspects of performance other than recall should be affected differently by shared and distinctive information, as should different components of recall performance itself (e.g., recall of content versus syntactic information from prose). The latter predictions are derived from the assumption that shared and distinctive information have different functions; if so, these differences should be manifested by indices of the functions served.

Data consistent with both implications of the above position have been obtained in explicit tests thereof by Einstein and Hunt (1980) and Hunt and Einstein (1981). Other data, from studies of the role of imagery in memory for verbal materials, also provide support for this framework and will be considered at length below.

In the Einstein and Hunt (1980) and Hunt and Einstein (1981) studies, which did not involve imagery manipulations, the primary measure of memory was free recall. Free-recall procedures entail a minimal amount of explicit cue information, limited usually to general shared information, such as "Recall the things you have just seen." Thus, free recall depends heavily upon the encoded trace information. To influence the relative encoding of shared and distinctive information, Einstein and Hunt manipulated orienting tasks and materials under incidental memory instructions.

Across these experiments, free recall was better when the encoding situation drew attention to both shared and distinctive information than when the situation favored only one type of information. For example, an orienting task requiring subjects to sort categorized word lists was intended to draw attention to the shared information among category members. On the other hand, a pleasantness rating task, which does not require attention to categorical relationships so much as to the particular meaning of a word was assumed less likely to activate shared information. As expected, subjects required to perform both tasks recalled more words than those required to perform either alone. Appropriate comparisons also were made to demonstrate that this result owed to the qualitative aspects of the tasks, not to the difference between one and two tasks.

Hunt and Einstein (1981) further found that subjects' recall of highly categorized lists was better following a pleasantness rating than following a sorting task. If the materials influence encoding of shared or distinctive information, this result is expected because highly categorized words should be represented richly by shared information. To require subjects to perform a pleasantness rating task on these materials is to add distinctive information to the shared information. The obverse finding was also obtained in that ad hoc categories, whose relationship is not obvious, were better recalled following sorting than pleasantness rating. These results suggest that the encoding of shared or distinctive information is influenced by the relationships among materials, but the encoding can be supplemented by the complementary type of information when the orienting task's influence is not redundant to the material's influence. The data clearly show that free recall is better under circumstances encouraging the encoding of both shared and distinctive information.

This same series of experiments produced data consistent with the assumption that shared and distinctive information operate independently in memory. Clustering scores, used as an index of relational processing, were always higher when the orienting tasks or materials encouraged encoding of shared information rather than distinctive information. Circumstances encouraging the encoding of shared information also produced higher levels of category recall than circumstances encouraging distinctive encoding, but the latter circumstances produced higher within-category recall than did the former. Finally, manipulations favoring distinctive encoding produced better recognition memory for a word embedded in categorically related distractors than did manipulations favoring encoding of shared information. All of these comparisons converge in support of the assumption that shared and distinctive information exert independent effects upon retrieval.

With support of the basic assumptions from this initial series of experiments, the theoretical framework outlined above has been applied with some success to a variety of memory problems. These include typicality effects in recall (Hunt & Einstein, 1981), differential effects of categorical and orthographic isolation

(Hunt & Mitchell, 1982), category size effects in recall (Hunt, Ausley, & Schultz, 1986; Hunt & Seta, 1984), and the generation effect (Gardiner & Hampton, 1985). In the following sections we shall discuss research on memory for concrete and abstract materials in light of the theoretical distinction between shared and distinctive information.

A Theoretical View of Imagery Effects in Terms of Shared and Distinctive Information

Concrete materials usually are remembered better than abstract materials, a fact that figures prominently in the ascription of visual imagery to memory traces. The concreteness effect, however, is not immune to the controversy surrounding the concept of imagery in memory, and, as we shall see shortly, concrete materials are not always remembered better than abstract ones. At a minimum, this failure to find the concreteness effect under all circumstances indicates that the psychological functions engaged by material concreteness are contextually sensitive. Our goal is to describe that functional sensitivity in terms of the processing of shared and distinctive information.

We begin by assuming that certain variables encourage the construction of mental images and, for that matter, other modality-specific "images" as well. The processing entailed in these constructions leaves residual information that is part of the memory for the event. We know, for example, that people are extremely accurate at incidental memory for the modality of a remembered event (Johnson, 1983; Lehman, 1982). We further assume that whatever information allows these judgments can be modeled as elements of the set representing that particular event. These elements may be conceptualized as perceptual, although the ontological status of the representation again is not at issue.

The elements representing the residual of imaginal processing (Marschark et al., in press) function as do the other elements of the representation. That is, the imaginal elements may be shared among events or may be specific to a particular event. Again, much of the theoretical analysis at this point hinges on the experimental delineation of the "event." An image may be constructed to represent a single sentence or an entire prose paragraph. In each case, however, the subject may be required to recall discrete sentences. In the case of the paragraph, the encoding with reference to imagery is wholistic, and the perceptual elements representing the paragraph may be shared by all sentences that are members of the paragraph. In this case, other elements of the representation of each sentence would have to serve as distinctive information to allow precise delineation of individual sentences. On other occasions, particularly with discrete list presentation, the perceptual elements of each list member may be quite distinctive.

Much of the data concerning the effects of concrete and abstract materials are therefore complicated by the unit of analysis question mentioned earlier. For that reason, some of the confusion associated with the presence and absence of concreteness in the empirical literature may be·resolved by adopting the shared–distinctive element framework.

Several investigators have implicitly considered the dichotomy of shared versus distinctive information attempting to account for concreteness effects in terms of differences in comprehensibility between concrete and abstract materials. Kieras (1978) and Schwanenflugel and Shoben (1983), for example, have outlined the *context availability* position. According to Kieras (1978, pp. 543–544), "the content from high-imagery sentences has much more overlap with permanent memory information" than does content from low-imagery sentences. This results in high-imagery sentences being easier to comprehend ("less structure has to be built") and to subsequently to recall ("there will be abundant retrieval paths from permanent memory into the new information"). In this view, high- and low-imagery information is assumed to involve common, amodal *formats* of representation, even though they may have qualitatively different configurations of item-specific and relational information relevant to them (see also, Marschark, 1985; Marschark et al., in press; Nelson, Reed, & McEvoy, 1977; Snodgrass, 1984).

Marschark (1985) elaborated the context availability position in terms of item-specific and relational processing, although these mechanisms are identical to those considered here as the processing of distinctive and shared information. His goal, however, was to account for imagery effects in terms of memory rather than comprehension differences between concrete and abstract verbal materials. Consistent with the present view, he suggested that processing of distinctive, individual item information could account for the imagery effects in the recall of word lists insofar as the construction of mental images at learning provides for retrieval paths to perceptual as well as verbal information in memory (cf. Kieras, 1978). Learning of individual sentences similarly was suggested to involve processing of distinctive, individual item information relevant to concepts and propositions within sentences, but also to entail processing of information common to those units, in determination of the meaning of the sentence. Memory for concrete and abstract sentences therefore may show evidence of equal integrative or "wholistic" processing. At the same time, concrete sentences, with the advantage of distinctive, sententially relevant images, may be better remembered overall (Brewer, 1975; Marschark & Paivio, 1977).

With multisentence prose, another level of analysis comes to bear as information shared among sentences compose the contextual relations or *macrostructure* of the text (Kieras, 1981; Kintsch & van Dijk, 1978). Information specific to particular words, propositions, or sentences will be less important than macrolevel information for recall here and so content recall for concrete and abstract prose will be roughly equivalent.*

---

*Although schema-guided content recall may not differ for concrete and abstract prose, Marschark (1978) found that syntactic information was relatively better retained in memory for abstract than concrete paragraphs.

In summary, Marschark's (1985) framework and the present position explicitly predict that concreteness effects will be most potent when context is at a minimum, as in word or sentence lists. In the absence of relational processing among items, information specific to individual items within lists will be most salient, and the advantage held by concrete stimuli in retrieval of perceptual as well as verbal/semantic information will result in a memory advantage. Concreteness effects should be less pronounced when linguistic units are presented in context, such as when sentences of words are presented in coherent paragraph order. In that case, the processing of information shared between units will result in abundant retrieval routes for abstract as well as concrete materials. Processing of distinctive information (e.g., proposition-specific images) will not be as central to subsequent recall as information relevant to the paragraph theme at this level and may even hurt performance if it is at the expense of processing contextual relationships.

Imagery Versus Processing of Shared and Distinctive Information in Memory for Prose

An explicit investigation of relational and item-specific processing in memory for prose was provided recently by Einstein, McDaniel, Bowers, and Stevens (1984). In two experiments, they increased subjects' processing of distinctive lexical information by having them fill in missing letters in a passage. Processing of information shared by sentences was increased by having them reorder sentences of a passage that had been scrambled or by presenting an ambiguous paragraph with a disambiguating title. Einstein et al. (1984) found that subsequent recall of the passages was related not so much to the processing difficulties created by the orienting tasks as to the type of information that was encoded under different processing manipulations. Good memory depended on the combined influence of shared and distinctive information and the processing of them. If materials elicited one type of processing, memory was best served by processing of the other, and vice versa (Einstein & Hunt, 1980; Hunt & Einstein, 1981).

Although Einstein et al. (1984) did not consider the possible interaction of imagery with the processing of shared and distinctive information, Marschark (1985) did so in his study of memory for high- and low-imagery prose. Concrete and abstract paragraphs equated for comprehensibility, syntactic structure, and conceptual structure were presented to subjects under a variety of conditions. In three experiments, Marschark consistently found equivalent recall of concrete and abstract sentences when they were presented in paragraph order. The usually robust advantage for concrete materials was obtained only when sentences of the paragraphs were presented in random order. These results were interpreted in the framework describe above: When presented in random order, the availability of both perceptual and semantic information in memory facilitated recall of high-imagery relative to low-imagery sentences. When presented in thematic order, however, recall of both material types was determined by the availability of thematically relevant information.

Marschark's (1985) finding of the absence of concreteness effects in memory for prose was replicated and extended recently by Bunn (1986). That study was primarily directed at the issue of individual differences in prose memory, but one result is of particular interest here. Bunn varied concreteness within subjects, presenting subjects with concrete and abstract paragraphs (multiple trials) in counterbalanced order. Considering the data from only the first presentation for all subjects (a between-subjects comparison comparable to that of Marschark, 1985), no concreteness effect was obtained in either gist or verbatim scoring of idea units recalled. In fact, abstract materials were slightly better remembered than the concrete ones, as had been found by Marschark (1985). Considering the data from the complementary, second-presented material set, however, a concreteness effect was obtained.

Although this reliable interaction does not follow from any other interpretation of concreteness effects with which we are familiar, it is entirely consistent with the present account. During the first presentation, subjects presumably engaged in "normal," thematic processing of the paragraphs, by attending to relationships among idea units, that is, to shared information. This strategy was eliminated following the first recall test, however, as subjects responded to the memory demands by engaging in a unit by unit encoding strategy (Marschark, 1979), that is, by attending to distinctive information. Concrete materials then held an advantage in recall insofar as unit-specific perceptual as well as nonperceptual information was available in memory, providing additional retrieval routes (Kieras, 1978; Marschark, 1985). Once again, we have an indication of the interaction of the memory "task" and the unit of analysis involved in encoding and retrieval.

The findings of Marschark (1985) and Bunn (1986) may seem counterintuitive because it is generally assumed that there have been ample demonstrations of imagery effects in previous studies of prose memory. In fact, there are only two other relevant studies of which we are aware, and both yielded results consistent with the present framework. One of these was Marschark's (1978, 1979)* earlier examination of the possibility that imagery effects in memory for prose might result, at least in part, from differences in the way that concrete and abstract sentences are processed at input rather than the form in which they might be stored. In presenting subjects with high- and low-imagery paragraphs, Marschark employed an auditory self-presentation procedure that yielded word by word processing latencies. In two experiments, he found that subjects receiving the high-imagery materials reported using imaginally based, comprehension-like strategies. These strategies were reflected in subjects' pausing longer following key content words than elsewhere in sentences. Subjects receiving the low-imagery materials, in contrast, generally reported using phrase by phrase, rote rehearsal strategies, and their latency data showed them to pause longer at gram-

---

*The 1979 published version of the 1978 dissertation did not include discussion of the recall findings.

matical boundaries of each sentence than elsewhere. Notwithstanding these processing differences, however, Marschark (1978) found that levels of content recall were almost identical for the high- and low-imagery materials.

Although consistent with the present theoretical framework, Marschark's (1978) recall findings seemed at the time to contradict previous findings of Yuille and Paivio (1969). Yuille and Paivio (1969) had been the first to extend imagery research to prose learning in their replication of the classic study by Pompi and Lachman (1967). Pompi and Lachman (1967) had reported that subjects receiving the words of a (high-imagery) story in prose form were more likely than subjects receiving the same words in random order to falsely recognize new words associated with the passage's theme. Further, recall of the organized word set was consistently superior to that of the random set. Pompi and Lachman concluded that meaning from a prose passage, unlike random word or sentence lists, is abstracted and stored in some integrated form.

Yuille and Paivio (1969) hypothesized that theme-preserving, complex images could have been the representational format indicated by Pompi and Lachman's findings. Accordingly, they predicted that the facilitative effects of prose organization should be directly related to passage concreteness and replicated the Pompi and Lachman study, using paragraphs varying in rated concreteness (presented one word at a time). As expected, recall of concrete words was significantly higher than recall of abstract words, and concrete materials were affected by the order manipulation to a greater extent than were the abstract materials. At the same time, however, examination of Yuille and Paivio's (1969) reported data indicates that for both syntactic and random presentations, the proportions of thematically consistent intrusion errors were greater for abstract than for concrete materials. This finding indicates that some form of semantically integrated representation was available for both material types (Anderson & Ortony, 1975) and is thus clearly inconsistent with the assumption of the dual coding model that abstract verbal material is stored verbatim (Paivio, 1971).

All of these results, however, are consistent with the present theoretical framework. In our view, the recall advantage for concrete over abstract words in Yuille and Paivio's experiment was a consequence of the processing of distinctive, individual item information at the level of individual words, elicited by their word by word presentation method. The rough equivalence of theme-related intrusions, like the comparable levels of recall in Marschark's (1978, 1985) and Bunn's (1986) studies, in contrast, is assumed to have been produced by the macrolevel processing of shared information.

Imagery Versus Processing of Shared and Distinctive Information in Memory for Sentences

Indications of imagery effects at the level of processing distinctive item information but not at the level of processing shared features are also available from several studies that have examined memory for phrases and sentences varying in rated imageability. Begg (1972), for example, examined memory for concrete and abstract adjective-noun phrases. Begg hypothesized that concrete phrases, such as "white horse," are stored in long-term memory as unitary images, whereas abstract phrases, such as "absolute truth," must be represented as verbatim linguistic strings. In three experiments, he presented subjects with lists of phrases or their component words, followed by cued or free recall. In accord with his assumptions, Begg found that in free recall subjects recalled the same proportion of concrete words and two-word concrete phrases (even though the latter contained twice as many words), whereas they recalled approximately equal numbers of abstract words from word and phrase lists (i.e., half as many phrases as words). In cued recall, Begg found that adjectives were effective recall cues for the concrete nouns but not for the abstract nouns.

Begg's (1972) encoding-specificity interpretation of his results were consistent with his hypothesis of differences in representation between (integrated) concrete and (independently stored) abstract verbal materials. Nonetheless, this conclusion has an important limitation. Begg's use of adjectives as recall cues was based on assumptions about the ways in which they would be represented in the images generated for concrete phrases and the verbatim strings of abstract phrases. The status of abstract adjectives as contiguity cues, however, follows only from the now questionable assumption of the "literal" encoding of abstract materials. Alternatively, if some transformed verbal representation or even an image were constructed for abstract phrases, then such cues would be ineffective [as, for example, in Marschark & Hunt's (1986) use of such cues in paired-associate learning]. The failure to find cueing effects with abstract materials in Begg's study (as well in prior studies involving abstract paired associates), therefore, may have been due to the use of inappropriate cues rather than a lack of integrative processing. In the present terms, Begg employed cues for the abstract phrases that assumed contiguity to be the only shared feature when, in fact, there may have been superseding features.

In fact, there is a variety of other evidence consistent with the view that abstract as well as concrete sentences can be retained in some integrated but nonimaginal format. One of the first such indications was provided by Franks and Bransford (1972), who demonstrated that that subjects spontaneously integrated nonconsecutive but semantically related abstract sentences into complex idea units (see also, Richardson, 1985). Unfortunately, those results were not compared to the earlier results of Bransford and Franks (1971) using concrete materials. Franks and Bransford's (1972) goal was to demonstrate that their 1971 results were better accounted for in terms of semantic integration than imaginal storage and thus only abstract materials were employed. From the present theoretical framework, however, we would expect that the false alarm rates in recognition of concrete and abstract sentences should either not differ or indicate an advantage for concrete sentences (the latter indicating the extent to which sentence-specific images are more directly analogous to original wording than are the representations of abstract sentences). Either finding would be contrary to the dual coding position from which (verbatim encoded) abstract sentences would be predicted to be more accurately recognized.

Additional evidence indicating that concrete and abstract materials may undergo similar integration is available from several studies that have obtained greater levels of overall recall but not integration for concrete than abstract sentences. Brewer (1975), for example, found that the frequencies of semantic substitutions (e.g., remembering "Russian is difficult to pronounce" as "Russian is hard to pronounce") in recall of concrete and abstract sentences were equally frequent when symmetrical synonym pairs were available for both types of material. Brewer's (1975) results, like those of Franks and Bransford (1972), are therefore clearly problematic for representational imagery theories like dual coding theory.

A similar conclusion was suggested by Marschark and Paivio (1977). In two of three experiments using different paradigms, they examined the extent to which recall of concrete and abstract sentences could be facilitated by nonverbatim, but semantically consistent retrieval cues. In the third experiment, they examined the extent to which cueing recall of sentence objects with whole-sentence frames compared to cueing with partial sentence frames (that is, whether cueing with the "whole" was better than the sum of cueing with its parts). As in the above studies, Marschark and Paivio obtained results indicating that concrete and abstract sentences did not differ in the degree to which they were represented in some integrated, wholistic form. Overall levels of recall were higher for the concrete than the abstract sentences. Insofar as these findings could not be easily accounted for in terms of any available models, Marschark and Paivio (1977) suggested that some semantic code might underly memory for both concrete and abstract sentences at a level different from that yielding evidence indicating functionally distinct processing systems (see similar conclusions by Nelson et al., 1977; Snodgrass, 1984). That is, both concrete and abstract sentences undergo similar processing of "shared" information at the level of individual sentences, but in the absence of a larger context (other than the list itself), sentence-specific imagery to concrete sentences provides for the creation of additional, distinctive retrieval routes for subsequent recall (Kieras, 1978; Schwanenflugel & Shoben, 1983).

In summary, previous research findings with regard to memory for concrete and abstract sentences provide an interesting pattern of results that appear to both support and contradict predictions from traditional imagery theories. A variety of studies have indicated that more concrete than abstract sentences are remembered, but others have failed to obtain differences at levels reflecting the extent of integrative processing. Although clearly inconsistent with interpretations of concreteness effects in terms of the retention of verbal and imaginal codes, this pattern of results is consistent with (and, in fact, has engendered) the present aim of accounting for those effects in terms of differences in shared and distinctive element processing. Further, such results suggest the possibility that similar patterns might be demonstrated in other recall paradigms for which imagery has served an explanatory function. What, for example, might happen if shared rather than distinctive information could be tapped in traditional learning tasks involving list of words and word pairs?

Concreteness Effects in Paired-Associate Learning:
"Now You See 'em, Now You Don't"

The demonstration of concreteness effects in paired-associate tasks was the major impetus behind the modern resurrection of imagery and dual coding theories. Not only have such effects been obtained across a variety of studies manipulating material concreteness and instructional variables, but specific, crucial tests of relevant theories have been made within the paradigm. Discussion of such findings is not necessary here (see Paivio, 1971, 1986, for reviews) beyond noting that such results are virtually always supportive of predictions made from dual coding theory and so have been taken as indicative of differences in the way that concrete and abstract verbal information are stored in memory.

Recently, however, we have conducted several experiments indicating that imagery effects can be attenuated or eliminated in paired-associate learning (Marschark & Hunt, 1985, 1986). One way in which this can be effected is by using free recall rather than cued recall following the standard paired associate learning task. Marschark & Hunt (1985) had subjects learn mixed (Experiment 1) or homogeneous (Experiment 2) lists of concrete and/or abstract paired associates, after which half of the subjects received a cued-recall test and half a free-recall test. Consistent with previous findings, significantly more concrete than abstract response items were recalled when cued with stimulus items, but the differences were much smaller and not reliable in the free-recall conditions. In a third experiment, subjects were engaged specifically in processing information relevant to individual items (rating individual item imageability) or information "shared" by the two terms (rating ease of integration) tasks. Imagery effects were obtained in both cued- and free-recall conditions under relational orienting instructions, but not in either under individual item instructions. Marschark and Hunt (1986) extended and replicated these findings, examining the effects of different shared-feature orienting tasks (Experiments 1–3), a priori relatedness of stimulus and response terms (Experiments 1 and 2), and the use of alternative retrieval cues (Experiment 3).

Our interpretation of these data is based on the functions of shared and distinctive information. Shared information delineates the class from which the target element is to be drawn. In the case of paired-associate lists in which the pairs bear no relationship to one another, the class delineation may be conceptualized as the individual pairs from which a response item must be drawn. Therefore, the important relationship to be established is between the members of each pair. As previously argued, such a relationship can be established regardless of concreteness. Once formed, however, distinctiveness can then exert its function. Delimitation of the class can be followed by more precise discrimination of members of the class. In paired-associate learning, this is the function that is served by concreteness: the specification of individual members of the pairs.

On the face of it, the interpretation of the paired-associate data contradicts the prose data of Marschark (1985). Remember that he found concreteness effects in prose memory only when the sentences were presented in scrambled orders, a manipulation presumed to preclude processing of shared information. It therefore appears that in prose a concreteness effect is found only when shared information is impoverished, but with paired-associates a concreteness effect is found only when shared information is available. The resolution of this apparent contradiction lies in the unit of analysis problem.

The dependent measure in relevant prose research is typically either the number of sentences or idea units recalled. With syntactically ordered prose, however, the encoding of the materials entails processing relationships among sentences (or idea units). The structure of normal prose draws attention to the relationship among these higher order units, sometimes at the expense of attention to individual sentences (Einstein et al., 1984). Because the concreteness manipulation is at the level of individual sentences, this potentially distinctive information is not as salient in normal prose as in scrambled prose. Here, the relationships among the individual sentences are very difficult to detect without special instructions (Einstein et al., 1984). Therefore, the encoding unit is the individual sentence, and the perceptual information accruing to the representation of the concrete sentences may be quite salient. Interestingly, in this case, the perceptual information could serve the function of shared information for elements of the sentence. By considering the potential psychological units in different situations and the different functions that the perceptual information associated with concrete materials may serve, any contradiction between the interpretation of the prose data and the paired-associate data is removed.

Lest one feel mildly deceived by a post hoc shell game, we would point out that the foregoing account has clear and easily tested implications. One prediction (as yet untested), for example, is that recall of individual words within sentences should not vary as a function of concreteness if the sentences are meaningful. If, however, the sentences are anomalous, a concreteness effect for the individual words should be present. This situation is analogous to normal versus scrambled prose in that anomalous sentences focus attention on individual words much as scrambled prose focuses attention on individual sentences.

Another paired-associate learning study consistent with our results as well as the sentence-level studies noted above was provided by Day and Bellezza (1983). In comparing the contributions to imagery effects of familiarity and concreteness, Day and Bellezza provided subjects with pairs of concrete and abstract words, together with instructions to form distinctive, imaginal mediators linking them. To their surprise, they found that even when the abstract pairs obtained higher rated imagery scores, concrete pairs were better remembered. This finding led Day and Bellezza to reject the dual coding explanation of imagery effects in paired-associate learning and to suggest, in its place, a schema theory that explicitly did not "represent relations among words or concepts" (p. 257).

Day and Bellezza's (1983) results, however, are entirely in accord with predictions from an account of imagery effects in terms of shared, relational information versus distinctive, item-specific information. As in the sentence memory studies by Brewer (1975) and Marschark and Paivio (1977), Day and Bellezza's mediational instructions can be seen to have increased the processing of shared information between the abstract words. The higher imagery ratings for related abstract pairs relative to unrelated concrete pairs (but, importantly, not relative to related concrete pairs) indicates that abstract and concrete verbal materials can receive comparable integrative, relational processing. Nonetheless, as in the sentence studies, there remains a recall superiority for concrete materials. Not only do individual concrete words retain an advantage in terms of the distinctive encoding of perceptual as well as nonperceptual information at the level of individual items (i.e., "dual coding"), but the identities of concrete words are more distinctly represented within the generated mediators than are the identities of abstract words (cf. Begg, 1972).

In short, there have now been several demonstrations indicating the viability of the shared–distinctive dichotomy in accounting for concreteness effects at the level of word pairs as well as in sentence and prose learning. Taken together, the paired-associate findings suggest the need to further reexamine imagery effects in traditional verbal learning paradigms in order to clarify the extent to which explanations thereof in terms of the "modality" of representation are either necessary or sufficient. At the very least, these results are consistent with the theoretical framework outlined above accounting for imagery effects in terms of the processing of shared and distinctive information and remove some of the theoretical constraints imposed by extensive paired-associate results indicating the inviolability of imagery and concreteness as explanatory devices.

Summary and Conclusions

Our goal in this chapter has been to present a general theoretical position with regard to memory and to extend this position to the effects of concreteness on memory for verbal materials. The impetus for this pursuit lies in our observations that (a) both similarity and differences among the same events facilitate memory, and (b) the effects of concreteness on memory appear better explained in terms of a processing model than in terms of a representational model (Marschark et al., 1986). To explain the independent effects of similarity and difference relationships, we have applied Tversky's (1977) set-theoretic model of similarity to memory. The additional assumptions required for the application of this model to memory are associated with retrieval processes. Retrieval is viewed as progressively finer delineation of information. Thus, retrieval of generic events can be accomplished by the activation of widely shared information in the encoded experience. More precise discrimination at retrieval requires the activation of less widely shared information in the encoded experience. Shared information functions to delineate a class of events, and distinctive information functions to specify a particular event in that class. On this view, both shared and distinctive information are important to memory.

The principles of memory emerging from this perspective are relationships among elements. These relationships theoretically govern memory functions irrespective of the particular elements related. The theoretical unit of analysis of therefore content free, allowing the theoretician flexibility comparable to that of the memory system in defining "events" at the time of retrieval. The value of this flexibility is an increased generality of the theoretical principles encompassed by the relationships. We can move across different materials unimpeded by debates about the ontological status of the memory trace. Because establishment of the *real* trace is complicated by the memory system's ability to define "events" in accord with retrieval demands, this approach allows us to describe particular aspects of the memory process without stumbling on the questions of the qualitative nature of the representation (see Marschark et al., in press, for further discussion).

Of course, relationships logically entail things related. We propose that the content-free theoretical elements be identified in particular situations with regard to the known encoding and retrieval contexts. That is, in a given experiment, the elements of the experience can be specified with regard to the encoding environment and the retrieval demands. For example, our analyses of concreteness effects assumed that certain elements of the set representing an event have been perceptual. From this assumption, one moves quickly to the relationships among the elements to describe memory performance. Other than the potential for relationship with elements of the same kind, no privileged functional status is granted to qualitatively specified elements. What matters is the relationship, not the things related.

Acknowledgments. Preparation of this report was supported in part by grant #RO1-NS-20064 to Marc Marschark from the National Institute for Neurological and Communicative Disorders and Stroke and an Excellence Fund Fellowship to R. Reed Hunt from the Research Council of the University of North Carolina at Greensboro. Order of authorship was determined arbitrarily.

References

Anderson, J. R. (1978). Arguments concerning representations for mental imagery. *Psychological Review, 85*, 249–277.

Anderson, J. R., & Bower, G. H. (1973). *Human associative memory.* Washington, DC: Winston.

Anderson, R. C., & Ortony, A. (1975). On putting apples into bottles—A problem of polysemy. *Cognitive Psychology, 7*, 167–180.

Begg, I. (1972). Recall of meaningful phrases. *Journal of Verbal Learning and Verbal Behavior, 11*, 431–439.

Begg, I. (1978). Imagery and organization in memory: Instructional effects. *Memory & Cognition, 6*, 174–183.

Bransford, J. D., & Franks, J. J. (1971). The abstraction of linguistic ideas. *Cognitive Psychology, 2*, 331–350.

Brewer, W. (1975). Memory for ideas: Synonym substitution. *Memory and Cognition, 3*, 458–464.

Bunn, C. (1986). Individual differences in spatial-imagery ability and memory for concrete and abstract prose. Unpublished honors thesis, Trent University, Peterborough, Ontario, Canada.

Craik, F. I. M., & Lockhart, R. S. (1972). Levels of processing: A framework for memory research. *Journal of Verbal Learning and Verbal Behavior, 11,* 671-684.

Day, J. C., & Bellezza, F. S. (1983). The relationship between visual imagery mediators and recall. *Memory and Cognition, 11,* 251-257.

Einstein, G. O., & Hunt, R. R. (1980). Levels of processing and organization: Additive effects of individual item and relational processing. *Journal of Experimental Psychology: Human Learning and Memory, 6,* 588-598.

Einstein, G. O., McDaniel, M. A., Bowers, C. A., & Stevens, D. T. (1984). Memory for prose: The influence of relational and proposition-specific processing. *Journal of Experimental Psychology: Learning, Memory, and Cognition, 10,* 133-143.

Epstein, M. L., Phillips, W. D., & Johnson, J. J. (1975). Recall of related and nonrelated word pairs as a function of processing level. *Journal of Experimental Psychology: Learning, Memory, and Cognition, 1,* 149-152.

Estes, W. K. (1950). Toward a statistical theory of learning. *Psychological Review, 57,* 94-107.

Foss, D. J., & Harwood, D. (1975). Memory for sentences: implications for human associative memory. *Journal of Verbal Learning and Verbal Behavior, 14,* 1-16.

Franks, J., & Bransford, J. D. (1972). The acquisition of abstract ideas. *Journal of Verbal Learning and Verbal Behavior, 11,* 311-315.

Gardiner, J. M., & Hampton, J. A. (1985). Semantic memory and the generation effect: Some tests of the lexical activation hypothesis. *Journal of Experimental Psychology: Learning, Memory, and Cognition, 11,* 732-742.

Hunt, R. R., & Elliott, J. M. (1980). The role of nonsemantic information in memory: orthographic distinctiveness effects on memory. *Journal of Experimental Psychology: General, 109,* 49-74.

Hunt, R. R., & Einstein, G. O. (1981). Relational and item-specific information in memory. *Journal of Verbal Learning and Verbal Behavior, 15,* 559-566.

Hunt, R. R., & Mitchell, D. B. (1978). Specificity in nonsemantic orienting tasks and distinctive memory traces. *Journal of Experimental Psychology: Human Learning and Memory, 4,* 472-481.

Hunt, R. R., & Mitchell, D. B. (1982). Independent effects of semantic and nonsemantic distinctiveness. *Journal of Experimental Psychology: Learning, Memory, and Cognition, 8,* 81-87.

Hunt, R. R., & Seta, C. E. (1984). Category size effects in recall: The roles of relational and individual item information. *Journal of Experimental Psychology: Learning, Cognition, and Memory, 10,* 454-464.

Hunt, R. R., Ausley, J. A., & Schultz, E. E. (1986). Shared and item-specific information in memory for event descriptions. *Memory and Cognition, 14,* 49-54.

Johnson, M. K. (1983). A modular model of memory. In G. H. Bower (Ed.), *The psychology of learning and motivation: Advances in research and theory* (Vol. 17 pp. 81-123). New York: Academic Press.

Kieras, D. E.(1978). Beyond pictures and words: Alternative information processing models for imagery effects in verbal memory. *Psychological Bulletin, 85,* 532-554.

Kieras, D. E. (1981). The role of major referents and sentence topics in the construction of passage macrostructure. *Discourse Processes, 4,* 11-15.

Kintsch, W., & van Dijk, T. A. (1978). Toward a model of text comprehension and production. *Psychological Review, 85*, 532–554.

Koffka, K. (1935). *Principles of gestalt psychology.* New York: Harcourt, Brace, & Co.

Lehman, E. B. (1982). Memory for modality: Evidence for an automatic process. *Memory and Cognition, 10*, 554–564.

Lockhart, R. S., Craik, F. I. M., & Jacoby, L. (1976). Depth of processing, recognition, and recall. In J. Brown (Ed.), *Recall and Recognition.* New York: Wiley.

Marschark, M. (1978). Prose processing: A chronometric study of the effects of imagability. Unpublished doctoral dissertation, University of Western Ontario, London, Ontario, Canada.

Marschark, M. (1979). The syntax and semantics of comprehension. In G. Prideaux (Ed.), *Perspectives in experimental linguistics.* Amsterdam: John Benjamins B.V.

Marschark, M. (1985). Imagery and organization in the recall of prose. *Journal of Memory and Language, 24*, 734–745.

Marschark, M., & Hunt, R. R. (1985). Imagery effects in paired associate learning: Now you see them, now you don't. Paper presented at the Canadian Psychological Association meetings, June 6–8, Halifax, Nova Scotia, Canada.

Marschark, M., & Hunt, R. R. (1986). Imagery effects in paired associate learning: Now you see them, now you don't, Part 2. Paper presented at the Canadian Psychological Association meetings, June 19–21, Toronto, Ontario, Canada.

Marschark, M., & Paivio, A. (1977). Integrative processing of concrete and abstract sentences. *Journal of Verbal Learning and Verbal Behavior, 16*, 217–231.

Marschark, M., Richman, C. L., Yuille, J. C., & Hunt, R. R. (in press). The role of imagery in memory: On shared and distinctive information. *Psychological Bulletin.*

Nelson, D. L., Reed, V. S., & McEvoy, C. L. (1977). Learning to order pictures and words: A model of sensory and semantic coding. *Journal of Experimental Psychology: Human Learning and Memory, 3*, 485–497.

Paivio, A. (1971). *Imagery and verbal processes.* New York: Holt, Rinehart, and Winston.

Paivio, A. (1983). The empirical case for dual coding. In J. Yuille (Ed.), *Imagery, memory, and cognition: Essays in tribute to Allan Paivio.* Hillsdale, NJ: Erlbaum Associates.

Paivio, A. (1986). *Mental representations: A dual coding approach.* New York: Oxford University Press.

Pompi, K. F., & Lachman, R. (1967). Surrogate processes in the short term retention of connected prose. *Journal of Experimental Psychology, 75*, 143–150.

Pylyshyn, Z. (1973). What the mind's eye tells the mind's brain: A critique of mental imagery. *Psychological Bulletin, 80*, 1–24.

Richardson, J. T. E. (1985). Imagery versus decomposition in the retention of complex ideas. *Memory and Cognition, 13*, 112–127.

Schwanenflugel, P., & Shoben, E. J. (1983). Differential context effects in the comprehension of concrete and abstract prose. *Journal of Experimental Psychology: Learning, Memory, and Cognition, 9*, 82–102.

Snodgrass, J. G. (1984). Concepts and their surface representations. *Journal of Verbal Learning and Verbal Behavior, 23*, 3–23.

Tulving, E. (1974). Cue-dependent forgetting. *American Scientist, 62*, 74–82.

Tversky, B. (1977). Features of similarity. *Psychological Review, 84*, 327–352.

Yuille, J. C., & Marschark, M. (1982). Imagery effects on memory: Theoretical interpretations. In A. Sheikh (Ed.), *Imagery: Current theory, research, and application.* New York: John Wiley & Sons.

Yuille, J. C., & Paivio, A. (1969). Abstractness and the recall of connected discourse. *Journal of Experimental Psychology, 82,* 467–471.

CHAPTER 7

Reversing the Picture Superiority Effect

Henry L. Roediger III and Mary Susan Weldon

Imaginal coding typically enhances retention. Pictures are remembered better than words; words for which subjects imagine referents are better remembered than words studied without such coding; concrete words are better retained than abstract words; and mnemonic devices employing imagery can produce dramatic effects on retention. These facts have long been noted (Paivio, 1971) and many contributions in this volume confirm the efficacy of imagery and imagination in remembering.

If we conceive the process of remembering as involving the broad stages of encoding, storage, and retrieval (Köhler, 1947; Melton, 1963), then it is fair to say that theories explaining the superior retention of information encoded imaginally have emphasized encoding and storage processes as the loci of the effects. For example, Paivio's (1969, 1986) dual code theory attributes the picture superiority effect to redundant coding, and Nelson's (1979) sensory-semantic model to pictures' superior sensory codes. Interestingly, the possible importance of retrieval factors has been relatively neglected.

In this chapter we present evidence that the neglect of the retrieval phase in such effects is unwarranted. In fact, we show that retrieval factors are critical in producing the "standard" imagery effects. We concentrate primarily on the picture superiority effect, the finding that pictures are better remembered than words, but at the end of the chapter we argue that our thesis also holds for other standard effects of imagery and mnemonic devices.

First, we briefly review evidence documenting the picture superiority effect. Next, in something of a detour to lay the groundwork of our argument, we review recent evidence showing important differences between certain classes of retention tasks. From this literature we hypothesize that one may in fact find a reversal of the usual picture superiority effect on certain tests, such that words are retained better than pictures. We present several experiments that illustrate superior retention for words than for pictures and then resurrect some older evidence bearing on this point. We conclude with a section summarizing our argument and extending it to other imagery manipulations and mnemonic techniques.

The Picture Superiority Effect

The first evidence suggesting that pictures or objects are remembered better than words was produced in a study by Kirkpatrick in 1894. He presented subjects with either objects or words and tested retention both immediately and 72 h later. At both intervals he found that the objects were better remembered than the words. This finding was replicated by Calkins (1898), who compared retention of pictures and words under better controlled conditions, but was then largely ignored by researchers interested in human learning and memory for some 60 years, until the important line of work initiated by Allan Paivio in the 1960s. In the past 20 years the superior retention of pictures relative to words on many tests of episodic memory has been reported with heartening regularity for a science often plagued with failures to replicate. Here we touch on only some features of this evidence and refer the reader to excellent discussions by Madigan (1983) and Paivio (1971, Chapter 7; 1986, Chapter 8) for more thorough reviews.

The general conclusion to emerge from the literature is that when subjects study a list of pictures and words, pictures are better remembered on tests of free recall (e.g., Paivio, Rogers, & Smythe, 1968), recognition (e.g., Madigan, 1983), serial recall (Herman, Broussard, & Todd, 1951), and paired-associate learning (Paivio & Yarmey, 1966), although some qualifications exist for each of these tasks. The general form of the qualification is that the picture superiority effect diminishes or evaporates under certain encoding conditions. Thus, for example, elaborative semantic or imaginal encoding of words can produce word recall equal to or better than picture recall (Durso & Johnson, 1980). At a very fast rate of presentation (5.3 items/sec), free recall of pictures and words is equivalent and serial recall of words exceeds that of pictures (Paivio & Csapo, 1969). In paired-associate learning pictures (P) produce better performance than words (W) when used as stimuli (P–P and P–W pairs lead to better performance than W–P and W–W pairs) but, when used as responses, pictures show no advantage to words and sometimes even produce slightly worse performance (see Paivio, 1971, p. 255; Postman, 1978). These exceptions must be viewed against a background of studies typically producing robust picture superiority effects. A typical example in free recall, from Paivio et al. (1968), is shown in the left panel of Figure 7.1.

Theorists' emphasis on encoding operations as the locus of the picture superiority effect seems natural, because in previous research with standard measures, variation in form of the test alone has never eliminated the picture superiority effect. That is, we can find no experiments using customary memory tests in which study conditions have been held constant and various forms of test have yielded both the picture superiority effect and its elimination or reversal across tests.

Recognition memory experiments with words as the test items are the most informative on this issue, because the format of the test item matches the study episode more closely for words than for pictures. Many popularly accepted notions about retrieval processes, such as the encoding specificity principle (Tulving & Thomson, 1973), would seem to predict that on a word recognition test, words should be remembered better than pictures. This is because there is

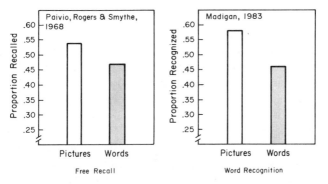

FIGURE 7.1. The picture superiority effect as shown in free recall (left panel; results from Paivio et al., 1968) and in word recognition (right panel; results from Madigan, 1983).

a greater match between the study and test episodes in the (study) word– (test) word case than in the picture–word case. Yet, several studies have shown that the picture superiority effect persists on word recognition tests (Borges, Stepnowsky, & Holt, 1977; Jenkins, Neale, & Deno, 1967; Madigan, 1983; Scarborough, Gerard, & Cortese, 1979; Snodgrass & McClure, 1975). For example, Madigan (1983) presented subjects words or pictures and then tested their recognition of the same words they had studied or the word labels of the studied pictures. Despite the fact that the symbolic modality was changed between study and test for picture items, subjects still recognized items studied as pictures about 15% better than items presented as words, even though words were tested in exactly the same form as their original presentation (see the right panel of Figure 7.1).

We should also note that in free recall, as well as in word recognition, subjects must reproduce pictorial information in a form different from that in which it was studied. That is, when subjects recall a series of words and pictures, they must produce verbal responses, and in some sense, therefore, words appear to enjoy the advantage of being recalled in the same form as presented, whereas pictures should suffer from being recalled in a different form. Yet despite the potential obstacle to picture retrieval that the different study and test formats may create, recall and recognition of pictures is superior to that of words. Thus, the picture superiority effect has proved to be robust across various retrieval tasks, even though they may seem to favor word retrieval. As Madigan notes, ". . . the effects of symbolic modality (verbal *versus* pictorial) are large, reliable and general ones, and as such ought to influence the development of theories of cognition and memory and demand satisfactory accounting for by any such theories" (1983, p. 65). The remainder of the chapter is directed toward this end.

Implicit Measures of Retention

In the past 10 years psychologists investigating memory have begun to explore a new set of measures, and we are still fumbling for an appropriate categorization or taxonomy of memory in light of new data. Graf and Schacter (1985) have provided the helpful classification of explicit and implicit measures of retention, which serves as at least a descriptive distinction. Explicit measures of retention are those in which people are asked to recollect some information; subjects know that their memories are being tested and they attempt conscious retrieval of the requested information. All the standard measures of episodic memory—free recall, cued recall, serial recall, frequency judgments, and various recognition procedures—would qualify as explicit measures of retention. Implicit measures of retention are those in which learning and retention are measured indirectly, usually through some form of repetition priming (the facilitation in processing a test stimulus because of its prior exposure, typically measured by improved accuracy or speed of responding). In these implicit tasks subjects are exposed to material (words, pictures, sentences) and then later given another task in which some form of these same items is repeated. In Table 7.1 we list the main tasks that have been used as implicit measures of memory, although the list is by no means exhaustive. Even Ebbinghaus's (1885/1964) savings method can be considered an implicit measure of retention (Roediger, 1985).

Implicit measures of retention have become of interest because they appear to reveal learning in cases where standard, explicit measures do not. For example, when patients classified as amnesic are given tests of verbal memory, their recall and recognition are notoriously poor. However, on implicit tests, such as completing fragmented words or producing the first word to come to mind to a three-letter stem (Warrington & Weiskrantz, 1970), these patients often show perfectly normal levels of priming. The implication of such results is that amnesics do not suffer difficulties in acquiring or storing information, as has long been thought; instead, the difficulty seems to be one of gaining conscious access to available information (as required on explicit tests). An ancillary implication, to state the case most forcefully, is that implicit measures of retention permit measurement of unconscious memories.

Although systematic use of such implicit measures in studying memory of normal subjects dates only to the past 10 years or less, many important discoveries have been made (see Jacoby & Witherspoon, 1982; Roediger & Blaxton, 1987, for partial reviews). Interestingly, manipulation of independent variables often

TABLE 7.1. Implicit Measures of Retention as Revealed Through Repetition Priming.

Measure	Sample references
1. Savings in relearning	Ebbinghaus (1885/1913)
2. Reading inverted text	Kolers (1976)
3. Perceptual identification	Jacoby and Dallas (1981)
4. Visual duration threshold	Winnick and Daniel (1970)
5. Lexical decision task	Scarborough, Gerard, and Cortese (1979)
6. Word stem completion	Warrington and Weiskrantz (1970)
7. Word fragment completion	Tulving, Schacter, and Stark (1982)
8. Anagram solution	Dominowski and Ekstrand (1967)
9. Spelling homophones	Jacoby and Witherspoon (1982)

exerts different effects on implicit tasks than on explicit tasks. For example, manipulations of "elaborative coding," such as varying orienting tasks in a levels of processing experiment or forming mental images, have large effects on explicit tasks but have little or no effect on perceptual identification or word stem completion (Graf & Mandler, 1984; Jacoby & Dallas, 1981). Other variables, such as the modality and typography of studied words, which have very little effect on long-term recall and recognition, can be shown to have sizeable effects on repetition priming in implicit tasks (Graf, Shimamura, & Squire, 1985; Jacoby & Dallas, 1981; Roediger & Blaxton, 1987a). Even more impressively, some variables that exert powerful effects in one direction on recognition and recall can be shown to exert equally powerful, but opposite effects on implicit measures (Blaxton, 1985; Jacoby, 1983).

The challenge of understanding powerful dissociations among measures of retention is paramount. Various researchers have suggested that the basic underlying distinction is between tasks requiring episodic or semantic memory (Tulving, 1983), or declarative and procedural memory (Cohen & Squire, 1980), or perhaps even implicit and explicit retention (measures requiring or not requiring conscious awareness). Here we argue that the best understanding of these dissociations currently lies in the distinction made by Jacoby (1983) between conceptually-driven and data-driven tests of retention. Briefly, some tests of retention, such as free recall, provide subjects with little overt "data" to guide retrieval and so subjects must rely on conceptual processes (organization, elaboration, and the like) to provide their own cues during retrieval. On the other hand, in such tasks as perceptual identification or word fragment completion, subjects are provided some form of "data" at test, with the requirement being to produce the first appropriate response that comes to mind. In these tasks, variation in the surface features between study and test presentations produces large effects on performance; therefore, the similarities in processing the "data" are critical. The distinction between data-driven and conceptually-driven processing depends both on the similarity of the "data" provided at study and test and on task requirements. In recognition memory tasks, for example, subjects are provided with "data" in the form of copy cues, but the task requirement to decide whether or not each item is a word from the studied list causes the subject to rely mostly on conceptually driven processing (Jacoby, 1983). However, the distinct terms "data-driven" and "conceptually-driven" processing should properly be considered to represent endpoints on a continuum rather than a strict dichotomy (Roediger & Blaxton, 1987b). For example, the type of processing required in recognition can be manipulated by task demands, as shown by Johnston, Dark, and Jacoby (1985).

According to this distinction between data-driven and conceptually-driven processing, study manipulations that vary elaboration of coding (levels of processing, forming images, generating words from impoverished cues) should produce large effects on conceptually-driven tasks but little or even reverse effects on data-driven tasks. On the other hand, various methods of manipulating the physical attributes of study stimuli (changing modality, typeface, etc.) should have large effects on data-driven tasks but little effect on conceptually-driven tasks. Roediger and Blaxton (1987b) have reviewed the body of evidence consistent with these predictions and have also elaborated the distinction between data-driven and conceptually-driven processes. Here we wish to invoke this distinction to set the stage for the current investigations. Briefly, we hypothesized that an implicit memory task that emphasized data-driven processing might reverse the usual superiority of pictures to words in tests of retention. If an exception were to be found to the usual "law" of the picture superiority effect, then perhaps it could serve as a tool to permit a new line of inquiry on picture/word effects.

Reversing the Picture Superiority Effect

The implicit, data-driven task we chose for this research was the word fragment completion task (Tulving et al., 1982). In this test subjects attempt to supply letters missing from words in order to form a complete word (e.g., _hi_b_e for "thimble"). On this test, some words have been presented during an earlier study phase and others have not. The latter set provides a baseline measure of completion to permit assessment of priming from prior study. The fragments are normed ahead of time so that each has a unique solution. Subjects taking the test in our experiments are not informed that some of the fragments are items studied earlier.

Previous research in our laboratory has shown that this test is quite sensitive to the physical format of presented information, unlike most studies of free and cued recall. For example, Roediger and Blaxton (1987b) showed greater priming of words presented visually than those presented auditorily. That is, significantly more fragments were completed when subjects had previously read the target words than if they had heard them. (Significant cross-modal priming did occur, however.) Similarly, Durgunoğlu and Roediger (1986) tested Spanish–English bilinguals on free recall and word fragment completion after they had studied a mixed list of Spanish and English words. Spanish words were remembered slightly better in free recall, probably because the subjects were Spanish-dominant bilinguals. However, on the English word fragment completion test subjects showed greater priming for words presented in English than for those studied in Spanish. In fact, no significant priming occurred in the cross-language condition. Thus, in both the cross-modal and cross-language experiments, the most priming was obtained from stimuli that most closely matched the word fragments in terms of surface features. The word fragment completion task is primarily data-driven in that it taps memory for the processing of the surface features more than the conceptual features of studied stimuli. These results led us to hypothesize that the picture superiority effect might be reversed when retention was measured by priming on the word fragment completion test, because fragment completion performance benefits most from studying physically similar stimuli, i.e., words.

Experiment 1

Our first experiment in attempting to reverse the customary picture superiority effect by using an implicit (data-driven) memory test is reported in detail elsewhere (Weldon and Roediger, 1987) and we only summarize the main points here. Subjects studied a mixed list of 42 pictures and words (half of each) presented for 5 sec per item and then, after a brief delay, received either a free-recall test or a word fragment completion test. In free-recall subjects were told to write the names of the studied pictures and words. In the fragment completion test subjects were instructed that they would see word frames and that they should complete each with a word, if possible. An example was given (_cc_rd_o_ for "accordion"). They were further told that the task was difficult and that they should continue trying throughout the 20-sec period provided for each fragment. The test was represented as a filler task to collect information for future research, with no mention made that some items had been studied previously. The fragments represented equal numbers of items studied as words and as pictures. In addition, one third of the fragments represented nonstudied items. The items were counterbalanced across the three conditions (word, picture, nonstudied) over subjects.

We expected to replicate the usual picture superiority effect for subjects who received the free recall test but hoped to reverse the effect on priming in word fragment completion. The results confirmed these expectations, as shown in Figure 7.2. On the left is free recall, showing that pictures were remembered better than words.* More interestingly, depicted on the right is the amount of priming in the word fragment completion task for both pictures and words. The bars represent the amount of facilitation (priming) from studying pictures and words beyond the base rate of completing nonstudied items (.38). Study of words produced much greater priming than study of pictures, 0.26–0.07. Thus, on the implicit memory test of word fragment completion, we reversed the usual picture superiority effect.

A critic might complain that our reversal of the picture superiority effect under these conditions was uninteresting because we merely contrived conditions that artificially favored word retrieval. That is, the word fragments provided at test obviously matched the stimuli studied as words better than those studied as pictures. It is therefore no surprise that word fragment completion reveals greater priming from words than pictures. However, this argument from our hypothetical critic evaporates when one considers the recognition memory results shown above on the right in Figure 7.1 (e.g., Madigan, 1983), where presentation of pictures produced superior recognition to presentation of words even when the recognition test was wholly composed of words. In such a recognition test the overlap between the surface features of study and test items is even

---

*All results described in the text were statistically significant at or beyond the .05 level of confidence by conventional tests, unless otherwise noted.

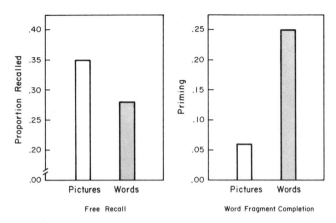

FIGURE 7.2. The picture superiority effect in free recall (left panel) was reversed when retention was measured by priming on the word fragment completion task (right panel). Priming is computed by subtracting the baseline completion rate for nonstudied items from the completion rate for studied items for each subject. Data from Weldon and Roediger (1987, Experiment 1).

greater than in the word fragment completion test, and yet the picture superiority effect still obtains. Although recognition may have what we are calling a data-driven component, under "standard" conditions in which items in recognition tests are paced slowly, recognition behaves largely as a conceptually-driven test (Jacoby, 1983; Johnston et al., 1985).

The reversal of the picture superiority effect we found in word fragment completion priming is therefore genuine and also helps point up a critical feature of the distinction between data-driven and conceptually-driven tasks: these tasks do not necessarily differ in the amount and kind of data presented at test but differ instead in terms of the processing requirements of the test. Conceptually-driven tasks require subjects to reflect on the meaning (or associations or images or elaborations) of a concept, whereas data-driven processing usually requires a response to the presented data without the necessity for higher level reflection.

Experiment 2

A potential problem with the interpretation of our results occurred to us. We obtained the picture superiority effect in free recall, whereas our reversal was obtained in the word fragment completion task. The difference we obtained between free recall and word fragment completion may have been resulted simply from different cueing properties in the two situations, rather than to differences in types of processing. That is, words were retained better than pictures in the word fragment completion task (a cued task), but pictures were retained better than words in free recall. Perhaps it is the case that words are simply remembered better than pictures on tests that involve cued recall. Of course, the picture superiority effect in word recognition (Madigan, 1983) would seem to argue against this possibility. However, we decided to test it directly by seeing if we could obtain both picture superiority and word superiority under identical cuing conditions by varying only the instructions telling subjects how to use the cues. We hoped to find that subjects given Implicit instructions would reveal greater priming for words than pictures, whereas those given Explicit instructions would remember pictures better than words.

In this experiment all subjects studied mixed lists of 26 pictures and 26 words for 5 sec each then received word fragments at test. Thirteen test fragments were nonstudied items, and all items were rotated so that they served as pictures, words, or nonstudied items an equal number of times across subjects in each test condition. The critical manipulation was the instructions given at test. Twenty-five subjects received Implicit retention instructions; i.e., they were told to try to solve each fragment with the first word that came to mind. They were told that they were helping prepare materials for future research and were not told that some of the fragments were items from the study list. This condition replicated the word fragment completion test condition in Experiment 1. After they finished the fragment completions, these subjects were given 7 min to free recall the pictures and words. The other half of the subjects received the same word fragments in the same order at test but were given Explicit retrieval instructions; i.e., they were told to use the fragments as retrieval cues to help them remember the pictures and words they had studied. All subjects were given 15 sec to complete each fragment. The manipulation of instructions permitted us to equate the cues in the implicit and explicit retrieval conditions to determine whether the presentation of such cues always leads to superior retention of words relative to pictures.

The fragment completion results are displayed in the left panel of Figure 7.3. First, notice that the reversal of the picture superiority effect reported in the first

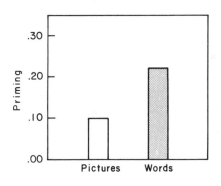
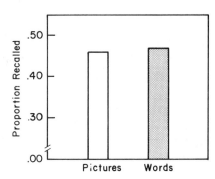

Standard Implicit Instructions   Explicit Cued Recall Instructions

FIGURE 7.3. The picture superiority effect was reversed on the implicit word fragment completion test (left panel), but pictures and words were retrieved equally well when the same cues were used on an explicit task (right panel).

experiment was replicated in the group that received Implicit fragment completion instructions: words produced significantly more priming than pictures. The baseline rate of completion was 0.32, and the total completion rates for words and pictures were 0.54 and 0.42, respectively. Interestingly, in this group the usual picture superiority effect was obtained on the free-recall test given after fragment completion. Proportions recalled were 0.37 for pictures and 0.26 for words. This picture superiority effect in free recall occurred despite the fact that subjects had received a second study opportunity during the fragment completion test for more of the original word items than picture items.

In the group that received the same fragment cues with the Explicit cued-recall instructions, the better performance obtained from studying words than pictures under Implicit instructions was eliminated. As shown in Figure 7.3, there was no significant difference between the number of pictures and words recalled. Although Explicit instructions altered the pattern of results, we had expected cued recall to produce a picture superiority effect. One possible—although speculative—interpretation of our failure to find the picture superiority effect in explicit cued recall with word fragment cues is that there is simply a strong and unavoidable data-driven component to such cues. That is, when impoverished data are provided to subjects, it may be difficult or impossible to override data-driven processing completely by explicit memory instructions. In fact, Blaxton (1985) developed a graphemic cued-recall test in which subjects were given words that looked and sounded like target words (for example, the word "chopper" as a cue for the target word "copper"). She showed that under explicit memory instructions, her graphemic cued recall task behaved like a data-driven task, because it was sensitive to the physical format of studied information but relatively unaffected by conceptual manipulations at study. Therefore, our word fragment cued-recall task, like Blaxton's graphemic cued-recall test, might have an inherently data-driven aspect.

Experiment 3

If the preceding reasoning were correct, then we failed to find the picture superiority effect in cued-recall in Experiment 2 because the cues we used (word fragments) had an inherent data-driven component that favored word recall. One way to test this idea was to develop another cued-recall task in which the cues would provide only a conceptual relation to the target words. Under these conditions, the picture superiority effect should emerge. Surprisingly, we could find no experiment appropriate to our needs in the literature, so we conducted a third experiment in which we provided extralist cues that shared no physical "data" with the targets. Instead, the cues were strong associates of the targets (e.g., "emergency" as a cue for "ambulance") with the latter concept presented either as a picture or a word in the study list. Thus, the cued recall task was conceptually-driven, because subjects were required to rely on associative information in order to use the cues to recall the targets. If our hypothesis is correct, i.e., that the word fragment completion task is too data-driven to permit a picture superiority effect under explicit cued-recall instructions, then removing the data-driven component of the cues should restore the picture superiority effect.

Forty subjects studied mixed lists of 30 pictures and 30 words, with study format counterbalanced across subjects. They then received the extralist cued-recall test, which contained 60 cue words associatively related to the studied items. Subjects were told to use these cues to help them remember the pictures and words, and to write each recalled item next to the cue. They were given 15 sec to attempt to recall an item for each cue.

Cued recall was significantly higher for pictures than words, with recall proportions of 0.72 for pictures and 0.56 for words. Thus, the picture superiority effect was obtained in cued recall with extralist associates as cues. This result suggests that the failure to find a picture superiority effect using word fragments as cues in the previous experiment probably owes to the inherently data-driven nature of the retrieval task, and not to any general absence of picture superiority effects in cued recall. Cued recall with associatively related items is a conceptually-driven task because it requires the use of information about an item's meaning and semantic relationships with other items. Therefore, because pictures induce more conceptual processing, pictures were remembered better than words on this cued recall test.

We emphasize that our hypothesis—that cued recall with word fragment cues is inherently data driven—is speculative and admittedly ad hoc at this point. A reasonable objection to the suggestion that explicit cued recall with word fragments is data-driven is that we also maintain that explicit word recognition is conceptually driven, and yet the word recognition test provides more data than a fragment completion test. One might argue that the recognition test should therefore be more data-driven than the cued fragment completion test with explicit memory instructions. However, the critical factor determining the degree to which a task is data-driven may be the degree to which it is *data limited*. Performance on data-limited tasks such as perceptual identification and word fragment completion may depend more heavily on recapitulation of perceptual rather than conceptual processes. These ideas require further research but open exciting possibilities for understanding the mechanisms underlying the distinction between conceptually and data-driven tasks.

Experiment 4

In the final part of this section on our own research, we raise one last question concerning our demonstration of a reversal of the usual picture superiority effect on priming in word fragment completion. One possible description of most of our results so far is that the picture superiority effect is obtained on explicit memory tests (free recall and extralist cued recall), but not on implicit memory tests (word fragment completion). Perhaps the explicit/implicit distinction provides at least a description of when the picture superiority effect will be found or reversed. On the other hand, we have argued that the proper distinction underlying our results and those of others is that between data-driven and conceptually-driven processing. A natural confounding has been built into most research, such that almost all explicit memory tests are what we would call conceptually-driven and almost all implicit memory tests (see Table 7.1) are data-driven. Blaxton (1985) has performed experiments in which she has developed variants on the standard tasks (that is, she developed a data-driven explicit task and a conceptually-driven implicit task); she has shown that the requirements of the task in terms of its data-driven or conceptually-driven component was the critically important feature, and not whether the task was implicit or explicit. We used the same logic in an experiment in which we sought to show that the picture superiority effect could be obtained or reversed on an implicit memory task depending on the type of data presented at test.

Subjects in this experiment studied a mixed list of words and pictures and then received one of two types of implicit memory tests (Weldon & Roediger, 1987, Exp. 4). One test was the word fragment completion task in which fragments representing studied items (pictures and words) were intermixed with fragments of nonstudied items. Other subjects took a newly developed picture fragment identification test in which their task was to name severely degraded pictures created by eliminating critical features. (These picture fragments were normed; several examples with their verbal labels appear in Figure 7.4.) As in word fragment completion, subjects taking the picture identification test were asked to identify fragments of items previously presented as pictures or words, as well as nonstudied items. As usual, subjects taking both types of test were given instructions to complete the word fragment or identify the picture fragment as quickly as possible, with no mention of the fact that some items had been studied previously.

Both tasks used in this experiment are implicit memory tasks, but the type of data provided should match features of the study episodes in different ways. The "data" in the word fragments match those in studied words much better than

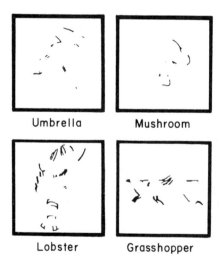

Umbrella   Mushroom

Lobster   Grasshopper

FIGURE 7.4. Examples of test items used in the picture fragment identification test.

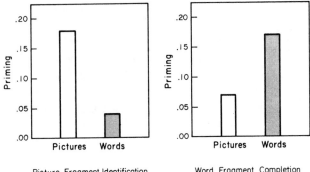

FIGURE 7.5. A picture superiority effect was found in the picture identification task, but greater priming (studied vs. nonstudied completion rates) occurred for words than pictures on the word fragment completion test.

those in pictures, but the converse was true of the picture fragment identification task. Here, match of the test stimuli was better with studied pictures than with studied words. Thus, despite the fact that both are implicit memory tasks, we predicted a picture superiority effect for the picture fragment identification task, but greater priming from words on the word fragment completion test (as in Figure 7.2).

The results followed our expectations quite well, as can be seen in Figure 7.5. The picture identification test did lead to greater priming from prior study of pictures than words, whereas words produced greater priming than pictures on the word fragment completion test. (Note that small cross-form priming was obtained on both tests, although it was reliable only on the word fragment completion test.) Because the picture superiority effect can be obtained or reversed on implicit memory tests, depending on the type of data provided at test, we conclude that a possible generalization from our earlier work—i.e., that picture superiority occurs only on explicit tests but is reversed on implicit tests—is inaccurate. (See Warren and Morton, 1982, for a similar demonstration with perceptual identification.) Instead, the critical determinant is the degree to which the retrieval test accesses the record of the type of processing performed during the study episode.

To summarize the main results and conclusions emerging from our experiments:

1. The picture superiority effect can be reversed by changing retrieval demands alone.
2. Fragment completion tests such as those used here are primarily data driven: that is, they tap memory for the processing of stimulus surface features.
3. Whereas conceptually-driven tests typically produce better retention for pictures than words, data-driven tests produce superior retention for those stimuli whose physical attributes most closely match those of the test stimuli.

Related Research

Our results above showed that words are retained better than pictures when memory is measured by an implicit, data-driven memory task of completing word fragments. Of course, our demonstration is limited to just this one measure—priming in word fragment completion. It would be comforting to know that our claims generalize to other tasks. Fortunately, some relevant evidence that converges with our conclusion does exist. However, the researchers who collected it were mostly concerned with other issues and did not consider their findings to show a reversal of the picture superiority effect, probably because the tasks used were considered to measure perception rather than memory. However, the work of Jacoby, Kolers, and others has convinced most researchers that priming in "perceptual" tasks can provide important information about memory (see Kolers & Roediger, 1984), so this evidence is relevant in the present context.

Wilma Winnick and Stephen Daniel (1970) reported what should properly be considered a landmark study. However, because of the language in which they cast their results, and perhaps because of the temper of the times, their report went largely unnoticed for a decade or more. Their Experiment 2 was remarkable because it clearly showed (a) the generation effect in free recall (Slamecka & Graf, 1978), (b) the reversal of the generation effect on a perceptual fluency test of implicit memory (Jacoby, 1983), (c) the picture superiority effect in free recall, and (d) reversal of the picture superiority effect on an implicit test. The latter two points are most relevant to present concerns, but we shall describe the experiment in its entirety to help resurrect it.

Winnick and Daniel (1970, Exp. 2) had subjects read four words aloud from each of three types of stimulus display, which instantiated one independent variable in their experiment. Subjects said the word when presented with (a) the word itself (e.g., "airplane"), (b) a picture of the named object, or (c) a definition of the object. Four other words from the same set were not presented but were used as a baseline for one of the tests. Items were counterbalanced across conditions over subjects and the three conditions of word naming were realized within subjects.

The other primary factor was the type of test given. Half the subjects received a free-recall test for the stimuli, whereas the other half were given a tachistoscopic word identification test. In the latter, the threshold for naming each word was measured by the ascending method of limits beginning with an exposure duration of 10 msec and increasing by 5 msec increments on each trial until subjects could identify the word. The measure of interest was the visual duration threshold, or the average amount of time subjects needed to identify words in the different conditions. The nonstudied control words were used as a baseline against which to measure priming in the various study conditions. Subjects were not informed that the studied words were to be presented during the threshold test, so this measure qualifies as an implicit measure of retention.

The results of Winnick and Daniel's experiment are shown in Figure 7.6. Consider first the free-recall results in the left panel. Labels that subjects generated

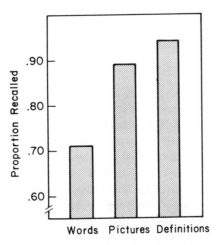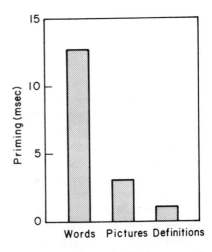

FIGURE 7.6. Results from Winnick and Daniel's (1970) Experiment 2. Words generated from pictures and definitions were better recalled than presented words (left panel). However, the amount of implicit retention revealed by priming (reduction in identification thresholds) in the tachistoscopic identification task was greater for words presented visually than those produced from pictures or definitions.

in response to a picture or a definition were better retained than studied words, revealing the picture superiority effect and the generation effect. The comparison of recall of words generated in response to pictures and to definitions raises an interesting thought concerning the picture superiority effect: perhaps the advantage in recall of pictures to words is not caused by some form of imaginal coding, which is the usual account, but should be considered instead a species of the generation effect. That is, good recall or recognition of words generated from pictures might be achieved by the same mechanisms producing the generation effect and not by dual coding in imaginal and verbal systems (Paivio, 1971). Words generated in response to definitions can be conceived as a relevant comparison condition for the usual picture presentation condition, because we may assume that processing occurs wholly within the verbal system. In this control case, recall of the generated responses is actually slightly superior to recall of words generated to pictures. The possibility that the picture superiority effect in recall and recognition is really a result of generation (rather than imaginal coding) is further discussed by Weldon and Roediger (1987) in light of new data on the issue. The main point to be taken from the left panel of Figure 7.6 for current purposes is that Winnick and Daniel did find superior free recall of pictures relative to words.

The right panel of Figure 7.6 shows the amount of priming on the tachistoscopic threshold measure. Priming here indexes the reduction in word recognition thresholds for the two study conditions relative to nonstudied words. On this measure, studied words showed considerable priming, but items generated from pictures or definitions did not. (Although the amount of priming for words may seem small — a 13-msec advantage over control words — this actually reflects considerable priming in the threshold task. Thresholds averaged about 62 msec in the control condition, so the priming from words represents about a 20% improvement.)

The overall pattern of results thus reflects a strong dissociation: the effect of the various study conditions on free recall was exactly reversed on the implicit threshold identification task (cf. Jacoby, 1983; also Blaxton, 1985). Pictures were remembered better than words on free recall, but words were retained better than pictures as measured by priming on the identification task. Thus the results anticipate our own shown in Figure 7.2 and we would argue that they support our reasoning; free recall is a conceptually-driven test, whereas tachistoscopic identification is data-driven. Of course, Winnick and Daniel (1970) did not discuss their results in any of the terms used here — most of which were not in use in 1970 — but instead discussed them in terms of the response availability and perceptual sensitization created by various conditions.

Another important aspect of the Winnick and Daniel results — noted rather belatedly by Morton (1979) — is that they call into question his logogen model. According to the original version of the model, logogens are abstract representations of words or concepts activated by any relevant source. The firing of a logogen leaves residual activation that then produces priming if the same stimulus is repeated after a short delay. Because the logogen is abstract, activation and priming should occur whenever the logogen is activated and by whatever means. However, the Winnick and Daniel (1970) results showed that priming occurred when subjects had previously seen words, but not when the equivalent concepts were generated from pictures or definitions. Morton (1979; Clarke & Morton, 1983) replicated Winnick's and Daniel's (1970) findings and extended them in important ways, causing changes in the logogen model, too (see also Jackson & Morton, 1984; Warren & Morton, 1982). Although providing details of this work is beyond the scope of this chapter, in general the results are consistent with the notion that priming in either visual or auditory identification or threshold tasks behaves in a "data-driven" fashion.

Another relevant set of experiments was reported by Scarborough et al. (1979). In their experiments subjects generated words in response either to the name of the word or to a picture representing the concept. A third set of control words was not presented. Later subjects saw the words generated at study presented in a lexical decision task (Experiments 1 and 2) or in a standard recognition memory procedure (Experiment 3). In the lexical decision task, words were mixed with nonwords, and subjects made word/nonword judgments about each item; in the recognition experiment words were mixed with distractors and subjects made old/new decisions about each item. The measure of interest in the lexical decision task was repetition priming, measured as the increased speed with which previously generated items were identified as words, relative to the nonstudied items. The measure of interest in the recognition memory task was, of course, the ability to discriminate old from new items as represented by d'.

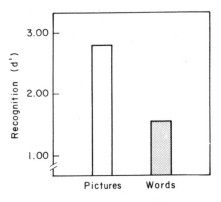
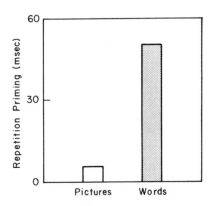

FIGURE 7.7. Results from Scarborough, Gerard, & Cortese (1979). Pictures were better recognized than words on a word recognition test (left panel; data from Experiment 3), but repetition priming (facilitation in decision times) in the lexical decision task was greater for items previously studied as words rather than pictures (right panel; data from Experiment 2). Only results from low-frequency items are given.

The results are presented in Figure 7.7 for low-frequency words. In the left panel are d' values and the usual finding was obtained: words generated in response to pictures were better recognized than those actually seen as words, even on a word recognition test. However, considering repetition priming in the lexical decision task as an implicit measure of retention, the picture superiority effect was reversed (see the right panel). Only a nonsignificant 5-msec priming effect was found for words generated in response to pictures, but prior naming of the word itself produced a 50-msec priming effect. Although Scarborough et al. (1979) did not explicitly note that they had reversed the picture superiority effect on some form of memory test, their interpretation of these results is generally similar to the one offered here. Somewhat curiously, the effects in the lexical decision task were not well replicated in one experiment with medium- and high-frequency words. However, Durso and Johnson (1979) also found greater repetition priming from words than from pictures on tasks requiring either naming or categorization of words. Therefore, the effect seems genuine.

Finally, we should note one other relevant experiment, albeit briefly. Kroll and Potter (1984, Exp. 5) employed a decision task in which subjects had to categorize pictures and words as representing "real objects" or not when pictures and names of objects were mixed with nonwords and nonsense "objects." The concepts representing pictures and words were sometimes repeated, and then either in the same form or a different form. In general, Kroll and Potter found strong repetition effects when the repetition occurred in the same surface form (picture–picture or word–word), but either no (word to picture) or slight (picture to word) priming was obtained with cross-form repetitions. In general, the results agree that these "priming" tasks are largely data-driven (enhanced by matching surface features) and little affected by conceptual processing (a correspondence in the underlying concepts).

Synopsis and Extensions

The superiority of pictures to words in retention has been considered as a general, established fact, as indeed it is in most episodic memory tests. However, the results from our experiments (Weldon & Roediger, 1987, and from others reviewed in the preceding section, show that on several implicit measures of retention, words produce superior performance (priming) relative to pictures. We suggested that the reason for the picture superiority effect on most explicit measures of retention is that these depend on conceptual information (elaborations, associations, images and the like) for good performance; in short, they are conceptually-driven. On the other hand, most implicit measures of retention require subjects to produce the first accessible response given some data-limited presentation. In these cases the match between surface features of the test items and the items studied earlier determines how good performance will be, with conceptual factors (elaboration, etc.) playing little or no role. Thus, when test items consist of words on these data-driven implicit tests, priming from prior study of words exceeds priming from prior study of pictures, thus reversing the usual advantage of pictures to words in tests of retention. Of course, if the "data" in the test are pictorial, then the picture superiority effect will still be found on data-driven tests (see Figure 7.5).

What implications do our results with data-driven tests, showing reversals of the usual picture superiority effect, have for theories of imagery in remembering? First, we believe that our results do point up a critical oversight in imagery research (and most other memory research) by neglecting task differences in remembering (Jenkins, 1979). Our results show that, on appropriate tests, words are retained better than are pictures and so there is nothing inherently more memorable – as a main effect across every retention test – in pictures than words. However, the implication of our results for specific theories of imagery in remembering may be less profound. In Paivio's (1971) dual code theory, our results could be interpreted as showing test conditions in which verbal coding can be more powerful than imaginal encoding. However, two codes would still be postulated. In terms of Nelson's (1979) semantic sensory model, implicit memory tests may tap the record of sensory features, whereas conceptually-driven tests would tap the semantic component. At this general level, our results would not be inconsistent with the main postulates of either theory.

The interpretation of our data offered above can be put into the more general terms of transfer-appropriate processing, in the various forms in which that idea has been raised (Morris, Bransford, & Franks, 1977; see also Kolers & Roediger, 1984; McDaniel, Friedman, & Bourne, 1978; Stein, 1978). The basic notion is that learning activities may be of many kinds (offering many possibilities for encoding material) and that performance on some test of retention or transfer will benefit to the extent that the kind of processing or the procedures required by the test recapitulate those of the original learning experience. (Many similar ideas exist in the psychology of learning and memory—stimulus generalization, the encoding specificity hypothesis—but we prefer the variants mentioned above because the emphasis is on a matching of processes or procedures rather than a matching of mental elements, structures, or contents.) Put in these broad terms, our argument is that most explicit, conceptually-driven retention tests favor processing of pictures because the procedures in picture encoding are conceptually richer. Similarly, for implicit tests that are data-driven and involve rapid processing of words, prior study of words will produce more priming than prior study of pictures.

The concept of transfer-appropriate processing is, we believe, fundamental to a proper understanding of learning and memory. Roediger and Blaxton (1987b) discuss these issues in more detail. We shall illustrate the applicability in the present context by reference to other work on imagery and mnemonics. Mnemonic devices have long been known to produce very high levels of recall on certain types of memory test (e.g., Bellezza, 1981; Bower, 1970; Yates, 1966). Critics of mnemonics have argued that their use is really quite limited, involving situations where people remember lists or series of elements. Another way of stating this criticism is that traditional mnemonic devices may provide appropriate transfer for only a few measures of retention, and for limited materials. That is, the encoding activities encouraged by mnemonics may require (even demand) appropriate forms of test to reveal their benefit and be useless for most practical purposes. However, we believe that suitable mnemonics can improve performance in many relevant situations, especially when people are required to recall information with little aid from external cues. Most common mnemonics provide the means of supplying a good set of self-generated cues.

An example of transfer-appropriate processing induced by mnemonics occurs in a comparison of the effectiveness of mnemonics in which different measures of recall were obtained. Roediger (1980) instructed subjects to use one of five mnemonic techniques to study and recall lists of 20 words. The techniques were (a) imagery—subjects were to imagine the referent of each word; (b) the link method—subjects were to imagine the object represented by each word and link it to the next; (c) the familiar method of loci; (d) a peg method involving a number–word rhyme scheme ("one is a gun," etc.); (e) a rehearsal control group who repeated each word until the next word was presented. After a small amount of training, subjects learned and recalled successively three lists of 20 words. On their test sheets they were given the numbers 1 to 20 in a column and asked to write down the appropriate word beside each number. However, they were further told that they should be sure to write down all words they could remember, either guessing at the proper locations when unsure or writing them at the bottom of the page.

The results were analyzed in terms of two measures. First, the total number of items recalled in any position was measured and is presented in the solid columns of Figure 7.8, with the bars representing averages across three lists. All four

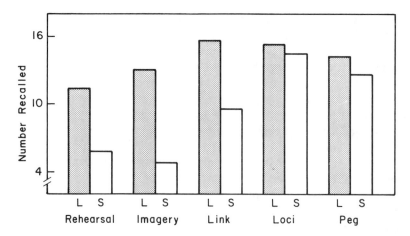

FIGURE 7.8. Results from Roediger (1980). The five groups using different learning strategies exhibited smaller differences when scored on total item recall (L for lenient scoring) than when scored by a strict positional criterion (S).

groups that used imagery recalled significantly more items than did the Rehearsal control group. Differences among the four groups using imagery were small, although the Link and Loci groups recalled significantly more words than the Imagery group (see Roediger, 1980 for further details). The situation is rather different when subjects' data were rescored by a strict positional criterion. By this measure, subjects were given credit for correctly recalling a word only when it appeared on their recall sheets next to the correct number. The results are shown in the open bars of Figure 7.8, where differences among conditions are much greater. Recall was low and did not differ between the Rehearsal and the Imagery groups, was better in the Link group, and was best in the Loci and Peg groups. Of course, in some sense these results are not surprising, because the Peg and Loci conditions encourage encoding of order information, whereas the simple Imagery and Rehearsal instructions do not. The link mnemonic encourages some attention to a fixed order, but not as much as the loci and peg systems.

The important point is that to see marked differences in effectiveness of the various mnemonics, one must test knowledge in an appropriate way. Simply by looking at the total number of items recalled, one might conclude that the mnemonics had little advantage over a simple instruction to form separate images (or to rehearse, for that matter). However, when order is taken into account, the peg and loci mnemonic techniques showed over a 100% advantage relative to the Imagery or Rehearsal control groups. One could imagine a further test that would show a marked advantage for only one of the five groups, although we know of no study documenting this point. Suppose subjects had been asked to produce the words associated with the various numbers when the numbers were given in a random order (what was the fourteenth word? the eighth? etc.)? Certainly one would predict the Peg group to perform much better than the other groups in terms of their speed and accuracy of response, because their encoding strategy uniquely promoted retention of this sort of information. Once again, appropriate retention tests may reveal transfer of the specific information learned, where inappropriate tests do not.

From the consideration of transfer-appropriate processing, successful mnemonics can probably be constructed for any retention test. One needs to ask, what are the critical requirements of the test or evaluation procedure, and what kind of learning activities would promote (transfer to) the particular test? An excellent example of this logic is given by Rohwer and Thomas (Chapter 20, this volume) in which they discuss the role of mnemonic strategies in promoting effective study in classroom settings. Traditional mnemonics such as the peg method, may be of little use in most educational applications. However, by considering the various task demands, learning, materials, subject characteristics, and learning strategies (Jenkins, 1979), one can develop efficient learning strategies with important practical applications (see Figure 20.1 in Rohwer and Thomas, Chapter 20, this volume). McDaniel and Pressley (1984) showed how the keyword method could be used to important benefit in an educational situation when put in an appropriate context. The concept of transfer-appropriate processing thus serves as a useful theoretical context for understanding many phenomena of learning and memory, and also serves the practical function of potentially guiding discovery of more efficient methods of instruction in educational and other applied situations.

Acknowledgments. This research was supported by NIH Grant RO1 HD15054 awarded by the National Institute for Child Health and Human Development.

References

Bellezza, F. S. (1981). Mnemonic devices: Classification, characteristics, and criteria. *Review of Educational Research, 51*, 247–275.

Blaxton, T. A. (1985). *Investigating dissociations among memory measures: Support for a transfer appropriate processing framework.* Unpublished doctoral dissertation, Purdue University, West Lafayette, IN.

Borges, M. A., Stepnowsky, M. A., & Holt, L. H. (1977). Recall and recognition of words and pictures by adults and children. *Bulletin of the Psychonomic Society, 9*(2), 113–114.

Bower, G. H. (1970). Analysis of a mnemonic device. *American Scientist, 58*, 496–510.

Calkins, M. W. (1898). Short studies in memory and association from the Wellesley College laboratory. *Psychological Review, 5*, 451–462.

Clarke, R. G. B., & Morton, J. (1983). The effects of priming in visual word recognition. *Quarterly Journal of Experimental Psychology, 35A*, 79–96.

Cohen, N. J., & Squire, L. R. (1980). Preserved learning and retention of pattern-analyzing skill in amnesia: Dissociation of knowing how and knowing that. *Science, 210*, 207–210.

Dominowski, R. L., & Ekstrand, B. R. (1967). Direct and associative priming in anagram solving. *Journal of Experimental Psychology, 74*, 84–86.

Durgunoğlu, A., & Roediger, H. L. (1986). Test differences in accessing bilingual memory. Manuscript submitted for publication.

Durso, F. T., & Johnson, M. K. (1979). Facilitation in naming and categorizing repeated pictures and words. *Journal of Experimental Psychology: Learning and Memory, 5,* 449–459.

Durso, F. T., & Johnson, M. K. (1980). The effects of orienting tasks on recognition, recall, and modality confusion of pictures and words. *Journal of Verbal Learning and Verbal Behavior, 19,* 416–429.

Ebbinghaus, H. (1964). *Memory: A contribution to experimental psychology.* (H. A. Ruger & C. E. Bussenius, Trans.). New York: Dover. (Original work published 1885.)

Graf, P., & Mandler, G. (1984). Activation makes words more accessible, but not necessarily more retrievable. *Journal of Verbal Learning and Verbal Behavior, 23,* 553–568.

Graf, P., & Schacter, D. L. (1985). Implicit and explicit memory for new associations in normal and amnesic subjects. *Journal of Experimental Psychology: Learning, Memory, and Cognition, 11,* 501–518.

Graf, P., Shimamura, A., & Squire, L. R. (1985). Priming across modalities and priming across category levels: Extending the domain of preserved function in amnesia. *Journal of Experimental Psychology: Learning, Memory, and Cognition, 11,* 386–396.

Herman, T., Broussard, I. G., & Todd, H. R. (1951). Intertrial interval and rate of learning serial order picture stimuli. *Journal of General Psychology, 45,* 245–251.

Jackson, A., & Morton, J. (1984). Facilitation of auditory word recognition. *Memory and Cognition, 12,* 568–574.

Jacoby, L. L. (1983). Remembering the data: Analyzing interactive processes in reading. *Journal of Verbal Learning and Verbal Behavior, 22,* 485–508.

Jacoby, L. L., & Dallas, M. (1981). On the relationship between autobiographical memory and perceptual learning. *Journal of Experimental Psychology: General, 111,* 306–340.

Jacoby, L. L., & Witherspoon, D. (1982). Remembering without awareness. *Canadian Journal of Psychology, 36,* 300–324.

Jenkins, J. J. (1979). Four points to remember: A tetrahedral model of memory experiments. In L. S. Cermak & F. I. M. Craik (Eds.), *Levels of processing in human memory.* Hillsdale, NJ: Erlbaum Associates.

Jenkins, J. R., Neale, D. C., & Deno, S. L. (1967). Differential memory for picture and word stimuli. *Journal of Educational Psychology, 58,* 303–307.

Johnston, W. H., Dark, V. J., & Jacoby, L. (1985). Perceptual fluency and recognition judgements. *Journal of Experimental Psychology: Learning, Memory, and Cognition, 11,* 3–11.

Kirkpatrick, E. A. (1894). An experimental study of memory. *Psychological Review, 1,* 602–609.

Köhler, W. (1947). *Gestalt psychology.* New York: Liveright.

Kolers, P. A. (1976). Reading a year later. *Journal of Experimental Psychology: Human Learning and Memory, 2,* 554–565.

Kolers, P. A., & Roediger, H. L. (1984). Procedures of mind. *Journal of Verbal Learning and Verbal Behavior, 23,* 425–449.

Kroll, J. F., & Potter, M. C. (1984). Recognizing words, pictures and concepts: A comparison of lexical, object and reality decisions. *Journal of Verbal Learning and Verbal Behavior, 23,* 39–66.

Madigan, S. (1983). Picture memory. In J. C. Yuille (Ed.), *Imagery, memory and cognition: Essays in honor of Allan Paivio* (pp. 65–89). Hillsdale, NJ: Erlbaum Associates.

McDaniel, M. A., & Pressley, M. (1984). Putting the keyword method in context. *Journal of Educational Psychology, 76,* 598–609.

McDaniel, M. A., Friedman, A., & Bourne, L. E., Jr. (1978). Remembering the levels of information in words. *Memory and Cognition, 6,* 156–164.

Melton, A. W. (1963). Implications of short-term memory for a general theory of memory. *Journal of Verbal Learning and Verbal Behavior, 2,* 1–21.

Morris, C. D., Bransford, J. D., & Franks, J. J. (1977). Levels of processing versus transfer appropriate processing. *Journal of Verbal Learning and Verbal Behavior, 16,* 519–533.

Morton, J. (1979). Facilitation in word recognition: Experiments causing change in the logogen model. In P. A. Kolers, M. E. Wrolstead, & H. Bouma (Eds.), *Processing of visible language* (Vol. 1, pp. 259–268). New York: Plenum Press.

Nelson, D. L. (1979). Remembering pictures and words: Appearance, significance, and name. In L. S. Cermak & F. I. M. Craik (Eds.), *Levels of processing in human memory.* Hillsdale, NJ: Erlbaum Associates.

Paivio, A. (1969). Mental imagery in associative learning and memory. *Psychological Review, 76,* 241–263.

Paivio, A. (1971). *Imagery and verbal processes.* New York: Holt, Rinehart & Winston.

Paivio, A. (1986). *Mental representations: A dual coding approach.* New York: Oxford University Press.

Paivio, A., & Csapo, K. (1969). Concrete-image and verbal mental codes. *Journal of Experimental Psychology, 80,* 279–285.

Paivio, A., & Yarmey, A. D. (1966). Pictures versus words as stimuli and responses in paired-associate learning. *Psychonomic Science, 5,* 235–236.

Paivio, A., Rogers, T. B., & Smythe, P. C. (1968). Why are pictures easier to recall than words? *Psychonomic Science, 11,* 137–138.

Postman, L. (1978). Picture-word differences in the acquisition and retention of paired associates. *Journal of Experimental Psychology: Human Learning and Memory, 4,* 146–157.

Roediger, H. L. (1980). The effectiveness of four mnemonics in ordering recall. *Journal of Experimental Psychology: Human Learning and Memory, 6,* 558–567.

Roediger, H. L. (1985). Remembering Ebbinghaus. *Contemporary Psychology, 30,* 519–523.

Roediger, H. L., & Blaxton, T. A. (1987a). Effects of varying modality, surface features, and retention interval on priming in word fragment completion. *Memory & Cognition,* in press.

Roediger, H. L., & Blaxton, T. A. (1987b). Retrieval modes produce dissociations in memory for surface information. In D. S. Gorfein & R. R. Hoffman (Eds.), *The Ebbinghaus centennial conference.* Hillsdale, NJ: Erlbaum Associates, in press.

Scarborough, D. L., Gerard, L., & Cortese, C. (1979). Accessing lexical memory: The transfer of word repetition effects across task and modality. *Memory and Cognition, 7,* 3–12.

Slamecka, N. J., & Graf, P. (1978). The generation effect: Delineation of a phenomenon. *Journal of Experimental Psychology: Human Learning and Memory, 4,* 592–604.

Snodgrass, J. G., & McClure, P. (1975). Storage and retrieval properties of dual codes for pictures and words in recognition memory. *Journal of Experimental Psychology: Human Learning and Memory, 1,* 521–529.

Stein, B. S. (1978). Depth of processing re-examined: The effects of precision of encoding and test appropriateness. *Journal of Verbal Learning and Verbal Behavior, 17,* 165–174.

Tulving, E. (1983). *Elements of episodic memory.* London: Oxford University Press.

Tulving, E., & Thomson, D. (1973). Encoding specificity and retrieval processes in episodic memory. *Psychological Review, 80*, 352–373.

Tulving, E., Schachter, D. L., & Stark, H. A. (1982). Priming effects in word-fragment completion are independent of recognition memory. *Journal of Experimental Psychology: Learning, Memory, and Cognition, 8*, 336–342.

Warren, C., & Morton, J. (1982). The effects of priming on picture recognition. *British Journal of Psychology, 73*, 117–129.

Warrington, E. K., & Weiskrantz, L. (1970). Amnesic syndrome: Consolidation or retrieval? *Nature*(London), *228*, 628–630.

Weldon, M. S., & Roediger, H. L. (1987). Altering retrieval demands reverses the picture superiority effect. *Memory & Cognition*, in press.

Winnick, W. A., & Daniel, S. A. (1970). Two kinds of response priming in tachistoscopic recognition. *Journal of Experimental Psychology, 84*, 74–81.

Yates, F. (1966). *The art of memory*. Chicago: University of Chicago Press.

PART II

Individual Differences

Who is likely to employ imagery and other mnemonics spontaneously? Who benefits from imagery and related mnemonic training? Why do some people benefit more than others? These are core questions addressed by the chapters in this section.

Katz (Chapter 8) provides a detailed perspective on three individual differences factors that determine the use of imagery. First of all, there are person differences in knowing how to carry out imaginal procedures. Katz reviews much of the literature documenting individual differences in knowing how and the ways these individual differences determine use of imagery and mnemonics. Knowing how turns out to be quite complicated, including individual differences in generating simple and complex images, in accessing images once they are generated, and in maintaining generated images. Second, people must know when to use imagery. Katz reviews virtually all of the relevant evidence. It is clear from this review that there are substantial gaps in this form of knowledge even for very mature learners. Third, Katz points out that what learners know about themselves can be an important determinant of imagery use. For instance, people who believe themselves to be high imagers are more likely in general to use imagery than are people who view themselves as low imagers. On the other hand, Katz is careful to point out how all of these individual differences factors interact with context, so that there are occasions when even people who see themselves as high imagers do not use imagery.

Denis (Chapter 9) reports on how individual differences in imagery abilities affect learning of prose in the absence of instructions to use imagery. In particular, high imagers process concrete prose differently than do people low in imagery. Highs also learn more concrete prose than do lows. Denis reports in depth on a series of studies conducted in his own laboratory confirming the processing characteristics of readers who are high and low in imagery ability.

Ernest (Chapter 10) reviews in detail the many studies of imagery use by the blind. There are some surprising findings summarized in this chapter. For instance, the blind often profit from instructions to use visual imagery. There are also many more similarities in the mental rotation skills of blind and sighted people than there are differences. On the other hand, there are findings that are consistent with the intuitive position that blind people might somehow compensate through other sensory systems. For instance, the blind seem to be skilled in using auditory imagery; haptic memory in the blind is at least as good (and probably better) than haptic memory in sighted individuals.

Siaw and Kee (Chapter 11) consider whether there are socioeconomic-status (SES) and ethnicity differences in imaginal and mnemonic functioning, especially in associative and free-recall tasks. They make the case very clearly that it is often impossible to separate unambiguously SES and ethnicity factors. They also touch on many methodological points relevant to the study of population differences. What is most striking about their chapter, however, is that individual differences in strategy use based on SES and ethnicity seem rather insignificant compared to the similarities in processing across populations.

Beuhring and Kee (Chapter 12) summarize the research on the development of elaborative propensity and present data that document the changes during adolescence in spontaneous use of elaboration. The investigators collected performance data, strategy report data, and metamemory data. What emerges are portraits of grade-school children who rarely use elaboration without instructions to do so and of 16- to 18-year-olds who use elaboration much more frequently.

Pressley, Borkowski, and Johnson (Chapter 13) also explore the development of imagery and elaboration skills, particularly in relationship to a position that they call the good strategy user model. Good strategy users know strategies; they know when and where to use the strategies that they possess; they tend to try to be strategic when facing a problem; and they have well developed knowledge bases. Pressley et al. outline the developmental data documenting that children are anything but good mnemonic strategy users, with striking gains in good mnemonic strategy use during the adolescent years. On the other hand, there is room for improvement even among adult learners. Pressley et al. take up the problems of autonomous use of imagery and elaboration, their use under instruction, and transfer of these types of strategies. They note developmental improvements in all of these areas.

In summary, although there are some individual differences that are telling with respect to mnemonic use (e.g., developmental status, high- and low-imagery ability), there are other factors that are not as potent as might have been expected (e.g., SES, blind versus sighted). Reading the chapters presented in this section will make apparent the many "type of learner" complexities that must be considered when drawing conclusions about the probable effectiveness of any given mnemonic intervention.

CHAPTER 8

Individual Differences in the Control of Imagery Processing: Knowing How, Knowing When, and Knowing Self

Albert N. Katz

Scientists have studied individual differences in imagery for well over a hundred years (e.g., Galton, 1880). During all this time, theorists have favored data-driven models in explaining imagery differences, such as those that assume the differences result from either the latency or the perceptual clarity with which images are formed. These data-driven models have had little to say about the role that prior knowledge or belief systems play in producing individual variability in image arousal or effectiveness. To emphasize the importance of concept-driven components, Katz (1983) proposed an interactive model in which he postulated that imaginal effectiveness results, in part, from the conjoint influence of three related knowledge states. These states can be characterized as "how-to knowledge," "when-to knowledge," and "self-knowledge." The goal of the interactive model is to understand when and how people use imagery mediators in their everyday activities. From this perspective, the research questions of interest revolve around the conditions under which imaginal processes are spontaneously employed. The present chapter is directed at separately examining the three knowledge states suggested by the model as they relate to memory-relevant situations. We should begin with a warning: imagery effects in memory have been widely discussed in the 15 years since the epochal book by Paivio (1971) and yet there is a relative paucity of research performed on the type of question to which we are directed by the interactional model. In this chapter the relevant literature is reviewed. The aim is not to provide conclusive evidence for the interactional model but to summarize and direct the reader to research questions and problems triggered by the model.

An Interactive Model of Imagery Differences

The basic assumption of the model is that most tasks do not have an obligatory mode of processing. That is, different operations applied to the same problem may prove effective in producing results, albeit not necessarily equally effective results (e.g., Simon, 1975; or the parallel race model suggested for imagery by Kosslyn, 1983). The problem becomes one of determining which process (or set of processes) will actually be employed by a participant in a given situation. The interactionist position is that use of imagery depends on a complex interaction of skill level, interpretation of the context, and personality factors. The model holds that certain contexts are more likely to induce or discourage the use of imagery, at least for some individuals. Thus the model directs research toward attempting to identify people who will use nonimagistic processes capable of performing so-called "prototypic" imagery tasks, such as mental rotation (cf. Cooper, 1976; Egan, 1979. Mumaw, Pelligrino, Kail, & Carter, 1984), and people who use imagery mediators in abstract logical tasks that many claim are not suited for imagery (cf. Burnett, McLane, & Dratt, 1979; Egan & Grimes-Farrow, 1982; Mathews, Hunt, & MacLeod, 1980).

The success in identifying different processing modes relevant to imagery is interpreted to indicate the presence of concept-driven mechanisms that control which processes are employed in a given situation. That is, the use or non-use of imagery processes is not considered to be determined solely by data-driven factors, such as referential concreteness (cf. Paivio, 1971) or structural limitations of the mental representation (cf. Kosslyn, 1983) but by concept-driven individual difference factors that interact with these other factors to determine strategic choice.

The individual differences are seen at the level of the three knowledge components depicted in Figure 8.1. Following Anderson (1976), a distinction is made between declarative knowledge (i.e., knowledge of facts) and procedural knowledge (i.e., knowledge about knowing how to do something). Facts, in the present use, refers to propositions held by a person, regardless of the accuracy with which they describe reality. Unlike Anderson we make a distinction between personal facts with autobiographical reference (e.g., "I form vivid images") and generic facts independent of the self (e.g., "vivid images are needed for memory"). Only a portion of our declarative knowledge involves the facts we know about imagery; this knowledge about imagery is presumably related to other facts represented in memory. Thus our knowledge about our imaginal skills will be embedded within the larger view that we hold about ourselves (such as "I am creative," or "I frequently fail to achieve the goals that I set for myself"). Similarly nonpersonal, generic knowledge of imagery will be related to other facts we hold regarding the world (such as "artists have well-developed imagery skills," or "imagery skills are useless in logical, reasoning situations"). Among the facts stored in the personal system are those related to episodes in which the person has used imagery, and among the facts in the generic systems are those related to conditions in which imagery is likely to be efficacious or not. I envision these two fact systems as being in communication with one another because it seems probable that one may form general inferences based on personally experienced episodes (e.g., "imagery doesn't work in context X, since it didn't work for me in a similar context two years ago"). Moreover, one can readily make personal inferences using, in part, generic information (e.g., "vivid imagers are creative; I am a vivid imager; therefore, I must be creative").

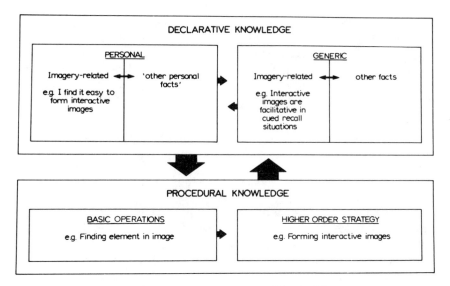

FIGURE 8.1. The components of the model.

These two fact systems are also in communication with a procedural knowledge system. We can think of these procedures as similar to a set of basic subprocesses from which higher order strategies are constructed. For imagery, these would be the processes involved in performing specific mental actions, such as those involved in forming an interactive image. A list of image procedures relevant to mnemonic activity will be described later. This procedural knowledge communicates with declarative knowledge to perform two functions. First, input from the declarative systems can serve to initiate procedural action. Anderson (1976) suggests that the procedural knowledge will be represented as production systems, that is, as condition–action pairs. When a given set of conditions are met a given action will ensue. In this model there is an operator that scans the active portion of the declarative knowledge systems and, when the antecedent facts are found, will initiate the action. Thus one can envision production systems such as: If the following declarative knowledge is activated (1) we are in context X, and (2) vivid imagery is effective in context X AND IF supportive personal declarative knowledge is activated (e.g., "I am a vivid imager") THEN generate image. The second function is involved in the acquisition of new knowledge. Presumably what we know depends, in part, on the success and failures associated with performing actions in different contexts (see, for instance, Pressley, Borkowski, & Schneider, in press, for experiments in which strategy–utility information is manipulated).

The noteworthy aspect of this model from an individual differences perspective on imagery is the emphasis given to concept-driven factors. The use of imagery is seen as a function of the declarative knowledge held by a person, and the set of procedural productions related to this knowledge. A central motif in the interactional approach is in understanding the interrelationships of the knowledge systems as they relate to imagery. People are seen as differing in the mental operators they can apply to imagery-related problems and in the skills with which these operators can be applied. Moreover, these skills are now seen as being closely tied to knowledge about when to use these skills.

Mnemonics and the Three Ks: Knowing How, Knowing When, and Knowing Oneself

Knowing How

It is assumed that a sophisticated participant has a developed base of imagery-based procedural knowledge, i.e., knowledge of how to perform imaginal acts. Kosslyn (1980, Chapter 5) iterates the primitive procedural knowledge from which more complex strategies are developed. These primitives include processes necessary for the generation, inspection, and transformation of images. Recent work (Kosslyn, Brunn, Cave, & Wallach, 1984) has been consistent with the interpretation that these primitive processes have psychological reality. Further research is needed to determine whether these primitives are inherent or acquired, and the degree to which the processes are modified by learning.

While it is possible that the primitive procedures suggested by Kosslyn might play some mnemonic function, the available evidence suggests that imagery facilitation of memory depends upon more complicated procedural strategies. The working hypothesis is that the integration and coordination of the primitives can be conceptualized in terms of learned skills. Like any other skilled activity, individual's could be ranked according to their proficiency at applying the skill. Skill differences should be reflected both by efficiency and by latency measures. Indeed Chase and Ericcson (1982) point to the speed of execution as one of the telling signs of level of skill acquisition. Unfortunately, there is relatively little research on the speed functions obtained on imagery tasks as a function of practice. The few reports that are available suggest that imagery differences can be conceptualized in skill terms. For instance, Wallace, Turner, and Perkins (reported by Wood, 1967) show the speed with which an imagery mnemonic was applied increased 75% with practice. Similarly, Corbett (1977) found that, even when an imagery mnemonic produces 100% recall, additional practice still resulted in faster retrieval. There are no studies in which persons differing in imagery level have been tested for differences in speed functions over practice, though a skills analysis would suggest that any advantage to high imagers should disappear with sufficient practice. In any event, the general point is that the use of imagery could be profitably analyzed in terms of a set of acquired skills. Consequently, individual differences in imagery, such as found with measures of vividness or spatial manipulation, should reflect, in part, skill differences in employing imagery procedures. This conclusion is reinforced by the observation that imagery plays an important role in the exceptional memory demonstrated by most, if not all, mnemonists (see Rawles, 1978 for an historical review). As Wilding and Valentine (1985) note, the evidence is that mnemonists do not have exceptional memory abilities but rather are highly skilled at deploying learned organizational strategies.

One practical problem for studying differences in skill levels is in first disentangling differences caused by differences in the declarative knowledge necessary to knowing when to apply a strategy, from differences in the procedural knowledge for doing so efficiently. The ideal design would be one in which persons would be equated for "when" knowledge, and then tested on parameters relevant to "how" or procedural knowledge. There is an existing literature that can be analyzed along these lines. The basic feature of these studies is that high- and low-ability imagers are tested under instructions to use imagery in a task. The assumption would be that when knowledge is equated because all participants know that imagery is called for; performance differences, therefore, are caused by differences in imagery proficiencies.

The findings are quite clear for the case in which participants are just told to use imagery to remember material; high and low imagers, defined by tests of imagery vividness, show no difference in memory performance (Danaher & Thorensen, 1972; Janssen, 1976; Rehm, 1973; Rimm & Bottrell, 1969). The picture is different when specific imagery mnemonics are applied. Both DiVesta and Sunshine (1974) and Delaney (1978) found that high imagers (defined by spatial visualization tests) performed better than low imagers even after both groups learned the same materials using the same mnemonic (the keyword technique in the Delaney study, and the one-bun mnemonic in DiVesta and Sunshine). Delaney (1978) also probed the strategies used by participants and found that high and low imagers did indeed use the same strategies. The conclusion that I draw from these studies is that high spatial visualizers are more skilled in applying imagery mnemonics that involve transforming information. Taken together with the null findings reported above, two tentative hypotheses are suggested. First, imagery vividness plays no, or a very minimal, role in overall memory recall skill differences, although there may be specific memory tasks where vividness may be of importance (see Slee, 1980). Day and Bellezza (1983) came to a similar conclusion based on a different data base. Second, for those contexts in which high and low imagers do not differ in their knowledge that imagery is appropriate, skill differences may emerge only when specific instructions or training on how to use imagery is given. Imagery instructions, to be effective, may have to specify the way imagery is to be employed, such as through emphasizing the need to maintain the image in a literal form or the need to transform information into an interactive image (e.g., see Pressley, Borkowski, & O'Sullivan, 1985).

In the sections that follow I will put forward some of the specific skills or imagery procedural knowledge that might be related to mnemonic functioning. The specific mnemonic skill functions examined follow from the suggestions of Reese (1977) and Begg (1982) that effective mnemonic imagery can be understood in terms of an organizational-redintegration principle. According to this position, imagery is an effective means of organizing separate pieces of information into larger, meaningful units; access of the unit is redintegrative in that once contacted in memory all of the organized information is available for use.

Skill in Generating Simple Images

One can argue that persons may differ in the proficiency to generate images of any sort, i.e., even images of single referent objects. There is some evidence for this position. Persons reliably differ in the speed with which they can generate images (Kosslyn, 1983, pp. 199–200). This difference is also related to some other individual difference variables: high imagers are faster at generating images to words than are low imagers (Ernest & Paivio, 1971); and amnesics are slower than their control group, especially after both groups have practiced (Howes, 1983).

Skill in Relational Imagery

Cued recall is better after participants image items interacting in some meaningful way than when the same items are imaged as separate units (e.g., Bower, 1970; see Begg, 1982). Indeed Reese (1977) argued that the effectiveness of the compound imagery found with virtually every mnemonic technique can be attributed to the organization of items that results from "imaging them as related or interacting" (p. 230). It can be hypothesized then that one skill that develops with practice is the skill to relate information imaginally. There is some available evidence that indicates that relational imagery does function as an individual difference variable. For instance, while young children can be taught to use keyword imagery mnemonics they only do so when given explicit illustration of the keyword and the definition. That is, children seem to have difficulty in generating interactive mental images, in contrast with typical adult performance (Pressley & Levin, 1978). Similar findings are observed for participants with low vocabulary ability (McGivern & Levin, 1983). Finally there is evidence from persons with amnesic pathologies. Baddeley and Warrington (1973) suggest that amnesics inability to benefit from instructions to use imagery is caused by a deficiency in generating meaningful interactive images. Howes (1983) found that with practice amnesics could produce interactive images, but even then did so more infrequently than the appropriate control group.

Skill in Accessing the Image

One important aspect of the organizational–redintegrative principle is that independent factors are responsible for the availability of a trace and the access to it. Consequently, even though two persons may be equally skilled in encoding information in terms of interactive images, they may differ with respect to the skill with which they can generate effective retrieval cues. There is a surprising lack of individual difference data on this important question. For instance, consider the keyword mnemonic. Participants are required to choose a keyword that sounds like the vocabulary item to be learned and then must form an interactive image involving the referrents of the keyword and the vocabulary item. Recall presumably involves using the keyword to access the interactive image that contains the vocabulary item. Pressley (Pressley & Levin, 1981; Pressley, Levin, Hall, Miller, & Berry, 1980) has shown that the nature of the chosen keyword is essential to the effectiveness of the mnemonic: if a poor cue is chosen, then access to an available image is impaired. The skills necessary to finding good retrieval cues remain to be studied in depth. The contribution of imagery skill factors in both cue selection and mnemonic effectiveness would be of special interest. Persons reliably differ in the ease with which they can classify parts of an image (Kosslyn, 1983); and it is this function that is involved in the generation of imaginal pegs or for creating bizarre images. Further experimental investigation of these individual differences in skills implicated in the retrieval of imaged information is clearly required.

Skills in Maintaining an Image in Memory

Reese (1977) argues that information learned by imagery mnemonics is forgotten by alterations in the memory trace over time. A similar interpretation could be given to Bower's (1972) observation that participants using imagery mnemonics made a greater number of intrusion errors than the comparison group, when the items to be remembered were similar in meaning (and presumably led to the generation of images easy to confuse with one another). The individual difference implication of this position would be that persons might differ in the skill with which they maintained the original encoding. A clear case of the maintenance of literal memory over extended time periods is provided in the analysis of the mnemonist S (Luria, 1968). To my knowledge, the only study of individual differences in image maintenance in normal populations has been performed in Kosslyns' laboratory (Kosslyn et al., 1984). In this study various tasks assumed to index the mental structures and processes posited for imagery by Kosslyn were completed by a sample of 50 persons. Performance on different tasks assumed to index the maintenance of images were correlated with one another but not with performance on tasks that indexed other aspects of imagery processing, such as those involved in mental rotation. Subsequent analysis indicated that people who had difficulty in image maintenance not only could not remember much information, but had a hard time using complex images in simple tasks.

Conclusions

A skills approach to imagery directs one to a componential analysis in which an individuals imagery "ability" would be decomposed into a set of more primitive skills. In a similar way one could decompose an imagery mnemonic intervention into a set of simpler components, as was done in Pressley and Levin (1978). The interactionist position would be to map the skill differences onto the task components. This approach can be contrasted with the standard individual differences approach to mnemonic instruction, which attempts to relate overall performance to global ability measures, such as measures of imagery (e.g., Delaney, 1978), vocabulary learning (e.g., McGivern & Levin, 1983), or scholastic ability (e.g., McDaniel & Pressley, 1984). Without the finer analysis suggested above aspects of these studies are difficult to interpret. For instance, it has been found that high spatial imagers recall more than do low spatial imagers, even after both groups are given instructions to use an imagery mnemonic (e.g., Delaney, 1978). This finding indicates that one or more of the skills measured by spatial visualization ability tests is involved in one or more of the components involved in the successful application of the keyword mnemonic. Without componential analysis, however, we are not enlightened to which skills or task components are involved. Similarly, the conflicting literature in which vocabulary ability has been shown both to interact (e.g., McDaniel & Pressley, 1984) and not interact (Pressley, Levin, Nakumura, Hope, Bishop, & Toye, 1980) with the imposition of a mnemonic technique may be due to the interaction of different skills and task operations. The model clearly mandates careful study of the interaction of specific vocabulary and imagery skills in all phases of mnemonic task implementation.

A second aspect of the skills approach is the emphasis given to extended practice. The assumption is that imagery skills, like other skills, improves with practice. A list of skills relevant to mnemonic performance has been suggested above. The list is meant as representative of the type of skill differences we are talking about and is not meant to be comprehensive. We assume that proficiency in applying these skills will increase with practice. This assumption has yet to be tested systematically. Training studies involving teaching the component skills of imagery should not only have theoretical implications as to the bases of so-called ability differences but may well have direct educational benefits.

Finally, it might be instrumental to draw a distinction between availability of procedural knowledge and the use of that knowledge. Knowing how to perform an imaginal operation is a prerequisite for imaginal mediation. Whether or not that knowledge will be applied, however, will largely be a function of declarative knowledge, i.e., knowing when to apply the procedures, and knowing personal characteristics of relevance. A metaphor might be in order. Fully functioning people know how to run, though they differ in the skill with which they do so. People also have declarative knowledge of running. Some of his knowledge is general (such as "people will cross a road more rapidly if they run than if they walk") and some of this knowledge is personal (such as "most people run faster than me"). Whether or not a person standing on the corner of the street will decide to cross the street in the midst of oncoming cars will depend on an interaction of all three knowledge states, i.e., the knowledge of how to run, the knowledge that the context calls for running (and not walking), and the knowledge that he or she is capable of running fast enough to make it across the street before the onrushing car will hit. It is to the role that declarative knowledge plays in imagery use that we now turn.

Knowing When

Psychologists have, by now, discovered many of the situations in which imagery processes are mnemonically effective. For instance, people remember more easy to image items than ones difficult to image, and more items when they are instructed to use imagery than when they are given instructions to use rote procedures (see Richardson, 1980 for a review). The questions of interest here is whether people differ in their knowledge of these situations, and whether this declarative knowledge actually guides the processes that are spontaneously engaged in everyday situations requiring memory. There is surprisingly little research on the use of mnemonics in everyday contexts, however. The little available empirical evidence suggests that mnemonic techniques are frequently employed, although it is not clear the extent to which this use has been prompted by explicit instructions. Gruneberg (1978) found that 30% of the students he surveyed used some mnemonic when studying for final exams, and, in anatomy classes, about 50% used a first-letter mnemonic. Similarly, Perlmutter (1978, p. 335) claims that "most subjects reported that they often used memory strategies." Harris (1980) also found high use of mnemonic intervention. However, he observed, that the most commonly employed mnemonics were external ones, such as the use of a notepad, that did not involve transforming the information. Mental and transformational techniques were much less frequently used, especially those with an imagery component. For instance, only 7% claimed to have ever used the peg technique and only between 17 and 23% ever used the method of loci. Questions remain. How often are imagery mnemonics used in everyday contexts? Do people know when the use of imagery mediators would be appropriate and when they might be inappropriate? What are the situations perceived as calling upon imaginal tools? Does this knowledge reliably differ between persons? From a functional perspective these might be the most important questions facing imagery researchers and yet, as Morris and Hampson (1983) point out, there has been virtually no direct research on these questions. The limited literature related to these questions will be reviewed here.

Survey Studies

The most detailed examination of spontaneous imagery use is provided in the introspective literature (see Yates, 1966), especially the psychological literature of the early 20th century. Imagery is claimed to be important for content that is unfamiliar (Woods, 1915), novel (Finkenbinder, 1914), requires effortful activity (Fisher, 1916), and for thinking that leads to a "conflict" in consciousness (Fox, 1914). Presumably, imaginal mnemonic mediation would occur to the extent that these conditions exist in contexts people perceive as requiring that information be remembered. Unfortunately little information is available on whether there are reliable individual difference in the knowledge that people hold regarding the usefulness of imagery in different contexts. The only study to address the question directly, Denis and Carfantan (1985), reported on a short questionnaire given to 148 University-level participants. They found that participants were highly sensitive to situations in which imagery mnemonics have been shown to be effective. For instance, 85.1% of the sample knew that memory is better for items presented as pictures than as words, and 89.9% knew that forming an image to verbally depicted items facilitated learning of the items. Once again individual difference data are not provided. This lack is especially pertinent here because 77% of the participants were females, and it is well established that females report more vivid images than do males (Ernest, 1977) and are more sensitive in monitoring memory performance (Chaffin, Crawford, Herrmann, & Deffenbacher, in press). An individual difference contribution is also suggested by the fact that 62.8% of the sample knew that high imagers perform better on word memory tests than do low imagers. It is tantalizing to speculate that the persons who claimed a relationship between memory and imagery level were themselves high imagers. We envision more studies of the sort initiated by Denis and Carfantan will be performed. These studies should incorporate individual difference variables and the monitoring of actual memory performance (e.g., Pressley, Levin, & Ghatala, 1984).

Data provided by Paivio and Harshman (1983) also provide some insight into the conditions calling for imagery. Paivio and Harshman analyzed the data of over 700 respondents to the Individual Difference Questionnaire (IDQ), a self-report instrument that includes a broad range of questions tapping imaginal abilities, habits, and preferences. The item frequency response rate was kindly provided to me by the authors. Consistent with Denis and Carfantan (1985), participants overwhelmingly claimed that imagery plays an important mnemonic function in their everyday life: over 90% claimed to use mental pictures to reminisce, over 85% used images to remember scenes and about the same percentage claimed to use mental images to remember, in general. While these scores are high, 10–15% of the sample claimed not to use images in these same situations.

Finally, in an ongoing project, I have attempted to examine individual differences in sensitivity to deployment of imagery as a function of task. One hundred university undergraduates completed a short task-specific questionnaire and the Individual Difference Questionnaire (Paivio and Harshman, 1983). The task-specific questionnaire consisted of the instructions employed in 22 different studies. The tasks were selected from various factor-analytic studies to reflect the use of mental operations that were "imagistic" or not, as determined by the loadings on imagery factors. Two seven-point rating scales followed each description; one scale indexed the frequency with which the participant thought they would use imagery processes in completing the task while the other scale indexed frequency of verbal mediation. Each task was clearly seen as requiring imagery processes or not. The frequency with which the tasks were rated as calling upon imagery correlated substantially and negatively with the reported frequency of verbal mediational requirements ($r = -.991$). The 22 tasks, the imagery ratings, and standard deviations given each task are provided separately for the high and low imagers (median split on the IDQ) in Table 8.1. Treating tasks as random

TABLE 8.1. Mean imagery ratings reported by high- and low-IDQ scorers when asked to rate the likelihood they would employ imagery processes for each of 22 different tasks.

	IDQ[a] Level	
Task	High	Low
1. Language Usage Test	1.93 (1.3)[b]	2.71 (1.9)
2. Verbal Reasoning Test	3.00 (1.9)	3.13 (2.0)
3. Remote Associate Test	3.02 (1.5)	3.21 (1.7)
4. Numerical Ability Test	3.20 (2.1)	3.02 (2.0)
5. Rating words along specific–general dimension	3.5 (1.8)	3.40 (1.9)
6. Spelling Test	3.49 (2.3)	3.56 (2.2)
7. Rating words along good–bad dimension	4.27 (1.6)	3.79 (2.1)
8. Rating words along boring–interesting dimension	4.38 (2.0)	4.15 (1.9)
9. Rating words along emotional–unemotional dimension	4.67 (1.8)	4.27 (1.9)
10. Rating words along abstract–concrete dimension	4.62 (1.9)	4.42 (1.8)
11. Reaction time to produce verbal associations	4.71 (2.0)	4.54 (2.0)
12. Ratings of the ease of producing verbal associates	4.89 (2.0)	4.42 (1.6)
13. Rating of words along tangible–intangible dimension	4.38 (1.8)	4.81 (1.9)
14. Rating of words along pleasant–unpleasant dimension	5.04 (1.6)	4.54 (1.9)
15. Ease of producing a label to a picture	5.11 (1.7)	4.69 (1.8)
16. Producing autobiographical memories	5.76 (1.2)	4.81 (1.8)
17. Mechanical Reasoning Test	5.71 (1.9)	6.00 (1.4)
18. Rating of the ease of forming images to words	6.13 (1.3)	5.79 (1.5)
19. Reaction time to form images to words	6.20 (1.1)	6.13 (1.4)
20. Memory for Designs Test	6.51 (0.8)	6.19 (1.3)
21. Abstract Reasoning Test	6.31 (1.3)	6.35 (1.4)
22. Space Relations Test	6.60 (1.1)	6.52 (1.2)

[a]Mean ratings of high-IDQ scores based on $N = 45$; for low-IDQ scores based on $N = 48$.
[b]Scores can vary from 1 = "use imagery never" to 7 = "use imagery all the time." The standard deviations are presented in parenthesis.

effects, and thus the average ratings as data points, two findings emerge. First, high and low imagers exhibited amazingly similar rankings of the different tasks in terms of how frequently imagery mediation would be required; the $r = .96$. Second, in general, high imagers claimed that they would use imagery mediation to a greater extent, $t(21) = 1.74$, $p < .05$, one tailed. Taken together, the data are most parsimoniously explained as indicating that most people know that imagery plays some mnemonic role, and that this role varies across different tasks. High and low imagers do not seem to differ in this declarative knowledge at least for the tasks sampled, although high imagers appear more willing to attempt imagery mediation for almost all tasks, perhaps because they see this knowledge as relevant to their self-schema.

Surprisingly, there are two crucial questions for which there is no evidence available at all. First, gross measures of whether or not a person employs imagery mnemonics tell us nothing about how or when the mnemonic is being employed. As shown above, there is evidence that most persons know imagery has a memory-enhancing function, and that different tasks call upon imagery processes to varying degrees. What we do not know is whether persons distinguish between the availability of imagery as a mnemonic and the usefulness of different imagery mnemonics in different contexts. For instance, do people know when it is useful to employ interactive imagery and when it is useful to employ separated imagery (cf. Begg, 1983)? Second, mnemonic intervention presumably should occur when a person knows that he or she is in a situation in which needed information is often forgotten. Studies to examine the interaction of beliefs held about these situations and the use of specific mnemonic coping techniques are required. There are a number of surveys now available that globally measure knowledge about memory failure (see Herrmann, 1984). Examination of the items from the various scales indicate that the type of information most suscepti-ble to memory lapse can be characterized as arbitrary (i.e., the label is not syste-matically linked to the referent object); not distinctive (such as remembering whether an act that is frequently performed has been done on a specific occa-sion), and literal (i.e., information where specific detail, not thematic knowledge, is required). These are exactly the type of situations in which trans-formational mnemonic techniques are most appropriate. Unfortunately, there has yet to be a report that has systematically explored the correspondences between the types of mnemonic activity employed in different real-world memory-relevant contexts. A large-scale study is required in which a wide range of memory-related situations can be sampled. These data subsequently should be examined to identify those situations in which memory failures are common and related to the type of mnemonic activity (if any) that a person may employ as a means of coping with these lapses of memory.

Posttask Questionnaires

There have been several studies in which participants are given a postlearning questionnaire to probe the type of mediator they have used to learn different stimulus items. The basic findings are:

1. Subjects frequently use mental imagery spontaneously, especially if the item is concrete; the use of imagery for concrete items increases over trials even when the subject has been given instructions to use a non-imagistic mnemonic strategy (Paivio, Smythe, & Yuille, 1968; see Paivio, 1971, pp. 361–366).
2. Imagery mediators are more likely to be reported after the administration of instructions to learn the material with the use of imagery mnemonics (Paivio & Yuille, 1967, 1969).
3. The recall of specific items is predicted by the number of participants who report they have used imagery in learning the item (Paivio, Yuille, & Smythe, 1966; Paivio et al., 1968).
4. The performance of specific subjects can be predicted by the number of imagi-nal mediators they claim to use; the greater the number of imagery mediators reported the better is the recall for concrete but not for abstract materials (Richardson, 1978).

Recently, the posttask questionnaire technique has been employed to discover when different strategies are employed, and why they may be effective. Pressley,

Levin and Ghatala (1984), for instance, found that adults initially adopt a mnemonic strategy suggested by the experimenter but abandon the strategy for a better one after practice with the learning task. That is, participants do not appear to come to a task with a sense of the appropriate mnemonic to use but are sensitive to "what works," after direct experience with specific tasks. Herrmann, Grubs, Sigmundi, and Grueneich (1983) report a similar finding: questions pertaining to the declarative knowledge of memory did not predict actual memory performance if the questions were asked before the memory tasks were performed; however there was considerable predictability if given 2 weeks after the tasks. This adult sensitivity can be contrasted with data based on the performance of children. Children are resistant to changing strategies and only do so when given very explicit feedback on their performance (Pressley, Ross, Levin, & Ghatala, 1984).

McDaniel and Kearney (1984) report further data consistent with the notion of task sensitivity. They asked adult participants to perform three learning tasks under one of four different instructional sets: uninstructed, imagery mnemonics, verbal elaboration mnemonics, and an organizational mnemonic. Following the learning tasks participants completed a set of questionnaires that probed the nature of the encoding strategies employed for each task. With the uninstructed subjects, the most frequently employed strategy differed across tasks. This suggests that participants attempt to shape the strategy they use to the task at hand. Subjects instructed to use a specific mnemonic technique actually tended to use the mnemonic. The pattern of recall for participants employing different strategies for different tasks indicates that for some tasks all encoding strategies are equally effective, whereas for some other tasks, certain strategies were more effective than others. Participants in the uninstructed condition spontaneously employed strategies that produced recall comparable to the recall observed for participants assigned to the most effective strategy for a particular learning task. Taken together these findings suggest that adult participants are sensitive to the fact that different tasks demand different processing strategies. Moreover, this sensitivity appears to act in a state rather than in a trait manner, i.e., knowledge of the mnemonic strategy to use is closely tied to practice on the task and is not based on an habitual preference to use a given strategy for all types of tasks.

Conclusion

When does a person choose to employ imagery mnemonics and when do they choose to use some other mnemonic intervention? The individual difference aspect of this question can be addressed from either a trait or a state perspective. The former approach would look for stable, habitual modes of reacting to memory failure situations. The general literature in which memory habits are surveyed tends to adopt this position implicitly (Herrmann, 1984). Indeed, people reliably differ in the situations they report as leading to memory failure on these metamemory surveys. These reports only correlate modestly with memory assessed in the laboratory (Herrmann, 1982). The more specialized literature on imagery effects indicates that most people believe that imagery plays some general mnemonic role, while, paradoxically, it also indicates that relatively few people actually claim to use imagery mnemonics habitually (cf. Harris, 1980). Moreover, high and low imagers do not differ in the declarative knowledge held about the situations calling for imagery use. Taken together, these findings suggest the knowledge that imagery is a mnemonically effective is equally available to persons' differing in imagery ability and, hence, is unlikely to be an important factor in the memory differences observed for these two groups of people. This general knowledge may be independent of strategy-specific knowledge regarding the appropriateness of different forms of imagery mediation for different tasks. Metamemory questionnaires sensitive to differences in strategy-specific knowledge are required before trait-based metacognitive differences can be completely discounted.

A state perspective, in contrast, would lead us to look for situational factors that induce imagery mnemonic use. Both the early introspective literature and the more recent studies employing posttask strategy measures indicate the presence of metacognitive differences at a state level. Sophisticated participants spontaneously modify strategy use as a function of task materials and the nature of the memory task involved; this modification is especially evident after direct practice with a strategy. The individual differences related to this meta-memorally based strategy choice have yet to be mapped out in detail.

Knowing Self

The final component of the interactional model is the declarative knowledge held by a person about her- or himself. Included in this knowledge would be beliefs about ones' abilities, personality, physical appearance, and social networks. The theory of self held by any person can be measured through responses given on self-report questionnaires. Thus a person who endorses an item such as "I have a good memory for faces" (Sehulster, 1981a) or an item such as "I often use mental images or pictures to help me remember things" (Paivio & Harshman, 1983) is telling us about his or her beliefs related to mnemonic functioning.

Two aspects of self theory should be emphasized. First, it is held that one's self-belief system is not epiphenomenal but plays a mediating role in how one encodes, stores, and retrieves information (see Schneider, 1985 for a review). For instance, questions taken from the IDQ, which I take to be, mainly, a measure of imagery self-belief, was the only self-report imagery test to correlate with performance tasks relevant to imagery in a recent study by Poltrock and Brown (1984). Along similar lines Sehulster (1981a) found that, from one's beliefs about their memory for trivia, one could predict memory performance in a task of the cued recall of trivial facts. Moreover, he found that beliefs about memory ability are reflected in the amount of money that people bet on their memory for trivia.

Second, it should be noted that the self is a richly integrated set of subsystems. Beliefs about memory or imagery, while conceptually distinct, have to be considered as parts of a larger whole. Two persons may have very similar beliefs, but the expression of these beliefs in performance may differ as a function of personality differences or different social comparison contexts. For instance, Katz (1984) identified four groups of people who gave distinct response patterns on a battery of cognitive tests. Two of these groups were characterized by the self-belief that they were highly dependent on imagery processes. The performance of one group of persons (labeled initiators) was characterized by fluidity of responding in figural divergent thinking tasks but poor performance in a task requiring the identification of a single correct answer. The performance of the second group (labeled esthetics) was characterized by preference for simple figures and high scores on a test of closure. These two groups also exhibited notable differences in personality, with the initiators characterized by such trait terms as ambitious, reflective, intellectually driven, and arrogant. In contrast, the esthetician is best characterized as rebellious, moody, dissatisfied, restless, self-critical, and nontrusting. The point of emphasis here is that both groups believe themselves to be high imagers. The way that they interpret and interact with other aspects of their environment, however, strongly suggests that they would call upon their imagery skills in different contexts, and put these skills to quite different use. Only when one examines the larger context would one ask such questions as: Does the social context in which a memory task is embedded differentiate between different groups of persons who perceive themselves as imagers? Likewise, can we predict on the conjoint basis of imagery belief and personality whether imagery skills will be employed in encoding information in an elaborative or discriminative fashion?

To date, the recent upsurge of interest in studying the self-concept by experimental psychologists has not led to attempts to identify systematically the major components of the self-belief systems related to imagery or to memory functioning or to relate these systems to the larger social-personological structure in which they are embedded. Sehulster (1981a, b) has provided the most comprehensive analysis of memory beliefs and even he has not systematically investigated how our memory beliefs are related to differences in type of information, intentionality, social setting and the like. There is no comparable published studies dealing specially with mnemonic imagery. Research is underway in my laboratory now that is aimed at identifying the declarative knowledge of imagery held by high and low imagers and in relating this knowledge to mnemonic activities. In the preliminary work, participants were given Gough's and Heilbrun's (1983) 300-item adjective checklist and asked to choose those items that they believe to be descriptive of high-imagery persons. The checklist has been used extensively as a means of assessing personality. These data therefore provide normative information regarding the general declarative knowledge held about the personality of the high-imagery person. The sample was also given the IDQ (Paivio & Harshman, 1983) to complete. Recall the argument that the responses given on the IDQ represent beliefs about imagery. We can therefore address the question whether people who hold the belief that they are highly imagistic and those who do not see themselves as imagistic differ in their declarative knowledge about high imagery persons. There is a final aspect to the procedure. After the completion of the adjective checklist the participant is given an incidental recall test. The rationale and the findings for the memory test are presented shortly.

The adjective choices made by each person can be combined into higher order scales. Among these scales are those that measure the basic needs or personality dispositions described by Murray (1938); such needs include the Need for Achievement, the Need for Affiliation, and the Need for Dominance. The 15 Murray Need Scales addressed by the adjective checklist were computed from the data in the recommended fashion (see Gough & Heilbrun, 1983). The raw scores for each person were converted to standard scores in order to control for individual differences in the number of adjectives different people were willing to apply to their description of a high-imagery person. These data are presented in the left-hand panel of Table 8.2. While the profile is within normal range, it can be seen that, on average, people believe high imagers to be somewhat low in the Need for Nurturance and slightly high in the needs for Autonomy and Exhibitionism. Examination of the standard deviations show considerable individual differences in the personality characteristics attributed to high-imagery persons. Can some of these differences be explained as a function of one's beliefs regarding person imagery level? The standardized personality scale scores for each person were correlated with their IDQ imagery scores. These data are presented in the right-hand panel, Table 8.2. As can be seen, higher scores on Achievement, Dominance, Affiliation, Exhibition, Aggression, and a lower score on the Abasement need scale are associated with the degree to which a person holds the belief that they are high imagers themselves. Thus high imagers are more likely than low imagers to hold the beliefs that high-imagery persons are hardworking, goal

TABLE 8.2. The mean personality profile attributed to high imagers and the relationship of attributed personality characteristics to beliefs held about imagery.

Personality need scales	Mean	SD	r (with IDQ)
Achievement	50.7	9.3	.22[a]
Dominance	49.7	9.6	.26[a]
Endurance	47.9	9.2	.14
Order	48.8	10.7	.07
Intraception	47.2	10.9	.03
Nurturance	39.3	7.0	.14
Affiliation	42.4	9.0	.30[a]
Heterosexuality	46.5	8.8	.19
Exhibition	55.1	8.7	.28[a]
Autonomy	56.2	7.1	.14
Aggression	54.0	8.0	.23[a]
Change	54.4	10.2	.09
Succorance	48.6	9.1	−.11
Abasement	50.0	9.1	−.23[a]
Deference	42.3	8.5	−.10

[a] $p < .05$.

directed, determined, ambitious, comfortable in social situations, forceful, manipulative, competitive and assertive. High and low imagers do not differ in their beliefs regarding such personality characteristics as persistence, fastidiousness, foresightedness, autonomy, or spontaneity.

Future research is envisioned to see whether persons who hold that they are high imagers will describe themselves in trait terms similar to those given for the ideal high imager. For instance, can one predict the likelihood that imaginal mediation will be spontaneously employed as a function of the correspondence between the personality profile obtained from self-reports on the adjective checklist and the ideal high-imager profile described above? Moreover, do problem-solving or memory contexts that emphasize the utility of personality characteristics, such as achievement or dominance, lead to the spontaneous use of imagery mediation by persons who believe themselves to be imagers, whereas contexts that emphasize such characteristics as persistence or autonomy do not? Although limiting factors doubtless exist, the interactional model, which emphasizes declarative knowledge of the self, clearly leads to the prediction that beliefs about imagery and about the self should contribute conjointly to imaginal use.

A critical experimental question is how one examines imaginal use that is based on self-belief in mnemonically relevant situations. The "obvious" technique would be to relate belief to memory performance, as Sehulster did with belief in trivia recall and performance on the recall of trivia from long-term memory. This approach is reasonable, for one way that belief systems develop is through the self-monitoring of performance: persons who perform well tend to develop a belief that they are good at doing the task. However, the social psychological and clinical literature is rich with observations that beliefs also develop in the absence of performance, i.e., through social contacts. Thus a person may believe that, compared to most persons, he or she has a poor memory or good "powers" of imagery. Consequently, measures other than scores on tests of memory alone will be required. Despite this caveat, there is at least one well documented phenomenon in which self-beliefs have been shown to have a direct effect on the recall of information. This phenomenon is called the self-reference effect and refers to the observation that items judged for self descriptiveness are recalled better on a subsequent incidental memory test than the same items judged on other dimensions, or with respect to persons other than the self (e.g., Bower & Gilligan, 1979; Rogers, Kuiper, & Kirker, 1977; see Rogers, 1981).

The interactional model would lead one to postulate recall differences to be observed between high- and low-imagery persons after they make self-referent decisions. Imagery-based differences could result from differences in the mental representations held by high and low imagers or from the greater use of mnemonically effective imagery strategies by high-imagery persons. In the former case, the argument would be that high imagers have a richer, personalized, integrated representation for the concept of "high imager." Structures of this sort are known to facilitate retrieval (Bellezza, 1984; Bower & Gilligan, 1979). Thus the engagement of these structures would benefit high- over low-imagery participants. Moreover, this benefit should be limited only to structures relevant to beliefs about imagery. An experimental test of this position is discussed in the next section.

Imagery differences arising from differences in the use of imagery mediation would work indirectly. That is, arousal of beliefs about imagery would be personally relevant to high imagers but not to low imagers. Consequently, high imagers would be more likely to employ mnemonically effective strategies when they make self-referent decisions and more likely to demonstrate superior incidental recall on a subsequent test. Evidence for this position is quite mixed. Studies directing persons to use imaginal strategies in self-referent tasks have generally failed to show superior recall compared to control groups not so instructed (e.g., Lord, 1980; Pressley, Levin, Kuiper, Bryant, & Michener, 1982), though there are some cases in which the predicted effect does emerge. The positive evidence has been more likely to emerge for pictorial stimuli and for situations in which the experimenter ensured that the self-referent task engaged belief systems (e.g., Miall, 1985; Mueller, Heesacker, & Ross, 1984; Yarmey & Johnson, 1982). Studies are required to examine directly the question. One test now underway in my laboratory involves probing participants for the strategies they employed while making self-referent decisions. The prediction is that participants who hold the belief that they are high imagers will employ imagery strategies, and that subsequent recall will be a direct function of the use of these strategies.

Imagery Belief Systems and the Self-Reference Effect

The model that we have developed (Katz, 1985) posits that the declarative knowledge (or beliefs) that we hold about ourselves is independent of generic knowledge. Individual differences in the self-referent effect would, in part, result from which of these two systems were engaged when performing a task. For simplicity's sake, we can discuss the relationship of ability level and declarative knowledge in terms of a 2 (ability level: high vs. low) × 2 (declarative knowledge: self vs. impersonal) matrix. High- and low-ability persons would both have access to consensual beliefs (i.e., generic declarative knowledge) about the personality traits relevant and not relevant to that ability, such as imagery. However, high- and low-ability persons should differ radically in whether or not they attribute these characteristics to their self-schema. The working hypothesis is that high-ability people are likely to see the relevant traits as being descriptive of themselves whereas the low-ability person is less likely to make that self-attribution. Therefore, high-ability persons would have the relevant information represented both generically and personally, whereas the low-ability person would have this same information represented only generically. There is no reason to expect the high- and low-ability person to differ systematically in the attribution of irrelevant traits to themselves. Thus irrelevant information should be represented generically for both high- and low-ability persons.

This model makes very explicit predictions regarding the conditions under which one would expect the self-reference effect to occur. Recall the premise that high-ability persons are more likely than low-ability persons to believe that the set of relevant ability traits are self-descriptive. Beliefs about nonrelevant items should be equally salient to the self-concepts of both high- and low-ability participants. When making self-referent decisions about trait terms, only the personal declarative system is engaged; hence, one would expect consequently an interaction between ability level and trait relevance: compared to those of low ability, high-ability persons should exhibit a superiority in the incidental recall of ability-relevant traits because of differential arousal of belief structures. In contrast, high- and low-ability persons should exhibit equal recall for traits not relevant to the ability. This predicted interaction has been observed with creative ability and traits relevant to beliefs about creative persons (Katz, 1985).

The question of immediate interest is whether the same interaction emerges with imagery ability. Preliminary data are very positive. Recall the study discussed above in which high- and low-IDQ imagery participants chose adjectives they believed to be descriptive of high-imagery persons. The results indicated that there was a set of personality characteristics that was seen as being important by high imagers, but less so by low imagers. There was also a set of personality characteristics that did not distinguish high and low imagers. From these data one could isolate the specific trait terms that significantly differentiated the high- and low-IDQ scorer. Recall also that, after making trait choices (phase 1), each participant was given an incidental memory test (phase 2). Would memory for traits vary as a function of beliefs about imagery and salience of traits to that belief? One can treat the memory data as representing the four cells of a 2 (IDQ: high vs. low) × 2 (traits: salient to high imagers vs. not salient). The data were scored as the total number of traits recalled conditionalized on the total number of salient and nonsalient traits chosen by each person; this measure controls for initial differences in the number of characteristic traits selected in phase 1. The recall data means and standard deviations for each of the four conditions are presented in Table 8.3. High and low IDQ imagers did not differ overall on the proportion of adjectives they recalled. Moreover, for both groups, adjectives checked as salient for high-imagery persons were more likely to be recalled than were items not checked as being salient. Of greater theoretical interest is the predicted interaction with IDQ imagery level: high-IDQ scorers recalled proportionately more of the salient items they had chosen as characteristic of high

TABLE 8.3. Mean proportion of trait terms recalled.

	Nature of trait terms	
IDQ level	Endorsed as characteristic of high imagers	Not endorsed as characteristic of high imagers
High mean	.10	.03
SD	.05	.03
Low mean	.06	.04
SD	.05	.03

imagery persons (i.e., themselves) than did low-IDQ scorers. High- and low-IDQ imagers did not differ in their recall of nonsalient items.

The favored explanation is that high- (but not low-) IDQ imagery scorers were, in fact, describing themselves when asked to choose adjectives characteristic of the "high-imagery" person. That is, the task activated beliefs relevant to the self for high-, but not for low-, IDQ imagers. At recall, high imagers had available the self-schema and hence showed facilitated recall only for traits consistent with it. The position suggests a further possibility: to the extent that context suggests that imagery is useful, high, but not low, imagers would have their self-schemata aroused. That is, for high imagers, certain contexts may automatically activate beliefs about one's imagery ability; these contexts would include those that arouse declarative knowledge of the appropriateness and utility of imagery (see McDaniel, Lapsley, & Milsead, 1985 for an example of automatic, obligatory processing of self-relevant information). To date, there are no studies that have examined the spontaneous arousal of self-schemata for persons differing in beliefs about imagery as a function of conditions believed to induce imagery processing, although there is some evidence that the recall of autobiographical information may involve the conjoint activity of imaginal operators and self-schematic content (see Helstrup, 1985).

Conclusions

The available evidence suggests that people differ in the declarative knowledge of imagery held as being personally relevant. People who believe themselves to be high imagers attribute different personality characteristics to high imagers in general than do people who do not believe themselves to be imaginal. As well, there is some evidence that arousal of beliefs about imagery mediates the recall of declarative knowledge relevant to imagery for the high-, but not the low-imagery person. Research is required to determine whether self-belief directly mediates recall or whether the recall is mediated by the activation of imagery strategies.

It should be emphasized that there is a large promissory note associated with the study of personally salient declarative knowledge of imagery. The underlying assumption is that knowledge of the self will be aroused and become involved in information processing only for certain contexts. Some of these contexts will be especially relevant to the use of imagery. Only those persons who believe themselves to be high imagers are likely to initiate imagery-based processing when confronted with these contexts. Persons who believe themselves to be high imagers may not initiate imagery processing if they believe the context calls for processes other than imagery. Similarly, persons who do not believe themselves to be high imagers may decide to use some other operation even if they do perceive the context as one in which imagery may prove useful. Consequently, spontaneous use of imagery mnemonics will be determined as a function of both self-beliefs and the nature of the context. The theoretical position clearly mandates the scaling of properties of the self related to imagery use and properties of the environment that are believed to arouse beliefs about the self, and about the appropriateness of imaginal action. Little work has been done yet on these questions, although Greenwald (1981) has outlined some of the conditions that may prove fruitful. For instance, Greenwald argues that the self is activated when a person is engaged in a persisting task. Such tasks include those that are related to one's work, hobbies, and other life pursuits. There is a not surprising paucity of memory studies in which ecologically relevant contexts such as these have been studied. What, for instance, do we know of the imaginal memory for persons engaged in activities requiring maintenance of a representation, such as may be involved in the color memory of professional decorators or the imaginal memory for persons engaged in professions requiring transformation of representation, such as may be required of architects. And yet, to the extent that a vocation is important to the beliefs held by a person, these would be the types of real-life situations in which questions about self-belief, imagery, and memory could be asked. Studies of this type are sorely lacking, although these are the types of study toward which an interactional model would direct us.

Summary and Conclusion

Fifteen years ago, Tulving and Madigan (1970, p. 477) wrote "We cannot help but feel that if there is ever going to be a genuine breakthrough in the psychological study of memory . . . it will, among other things, relate the knowledge stored in an individual's memory to his knowledge of that knowledge." Clearly, as this review has shown, research has been done on this topic in the intervening years. Much more needs to be done. The interactional model has been offered as a framework with which to study our knowledge of imaginal operations and the relationship of this knowledge to spontaneous mnemonic activity. The aim has been to demonstrate that separate knowledge factors, capable of experimental disentanglement, play distinguishable roles in when and how mnemonic intervention occurs. I would like to conclude by briefly addressing three general issues that, within the framework of the model, deserve special emphasis.

Use Versus Utility of Strategy Employment

In this chapter the emphasis has been on the conditions under which an imaginal strategy is used spontaneously. The utility or usefulness of the strategy may be somewhat unrelated to use, however. Richardson (1985), for instance, has shown that instructions to use imagery increase the likelihood that people will attempt to employ images in memorizing both concrete and abstract words. However, the increased use of imagery was effective only with the concrete words and was ineffective for the abstract words presented. Almost certainly there are other situations in which imagery use will be unrelated to imaginal effectiveness. Nevertheless, it is probable that in everyday, memory-related situations, imagery use and utility are not totally independent because a metacognitive aspect of strategy use would be knowledge of those conditions in which strategy use was efficacious. Research should be directed at discovering the individual differences and the environmental contexts associated with learning use–utility contingencies (see Pressley et al., in press, for initial research in this direction). Moreover, research is required to determine how a strategy choice is made when one is faced with a novel context in which past experience with the use of an imaginal strategy would be an imperfect predictor of imagery utility.

Concept-Driven Versus Data-Driven Theorizing

The interactional model emphasizes the role that prior knowledge plays in imagery mediation. This emphasis on concept-driven factors can be contrasted with the more usual data-driven approach to individual differences in imagery. For instance, one traditional view is that perceptual and imaginal operations tap a common set of processes. One cannot deny that, at some level, perception has to be data driven. To the extent that perceptual differences are tied to data-driven processing, then it may be assumed that some proportion of observed imagery differences are also driven by the analyses made on perceptual or perceptual-like input. The emphasis here on concept-driven processing was meant to redress what I felt was an imbalance in favor of data-driven models of imaginal differences. The assumption is that both data-driven and concept-driven factors must be considered. The empirical questions arise in determining the conditions under which either data-driven or concept-driven factors assume greater importance. Kaufmann (1985), for instance, postulates two dimensions of importance: task concreteness and the degree of programming in the task environment. According to this model imagery will be more useful as conditions become increasingly more concrete (i.e., deal with information pertaining to physical objects, or events) and less programmed (i.e., novel in the sense of not being associated with well-established strategies for solution). To these dimensions one may also wish to add the perceived goal of the task (see Slee, 1980). Some tasks demand maintenance of content (representational images) and some transformation of content (transformational images). A task for empirical investigation is the systematic evaluation of these parameters and the relationship of each with demands for data versus concept-driven processing.

Interactive Predictions

Finally, it should be emphasized that the model is interactive. The information derived from the combination of different knowledge states is nonadditive. The analogue would be to the metaphor literature in which the separate knowledge held about objects is an imperfect predictor of the interpretation given to the combination of these objects (such as when our knowledge of Sylvester Stallone and of cars is combined in: "Sylvester Stallone is the TransAm of Actors"). Arousal of personal and generic declarative knowledge is assumed to also lead to the emergence of hitherto unrelated knowledge. Thus the interactional approach suggests, in general, an ipsative examination of imagery differences. Each individual's knowledge systems should be mapped and differences at this level related to more general nomethetic principles (see Trick & Katz, 1986, for one such example).

Keeping this caveat in mind, some general interactive predictions directly emerge from the model. For instance, the model leads to the prediction that imagery skill can be facilitative in some contexts, but detrimental in others. Consider the case where two persons both employ the use of relational imagery in committing information to memory. The person who is high in the skill will form much better interactive images than the low-skill person. If, as claimed by some (e.g., Baker & Santa, 1977), interactive imagery reduces recognition memory scores by "messing up" the memory trace of each item interacting in the image, then the highly skilled relational imager can be predicted to show inferior performance in recognition memory tests. In contrast, the same high imagers should show superior performance in cued-recall tests, because of the superiority they would show in redintegration. Extending this laboratory prediction to the real-life situation, one should be able to disentangle the influence of generic declarative knowledge (such as the knowledge involved in knowing the context in which the encoded information is likely to be called upon) and of personal declarative knowledge (such as the knowledge that one is skilled in forming interactive images and, hence, the likelihood of interactive images being formed without explicit instructions to do so). I assume that, in the everyday contexts in which mnemonic functioning is expressed, interactive combinations of information from different knowledge states may, in fact, be the norm. Our short-term goal is in confirming the functional separation of knowledge states related to imagery, and mapping out the fine-grained details of these states. Our longer goal will be to understand how and when these factors will interact.

Acknowledgments. Preparation of this chapter was supported by the Natural Sciences and Engineering Research Council of Canada operating grant A7040. I also would like to acknowledge the support given to me by a leave fellowship from the Social Sciences and Humanities Research Council of Canada. The support of the Institute of Personality Assessment and Research, University of California, Berkeley, where a first draft of the manuscript of this paper was written, is also gratefully acknowledged. Finally, I would like to thank the editors and several colleagues for feedback given on an earlier draft of the manuscript. Special thanks are due Drs. J. Clark, T. Helstrup, J. Howes, G. Kaufmann, and A. Paivio, and Mr. A. Patrick for their helpful comments and criticisms.

References

Anderson, J. (1976). *Language, memory and thought*. Hillsdale, NJ: Erlbaum Associates.

Baddeley, A., & Warrington, E. (1973). Memory coding and amnesia. *Neuropsychologia*, *11*, 159–165.

Baker, L., & Santa, J. (1977). Context integration and retrieval. *Memory and Cognition*, *5*, 308–314.

Begg, I. (1982). Imagery, organization, and discriminative processes. *Canadian Journal of Psychology, 36*, 273–290.

Begg, I. (1983). Imagery instructions and the organization of memory. In J. Yuille (Ed.), *Imagery, memory and cognition* (pp. 91–115). Hillsdale, NJ: Erlbaum Associates.

Bellezza, F. (1984). The self as a mnemonic device: The role of internal cues. *Journal of Personality and Social Psychology, 47*, 506–516.

Bower, G. (1970). Imagery as a relational organizer in associative learning. *Journal of Verbal Learning and Verbal Behavior, 29*, 529–533.

Bower, G. (1972). Mental imagery and associative learning. In L. W. Gregg (Ed.), *Cognition in learning and memory*. New York: Wiley.

Bower, G., & Gilligan, S. (1979). Remembering information related to one's self. *Journal of Research in Personality, 13*, 420–432.

Burnett, S., McLane, D., & Dratt, L. (1979). Spatial visualization and sex differences in quantitative ability. *Intelligence, 3*, 345–354.

Chaffin, R., Crawford, M., Herrmann, D., & Deffenbacker, K. (in press). Gender differences in the perception of memory abilities in others. *Human Learning*.

Chase, W., & Ericsson, K. (1982). Skill and working memory. In G. Bower (Ed.), *The psychology of learning and motivation* (Vol. 16, pp. 1–58). New York: Academic Press.

Cooper, L. (1976). Individual differences in visual comparison processes. *Perception and Psychophysics, 19*, 433–444.

Corbett, A. (1977). Retrieval dynamics for rote and visual image mnemonics. *Journal of Verbal Learning and Verbal Behavior, 16*, 233–246.

Danaher, B., & Thorensen, C. (1972). Imagery assessment by self-report and behavioral measures. *Behavior Research and Therapy, 10*, 131–138.

Day, J., & Bellezza, F. (1983). The relation between visual imagery mediators and recall. *Memory and Cognition, 11*, 251–257.

Delaney, H. (1978). Interaction of individual differences with visual and verbal elaboration instructions. *Journal of Educational Psychology, 70*, 306–318.

Denis, M., & Carfantan, M. (1985). People's knowledge about images. *Cognition, 20*, 49–60.

DiVesta, F., & Sunshine, P. (1974). The retrieval of abstract and concrete materials as function of imagery, mediation and mnemonic aids. *Memory and Cognition, 2*, 340–344.

Egan, D. (1979). Testing based on understanding: Implictions from studies of spatial ability. *Intelligence, 3*, 1–15.

Egan, D., & Grimes-Farrow, D. (1982). Differences in mental representations spontaneously adopted for reasoning. *Memory and Cognition, 10*, 297–307.

Ernest, C. (1977). Imagery ability and cognition: A critical review. *Journal of Mental Imagery, 2*, 181–216.

Ernest, C., & Paivio, A. (1971). Imagery and verbal associative latencies as a function of imagery ability. *Canadian Journal of Psychology, 25*, 83–90.

Finkenbinder, O. (1914). The remembrance of problems and of their solutions: A study in logical memory. *American Journal of Psychology, 6*, 400–413.

Fisher, C. (1916). The process of generalizing abstraction, and its product, the general concept. *Psychological Monographs, 21*, 150–180.

Fox, C. (1914). The conditions which arouse mental images in thought. *British Journal of Psychology, 6*, 420–431.

Galton, F. (1880). Statistics of mental imagery. *Mind, 5*, 301–318.

Gough, H., & Heilbrun, A. (1983). *The adjective check list manual*. Palo Alto, CA: Consulting Psychologist Press.

Greenwald, A. (1981). Self and memory. In G. Bower (Ed.), *The psychology of learning and memory* (Vol. 15, pp. 201–236). New York: Academic Press.

Gruneberg, M. (1978). The feeling of knowing, memory blocks and memory aids. In M. Gruenberg & P. Morris (Eds.), *Aspects of Memory* (pp. 186–209). London: Methuen.

Harris, J. (1980). Memory aids people use: Two interview studies. *Memory and Cognition*, *8*, 31–38.

Helstrup, T. (1985). Self, imagery and memory: How are they related? Unpublished manuscript, University of Bergen, Bergen, Norway.

Herrmann, D. (1982). Know thy memory: The use of questionnaires to assess and study memory. *Psychological Bulletin*, *92*, 434–452.

Herrmann, D. (1984). Questionnaires about memory. In J. Harris & P. Morris (Eds.), *Everyday Memory* (pp. 133–151). London: Academic Press.

Herrmann, D., Grubs, L., Sigmundi, R., & Grueneich, R. (1983). Awareness of memory aptitude as a function of memory experience. Paper presented at the British Psychological Society Meeting, York, England, April 1983.

Howes, J. (1983). Effects of experimenter- and self-generated imagery on the Korsakoff patient's memory performance. *Neuropsychologia*, *21*, 341–349.

Janssen, W. (1976). Selective interference in paired-associate and free recall learning: Messing up the image. *Acta Psychologica*, *40*, 35–48.

Katz, A. (1983). What does it mean to be a high imager? In J. Yuille (Ed.), *Imagery, memory and cognition* (pp. 39–63). Hillsdale, NJ: Erlbaum Associates.

Katz, A. (1985). Self-reference in the encoding of creative-relevant traits. Unpublished manuscript, University of Western Ontario, London, Ontario, Canada.

Katz, A. N. (1984). Creative styles: Relating tests of creativity to the work patterns of scientists. *Personality and Individual Differences*, *5*, 281–292.

Kaufmann, G. (1985). Mental imagery and cognition. Unpublished book manuscript, University of Bergen, Bergen, Norway.

Kosslyn, S. (1980). *Image and mind*. Cambridge, MA: Harvard University Press.

Kosslyn, S. (1983). *Ghosts in the mind's machine*. New York: Norton.

Kosslyn, S., Brunn, J., Cave, K., & Wallach, R. (1984). Individual differences in mental imagery ability: A computational analysis. *Cognition*, *18*, 195–243.

Lord, C. (1980). Schemas and images as memory aids: Two modes of processing social information. *Journal of Personality and Social Psychology*, *38*, 257–269.

Luria, A. (1968). *The mind of a mnemonist*. New York: Avon.

Mathews, N., Hunt, E., & MacLeod, C. (1980). Strategy choice and strategy training in sentence–picture verification. *Journal of Verbal Learning and Verbal Behavior*, *19*, 531–548.

McDaniel, M., & Kearney, E. (1984). Optimal learning strategies and their spontaneous use: The importance of task-appropriate processing. *Memory and Cognition*, *12*, 361–373.

McDaniel, M., & Pressley, M. (1984). Putting the keyword method in context. *Journal of Educational Psychology*, *76*, 598–609.

McDaniel, M., Lapsley, D., & Milstead, M. (1985). The encoding of self-features in memory: Release from proactive interference. Unpublished manuscript, University of Notre Dame, Notre Dame, IN.

McGivern, J., & Levin, J. (1983). The keyword method and children's vocabulary learning: An interaction with vocabulary knowledge. *Contemporary Educational Psychology*, *8*, 46–57.

Miall, D. (1985). Emotion and the self: The context of remembering. Unpublished manuscript, College of St. Paul and St. Mary, Cheltenham, England.

Morris, P., & Hampson, P. (1983). *Imagery and consciousness.* London: Academic Press.

Mueller, J., Heesacker, M., & Ross, M. (1984). Body-image consciousness and self-reference effects in face recognition. *British Journal of Social Psychology, 23,* 277–279.

Mumaw, R., Pellegrino, J., Kail, R., & Carter, P. (1984). Different slopes for different folks: Process analysis of spatial aptitude. *Memory and Cognition, 12,* 515–521.

Murray, H. (1938). *Exploration in personality.* New York: Oxford University Press.

Paivio, A. (1971). *Imagery and verbal processes.* New York: Holt, Rinehart and Winston.

Paivio, A., & Harshman, R. (1983). Factor analysis of a questionnaire on imagery and verbal habits and skills. *Canadian Journal of Psychology, 37,* 461–483.

Paivio, A., & Yuille, J. (1967). Mediation instructions and word attributes in paired-associate learning. *Psychonomic Science, 8,* 65–66.

Paivio, A., & Yuille, J. (1969). Changes in associative strategies and paired-associate learning as a function of word imagery and type of learning set. *Journal of Experimental Psychology, 79,* 458–463.

Paivio, A., Smythe, P., & Yuille, J. (1968). Imagery versus meaningfulness of nouns in paired-associate learning. *Canadian Journal of Psychology, 22,* 427–441.

Paivio, A., Yuille, J., & Smythe, P. (1966). Stimulus and response abstractions, imagery and meaningfulness and reported mediators in paired-associate learning. *Canadian Journal of Psychology, 20,* 362–377.

Perlmutter, M. (1978). What is memory aging the aging of? *Developmental Psychology, 14,* 330–345.

Poltrock, S., & Brown, P. (1984). Individual differences in visual imagery and spatial ability. *Intelligence, 8,* 93–138.

Pressley, M., & Levin, J. (1978). Developmental constraints associated with children's use of the keyword method of foreign language vocabulary learning. *Journal of Experimental Child Psychology, 26,* 359–372.

Pressley, M., & Levin, J. (1981). The keyword method and recall of vocabulary words from definitions. *Journal of Experimental Psychology: Human Learning and Memory, 7,* 72–76.

Pressley, M., Borkowski, J., & O'Sullivan, J. (1985). Children's metamemory and the teaching of memory strategies. In D. Forrest-Pressley, G. MacKinnon, & T. Waller (Eds.), *Metacognition, cognition and human performance, Vol. 1: Theoretical perspectives* (pp. 111–153). New York: Academic Press.

Pressley, M., Borkowski, J., & Schneider, W. (in press). Good strategy users coordinate metacognition, strategy use, and knowledge. In R. Vasta & G. Whitehurst (Eds.), *Annals of child development* (Vol. 4). New York: JAI Press.

Pressley, M., Levin, J., & Ghatala, E. (1984). Memory-strategy monitoring in adults and children. *Journal of Verbal Learning and Verbal Behavior, 23,* 270–288.

Pressley, M., Levin, J., Hall, J., Miller, G., & Berry, J. (1980). The keyword method and foreign word acquisition. *Journal of Experimental Psychology: Human Learning and Memory, 6,* 163–173.

Pressley, M., Levin, J., Kuiper, N., Bryant, S., & Michener, S. (1982). Mnemonic versus nonmnemonic vocabulary-learning strategies: Additional comparisons. *Journal of Educational Psychology, 74,* 693–707.

Pressley, M., Levin, J., Nakamura, G., Hope, D., Bishop, J., & Toye, A. (1980). The keyword method of foreign vocabulary learning: An investigation of its generalizability. *Journal of Applied Psychology, 65,* 635–642.

Pressley, M., Ross, K., Levin, J., & Ghatala, E. (1984). The role of strategy utility knowledge in children's strategy decision making. *Journal of Experimental Psychology, 38,* 491–504.

Rawles, R. (1978). The past and present of mnemotechny. In M. Gruneberg, P. Morris, & R. Sykes (Eds.), *Practical aspects of memory* (pp., 164–171). London: Academic Press.

Rehm, L. (1973). Relationships among measures of visual imagery. *Behavior Research and Therapy, 11*, 265–270.

Reese, H. (1977). Toward a cognitive theory of mnemonic imagery. *Journal of Mental Imagery, 1*, 229–244.

Richardson, J. (1978). Reported mediators and individual differences in mental imagery. *Memory and Cognition, 6*, 376–378.

Richardson, J. (1980). *Mental imagery and human memory.* New York: St. Martin's Press.

Richardson, J. (1985). Converging operations and reported mediators in the investigation of mental imagery. *British Journal of Psychology, 76*, 205–214.

Rimm, D., & Bottrell, J. (1969). Four measures of visual imagination. *Behavior Research and Therapy, 7*, 63–69.

Rogers, T. (1981). A model of the self as an aspect of the human information processing system. In N. Cantor & J. Kihlstrom (Eds.), *Personality, cognition and social interaction* (pp. 193–214). Hillsdale, NJ: Erlbaum Associates.

Rogers, T., Kuiper, N., & Kirker, W. (1977). Self-reference and the encoding of personal information. *Journal of Personality and Social Psychology, 35*, 677–688.

Schneider, W. (1985). Developmental trends in the metamemory-memory behaviour relationship: An integrative review. In D. Forrest-Pressley, G. MacKinnon, & T. Waller (Eds.), *Metacognition, cognition and human performance, Vol. 1: Theoretical perspectives* (pp. 57–109). New York: Academic Press.

Sehulster, J. (1981a). Structure and pragmatics of a self-theory of memory. *Memory and Cognition, 9*, 263–276.

Sehulster, J. (1981b). Phenomenological correlates of a self theory of memory. *American Journal of Psychology, 94*, 527–537.

Simon, H. (1975). The functional equivalance of problem solving skills. *Cognitive Psychology, 7*, 268–288.

Slee, J. (1980). Individual differences in visual imagery ability and the retrieval of visual appearance. *Journal of Mental Imagery, 4*, 93–113.

Trick, L., & Katz, A. (1986). The domain interaction approach to metaphor processing: Relating individual differences and metaphor characteristics. *Journal of Metaphor and Symbolic Activities, 1*, 185–213.

Tulving, E., & Madigan, S. (1970). Memory and verbal learning. In P. Mussen & M. Rosezweig (Eds.), *Annual Review of Psychology* (Vol. 20, pp. 437–484). Palo Alto, CA: Annual Reviews.

Wilding, J., & Valentine, E. (1985). One man's memory for prose, faces and names. *British Journal of Psychology, 76*, 215–219.

Wood, G. (1967). Mnemonic systems in recalls. *Journal of Educational Psychology, 58*, 1–27.

Woods, E. (1915). An experimental study of the process of recognizing. *American Journal of Psychology, 26*, 313–387.

Yarmey, A. D., & Johnson, J. (1982). Evidence for the self as an imaginal prototype. *Journal of Research in Personality, 16*, 238–246.

Yates, F. A. (1966). *The art of memory.* London: Routledge and Kegan Paul.

CHAPTER 9

Individual Imagery Differences and Prose Processing

Michel Denis

The revival of interest in imagery within the field of cognitive psychology forced researchers involved in the study of prose processing mechanisms to take into account the potential role of visual imagery in comprehension and memory for texts. The growth of this field of study was to a great extent fostered by the existence of a considerable body of research on text processing (cf. Kintsch & van Dijk, 1978; van Dijk & Kintsch, 1983). More recently, assumptions regarding the role of "mental models" (Garnham, 1981; Johnson-Laird, 1983) or "situation models" (Kintsch, 1985; Perrig & Kintsch, 1985) in prose comprehension have placed increasing emphasis on imagery processes. Visual imagery appears as a likely candidate for the construction of models of spatial configurations described in a text (e.g., Mani & Johnson-Laird, 1982; Perrig & Kintsch, 1985). An overview of the literature on this issue shows that the intersection of imagery research and prose processing studies has indeed produced valuable empirical and theoretical findings and has been beneficial to both fields (for a more comprehensive review, see Denis, 1984).

This chapter reviews some of the most widely employed empirical approaches to effects of imagery on prose processing. Special emphasis is placed on approaches taking individual imagery differences into account. Findings from a research program on the role of individual imagery characteristics on the processing of narratives are presented. The chapter also reports and discusses results from a new experiment on the processing of descriptive prose.

The Effects of Imagery Instructions on Prose Memory

To investigate the possible effects of imagery on the processing of connected prose, the most commonly used paradigm consists of instructing subjects to read prose material while generating detailed visual images of its content (e.g., the characters, their actions, the objects and scenery). The subjects are then tested for recall or recognition, and their retention scores are compared with those of control subjects who have not been given imagery instructions. Note that this paradigm does not imply that control subjects do not also make use of some imagery. In fact, it seems likely that most adults do use some imagery spontaneously when reading or studying text (e.g., Paivio, 1986). Instead, imagery instructions merely maximize the probability of subjects using imagery-based strategies extensively.

In general, visualization instructions during reading facilitate prose retention, both in adults (Anderson & Kulhavy, 1972; Giesen & Peeck, 1984; Perrig, in press; Rasco, Tennyson, & Boutwell, 1975) and in children (Levin, 1973; Levin & Divine-Hawkins, 1974; Maher & Sullivan, 1982). Developmental studies have shown that 8- to 9-year-old children can be trained to use imagery strategies during text reading or listening (Lesgold, McCormick, & Golinkoff, 1975; Pressley, 1976), whereas imagery instructions are generally ineffective with younger subjects, unless the experimenter uses pictorial material designed to "aid" children in elaborating visual images (Guttman, Levin, & Pressley, 1977; Ruch & Levin, 1979).

The positive effects of imagery instructions on prose memory are now well established, but what remains open to interpretation are the specific mechanisms producing these effects. Considering the available evidence, two major factors can account for the efficiency of imagery during prose reading. First of all, imagery helps readers to encode semantic information more extensively. The semantic processing of sentences, which is responsible for the storage of some abstract (propositional) information, is supplemented by the elaboration of representations having structural characteristics in common with perception. For instance, according to Perrig and Kintsch's (1985) theoretical model, a text describing a spatial configuration is likely to elicit readers' visual imagery, used for the elaboration of a mental map of the configuration (a "situation model"), in addition to the propositional textbase. This model is expected to be of special use for some types of further requirements; in particular, inferences concerning the locations of elements in the configuration would to a large degree rely on the retrieval of information encoded in this model.

Second, images reflect not disparate collections of objects and characters, but structured scenes in which these objects and characters interact. Images elaborated during the reading of concrete prose thus combine meaningful components into highly integrated configurations. Word-memory studies have reliably demonstrated visual imagery to be a highly effective means for combining information and coding compound scenes (Begg, 1978; Paivio & Begg, 1981). Inasmuch as imagery is a process particularly suited to interrelating units of information into more highly organized structures, it is likely to enhance coding efficiency, because later retrieval of a given unit will lead to the other units composing the configuration.

Another critical question involves the exact locus of imagery effects in prose memory. At which representational level of prose will facilitation appear? More precisely, whereas images are clearly facilitative in the processing of episodes, what role should be attributed to them in the encoding of macrostructures? Although the issue has been introduced only just recently (Denis, 1984; Perrig, in press), and still deserves more investigation, it is likely that certain representational levels in prose processing are more involved than others with imagery effects. Perrig (in press) has presented empirical evidence that in the processing of narratives, visual imagery essentially improves content organization, and thus recall, of microelements (sentences), but not the thematic organization of the text. The macrostructure, which contains the most important ideas of the whole text, mainly includes nonfigurative meaning components, based on knowledge about causal relationships, goals, motives, etc., all of which cannot be expressed easily in visual images. Imagery is therefore of no use in the construction of the macrostructure. On the other hand, the organization of microelements may benefit more from imaginal encoding, especially in the case of concrete information. These notions are in line with the distinction between prose-learning strategies suited to the processing of the main ideas of a text (directed toward identifying, analyzing, or integrating information within the text's macrostructure), and complementary, microstructure strategies, intended for the processing of details (Levin, 1982).

In a similar vein, Marschark (1985) developed the idea that in the memory of verbal material, imagery has its most potent effects when context is at a minimum, as in word or sentence lists; on the other hand, imagery effects are assumed to be less pronounced when linguistic units are presented in some context, as in meaningful paragraphs or prose passages. Actually, Marschark (1985) found evidence that the paragraph context attenuates differences in recall between concrete (high-imagery) and abstract (low-imagery) materials. This finding makes sense if one accepts the idea that relational processing among sentences at the macrolevel of the text is equivalent for both material types and provides equally rich retrieval contexts for concrete and abstract materials. In short, the line of argument is that in text memory the occurrence of imagery effects depends to a great extent on a relative lack of macrolevel (or contextually related) processing.

Finally, certain methodological problems associated with paradigms using imagery instructions should not be overlooked. In the majority of published studies, this paradigm explicitly involves a learning set; that is, both the subjects in the control and those in the experimental conditions are forewarned that they are to have a typical retention test and are encouraged to read the material with this in mind. Therefore, what is investigated is in fact the effects of imagery on intentional learning from prose material. Furthermore, in some studies, imagery elaboration is explicitly presented to the subjects as a strategy that should enhance their learning from the text (Rasco et al., 1975). In this case, the facilitation produced by imagery instructions may well include a component arising from expectancy effects.

Individual Imagery Differences and Prose Memory

Much less attention has been paid to the potential incidence of individual imagery characteristics on the retention of prose in the absence of any imagery instructions. Imagery abilities vary across individuals; the role of this variable has been documented in several word-memory studies (Ernest, 1977; Ernest & Paivio, 1971; Hishitani, 1985). Taking advantage of individual differences to visualize the content of concrete prose should be a valuable means of investigating the effects of imagery activity in text processing.

Despite the difficulties inherent in the measurement of individual imagery characteristics, including the selection of appropriate psychometric instruments, the study of individual differences should help to minimize other methodological difficulties, such as those resulting from the expectancy effects potentially associated with imagery instructions. This is true because all subjects are exposed to the very same instructions, and these instructions do not refer to imagery activity. Furthermore, when appropriate precautions are taken, reading instructions can be formulated in such a way (e.g., by using comprehension instructions) that their elicitation of intentional learning sets is highly improbable.

A small number of studies have investigated the effects of individuals' imagery characteristics on memory for text (Chaguiboff & Denis, 1981; Denis, 1982). In these studies, Marks' (1973) Vividness of Visual Imagery Questionnaire (VVIQ) was used to determine subjects who were likely to generate visual images from verbal descriptions. It was assumed that high scorers on this questionnaire, or "high imagers" (HIs), would have a greater tendency to construct visual images of prose content than would low scorers, or "low imagers" (LIs).*

In the Chaguiboff and Denis (1981) study, the subjects read a 2000-word narrative (about an automobile trip) at their own pace and then had to supply recognition responses to concrete nouns (half of them extracted from the text, half distractors). Subjects classified as HIs not only had higher recognition scores than LIs but also produced significantly faster responses than LIs when they were correct. In another condition in the same study, recognition responses were solicited to drawings representing the objects denoted by the nouns. In this condition, response latencies were not substantially affected for HIs, whereas they increased significantly for LIs. This finding suggested that LIs had special difficulties in matching probes having a figural content with their own memory representations of the text. A likely explanation was that LIs' memory representations were rather poor in figural content, as compared to HIs. These findings thus support the idea that differential encoding processes are developed during reading, with HIs being more inclined to construct visual images of the episodes than LIs.

The assumption that HIs were involved in additional processing was equally confirmed by the analysis of spontaneous reading times. HIs had significantly longer reading times for the text than LIs (the difference being about 10%). This finding can be accounted for if one assumes that (a) total reading time of concrete episodes includes a component that is devoted to elaborating and maintaining visual images (in fact, the sum of microcomponents distributed all along the reading period) and (b) HIs spend longer on these processes than LIs. In addition, the

---

*In the French version of the VVIQ, higher scores indicate higher imagery vividness.

increase in recognition scores associated with being a high imager was proportionally greater than the increase in reading times. This finding weakens the potential argument that the difference between HIs' and LIs' performances was simply an artifact of longer total reading time by HIs.

The finding that HIs take more time to read concrete prose when they read at their own pace was replicated in another study especially designed to examine reading time, which used a new narrative describing a farmer who rides to a village and then meets with a series of incidents traveling home (Denis, 1982). Again, HIs took longer to read than LIs. In addition, HIs also obtained significantly higher scores on a recognition test of text content. This result provided support for the inference that HIs did in fact spontaneously engage in more imagery activity during reading than did LIs, and that the extra time devoted to reading by HIs at least partly reflects the extra imagery processing they developed when reading highly imageable material. Again, the difference between HIs' and LIs' retention scores was greater than their difference in reading times.

A control experiment was devised in order to evaluate the potential argument that HIs have longer reading times simply because they are slower readers in general. Results showed that HIs and LIs did not differ in their reading times when they were asked to read a highly abstract, nonimageable text. Furthermore, there was no difference between HIs and LIs on the recognition test administered after reading the abstract text. Thus, individual imagery characteristics apparently affected processing of verbal material only insofar as this material was likely to elicit visual imagery.

Additional experiments were performed with the purpose of influencing imaginal processing during text reading through very simple instructional manipulations. A new sample of subjects was presented with the previously used narrative and was instructed to read it as fast as possible. The assumption was that these instructions would incite HIs to decrease the amount or frequency of their imagery activity. Actually, HIs now had significantly shorter reading times than before, whereas LIs' reading times were not substantially modified. Perhaps the most salient finding was that despite significant modification in their reading behavior, HIs' recognition scores remained significantly higher than those of LIs.

In the final experiment of this series, subjects were asked to construct visual images of characters and events for every sentence as they were reading the narrative. These imagery instructions produced a moderate increase in HIs' reading times, whereas LIs' reading times increased considerably, the end result being no significant difference in overall reading times between HIs and LIs. Furthermore, imagery instructions significantly improved recognition scores, yielding equivalent, relatively high performances for HIs and LIs.

The fact that imaging while reading takes time was confirmed more recently by Giesen and Peeck (1984), who found that subjects receiving instructions to elaborate visual images while reading used significantly more reading time than subjects in a control condition; their performance was also better on questions dealing with concrete and spatial information, whereas no differences were found for retention of abstract content.

The experiments reported above clearly suggest that individual imagery characteristics have a measureable impact on prose retention, and that these effects are mediated by differential encoding processes taking place during reading. Furthermore, reading time (more precisely, the difference between HIs' and LIs' reading times) emerges as a valuable tool in measuring increments in imagery activity generated by HIs while they read narrative prose.

Imagery Differences and the Reading of Character Descriptions in Prose: A New Experiment

A new experiment outlined here was aimed at evaluating the robustness of the findings from the Denis (1982) studies, with the following methodological modifications. In this experiment, the manipulations were made in a within-subject experiment; consequently, each subject was presented with several different texts. Instead of narratives, the four texts used were descriptions of imaginary characters. The descriptions contained both highly concrete (HC) and moderately concrete (MC) passages, which provided a means of evaluating the effects of imaging on different types of passages.

All of the 96 subjects who participated in the experiment were first tested in self-paced (SP) reading conditions for two texts. They were instructed to read in an ordinary fashion, at their own pace, without rereading. When the subjects had completed their reading of these two texts, they received one of three sets of instructions. One group of subjects was simply told to read the two other texts as before. Because these subjects were in the self-paced reading conditions throughout the experiment, they constituted the SP–SP group. The second group of subjects was instructed to read the texts as fast as possible, so as to reach the end of each text in as short a time as possible. Because these subjects successively received self-paced, then fast reading (FR) instructions, they constituted the SP–FR group. The third group of subjects was instructed to elaborate visual images which were as detailed and vivid as possible for characters, actions, and scenes presented in the texts. Because these subjects successively received self-paced reading, then imagery (IM) instructions, they constituted the SP–IM group.

After each of the subjects finished reading the four texts, they completed a two-alternative forced-choice test on the characters described in the texts. Each item referred to a piece of information that had been mentioned explicitly in one of the texts. There were 48 items on the test, half tapping HC and half tapping MC passages of the texts. The subjects who participated in the experiment had completed the VVIQ in a classroom setting 1 week before the experimental session.

Preliminary analyses were conducted on reading time data for subjects from the SP–SP group, who were not requested to modify their reading strategy in any way during the entire course of the experiment. There were no reading time differences for the four texts. In addition, there was no significant difference in reading time between the HC and MC passages. Finally, there was no overall effect of the position of the texts in the experimental sequence, that is, from the first to the last (fourth) text. Similar analyses were performed on retention scores. Here again, the mean scores were not significantly different for the four texts. HC and MC passages produced virtually identical proportions of correct responses. Furthermore, the position of the texts in the experimental sequence had no detectable effects.

To recapitulate, the preliminary analyses lent support to the assumption that the four texts were roughly equivalent, at least for the measures investigated here. Furthermore, the serial position of the texts in the experimental session did not appear to affect these measures substantially.

Overall Effects of Individual Imagery Characteristics on Reading Times

An analysis was designed to confirm the previously established effects of individual imagery characteristics on reading times. In order to measure such an effect over as large a sample as possible, the analysis was performed on the first and the second texts read by the subjects in all three groups, that is, the part of the experiment where reading conditions were identical for the three groups, when all subjects were involved in self-paced reading.

The 96 subjects were classified as HIs or LIs according to whether their VVIQ scores were above or below the entire group's median. HIs' spontaneous reading times were longer than LIs' times, 69.7 vs. 63.9 sec, respectively (means per page), although this difference failed to reach significance at the conventional probability level. The same type of comparison was then repeated by contrasting more extreme VVIQ scorers. Mean reading times were 74.9 sec per page for the 24 highest HIs, and 62.3 sec for the 24 lowest LIs. Not surprisingly, the contrast was more marked than in the previous analysis. The difference between HIs' and LIs' reading times was significant. The effect was consistent over both types of pages.

Overall Effects of Individual Imagery Characteristics on Retention Scores

The whole population was again split at the median of VVIQ scores, and the mean proportions of correct responses per page on the retention test were then compared in HIs and LIs. Mean retention scores were .68 for HIs vs. .62 for LIs. This difference was significant. There was a slight, nonsignificant superiority of HIs over LIs as concerns HC pages (.66 vs. .61), whereas the difference was clearer as concerns MC pages (.71 vs. .63). Restricting the analysis to the highest HIs and lowest LIs did not substantially affect the contrast between mean retention scores.

Comparison of HIs' and LIs' Reading Times in the Three Experimental Conditions

The next step in the analysis consisted in evaluating to what extent reading instructions designed to affect subjects' reading speed did in fact influence HIs' and LIs' reading time patterns. The SP–SP, SP–FR, and SP–IM groups were henceforth treated independently. Within each of these groups, the most salient comparison involved reading times for the first two texts versus those for the last two texts, with HIs and LIs analyzed separately.

The first operation consisted in defining within each group those subjects who could be considered as HIs and LIs. Instead of maintaining all 96 subjects and splitting them according to the overall median of VVIQ scores (thus resulting in analysis difficulties, such as unequal numbers of subjects in different subgroups), it seemed preferable to rely on comparisons between equal subsets of subjects on each side of the median, in all three experimental groups.

In each of these groups, 10 subjects were drawn randomly from those whose VVIQ scores were above the overall median, and 10 from those whose scores were below that median. Means and standard deviations of VVIQ scores were controlled for homogeneity in the three resulting subgroups of HIs and in the three subgroups of LIs. A further check was made that the mean reading times per page for the first two texts were of comparable magnitudes in the three sub-groups of HIs, as well as in the subgroups of LIs. An analysis of variance did not reveal any significant difference among the subjects from the three groups. Thus it was assumed that for the part of the experiment common to the three groups, there was a satisfying level of similarity across the three subgroups of HIs as well as across those of LIs. The analysis showed significant effects of individual imagery characteristics, with HIs having longer reading times than LIs on the average, 71.5 vs. 61.8 sec, respectively.

Figure 9.1 shows the mean reading times for HIs and LIs, in each group, for the first two and the last two texts. Relative changes (decrease or increase) in reading times from the first two to the last two texts were analyzed using t tests.

Not surprisingly, as concerns subjects of the SP–SP group, there was no significant change in reading times from the first to the last part of the experiment, either for HIs or LIs.

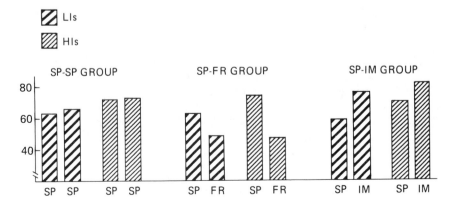

FIGURE 9.1. The mean reading times (sec) of LIs and HIs in the three groups of the experiment.

Subjects in the SP–FR group on the average showed a significant decrease in their reading times after fast reading instructions. The decrease was significantly more marked in HIs than in LIs (-35.8 vs. -24.3%). As a result, under fast reading instructions, both HIs and LIs had highly comparable reading times, 46.8 and 48.1 sec, respectively.

Subjects in the SP–IM group on the average showed a significant increase in their reading times after imagery instructions. The increase in reading times was larger in LIs than in HIs ($+28.4$ vs. $+19.8\%$), but the difference did not reach significance. Detailed analysis showed that this increase was actually greater in LIs than in HIs, but only for the HC pages ($+34.9$ vs. $+19.8\%$), whereas there was no significant difference as concerns MC pages ($+21.4$ vs. $+20.5\%$). On the other hand, while LIs' lengthening of their reading times was more marked for HC than for MC pages, HIs lengthened their reading times in a quite similar fashion for both kinds of pages. Finally, under imagery instructions, both LIs and HIs attained reading times which did not significantly differ from each other, 76.0 and 82.2 sec, respectively.

Comparison of HIs' and LIs' Retention Scores in the Three Experimental Conditions

Identical comparisons as above were made for retention scores. A preliminary analysis of retention scores for the first two texts (when all subjects were under self-paced reading instructions) was performed. As expected, no difference was found across the mean retention scores of the three groups. The only significant factor was subjects' imagery characteristics, with HIs attaining higher scores than LIs, .69 vs. .61, respectively. There was no reliable difference between retention scores for HC and MC pages.

Figure 9.2 shows the mean retention scores for HIs and LIs, in each group, for the first two and the last two texts. Variations in scores (decrease or increase) from the first two to the last two texts were analyzed using t tests.

As concerns subjects in the SP–SP group, no substantial difference was found in retention scores between the first two and the last two texts, either for HIs or LIs.

In the SP–FR group, there was a significant overall decrease in retention scores after fast reading instructions. This decrease was similar in magnitude in both HIs and LIs, with retention scores remaining substantially higher in HIs than in LIs after fast reading instructions, .57 vs. .45, respectively, for both HC and MC pages.

In the SP–IM group, as expected, instructions to image resulted overall in significantly higher retention scores. This effect, in fact, was essentially a result of HC pages. As concerns these pages, imagery instructions significantly favored retention scores. While the score increase was apparently twice as high in HIs than in LIs, there was no significant difference between both groups, who attained similarly high levels of retention, .78 and .73, respectively. As concerns MC pages, imagery instructions only favored HIs, whose scores slightly

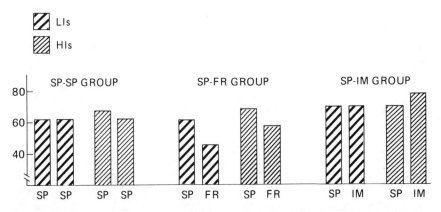

FIGURE 9.2. The mean retention scores (percentage correct) of LIs and HIs in the three groups of the experiment.

increased, while those of LIs slightly decreased; as a result, under imagery instructions, HIs had significantly higher retention scores than did LIs, .76 vs. .65, respectively. Put in another way, the apparent overall stability of LIs' scores seems in fact to result from the combined effects of an increase for HC pages and a decrease for MC pages. In contrast, HIs' scores increased for both HC and MC pages.

Summary and Discussion

The present experiment provided a confirmation of the finding that individuals characterized as HIs spend more time reading concrete prose (in this case, prose describing characters) than LIs (Denis, 1982). The extra time is assumed to reflect extra imagery generated by HIs (i.e., elaboration and inspection of visual images of the scenes described). Visual images, in addition, are likely to favor encoding of additional information. Consistent with this claim, readers who are disposed to use imagery retrieve information more accurately than people less prone to imaging. In self-paced reading conditions, these effects were obtained for both highly concrete and less concrete (although not totally abstract) passages.

Under fast reading instructions, both HIs and LIs reduced their reading times to comparable values, with HIs reducing their times more markedly than LIs. This finding supports the hypothesis that the drop in time used for elaborating and maintaining images may be a factor responsible for decreasing the total reading time in HIs.

Imagery instructions led both groups of subjects to increase their reading times to maximal, similar values, with LIs increasing their times more sharply than HIs. This is an indication that such instructions probably encourage HIs to develop additional imagery activity; on the other hand, LIs apparently are able to use a type of activity they would not spontaneously employ. It is interesting to note that under imagery instructions, LIs lengthened their reading times more for very concrete passages compared to less concrete passages. People not spontaneously inclined to imaging nevertheless were capable of engaging themselves in imaginal processing when they were required to do so, but this apparently was easier for them with materials more likely to elicit images. In contrast, HIs lengthened their reading times in similar proportions for both kinds of passages.

With respect to retention, HIs again showed a superiority over LIs under self-paced reading instructions. Fast reading instructions produced a strong decrease in retention scores in both HIs and LIs, but scores remained substantially higher in HIs than in LIs, for both concrete and moderately concrete passages. Instructions to image while reading produced overall higher retention scores, but this effect was not equivalent across subjects or parts of texts. Imagery instructions produced longer reading times in both HIs and LIs for highly concrete prose, but significant increases in retention were only observed for HIs. The HIs responded to instructions, with a clear effect on memory performance. In contrast, the LIs, who responded equally to instructions (as is shown by the increase in their reading times), did not benefit much from this extra processing (as is shown by the low level of improvement in their retention). It therefore seems that LIs' extra processing did not actually result in effective visual imagery. With less concrete passages, there was no evidence that imagery instructions were beneficial for LIs. In short, the extra processing produced by imagery instructions favored the encoding of highly concrete passages but did not have a significant impact on the encoding of less concrete passages.

Conclusions

On the whole, the experiment reported in this chapter clearly indicates that HIs are in a more favorable position than LIs for prose processing and memory not only in self-paced, "natural" reading conditions, but also in constrained conditions (such as fast reading conditions), as well as in conditions where they are required to use the reading strategy they would have chosen spontaneously.

A number of questions emerge from these findings. First, given that some people tend spontaneously to elaborate visual images and are able to make proficient use of them in the processing of concrete prose, one may legitimately wonder about the usefulness of such a processing strategy for individuals whose "cognitive style" is not consistent with imagery production. The above experiment showed that the effectiveness of imagery-based processing strategies was rather low for LIs and that these strategies only had effects, if at all, on those parts of prose material which were easier to convert into images. However, while the effects on retention were low, they were not totally absent, and room certainly remains for further speculations about the utility of promoting imagery-based strategies in inefficient prose learners. For instance, given the number of valuable methods designed to improve prose processing in children, especially those involving the use of illustrations and picture-based strategies (e.g., Levin, 1982;

Pressley & Miller, 1987), it would be of special interest to establish whether the effectiveness of these strategies is dependent upon individual imagery differences. In particular, one interesting possibility to test empirically would be whether LIs especially benefit from pictures embedded in text.

Second, this question also points to the issue of people's ability to evaluate the efficiency of the processing strategies they are likely to use, and more generally the issue of the use of metacognitive information in the regulation of cognitive activities (cf. Katz, 1983; Pressley, Levin, & Ghatala, 1984). In this respect, one should note that there is a widespread agreement among individuals that imagery is useful in learning and memory (Denis & Carfantan, 1985), and this is true for people having either high- or low-imagery abilities (Denis & Carfantan, in press). This gives support to the idea that subjects' statements about the usefulness of imagery should not be taken as reliable indicators of the likelihood of their making actual use of imagery in cognitive processing. Furthermore, valuable information certainly could be gathered from experiments in which subjects were given explicit performance feedback after having used imagery strategies or not, in order to provide them with objective knowledge about the efficacy of these strategies (see Pressley, Ross, Levin, & Ghatala, 1984).

Last, one may speculate about which "components" of imagery abilities are assumed to be the most useful in the processing of prose. In the present experiment, vividness of visual imagery proved to be a reliable variable. Employing more objective measures of individuals' imagery abilities should also extend our knowledge of specific imagery components involved in prose processing and memory.

Acknowledgments. The research reported in this chapter was conducted in the Laboratoire de Psychologie, Université de Paris VIII, and was aided by the Equipe de Recherche Associée au CNRS No. 235, and by the Action Thématique Programmée CNRS No. 60/83 (Aspects cognitifs et neurobiologiques du langage). Jean-Claude Verstiggel efficiently contributed to the collection and analysis of the data. The assistance of Connie Greenbaum was greatly appreciated in the preparation of the manuscript.

References

Anderson, R. C., & Kulhavy, R. W. (1972). Imagery and prose learning. *Journal of Educational Psychology, 63,* 242–243.

Begg, I. (1978). Imagery and organization in memory: Instructional effects. *Memory and Cognition, 6,* 174–183.

Chaguiboff, J., & Denis, M. (1981). Activité d'imagerie et reconnaissance de noms provenant d'un texte narratif. *L'Année psychologique, 81,* 69–86.

Denis, M. (1982). Imaging while reading text: A study of individual differences. *Memory and Cognition, 10,* 540–545.

Denis, M. (1984). Imagery and prose: A critical review of research on adults and children. *Text, 4,* 381–401.

Denis, M., & Carfantan, M. (1985). People's knowledge about images. *Cognition, 20,* 49–60.

Denis, M., & Carfantan, M. (in press). What people know about visual images: A metacognitive approach to imagery. In D. G. Russell & D. F. Marks (Eds.), *Imagery 2.* Dunedin, New Zealand: Human Performance Associates.

Ernest, C. H. (1977). Imagery ability and cognition: A critical review. *Journal of Mental Imagery, 1,* 181–215.

Ernest, C. H., & Paivio, A. (1971). Imagery and verbal associative latencies as a function of imagery ability. *Canadian Journal of Psychology, 25,* 83–90.

Garnham, A. (1981). Mental models as representations of text. *Memory and Cognition, 9,* 560–565.

Giesen, C., & Peeck, J. (1984). Effects of imagery instruction on reading and retaining a literary text. *Journal of Mental Imagery, 8*(2), 79–90.

Guttmann, J., Levin, J. R., & Pressley, M. (1977). Pictures, partial pictures, and young children's oral prose learning. *Journal of Educational Psychology, 69,* 473–480.

Hishitani, S. (1985). Imagery differences and task characteristics in memory. In D. F. Marks & D. G. Russell (Eds.), *Imagery 1* (pp. 5–13). Dunedin, New Zealand: Human Performance Associates.

Johnson-Laird, P. N. (1983). *Mental models.* Cambridge, England: Cambridge University Press.

Katz, A. N. (1983). What does it mean to be a high imager? In J. C. Yuille (Ed.), *Imagery, memory and cognition: Essays in honor of Allan Paivio* (pp. 39–63). Hillsdale, NJ: Erlbaum Associates.

Kintsch, W. (1985). Memory for prose. Paper presented at the Symposium on Structure and Function of Human Memory, In Memoriam Hermann Ebbinghaus, July 1–6, Berlin, GDR.

Kintsch, W., & van Dijk, T. A. (1978). Toward a model of text comprehension and production. *Psychological Review, 85,* 363–394.

Lesgold, A. M., McCormick, C., & Golinkoff, R. M. (1975). Imagery training and children's prose learning. *Journal of Educational Psychology, 67,* 663–667.

Levin, J. R. (1973). Inducing comprehension in poor readers: A test of a recent model. *Journal of Educational Psychology, 65,* 19–24.

Levin, J. R. (1982). Pictures as prose-learning devices. In A. Flammer & W. Kintsch (Eds.), *Discourse processing* (pp. 412–444). Amsterdam: North-Holland.

Levin, J. R., & Divine-Hawkins, P. (1974). Visual imagery as a prose-learning process. *Journal of Reading Behavior, 6,* 23–30.

Maher, J. H., Jr., & Sullivan, H. (1982). Effects of mental imagery and oral and print stimuli on prose learning of intermediate grade children. *Educational Communication and Technology, 30,* 175–183.

Mani, K., & Johnson-Laird, P. N. (1982). The mental representation of spatial descriptions. *Memory and Cognition, 10,* 181–187.

Marks, D. F. (1973). Visual imagery differences in the recall of pictures. *British Journal of Psychology, 64,* 17–24.

Marschark, M. (1985). Imagery and organization in the recall of prose. *Journal of Memory and Language, 24,* 734–745.

Paivio, A. (1986). *Mental representations: A dual coding approach.* New York: Oxford University Press.

Paivio, A., & Begg, I. (1981). *Psychology of language.* Englewood Cliffs, NJ: Prentice-Hall.

Perrig, W. J. (in press). Imagery and the thematic storage of prose. In D. G. Russell & D. F. Marks (Eds.), *Imagery 2*. Dunedin, New Zealand: Human Performance Associates.

Perrig, W., & Kintsch, W. (1985). Propositional and situational representations of text. *Journal of Memory and Language, 24*, 503–518.

Pressley, G. M. (1976). Mental imagery helps eight-year-olds remember what they read. *Journal of Educational Psychology, 68*, 355–359.

Pressley, M., Levin, J. R., & Ghatala, E. S. (1984). Memory strategy monitoring in adults and children. *Journal of Verbal Learning and Verbal Behavior, 23*, 270–288.

Pressley, M., & Miller, G. E. (1987). The effects of illustrations on children's listening comprehension and oral prose memory. In D. M. Willows & H. A. Houghton (Eds.), *The psychology of illustration*, Vol. 1, *Basic Research*. New York: Springer-Verlag.

Pressley, M., Ross, K. A., Levin, J. R., & Ghatala, E. S. (1984). The role of strategy utility knowledge in children's strategy decision making. *Journal of Experimental Child Psychology, 38*, 491–504.

Rasco, R. W., Tennyson, R. D., & Boutwell, R. C. (1975). Imagery instructions and drawings in learning prose. *Journal of Educational Psychology, 67*, 188–192.

Ruch, M. D., & Levin, J. R. (1979). Partial pictures as imagery-retrieval cues in young children's prose recall. *Journal of Experimental Child Psychology, 28*, 268–279.

van Dijk, T. A., & Kintsch, W. (1983). *Strategies of discourse comprehension*. New York: Academic Press.

CHAPTER 10

Imagery and Memory in the Blind: A Review

Carole H. Ernest

This chapter reflects the position that the examination of individual or group differences is useful in determining the limits and limitations of human cognitive functioning. This selective review of the literature on imagery and memory in the blind was motivated by three broad questions. First, in the absence of vision, and presumably visual images, are congenitally or early-blind individuals disadvantaged on learning and memory tasks presumed to require visual-imaginal processes? Second, given some investigators' definition of imagery ability as visuospatial skill (see Ernest, 1977), can forms or shapes and information about their spatial orientation be processed or remembered as well by those lacking visual experience as those with it? Finally, do the blind compensate for their lack of vision by developing nonvisually based strategies or skills (e.g., auditory, tactile, haptic, self-referent) as aids to memory?

The predominant but not sole emphasis in this review is on research (a) published within the past 15 years that, (b) included both blind and sighted individuals who, (c) were at least 10 years of age, and (d) were tested under identical experimental conditions. The relevant literature is presented in two main sections—Verbal Recall of Linguistic Stimuli, where the paired-associate and free-recall literature are examined, and Haptic Memory for Figural-Spatial Information, where the literature on shape recognition memory and mental rotation is examined individually. It should be noted that many of the theoretical issues addressed in the studies reviewed are not presented here; neither are the theoretical or organizing frameworks provided here necessarily central in the studies examined. Each section, or subsection, ends with "Summary and Comment" statements. The intent of the commentary is to elaborate particularly on some of the more provocative, or unexpected, findings by briefly examining related research in the blind–sighted literature. The chapter concludes with Final Comments, wherein a general overview of the findings is provided and suggestions are made for further research with the blind and sighted.*

---

*The congenitally and early blind discussed here are not necessarily totally blind; they may have some light perception or even minimal form perception. The present review therefore seeks consistencies or general patterns in the literature for each of

Verbal Recall of Linguistic Stimuli

In 1971, Paivio suggested that although the congenitally blind may be deficient in visual imagery, their imagery based on intact sensory modalities should not differ from that of the sighted. He proposed that the "concrete" words of the congenitally blind were not those whose referents could be visualized but were those that could be heard, felt, or otherwise experienced. In other words, "purely visual words would be effectively abstract" for the blind (Paivio, 1971, p. 518). Rating data have subsequently confirmed that direct sensory experience does provide an important imaginal attribute of words for the blind as well as the sighted (Cornoldi, Calore, & Pra-Baldi, 1979; Sholl & Easton, 1986).

Paivio's views have been expressed as the modality-specific imagery hypothesis. This hypothesis is an extension of the dual coding hypothesis (now dual coding theory; see Paivio, 1983) which states that concrete words are remembered better than abstract words because two symbolic systems, an imagery and a verbal system, are available to encode concrete words, whereas the verbal symbolic system primarily is relevant to the encoding of abstract words. Its conceptual-peg corollary states that, in the paired-associate paradigm, stimulus imagery is more important to recall than response imagery because the stimulus serves as a conceptual "peg" from which the response term can be "hung." Specific predictions that can be derived from the modality-specific imagery hypothesis, and that are relevant to the studies examined here, follow:

1. The blind should be deficient, relative to the sighted, in their memory for words rated high in visual image-evoking capacity.
2. High–low differences in the visual image-evoking capacity of words should influence the recall of the sighted, but not the blind.
3. The blind (but not the sighted) should recall more words high in auditory or tactile imagery than words high in visual imagery.
4. Both the blind and the sighted should be influenced by high–low differences in words' auditory or tactile imagery.
5. Recall should be enhanced in the blind when the stimulus terms in a paired-associate task are high in auditory relative to visual imagery.

Studies using high- or low-imagery words as defined by the Paivio, Yuille, and Madigan (1968) norms, rather than norms based on specific modality imagery (e.g., Yuille & Barnsley, 1969), are interpreted here as primarily (but not solely) indexing the visual image-evoking capacity of words.

To anticipate the findings, some support exists for the predictions, the conceptual-peg corollary (prediction 5) excepted. Unexpected findings include occasional facility of the blind with "visual" words, reports of visual imagery by

---

the areas investigated, irrespective of variations across studies in the degree of blindness experienced by subjects. Indeed, many investigators simply do not report such information.

the blind, the facility of the blind with imagery instructions, and "deficiencies" in the sighted's use of auditory imagery.

The *paired-associate* study that motivated much of the research in this area was Paivio and Okovita's (1971). They selected noun pairs that were all high in rated visual imagery, but half were also high, or low, in rated auditory imagery. Although the sighted recalled significantly more than the blind, high-auditory pairs were learned better than low-auditory pairs by both groups of adolescents; the difference, however, was significant only for the blind. The two groups' performance did not differ with high-auditory words, a somewhat surprising finding given the potential availability of two imaginal encodings (auditory and visual) for the sighted. The sighted did excel when the pairs were low in auditory imagery, however, presumably because the high visual referent characteristics of the low-auditory words were used to aid their recall. In their second experiment, word pairs were high in either visual imagery (but low in auditory and tactile imagery) or auditory imagery (but low in visual and tactile imagery). The blind, who excelled generally (perhaps because some had participated in the first experiment), recalled significantly more high-auditory than high-visual pairs, with the reverse occurring among the sighted. The benefits accruing to the blind from high auditory imagery (in both experiments) were interpreted as reflecting the expected "positive mnemonic effectiveness of modality specific imagery" (p. 509). Unexpectedly, however, the two groups performed comparably on the visual pairs in the second experiment and the sighted recalled significantly fewer auditory words than the blind.

Using the words from Paivio and Okovita's second experiment, and testing only the blind, Hans (1974) found little support for the modality-specific imagery hypothesis or its conceptual-peg corollary. Although high-auditory pairs were recalled best (but only marginally better than high-visual pairs), visual–auditory pairs were not recalled less well than auditory–visual pairs. Indeed, subjects' recall tended to be higher when both stimulus and response terms were high in visual (or auditory) imagery than when one member of the pair was high in auditory imagery. The blinds' verbal reports that unimodal pairs were easier to learn than bimodal pairs (which did not "make any sense"), suggested to Hans that the blind were not using modality-specific imagery. Zimler and Keenan (1983, Exp. 1) also failed to support the corollary in a study in which subjects were instructed to generate "imaginal scenes" involving the word pairs. They replicated the significantly poorer performance of sighted subjects, relative to the blind, on auditory pairs (reported earlier by Paivio and Okovita, 1971), but they also found that their blind subjects (adults and children) recalled significantly fewer visual pairs than the sighted. (There was no main effect for sightedness.) Blind adults, however, recalled significantly more visual than auditory pairs, with blind children showing the same result as a trend. Perhaps Zimler and Keenan's failure to control for their words' tactile imagery is relevant to the latter result.

Learning under standard paired-associate instructions versus instructions "to remember the list by imagining a relationship between the words in each pair"

(p. 424) was examined by Jonides, Kahn, and Rozin (1975) using word pairs high or low in rated imagery (and manual rather than oral responding). Both subject groups—but particularly the blind—and both word types profited significantly from imagery relative to standard instructions. The authors' conclusion that "imagery instructions have substantial mnemonic value in the absence of vision" (p. 425) seems reasonable in view of the fact that their imagery instructions could have evoked the generation of nonvisual mediators (e.g., auditory, tactile) in the blind. Trends in the data did show, however, that the advantage in learning high- relative to low-imagery words was almost twice as great for the sighted than the blind. Also, the sighted–blind difference (favoring the sighted) was clearly greater for high- than low-imagery words.

Marchant and Malloy's (1984) study also included an instruction variable— repetition followed by imagery instructions that emphasized the generation of visual, auditory, and tactile imagery. Word pairs were selected to be high in rated visual, auditory, or tactile imagery (and low in the other two modalities), or low in all three (i.e., abstract). Consistent with Jonides et al. (1975), imagery instructions enhanced recall for all word types and for both the blind and the sighted. However, the blind recalled significantly fewer visual words (but not other word types) than the sighted, regardless of instructions. Under repetition instructions, there was a tendency for the blind to recall more abstract than visual words and to recall auditory words best; that tendency was reversed for the sighted. However, no comparisons with abstract word recall were reported as significant for the blind or sighted.

Self-report data in the Marchant and Malloy (1984) study indicated that under imagery instructions the blind generated significantly fewer images to visual pairs than did the sighted and the proportion of all images generated by the blind that were judged to be visual was significantly lower than for the sighted when the word pairs were visual (10 vs. 33%) and auditory (5 vs. 19%) but not tactual (0 vs. 8%). The blind and sighted did not differ in the proportion of auditory or tactile images generated to the visual, auditory, or tactile word pairs. A final result of interest is the judged modality of the images generated to low-imagery or abstract words: the majority were tactile for the blind (34%) but visual for the sighted (18%).

A variant on the standard paired-associate procedure was used in recent studies by Kerr (1983, Exp. 3) and Zimler and Keenan (1983, Exp. 3). The task, first developed by Neisser and Kerr (1973), requires subjects to generate an image to pairs of sentences describing some scene. The second sentence of each pair always contains a "target" noun, which is subsequently and unexpectedly probed for recall by re-presenting the initial sentence. The main manipulation is the "location" of the target item in the scene described by the sentence. It can be a visible and central part of the scene (the "pictorial" condition), concealed or occluded, or separate and spatially distant from the scene described in the first sentence. For incidental cued recall, a type-of-imagery main effect emerged in both studies, although they disagreed on the locus of the differences [i.e., pictorial = concealed > separate in Kerr (1983); pictorial > separate = concealed in Zimler & Keenan (1983)]. More importantly, they agreed that the blind and sighted showed the same recall pattern under the different imagery conditions. Only Kerr (1983) reported that image generation times were significantly longer in the blind than the sighted, perhaps (as she suggested) because of two particularly slow subjects.

Three studies using the *free-recall* paradigm can be interpreted within the framework of the modality-specific imagery hypothesis. In Craig's (1973) study, lists of high-imagery words were recalled significantly better than low-imagery lists by both the blind and the sighted. However, the data did show that the sighted were more influenced by variations in word imagery than were the blind, and blind–sighted differences (favoring the sighted) were greater for high- than for low-imagery word lists (see also Jonides et al. 1975). The orienting task in Cornoldi's et al. (1979) study of incidental free recall required blind and sighted subjects to rate the image-evoking capacity of nouns from each of three categories: high-imagery words whose referents could have been experienced by the blind (e.g., stone), high-imagery words unlikely to have been experienced (e.g., tiger), and low-imagery or abstract words (e.g., piece). The rating data confirmed speculations that the images of the blind are based on nonvisual sensory experience and/or verbal knowledge (Bugelski, 1971; Paivio, 1971). A significant interaction revealed equivalent imagery ratings by the blind and sighted for high-imagery experienced words, higher ratings by the sighted for high-imagery nonexperienced words, and slightly higher ratings by the blind for abstract words. The lowest ratings by the blind were for high-imagery nonexperienced words; they were for abstract words by the sighted. Given the latter, it is interesting that the greatest blind–sighted difference in recall was for abstract words where the blind clearly excelled under incidental and, in a subsequent experiment, intentional recall. The sighted, on the other hand, were marginally superior in their recall of both high-imagery word types, particularly under incidental recall conditions.

Sighted individuals' relatively poor recall of words with auditory referents reported by Zimler and Keenan (1983) in their first experiment was replicated in their free-recall study (Exp. 2) using the same subjects. This study also examined the organizational strategies of the blind and sighted. The words in each list represented each of three attributes—the visual but nontangible attribute of red (e.g., cherry), the auditory attribute of loudness (e.g., thunder), and the combined visual and haptic attributes of roundness (e.g., wheel). As expected, the blind recalled significantly fewer "red" than "loud" words and the proportion of "loud" words recalled was significantly greater for the blind than the sighted, particularly children. Unexpectedly, the blind and sighted did not differ in their recall of "red" (or "round") words. Only the "red" category revealed differences between the blind and sighted in category labeling accuracy and clustering. Blind children were less able to identify the feature common to the "color" words, and in their recall they clustered "red" words less than sighted children. The fact that blind adults clustered "red" words more than sighted adults was unexpected. Nevertheless it did suggest to the authors that the "deficiency" experienced by blind children was not permanent but reflected a developmental lag in learning about the visual world through verbal instruction.

Summary and Comment

With the exception of the conceptual-peg corollary, most predictions derived from the modality-specific imagery hypothesis received some support, although frequently only as nonsignificant trends that were not necessarily discussed by the authors. With two exceptions (Paivio & Okovita, 1971, Exp. 2; Zimler & Keenan, 1983, Exp. 2), the blind were inferior, relative to the sighted, in their recall of highly visual words (Marchant & Malloy, 1984; Paivio & Okovita, 1971, Exp. 1; Zimler & Keenan, 1983, Exp. 1) and words high in imagery as defined by the Paivio et al. (1968) norms (Cornoldi et al., 1979; Craig, 1973; Jonides et al., 1975). Although the blind did show (nonsignificant) recall differences in response to variations in the (visual) image-evoking capacity of words, high–low recall differences tended to be greater in the sighted than the blind (Craig, 1973; Jonides et al., 1975; Marchant & Malloy, 1984). Consistent with the third prediction, the blind showed some (albeit weak) superiority in the recall of tactile word pairs (Marchant & Malloy, 1984) and auditory words or word pairs over their visual counterparts (Hans, 1974; Marchant & Malloy, 1984; Paivio & Okovita, 1971, Exp. 2; Zimler & Keenan, 1983, Exp. 2), Zimler and Keenan's (1983) first experiment excepted. Finally, although high–low variations in words' auditory imagery were reflected in recall differences for the sighted and particularly the blind in Paivio and Okovita (1971, Exp. 1), no such evidence was found in Marchant and Malloy (1984) for auditory or tactile words.

Rather unexpected was the difficulty experienced by the sighted in using auditory referential imagery as a coding device in memory. Except under circumstances where the sighted (and blind) were explicitly instructed to use auditory imagery (Marchant & Malloy, 1984, where the two groups were equivalent in auditory word recall), they neglected to use it to advantage (Paivio & Okovita, 1971, Exps. 1 & 2; Zimler & Keenan, 1983, Exps. 1 & 2). The blind also showed occasional facility with high-visual words, either relative to the sighted (Paivio & Okovita, 1971, Exp. 2), to high-auditory pairs (Zimler & Keenan, 1983, Exp. 1), or to pairs containing one auditory term (Hans, 1974). It is conceivable that some of these inconsistencies with the modality-specific imagery hypothesis or, indeed, some of the very weak effects in its support, can be attributed to variations across studies in the criteria used for selecting "imagery" words or for "matching" blind and sighted subjects.

Also unexpected were blind subjects' reports of visual imagery (Marchant & Malloy, 1984) and evidence that the blind and sighted profited similarly from instructions to use imagery in learning (Jonides et al., 1974; Kerr, 1983, Exp. 3; Marchant & Malloy, 1984; Zimler & Keenan, 1983; Exp. 3). Blind individuals' occasional reports of images judged to be visual led Marchant and Malloy (1984) to suggest that the cognitive systems used to create visual imagery are possibly intact in the blind, but lacking training or experience. Schlaegel (1953) also reported that a few of his subjects who were totally blind before the age of six reported visual images as the initial image to a series of words and phrases. However, subsequent interviews with these individuals persuaded Schlaegel that "what they meant by 'see' was not a visual image but that they thought of the characteristics of the object named" (p. 274). Bugelski (1971) and Johnson (1980) have also questioned the existence of visual images in their blind subjects. Bugelski (1971, p. 61) suggested that the blind "simply translated visual words into nonvisual ones" (e.g., "lightning" into "fast," "shadow" into "to follow," etc.). Johnson (1980) similarly questioned the meaning of his results when he found that the responses of blind (before the age of 1 year) and sighted adolescents to a measure of verbal originality did not differ in the incidence of visual images. He pondered whether "perhaps what the blind adolescents meant by 'see' may have been some characteristics of the particular word stimulus rather than a visual image" (p. 178). Despite these arguments, it should nevertheless be considered that some visual imagery may occur in the blind, even the congenitally blind, if they have minimal contrast or form perception (see Kerr, Foulkes, & Schmidt, 1982).

The mnemonic advantage to the blind of imagery instructions has been interpreted in several ways. Jonides et al. (1975) and Zimler and Keenan (1983, Exp. 1) suggested that the blind may engage in the elaboration of abstract or semantic representations. Kerr (1983, Exp. 3) emphasized the ability of the blind to encode the spatial and interactive (but not visual-pictorial) characteristics of a scene and suggested that these characteristics influenced recall not only in the blind but also in the sighted. On the other hand, Zimler and Keenan (1983, Exp. 3) proposed that the haptic images of the blind preserved the same information as the visual images of the sighted. All of these interpretations imply that the ability to use visual imagery is a sufficient but not a necessary cognitive requirement of "visual imagery" tasks.

Although direct, tangible experience with nouns' referents seems to define their image-evoking capacity for both the blind and sighted (Cornoldi et al., 1979), such experience appears not to be necessary for the development of color concepts (see Zimler & Keenan, 1983, Exp. 2). This result confirms Marmor's (1978) findings that "lack of visual experience need not preclude an accurate understanding of color relations" (p. 275). In this study, early blind, late blind, and sighted college students rank ordered, on the basis of similarity, 36 pairs of color names derived from the nine colors comprising the color spectrum. Using multidimensional scaling techniques, a two-dimensional color space summarized the rankings for all three groups. When asked what strategies they used in their ranking, 31% of the early blind, 25% of the late blind, and 44% of the sighted reported using a "spectral model" (e.g., rainbow). The performance of these subjects, however, could not be distinguished from nonspectral model subjects. The early blind reported learning about colors from "chance conversations in which colorful objects and events like rubies and sunsets were discussed, and conversations about how to dress to please the sighted public" (Marmor, 1978, p. 224).

However, Marmor also suggests that other potential sources of information about color relations include books, school curricula, dictionary definitions, and grammar (e.g., "bluish"). Her point that "judging the similarities between color could become a simple logical exercise" (p. 277) is reinforced by her finding that WAIS verbal intelligence test scores (but not sex or age at onset of blindness) significantly predicted the variance accounted for by a two-dimensional solution for all three groups of individuals.

Haptic Memory for Figural-Spatial Information

The first section of this review concentrated on the learning and memory literature in which linguistic stimuli varied predominantly in their visual and/or auditory image-evoking capacities. Memory for nonlinguistic information acquired through the sensory modality of touch is the focus of the present section. The relevant literature is organized around the two paradigms of recognition memory and mental rotation. The first subsection examines recognition memory for unfamiliar shapes whose features are acquired only through haptic (i.e., touch and movement) exploration, whereas the second subsection primarily examines memory for shapes (familiar or unfamiliar) that vary in their orientation from the upright. As before, the self-reported and inferred strategies of the blind and sighted are emphasized, when such evidence is reported. The general findings in this section are that the speed or accuracy advantage of the blind found in the recognition memory studies occasionally becomes a speed or accuracy disadvantage in the orientation or rotation studies. Also, although the strategies of the blind and sighted may not differ appreciably when based on self-reports, they do when strategies are inferred or observed from performance.

Recognition Memory

It seems reasonable to assume that, relative to sighted individuals, tactile memory for shape should be equivalent or even enhanced in the blind by virtue of their greater experience in encoding such information haptically. However, if tactile encoding is more efficient in the blind (or if tactual inputs are recoded visually by the sighted), the blind may be expected to suffer greater *modality-specific interference* than the sighted if required to engage in some irrelevant tactile task while holding relevant tactile information in memory. The phenomenon of modality-specific interference has been amply demonstrated in the visual and auditory modalities (see Brooks, 1968; Segal & Fusella, 1970) and is interpreted to mean that similar mental mechanisms underlie imaging and perceiving. In short, if one's memory images are haptic, their retrieval may be interfered with more by a concurrent (and irrelevant) haptic task than one tapping a different modality. The findings, in preview, suggest that any retention differences favoring the blind may be most evident under difficult response conditions. The findings also provide no evidence of differential interference effects in the blind and sighted.

Millar (1974), for example, reported "enhancement" in the blind in the form of shorter response latencies in a yes–no comparison task, but no evidence for relatively greater modality-specific interference (or facilitation). In one experiment (Millar, 1974, Exp. 1), blind and sighted 9½ to 10 year olds explored three-dimensional nonsense shapes tactually (in a closed unit) followed by immediate responding or 5, 10, or 30 sec of unfilled delays or "distractor" activities. The faster response latencies of the blind were accompanied by more errors, but error rates were too low to permit analysis. Interference occurred in the sense that responses were significantly slower when intervals were filled with movement distractors (i.e., barrel nesting) than movement rehearsal (i.e., finger tracing the standard) but modality-specific effects were not obtained. That is, movement rehearsal latencies were not facilitative relative to unfilled delays and verbal distractors (i.e., counting backwards) were not less disrupting than movement distractors. Nevertheless, the effects obtained were true for both the blind and sighted. A similar pattern emerged with even younger children (Exp. 3), whose correct response latencies were significantly faster than the sighted but whose errors were now significantly greater, particularly in the 10-sec condition. Although verbal and movement distractors led to more errors than the other two conditions, the effect again was common to both the blind and the sighted. Millar (1974) dismissed the apparent speed–accuracy tradeoff in her studies as reflecting either visual recoding by the sighted or a retention superiority by the blind. Instead she attributed it to response strategy differences, that is, a speed bias in the blind given their greater acquaintance with "relatively slow tactile inputs" (p. 263).

The absence of differential interference effects has also been reported by Hampson and Duffy (1984) using a haptic version of Brooks' (1968) selective interference task. Subjects categorized the corners of memorized abstract shapes as top/bottom or middle (for example) by responding "yes" or "no" either verbally, spatially (by typing), or by tapping. Although modality-specific interference occurred in the expected fashion, it occurred regardless of whether the adolescent subjects were sighted, blindfolded sighted, or blind. Interestingly, the sighted who explored the shapes visually rather than tactually yielded somewhat longer response times than the other two groups, who did not differ.

Contrary to Millar's (1974) speculations, retention differences favoring the blind have indeed been found when variations in task difficulty are introduced. Davidson, Barnes, and Mullen (1974) gave blindfolded sighted and blind adolescents three-dimensional unfamiliar forms to explore with their preferred hand. When the subsequent matching task included three comparison figures (standard + two lures), the blind and sighted did not differ in accuracy. However, under the more difficult task of selecting from among five comparison figures, significantly fewer errors were made by the blind. Davidson et al. (1974) speculated that the blind may use more efficient haptic scanning strategies than the sighted in unfamiliar form matching.

Summary and Comment

The evidence from these few recognition memory studies favors "enhancement" more than "equivalence" when comparing the blinds' tactually derived memories of shape with those of the sighted. The memory advantage experienced by the blind under difficult response conditions (Davidson et al., 1974) replicates that of Davidson and Whitson (1974) using a curvature matching task in which the number of comparison items was one, three, or five. The blind made significantly fewer errors than the sighted in the more difficult three- and five-item comparison conditions. Davidson's et al. (1974) speculation that the haptic scanning strategies of the blind may be more efficient than the sighted was based on previous evidence from Davidson (1972) and Davidson and Whitson (1974). In these studies, not only were the blind more accurate than the sighted in their judgments of curvature, but they used predominantly a scanning strategy called "gripping," a strategy that significantly improved the performance of sighted subjects when they were instructed to use it, particularly in the more difficult comparison conditions (Davidson & Whitson, 1974). Davidson (1972) described the gripping strategy of the blind in curvature matching as permitting a global, simultaneous apprehension of stimulus features, whereas the strategies of the sighted were more oriented to the successive examination of stimulus attributes.

Hampson's and Duffy's conclusion that "the organization of features within objects can be learned in a similar fashion and result in equivalent representations in the blind and sighted" (1984, p. 419) is consistent with Kerr's (1983, Exp. 2) results concerning the mental representations of common objects in the blind and sighted. Using a variation of Kosslyn's (1975, Exp. 1) image-scanning task, subjects imaged familiar "target" objects (e.g., breadbox) in their appropriate size relative to a small or large object (paperclip or car). The task was to indicate whether a named property was or was not part of the target. Although response times tended to be longer for the congenitally blind than the sighted — perhaps because of the sighted's verbal and haptic prior knowledge of the objects — responses were significantly longer to relatively small targets for both groups. Based on young children's descriptions of common objects, Anderson (1984) has similarly concluded that the blinds' mental images of objects do not deviate from those acquired by the sighted through vision.

Although neither blind children nor adolescents experienced more modality-specific interference than their sighted counterparts in the studies reviewed above, there is evidence that the blind may suffer greater interference under nonfigural recall conditions. Millar (1975) had children reproduce a "near" and "far" location on a five-sided open maze. The relative difficulty of the blind in reproducing the more distant position, regardless of recall starting point, led her to infer that the sighted used visual representations in performing the task, whereas the blind "relied on haptic memory which decays with time or is interfered with by subsequent movements" (p. 456). Further, Shagan and Goodnow (1973) have shown that reproductions of distance by the blind (males and females) are more negatively affected by an intervening digit classification task than is found in the sighted, particularly sighted males. Even in the absence of an intervening task, however, the blind tend to have difficulty reproducing distance information (as reflected in arm movement responses) both relative to the sighted (Hermelin & O'Connor, 1975; Shagan & Goodnow, 1973) and to the blind who have had visual experience (Colley & Colley, 1981). Although the blinds' relatively poor motor or movement memory has been attributed to their inability to use visual images as mediators, other explanations emphasize the role of prior visual experience in the establishment of an external (rather than egocentric) frame of reference (see Dodds & Carter, 1983, for a recent statement of this position). These views are particularly relevant to the literature on mental rotation in the blind and sighted, which follows.

Mental Rotation

Mental rotation tasks typically are comparison tasks in which judgments of the identity of two forms are made under circumstances where the forms differ in their spatial orientation. The two forms may be physically present (e.g., Shepard & Metzler, 1971) or one of them may be retrieved from semantic memory under those circumstances where the forms are highly familiar (e.g., single letter). Performing such tasks is assumed typically to require the mental manipulation of images in two- or three-dimensional space, although other interpretations have been proposed. Behavioral measures of mental rotation phenomena emphasize either accuracy (e.g., the Mental Rotations Group Test, Vandenberg & Kuse, 1978) or response latencies in making correct judgments (e.g., Shepard & Metzler, 1971), frequently in relation to the degree of angular disparity between the standard and the comparison figures.

The central question addressed here is whether the absence of sight, and presumably of visual images, quantitatively and/or qualitatively influences the performance of the blind on such tasks. A negative quantitative influence would be defined as more errors or longer latencies or both; a qualitative difference would be defined as the absence of the typical (i.e., sighted) function relating angular discrepancy or orientation to performance. In general, the results reported here suggest that congenital blindness does not preclude responding in "typical" fashion but that having or having had visual experience does make mental rotation, or judgments based on orientation, easier.

These were the conclusions of Marmor and Zaback (1976) whose response latency task was a tactile variation of the classic Shepard and Metzler (1971) paradigm. Pairs of simple cone-shaped stimuli, with a "bite" missing, were simultaneously presented to the left and right hands. The left-hand stimulus was always in an upright (i.e., 0°) position, whereas the right-hand stimulus could be presented at 0° or rotated to 30°, 60°, 120°, or 150° in a clockwise direction. For early blind subjects (blind before 6 months), errors were significantly greater and response latencies at the unrotated position longer than for the late blind (after 6 years) or (blindfolded) sighted, who differed little. Although all groups showed significant linear increases in reaction time (RT) as a function of the angular discrepancy between stimuli, they differed in speed of mental rotation; early blind rotated at a rate of 59° per second, which differed significantly from the late blind (114° per sec) and sighted (233° per sec), who did not differ. Evidence that mental rotation was indeed involved was reinforced by the subjective reports of all groups (i.e., 69% of the sighted, 94% of the late blind, and 63% of the early blind), although the absence of such reports was not reflected in different response patterns. Interestingly, a few subjects (sighted and early blind) reported using a verbal rule or logical reversal strategy similar to Just and Carpenter's (1985) orientation-free description. This was used as well as, or instead of, mental rotation.

Only a single highly familiar stimulus was used in Carpenter and Eisenberg's (1978) mental rotation task. The single letters P and F were presented at orientations from 0° to 300° in 60° steps. Blind students participated in experiment 1 and (blindfolded) sighted students in experiment 3. Error rates were low for both groups, who yielded reaction times that significantly increased from 0° to 180° and then decreased to 300°. Although data from the two experiments were not analyzed together, the blind were generally faster responders (particularly at 0°) and the *RT* functions of the sighted showed greater curvilinearity. This was reflected particularly in small *RT* differences between the 0° and 60° rotations. Carpenter and Eisenberg (1978) suggested that this may have resulted from the sighted's greater familiarity with letters that are not perfectly upright. However, other evidence (from Carpenter and Eisenberg's Exp. 4) suggested that the sighted used different frames of reference in making their judgments than did the blind. For example, some of the curvilinearity in the sighted *RT* functions could be attributed to varying their frame of reference as a function of initial hand position, whereas hand position was not a factor for the blind. Carpenter and Eisenberg suggest that "perhaps the body or cues on the table or in the room" (p. 123) serve as the frame of reference for the blind.

With respect to strategies, the self-reports of subjects were similar to those reported by Marmor and Zaback (1976). The majority of the sighted and blind reported mentally rotating or "twisting" the letters in their minds, although some made their decisions on the basis of an analysis of stimulus features. The *RT* functions of those reporting nonrotation or orientation-free strategies (two of the blind and one of the sighted) did not, however, differ from those using a mental rotation strategy.

The accuracy studies of rotation or orientation phenomena that follow are of two types—those in which subjects must identify or haptically recognize the correct response, and those requiring its reproduction. Experiments by O'Connor and Hermelin (1975) represent the first type. In one experiment, subjects haptically (or visually) explored two shapes and attempted to identify the form that would result if they were juxtaposed. Half of the time one of the shapes had to be rotated mentally 180° before a decision could be made. Only the unblindfolded sighted, who made significantly fewer errors than the blind and blindfolded sighted, were influenced by the rotation variable. However, both the blind and blindfolded sighted behaved similarly when the input was tactual.

Although these results suggested to the authors that the touch modality was less sensitive to orientation features than the visual modality (see also Pick, Klein, & Pick, 1966), other studies suggested otherwise. In their second experiment, for example, subjects judged whether a plastic hand presented in one of six orientations, covering two dimensions, was a left or right hand. The blind and blindfolded tactually explored each stimulus; the sighted simply looked at the stimulus. The three groups differed significantly in errors in the order of blind, blindfolded, and sighted. Although the orientation factor was significant, there was no interaction with subject groups. O'Connor and Hermelin suggested that the availability of visual schemata, such as would exist in the blindfolded and the sighted, clearly enhances performance, although not differentially with respect to orientation.

Adult subjects tactually explored random shapes with either the left or right hand in Dodds' (1983) study and subsequently attempted to select the target from an array of three shapes. Orientation differences between the target and its comparison proved to influence performance significantly, with accuracy generally declining from 0° to 315°; sightedness, however, was not significant, nor did it interact with orientation. Sightedness did interact with the hand used for exploration, however. Although the adventitiously (or late) blind, congenitally blind, and sighted (who were matched for handedness) did not differ when the right hand was used, the sighted were significantly more accurate than the combined blind groups when tactual exploration involved the left hand. The interaction also reflected a right-hand superiority in the two blind groups but a left-hand superiority in the sighted. Given the preferential access of the left hand to the right (spatial) hemisphere of the brain, and the right hand to the left (verbal) hemisphere, Dodds (1983) speculated that sighted subjects likely used a mixed strategy in performing the task—a spatial strategy with the left hand and a verbal labeling strategy with the right hand—whereas the blind groups used a consistent verbal strategy regardless of hand. Although other interpretations are possible (see "Summary and Comment" section below), the important result for present purposes is that orientation effects were similar in the blind and the sighted.

In one of Millar's (1976) experiments, headed matchsticks were presented in one of eight orientations (0° to 315° in 45° steps) to three age groups of totally blind and (blindfolded) sighted children. Subjects' task was to feel the standard on each trial and select it from among eight alternatives. This recognition task was followed by a more difficult Piaget-type perspective change task in which a standard matchstick was always presented vertically, but subjects had to select from the alternatives the one the standard would look like if it were to be viewed from each of seven locations around the table (45° to 315° in 45° steps). Age and task yielded significant effects; sightedness did not. Also, although degree of rotation significantly influenced accuracy, it was not in the direction of increased errors with further test positions. Instead, orthogonals (i.e., 90°, 180°, 270°) were easier than obliques, regardless of age, task, or sightedness. Age of onset of blindness did prove to be important, however, in the one group where it could be examined. When data from the oldest group (mean age of 10 years) were analyzed separately, the late blind (occurring between 2 and 6 years) did significantly better than the early blind (from birth) on the perspective change task, but there were no differences on the recognition task. Thus, the prior visual experiences of the blind proved to be important for overall accuracy in a perspective change task, perhaps because (as reported by Millar) these individuals often report actively attempting to maintain information in memory visually (see also Marmor & Zaback, 1976). This "visual" effect nevertheless occurred independently of degree of rotation.

Millar (1976) used a reproduction index of memory in her second experiment. In a rotation task, a square base containing a raised vertical line was rotated clockwise between the palms of subjects' hands. When it reached one of seven test positions (45° to 315°), the subject's task was to imagine, and draw, the direction of the line. A perspective move task required subjects to move physically to one of the seven test positions around the table before reproducing the vertical line's direction. The most important result for present purposes was that sighted subjects' performance was not influenced by degree of rotation whereas the blinds' was. Although the blind did not differ significantly from the sighted on orthogonals, they did significantly worse on the oblique test positions. The blind also had more difficulty with far than near orthogonal test positions.

Cleaves and Royal (1979) also used a reproduction form of recall. Their adult subjects—who were either congenitally blind, late blind (after 11 years), or sighted—learned two simple finger T mazes, each with three direction changes, and a five-turn complex maze. Subsequently, subjects pointed to the location of the goal, the first turn, and the second turn, the nonpointing finger always in the start hole "as a stable reference point" (p. 15). Pointing was done under each of three conditions: imagining the maze in the same (unrotated) plane as during the learning trials, rotated left to right through its vertical axis (horizontal rotation), or "flipped downward" around its horizontal axis (vertical rotation). The three subject groups did not differ in the number of trials to criterion in the learning phase of the task, although the congenitally blind did take significantly longer to track each maze, with the late blind the fastest (significantly) of all. Localization displacement errors were significantly greater in the congenitally blind than the other two groups. However, both the early blind and the sighted found the vertical rotation condition the most difficult, followed by the horizontal and unrotated conditions; their error patterns were essentially identical (i.e., no interaction). The late blind, with the lowest error magnitude of all, were significantly better than the sighted in the vertical rotation condition only; their horizontal and vertical errors did not differ.

Summary and Comment

The similarities between the blind and sighted in rotation tasks are more striking than the differences, and the differences that do emerge seem to represent primarily quantitative rather than qualitative differences in performance. For example, the blind occasionally made more errors in their judgments than the blindfolded sighted (Cleaves & Royal, 1979; Marmor & Zaback, 1976; Millar, 1976, Exp. 2; O'Connor & Hermelin, 1975, Exp. 2), but not usually (Carpenter & Eisenberg, 1978; Dodds, 1983; Millar, 1976, Exp. 1; O'Connor & Hermelin, 1975, Exp. 1). The basis for some of the inconsistency is not immediately clear. Marmor and Zaback's (1976) requirement that their subjects use both hands simultaneously in tactually scanning pairs of shapes may be relevant given Dodds' (1983) evidence for a left-hand inefficiency in the blind when exploring shapes, as might O'Connor and Hermelin's task requirement that subjects distinguish left from right.

Dodds (1983) had dismissed the left hand inefficiency of the blind as reflecting "the right hemisphere's failure to develop spatial processing functions as a consequence of the absence of visual input since the right-hand superiority of the adventitiously blinded group was equal to that of the congenitally blind group" (p. 17). Nevertheless, the relatively poor left-hand performance of the blind may reflect less efficient right-hemispheric figural-spatial processing than in the sighted given recent dichotic listening evidence that the congenitally blind (particularly adults) process linguistic information equally well in the right as in the left hemisphere of the brain (Karavatos, Kaprinis, & Tzavaras, 1984; Larsen & Hakonsen, 1983). Karavatos et al. attributed this "bilateralization" of language effect to efficiency with the braille system because the learning and reading of braille seems to be predominantly a right-hemisphere activity (Hermelin & O'Connor, 1971a, 1971b; Rudel, Denckla, & Spalten, 1974). Importantly, Dodds' blind subjects were all competent braille readers.

Some inconsistencies also emerged in the rotation task latency measures. The response latencies of the blind were faster than the sighted when the task required the retrieval of highly overlearned stimuli (e.g., letters) from semantic memory (Carpenter & Eisenberg, 1978), but slower when simultaneously received haptic inputs had to be compared (Marmor & Zaback, 1976). Importantly, the (early) blind and blindfolded sighted responded similarly to the rotation or orientation factor (Carpenter & Eisenberg, 1978; Dodds, 1983; Marmor & Zaback, 1976; Millar, 1976, Exp. 1; O'Connor & Hermelin, 1975) but with one exception—when the blind had to reconstruct oblique positions in space (Millar, 1976, Exp. 2). This result reinforces Carpenter and Eisenberg's (1978) speculation that the frame of reference used by the blind and sighted as a mnemonic device may differ.

Indeed, research relevant to the processes involved in coding spatial position suggests that the frame of reference of the blind is egocentric or self-referent; it tends to be externally based for the sighted or for those who have had the experience of sight (Millar, 1979, 1981). Millar (1979), for example, reported that, contrary to the sighted or to the blind with minimal visual experience, congenitally totally blind children failed to use external cues as aids in moving small objects from their positions on a background geometric form to the same locations on a nearby identical form; this failure to use external cues occurred even when the salience of the forms was increased. Millar argued that "visual experience affects coding by drawing attention to external cues, and by providing more adequate spatial information than other sources usually available to the blind. In its absence, movement coding and self-reference can become preferred strategies" (p. 11). The blinds' preference for self-referent coding strategies is, however, even more broadly apparent. It is apparent in their mental representations of the environment (Byrne & Salter, 1983; Dodds, Howarth, & Carter, 1982); in their mental representations of common objects, for which the blind verbally report significantly more egocentric (but not perceptual or functional) attributes than the sighted (Anderson, 1984); and in their dreams, which are set more frequently in known than in novel locations in the congenitally blind (Kerr et al., 1982).

Final Comments

Three general but not necessarily independent conclusions can be drawn from this review. First, and as suggested by the modality-specific imagery hypothesis, auditory imagery is a more effective mediator of verbal recall for the congenitally or early blind than is visual imagery. Moreover, the efficacy of auditory imagery is greater in the blind than the sighted, whereas the sighted use visual imagery as a mediator of recall more effectively than do the blind. Second, haptic memory in the blind is at least equivalent, if not superior, to that of the sighted unless the task involves a spatial rotation component; then the advantage of having normal visual experience is clearly facilitative. Third, the inferred strategies of the blind and sighted are more different than they are similar. In the sighted they are primarily visual and externally derived; in the blind they are predominantly auditory, kinaesthetic, and based on internal cues. Indeed, the strategies of the blind may be generally described as self-referent.

Self-reference as a coding device in memory is not new. The self-reference effect in the sighted (Rogers, Kuiper, & Kirker, 1977) refers to the fact that words judged for the appropriateness of their descriptions of oneself are remembered better than words judged on some other basis, such as their meaning. Bellezza (1984) has interpreted this effect to mean that "the self provides a set of organized internal cues in the form of personal experiences that can mediate recall" (p. 506). In the present context, however, the congenitally blinds' self-referent rather than external frame of reference for coding spatial information such as orientation appears to be detrimental, not facilitative, to performance.

The present review nevertheless also suggests that the dominance of the visual modality in the sighted may limit their access to the mnemonic potential of other sensory modalities, such as the auditory and tactual–kinaesthetic. Indeed, research on the mnemonic effectiveness of kinaesthetic or motor imagery in the sighted is rather sparse. Although Aylwin (1977) has suggested that visual and kinaesthetic imagery tap different aspects of the semantic memory system, recent work by Saltz (see Saltz & Donnenwerth-Nolan, 1981) is particularly encouraging in its *comparison* of visual and motor imagery in memory. In Saltz and Donnenwerth-Nolan (1981), both visualization and active motor enactment significantly (and independently) enhanced subjects' memory for sentences over a control condition, although visual imagery was mnemonically more effective than motoric imagery. The authors proposed a "specificity-distinctiveness" explanation for the facilitation following motor enactment—that is, "since motor imagery is assumed to be part of the meaning of many verbal concepts, the enactment of the appropriate motoric responses should increase the specificity with which these concepts are registered" (p. 331). This explanation may also be pertinent to Ernest's (1983a) report of small but significant correlations (for males only) between self-ratings of kinaesthetic imagery vividness and recognition memory for concrete words. In this study, no other imagery modalities, including the visual, yielded significant correlations. Regardless of their interpretation, these studies suggest a potential avenue for further research in the sighted, as well as the blind.

References to sex differences have been rare in this review. Given the writer's long-standing research interest in this area, the omission has not been deliberate. Many authors of both the "core" and "related" papers discussed here reported the sex of their subjects, and some matched their blind and sighted subjects on this factor. However, their analyses did not include an examination of sex differences within the two groups, with but three exceptions. Marmor and Zaback (1976) reported a significant Sex × Rotations interaction for the sighted but not the blind in one of their analyses, although the nature of the interaction was not described. In their study on the effects of an intervening task on the reproduction of arm movements, Shagan and Goodnow (1973) reported that sighted females' performance was more similar to that of the blind (male and female) than of sighted males. No sex differences emerged for the blind in Larsen and Hakonsen's (1983) dichotic listening study but a trend (direction unspecified) did emerge for the sighted.

If further research should reveal that sex differences do exist in the blind, and in a manner similar to those reported for the sighted, one might expect to find a female superiority on learning and memory tasks (Ernest, 1983a; Maccoby & Jacklin, 1974); a male superiority on mental rotation tasks (Kail, Carter, & Pellegrino, 1979; Tapley & Bryden, 1977); and sex differences in the use of organizational strategies (Cox & Waters, 1986), spatial problem-solving strategies (Allen & Hogeland, 1978; Linn & Petersen, 1985), and in the lateralization of brain function (Ernest, 1983b; McGlone, 1980). On the other hand, if there is a relative absence of sex differences in the blind, this has important implications for the interpretation of cognitive sex differences in the sighted. For example, although there are several biologically oriented explanations for sex differences in spatial ability (see McGee, 1979), environmental interpretations include differences in child-rearing practices, such as the greater encouragement of exploratory activity for boys than girls (Sherman, 1978). Clearly the blind, both male and female, are limited in their physical interactions with the environment.

Acknowledgments. Preparation of this chapter was supported by a grant from Trent University's Committee to Aid Research in the Sciences (NSERC funds).

I am grateful to Susan Lederman for her comments on an earlier draft of the manuscript and to Mike Pressley and Mark McDaniel for their editorial guidance and constructive criticisms.

References

Allen, M. J., & Hogeland, R. (1978). Spatial problem-solving strategies as functions of sex. *Perceptual and Motor Skills, 47*, 348–350.

Anderson, D. W. (1984). Mental imagery in congenitally blind children. *Journal of Visual Impairment and Blindness, 78*, 206–210.

Aylwin, S. (1977). The structure of visual and kinaesthetic imagery: A free association study. *British Journal of Psychology, 68*, 353–360.

Bellezza, F. S. (1984). The self as a mnemonic device: The role of internal cues. *Journal of Personality and Social Psychology, 47*, 506–516.

Brooks, L. R. (1968). Spatial and verbal components of the act of recall. *Canadian Journal of Psychology, 22*, 349–368.

Bugelski, B. R. (1971). The definition of the image. In S. J. Segal (Ed.), *Imagery: Current cognitive approaches* (pp. 49–68). New York: Academic Press.

Byrne, R. W., & Salter, E. (1983). Distances and directions in the cognitive maps of the blind. *Canadian Journal of Psychology, 37*, 293–299.

Carpenter, P. A., & Eisenberg, P. (1978). Mental rotation and the frame of reference in blind and sighted individuals. *Perception and Psychophysics, 23*, 117–124.

Cleaves, W. T., & Royal, R. W. (1979). Spatial memory for configurations by congenitally blind, late blind, and sighted adults. *Journal of Visual Impairment and Blindness, 73*, 13–19.

Colley, A., & Colley, M. (1981). Reproduction of end-location and distance of movement in early and later blinded subjects. *Journal of Motor Behavior, 13*, 102–109.

Cornoldi, C., Calore, D., & Pra-Baldi, A. (1979). Imagery ratings and recall in congenitally blind subjects. *Perceptual and Motor Skills, 48*, 627–639.

Cox, D., & Waters, H. S. (1986). Sex differences in the use of organization strategies: A developmental analysis. *Journal of Experimental Child Psychology, 41*, 18–37.

Craig, E. M. (1973). Role of mental imagery in free recall of deaf, blind, and normal subjects. *Journal of Experimental Psychology, 97*, 249–253.

Davidson, P. W. (1972). Haptic judgments of curvature by blind and sighted humans. *Journal of Experimental Psychology, 93*, 43–55.

Davidson, P. W., Barnes, J. K., & Mullen, G. (1974). Differential effects of task memory demand on haptic matching of shape by blind and sighted humans. *Neuropsychologia, 12*, 395–397.

Davidson, P. W., & Whitson, T. T. (1974). Haptic equivalence matching of curvature by blind and sighted humans. *Journal of Experimental Psychology, 102*, 687–690.

Dodds, A. G. (1983). Mental rotation and visual imagery. *Journal of Visual Impairment and Blindness, 77*, 16–18.

Dodds, A. G., & Carter, D. D. (1983). Memory for movement in blind children: The role of previous visual experience. *Journal of Motor Behavior, 15*, 343–352.

Dodds, A. G., Howarth, C. I., & Carter, D. C. (1982). The mental maps of the blind: The role of previous visual experience. *Journal of Visual Impairment and Blindness, 76*, 5–12.

Ernest, C. H. (1977). Imagery ability and cognition: A critical review. *Journal of Mental Imagery, 1*, 181–216.

Ernest, C. H. (1983a). Imagery and verbal ability and recognition memory for pictures and words in males and females. *Educational Psychology*, *3*, 277–244.

Ernest, C. H. (1983b). Spatial-imagery ability, sex differences, and hemispheric functioning. In J. C. Yuille (Ed.), *Imagery, memory and cognition: Essays in honor of Allan Paivio* (pp. 1–38). Hillsdale, NJ: Erlbaum Associates.

Hampson, P. J., & Duffy, C. (1984). Verbal and spatial interference effects in congenitally blind and sighted subjects. *Canadian Journal of Psychology*, *38*, 411–420.

Hans, M. A. (1974). Imagery and modality in paired-associate learning in the blind. *Bulletin of the Psychonomic Society*, *4*, 22–24.

Hermelin, B., & O'Connor, N. (1971a). Right and left handed reading of braille. *Nature*(London), *231*, 470.

Hermelin, B., & O'Connor, N. (1971b). Functional asymmetry in the reading of braille. *Neuropsychologia*, *9*, 431–435.

Hermelin, B., & O'Connor, N. (1975). Location and distance estimates by blind and sighted children. *Quarterly Journal of Experimental Psychology*, *27*, 295–301.

Johnson, R. A. (1980). Sensory images in the absence of sight: Blind versus sighted adolescents. *Perceptual and Motor Skills*, *51*, 177–178.

Jonides, J., Kahn, R., & Rozin, P. (1975). Imagery instructions improve memory in blind subjects. *Bulletin of the Psychonomic Society*, *5*, 424–426.

Just, M. A., & Carpenter, P. A. (1985). Cognitive coordinate systems: Accounts of mental rotation and individual differences in spatial ability. *Psychological Review*, *92*, 137–172.

Kail, R., Carter, P., & Pellegrino, J. (1979). The locus of sex differences in spatial ability. *Perception and Psychophysics*, *26*, 182–186.

Karavatos, A., Kaprinis, G., & Tzavaras, A. (1984). Hemispheric specialization for language in the congenitally blind: The influence of the braille system. *Neuropsychologia*, *22*, 521–525.

Kerr, N. H. (1983). The role of vision in "visual imagery" experiments: Evidence from the congenitally blind. *Journal of Experimental Psychology: General*, *112*, 265–277.

Kerr, N. H., Foulkes, D., & Schmidt, M. (1982). The structure of laboratory dream reports in blind and sighted subjects. *Journal of Nervous and Mental Disease*, *170*, 286–294.

Kosslyn, S. M. (1975). Information representation in visual images. *Cognitive Psychology*, *7*, 341–370.

Larsen, S., & Hakonsen, K. (1983). Absence of ear asymmetry in blind children on a dichotic listening task compared to sighted controls. *Brain and Language*, *18*, 192–198.

Linn, M. C., & Petersen, A. C. (1985). Emergence and characterization of sex differences in spatial ability: A meta-analysis. *Child Development*, *56*, 1479–1498.

Maccoby, E. E., & Jacklin, C. N. (1974). *The psychology of sex differences*. Stanford, CA: Stanford University Press.

Marchant, B., & Malloy, T. E. (1984). Auditory, tactile and visual imagery in PA learning by congenitally blind, deaf, and normal adults. *Journal of Mental Imagery*, *8*, 19–32.

Marmor, G. S. (1978). Age at onset of blindness and the development of the semantics of color names. *Journal of Experimental Child Psychology*, *25*, 267–278.

Marmor, G. S., & Zaback, L. A. (1976). Mental rotation by the blind: Does mental rotation depend on visual imagery? *Journal of Experimental Psychology: Human Perception and Performance*, *2*, 515–521.

McGee, M. G. (1979). Human spatial abilities: Psychometric studies and environmental, genetic, hormonal, and neurological influences. *Psychological Bulletin*, *86*, 889–918.

McGlone, J. (1980). Sex differences in human brain asymmetry: A critical survey. *The Behavioral and Brain Sciences, 3*, 215–263.

Millar, S. (1974). Tactile short-term memory by blind and sighted children. *British Journal of Psychology, 65*, 253–263.

Millar, S. (1975). Spatial memory by blind and sighted children. *British Journal of Psychology, 66*, 449–459.

Millar, S. (1976). Spatial representation by blind and sighted children. *Journal of Experimental Child Psychology, 21*, 460–479.

Millar, S. (1979). The utilization of external and movement cues in simple spatial tasks by blind and sighted children. *Perception, 8*, 11–20.

Millar, S. (1981). Self-referent and movement cues in coding spatial location by blind and sighted children. *Perception, 10*, 255–264.

Neisser, U., & Kerr, N. (1973). Spatial and mnemonic properties of visual images. *Cognitive Psychology, 5*, 138–150.

O'Connor, N., & Hermelin, B. (1975). Modality-specific spatial coordinates. *Perception and Psychophysics, 17*, 213–216.

Paivio, A. (1971). *Imagery and verbal processes.* New York: Holt, Rinehart, & Winston.

Paivio, A. (1983). The empirical case for dual coding. In J. C. Yuille (Ed.), *Imagery, memory and cognition: Essays in honor of Allan Paivio* (pp. 307–332). Hillsdale, NJ: Erlbaum Associates.

Paivio, A., & Okovita, H. W. (1971). Word imagery modalities and associative learning in blind and sighted subjects. *Journal of Verbal Learning and Verbal Behavior, 10*, 506–510.

Paivio, A., Yuille, J. C., & Madigan, S. A. (1968). Concreteness, imagery, and meaningfulness values for 925 nouns. *Journal of Experimental Psychology Monograph Supplement, 76*(1, Pt. 2), 1–25.

Pick, H. L., Klein, R. E., & Pick, A. D. (1966). Visual and tactual identification of form orientation. *Journal of Experimental Child Psychology, 4*, 391–397.

Rogers, T. B., Kuiper, N. A., & Kirker, W. S. (1977). Self-reference and the encoding of personal information. *Journal of Personality and Social Psychology, 35*, 677–688.

Rudel, R. G., Denckla, M. B., & Spalten, E. (1974). The functional asymmetry of braille letter learning in normal, sighted children. *Neurology, 24*, 733–738.

Saltz, E., & Donnenwerth-Nolan, S. (1981). Does motoric imagery facilitate memory for sentences? A selective interference test. *Journal of Verbal Learning and Verbal Behavior, 20*, 322–332.

Schlaegel, T. F. (1953). The dominant method of imagery in blind as compared to sighted adolescents. *Journal of Genetic Psychology, 83*, 265–277.

Segal, S. J., & Fusella, V. (1970). Influence of imaged pictures and sounds on detection of visual and auditory signals. *Journal of Experimental Psychology, 83*, 458–464.

Shagan, J., & Goodnow, J. (1973). Recall of haptic information by blind and sighted individuals. *Journal of Experimental Psychology, 101*, 221–226.

Shepard, R. N., & Metzler, J. (1971). Mental rotation of three-dimensional objects. *Science, 171*, 701–703.

Sherman, J. A. (1978). *Sex-related cognitive differences.* Springfield, IL: Charles C Thomas.

Sholl, M. J., & Easton, R. D. (1986). Effect of referent object familiarity on verbal learning in the sighted and the blind. *Journal of Experimental Psychology: Learning, Memory, and Cognition, 12*, 190–200.

Tapley, S. M., & Bryden, M. P. (1977). An investigation of sex differences in spatial ability: Mental rotation of three-dimensional objects. *Canadian Journal of Psychology, 31*, 122–130.

Vandenberg, S. G., & Kuse, A. R. (1978). Mental rotations, a group test of three-dimensional spatial visualization. *Perceptual and Motor Skills, 47*, 599–604.

Yuille, J. C., & Barnsley, R. H. (1969). Visual, auditory and tactile imagery in paired associate learning. Paper presented at the XIX International Congress of Psychology, July, London, England.

Zimler, J., & Keenan, J. M. (1983). Imagery in the congenitally blind: How visual are visual images? *Journal of Experimental Psychology: Learning, Memory, and Cognition, 9*, 269–282.

CHAPTER 11

Development of Elaboration and Organization in Different Socioeconomic-Status and Ethnic Populations

Susan Nakayama Siaw and Daniel W. Kee

Introduction and Historical Perspectives

This chapter provides a review of studies that have compared the development of mnemonic strategies in the learning and memory of different American ethnic and socioeconomic-status (SES) populations. During the past 20 years, there has been substantial growth in memory development research. Although reviews of this literature frequently provide analyses of memory development in different cultures (see Kail & Hagen, 1977; Pressley & Brainerd, 1985), American subcultural groups are rarely considered in these reviews (see Kail & Hagen, 1982, for an exception). Thus, this chapter augments extant reviews of the memory development literature by synthesizing comparative studies of mnemonic strategy development in American subcultural populations.

Research concerned with population comparisons has been motivated by both applied and theoretical issues. For example, the civil rights movement of the 1960s focused societal attention on the discrepancies in school achievement between rich and poor and white and black children. In response, educational research was initiated to determine whether such school achievement differences could be attributed to corresponding differences in basic learning and memory processes (see Rohwer, 1971).

Jensen's two-level theory of mental abilities provided another motivation for research in this area (see Jensen, 1969). Level I ability involves rote, associative processing and is utilized on such tasks as forward digit span. Level II ability involves conceptual processing and is measured by such tasks as the Raven Progressive Matrices. According to Jensen's model, children from different populations are expected to perform similarly on level I tasks, but population differences are expected to appear on level II tasks with increasing age. Jensen (1969) initially proposed that level II ability develops sooner and faster in higher SES than in lower SES populations. He later suggested that his predictions concerning level II ability were more applicable to ethnic rather than to SES differences (Jensen & Figueroa, 1975).

The majority of memory research concerning the aforementioned applied and theoretical issues have limited their comparisons to mnemonic strategy development in paired-associate and free-recall learning. Because the questions addressed by studies using these different methods are not identical, our review treats each separately, beginning with research in associative memory.

Mnemonic Strategy Development in Associative Memory

The associative memory studies considered in this first section were largely motivated by the schooling issues identified above. The paired-associate method used in these studies required the learning of pairs of items, frequently concrete nouns such as **arrow**–glasses, by the study–test method. There is substantial evidence that mental elaboration often accompanies successful paired-associate performance (e.g., Pressley, 1982; Rohwer, 1973). Mental elaboration consists of creating a shared semantic context for the to-be-remembered (TBR) items. For example, a subject could relate the TBR items in a sentence or form an interactive image of the item referents engaged in an interaction (e.g., the **arrow** smashes the **glasses**). Although young children usually do not use elaboration unless instructed to do so (i.e., they are production deficient; Flavell, 1970), the spontaneous use of elaboration appears during adolescence (see Pressley, 1982; Pressley, Levin, & Bryant, 1983).

Population Comparisons in Childhood Under Standard Learning Instructions

A number of early studies examined the paired-associate performance of children under standard conditions consisting of TBR pairs presented by themselves (as opposed to an elaborative context) in conjunction with instructions to simply memorize the pairs (i.e., no special mnemonics suggested). A frequent comparison was between black and white children. These groups were selected because they represented populations that usually differed on standard indices of school achievement. Recall that researchers wanted to determine whether the groups also differed in basic learning and memory skills. In an early study, Semler and Iscoe (1963) found differences favoring white children at ages five and six but not between ages seven and nine. The findings of Semler and Iscoe, however, may not reflect ethnic group differences per se, because the children in the black sample were lower in SES than their white cohorts. A similar pattern of paired-associate performance was reported by Rohwer, Ammon, Suzuki, and Levin (1971) in a study that deliberately sampled from low-SES black and high-SES white populations. These populations provide a contrast between groups known to differ in school achievement. In the Rohwer et al. study, paired-associate differences favoring the high-SES white children were detected at the kindergarten level, but not at grades 1 or 3.

A minority of studies have examined ethnic group comparisons with SES held constant. For example, an early study by Jensen (1963) indicated equivalent paired-associate performance for fourth and sixth grade low-SES white and low-SES Mexican–American children. A comprehensive study by Kee and Rohwer (1973) examined the paired-associate performance of second grade low-SES children from white, black, Chinese–American, and Mexican-American groups. They observed equivalent levels of performance between the groups in both acquisition and retention.

Finally, a number of studies have compared paired-associate performance of children from different SES groups within various ethnic groups. For example, Williams, Williams, and Blumberg (1971) indicated similar SES differences within white (Exp. 1) and black (Exp. 2) groups such that performance favored the middle-SES children at the second grade, but not at the older grades of four and six. Reliable SES differences, however, have not been reported consistently in other studies within black and white groups (e.g., Green & Rohwer, 1971; Hall & Kaye, 1977; Rapier, 1968; Rohwer & Lynch, 1968; Rohwer, Lynch, Levin, & Suzuki, 1968).

Elaborative Facilitation During Childhood in Different Populations

Because preschoolers and young children are known to be production deficient or inefficient (i.e., they use the strategy poorly) in elaboration, a number of studies have examined the extent to which children from different populations benefit from presenting the TBR items in verbal (e.g., pairs embedded within a meaningful phrase or sentence) and/or pictorial (e.g., noun referents depicted in static or action sequences) elaborations. For example, Rohwer et al. (1971) compared the performance of high- and low-SES children from grades 1, 3, and 6. Children from both SES groups benefitted from the provision of either verbal or pictorial elaborations. Similarly, Kee and Rohwer (1973) reported that low-SES second-grade children from white, black, Chinese–American, and Mexican–American groups showed virtually identical patterns of performance improvement due to verbal and pictorial elaborations. Also, Rohwer and Ammon (1971) have demonstrated that second-grade low-SES black and high-SES white children show posttest benefits resulting from elaboration training consisting of 30-min training sessions administered on five consecutive days.

Some studies have also examined the effectiveness of instructions to elaborate in different populations. For example, Rohwer and Bean (1973) report that both low-SES and middle-SES children at grades 1, 3, and 6 show similar patterns of facilitation as a function of verbal elaboration instructions. Furthermore, Guy (1973) examined the effectiveness of both verbal and imagery elaboration instructions in a study that included low-SES black and high-SES white children in the sixth grade. Children in both populations showed similar patterns of elaborative facilitation. Thus, during the childhood period, it appears that children from diverse populations show similar patterns of performance improvement when task conditions provide or prompt the use of elaboration in associative learning.

Spontaneous Elaboration During Adolescence

Elaborative propensities are presumed to increase markedly during the adolescence years, although there appear to be substantial individual differences in spontaneous elaboration (see Pressley, 1982, for a review). Rohwer and Bean (1973) suggested that SES may be a subject factor associated with the emergence of the spontaneous use of elaboration. This conclusion was based on their detection of different patterns of elaborative facilitation for eleventh grade adolescents from low-SES (Exp. 1) and middle-SES (Exp. 2) populations. For example, the performance of the high-SES adolescents in a standard control condition did not differ from elaboration conditions in which subjects were instructed either to elaborate pairs verbally or to memorize pairs presented in verbal elaborations. Presumably, subjects did not benefit from the elaboration conditions because they spontaneously engaged in strategic activity similar to that suggested by the elaboration conditions. This interpretation was bolstered by the finding that performance in a repetition-control condition was inferior to the three forenamed conditions, thereby suggesting that the rote rehearsal of pairs interfered with their elaborative activities. In contrast, adolescents from the low-SES population showed substantial performance improvement in the elaboration conditions relative to the control condition. Also, performance in the control and repetition conditions were identical. This pattern of results for the low-SES eleventh grade adolescents resembled the performance of younger grade children also sampled in the study. There is some suggestion in subsequent studies, however, that SES per se may not be the critical factor governing the emergence of elaborative propensities in adolescence (see Rabinowitz & Chi, 1987; Rohwer, Raines, Eoff, & Wagner, 1977). For example, amount of past experience with pair members may be the more critical factor influencing probability of spontaneous elaboration, and being raised in a higher SES group may afford one with richer and more varied experiences with pair members.

In another study, Guy (1973) found that black and white eleventh grade adolescents may also differ in elaborative propensities. However, ethnic group membership and SES covaried in her study, thereby beclouding an interpretation of the population differences. In another study, Kennedy and Suzuki (1977) compared the performance of twelfth grade Mexican–American and Anglo–American adolescents. Evidence for spontaneous elaboration was reported for both populations.

The studies just reviewed are limited, however, because spontaneous elaboration was inferred from comparisons of performance under standard instructions versus elaboration and repetition instructions. For example, if performance in the elaboration and standard instructions conditions did not differ, and if repetition instructions decreased performance, spontaneous elaboration in the standard instructions condition was inferred. Thus, the aforementioned evidence for spontaneous elaboration is indirect and may not be sensitive to variations in the nature of strategies employed by subjects from different populations. A more complete and decisive characterization of spontaneous elaboration would be provided by using a direct measure of subjects' strategy use during learning (see Beuhring & Kee, Chapter 12, this volume). This kind of analysis would provide more direct evidence concerning the occurrence and kind of associative strategies used by children from different SES and ethnic groups.

Summary and Recommendations

The following conclusions are suggested by the associative memory studies reviewed: 1. During childhood, the performance of children from diverse populations does not differ consistently, and 2. all populations examined showed similar patterns of elaborative facilitation during childhood. Many of the populations compared (e.g., low-SES vs. high-SES, white vs. black) are known to differ in school achievement. Thus, some theorists have argued that the absence of paired-associate performance differences between the groups implies that these groups do not differ in "new" learning ability and that the school achievement differences typically observed should be attributed, at least in part, to variations in knowledge base resulting from differences in previous learning opportunities (see Rohwer, 1971). A different perspective is offered by Jensen's views of mental abilities. Recall that different populations, such as low- versus high-SES, are expected to differ on tasks that require conceptual abilities, but not rote-associative abilities. Thus, the similarity of paired-associate performance across the different populations could be interpreted as a reflection of the rote-associative nature of associative memory tasks. This view, however, should not be accepted uncritically (see Mandler, 1979; Rohwer, 1971), especially because there is substantial evidence that successful paired-associate performance is anything but rote (see Pressley, 1977, 1982; Reese, 1977; Rohwer, 1973).

Two important issues should be considered in future associative studies of mnemonic development in different populations. First, applied studies are required that evaluate the effectiveness of elaboration mnemonics on the learning of school-relevant content. For example, considerable research has demonstrated the effectiveness of the "keyword" method in foreign language vocabulary learning (see Paivio & Desrochers, 1981; Pressley, Levin, & Delaney, 1982). This method is based on the elaboration mnemonic, and an important extension of the population comparison research is to assess the effectiveness of the keyword method with children from different ethnic and SES groups. Because of the increasing numbers of children with English as a second language in our school systems, it would be particularly useful to demonstrate the effectiveness of the keyword method in facilitating the acquisition of an English vocabulary in limited-English-speaking populations. Second, there is a paucity of evidence concerning the development of spontaneous elaboration in different populations. Studies are needed that provide a direct assessment of the nature of individual differences in elaborative propensities for children from different populations. Furthermore, the role of both memory knowledge (see Beuhring & Kee, Chapter 12, this volume; Borkowski & Krause, 1983) and attentional capacity (see Gutentag, 1984) should be carefully considered.

Mnemonic Strategy Development in Free-Recall Learning

The free-recall task provides a measure of developmental changes in the use of organization in different populations. This task consists of the presentation of TBR items during a study trial, which is then followed by a request for recall of those items during a test trial. Typically, the experimenter constructs lists of TBR items that belong to specific categories (e.g., types of clothing, animals, and food) and presents the items in a random order during the study trial. The extent to which a subject recalls items from these experimenter-selected categories in succession is called *clustering*. Clustering reflects the degree of organization engaged in and is usually associated with higher recall (see Murphy, 1979, for a detailed treatment of different clustering measures).

The free-recall studies considered in this section were largely motivated by both the theoretical and applied issues described in the introduction. For example, whereas developmental research demonstrates that clustering increases with age (e.g., Kee & Bell, 1981), Jensen (1969, Jensen & Figueroa, 1975) suggested that developmental clustering rates may differ between populations. Jensen predicted that higher SES or white children are more likely to cluster in free recall, because clustering presumably involves level II processing, which supposedly develops sooner in these populations (Jensen & Frederiksen, 1973). In contrast, he predicted that low-SES or black children would be less likely to use level II processing on a free-recall task and so would exhibit lower levels of clustering. Unlike the associative memory studies just reviewed, comparative studies of free-recall learning have focused primarily on black and white children from different SES backgrounds.

Population Comparisons in Childhood

Taxonomic Organization in Free-Recall

The majority of free-recall studies relevant to this review have focused on the use of taxonomic clustering of a TBR list composed of randomly presented taxonomically related items. In comparisons on this task of low-SES black versus middle-SES white children from kindergarten through the third grade, population differences in recall and taxonomic clustering have not been detected (Glasman, 1968; Irwin, Gerdes, & Rohwer, 1971; Jensen & Frederiksen, 1973; Peterson, 1972; Schultz, Charness, & Berman, 1973). Other studies with young children, which deliberately held ethnicity or SES constant, have also failed to detect population differences. For example, no population differences have been demonstrated in recall and taxonomic clustering in black and white low-SES and middle-SES children around 6 and 7 years of age in three studies (Grimmett, 1975; Hall & Kaye, 1977; Siaw, 1984). Only one study (Hall & Kaye, 1980) suggested that 7- and 8-year-old white or middle-SES children recall more items from a randomly presented taxonomically related list than black or lower-SES 7- and 8-year-olds. It is noteworthy that the Hall and Kaye (1980) report is a longitudinal extension of a cross-sectional study (Hall & Kaye, 1977) and that the population differences in young children were demonstrated in only one of four cohorts. Considered together then, the majority of studies indicate no population differences in free recall and taxonomic clustering of a randomly presented categorized list in children below the fourth grade.

In contrast to the similarity of performance across populations below the fourth grade, greater recall and taxonomic clustering favoring middle-SES white over low-SES black children has been reported for fourth graders (Jensen & Frederiksen, 1973) and fifth graders (Glasman, 1968). It will be recalled that this outcome was predicted by some of Jensen's ideas about population differences in level II abilities with increasing age. Furthermore, the population differences reported in these two early studies were responsible for catalyzing many of the studies reviewed in this section designed to characterize the development of organization strategies in different populations. Nevertheless, the population differences in recall and clustering reported in these early studies were not reliably detected in subsequent studies. For example, studies comparing low-SES black and middle-SES white children between the fourth and seventh grades have not detected population differences in recall or taxonomic clustering (Gerdes, 1971; Peterson, 1972; Schultz, Foster, & Loney, 1977) or have found that middle-SES white subjects demonstrate higher taxonomic clustering than low-SES black subjects in the absence of recall differences (Irwin et al., 1971). Other studies have attempted to hold ethnicity and/or SES constant and have also demonstrated no differences between black and white low- and middle-SES fourth and fifth graders (Hall & Kaye, 1980; Mensing & Traxler, 1973; Schultz et al., 1973; Siaw, 1984). Considered together, the majority of studies suggest that there are no population differences in free-recall performance at the older age levels sampled in these studies.

Alternate Modes of Organization

As a result of early studies that detected population differences in recall and taxonomic clustering favoring middle-SES white children (e.g., Jensen & Frederiksen, 1973), some investigators questioned whether studies that focus solely on taxonomic clustering provide a complete picture of the organization and recall abilities of children from different populations. For example, it is possible that children of different ages or from different populations prefer to use nontaxonomic modes of organization. These alternate forms of organization would not be detected in standard analyses of taxonomic clustering. One alternate form of organization relies on thematic relationships between TBR items. For example, a barn and a cowgirl belong to the thematic group "farm." There is some suggestion that young children are more likely than older children to cluster on the basis of thematic relationships (Ceci & Howe, 1978; Denney & Ziobrowski, 1972; Worden, 1976). Recent studies by Orasanu, Lee, and Scribner (1979) and Siaw (1984) provide evidence concerning the use of thematic organization by children from different populations.

Orasánu and her colleagues demonstrated that low-SES black and middle-SES black children show a greater preference for sorting and clustering by thematic categories than middle-SES white children do at the first and fifth grade levels. In their study, subjects were presented with stimuli that were drawn from taxonomic categories. The subjects were asked to sort the TBR items into groups, and clustering was based on each subject's groups. There was some indication that the low-SES and middle-SES black children showed a greater preference for sorting and clustering the pictures into thematic categories than middle-SES white children, who preferred taxonomic organization. However, the black children's preference for thematic organization appeared to decrease with increased age and SES level. It is noteworthy that although the children from the populations sampled in this study may have approached the free-recall task using alternate modes of organization, there were no ethnic or SES differences in level of recall and clustering. A similar pattern of results is reported by Bjorklund and Weiss (1985), who found that low-SES white children demonstrated more thematic clustering than higher-SES white children, who engaged in more taxonomic clustering. Level of recall did not differ between SES groups in this study. A recent study of low-SES children (Gildemeister & Friedman, 1981), however, suggests that thematic organization is not always preferred over taxonomic organization by low-SES subjects.

Siaw extended previous research by examining taxonomic and thematic clustering in black and white 7- and 9-year-olds from both low- and middle-SES populations. Also, whereas previous studies measured thematic clustering of lists that were composed of items drawn from taxonomic categories, Siaw used TBR items that were cross-classified by taxonomic and thematic categories. For example, the item "fire truck" belongs to both the vehicle category (taxonomic) and the fire station category (thematic). Items were presented in a random order and recall was requested for a total of three trials. Siaw found that taxonomic clustering increased with age whereas thematic clustering was at chance for both age groups. There were no ethnic or SES differences detected in either type of clustering or in level of recall.

The thematic organization of the list in the Siaw (1984) study was "built in" via experimenter selection of potentially thematically related stimuli. Thematic organization can also be imposed by the subject via narratives that link TBR items together. One method that provides some indication that subjects may be employing narratives as a mnemonic strategy involves measuring subjective organization over trials. To our knowledge, no comparative study has addressed the issue of subjective organization, although a study by Irwin et al. (1971) suggests that low-SES black and middle-SES white children from kindergarten and the fifth grade exhibit an equally low incidence of spontaneously generated thematically based narratives between contiguously presented items. This finding is consistent with the associative memory studies reviewed above, which indicated that during childhood children from diverse populations are similarly production deficient or inefficient (i.e., they use the strategy poorly) in their use of elaboration.

Facilitation of Organization in Different Populations

Several lines of research have been concerned with factors that may influence the use of organization in free recall by different populations. Questions addressed by this research include:

1. Are taxonomic categories equally available as a basis for organization in different populations?
2. To what extent can the use of organization be affected by using stimulus lists that are biased in favor of one population?
3. To what extent can subjects from different populations profit from prompts to use organization as a mnemonic strategy?

A review of research addressing each of these questions follows.

The question of population differences in the availability of taxonomic categories in the repertoires of children from different populations was prompted by the early findings that low-SES black children exhibited less taxonomic clustering in free recall than middle-SES white children (e.g., Jensen & Frederiksen, 1973). The release from proactive interference (PI) task, which measures automatic, unconscious encoding of different conceptual categories, is a useful paradigm for assessing the availability of taxonomic categories in the repertoires of subjects from different populations. The PI task (Wickens, 1970) consists of four or five trials, each trial involving a brief presentation of a few TBR items, a filled retention interval to prevent rehearsal, and a recall test of the TBR items for that trial. When the TBR items are drawn from the same category for several trials (e.g., animals), performance may decline markedly over trials. This decline is referred to as "buildup of PI" and is attributed to the subjects' automatic encoding of the common concept for the items (in this case, "animals"). If the TBR items are drawn from a different category (e.g., clothing) on a later trial, significant improvement in performance may be observed. This is called "release from PI" and is attributed to the subjects now shifting their encoding to the new concept (in this case, to the concept "clothing"). In a series of PI studies by Kee and his associates, low-SES black and middle-SES white children from the second and fourth grade levels served as subjects, and TBR items were drawn from conceptual categories identical or similar to those used in previous free recall studies. There were no population differences in buildup or release from PI detected when items were presented pictorially (Kee & Helfend, 1977), aurally (Nakayama & Kee, 1980), or via print (Kee, Siaw, Cervantes, & Osaze, 1984). Thus, the population differences in taxonomic clustering that were detected in early free recall studies did not result from population differences in the availability of taxonomic categories in memory.

One limitation to the general statement that taxonomic categories are equally available in different populations is that stimuli in the aforementioned PI studies were generally selected to be typical or high frequency exemplars of taxonomic categories. Typicality judgments, however, vary with age, and there are also age differences in taxonomic category boundaries and members included within a category (Bjorklund, 1985). At present, we know very little about population differences in typicality, category boundaries, and category members, although Glasman (1968) provides preliminary evidence that black children may have more limited knowledge of taxonomic category members than white children with increasing age. In her study, Glasman provided taxonomic category labels to low-SES black and middle-SES white kindergarteners and fifth graders and asked each subject to provide as many exemplars as possible to each category label. The number of exemplars generated by the children increased with age, but whereas low-SES black and middle-SES white kindergarteners provided an equal number of category exemplars to the labels, middle-SES white fifth graders provided significantly more category exemplars than the low-SES black fifth graders did.

A second limitation of these studies of category availability is that there has been little differentiation between availability and accessibility of categories in different populations. For example, population differences that may be detected in clustering in free recall may result either from the unavailability of the categories in the subjects' repertoires or from the inability to access available categories (see Rabinowitz & Chi, 1987). Gerdes' (1971) free-recall study, which included population comparisons of the number of categories represented in recall and the average number of items remembered per category provides preliminary evidence on this issue. Gerdes, who tested seventh grade low-SES black and middle-SES white subjects and used high-frequency category exemplars as stimuli, did not detect any population differences on these measures in a standard condition. This suggests that the two populations accessed categories and items to the same degree under standard instructions. However, parity between populations in availability was not supported, for in conditions where the children were prompted to use the categories to aid recall, Gerdes found that middle-SES white children recalled more items per category but did not have more categories represented in their recall than low-SES black children did. In other words, if one makes the assumption that providing category prompts makes any available categorized items more accessible, then this pattern of results is consistent with the interpretation that middle-SES white children have a larger number of category exemplars available than low-SES black children do.

A second line of research investigating factors that may influence the use of organization by different populations are studies that utilize stimulus lists that are deliberately biased in favor of one population. The rationale behind these studies is that populations may differ in their knowledge of experimenter-selected taxonomic categories and so performance differences result from content of stimulus lists rather than differences in the ability to cluster. Franklin and Fulani (1979) constructed lists of taxonomically related items that were referred to as "black categories" (types of drugs, dances, and soul food) and "universal categories" (types of tools, tableware, and clothing). Subjects were low-SES black and middle-SES white adolescents, which is noteworthy, because adolescents have rarely been included in past free-recall comparative studies. Their study is also noteworthy because it provides one of the only reports of low-SES black subjects clustering more than middle-SES white subjects. Moreover, this population difference was detected for clustering based on both black and universal categories, although there was no population difference in level of recall. A different pattern of results was obtained by Schultz et al. (1977). They presented items from black familiar and white familiar taxonomic categories to fourth and sixth grade low-SES black and middle-SES white children and found that both low-SES black and middle-SES white subjects demonstrated higher clustering of the white familar than the black familar categories. There were no population differences in the two types of clustering or level of recall detected in this study. Considered together, the Franklin and Fulani and the Schultz et al. studies suggest that subjects from different populations generally perform similarly when asked to recall TBR stimuli assumed to favor a given population.

The third type of study that has been conducted to examine factors affecting the use of organization in different populations involves the effects of prompting subjects to use organization. Studies have been conducted to assess whether populations differ in their sensitivity to such prompts. Two major types of prompts that have been studied are blocking and instructions to use organization.

Blocking

Investigators have blocked items together by taxonomic categories or themes either by presenting items that belong to the same groups in succession or by requiring subjects to sort items into their appropriate category during the study period. Studies investigating the effects of blocking by taxonomic categories have yielded consistent results for young subjects but mixed results for older subjects. Studies by Grimmett (1975) with low-SES black and white first graders, Jensen and Frederiksen (1973) with low-SES black and middle-SES white second graders, and Siaw (1984) with low- and middle-SES black and white first and second graders consistently demonstrate that blocking by taxonomic categories during the study trial raises taxonomic clustering but does not raise recall relative to a control condition where items are presented in a random order. The increased clustering was not associated with higher recall as is typically found in the performance of older subjects.

For older subjects, blocking by taxonomic category significantly raised taxonomic clustering for low- and middle-SES black and white children from the fourth and fifth grades (Siaw, 1984) and low-SES black and middle-SES white fourth graders (Jensen & Frederiksen, 1973). In these studies, there were no differences in the benefits of taxonomic blocking on taxonomic clustering associated with ethnicity or SES. A study by Gerdes (1971) found that both low-SES black and high-SES white seventh graders increased taxonomic clustering following blocked presentation; however, the high-SES white children appeared to cluster more than the low-SES black children.

It is clear that blocking by taxonomic category raises clustering for older subjects from all populations in these three studies, but the results suggest that increased clustering does not always mediate greater recall for all of these populations. In the Gerdes study, blocking facilitated recall for the high-SES white but not the low-SES black seventh graders. In the Siaw study, blocking was more helpful in raising recall for the low- and middle-SES white children than for the low- and middle-SES black children. Finally, Jensen and Frederiksen found that blocking increased recall for both low-SES black and middle-SES white fourth graders, and although blocking appeared to be more beneficial for the low-SES black fourth graders, this effect was not significant.

Several studies have included conditions in which items were blocked thematically. Gerdes (1971) presented low-SES black and middle-SES white seventh graders with TBR items embedded within short titled narratives, e.g., "The story about Tom's trip to the zoo—when Tom went to the zoo, he saw a famous **giraffe** wearing a **vest**. First it blew up a **balloon** with a **strawberry** inside, but its best act was to play the **harmonica** while standing on its **elbow**." This manipulation raised thematic clustering for both populations relative to a no-narrative control group, but the facilitative effect of this manipulation on recall was limited to the middle-SES white children. Whereas the Gerdes study arranged TBR items into novel thematic groupings specific to their study, Siaw (1984) presented low- and middle-SES 7- and 9-year-olds with blocked items that possessed more universally agreed upon thematic relationships (e.g., a school bus, school sweater, pencil, student, and classroom are thematically related "school" items). This blocked condition raised thematic clustering for all subjects except 7-year-old white children. Recall was facilitated for the 9-year-olds, but not for the 7-year-olds, and this was not associated with ethnic or SES differences.

Instructions to Organize

Other studies have been concerned with population differences in the ability to profit from instructions to use organization. The approaches used in these studies vary widely and include describing the organizational structure of the list, providing explicit instructions to form narratives, and indirectly prompting organization by training skills assumed to underlie use of organization.

Schultz et al. (1973) provided taxonomic category labels during the study trial to first and fourth grade low- and middle-SES subjects from a predominantly white population. This condition generally raised recall and clustering, but there was some suggestion that this condition raised recall more for the middle-SES subjects, although this did not reach significance. Gerdes (1971) presented taxonomic category labels during the study and/or test trial to low-SES black and middle-SES white seventh graders. Test cues were helpful for the two populations in raising recall and clustering, but study cues were more helpful for the middle-SES white than for the low-SES black children in raising recall relative to a control condition in which no cues are provided.

Irwin et al. (1971) asked low-SES black and high-SES white kindergarteners and fifth graders to construct narratives linking sets of five contiguously presented items. Clustering in recall was based on each five-item group. These investigators found no population differences in performance at the kindergarten level. In contrast, it appeared that high-SES white children benefitted more from instructions to make up narratives than the low-SES black children did.

Finally, Peterson (1972) indirectly prompted organization by training low-SES third and sixth graders from a predominantly black population and middle-SES third and sixth grade white children in skills assumed to underlie organization. Children received either no training or four days of training in classification or class inclusion skills. Before training, there were no population differences in performance. Following training, there were no population differences at the third grade level, but at the sixth grade level, middle-SES white subjects demonstrated more taxonomic clustering than low-SES black subjects. There were no population effects detected in recall for the sixth graders, and there were no effects associated with type of training.

In summary, studies that tested the effects of various types of instructions to use organization have demonstrated that children from different populations exhibit similar benefits from the prompts or have found slight differences favoring middle-SES white subjects over low-SES black subjects. Because SES usually covaried with ethnicity in these studies, our understanding of developmental changes in the effects of prompting within different populations is limited. These studies also suggest that differences in the ability to benefit from category prompts in the populations tested become more pronounced with age. It is also noteworthy that in these available studies, population differences in recall were often not accompanied by differences in clustering and vice versa. Because only global clustering measures were analyzed, a more complete understanding of population differences would be provided in future work by indepth analyses of organizational strategies. This also suggests that the population differences may be influenced by other factors, e.g., attentional capacity or knowledge, which should be examined in future studies (see Pressley, Borkowski, & Schneider, in press).

Summary and Recommendations

The following conclusions are suggested by the free-recall studies reviewed: 1. During childhood, the performance of children from diverse populations on a standard free-recall task does not differ consistently. 2. Providing organization via blocking by categories generally raises recall and clustering for subjects from different age groups and populations. Differences, if any, were apparent by around the fifth grade and tended to favor low- or middle-SES white subjects over low- and middle-SES black children. 3. Instructions to use organization generally raises clustering and recall for subjects from different age groups and populations. Differences, if any, were apparent by around the fifth grade and tended to favor middle-SES white over low-SES black children.

Some theorists, such as Jensen, have argued that children from the populations compared in these studies (black versus white; low versus middle SES) differ in level II ability with increasing age and should demonstrate differences in spontaneous use of clustering with increasing age. Results of studies using the standard free-recall procedure do not provide support for this argument. However, because the majority of comparative subjects have focused on elementary school children, and because Jensen predicts that population differences appear with increasing age, future comparative studies should focus on the use of organization by older subjects.

Reviews of studies concerned with the effects of prompts to use organization indicate that all populations tested have benefitted from blocking and instructions to use organization. This suggests that children are production deficient or inefficient in their use of organization as a mnemonic strategy, which parallels the production deficiency or inefficiency in elaboration typically demonstrated by children in the associative memory research. Population differences in sensitivity to various types of prompts favoring white or middle-SES children over black or low-SES children were detected in some studies. These population differences were not consistently demonstrated, however, and our understanding is limited by the small number of available studies in this area and the typical confounding between ethnicity and SES.

Conclusions

There are production deficiencies and inefficiencies in memory strategy utilization during childhood. The studies reviewed in this chapter illustrate the generality of these production deficiencies and inefficiencies to various SES and ethnic populations. Indeed, performance similarities between diverse populations were observed in both baseline performance and the extent of performance improvements because of manipulations designed to encourage strategy utilization. Some suggestion of differential performance improvement was indicated in the free-recall literature. However, whether these differences should be attributed to SES, ethnicity, or some other individual difference factor is unclear at present. Population differences were also suggested during the adolescence period in the spontaneous use of elaboration. The apparent population differences in elaborative propensities, however, cannot be simply attributed to variation in either SES or ethnicity. It is important to keep in mind that most of the comparative studies cited in this review have utilized relatively rough estimates of SES (e.g., level of parents' education or place of residence). Recent critiques of such SES estimates suggest that future studies in this area should attempt to delineate SES via more sensitive measures (see Gottfried, 1985).

A number of factors are presumed to affect efficient strategy utilization. These factors include metamemory, knowledge, and attentional capacity (Borkowski & Krause, 1983; Gutentag, 1984; Pressley et al., in press). The quality of the child's environment may influence development within these domains, which in turn may influence strategy utilization. Indeed, the child's environment and these aforementioned factors seem interrelated, as stated by Borkowski and Krause (1983): "An enriched metamemory and the efficient use of study strategies lead to differential accumulation of information about the world, which in turn provides the semantic networks necessary for advanced learning and creativity" (p. 391). Following this line of thinking, it seems reasonable to hypothesize that if reliable population differences are detected in future work, a major factor influencing these differences would be "... the quality of early environments as they influence the development of semantic networks and learning strategies that make learning and retrieval more efficient" (Borkowski & Krause, p. 393).

It will also be important to examine the performance of various American sub-cultural groups with paradigms other than paired-associates and free recall. The use of elaboration and organization on other memory tasks as well as the use of other types of mnemonic techniques by different populations should be investigated. For example, in exploratory studies that examined memory for prose by children from different populations (Kee, Siaw, & Carter, 1985; Rohwer & Harris, 1975), there is some suggestion of population differences in memory for the gist of prose passages. Replication of any demonstrated differences as well as ways to ameliorate these differences should be a goal for future research. Historically, comparative research was initiated to better understand differences in school achievement between children from different populations. In this regard, it will be important to focus on mnemonic strategy utilization with school-relevant material by different populations.

Acknowledgments. The preparation of this chapter was facilitated by an Affirmative Action Faculty Development Award, California State Polytechnic University, Pomona, to S. N. Siaw and a President's Summer Grant and an Affirmative Action Faculty Development Award, California State University, Fullerton, to D. W. Kee.

References

Bjorklund, D. F. (1985). The role of conceptual knowledge in the development of organization in children's memory. In C. J. Brainerd & M. Pressley (Eds.), *Basic processes in memory development: Progress in cognitive development research* (pp. 103–142). New York: Springer-Verlag.

Bjorklund, D. F., & Weiss, S. C. (1985). The influence of socioeconomic status on children's classification and free recall. *Journal of Educational Psychology, 77,* 119–128.

Borkowski, J. G., & Krause, A. (1983). Racial differences in intelligence: The importance of the executive system. *Intelligence, 7,* 379–395.

Ceci, S. J., & Howe, M. J. A. (1978). Age-related differences in free recall as a function of retrieval flexibility. *Journal of Experimental Child Psychology, 26,* 432–442.

Denney, N. W., & Ziobrowski, M. (1972). Developmental changes in clustering criteria. *Journal of Experimental Child Psychology, 13,* 275–282.

Flavell, J. H. (1970). Developmental studies of mediated memory. In H. W. Reese & L. P. Lipsett (Eds.), *Advances in child development and behavior* (Vol. 5, pp. 181–211). New York: Academic Press.

Franklin, A. J., & Fulani, L. (1979). Cultural content of materials and ethnic group performance in categorized recall. In A. W. Boyd, A. J. Franklin, & J. F. Yates (Eds.), *Research directions of black psychologists* (pp. 229–240). New York: Basic Books.

Gerdes, B. (1971). *The relationship of provided organization to free recall learning in two populations.* Unpublished doctoral dissertation, University of California, Berkeley.

Gildemeister, J. E., & Friedman, P. (1981). *Organization in recall of urban third and fifth graders.* Paper presented at the 89th meeting of the American Psychological Association, August 24–28, Los Angeles, CA.

Glasman, L. D. (1968). *A social class comparison of conceptual processes in children's free recall.* Unpublished doctoral dissertation, University of California, Berkeley.

Gottfried, A. (1985). Measures of socioeconomic-status in child development research: Data and recommendations. *Merrill Palmer Quarterly, 31,* 85–92.

Green, R. B., & Rohwer, W. D., Jr. (1971). SES differences on learning and ability tests in black children. *American Educational Research Journal, 8,* 601–609.

Grimmett, S. A. (1975). Black and white children's free recall of unorganized and organized lists: Jensen's Level I and Level II. *Journal of Negro Education, 44,* 24–33.

Gutentag, R. E. (1984). The mental effort requirement of cumulative rehearsal: A developmental study. *Journal of Experimental Child Psychology, 37,* 92–106.

Guy, K. (1973). *Population differences in aural and pictorial-imaginal elaboration of a paired-associate list.* Unpublished master's thesis, University of California, Berkeley.

Hall, V. C., & Kaye, D. B. (1977). Patterns of early cognitive development among boys in four subcultural groups. *Journal of Educational Psychology, 69,* 66–87.

Hall, V. C., & Kaye, D. B. (1980). Early patterns of cognitive development. *Monographs of the Society for Research in Child Development, 45* (Serial No. 184).

Irwin, M. H., Gerdes, B. J., & Rohwer, W. D., Jr. (1971). *SES, age, and facilitation of free recall learning.* Paper presented at the meeting of the American Educational Research Association, April, New York, NY.

Jensen, A. R. (1963). Learning abilities in Mexican-American and Anglo-American children. *California Journal of Educational Research, 12,* 147–159.

Jensen, A. R. (1969). How much can we boost IQ and scholastic achievement? *Harvard Educational Review, 39,* 1–123.

Jensen, A. R., & Figueroa, R. A. (1975). Forward and backward digit span interaction with race and IQ: Predictions from Jensen's theory. *Journal of Educational Psychology, 67,* 882–893.

Jensen, A. R., & Frederiksen, J. (1973). Free recall of categorized and uncategorized lists: A test of the Jensen hypothesis. *Journal of Educational Psychology, 65,* 304–312.

Kail, R. V., & Hagen, J. W. (Eds.) (1977). *Perspectives on the development of memory and cognition.* Hillsdale, NJ: Erlbaum Associates.

Kail, R. V., & Hagen, J. W. (1982). Memory in childhood. In B. B. Wolman (Ed.), *Handbook of developmental psychology* (pp. 350–360). Englewood Cliffs, NJ: Prentice-Hall.

Kee, D. W., & Bell, T. (1981). The development of organizational strategies in the storage and retrieval of categorical items in free-recall learning. *Child Development, 52,* 1163–1171.

Kee, D. W., & Helfend, L. (1977). Assessment of taxonomic encoding categories in different populations. *Journal of Educational Psychology, 69,* 344–348.

Kee, D. W., & Rohwer, W. D., Jr. (1973). Noun-pair learning in four ethnic groups: Conditions of presentation and response. *Journal of Educational Psychology, 65,* 226–232.

Kee, D. W., Siaw, S. N., & Carter, L. (1985). Population differences in constructive memory. *Contemporary Educational Psychology, 10,* 268–274.

Kee, D. W., Siaw, S. N., Cervantes, M., & Osaze, J. (1984). Automatic conceptual encoding of printed verbal material: Assessment of population differences. *Journal of Contemporary Educational Psychology, 9,* 74–83.

Kennedy, S. P., & Suzuki, N. S. (1977). Spontaneous elaboration in Mexican-American and Anglo-American high school seniors. *American Educational Research Journal, 14,* 383–388.

Mandler, J. (1979). Organization and repetition: Organizational principles with special reference to rote learning. In L. Nilsson (Ed.), *Perspectives on memory research: Essays in honor of Uppsala University's 500th anniversary* (pp. 293–327). Hillsdale, NJ: Erlbaum Associates.

Mensing, P. M., & Traxler, A. J. (1973). Social class differences in free recall of categorized and uncategorized lists in black children. *Journal of Educational Psychology, 65,* 378–382.

Murphy, M. D. (1979). The measurement of category clustering in free recall. In C. R. Puff (Ed.), *Memory organization and structure* (pp. 51–83). New York: Academic Press.

Nakayama, S. Y., & Kee, D. W. (1980). Automatic encoding of superordinate and subordinate taxonomic categories in different populations. *Journal of Educational Psychology, 72,* 386–393.

Orasanu, J., Lee, C., & Scribner, S. (1979). The development of category organization and free recall: Ethnic and economic group comparisons. *Child Development, 50,* 1100–1109.

Paivio, A., & Desrochers, A. (1981). Mnemonic techniques in second-language learning. *Journal of Educational Psychology, 73,* 780–795.

Peterson, R. S. (1972). *The effects of categorization training and class inclusion training on children's use of categories in free recall.* Unpublished doctoral dissertation, University of California, Berkeley.

Pressley, M. (1977). Imagery and children's learning: Putting the picture in developmental perspective. *Review of Educational Research, 49,* 319–370.

Pressley, M. (1982). Elaboration and memory development. *Child Development, 53,* 296–309.

Pressley, M., Borkowski, J. G., & Schneider, W. (in press). Good strategy users coordinate metacognition, strategy use, and knowledge. In R. Vasta & G. Whitehurst (Eds.), *Annals of child development* (Vol. 4). Greenwich, CT: JAI Press.

Pressley, M., & Brainerd, C. J. (Eds.). (1985). *Cognitive learning and memory in children.* New York: Springer-Verlag.

Pressley, M., Levin, J. R., & Bryant, S. L. (1983). Memory strategy instruction during adolescence: When is explicit instruction needed? In M. Pressley & J. R. Levin (Eds.), *Cognitive strategy research* (pp. 25–50). New York: Springer-Verlag.

Pressley, M., Levin, J. R., & Delaney, H. D. (1982). The mnemonic keyword method. *Review of Educational Research, 52,* 61–91.

Rabinowitz, M., & Chi, M. T. H. (1987). An interactive model of strategic processing. In S. J. Ceci (Ed.), *Handbook of cognitive, social, and neuropsychological aspects of learning disabilities* (Vol. 2, pp. 83–102). Hillsdale, NJ: Erlbaum Associates.

Rapier, J. L. (1968). Learning abilities of normal and retarded children as a function of social class. *Journal of Educational Psychology, 59,* 102–110.

Reese, H. W. (1977). Imagery and associative memory. In R. V. Kail & J. W. Hagen (Eds.), *Perspectives on the development of memory and cognition* (pp. 113–175). Hillsdale, NJ: Erlbaum Associates.

Rohwer, W. D., Jr. (1971). Learning, race, and school success. *Review of Educational Research, 41,* 191–210.

Rohwer, W. D., Jr. (1973). Elaboration and learning in childhood and adolescence. In H. W. Reese (Ed.), *Advances in child development and behavior* (pp. 1–57). New York: Academic Press.

Rohwer, W. D., Jr., & Ammon, M. S. (1971). Elaboration training and paired associate learning efficiency in children. *Journal of Educational Psychology, 62*, 376–383.

Rohwer, W. D., Jr., & Bean, J. P. (1973). Sentence effects and noun-pair learning: A developmental interaction during adolescence. *Journal of Experimental Child Psychology, 15*, 521–533.

Rohwer, W. D., Jr., & Harris, W. J. (1975). Media effects on prose learning in two populations. *Journal of Educational Psychology, 67*, 651–657.

Rohwer, W. D., Jr., & Lynch, S. (1968). Retardation, school strata, and learning proficiency. *American Journal of Mental Deficiency, 73*, 91–96.

Rohwer, W. D., Jr., Ammon, M. S., Suzuki, N., & Levin, J. R. (1971). Population differences and learning proficiency. *Journal of Educational Psychology, 62*, 1–14.

Rohwer, W. D., Jr., Lynch, S., Levin, J. R., & Suzuki, N. (1968). Grade level, school strata, and learning efficiency. *Journal of Educational Psychology, 59*, 26–31.

Rohwer, W. D., Jr., Raines, J. M., Eoff, J., & Wagner, M. (1977). The development of elaborative propensity in adolescence. *Journal of Experimental Psychology, 23*, 472–492.

Schultz, C. B., Foster, M. R., & Loney, E. A. (1977). *The effect of culturally indigenous word lists on recall and clustering by lower-class blacks and middle-class whites: An exploratory study.* Paper presented at the meeting of the American Educational Research Association, April, New York, NY.

Schultz, T. R., Charness, M., & Berman, S. (1973). Effects of age, social class, and suggestion to cluster on free recall. *Developmental Psychology, 8*, 57–61.

Semler, I. J., & Iscoe, I. (1963). Comparative and developmental study of the learning abilities of Negro and white children under four conditions. *Journal of Educational Psychology, 54*, 38–44.

Siaw, S. N. (1984). Developmental and population comparisons of thematic and taxonomic organization in free recall. *Journal of Educational Psychology, 76*, 755–765.

Wickens, D. (1970). Encoding categories of words: An empirical approach to meaning. *Psychological Review, 77*, 1–15.

Williams, J., Williams, D. V., & Blumberg, E. L. (1973). Visual and aural learning in urban children. *Journal of Educational Psychology, 64*, 353–359.

Worden, P. (1976). The effects of classification structure on organized free recall in children. *Journal of Experimental Child Psychology, 22*, 519–529.

CHAPTER 12

Elaborative Propensities During Adolescence: The Relationships Among Memory Knowledge, Strategy Behavior, and Memory Performance

Trisha Beuhring and Daniel W. Kee

Introduction

Much of the developmental improvement in memory performance can be attributed to age-related changes in children's effective use of appropriate memory strategies. A number of factors are presumed to influence these strategic applications (see Guttentag, 1985; Pressley, Borkowski, & Schneider, in press) including metamemory (see Schneider, 1985). The present chapter reports experiments which illustrate the relationship between developmental improvements in metamemory, strategic behavior and memory performance.

A variety of strategies are known to improve memory performance. Among these, mental elaboration has been studied extensively, usually in the context of associative learning (see Pressley, 1982; Rohwer, 1973). When learning noun pairs, for example, an elaborative event can be created that unites the otherwise unrelated pair members (e.g., chain–jar: the CHAIN is inside the JAR).

Especially substantial increases in paired-associate performance have been reported during adolescence (e.g., Rohwer & Bean, 1973). Recent reviewers concluded that age-related increases in elaborative propensity are responsible (see Pressley, 1982; Rohwer, 1973). Support for this hypothesis is provided by both experimental evidence and subject strategy reports. For example, older adolescents are more likely than grade-school children to report the use of elaboration while studying noun pairs; they are also less likely to report the use of an inefficient strategy, such as rehearsal, or to fail to use any strategy at all (e.g., Pressley & Levin, 1977). Conversely, experimental evidence indicates that the typically poor performance of children and young adolescents can be greatly improved by instructing them to elaborate an interaction for the noun pair or by presenting the pair members in an elaborative episode (e.g., Rohwer & Bean, 1973).

Both types of evidence may be limited, however, because they are based on only *delayed* measures of the students' strategic activities. For example, experimental studies infer the nature of spontaneous strategic behavior from the effect of strategy instructions on cued recall. Studies of subject reports are limited because these reports are usually obtained *after* the students' finish studying all the pairs on the learning list. Consequently, the accuracy and completeness of the reports depends on the accuracy and completeness of the students' memory for the strategies they used to learn each pair.

One purpose of the experiments reported in this chapter was to provide a more accurate and direct assessment of the nature of the memory strategies that are used by different aged students to master an associative memory task. This was accomplished by having students verbalize their strategies for each pair during the study trial rather than afterwards.

Developmental differences in the propensity to elaborate are presumably related to developmental differences in the extent of students' knowledge about memory-relevant processes, or metamemory (see Schneider, 1985). For example, Waters (1982) reported that eighth and tenth graders who recognized that elaboration aids memory performance were more likely to use elaboration on a paired-associate task and had a higher level of cued recall than students who lacked such knowledge. Despite the within-grade metamemory–elaboration relationship, a developmental increase in the use of elaboration was not observed and there was no evidence of an increase in metamemory knowledge itself, probably because the age range Waters sampled was quite narrow. Consequently, the presumed developmental relationship between metamemory and elaboration could not be assessed.

According to Schneider (1985), the strength of evidence regarding a connection between metamemory and strategic behavior depends on such factors as the directness of the strategy measure used (also see Flavell & Wellman, 1977), the thoroughness and reliability of the metamemory assessment (also see Kurtz, Reid, Borkowski, & Cavanaugh, 1982), and whether the metamemory assessment was made before, during, or after the memory task. The study by Waters (1982), for example, relied on a postlearning interview rather than on a more direct, concurrent measure of strategy use. Her metamemory assessment was also limited to a single question that measured the subjects' ability to correctly select elaboration as the best memory strategy over rehearsal and careful reading. Furthermore, the order of metamemory assessment and paired-associate learning was not counterbalanced in her study. Therefore, Waters may have been tapping a reactive situation in which the paired-associate memory experience could very well have enhanced metamemory about the task and vice versa.

A second purpose of the experiments was therefore to provide a more complete and decisive analysis of the relationship between metamemory and associative strategy use. In addition to the *concurrent* and so more direct measure of mnemonic activity discussed above, a comprehensive metamemory questionnaire was used. This metamemory questionnaire was composed of relevant items from the frequently used Kreutzer, Leonard, and Flavell (1975) metamemory test, with additional items created to provide a detailed appraisal of subjects' specific knowledge about the relative effectiveness of different kinds of elaborations on cued recall. A composite metamemory score based on these items provided a more thorough and reliable measure of task-appropriate knowledge. The order of metamemory assessment and paired-associate learning was also counterbalanced in the present study. Finally, the relationship between metamemory and the tendency to elaborate was examined using regression analyses instead of the more typical chi-square and ANOVA. This approach takes individual differences into account rather than treating them as group error variance.

Description of Experimental Procedures

Our subjects were 32 10–11 year olds and 32 16–18 year olds from Los Angeles, California. Equal numbers of males and females were tested within each group. These age groups were selected because they bracket the period associated with some of the largest age-related improvements in paired-associate performance (see Rohwer, 1973).

The principal factors in our between-groups experimental design were age (younger vs. older), measurement order (metamemory interview before vs. after the memory task), lists (two lists for the memory task), and sex. Because list and sex had no significant effect, only grade and measurement order were included in the analyses reported.

The paired-associate materials used were comprised of two lists of 36 unrelated noun pairs that Rohwer (1980) found to be similarly difficult for both fifth and eleventh graders, presented at a 15-sec rate per pair for a single study trial. Participants were told they should study the pairs in such a way that they could later recall the second noun in each pair when given the first noun as a cue. They were also told to verbalize all their thoughts while studying. Care was taken not to give examples of the study strategies they should report. Instead, the procedure was likened to asking them to think out loud or to sing a song they had previously just been "singing in their head." It was further explained that the purpose of this procedure was to find out what students really do to learn this material. It was emphasized that there was no right or wrong way to study the pairs. Cued recall of the second noun in each pair was the measure of associative memory on the test trial.

Metamemory was assessed during an interview that was structured around nine items. Each item presented a sample memory task and required students to either (a) recommend the single best memory strategy for the task, (b) judge the relative effectiveness of different memory strategies that were provided for them, or (c) judge the relative ease with which different paired-associate lists could be learned (the lists favored the production of different strategies). Students were also required to explain their judgments.

Five of the items were chosen from Kreutzer et al. (1975) for their specific and general relevance to associative memory tasks. Opposites–Arbitrary measured awareness that preexisting associations would aid subsequent memory for item pairs. Story–List measured awareness that elaboration formed associations that would aid subsequent memory for a series of items. Study–Plan assessed knowledge of the different strategies that could be used to aid memory for a list of categorizable items. Retrieval-Event assessed knowledge that memory for a target fact could be cued by recalling a related piece of information. Savings measured awareness that apparently forgotten material may still be available for retrieval.

The other four items were designed to assess task-specific knowledge about the nature of effective associations. Research findings and pretesting with first-year college students suggested the strategy comparisons. Elaboration–Rehearsal measured awareness that elaborated interactions provided associations whereas side by side relationships and rehearsal did not. Elaboration–Structural assessed knowledge that elaborated interactions are specific to a pair and so would be more effective than associations based on letters or rhymes. Elaboration–Shared Attribute assessed knowledge that elaborations are more pair specific than associations based on an attribute the nouns share and so elaboration should be more effective even when the interactions are implausible. Retrieval–Elaboration was designed to measure awareness that elaborations related to the stimulus noun would be better than response-related ones because the stimulus would be more likely to cue the mediating interaction. A detailed description of our meta-memory assessment procedures is included in the Appendix.

Experimental Findings

Study Strategies

Age differences in the use of associative study strategies were examined to verify the occurrence and nature of the developmental trend that our study was designed to explain. The meaningfulness of this and subsequent analyses rests on the assumption that students' study trial verbalizations are an accurate and non-reactive measure of the memory strategies they have used. Both direct and indirect evidence supports this view (also see Ericsson & Simon, 1980). For example, the age difference in our students' cued-recall memory was similar to that reported by Rohwer (1980) for similarly aged students who learned the same paired-associate lists but without having to verbalize their strategies. The 11- and 17-year-old subjects in that study recalled an average of 8.3 and 20.3 pairs, respectively. The corresponding young and old subjects in this study recalled an average of 9.5 and 23.4 pairs, respectively. Postlearning interviews also suggested that the measure was nonreactive. A majority of students in both grades stated that verbalizing their strategies neither helped nor hindered their learning of the noun pairs. They also stated that they seldom failed to verbalize either their imagined or their verbal associations.

We classified verbalized strategies for each pair into one of three categories: Rehearsal, Elaboration, and Other Associative Strategies. In accord with the literature (e.g., Begg & Young, 1977; Rohwer, 1973; Rohwer, Raines, Eoff, & Wagner, 1977), Rehearsal was defined as the repetition of a noun pair with or without a conjunction (e.g., "The CATTLE and the BAY") and Elaboration was defined as the description of a direct interaction between the members of a noun pair (e.g., "The CATTLE swam in the BAY"). Strategies that provided associations other than a direct interaction were grouped together in a category of Other

Associative Strategies (e.g., identifying an attribute the nouns shared in common, such as color or shape; indicating that the pair members were owned by the same person; forming an interaction between the stimulus and a new, intermediate, response that would cue the actual response because of some preexisting association with it).

Analyses of the pair by pair strategy verbalizations, which are summarized in Table 12.1, both confirmed and refined previous conclusions about the existence of a developmental increase in the tendency to elaborate. There was an age-related decrease in the tendency of students to rely solely on rehearsal and a corresponding increase in the tendency to use elaboration and other associative strategies instead. Although the sizeable increase in the tendency to elaborate was expected, the increase in the number of other associations was not. As can be seen in Table 12.1, 9- and 10-year-old subjects usually elaborated if they produced any association at all, whereas the 16- to 18-year-old subjects were almost as likely to produce indirect associations as to elaborate. Because of the saliance of the developmental increase in the use of other associative strategies, this category of strategy use was included in subsequent analyses concerned with predicting cued recall from study strategies and examining the relationship between metamemory and strategic behavior.

Predicting Associative Recall From Study Strategies

Multiple regression was used to evaluate the relationship between reported strategy use and cued recall performance. The predictors were forced into the equation in a theoretically logical sequence: (1) number of elaborations, (2) number of other associative strategies, and (3) age level. Differences in the tendency to elaborate explained 42% of the variance in cued recall. An additional 29% of the variance was accounted for by the use of other associative strategies. Finally, other age-related differences that may influence associative performance accounted for less than 4% of the remaining variance. Nearly all of the developmental increase in cued recall could therefore be explained by the use of elaboration and other associative study strategies.

TABLE 12.1. Age differences in the use of study strategies.

	Age	
	Young	Old
Number of rehearsals	24.13	8.31
Number of elaborations	6.97	13.53
Number of other associations	2.16	11.19

Note: $n = 32$ per age level: Young, 10–11 years; old, 16–18 years. Technically, a total of 36 strategies could be produced, one for each pair studied. In practice, the total was less because an average of 2.73 and 3.03 strategies were unscorable for each grade, respectively.

An analysis was also conducted within age levels. The relative contributions of elaboration and other associative strategies to the prediction of cued recall differed markedly for each age group. Specifically, the number of elaborations produced by 10- and 11-year-olds subjects accounted for 66% of the variance in their cued-recall but the number of other associative strategies was so low that it accounted for none of the remaining variance. By contrast, the number of elaborations produced by the 16- to 18-year-old subjects accounted for only 13% of the variance in their cued-recall, whereas the number of other associations they produced explained an additional 26% of the variance.

The developmental elaboration hypothesis suggests that during adolescence subjects become more production efficient in the use of elaboration (Rohwer, 1973). Our results suggests that, although this is the case, subjects also increase their propensities to use other kinds of associative strategies that are less direct and pair specific. Furthermore, these associative strategies appear to be effective in facilitating paired-associate performance. Characterizations of developmental changes in paired-associate performance may therefore need to be revised to take into account the significant increase in the use of mnemonic strategies other than elaboration.

Postlearning interviews suggested that variations in the subjects' "knowledge base" (Pressley, Borkowski, & Schneider, in press) might contribute to both the developmental increase in the use of these other associative strategies and the propensities of subjects to select an alternate strategy over elaboration for a given pair. For example, many of our subjects reported that they resorted to other kinds of associations when they could not think of a "realistic" elaboration. Thus, the inaccessibility of relevant "event" knowledge for elaborative coding (see Rohwer, Rabinowitz, & Dronkers, 1982) apparently prompted subjects to apply alternate strategies. Of course, this action was driven by the mistaken assumption that only "realistic" elaborations would be useful (see Wollen & Margres, Chapter 5, this volume, as well as Einstein and McDaniel, Chapter 4, this volume). However, if subjects were successful in establishing unrealistic elaborations for pair members prior to resorting to nonelaborative strategies, the apparent effectiveness of "other associative strategies" in predicting recall might actually result from elaboration.

Metamemory

Metamemory judgments in previous studies have typically been scored as either reflecting accurate knowledge or not. The variety of judgments made by students in this study, however, indicated that a more refined scoring system would be necessary. Four to five categories of knowledge were therefore defined for each item in the metamemory scale. Whenever possible, the choice of categories and their rank ordering was based on theory or research as indicated in the Appendix. Each category was defined by the combination of an objective judgment (e.g., which of two strategies would help memory the most) and a justification or related set of justifications for such a judgment.

One category was reserved for justifications that reflected no appropriate knowledge regardless of the objective choice made. Another category was reserved for the only combination of judgment and justification that reflected completely accurate knowledge. The intermediate scoring categories were defined in such a way that there appeared to be meaningful differences between them, and all judgments could be classified. The Appendix provides more detailed definitions of the scoring categories for each item.

The Nature of Metamemory Development

Developmental and individual differences on the metamemory items are summarized in Table 12.2. The developmental trend appears as an age difference in the distribution of scores rather than as a discrete jump from no relevant knowledge

TABLE 12.2. Distribution of metamemory scores by item and age level.

Metamemory item	Score					Mean
	0	1	2	3	4	
Opposites–Arbitrary						
Young	3	3	13	13	–	2.13
Old	1	1	4	26	–	2.72
Story–List						
Young	1	8	7	16	–	2.19
Old	2	3	4	23	–	2.51
Study Plan						
Young	8	6	10	8	0	1.56
Old	1	2	7	17	5	2.72
Retrieval of Event						
Young	2	15	2	13	–	1.81
Old	1	3	2	26	–	2.66
Savings						
Young	9	0	0	23	–	2.16
Old	0	1	1	30	–	2.91
Elaboration–Rehearsal						
Young	14	13	3	1	1	.81
Old	5	8	3	10	6	2.13
Elaboration–Structural						
Young	9	8	12	3	–	1.28
Old	1	0	15	16	–	2.44
Elaboration–Shared Attribute						
Young	16	6	7	2	1	.94
Old	5	5	17	3	2	1.75
Retrieval of Elaboration						
Young	9	23	0	0	–	.72
Old	1	22	4	5	–	1.41

Note: Young, 10–11 years; old, 16–18 years. The scoring range was 0 to 3 for six of the nine items and 0 to 4 for the remaining three items. Only five items contributed to the composite metamemory score used in the regression analyses: Opposites–Arbitrary, Retrieval of Event, Elaboration–Rehearsal, Elaboration–Structural, and Elaboration–Shared Attribute.

to accurate knowledge (from zero to the highest score). The definitions of the intermediate scores (see Appendix) suggest that the transition between these extremes is marked by the gradual acquisition and refinement of knowledge.

One of the most interesting transitional degrees of knowledge in light of the elaborations produced by subjects during the memory task was the belief that unrealistic elaborations would not help memory despite the fact that they are actually quite effective. On the Metamemory Assessment, for example, the 16- to 18-year-olds, often recognized or produced unrealistic elaborations but then explicitly rejected them as useless (e.g., Elaboration–Rehearsal, score 1; Elaboration–Shared Attribute, score 3; Retrieval of Elaboration, score 1). This belief was implied even more often than it was expressed. Students in both age groups frequently produced or recognized familiar associations but not unlikely ones (e.g., Elaboration–Rehearsal, score 1).

In summary, the older subjects expressed far more knowledge about associative memory than the younger ones. This outcome is in contrast to Waters' (1982) findings, which were based on a narrow age group contrast, and is consistent with the hypothesis that significant metamemory development occurs during adolescence.

Regression analyses were used to predict strategic activities from a composite metamemory score based on five of the nine questionnaire items (the Appendix provides details about the nature and reliability of the metamemory score). For this analysis other types of associative strategies were combined with elaborations to obtain the dependent measure of number of associations. Metamemory scores explained 50% of the variance in the total number of associations reported by students while studying. Other age-related differences accounted for only 4 of the remaining variance. Most of the age-related increase in the tendency to use associative study strategies could therefore be predicted by the developmental increase in relevant metamemory knowledge.

Metamemory scores also explained nearly a third of the variance in the number of associations produced by students within each age group. In fact, the com-

TABLE 12.3. Age differences in the use of study strategies.

	Age	
	Young	Old
No-strategy instructions		
Number of Rehearsals	26.06	7.98
Number of Elaborations	5.38	15.75
Number of Other Assns.	2.00	8.44
Elaboration instructions		
Number of Rehearsals	1.38	.44
Number of Elaborations	25.44	24.94
Number of Other Assns.	6.50	9.44

Note: $n = 16$ per age (young, 10–11 years; old, 16–18 years) in each instructional condition.

TABLE 12.4. Recall performance by strategy instruction and age.

Instructions	Age		
	Young	Old	*M*
No strategy	9.50	24.44	16.97
Elaboration	20.63	26.63	23.63
M	15.05	25.53	

Note: $n = 16$ per age (young, 10–11 years; old, 16–18 years).

posite metamemory scores predicted individual differences equally well within these age levels despite the considerable difference between them in both the frequency and the diversity of their associative strategies.

A Followup Experiment

Experimental studies indicate that age differences in paired-associate recall are usually attenuated when subjects are instructed to elaborate, presumably because the instructions prompt younger subjects (who never or seldom use this strategy) to apply this strategy as consistently as older subjects (e.g., Pressley, Levin, & Bryant, 1983; Rohwer & Bean, 1973). A followup experiment was conducted to verify this hypothesis directly and to examine the extent to which paired-associate performance under elaboration instructions could be predicted by reported strategy use and metamemory.

Subjects in the first study returned a month later for another test on a different paired-associate list. Half of the subjects in each grade were given conventional learning instructions and half were told to produce an elaborative interaction between members of each pair. All methods and procedures were identical to the first experiment, except the metamemory questionnaire was not readministered.

The age-related pattern of strategy use observed in the initial experiment was replicated under the conventional instruction condition, as summarized in Table 12.3. With elaboration instructions, however, the pattern of strategy use by both age groups appears quite similar, particularly for the number of elaborations. This finding directly supports the hypothesis that instructions to elaborate are associated with corresponding increases in elaborative strategy use. The relatively high frequency of other associative strategies even under elaboration instructions is consistent with the earlier hypothesis that variations in knowledge base, coupled with an erroneous belief that only realistic associations work, may contribute to the tendency to select alternative strategies over elaboration.

Cued recall performance is presented in Table 12.4. Instructions to elaborate significantly increased the cued-recall performance of the 10–11 year-olds, but not the 16–18 year olds. The form of this interaction, as noted earlier, has traditionally been taken as evidence to support the developmental elaboration hypothesis (e.g., Rohwer, 1973).

A multiple-regression analysis was used to determine the significant predictors of cued-recall performance under elaboration instructions. The predictor variables were entered into the regression equation in the following order: (1) number of associative strategies (including elaboration and other); (2) metamemory score; and (3) age level. Although all subjects were instructed to use elaboration, individual differences in the number of overall strategies produced while studying accounted for 23% of the overall variance in cued recall. After differences in the number of study strategies were controlled, metamemory scores accounted for 12% of the remaining variance in cued recall. Like the findings from the primary experiment, age was no longer a major factor in accounting for differences in cued recall.

The finding that metamemory accounts for significant variance in cued recall under elaboration instructions (which presumably equates subjects for the type of study strategy used) even after the number of associative strategies has been entered into the regression equation (which controls for differences in how well instructions have been followed) suggests that metamemory is predicting developmental differences in other subject processes, such as retrieval. Indeed, whereas most elaboration research has focused on subject activities at study, evidence indicates that test trial mnemonic activities can affect recall as well (Kee, 1976; Pressley & Levin, 1980; Pressley & MacFadyen, 1983).

Conclusions

The results of this study accord well with current views about the nature of the developmental increase in associative memory during adolescence (Pressley, 1982; Rohwer, 1973, 1980). There were sizeable developmental increases in the use of elaboration and other associative study strategies and these increases accounted for nearly all of the corresponding increase in paired-associate recall.

The developmental increase in the use of associative strategies could in turn be attributed most directly to an age-related increase in relevant metamemory knowledge, particularly knowledge about the relative effectiveness of various study strategies under different conditions. In contrast to other studies, this finding provides unambiguous support for the theoretical relationship between developmental improvements in metamemory and strategic behavior (Schneider, 1985).

The nature of the students' metamemory judgments, together with the unusual strength of the metamemory–behavior relationship, suggests that future research should focus on measuring knowledge about production rules rather than on measuring declarative or factual knowledge per se. Interestingly, the most influential production rule in this study appears to have been an erroneous one, namely that elaboration was the best strategy for the task only when it produced a realistic association. Although theory and experimental evidence indicate that improbable associations work quite well (e.g., Kee & Nakayama, 1982; Rohwer, 1973; Rohwer & Bean, 1973), most students denied their effectiveness either explicitly or implicitly during the metamemory and postlearning interviews.

During the postlearning interviews, for example, mixed-strategy students who said they preferred elaboration also indicated they refused to use it consistently because elaboration often produced an improbable association (e.g., "I could have thought of an APRICOT stuck in a HORN but that wouldn't have worked"). They mistakenly believed it would be more effective to produce a less specific, but realistic, association instead. Similarly, some students who said they preferred any associative strategy to rote rehearsal nevertheless indicated they resorted to rehearsal whenever they could not think of a realistic association for the pair.

The same production rule was expressed in a variety of ways during the metamemory interview. Students typically recognized or produced the elaboration strategy only when it resulted in realistic interactions; they often explicitly rejected elaboration when it produced improbable interactions instead. The fact that the scoring of the metamemory judgments took this erroneous production rule into account (see Appendix) may explain the unusual strength of the relationships that were observed between individual and developmental differences in metamemory and strategic behavior.

Illuminating the production rules that guide students' behavior may suggest educational interventions in addition to providing theoretical insights into the nature of the metamemory–behavior relationship. The findings reported here suggest that instructional treatments that highlight erroneous production rules and then contradict them may be more effective for adolescents than instructional treatments that merely teach the appropriate strategy itself.

The educational interventions to which students have already been exposed may in turn provide hints about the normal course of metamemory development. Although mixed-strategy students in this study usually said they had discovered the elaboration strategy on their own, students who used elaboration consistently often reported they had been taught the strategy by a teacher, friend, or relative. Some students also reported acquiring the strategy in a study skills class or from educational TV programming. Particularly noteworthy is the observation by older students that they had learned the strategy sometime between ages 11 and 15. This period corresponds well with the age-range during which the propensity to elaborate on laboratory tasks begins to increase dramatically. Thus, if appreciation of the elaboration strategy is related to students' previous educational experiences, then differences in such experiences may provide some insight into the nature of individual and developmental differences in metamemory development itself.

Appendix

Description and Scoring of the Metamemory Interview

Opposites–Arbitrary

Asked students to judge whether it would be easier to learn pairs of opposites (black–white, left–right, day–night, happy–sad) or arbitrary pairs of names and actions (Mary–walk, Charley–jump, Anne–sit, Joe–climb). This measured awareness that preexisting associations would aid cued-recall memory (Kreutzer et al., 1975).

0 - The reason for choosing either/neither list did not refer to associations.
1 - Opposites would be easier (but the reason was unclear or the student was unsure).
2 - Opposites would be easier (because they provide better associations than the arbitrary pairs).
3 - Opposites would be easier (because they provide associations while the arbitrary pairs do not).

Story–List

Asked the student to judge whether telling a story about a man getting dressed for work would make it easier or harder to recall seven target nouns (bed, tie, coat, hat, table, dog, car). This measured awareness that elaborating a chain of association will aid free recall memory for a list of items (Kreutzer et al., 1975).

0 - The reason for either decision did not refer to associations.
1 - Story would make it harder (because it adds more words to be recalled).
2 - Story would make it easier (but the reason was unclear or the student was unsure).
3 - Story would make it easier (because it provides a thematic association for the target words).

Study Plan

Asked the student to recommend how to learn nine categorizable words (hat, jacket, sock, nose, hand, foot, apple, hotdog, pie). This assessed knowledge of the strategies that can be used to remember a categorizable list for free recall (Kreutzer et al., 1975).

0 - Only recommended rehearsal or an implausible strategy.
1 - Only recommended alphabetization of the words.
2 - Categorized sometimes or associated some items by elaboration.
3 - Categorized all items or associated all items in sets by using several elaborations.
4 - Elaborated the items within each category or joined all items by one elaboration.

Retrieval of Event

Asked student to recommend all the ways in which a friend could try to remember which Christmas s/he got a puppy as a gift. This assessed knowledge that memory for a target fact can be cued by recalling a related piece of information (Kreutzer et al., 1975).

0 - Only recommended thinking hard or an implausible retrieval strategy.

1 - Only recommended using external memory aids (e.g., a calendar or asking parents).
2 - Recommended successive elimination (remembering each preceeding Christmas in turn).
3 - Recommended remembering an associated fact to use as a retrieval cue (e.g., the friend's age that Christmas).

Savings

Asked the student to judge whether a list of birds would be learned more easily by a new learner or by a relearner who knew them once but forgot them. This measured awareness that apparently forgotten facts may still be in memory and are therefore worth trying to retrieve (Kreutzer et al., 1975).

0 - Makes no difference.
1 - Easier for the new learner (because the relearner will be confused by intervening learning).
2 - Easier for the relearner (but the reason was unclear or the student was unsure).
3 - Easier for the relearner (because the list is still in memory and so is still available to be recalled).

Elaboration–Rehearsal

Asked the student to judge the relative ease of learning three lists composed of the same noun pairs connected either by a conjunction, a locational preposition, or an interactive preposition (the MOP and/by/in the PAN, the JACKET and/by/in the BAG, the WATCH and/by/in the ROBE, the NICKEL and/by/in the SNAKE). Empirically, the first two are equivalent to rote rehearsal and the third is equivalent to elaboration (Begg & Young, 1977). Consequently this assessed knowledge that interactions provided an association that would aid cued-recall memory and side by side relationships did not.

0 - The reason for any ordering of the lists did not refer to associations.
1 - Conjunction and/or locational list(s) would be easiest (because they form associations while the interactions do not, or all three form associations but the interactions do not help memory because they are not realistic).
2 - Interaction list would be easiest (because it forms better associations than locational prepositions and conjunctions).
3 - Interaction list would be easiest (because it forms better associations than locational prepositions, whereas the conjunctions form no association at all).
4 - Interaction list would be easiest (because it forms associations, whereas the locational prepositions and conjunctions do not).

Elaboration–Structural

Asked students to judge the relative ease with which they could learn three lists of noun pairs for which the most readily implied association was either phonetic (goat–coat, money–honey, cart–heart, dirt–skirt), orthographic (phone–purse, coin–coat, rose–radio, horse–hose), or an elaborated interaction (bug–garden, coin–purse, bee–rose, water–plant). This assessed awareness of the implied association and knowledge that interactions were pair specific and so would aid cued recall more than the less specific letter or rhyme associations (see Paivio, 1971; Rohwer, 1973).

0 - The reason for any ordering of the lists did not refer to associations.
1 - Phonetic and orthographic lists would be easiest (because they provided associations, whereas the elaboration list did not).
2 - Phonetic and/or orthographic list would be easiest (because these associations were better than the recognized elaborations).
3 - Elaboration list would be easiest (because interactions are better than structural associations).

Elaboration–Shared Attribute

Asked the student to judge the relative ease of learning three lists of noun pairs for which the most readily implied association was either an attribute they shared in common (wire–thread, milk–snow, buzzer–trumpet, key–penny), a realistic interaction (scissors–pants, horse–corn, towel–glass, pencil–napkin), or an interaction that was very unlikely to occur (ball–jar, lion–sweater, teeth–chair, needle–sponge). This assessed both awareness of the implied associations and knowledge that pair–specific interactions would aid cued-recall more than general associations whether the interactions were plausible or not (see Rohwer, 1973).

0 - The reason for any ordering of the lists did not refer to associations.
1 - Shared attributes list would be easiest (because it provided associations, whereas the other lists did not).
2 - Shared attribute list would be easiest (because it was easier to think of associations for those pairs *or* because its associations were better than any type of interaction).
3 - Only the Realistic Elaboration list would be better than the Shared Attribute one (because only realistic interactions were better; unrealistic interactions would not help memory).
4 - Both Elaboration lists would be easier than the Shared Attribute one (because interactions always provided better associations, whether realistic or not).

Retrieval of Elaboration

Asked the student to judge whether it would be easier to recall a list of pairs when the nouns were associated either by a stimulus-related verb or by a response-related verb (the KNIFE cuts/beats the DRUM, the MATCH burns/stirs the PAINT, the CARPENTER builds/climbs the LADDER, the PIG eats/breaks the CANDY). This measured awareness that interactions related to the stimulus would help memory more than response-related interactions because the stimulus would be more likely to cue the mediating interaction in the former case (see Ehri & Rohwer, 1969; and Hasher, Griffen, & Johnson, 1977).

0 - The reason for choosing either/neither list did not refer to associations.
1 - Chose either list (because its associations seemed more realistic).
2 - Response-related list would be easiest (because these verbs were more likely to cue the response).
3 - Stimulus-related list would be easiest (because these stimuli were more likely to cue the mediating interactions that cue memory for the response).

Reliability of Scale and Selection of Item Subset for Analysis

Cronbach's alpha provided an estimate of the Metamemory Scale's reliability based on the intercorrelations among the nine items (see Cudeck, 1980; Nunnally, 1967). The scale was more reliable for the younger students ($\alpha = .76$) than for the older students ($\alpha = .47$), even though it was reliable for the sample as a whole ($\alpha = .80$). In part, this difference in reliability arose from the restricted range of older subjects' scores on the Kreutzer et al. (1975) items, which were originally designed for younger children.

Subsets of items were analyzed to see whether a more focused measure might have a greater reliability. A final set of five items that focused directly on knowledge of associative strategies (Opposites–Arbitrary, Elaboration–Structural, Elaboration–Rehearsal, Elaboration–Shared Attribute, and Retrieval Event) proved to be the most reliable for older subjects ($\alpha = .57$) without significantly reducing reliability for the younger subjects ($\alpha = .72$) or for the sample as a whole ($\alpha = .78$).

Examination of the intercorrelations among the items justified combining them to obtain a composite metamemory score for use in our analyses (see Nunnally, 1967; Kurtz et al., 1982). Analyses conducted with both the full scale and the subset of five items led to identical conclusions. Therefore, only the outcomes for the more reliable subscale are reported in the chapter. Also, standardizing the scores to control for differences in item difficulty and scoring range made little difference, so only the analyses of the more meaningful assigned scores are reported.

Acknowledgments. This report is based on a Ph.D. dissertation completed at the University of Southern California by the first author, under the direction of the second author. The preparation of this paper was supported by various grants from the California State University, Fullerton, to the second author. Special thanks to Professor Robert Cudeck for his advice on aspects of the statistical procedures used, and to Sue Houghton for her help and efficient word processing.

References

Begg, I., & Young, B. J. (1977). An organizational analysis of the form class effect. *Journal of Experimental Child Psychology, 23,* 503–519.
Cudeck, R. (1980). A comparative study of indices for internal consistency. *Journal of Educational Measurement, 17,* 117–130.

Ehri, L. C., & Rohwer, W. D., Jr. (1969). Verbal facilitation of paired-associate learning as a function of syntactic and semantic relations. *Journal of Verbal Learning and Verbal Behavior, 8*, 773–781.

Ericsson, K. A., & Simon, H. A. (1980). Verbal reports as data. *Psychological Review, 87*, 215–251.

Flavell, J. H., & Wellman, H. M. (1977). Metamemory. In R. V. Kail & J. W. Hagen (Eds.), *Perspectives on the Development of Memory and Cognition*. New Jersey: Erlbaum Associates.

Guttentag, R. E. (1985). Memory and Aging: Implications for theories of memory development during childhood. *Developmental Review, 5*, 56–82.

Hasher, L., Griffin, M., & Johnson, M. K. (1977). More on interpretive factors in forgetting. *Memory and Cognition, 5*, 41–45.

Kee, D. W. (1976). Storage and retrieval of noun pairs in children's recognition memory: Analysis of presentation made and elaboration effects. *Journal of Experimental Psychology: Human Learning and Memory, 2*, 623–632.

Kee, D. W., & Nakayama, S. (1982). Children's noun-pair retention: Assessment of pictorial elaboration and bizarreness effects. *Journal of Educational Psychology, 74*, 351–359.

Kreutzer, M. A., Leonard, C., & Flavell, J. H. (1975). An interview study of children's knowledge about memory. *Monograph of the Society for Research in Child Development, 40*(1, Whole Serial No. 159).

Kurtz, B. E., Reid, M. K., Borkowski, J. G., & Cavanaugh, J. C. (1982). On the reliability and validity of children's metamemory. *Bulletin of Psychonomic Society, 19*, 137–140.

Nunnally, J. C. (1967). *Psychometric theory*. New York: McGraw-Hill.

Paivio, A. (1971). *Imagery and verbal processes*. New York: Holt, Rinehart & Winston.

Pressley, M. (1982). Elaboration and memory development. *Child Development, 53*, 296–309.

Pressley, M., & Levin, J. R. (1977). Developmental differences in subjects' associative-learning strategies and performance: Assessing a hypothesis. *Journal of Experimental Child Psychology, 24*, 431–439.

Pressley, M., & Levin, J. R. (1980). The development of mental imagery retrieval. *Child Development, 51*, 558–560.

Pressley, M., & McFadyen, H. (1983). Mnemonic mediator retrieval at testing by preschool and kindergarten children. *Child Development, 54*, 474–479.

Pressley, M., Borkowski, J., & Schneider, W. (in press). Good strategy users coordinate metacognition, strategy use and knowledge. In R. Vasta & G. Whitehurst (Eds.), *Annals of child development* (Vol. 4). Greenwich, CT: JAI Press.

Pressley, M., Levin, J. R., & Bryant, S. (1983). Memory strategy instruction during adolescence: When is explicit instruction needed? In M. Pressley & J. R. Levin (Eds.), *Cognitive strategy research*. New York: Springer-Verlag.

Rohwer, W. D., Jr. (1973). Elaboration and learning in childhood and adolescence. In H. W. Reese (Ed.), *Advances in child development and behavior* (Vol. 3). New York: Academic Press.

Rohwer, W. D., Jr. (1980). An elaborative conception of learner differences. In R. E. Snow, P. A. Frederico, & W. E. Montague (Eds.), *Aptitude, learning and instruction*. New Jersey: Erlbaum Associates.

Rohwer, W. D., Jr., & Bean, J. F. (1973). Sentence effects and noun-pair learning: A developmental interaction during adolescence. *Journal of Experimental Child Psychology, 15*, 521–533.

Rohwer, W. D., Jr., Rabinowitz, M., & Dronkers, N. F. (1982). Event knowledge, elaborative propensity, and the development of learning proficiency. *Journal of Experimental Child Psychology, 33*, 492–503.

Rohwer, W. D., Jr., Raines, J. M., Eoff, J., & Wagner, M. (1977). The development of elaborative propensity in adolescence. *Journal of Experimental Child Psychology, 23*, 472–492.

Schneider, W. (1985). Developmental trends in metamemory–memory behavior relationship: An integrative review. In D. L. Forrest-Pressley, G. E. MacKinnon, & T. G. Waller (Eds.), *Cognition, metacognition, and human performance* (Vol. 1, pp. 57–109). New York: Academic Press.

Waters, H. S. (1982). Memory development in adolescence: Relationships between metamemory strategy use, and performance. *Journal of Experimental Child Psychology, 33*, 183–195.

CHAPTER 13

The Development of Good Strategy Use: Imagery and Related Mnemonic Strategies

Michael Pressley, John G. Borkowski, and Carla J. Johnson

Although most research on mnemonics has been done with adults, there are replicable developmental shifts in mnemonic skills. The analysis of age-related changes in mnemonic skills has increased understanding of theoretical issues, such as the nature of production deficiencies (Flavell, 1970) and imaginal representations (e.g., Bruner, Olver, & Greenfield, 1966; Kosslyn, 1980; Paivio, 1971, 1986), and holds promise for enhancing children's associative learning and memory processes in classroom contexts.

The major goal of this chapter is to provide a brief overview of the development of imagery and imaginal mnemonic skills. A second purpose is to discuss the probable origins of mnemonic skills in children and adolescents in light of a contemporary model of competent strategy use. The link between developmental trends in children's imagery use and the emerging hypotheses about the factors that facilitate or impede the development of these skills will become obvious after consideration of the nature of good strategy use (Pressley, Borkowski, & Schneider, in press-a).

The Good Strategy User

A proficient strategy user knows and can execute a variety of strategies that accomplish many specific cognitive goals. For instance, imagery strategies are available to augment learning of simple (e.g., letter–sound associations; Ehri, Deffner, & Wilce, 1984) as well as complex tasks (e.g., prose; Pressley, 1976). In addition to processing a variety of specific basic-level strategies, good strategy users execute higher order strategic plans. That is, they coordinate and sequence basic-level imagery strategies and combine them with other procedures. For instance, a highly strategic reader trying to understand and remember textbook content might first preview the chapter by reading headers and looking at pictures, followed by reading with imaginal coding and paraphrasing. Higher order plans always include monitoring strategies. The good reader would monitor whether the text was being understood and remembered in the process of executing this series of basic-level strategies. Monitoring might be accomplished by frequent self-testing, with the reader self-questioning after every page or two to determine whether the content could be recalled.

Appropriate use of strategies and the creation of higher order strategic sequences can occur only when learners possess detailed knowledge about how, when, and where to use strategies. This type of metamemorial information is referred to as *specific strategy knowledge* (Pressley, Borkowski, & O'Sullivan, 1984, 1985). The importance of specific strategy knowledge is well documented. For instance, there are repeated demonstrations of a positive relationship between knowing the value of a strategy (one aspect of specific strategy knowledge) and its subsequent application (e.g., Black & Rollins, 1982; Borkowski, Levers, & Gruenenfelder, 1976; Cavanaugh & Borkowski, 1979; Kennedy & Miller, 1976; Lawson & Fuelop, 1980; Paris, Newman, & McVey, 1982; Ringel & Springer, 1980). We emphasize that this form of metamemory – specific strategy knowledge – is intricate and detailed. For instance, consider what can be known about the strategic value of retrieval cues (Beal, 1985; Fabricius & Wellman, 1983). Good strategy users know that retrieval cues are associated with targets and that they should be unambiguous (i.e., not equally relevant to targets and nontargets). The good strategy user also knows how far the retrieval strategy can be "stretched," yet still work; whether the retrieval strategy is fun or easy to use; as well as relevant episodic information, such as the circumstances and occasions in which the strategy was acquired.

In addition to knowing about the attributes of specific strategies, good strategy users possess general knowledge about cognitive activities and general tendencies that support the use of specific strategies. This type of general knowledge includes understanding that personal effort can increase success, especially if that effort is channeled through task-appropriate strategies (e.g., Clifford, 1984) and that strategies must be shielded from competing behaviors, distractions, and emotions. These specific pieces of general knowledge motivate, respectively, the general tendencies to look for strategic options when faced with a challenge and to keep focused and calm when performing a task (e.g., Kuhl, 1985). These pieces of general knowledge and these general tendencies facilitate planful, controlled thinking and action.

Although the emphasis throughout this chapter is on strategy use, strategy implementation cannot be isolated from nonstrategic knowledge. Mature thinkers possess well-integrated scripts that encode knowledge about virtually every aspect of their lives, from eating at a restaurant to shoveling snow off the driveway (e.g., Mandler, 1983). They also have a host of interrelated associations (e.g., Anderson, 1983) as well as a great deal of hierarchically arranged, categorical information (e.g., Mandler, 1983). Although this information commonly is possessed by mature and intelligent adults, each person also has personalized, episodic information encoded in these scripts, associative networks, and categorical structures (e.g., Tulving, 1983).

The nonstrategic knowledge base relates to good strategy use in three ways:

1. Knowledge can diminish the need to use strategies. New information to be learned may be easy to acquire if the learner possesses a well-developed, relevant knowledge base. In this instance, there is little need to execute the strategies that are essential to learning in the absence of a rich knowledge base.

2. Congruence between the knowledge base and some content to be learned primes the use of strategies for material not so obviously related. For instance, a learner may realize that memorization of highly related paired-associate items, such as CAT–DOG, is easy because of the semantic relationship between the paired items. This realization may prime the search for semantic relationships for other pairings that are not so obviously related (e.g., TUR-KEY–ROCK). The learner would intentionally take special steps to facilitate acquisition of this nonobvious association (e.g., form an image of a turkey with rocks in its gizzard). The use of the elaboration strategy probably would not have occurred without prior exposure to highly related pairings that were highly congruent with the knowledge base.
3. Nonstrategic knowledge enables the use of specific strategies. For instance, many classification strategies cannot be executed in the absence of knowledge of category boundaries that are necessary to group items into their respective classes.

The components of good strategy use – specific strategy knowledge, general knowledge about cognitive activities, and domain-specific knowledge – combine to produce finely articulated cognitive performance. When confronted with a task, the good strategy user knows that effort is required and so gets set to attend selectively and work hard. Specific strategy knowledge then permits the selection of appropriate strategies, although strategy use may be bypassed if the material is easily assimilated because it is congruent with some part of the learner's knowledge base. A good deal of planning and sequencing of strategies may occur for particularly complex tasks. Explicit monitoring of performance throughout the execution sequence allows ineffective strategies to be abandoned and replaced with more effective ones.

Is it possible for the human mind to do so much simultaneous coordination and monitoring? After all, human beings (e.g., Kahneman, 1973) and children in particular (e.g., Case, 1985) are limited in how much mental activity they can perform at any one time. Fortunately, much of the mental activity associated with good strategy use can be done sequentially (i.e., components in higher order sequences are executed one component at a time) so that the burden on consciousness is more apparent than real. Furthermore, the good strategy user deploys many of these components in an automated fashion so that execution requires little conscious attention or effort (e.g., Ackerman & Schneider, 1985; Hess & Radke, 1981). In summary, the automatic coordination of components that can be executed efficiently is the hallmark of the good strategy user.

The Development of Imagery and Other Mnemonic Skills

Many adults are not good mnemonic strategy users. From this perspective, it is not surprising that children usually fail to use imagery and mnemonic coding techniques (Pressley, 1982). From another perspective, theories of cognitive development often include the assumption that the thinking of young children is highly imagistic (e.g., Bruner et al., 1966). In this vein, there is evidence supporting the claim that young children often represent concepts in an imagistic fashion (e.g., Kosslyn, 1976, 1980) and that imagery sometimes mediates children's execution of important cognitive tasks, such as reading (e.g., Sadoski, 1983, 1985). Nonetheless, the research evidence is overwhelming that children do not use imaginal coding to the extent that they could, with both research on spontaneous use of imagery and its use following instruction supporting this conclusion. Research on both autonomous and instructed use of imagery is taken up in this section.

Imagery and Related Mnemonic Strategies

Autonomous Use

There is a general developmental increase in the use of elaboration strategies (e.g., interactive imagery and sentences associating the two items), especially between the late grade-school years and adolescence (Kemler & Jusczyk, 1975; Kennedy & Suzuki, 1977; Pressley & Levin, 1977a; Rohwer & Bean, 1973; Rohwer, Raines, Eoff, & Wagner, 1977). One of the most impressive pieces of evidence consistent with this conclusion is provided by Beuhring and Kee in Chapter 12, this volume. As 10–12 year olds and 16–18 year olds studied paired associates, they verbalized what they were doing to learn the pairs (Ericsson & Simon, 1983). The results most relevant to this discussion were obtained when subjects were left to their own devices to learn the paired associates. There was a marked decline in the use of simple rehearsal with increasing age, accompanied by a striking developmental increase in the use of elaboration and other associative strategies. Whereas two thirds of the pairings were rehearsed by 10–12 year olds, only one third of the pairings were rehearsed by 16–18 year olds. Conversely, one third of the pairings were encoded using elaboration and related associative strategies by younger children, whereas two thirds of the pairs were learned in this fashion by older subjects. It should be emphasized, however, that there was room for additional elaborative activity even among the older subjects. This finding is consistent with previous research on the use of elaboration by mature learners.

Nonetheless, it must be emphasized that even some very young children probably use mnemonics. For example, a 6 year old in the study by Pressley and Levin (1977b) comes to mind. As picture pairs were presented, he shouted meaningful sentences that contained the paired items. Not surprisingly, this child remembered more of the pairings than any of his classmates, none of whom showed any sign of using elaboration. Whether the strategy was used intentionally by the 6 year old could not be discerned, nor was it determined whether the child anticipated the positive memorial consequences of his verbal elaborative activity.

Intentionality and anticipation of results is more likely when young children use well-known mnemonic poems, such as "30 Days Hath September," and mnemonic sentences that are passed from generation to generation (Brett, 1981). For example, "A rat in Tom's house might eat the ice cream" can be used to remember the spelling of "arithmetic." Formal study of children's deployment of these mnemonic devices is needed, focusing especially on children's understanding of the utility of the strategies. A particular interesting question is the extent that young children understand the coding principles that account for the potency of these literary mnemonics.

Strategy Use Following Instruction

Beuhring and Kee also provided data demonstrating that elaboration is a strategy that can be taught to children and adolescents. Following explicit instruction to use elaboration for paired-associate learning, more than two thirds of the pairs at both age levels were learned using the trained strategy, with the preponderance of the remaining items encoded via other associative strategies. Young learners can elaborate even though they do not do so autonomously.

There have been a number of experiments designed to determine when children can execute and benefit from mnemonics, such as simple imaginal and verbal elaboration. In recent years research has centered on children's use of the mnemonic keyword method. See, for instance, Chapter 16, by Mastropieri, Scruggs, and Levin, in this volume.

The keyword technique can be adapted to a variety of learning tasks with an associative component (Levin, 1985a; Pressley, Levin, & Delaney, 1982). These include acquisition of social studies and science facts, although the bulk of research has been concerned with first- and second-language vocabulary learning. For instance, to learn that the German word *Kürbis* means pumpkin, the anglophone learner could first establish an acoustic link between *Kürbis* and a concrete English word (e.g., curb), and then imagine an interaction between the keyword and the definition referent. In this case, an effective image (i.e., one that would enhance learning) would be a pumpkin sitting on a street curb.

At what developmental levels can children be taught to use elaborative procedures? The answer is complex. For instance, there are striking differences in the development of imaginal versus verbal elaboration of paired associates. Although preschool children experience great difficulty generating interactive images that embed paired associates, they can easily generate elaborative sentences that facilitate learning (e.g., Levin, McCabe, & Bender, 1975). The ability to generate interactive elaborative images develops during the grade-school years, paralleling developmental improvements from 5 to 12 years of age in other imagery-mediated tasks (e.g., Dean, 1976). During the early grade-school years, children's generation of imaginal elaborations is more certain when the items to be associated are presented pictorially rather than verbally, when there are obvious semantic relationships between the items to be associated, and when the pace of learning is relatively slow. These constraints do not hold by the end of grade-school years (e.g., Pressley & Levin, 1977b, 1978).

It should be emphasized as well that the developmental improvement in execution of imagery skills is not confined to elaboration of simple associative tasks. In particular, there are clear develomental improvements in children's ability to generate images that represent the content of prose. One study did more than any other to stimulate research on this problem.

By 1975, it was well established that children younger than 7 or 8 years of age could not generate representational images of prose or could do so only with great difficulty (Shimron, 1975). Guttmann, Levin, and Pressley (1977) proposed that less than complete pictures might prompt imaginal representations of connected materials that would not occur without external support and so improve children's learning of prose. To evaluate this hypothesis, Guttmann et al. (1977) created "partial pictures" to accompany short stories presented to children. In the partial picture condition, the sentence, "One evening Sue's family sat down to eat a big turkey dinner," was accompanied by the partial picture in Figure 13.1 (colored in the experiment) and an instruction to create an internal imaginal representation of the complete prose content. The partial pictures reiterated the content of the accompanying text except for one object that was occluded in the illustration. Cued recall of this object was the critical dependent variable. Performance in the partial picture condition was compared to performance (a) when children viewed complete pictures that included the objects to be recalled, (b) when children were given imagery instructions and no pictures, and (c) when children learned the prose without pictures or imagery instructions.

Across three experiments the conclusion that emerged was that partial pictures stimulated representational imagery when a simple imagery instruction failed to do so. When the data from Guttmann et al. (1977) are combined with outcomes in followup studies (Digdon, Pressley, & Levin, 1985; Purkel & Bornstein, 1980; Ruch & Levin, 1979), it is apparent that partial pictures do not stimulate imagery in preschool children, but do so with 5–7 year olds. Nonetheless, children's imagery skills continue to develop during the later grade-school years. Imagery instructions alone significantly facilitated the prose learning of 10–12 year olds but failed with 6–8 year olds (Levin, Bender, & Pressley, 1979). (See Pressley, 1977, and Pressley and Miller, 1987, for reviews of the relevant studies.)

FIGURE 13.1. Partial picture accompanying, "One evening Sue's family sat down to eat a big turkey dinner." From Guttmann et al. (1977). Copyrighted by the American Psychological Association. Reprinted by permission.

Before this subsection is closed, it should also be mentioned that even on those occasions when children execute imagery strategies, performance sometimes fails to improve significantly. Again, this pattern occurs more often with younger than with older children. For instance, Pressley and Levin (1980) demonstrated that even when young grade-school children generated mnemonic mediators to learn material, they sometimes failed to make use of the mediators at testing. Grade 1 (6–7 year olds) and grade 6 (11–12 year olds) subjects learned picture paired associates either under an instruction to generate interactive images or under a control instruction. At testing, imagery subjects in the first grade recalled more than control subjects only if they were told to think back to the images they had constructed during the study period. That is, grade 1 subjects failed to retrieve the mediators spontaneously, whereas Grade 6 subjects required no reminders at testing.

Short-Term Memory and Imagery Strategy Use

How can the development of imaginal skills be explained? Surprisingly, there has been remarkably little work aimed at explicating the mechanisms that account for age-related improvements in children's imagery. An information-processing hypothesis is now being evaluated—that children's imagery-generation skills are tied to how much information is held and coordinated in consciousness at any one time (i.e., short-term memory; Case, 1985, Chapter 13; Dempster, 1985). Since short-term memory is severely limited, only a few storage and processing activities can be carried out simultaneously. In this sense, short-term memory capacity is critical to imagery because the creation of imaginal representations requires that the learner perform several activities at once. Consider the specific case of imaginal coding of sentences. The learner must (a) hold the sentence in memory, (b) retrieve or construct images of each object and event represented in the sentence, and (c) combine the component images into a coherent representation of the sentence meaning.

Pressley, Cariglia-Bull, and Deane (1986) recently produced data consistent with the position that children's short-term memory capacity may be an important determinant of whether they benefit from an imagery strategy. Their study included children from 6 to 12 years of age. Short-term memory capacity (as measured by a battery of tasks, each tapping different aspects of short-term memory) predicted learning of sentences when children used imagery to code the materials better than it predicted learning of sentences when children were left to their own devices to memorize the materials. Short-term memory was a significant predictor of recall in the imagery condition even with age and general verbal ability controlled statistically. Short-term memory failed to predict recall in the control condition when either age or general verbal ability was taken into account. In short, all of the evidence produced by Pressley et al. (1986) pointed to short-term memory as an important determinant of imagery strategy execution. A more surprising outcome was that general verbal ability was also an important predictor of performance in the imagery condition, and much more so than in the control condition.

In short, age is by far the most frequently investigated individual differences variable in studies of children's imagery and mnemonics, with frequent reports that imagery instructions are effective with older but not younger children. The next step is to determine the variables that age indexes that are the underlying determinants of these developmental shifts. Pressley's et al. (1986) data suggest that both short-term memory and general verbal competence are two variables that should be explored in detail.

Transfer of Imagery Strategies Following Instruction

One of the most frequently noted performance shortfalls is the failure to transfer strategies following instruction (e.g., Brown, Bransford, Ferrara, & Campione, 1983). Failures to transfer mnemonic strategies are more likely with younger than with older subjects, with some evidence that adolescence is the developmental period when improvements in transfer skills are especially striking.

Pressley and Dennis-Rounds (1980) presented two associative learning tasks (learning city–product pairings and acquisition of the meanings of Latin vocabulary) to 10–13 year olds and 16–18 year olds. There were four conditions in each experiment. In three conditions, subjects were instructed to use the mnemonic keyword method to acquire the items on the first task, the learning of products that were produced in particular cities. In the fourth condition the subjects were given no strategy instruction, but instead were permitted to learn vocabulary in any way that they wished. Consistent with other results, keyword-instructed subjects outperformed the control subjects at both the younger and older age levels.

The most critical manipulation occurred with the presentation of the second task, learning the meaning of Latin words. Control subjects and one group of subjects who had been trained to use the keyword method for the city–product task were presented the Latin words and told to learn them but were provided no strategy instructions. One of the two remaining groups that had previously received keyword training was given more keyword method instruction, specifically on how to use the method to learn Latin words. In the remaining condition that had keyword instruction for the cities task, subjects were given a very general instruction to use the keyword strategy for the Latin task. These subjects were told, "Do about the same thing as you did to remember what the cities were known for" (p. 578).

The most important result on the Latin task was that the older adolescents transferred the keyword strategy. That is, older subjects who were provided keyword training for the city–product task, but no additional keyword training, outperformed control subjects during the learning of Latin words. Younger subjects, who received the general instruction to use keyword on the Latin task, outperformed control subjects, but there was no evidence of spontaneous transfer of the keyword strategy (i.e., the performance levels were almost identical in the control condition and in the condition in which subjects received keyword training only for the city–products task). Although transfer was more evident among the older adolescents than among the 10–13 year olds (i.e., strategy use occurred without prompting among the older subjects), it should be pointed out that at both age levels maximum performance on the Latin task was found when subjects were explicitly instructed on how to apply the method with Latin words. Transfer of the strategy was apparently far from complete even for the 16–18 year olds.

Less than maximum transfer (when transfer occurs at all) is the rule, even with mature subjects. One of the most thorough examinations of this phenomenon was conducted by Pressley and Ahmad (1986). The study was motivated by the observation that introductory psychology students at Western Ontario reported using imagery as a principle mediator for learning following participation in a laboratory exercise that provided practice with the "one-is-a-bun" pegword mnemonic. Pressley and Ahmad's (1986) experiment—designed to test the hypothesis that use of the keyword method would increase following exposure to a different, yet related, imagery strategy—included six conditions, with the learning of Latin words as the criterion task. Rehearsal control subjects were taught to say the Latin words and their meanings over and over, an instruction presumed to be antagonistic to the development of elaboration strategies (e.g., Rohwer & Bean, 1973). No strategy controls were left to their own devices to learn vocabulary. "Hint" subjects were given the general instruction to use "association, imagery, and/or mnemonics" to learn vocabulary. Although pegword experience subjects were provided no instructions as to how to encode the Latin words, they were given some practice with the "one-is-a-bun" mnemonic for list learning. Pegword experience + hint subjects were exposed to the pegword procedure and were given the hint about imagery before they studied the Latin words. In the sixth condition, subjects were explicitly taught to use the keyword method to learn the Latin vocabulary.

Both recall and self-report data were used to infer strategy use. The most important results were the following: (a) the hint had little effect (i.e., strategy use in the hint and control conditions was statistically comparable, as was strategy use in the pegword experience and pegword experience + hint conditions); (b) pegword experience stimulated use of keyword–mnemonic imagery on the Latin task (i.e., strategy use in the pegword experience condition was greater than in the control condition); and (c) pegword experience did not result in strategy use comparable to that in the keyword-instructed condition.

It should be emphasized, however, that the generalization that occurred in the pegword experience condition was impressive because of the notable processing differences between the pegword and the keyword situations. The pegword mnemonic is structured for application with lists of single items; keyword applies to single paired materials (e.g., foreign vocabulary and their meanings). Pegwords are encoded into long-term memory as part of the "one-is-a-bun" poem and can be reused with any list of single items; keywords must be generated on a case by case basis. Retrieval with keyword mnemonics goes from vocabulary item to keyword to meaning, whereas retrieval with the pegword system goes from list position numbers (subjects often have to generate these on their own) to pegwords to items.

There is, however, a common skill required in the pegword and keyword techniques—the use of proxies in interactive relationships with content to be remembered (list items, definitions). A pegword is a proxy for a list position number, whereas a keyword is a proxy for an acoustically similar vocabulary item. The pegword experience may have induced the rule, "use a proxy in interaction with what must be remembered." Regardless of the exact mechanism mediating transfer, the transfer reported by Pressley and Ahmad (1986) is the most impressive demonstration of elaborative generalization to date. Other reports of elaborative strategy transfer (e.g., O'Sullivan & Pressley, 1984; Pressley & Dennis-Rounds, 1980) were from one task perfectly matched to the keyword technique to another task perfectly matched to the strategy, as from one form of paired-associate learning (e.g., city–product learning) to another form of paired-associate learning (e.g., acquiring Latin meanings).

Thus far, we have reviewed data substantiating age-related increases in autonomous generation of mnemonics and age-related increases in susceptibility to instructions to use imagery and mnemonics. There are other developments in the use of mnemonic skills that are relevant to other aspects of the good strategy user model.

Specific Strategy Knowledge

Katz (Chapter 8, this volume) makes a convincing case that adults know a good deal about when to use certain imagery and mnemonic strategies. Unfortunately, the evaluation of mature learners' knowledge about other aspects of strategy deployment is far from complete. Even less is known concerning children's specific strategy knowledge about mnemonic skills. The most complete set of data on the problem is summarized by Beuhring and Kee (Chapter 12, this volume). In general, knowledge about elaboration (especially knowledge about the utility of elaboration) increases between the late grade-school years and late adolescence. For instance, older subjects in Beuhring's and Kee's study recognized the advantages associated with elaboration compared to rehearsal, even though the younger subjects failed to do so. There was also a developmental increase in recognition of the efficacy of an interactive relationship compared to other semantic relationships.

Transfer of Specific Strategies

Although utility information is certainly an important part of specific strategy knowledge, it is not all that a learner needs to know for appropriate strategy use to occur. As Katz points out, knowing when to use a strategy is also quite critical. So is knowing how to make slight changes in a strategy so that it fits new situations. It fact, it has been recognized for a long time that generalized use of strategies (i.e., transfer) depends heavily on what we refer to as specific strategy knowledge (e.g., Gagné, 1977; House, 1982; Thorndike & Woodworth, 1901).

Although they did not attempt to assess their subjects' knowledge of how, when, and where to use mnemonic strategies, O'Sullivan and Pressley (1984) provided evidence consistent with two hypotheses: (a) that children do not possess detailed metamemorial knowledge about individual strategies, especially about application of mnemonic strategies; and (b) that providing specific strategy knowledge to children increases their generalized use of mnemonic strategies.

O'Sullivan and Pressley required 10–12 year olds and young adults to learn two types of materials, both of which had an associative component. The first task was learning a list of city–product pairings (e.g., submarines are manufactured in Long Beach). The second was memorization of the meanings of Latin vocabulary.

Control subjects in the study learned both sets of materials with no strategy instructions. Subjects in all other conditions learned the city–product pairings using the keyword method, which effectively mediates learning of both types of materials (e.g., Pressley & Dennis-Rounds, 1980). Keyword training for the city–product task varied, however, with respect to how explicitly subjects were told how, where, and when keyword mnemonics would be helpful. In the most explicit condition, this information was conveyed both verbally and through several examples. In the least explicit keyword condition, specific strategy knowledge was not provided at all. The most important dependent variable in the study was whether subjects transferred the keyword strategy to the Latin vocabulary task, which also benefitted from keyword application (e.g., Pressley & Dennis-Rounds, 1980). In general, children were more likely to transfer when keyword instructions explicitly contained a lot of specific strategy knowledge. Adults' transfer was high, however, regardless of the explicitness of strategy information included in the instructions. This pattern of outcomes suggested that the adults previously abstracted more knowledge about a strategy from the simple strategy directions and practice than did the children. Thus, the explicit provision of specific strategy information was much more crucial with children, a finding compatible with other metamemory data.

For instance, Pressley, Levin, and Ghatala (1984a) required adults and 10- to 12-year-old children to try two different strategies (the keyword method and verbal rehearsal of the word and its meaning) to learn the meanings of Latin vocabulary items. During the course of trying both strategies and being tested on the items that were learned with them, adults abstracted that the keyword method produced learning superior to that produced by rehearsal. The adults also used this information in making a decision about how to study another list of vocabulary. Although children realized that the keyword method was a more viable strategy, they typically underestimated the size of the keyword advantage. Moreover, they did not realize that the information about differential strategy use should be used to decide which of the two strategies to use on another vocabulary learning task. Pressley, Ross, Levin, and Ghatala (1984) replicated these deficiencies exhibited by children. In short, adults are more certain than children to acquire specific strategy knowledge that they subsequently use to regulate cognition.

Metamemory as a Framework for Acquiring and Understanding New Strategies

A rich metamemorial knowledge base about "other" strategies probably supplies information about a range of essential attributes necessary for understanding the utility of a new strategy (Borkowski, Milstead, & Hale, in press). Borkowski and his associates have provided support for this claim, demonstrating the importance of prior metamemory for acquisition of new mnemonic strategies.

Kurtz, Reid, Borkowski, and Cavanaugh (1982) taught a totally new elaboration procedure to 7–8 year olds using self-instructional procedures. Durable use of the strategy (i.e., maintenance) was predictable from the children's knowledge of organizational and rehearsal strategies ($r = .50$). Additional support for the linkage between specific strategy knowledge in general and acquisition of new strategies was provided by Borkowski, Peck, Reid, and Kurtz (1983). Children were selected on the basis of their cognitive tempos, so as to form impulsive and reflective subgroups. There were clear differences in metamemorial knowledge about strategies associated with cognitive tempo, with knowledge about other strategies predicting long-term use of a newly acquired reading strategy even when tempo and general intelligence were controlled statistically (Kurtz & Borkowski, 1985). Finally, Borkowski and Peck (1985) established that metamemory was among several variables (perceptual efficiency and general knowledge were the others) that distinguished gifted from average children. Most critical to the present discussion, metamemory about other strategies predicted gifted children's transfer of a newly acquired strategy.

General Knowledge and General Tendencies

There are a few general inhibitors of children's strategy use that have been studied intensively, although usually not in the specific context of mnemonic strategy use. For instance, there is growing evidence that anxiety can disrupt efficient execution of strategies (e.g., Tobias, 1977, 1985). Impulsivity is also incompatible with good strategy execution (e.g., Kendall & Braswell, 1985; Meichenbaum, 1977). So are dysfunctional attributions about academic achievement, such as beliefs that poor performances are tied to low ability and that good performances are a consequence of luck or an easy test (e.g., Dweck & Elliot, 1983). Fortunately, treatments are available to reduce these tendencies and eliminate their debilitating consequences (e.g., Buxton, 1981; Clifford, 1984; Pressley, Reynolds, Stark, & Gettinger, 1983).

Particularly relevant to this chapter, Reid and Borkowski (1985) were able to show that reattribution training, aimed at changing one general tendency believed to be a determinant of good strategy use (beliefs about self-efficacy), could be an important component in teaching mnemonic and other memory strategies. They studied the effects of two different approaches to strategy training on the long-term use of strategies by hyperactive children. The two experimental regimens differed only in that one contained an attribution retraining component—in which the importance of effort in improving performance was repeatedly explained and demonstrated—whereas the other did not.

In a self-control training condition (Brown et al., 1983), the instructor modeled self-verbalization procedures for the child (e.g., "Look to see how the problem might be solved"; "Stop and think before responding"). The self-instructions were intended to control the tempo of the hyperactive students, thus setting the stage for teaching two learning strategies, an interrogative–elaborative procedure for associative learning and a clustering–rehearsal procedure for sort–recall readiness.

In a self-control plus attribution training condition, subjects received the same self-control instructions as well as the training of specific learning strategies. In addition, they received attribution retraining, including training about the causes of success and failure and feedback about the relationship between strategy use and successful paired-associate learning. Explicit emphasis was placed on the causes of good and poor performance, on how learning a particular pairing was greatly dependent on whether the elaborative strategy had been used to learn the item. Subjects in a third condition were taught both the elaboration and rehearsal–clustering procedures but did not receive self-control or attributional training.

The most important results were obtained on a 10-month followup of training effectiveness. Hyperactive children in the self-control plus attribution condition continued to use the elaboration and rehearsal–clustering strategies, more so than subjects in the other two conditions. Attributional beliefs and metamemory were also permanently altered in this condition compared to the other two treatments. In particular, children who had received attributional retraining understood better that their behavior was controllable. An important finding was that impulsivity decreased in children who were most hyperactive at the beginning of the study as a consequence of self-control plus attribution training.

There are two points about attribution retraining that deserve emphasis. First, general effort attributions that follow Weiner's (1985) model are discussed in the literature far more often that are strategic–effort attributions. Knowing that hard work is an important determinant of achievement is different, however, from understanding that hard work is most likely to pay off if it is channeled through appropriate cognitive tools, such as strategies. Many tales can be told about hard work followed by failure. Task persistence following failure despite great effort is more likely if the learner believes that failure has occurred because effort has been misdirected, rather than holding the belief that personal effort would have never paid off, perhaps because of a lack of ability. Believing that effort must be channeled through appropriate tools fuels the search for alternative strategies when failure occurs (Clifford, 1984).

The second point centers on the difficulty of establishing attributions that enhance the belief that strategies play an important role in self-regulation. Inculcation of these appropriate beliefs requires extensive, explicit training, especially with young children. Ghatala, Levin, Pressley, and Goodwin (1986) have shown that the chain of behaviors from strategy use to attributions about strategies to strategy regulation is very fragile in 6–7 year olds.

Effects of the Nonstrategic Knowledge Base

Given the dearth of information about the interplay between the knowledge base and strategy use, it is not surprising that this problem has not been explored in much detail with respect to mnemonics. The data that are available, however, suggest important relationships between strategic and nonstrategic factors.

The earliest developmental study to deal with this problem was Pressley and Levin (1977b). In that experiment, children benefitted differentially from a mnemonic imagery strategy depending on situational factors, including the degree of accessible and relevant linking relationships in the knowledge base. Pressley and Levin (1977b) first presented concrete paired associates to samples of grade 2 and grade 6 subjects who were instructed to generate internal images containing the paired items in interaction. Subjects were timed as they generated elaborations. Grade 6 children generated an image in less than 5 sec for each pair. In contrast, grade 2 children generated images in under 5 sec for pairs with obvious associations but required between 5 and 8 sec to generate relationships for not so obviously related items.

Next, new samples of children were presented the pairs at either a 6-sec or a 12-sec rate, with the instruction either to learn the associations using interactive imagery or simply to try hard to remember the pairings (i.e., a no-strategy control direction). At the grade 6 level, the imagery instruction promoted learning of both the obviously related and the not so obviously related pairs regardless of the rate of presentation. At the second-grade level, the imagery instruction was potent for both pair types at the slower rate of presentation. In contrast, when the pairs were presented at the 6-sec rate, grade 2 children benefitted from the imagery instruction only for items that were obviously related. Pressley and Levin's (1977b) data were consistent with the conclusion that young children's consistent use of imagery to mediate learning depends in part on the ready availability of elaborative relationships in the knowledge base.

Rohwer, Rabinowitz, and Dronkers (1982) provided an analytical developmental investigation of the dependence of mnemonic strategy use on the knowledge base. Fifth-grade students were presented one of two types of paired associates to remember, ones closely related in the knowledge base (e.g., ranch–cowboy) and ones not so closely related (e.g., ranch–floor). Subjects were presented the pairs and were provided either an instruction to learn them by generating verbal elaborations (little stories joining the paired items) or a no-strategy control instruction. The most important result was that verbal elaboration instruction affected learning of unrelated pairs but did not affect the learning of related materials. Rohwer et al. (1982) reasoned that if fifth graders used elaboration autonomously, the instruction to use verbal elaboration should have had little or no impact. Thus, the superior learning of unrelated pairs given the elaboration instruction suggested that the fifth graders were not elaborating these items. The failure to find an effect of instruction with related pairs suggested that items that were congruent with the knowledge base produced automatic semantic elaboration of these items.

One of the most interesting outcomes in Rohwer's et al. (1982) study is consistent with other data pointing to adolescence as a critical period in the development of elaborative skills. With adolescents as subjects, instructions to elaborate had little impact on the learning either of closely related or unrelated pairs. The generally high performance of the adolescents, compared especially to younger subjects who were not provided instructions to elaborate, was interpreted as evidence of autonomous use of the strategy by the older subjects. Of course, such an interpretation would benefit from more direct measures of both strategic activities and use of the knowledge base. Along these lines, Beuhring and Kee (Chapter 12, this volume) collected concurrent self-reports during associative learning. We believe that such secondary measures of elaborative processes will be common in future research on elaborative strategy by knowledge base interactions.

Summary: The Development of Mnemonic Skills

The development of imagery and mnemonic skills is complex, as should be apparent from the cursory overview of relevant issues and data base presented in this review. Several general conclusions and trends should be emphasized.

1. There are clear developmental increases in the uninstructed use of elaborative mnemonic strategies, with especially dramatic increases between late childhood (i.e., 11–12 years of age) and late adolescence (i.e., 17–18 years of age). Autonomous use of elaboration occurs first with familiar materials that elicit ready associations and then spreads to other materials (e.g., Rohwer et al., 1982; cf. Bjorklund, 1985). The variety of elaborative mnemonics used by children increases with age as well, a point supported by Beuhring's and Kee's data. Older subjects not only used more elaboration but also exploited many types of associative–semantic relationships between the paired items. In contrast, younger subjects constructed simple interactive elaborations if they elaborated at all. Whether this increased variety of mnemonics owes to a richer knowledge base, a deeper understanding of how an elaborative strategy can be stretched, or both is not possible to determine at this time.

2. There are clear developmental improvements in children's generation of imaginal mediators in response to instructions. Preschoolers do not generate their own imaginal mediators even when they are provided prompting. Generation skills emerge during the early grade-school years and are first apparent when the task is structured to keep short-term memory demands low, such as when part of the image is provided in the form of an illustration. Thus, children generate imaginal representations of prose given partial pictures before they can generate realistic internal images on their own (Guttmann et al., 1977). Before children can use the imagery keyword method with verbal materials alone, they can do so given picture of keywords and meaning referents (Pressley & Levin, 1978). This steady improvement in children's response to instruction probably results in part from developmental increases in functional short-term memory (Case, 1978, 1985; Pressley et al., 1986).

3. Generalization of instructed strategies increases with age. As is the case with autonomous use of imagery and mnemonics, adolescence is an important period for the development of mnemonic generalization. One possible explanation of this development of generalization propensity is that metacognition about elaboration undergoes significant changes during adolescence. This

hypothesis is consistent with data reported by O'Sullivan and Pressley (1984), Borkowski and his associates (e.g., Kurtz & Borkowski, 1985), and Beuhring and Kee (Chapter 12, this volume), although the problem requires additional study before a definitive conclusion can be drawn. Given the prominence of metacognitive theories of transfer (e.g., Brown et al., 1983), as well as contemporary interest in transfer as a developmental problem, the development of metacognitive–elaborative strategy use relationships is likely to receive additional research attention.

4. Despite the fact that imagery and mnemonic-generation skills develop slowly, it is always possible to obtain positive imagery and mnemonic benefits by providing prompts (e.g., pictures). For instance, the provision of pictures representing the content of prose facilitates learning at all ages (Levie, 1987; Levie & Lentz, 1982; Pressley & Miller, 1987). Provision of keyword mnemonic pictures has dramatic effects even with 3–5 year olds who are especially inefficient at acquiring vocabulary-meaning associations (Pressley, Samuel, Hershey, Bishop, & Dickinson, 1981). If the goal is simply to build up an associative knowledge base, providing pictorial mediators is a solution that can be implemented at almost any age. Some of the most dramatic effects have been obtained with disadvantaged learners, including learning-disabled and mentally retarded subjects (Mastropieri et al., Chapter 16; Pressley, Johnson, & Symons, in press).

New Directions for Developmental Imagery and Mnemonics Research

It would be difficult to read a volume such as this one without concluding that extensive research on imagery and mnemonics is justified, both on theoretical and pragmatic grounds. Past research has been limited in several respects: few tasks studied (e.g., paired-associate learning, vocabulary learning, sentence learning); few strategies examined (e.g., imaginal elaboration, keyword method, representative images of sentences); only normal participants in most studies, with important differences in general tendencies (e.g., anxiety, impulsivity); and knowledge bases generally ignored. Future work should be more broadly conceived, and we believe that the good strategy user model suggests a number of task and person variables that can be studied profitably. Given the breadth of the model, we do not advocate attempts to construct a single experiment or even a series of experiments on the entire framework. Rather, each component should be investigated intensively, with theoretically interesting and practically important interactions between components receiving attention.

First of all, a wider variety of mnemonic strategies need to be explored, each in great detail. It is simply amazing that 2000 years after Simonides used the method of loci to recall a list of guests (ones who were crushed by the falling roof of a banquet hall), we know almost nothing about children's ability to use that same method. The use of imagery–organizational strategies during reading has hardly been studied (Pressley, 1977). Yōdai mnemonics have been developed in Japan to assist children's learning of a number of content areas (Higbee & Kunihira, 1985), but systematic evaluation of that technique has not followed (Levin, 1985b; Pressley, 1985). We know nothing about whether children can use imagery in a prospective fashion (Ceci & Bronfenbrenner, 1985), such as constructing an image to serve as a reminder of tasks that should be performed over the course of a day. There is ample work to be done in establishing the range of imaginal and mnemonic procedures that children can carry out.

Children's monitoring strategies, especially as they are applied to keeping track of the use of mnemonic strategies, deserve additional attention. Preliminary data suggest that children's all too uncertain monitoring of mnemonic and imagery strategies (e.g., Pressley et al., 1984a; Pressley, Ross, Levin, & Ghatala, 1984b) can be improved through instruction (Ghatala et al., 1986; Ghatala, Levin, Pressley, & Lodico, 1985; Lodico, Ghatala, Levin, Pressley, & Bell, 1983). Finally, there is virtually no work on children's use of higher order strategic plans that include coordinated imagery strategies as components. Given the likelihood that imagery execution in the context of higher order frameworks is likely to produce more durable use of imagery (Brown et al., 1983; Elliott-Faust & Pressley, 1986; Meichenbaum, 1977), research on regulation by higher order strategies should be a high priority. There is additional motivation for this work, because the study of other strategies embedded in higher order structures has produced enormous theoretical and practical payoffs in classroom settings (e.g., Palincsar & Brown, 1984).

Our understanding of children's specific strategy knowledge is also very incomplete. Are some children more likely than others to acquire the understanding of when to use strategies? If so, why? Are some children more likely to use specific strategy knowledge that they possess? Can children be taught to abstract metacognitive information about strategies (e.g., Ghatala et al., 1986) or should it be provided for them (O'Sullivan & Pressley, 1984)? What metacognitive information should be taught to maximize durable and general use of strategies?

Beyond knowledge of specific strategies, there is also a need to understand more fully the general tendencies that learners possess that will affect their use of strategies, with emphasis on how to prevent the development of characteristics that interfere with efficient cognition and on how to promote desirable general tendencies. We suspect that many of these tendencies are generalizations of specific experiences and skills. Thus, the teaching of specific strategies may be a good point at which to intervene. By emphasizing the benefits that follow use of each specific strategy as it is taught, learners should eventually abstract the belief that each strategy has unique benefits and that competent performance is largely a function of what the learner selects to do during the acquisition process. This type of knowledge should motivate intellectual effort and attempts to find strategies that match the requirements of new learning challenges.

Control of general emotional and impulsive distractions is an area of great concern, with most efforts aimed at reducing disruptive general tendencies once they have developed (e.g., Covington, 1984; Kendall & Braswell, 1985). It seems to us that preventative work in this area is also desirable. We emphasize that action control (following Kuhl's, 1985, terminology) is only a setting condition for effective strategy use (Keogh & Barkett, 1980; Whalen & Henker, 1980). Still, it is disturbing that we can identify little research that has been focused on teaching children, from an early age, the benefits of reflective cognition. Based on social learning principles alone (Rosenthal & Zimmerman, 1978), we would expect that years of modeling and teaching of emotionally controlled performance would have long-term positive effects, at least for some children. Perhaps children could be exposed for a long time to teachers who deliberately act out the contents of cognitive behavior modification models (e.g., Meichenbaum, 1977). That is, they make clear how they are processing information and what the positive consequences are that follow effective processing. They would make obvious how calmly, deliberately, and attentively a successful thinker carries out problem solving and learning tasks.

Development of the knowledge base goes hand in hand with development of strategic competence. What prompts children to use knowledge at all? Does "automatic" use of available knowledge increase with development? What types of cues must be present for an available knowledge base to be activated? Are different types of cues necessary for different types of knowledge representations (e.g., associative cues for associative networks, pattern cues for schematic knowledge, visual cues for information coded as images), as might be suggested by Tulving's (1983) encoding specificity model? Especially interesting are problems of coordination between knowledge and strategies. When and how do children learn to coordinate the knowledge base and strategic processing? For instance, what prompts a child, who is an expert at computer programming, to abandon conventional wisdom in favor of using strategic problem solving to try to identify a new method for accomplishing a programming goal? We know nothing about when and why experts rely on strategies rather than on their knowledge (Gick, 1986), even though it seems likely that this is an ecologically valid setting for strategy use. The questions of when and how experts initiate strategy use and how that strategy use depends on the knowledge base should be studied in greater detail.

Even though the dynamics of knowledge base and strategy interactions have not been mapped out, the good strategy user model suggests that every effort should be made to build upon the knowledge base. The more children know, the less reliant they should be on strategies to generate solutions. That is one reason why we are so enthusiastic about providing mnemonic mediational aids to children who cannot generate mnemonic mediators on their own. The aids include pictures that contain transformational mnemonic representations that permit rapid acquisition of large quantities of knowledge (Pressley, 1983; Pressley & Miller, 1987). It seems to us that widespread use of mnemonic pictures as a way to build children's knowledge is a very real possibility in the not too distant future (Pressley, Johnson, & Symons, in press).

Finally, good thinking is often efficient to the point of automaticity. An important individual difference among children is whether they can carry out strategies quickly and effortlessly. Learners who do so are much better off than those who must execute each step with conscious effort. Much work needs to be done examining the relative efficiency of child strategy users. More work is needed on how strategy use proceeds from being clumsy and deliberate to being smooth and automatic (e.g., Corbett, 1977; Polya, 1981). In short, research on the development of mnemonic skills should be aimed at determining how nonstrategic knowledge, metacognition about strategies, and strategies are intertwined.

Acknowledgments. Writing of this chapter was supported by a grant to the first author from the Natural Sciences and Engineering Research Council of Canada. John Borkowski's participation was supported by NIH Grant HD-17648 and HD-21218.

References

Ackerman, P. L., & Schneider, W. (1985). Individual differences in automatic and controlled information processing. In R. F. Dillon (Ed.), *Individual differences in cognition* (Vol. 2, pp. 35–66). Orlando, FL: Academic Press.

Anderson, J. R. (1983). *The architecture of cognition.* Cambridge, MA: Harvard University Press.

Beal, C. R. (1985). Development of knowledge about the use of cues to aid prospective retrieval. *Child Development, 56,* 631–642.

Bjorklund, D. F. (1985). The role of conceptual knowledge in the development of organization in children's memory. In C. J. Brainerd & M. Pressley (Eds.), *Basic processes in memory development: Progress in cognitive developmental research* (pp. 103–142). New York: Springer-Verlag.

Black, M. M., & Rollins, H. A. (1982). The effects of instructional variables on young children's organization and free recall. *Journal of Experimental Child Psychology, 31,* 1–19.

Borkowski, J. G., & Peck, V. (1985). Causes and consequences of metamemory in gifted children. In R. Sternberg & J. Davidson (Eds.), *Conceptions of giftedness.* Cambridge: Cambridge University Press.

Borkowski, J. G., Levers, S. R., & Gruenenfelder, T. M. (1976). Transfer of mediational strategies in children: The role of activity and awareness during strategy acquisition. *Child Development, 47,* 779–786.

Borkowski, J. G., Milstead, M., & Hale, C. (in press). Components of children's metamemory: Implications for strategy generalization. In F. Weinert & M. Perlmutter (Eds.), *Memory development: Universal changes and individual development.* Hillsdale, NJ: Erlbaum Associates.

Borkowski, J. G., Peck, V., Reid, M., & Kurtz, B. (1983). Impulsivity and strategy transfer: Metamemory as mediator. *Child Development, 54,* 459–473.

Brett, S. (Ed.) (1981). *The Faber book of useful verse.* London: Faber and Faber.

Brown, A. L., Bransford, J. D., Ferrara, R. A., & Campione, J. C. (1983). Learning, remembering, and understanding. In J. H. Flavell & E. M. Markman (Eds.), *Handbook of child psychology: Vol. III: Cognitive development* (pp. 177–266). New York: John Wiley & Sons.

Bruner, J. S., Olver, R. R., & Greenfield, P. M. (1966). *Studies in cognitive growth.* New York: Wiley.

Buxton, L. (1981). *Do you panic about maths?: Coping with math anxieties.* London: Heinemann Educational Books.

Case, R. (1978). Intellectual development from birth to adulthood: A neo-Piagetian interpretation. In R. S. Siegler (Ed.), *Children's thinking: What develops?* (pp. 37–72). Hillsdale, NJ: Erlbaum Associates.

Case, R. (1985). *Intellectual development: Birth to adulthood.* Orlando, FL: Academic Press.

Cavanaugh, J. C., & Borkowski, J. G. (1979). The metamemory-memory "connection": Effects of strategy training and maintenance. *Journal of General Psychology, 101,* 161–174.

Ceci, S. J., & Bronfenbrenner, U. (1985). "Don't forget to take the cupcakes out of the oven": Prospective memory, strategic time monitoring, and context. *Child Development, 56,* 152–164.

Clifford, M. M. (1984). Thoughts on a theory of constructive failure. *Educational Psychologist, 19,* 108–120.

Corbett, A. T. (1977). Retrieval dynamics for rote and visual image mnemonics. *Journal of Verbal Learning and Verbal Behavior, 16,* 233–246.

Covington, M. V. (1984). Anxiety management via problem-solving instruction. In H. M. Van der Ploeg, R. Schwarzer, & C. D. Spielberger (Eds.), *Advances in test anxiety research* (Vol. 1, pp. 39–52). Hillsdale, NJ: Erlbaum Associates.

Dean, A. L. (1976). The structure of imagery. *Child Development, 47,* 949–958.

Dempster, F. N. (1985). Short-term memory development in childhood and adolescence. In C. J. Brainerd & M. Pressley (Eds.), *Basic processes in memory development: Progress in cognitive development research* (pp. 209–248). New York: Springer-Verlag.

Digdon, N., Pressley, M., & Levin, J. R. (1985). Preschoolers' learning when pictures do not tell the whole story. *Educational Communication and Technology Journal, 33,* 139–145.

Dweck, C. S., & Elliot, E. S. (1983). Achievement motivation. In E. M. Hetherington (Ed.), *Handbook of child psychology: Vol. IV: Socialization, personality, and social development* (pp. 643–691). New York: John Wiley & Sons.

Ehri, L. C., Deffner, N. D., & Wilce, L. S. (1984). Pictorial mnemonics for phonics. *Journal of Educational Psychology, 76,* 880–893.

Elliott-Faust, D. J., & Pressley, M. (1986). How to teach comparison processing to increase children's short- and long-term listening comprehension monitoring. *Journal of Educational Psychology, 78,* 27–33.

Ericcson, A., & Simon, H. A. (1983). *Verbal protocol analysis.* Cambridge, MA: The MIT Press.

Fabricius, W. V., & Wellman, H. M. (1983). Children's understanding of retrieval cue utilization. *Developmental Psychology, 19,* 15–21.

Flavell, J. H. (1970). Developmental studies of mediated memory. In H. W. Reese & L. P. Lipsitt (Eds.), *Advances in child development and behavior* (Vol. 5, pp. 182–211). New York: Academic Press.

Gagné, R. M. (1977). *The conditions of learning* (3rd ed.). New York: Holt, Rinehart, and Winston.

Ghatala, E. S., Levin, J. R., Pressley, M., & Goodwin, D. (1986). A componential analysis of the effects of derived and supplied strategy-utility information on children's strategy selection. *Journal of Experimental Child Psychology, 41,* 76–92.

Ghatala, E. S., Levin, J. R., Pressley, M., & Lodico, M. G. (1985). Training cognitive strategy monitoring in children. *American Educational Research Journal, 22,* 199–216.

Gick, M. L. (1986). Problem solving strategies. *Educational Psychologist, 21,* 99–120.

Guttmann, J., Levin, J. R., & Pressley, M. (1977). Pictures, partial pictures, and young children's oral prose learning. *Journal of Educational Psychology, 69,* 473–480.

Hess, T. M., & Radke, R. C. (1981). Processing and memory factors in children's reading comprehension skill. *Child Development, 52,* 479–488.

Higbee, K. L., & Kunihira, S. (1985). Cross-cultural applications of Yōdai mnemonics in education. *Educational Psychologist, 20,* 57–64.

House, B. J. (1982). Learning processes: Developmental trends. In J. Worell (Ed.), *Psychological development in the elementary years* (pp. 187–232). New York: Academic Press.

Kahneman, D. (1973). *Attention and effort.* Englewood Cliffs, NJ: Prentice-Hall.

Kemler, D. G., & Jusczyk, P. W. (1975). A developmental study of facilitation by mnemonic instruction. *Journal of Experimental Child Psychology, 20,* 400–410.

Kendall, P. C., & Braswell, L. (1985). *Cognitive-behavioral therapy for impulsive children.* New York: The Guilford Press.

Kennedy, B. A., & Miller, D. J. (1976). Persistent use of verbal rehearsal as a function of information about its value. *Child Development, 47,* 566–569.

Kennedy, S. P., & Suzuki, N. S. (1977). Spontaneous elaboration in Mexican-American and Anglo-American high school seniors. *American Educational Research Journal, 14,* 383–388.

Keogh, B. K., & Barkett, C. J. (1980). An educational analysis of hyperactive children's achievement problems. In C. K. Whalen & B. Henker (Eds.), *Hyperactive children: The social ecology of identification and treatment* (pp. 259–282). New York: Academic Press.

Kosslyn, S. M. (1976). Using imagery to retrieve semantic information: A developmental study. *Child Development, 47,* 434–444.

Kosslyn, S. M. (1980). *Image and mind.* Cambridge, MA: Harvard University Press.

Kuhl, J. (1985). Volitional mediators of cognition-behavior consistency: Self-regulatory processes and action versus state orientation. In J. Kuhl & J. Beckmann (Eds.), *Action control: From cognition to behavior* (pp. 101–128). New York: Springer-Verlag.

Kurtz, B. E., & Borkowski, J. G. (1985). Metacognition and the development of strategic skills in impulsive and reflective children. Paper presented at the biennial meeting of the Society for Research in Child Development, Toronto, Ontario, Canada.

Kurtz, B., Reid, M., Borkowski, J. G., & Cavanaugh, J. (1982). On the reliability and validity of children's metamemory. *Bulletin of the Psychonomic Society, 19,* 137–140.

Lawson, M. J., & Fuelop, S. (1980). Understanding the purpose of strategy training. *British Journal of Educational Psychology, 50,* 175–180.

Levie, W. H. (1987). Research on pictures: A guide to the literature. In D. M. Willows & H. A. Houghton (Eds.), *The psychology of illustration: Volume 1. Basic research.* New York: Springer-Verlag.

Levie, W. H., & Lentz, R. (1982). Effects of text illustrations: A review of research. *Educational Communication and Technology Journal, 30,* 195–232.

Levin, J. R. (1985a). Educational applications of mnemonic pictures: Possibilities beyond your wildest imagination. In A. A. Sheikh (Ed.), *Imagery in education: Imagery in the educational process* (pp. 63–87). Farmingdale, NY: Baywood.

Levin, J. R. (1985b). Yōdai features = mnemonic procedures: A commentary on Higbee and Kunihira. *Educational Psychologist, 20,* 73–76.

Levin, J. R., Bender, B. G., & Pressley, M. (1979). Pictures, imagery, and children's recall of central versus peripheral sentence information. *Educational Communication and Technology Journal, 27,* 89–95.

Levin, J. R., McCabe, A. E., & Bender, B. G. (1975). A note on imagery-inducing motor activity in young children. *Child Development, 46,* 263–266.

Lodico, M. G., Ghatala, E. S., Levin, J. R., Pressley, M., & Bell, J. A. (1983). The effects of strategy-monitoring on children's selection of effective memory strategies. *Journal of Experimental Child Psychology, 35,* 263–277.

Mandler, J. M. (1983). *Stories, scripts, and scenes: Aspects of schema theory.* Hillsdale, NJ: Erlbaum Associates.

Meichenbaum, D. M. (1977). *Cognitive behavior modification.* New York: Plenum Press.

O'Sullivan, J. T., & Pressley, M. (1984). Completeness of instruction and strategy transfer. *Journal of Experimental Child Psychology, 38,* 275–288.

Paivio, A. U. (1971). *Imagery and verbal processes.* New York: Holt, Rinehart, & Winston.

Paivio, A. U. (1986). *Mental representations: A dual-coding approach.* New York: Oxford University Press.

Palincsar, A. M., & Brown, A. L. (1984). Reciprocal teaching of comprehension-fostering and monitoring activities. *Cognition and Instruction, 1,* 117–175.

Paris, S. G., Newman, R. S., & McVey, K. A. (1982). Learning the functional significance of mnemonic actions: A microgenetic study of strategy acquisition. *Journal of Experimental Child Psychology, 34,* 490–509.

Polya, G. (1981). *Mathematical discovery: On understanding, learning, and teaching problem solving* (comb. ed.). New York: John Wiley.

Pressley, G. M. (1976). Mental imagery helps eight-year-olds remember what they read. *Journal of Educational Psychology, 68,* 355–359.

Pressley, M. (1977). Imagery and children's learning: Putting the picture in developmental perspective. *Review of Educational Research, 47,* 586–622.

Pressley, M. (1982). Elaboration and memory development. *Child Development, 53,* 296–309.

Pressley, M. (1983). Making meaningful materials easier to learn: Lessons from cognitive strategy research. In M. Pressley & J. R. Levin (Eds.), *Cognitive strategy research: Educational applications* (pp. 239–266). New York: Springer-Verlag.

Pressley, M. (1985). More about Yōdai mnemonics: A commentary on Higbee and Kunihira. *Educational Psychologist, 20,* 69–72.

Pressley, M., & Ahmad, M. (1986). Transfer of imagery-based mnemonics by adult learners. *Contemporary Educational Psychology, 11,* 150–160.

Pressley, M., & Dennis-Rounds, J. (1980). Transfer of a mnemonic keyword strategy at two age levels. *Journal of Educational Psychology, 72,* 575–582.

Pressley, M., & Levin, J. R. (1977a). Developmental differences in subjects' associative learning strategies and performance: Assessing a hypothesis. *Journal of Experimental Child Psychology, 24,* 431–439.

Pressley, M., & Levin, J. R. (1977b). Task parameters affecting the efficacy of a visual imagery learning strategy in younger and older children. *Journal of Experimental Child Psychology, 24,* 53–59.

Pressley, M., & Levin, J. R. (1978). Developmental constraints associated with children's use of the keyword method of foreign language vocabulary learning. *Journal of Experimental Child Psychology, 26,* 359–372.

Pressley, M., & Levin, J. R. (1980). The development of mental imagery retrieval. *Child Development, 51,* 558–560.

Pressley, M., & Miller, G. E. (1987). The effects of illustrations on children's listening comprehension and oral prose memory. In H. A. Houghton & D. M. Willows (Eds.), *The psychology of illustration: Volume 2. Educational issues.* New York: Springer-Verlag.

Pressley, M., Borkowski, J. G., & O'Sullivan, J. T. (1984). Memory strategy instruction is made of this: Metamemory and durable strategy use. *Educational Psychologist, 19*, 94–107.

Pressley, M., Borkowski, J. G., & O'Sullivan, J. T. (1985). Children's metamemory and the teaching of memory strategies. In D. L. Forrest-Pressley, G. E. MacKinnon, & T. G. Waller (Eds.), *Metacognition, cognition, and human performance* (pp. 111–153). New York: Academic Press.

Pressley, M., Borkowski, J. G., & Schneider, W. (in press-a). Cognitive strategies: Good strategy users coordinate metacognition and knowledge. In R. Vasta & G. Whitehurst (Eds.), *Annals of child development* (Vol. 4). Greenwich, CT: JAI Press.

Pressley, M., Cariglia-Bull, T., Deane, S. (1986). *Short-term memory as a predictor of the effectiveness of a prose imagery strategy.* Technical Report. London, Ontario: Department of Psychology, University of Western Ontario.

Pressley, M., Johnson, C. J., & Symons, S. (in press-b). Elaborating to learn and learning to elaborate. *Journal of Learning Disabilities.*

Pressley, M., Levin, J. R., & Delaney, H. D. (1982). The mnemonic keyword method. *Review of Educational Research, 52*, 61–92.

Pressley, M., Levin, J. R., & Ghatala, E. S. (1984a). Memory strategy monitoring in adults and children. *Journal of Verbal Learning and Verbal Behavior, 23*, 270–288.

Pressley, M., Reynolds, W., Stark, K. D., & Gettinger, M. (1983). Cognitive strategy training and children's self-control. In M. Pressley & J. R. Levin (Eds.), *Cognitive strategy research: Psychological foundations* (pp. 267–300). New York: Springer-Verlag.

Pressley, M., Ross, K. A., Levin, J. R., & Ghatala, E. S. (1984b). The role of strategy utility knowledge in children's strategy decision making. *Journal of Experimental Child Psychology, 38*, 491–504.

Pressley, M., Samuel, J., Hershey, M. M., Bishop, S. L., & Dickinson, D. (1981). Use of a mnemonic technique to teach young children foreign language vocabulary. *Contemporary Educational Psychology, 6*, 110–116.

Purkel, W., & Bornstein, M. H. (1980). Pictures and imagery both enhance children's short-term and long-term recall. *Developmental Psychology, 16*, 153–154.

Reid, M. K., & Borkowski, J. G. (1985). *The influence of attribution training on strategic behaviors, self-management, and beliefs about control in hyperactive children.* Unpublished manuscript. South Bend, IN: University of Notre Dame.

Ringel, B. A., & Springer, C. J. (1980). On knowing how well one is remembering: The persistence of strategy use during transfer. *Journal of Experimental Child Psychology, 29*, 322–333.

Rohwer, W. D., Jr., & Bean, J. P. (1973). Sentence effects and noun-pair learning: A developmental interaction during adolescence. *Journal of Experimental Child Psychology, 15*, 521–533.

Rohwer, W. D., Jr., Rabinowitz, M., & Dronkers, N. F. (1982). Event knowledge, elaborative propensity, and the development of learning proficiency. *Journal of Experimental Child Psychology, 33*, 492–503.

Rohwer, W. D., Jr., Raines, J. M., Eoff, J., & Wagner, M. (1977). The development of elaborative propensity during adolescence. *Journal of Experimental Child Psychology, 23*, 472–492.

Rosenthal, T. L., & Zimmerman, B. J. (1978). *Social learning and cognition.* New York: Academic Press.

Ruch, M. D., & Levin, J. R. (1979). Partial pictures as imagery-retrieval cues in young children's prose recall. *Journal of Experimental Child Psychology, 28,* 268–279.

Sadoski, M. (1983). An exploratory study of the relationship between reported imagery and the comprehension and recall of a story. *Reading Research Quarterly, 19,* 110–123.

Sadoski, M. (1985). The natural use of imagery in story comprehension and recall: Replication and extension. *Reading Research Quarterly, 20,* 658–667.

Shimron, J. (1975). Imagery and the comprehension of prose by elementary school children. (Doctoral dissertation, University of Pittsburgh, 1974). *Dissertation Abstracts International, 36,* 795-A (University Microfilms No. 75-18,254).

Thorndike, E. L., & Woodworth, R. S. (1901). The influence of improvement in one mental function upon the efficiency of other functions. *Psychological Review, 8,* 247–261, 384–395, 553–564.

Tobias, S. (1977). A model for research on the effect of anxiety on instruction. In J. E. Sieber, H. F. O'Neil, Jr., & S. Tobias (Eds.), *Anxiety, learning, and instruction* (pp. 223–240). Hillsdale, NJ: Erlbaum Associates.

Tobias, S. (1985). Test anxiety, interference, defective skills, and cognitive capacity. *Educational Psychologist, 20,* 135–142.

Tulving, E. (1983). *Elements of episodic memory.* New York: Oxford University Press.

Weiner, B. (1985). *Human motivation.* New York: Springer-Verlag.

Whalen, C. K., & Henker, B. (1980). The social ecology of psycho-stimulant treatment: A model for conceptual and empirical analysis. In C. K. Whalen & B. Henker (Eds.), *Hyperactive children: The social ecology of identification and treatment* (pp. 3–51). New York: Academic Press.

PART III

Applications

The 2000-year history of imagery and related mnemonics has largely been a tale of people finding ways to improve learning of material that they have found otherwise difficult to acquire (Fenaigle, 1813; Yates, 1966). It has only been in the last 30 years that formal evaluations of mnemonic applications have been attempted, with much of this work stimulated by Miller, Galanter, and Pribram's (1960) analysis of mnemonic imagery as a psychological plan. Given the excitement generated by applied research on imagery and mnemonics, it seems likely that this type of research will flourish in the years to come. The chapters presented here review the best applied work that is currently available.

Richardson, Cermak, Blackford, and O'Connor (Chapter 14) explore how mnemonics and imagery can be used in cognitive rehabilitation following brain injury. The challenges for researchers interested in this problem are many. First of all, there are a host of types of injury. Second, there are rarely enough patients in any particular category to permit large-scale experimentation. Third, this type of work requires sophisticated understanding of both neuropsychology and contemporary cognitive psychology. It is, therefore, not surprising that Richardson et al. review many intensive, interdisciplinary studies of a few patients. Richardson et al. conclude that the training of specific memory skills must take account of the specific information processing characteristics of the patient and must be embedded in a larger training program that includes teaching patients to self-regulate their learning.

Turnure and Lane (Chapter 15), as well as Mastropieri, Scruggs, and Levin (Chapter 16), explore the utility of imagery and mnemonic training for special education. Both chapters are sanguine about this possibility. Turnure and Lane review briefly the types of special populations that benefit from mnemonics as well as some of the more popular approaches used in this type of research. They pay particular attention to relating the work on mnemonics to Sternberg's componential analysis of performance and to analyzing the problem of strategy generalization when special populations are the learners. A particular strength of Mastropieri's et al. chapter is that they review an impressive body of literature documenting the effectiveness of mnemonic interventions compared to other educational procedures that are currently in use with learning disabled students.

Mastropieri et al. cover most of the literature documenting that mnemonics can be used to teach vocabulary, content-area facts, and prose materials to handicapped learners. It is clear from both Turnure and Lane and Mastropieri et al. that mnemonic interventions deserve a place in the education of people who otherwise experience difficulty mastering academic content.

Mnemonic educational interventions are useful for very capable learners as well as for students who are considered academically impaired. Consistent with this conclusion, Snowman (Chapter 17) describes his efforts to train university students to mediate learning from prose. Snowman teaches students the coordinated use of two learning tactics, a scheme for parsing prose into main and supporting ideas and loci mnemonics. His chapter summarizes some of his own research documenting the efficacy of this combined approach, concluding with a discussion of research aimed at enhancing transfer of trained mediational strategies.

McCormick and Levin (Chapter 18) review in detail the literature documenting that mnemonics are helpful in the learning of prose material. Their chapter includes discussions of ecologically valid demonstrations of mnemonically mediated prose learning (e.g., Snowman's work), as well as coverage of extremely well-controlled laboratory studies. They touch on a variety of contemporary issues in this research domain, including differences between illustration and imagery effects, whether mnemonics can be trained in classrooms, the relative benefits of mnemonics for learning from listening versus learning from reading, the types of materials that can be learned with imagery and related procedures, and the range of dependent measures that can be used in the study of mnemonics. In short, McCormick and Levin touch on all of the important concerns for researchers who are trying to devise ways to improve prose learning through mnemonic interventions.

Higbee (Chapter 19) discusses a type of mnemonic that has been used in Japan for some time, Yōdai mnemonics. These mnemonics are especially suited to teaching complex procedures, such as mathematical computational schemes. Although there have been only a few formal evaluations of these procedures, the available data suggest that they are very potent in actual classrooms. The chapter includes detailed presentation of sample Yōdai mnemonics and the analysis of these mnemonic procedures in familiar information processing terms — such as meaningfulness, organization, association, attention, and visualization. Higbee also makes clear how Yōdai mnemonics contrast with other procedures that are aimed more at enhancing memory for specific facts.

The applications section concludes with Chapter 20, Rohwer and Thomas' contribution, which offers a number of distinctions that need to be considered in designing mnemonic interventions. A main strength of this chapter is that it attempts to evaluate the role that mnemonics may play in the larger educational scene.

In short, there can be little doubt that mnemonics researchers have spent a lot of energy determining how imagery and mnemonics may be useful in the educational process. There is enough research currently available to guide curriculum designers as they prepare mnemonically based materials for dissemination in educational settings. There are also enough new research ideas offered in these chapters to keep educational researchers busy for some years to come.

References

Fenaigle, G. von (1813). *The new art of memory.* London: Sherwood, Neely, & Jones.

Miller, G., Galanter, E., & Pribram, K. (1960). *Plans and the structure of behavior.* New York: Holt, Rinehart, & Winston.

Yates, F. A. (1966). *The art of memory.* Chicago: The University of Chicago Press.

CHAPTER 14

The Efficacy of Imagery Mnemonics Following Brain Damage

John T. E. Richardson, Laird S. Cermak,
Susan P. Blackford, and Margaret O'Connor

As other contributions to this volume admirably demonstrate, experimental research on the effects of administering training or instructions to subjects to use mental imagery in learning verbal material has often produced consistent, reliable, and substantial improvements in their retention. It is clearly possible to enhance an individual's performance in learning and remembering by manipulating the encoding strategies that are employed. This has led to the application of imagery techniques as memory aids for cognitively impaired people, although the success of this application is much more controversial than is the case with normal individuals.

This chapter reviews research endeavors and clinical applications of mental imagery with brain-damaged patients. Our discussion is concerned with the practical effectiveness of imagery mnemonic techniques in dealing with cases of acquired memory dysfunction, and with the extent to which such techniques constitute a reasonable basis for developing programs of remediation and rehabilitation in patients who suffer from disorders of memory following neurological damage. The usefulness of mnemonic training in cases of organic dysfunction is a matter that also arises implicitly in Chapter 10, this volume, by Carole Ernest on learning and memory in the blind and the deaf, and also in the chapters by Turnure and Lane (Chapter 15) and by Mastropieri, Scruggs, and Levin (Chapter 16) on special education.

We shall start by considering the various patient populations who tend to demonstrate impaired memory function and the attempts to date to alleviate such impairment by means of training or instructions in the use of mental imagery. In the light of this evidence, we shall then consider the factors that influence the usefulness of mental imagery as a therapeutic device. These include characteristics of the patients themselves, characteristics of the memory tasks, and factors inherent in the different imagery techniques that render them more or less effective. Finally, we shall discuss clinical attempts by Laird Cermak, Susan Blackford, and Margaret O'Connor to use mental imagery with patients at the Boston Veterans Administration Medical Center.

Imagery, Memory, and Brain Damage

Impaired memory function is a frequent outcome of brain damage; indeed, it is often itself a reliable sign that such damage has occurred. There are, however, three main categories of patients in whom disorders of learning and memory are particularly significant (Richardson, 1982):

1. Memory dysfunction is often demonstrated following physical injury to the brain. In wartime, traumatic damage is typically associated with open wounds resulting from weapons or shrapnel. In peacetime, such damage is more likely to take the form of "closed" head injuries in which the contents of the skull are not exposed; these are a frequent outcome of domestic, occupational, recreational, and road accidents.
2. Memory dysfunction may also be a consequence of endogenous neurological diseases, especially those of a histopathological nature (such as cerebral tumors), and also those associated with the vascular system (such as cerebral thrombosis or hemorrhage). This category includes both the normal degenerative processes that are characteristic of old age and more chronic conditions, such as senile and presenile dementia.
3. Finally, the treatment of neurological disease or of the complications arising out of brain damage may necessitate surgical intervention, which can itself give rise to certain cognitive deficits. Disorders of memory are demonstrated particularly after operations upon the cortical and subcortical structures of the temporal lobes, which may be required to relieve chronic intractible epileptic or depressive conditions.

The first investigation of the practical usefulness of imagery mnemonics in neurological patients was carried out by Patten (1972), who taught a variety of mnemonic devices to four patients with verbal memory deficits attributed to focal lesions of the left cerebral hemisphere. These devices included a complex peg-word mnemonic in which concrete nouns (e.g., TEACUP, RADIO) were associated with the digits 1 to 10 and then used as mental "pegs" for remembering lists or sequences of words, as well as the use of more loosely structured interactive imagery. All four patients were able to use these techniques to improve their memory performance. They subsequently reported that they were able to rely upon their own memory skills rather than those of others in everyday life, and that they experienced an enhanced level of self-esteem as a result.

However, Patten mentioned that no such benefits were obtained from memory training in three other patients with more diffuse lesions in the midline structures of the brain. He commented:

None of these patients could form vivid visual images, none had any recent memory modality preserved, none were aware of their memory defect or interested in improving it. . . . Each of the cases in which memory therapy was successful was able to overcome a verbal memory defect by the strategy of encoding in the preserved, or relatively preserved visual modality. (p. 31)

It is possible that the degree of memory impairment was more severe in the patients with midline lesions than in those with damage confined to the left hemisphere. Therefore, these results suggest that the beneficial effect of the peg-word system may be limited to a carefully selected group of patients with deficits of verbal memory.

Studies of Amnesia and Korsakoff's Syndrome

A pronounced disorder of memory function in the absence of any general intellectual impairment is clinically described as "amnesia." Such a condition may arise from a variety of causes but is a central feature of Korsakoff's syndrome, which results from chronic alcoholism. Attempts to train Korsakoff patients and other cases of amnesia in the use of mental imagery have unfortunately produced rather mixed results.

Baddeley and Warrington (1973) found that a heterogeneous sample of six amnesic patients showed improved recall as a result of either phonemic similarity or taxonomic categorization in the stimulus material. However, when instructed to make up complex visual images in order to learn groups of four words describing objects in a physical scene, they showed no such improvement in performance, unlike a matched sample of control patients suffering from peripheral nerve lesions. These results suggested that the amnesic patients were specifically impaired in the use of mental imagery as a form of coding in long-term memory. Nevertheless, in contrast to the patients who had failed to benefit from Patten's (1972) "memory therapy," all of the amnesic subjects in this study claimed to be able to form the relevant images. Baddeley and Warrington concluded that their patients were not impaired in the construction of mental images per se but had failed to gain the normal benefit from constructing an interactive relationship or episode. However, this idea was refuted by a subsequent, unpublished study by Brooks and Baddeley in which a heterogeneous group of amnesic patients was found to have no difficulty in producing simple drawings to illustrate the interactive images that they had generated to link pairs of unrelated words yet still showed no benefit from the use of mental imagery (Baddeley, 1982).

Cermak (1975) hypothesized that amnesic patients might be able to benefit from less complex interactive images than those demanded in the study by Baddeley and Warrington. He compared six Korsakoff patients with six alcoholic controls in their learning and retention of lists of five paired associates under rote learning and interactive imagery instructions. Both groups of subjects showed enhanced performance as a result of the imagery instructions in both recognition and free recall, although the performance of the Korsakoff patients was still significantly poorer than that of the controls. In absolute terms, the Korsakoff patients demonstrated a greater amount of improvement, but this was because the alcoholic controls approached a ceiling on all of the performance measures employed. Cermak concluded that Korsakoff patients were capable of forming and utilizing images as aids to retrieval, and that imagery constituted a useful device for facilitating amnesic patients' storage and retrieval of verbal information.

Subsequently, Cermak (1976) described a single case of amnesia resulting from encephalitis and compared his performance with that of the Korsakoff patients. Although initially more impaired in his learning of paired associates, this patient showed an even greater improvement when given interactive imagery instructions, such that his performance approached that of the alcoholic controls. In both of Cermak's studies, the subjects were provided with specific mental images by the experimenter and were reminded to use the relevant images at the time of recall. More recently, Cermak (1980) suggested that these were crucial aspects of his experimental procedure and that without being reminded to use mental imagery both in learning and at retrieval amnesic patients would show no improvement in their performance (cf. Crovitz, 1979).

Kapur (1978) examined the possibility that Korsakoff patients were deficient in the ability to construct mental images. In his experiment, each patient was required to imagine a seven-letter word and to indicate, starting from the end of the word and working backwards, whether each of the letters was large or small in size. The Korsakoff patients were able to indicate the correct letter sizes as well as the alcoholic controls in terms of both their speed and their accuracy. Kapur therefore concluded that the difficulty that Korsakoff patients demonstrated with imagery instructions resulted from a failure to utilize an image rather than a failure to form one.

Cutting (1978) compared a group of 10 Korsakoff patients with 10 alcoholic controls in learning lists of 10 paired associates. The controls showed improved performance as a result of interactive images that were either generated by each subject or provided by the experimenter, but the Korsakoff patients showed no such improvement: indeed, they showed no evidence of any learning at all under any of the relevant conditions. Cutting ascribed the Korsakoff patients' failure to utilize mental imagery to a deficit in their capacity for active mental operations, arguing that such patients were adept only at passive cognitive tasks.

Gianutsos (1981) achieved rather better success with a single case of amnesia caused by encephalitis, who initially demonstrated a pronounced difficulty in acquiring new information. His recall of word lists was measured both with immediate testing and after an interval occupied by an irrelevant distractor task in order to produce independent measures of the short-term and long-term components of recall. Practice in memory span was found to enhance short-term storage, but not long-term storage, whereas training in the use of mental imagery or simple stories as mediating devices produced the opposite pattern of results. The effect of such mnemonic elaboration was relatively modest, although it did seem to be maintained following the discontinuation of training. However, it is unclear from Gianutsos' paper whether the patient was explicitly instructed to try to generalize the elaborative strategies that he had been taught. Moreover, it was subsequently found that other techniques were necessary to alleviate this patient's memory disorder on his return to work as a college professor (Gianutsos & Grynbaum, 1983).

In the light of the disappointing results obtained by Baddeley and Warrington (1973), Cermak (1975), and Cutting (1978), Kovner, Mattis, and Goldmeier (1983) suggested that amnesics were deficient in the ability to organize familiar items into context-dependent combinations and needed the support of a clear mnemonic structure if mental imagery were to be beneficial. They compared a heterogeneous group of five amnesic patients with a control group of normal volunteers in their learning of lists of unrelated words presented repeatedly over successive weekly sessions. When provided with a bizarre story that linked the items to be read and that they were instructed to visualize, both groups showed substantial (and roughly equivalent) amounts of learning, although the amnesics were impaired throughout relative to the controls. In the absence of an opportunity to image a bizarre story but with an equivalent level of feedback and correction, the controls showed a similar (although poorer) pattern of performance, whereas the amnesics showed no sign of any learning over the eight sessions. Kovner et al. suggested that their mnemonic technique provided the subjects with artificial "chunks" of information that could be encoded and transferred relatively normally into long-term memory. A follow-up study with just two of these amnesic patients (Kovner, Mattis, & Pass, 1985) produced similar effects of both bizarre and nonbizarre stories in extended testing over 7 weeks: indeed, these two patients were able to learn up to 120 words using such methods.

In short, it would appear that imagery instructions must be supported by explicit mnemonic structure at the time of learning or by prompting at the time of recall if they are to be of any benefit to amnesic patients.

Studies of the Effects of Unilateral Temporal Lobectomy

As mentioned earlier, an iatrogenic cause of memory dysfunction is the use of temporal lobectomy for the relief of chronic epilepsy. Typically, patients with lesions of the left temporal lobe are impaired in verbal memory tasks but not in nonverbal memory tasks; conversely, patients with lesions of the right temporal lobe tend to be impaired in nonverbal memory tasks but not in verbal memory tasks (Milner, 1971). A number of studies have shown that training or instructions in the use of mental imagery may be of benefit to both groups of patients.

Jones (1974) asked patients who had undergone unilateral anterior temporal lobectomy to learn three lists of 10 concrete and abstract paired associates over three trials. The first list was learned under standard instructions with no reference to any particular mnemonic technique; for the second list, the concrete pairs were accompanied by relevant drawings as interactive mediators, which the subjects were instructed to visualize; and the third list was accompanied by instructions to the subjects to make up their own interactive images. In the case of the concrete pairs, the patients with lesions of the left temporal lobe showed a significant impairment compared to a group of normal controls, but the patients with lesions of the right temporal lobe did not. All three groups of subjects showed a similar improvement in recall after training and instructions in the use of mental imagery. In particular, and in accordance with Patten's (1972) original findings, the patients with lesions of the left temporal lobe produced enhanced performance under imagery instructions; however, they were still significantly poorer in their level of recall than the control group. In the case of the abstract pairs, the three groups showed the same relative levels of performance as in the case of the concrete pairs, but no improvement as a result of imagery mnemonic instructions.

Jones also examined the effects of mental imagery on the memory abilities of two patients (H.M. and H.B.) with bilateral lesions of the temporal lobes, which normally lead to a severe and generalized memory loss (Milner, 1973). One case had undergone bilateral mesial temporal lobectomy, and the other was a case of a bilateral tumor tested subsequent to unilateral temporal lobectomy. Neither of these patients showed any retention even under instructions to use mental imagery, although they were apparently able to form vivid visual images in response to experimental instructions. They appeared to forget that they had previously formed a visual association linking the items to be remembered and so were unable to utilize their newly formed images at the time of recall. Furthermore, even when reminded that he had done so, H.M. could not retrieve his previous image and instead conjured up an entirely new one.

In the light of previous research on the effects of unilateral temporal lobectomy upon nonverbal memory, Jones had anticipated that the effective use of mental imagery should depend upon the integrity of the right temporal lobe, and that patients with lesions of that lobe should therefore derive less help from the use of an imagery mnemonic. However, that group of patients in her study not only achieved a normal level of performance in absolute terms, but they also seemed able to employ mental imagery just as efficiently as the normal controls. Moreover, their level of recall was also unrelated to the amount of temporal neocortex that had been excised and to the extent of the encroachment upon the hippocampus. She suggested that the anticipated effects had been masked by a ceiling effect in her data, and that they would become more apparent in a more difficult learning task.

Accordingly, Jones-Gotman and Milner (1978) carried out another study in which all of the subjects were given interactive imagery instructions for a single presentation of a list of 60 concrete paired associates. The patients with lesions of the right temporal lobe achieved better performance than those with lesions of the left temporal lobe, even though the latter excluded cases of severe memory impairment. However, both groups were significantly impaired in comparison to a group of normal controls on both immediate recall and after a 2-hr delay. The patients with lesions of the right temporal lobe also showed more forgetting during the interval between the two tests, and their level of performance was inversely related to the amount of hippocampal removal (though not to the extent of neocortical excision). This appeared to support the hypothesis that the right hippocampus was important in imagery-mediated verbal learning.

In a subsequent experiment with a subsample of the patients with lesions of the right temporal lobe, Jones-Gotman and Milner (1978) found no evidence for an impairment in the learning of abstract paired associates under either rote learning or verbal mediation instructions, and no correlation between memory performance and the amount of hippocampal removal. Unfortunately, their main study contained no control data on the levels of performance to be expected under standard instructions. Their results, therefore, confound the effects of imagery instructions with differences in their subjects' absolute level of learning ability and cannot be taken as unequivocal support for their idea that the right hippocampal region is important in image-mediated verbal learning.

A further study was carried out by Jones-Gotman (1979) in which an incidental learning paradigm was used to control for differences in the subjects' spontaneous learning strategies. They were presented with a list of 40 unrelated concrete and abstract words to be rated along a seven-point scale either in terms of the ease with which they could be visualized or in terms of the ease with which they could be pronounced. In an unanticipated immediate test of free recall, patients with lesions of the left temporal lobe were impaired in comparison to a group of normal controls, but patients with lesions of the right temporal lobe were not. All three groups remembered more concrete words than abstract words, and they remembered more words that they had rated on ease of visualization than ones that they had rated on ease of pronunciation. In a second recall test administered after a 2-hr delay, the same pattern of results emerged, except that the patients with lesions of the right temporal lobe were significantly impaired on those words which they had rated on ease of visualization, although not on those words which they had rated on ease of pronunciation. Finally, Jones-Gotman showed that the level of performance of patients with lesions of the right temporal lobe on concrete words that they had rated on their ease of visualization was inversely related to the extent of hippocampal removal in both immediate and delayed recall.

Jones-Gotman concluded that patients with lesions of the right temporal lobe were able to use visual imagery, although less efficiently than normal subjects. More specifically, although they achieved normal levels of performance on immediate testing, their images apparently became less accessible during the interval between the two recall tests, and this was associated with the extent of damage to the right hippocampal region. However, Jones-Gotman's study suffers from a number of problems that prevent one from accepting these conclusions uncritically. First, the task of rating individual items on their ease of visualization does not seem to be one that promotes the sort of interactive imagery which would promote efficient learning (Richardson, 1979a). It follows that Jones-Gotman's results may well be quite irrelevant to the more effective uses of mental imagery. Second, all her patients had suffered from neurological disorders of long standing (usually intractable epilepsy), and there was no guarantee that the area of diseased tissue was confined to those regions that had been surgically removed. Instead, those patients who required more extensive excision of cortical and subcortical tissue might well have suffered more extensive neurological damage not confined to the right hippocampal region. Third, the rating task was self-paced, with the result that the total exposure to the stimulus material might have varied considerably from one subject to another. Jones-Gotman did not report any data on this point, but it is possible that the three groups of subjects differed not merely in the overall time taken to rate the 40 words, but also specifically in the amount of time and effort spent in considering their ease of visualization.

Studies of the Effects of Closed Head Injury

Closed head injuries also may give rise to disturbances of learning and remembering. Apart from the initial phenomena of retrograde and anterograde amnesia, most patients demonstrate an impairment of memory that persists beyond the immediate period of recovery. A primary goal in the rehabilitation of head-injured patients is therefore the development of techniques for enhancing the acquisition of new information.

Glasgow, Zeiss, Barrera, and Lewinsohn (1977) studied the efficacy of various mnemonic techniques in two cases of closed head injury. One patient with predominantly left-sided brain damage and an expressive speech deficit was taught to use mental imagery in order to remember names paired with faces. The procedure required him to translate each name into a concrete noun and then to associate a mental image of this concrete noun with one of the prominent facial features represented in the corresponding picture. He found this procedure to be fairly useful in learning a small number of face–name pairs involving very simple, pictureable names (e.g., Mr. Fox). However, it was of little value in learning the more complex names encountered by this patient in everyday life, though a simplified imagery–rehearsal strategy did prove to be helpful for this purpose.

Crovitz, Harvey, and Horn (1979) explored the effects of instructing two other head-injured patients in the use of bizarre imagery to remember sequences of common words. One of these subjects showed some improvement in performance, but only when the bizarre images were supplied by the experimenter; he did appear to be able to generate his own images, but failed to use them to mediate his own retention (see also Crovitz, 1979). The other subject experienced some initial difficulty in using bizarre mediators provided by the experimenter but subsequently was able to achieve some improvement using self-generated images.

Crosson and Buenning (1984) reported the results of a memory remediation program devised for a single case of closed head injury. They focused upon the patient's retention of short paragraphs of text, which was highly relevant to his work as a consultant. His ability to recall the gist of such paragraphs was improved to within normal levels by the use of visual imagery and other mnemonic devices based upon feedback, concentration, and selective questioning. Visual imagery and selective questioning appeared to be the more effective strategies, and there was some evidence that the resulting improvement generalized to other memory tasks. However, at a follow-up examination 9 months later, his recall performance was only slightly increased, and the patient seemed to have abandoned the use of mnemonic strategies in favor of external memory aids, such as a note pad. Crosson and Buenning suggested that this was because of the patient's failure to practice the mnemonic strategies that had proved helpful, and that it was necessary to teach patients to generalize the use of such techniques beyond the immediate circumstances of training.

A formal experimental investigation of the value of imagery mnemonic instructions was reported recently by Richardson and Barry (1985). They tested 48 subjects with minor closed head injuries and a similar number of control patients, who were other accident victims admitted to a hospital for orthopaedic treatment. Each subject was presented with five lists of 10 concrete words and five lists of 10 abstract words (matched for frequency of usage) in a randomized sequence for immediate free recall, followed by a final, unanticipated recall test on all of the words presented. Half of the head-injured patients and half of the control patients were given standard instructions that did not specify any particular technique for learning the lists; the rest of the subjects were given additional instructions to make up mental images that related together the things described by the words in each list.

The results are shown in Table 14.1. Under standard instructions, the patients with head injuries were impaired relative to the control patients in the recall of concrete material, but not in the recall of abstract material. The control patients showed the normal advantage in the recall of concrete material that is typically demonstrated in formal laboratory experiments, but the patients with head injuries did not. These results replicated those of an earlier study by Richardson (1979b). However, under imagery instructions, the patients with head injuries were not impaired relative to the control patients in the recall of either concrete or abstract material, and both groups of patients showed the usual pattern of better recall on concrete material than on abstract material.

In short, the effect of imagery instructions in the case of patients with minor closed head injury is to enhance their performance to the level demonstrated by normal controls. Imagery instructions may also be effective in the case of patients with more severe head injuries, but such patients seem to encounter great difficulty in transferring these strategies to everyday learning situations.

Studies of Cerebral Vascular Disease

Patients suffering from cerebral vascular disease also tend to demonstrate disorders of learning and memory. Lewinsohn, Danaher, and Kikel (1977) studied the effectiveness of bizarre visual imagery as a mnemonic device in helping such patients to learn a list of 15 concrete paired associates and a set of 15 face–name

TABLE 14.1. Mean percentage correct in free recall for head-injured patients and orthopaedic controls on concrete and abstract material under standard learning instructions and imagery mnemonic instructions.

	Standard instructions		Imagery instructions	
	Concrete	Abstract	Concrete	Abstract
Controls	35.3	27.1	39.4	29.5
Head-injured	25.5	25.4	37.5	28.3

Note: Data from "The Effects of Minor Closed Head Injury Upon Human Memory: Further Evidence on the Role of Mental Imagery," by J. T. E. Richardson and C. Barry, 1985, Cognitive Neuropsychology, 2, 149–168. Copyright 1985 by Lawrence Erlbaum Associates Limited. Adapted by permission.

associations. (Their total sample of 19 "brain-injured" subjects also included one case of traumatic brain damage and four patients who had undergone surgical removal of cerebral tumors. No information was provided concerning the exact sites of their lesions, but their average performance on the Vocabulary Subtest of the Wechsler Adult Intelligence Scale was within the normal range.) Both on immediate testing and after a delay of 30 min, a program of imagery training enhanced performance to approximately the same extent in both the brain-damaged patients and normal controls. In particular, one third of the patients assigned to a control condition failed to learn the list of paired associates within 10 trials, whereas all of the patients given training in the use of mental imagery were able to do so. However, this sort of training was somewhat less effective in the face–name task, and it produced no facilitation at all when the subjects were retested on and relearned the same materials after a further interval of 1 week. These results suggest that imagery mnemonics may be of only limited value in setting up permanent memories, especially in those areas which are relevant to everyday interactions.

Gasparrini (1978; Gasparrini & Satz, 1979) investigated 30 patients with verbal memory deficits following cerebral vascular accidents in the left hemisphere. Once again, no information was provided concerning the exact sites of their lesions, but the patients were described as being "mildly to moderately aphasic." Using a within-subjects comparison, training in the use of interactive imagery was found to produce better performance in paired-associate learning than training in verbal mediation. However, in a between-subjects comparison, instructions to use mental imagery only produced better performance than instructions to use rote repetition in a training phase wherein the learning of each paired associate was carefully monitored: because of considerable variation within each of the treatment groups, training in the use of imagery did not lead to any significant enhancement of performance on other materials or learning tasks.

Finally, Wilson (1982) reported a case study of a patient who demonstrated a severe memory deficit as a result of a bilateral cerebral vascular accident involving both posterior cerebral arteries. Computerized tomography indicated that there was a greater degree of damage in the left cerebral hemisphere, but there was no evidence of dysphasia, dyslexia, or dysgraphia. Wilson presented this patient with "pictures" of names as an aid to recall; for instance, the name "Barbara" was depicted as a barber holding the letter A. The patient was able to learn 12 different names, just 2 weeks after training in visualization had begun. Remarkably, 3 months later he was able to recall 10 of the names on the first retest and two more with a prompt. On a second retest, he remembered all 12 names. The names chosen were those of the patient's therapists, but it is unclear whether he ever connected the names with the actual people.

However, Wilson herself suggested that the subject actually used this procedure as an opportunity to employ a verbal mediation strategy. On the one hand, the names that he remembered most easily were those with a "wordy" description (e.g., "RUSH for all you're WORTH" for Dr. Rushworth); on the other hand, those that took longest to retrieve tended to be those that he found easier to draw (e.g., Dr. Hunt, Mrs. Long). Moreover, this patient was unsuccessful at memorizing a shopping list by means of a pegword mnemonic (the "one is a bun" method described by Lorayne, 1979), and as a result actually produced even poorer performance in tests of free recall. In contrast, he rapidly reached 100% success using a first-letter mnemonic aid (e.g., "GO SHOPPING" = grapes, oranges, sugar, etc.), and this list was recalled perfectly 3 months later. Apparently, the retention of this mnemonic was sufficient to cue the list at the time of retrieval.

Once again, therefore, imagery instructions may give rise to clear improvements in the performance of patients with cerebral vascular disease in experimental tasks, but their value in everyday learning situations is somewhat questionable.

Studies of Normal Aging

The final topic that needs to be mentioned is the use of imagery mnemonic techniques in retraining the elderly, who demonstrate poorer performance across a wide range of learning tasks (Craik, 1977). Although it is possible to attribute this deficit at least in part to the imposition of normative expectations upon the aging individual, it is generally and most plausibly interpreted as the product of actual physiological degeneration.

In the absence of any particular instructions, Hulicka and Grossman (1967) found that elderly subjects were much less likely to report the use of imaginal mediators in paired-associate learning than young subjects (see also Hulicka, Sterns, & Grossman, 1967). Under imagery instructions, the older subjects showed a greater improvement in their recall than the younger subjects, although they were still considerably impaired in their level of performance. This pattern of results was replicated in subsequent studies (Canestrari, 1968; Rowe & Schnore, 1971; and cf. Caird & Hannah, 1964). Finally, Hulicka and Grossman found a greater improvement in the case of older subjects as a result of mediators generated by the subjects themselves than as a result of mediators provided by the experimenter.

The latter result was also obtained in a subsequent investigation by Treat and Reese (1976). However, these researchers found a three-way interaction between the effects of age, instructions, and anticipation (retrieval) time. In the younger subjects, imagery instructions led to enhanced performance with a short (2 sec per pair) anticipation interval, but not with a long (6 sec per pair) anticipation interval. However, in the older subjects, imagery instructions led to enhanced performance only with the longer anticipation interval. The older subjects were generally impaired relative to the younger subjects, but not under imagery instructions and the longer anticipation interval. In other words, for the older subjects, a longer retrieval time was necessary for imagery instructions to be beneficial, but under these circumstances the performance of the older subjects was raised to the same level as that of the younger subjects (see also Thomas & Ruben, cited by Poon, Walsh-Sweeney, & Fozard, 1980).

Following up these results, Treat, Poon, and Fozard (1978) compared the effects of practice upon self-paced paired associate learning in young and old subjects. The younger subjects generally produced superior performance to the older subjects but showed no improvement as a result of instructions to use either self-generated or experimenter-generated imagery; this was taken to suggest that young subjects spontaneously employed fairly efficient learning strategies. The older subjects found subject-generated imagery more beneficial than experimenter-generated imagery, and both techniques produced better performance than standard learning instructions. However, all of the elderly subjects demonstrated a substantial improvement in performance across three learning sessions at intervals of 2 weeks, with the result that there was no significant difference among the treatment groups by the end of the third session. These results suggested that older subjects could benefit from instructions to use self-generated imagery, but that they could also spontaneously develop appropriate and efficient mnemonic strategies, given sufficient practice and experience with the learning task.

Robertson-Tchabo, Hausman, and Arenberg (1976) investigated the use of the method of loci as a mnemonic technique in the free recall of lists of unrelated words. Elderly subjects were found to improve their performance in learning different lists in three experimental sessions, with no evidence of any proactive interference among the lists. However, in a final posttest, most of the subjects failed to use the mnemonic unless specifically instructed to do so. Hellebusch (1976) similarly explored the value of the pegword system ("one is a bun," etc.) in free recall. Both young and old subjects showed improved short-term retention as a result of this technique, although the older subjects were still impaired relative to the younger subjects. This improvement extended to a long-term retention test administered 2 weeks later in the case of the younger subjects, but not in the case of the older subjects. Moreover, subjective reports indicated that the older subjects were less likely to transfer the mnemonic technique that they had been taught to new lists of words learned under either paced or self-paced conditions. Finally, even the modest improvement demonstrated by the elderly subjects in this study was not replicated in a subsequent experiment by Mason and Smith (1977).

Most of the studies reviewed in this section suggest that mnemonic aids based upon the use of mental imagery can be used to improve the performance of older subjects. However, as Poon et al. (1980) pointed out, "The evidence suggests that expectations of the time needed by the elderly to acquire and demonstrate proficiency with a mnemonic technique may need to be extended, particularly if the technique and stimuli are novel to the elderly learner" (p. 475). It has also been pointed out that elderly subjects appear to be deficient precisely in the area of nonverbal encoding, and that it may therefore be more reasonable to try to train such individuals in the use of verbal mnemonic techniques (Winograd & Simon, 1980; cf. Cermak, 1980).

Patient Variables

In evaluating any therapeutic approach, it would be unreasonable to expect all potential candidates for remediation or rehabilitation to demonstrate a similar and substantial facilitation. Certainly, the most obvious conclusion to be drawn from the various case studies that have been carried out is that there exist considerable individual differences in the benefit to be gained from training in the use of mental imagery following brain damage (cf. Levin, Benton, & Grossman, 1982, p. 218). The question therefore arises as to which categories of brain-damaged patients are likely to benefit from the use of imagery mnemonic techniques.

First of all, it is obvious that the value of such techniques depends upon the integrity of those areas of the brain that are needed to subserve them. Unfortunately, exactly which areas subserve the construction and retention of mental images is currently a matter of conjecture and debate. It used to be received wisdom in clinical neuropsychology that the right cerebral hemisphere, and specifically the right hippocampal region, contained the seat of mental imagery. An immediate corollary of this idea was that patients with left-hemisphere involvement should be able to overcome their verbal memory problems by using the preserved right-hemisphere faculty of mental imagery. It is true that some studies have shown that patients with left-hemisphere damage may benefit from training in the use of mental imagery (e.g., Jones, 1974; Jones-Gotman, 1979; Jones-Gotman & Milner, 1978; Patten, 1972; Wilson, 1982), and this might be attributed to their use of the intact right hemisphere. There is also evidence that patients with more severe forms of amnesia and more medial or bilateral damage have much more difficulty in using mental imagery unless the task is highly structured and the memory load is minimal (e.g., Cermak, 1975; Cutting, 1978; Jones, 1974; Patten, 1972). However, the idea of a right-hemisphere locus for mental imagery seems to be contradicted by the findings of Jones (1974) that patients with lesions of the right temporal lobe show a normal advantage in learning concrete rather than abstract material, and that they show a normal benefit from imagery mnemonic instructions (Richardson, 1980, pp. 139–140). Moreover, recent analyses have tended to emphasize the importance of structures within the left cerebral hemisphere in imaginal functioning (Erlichman & Barrett, 1983; Farah, 1984, in press; Farah, Gazzaniga, Holtzman, & Kosslyn, 1985; Kosslyn, Holtzman, Farah, & Gazzaniga, 1985).

Nevertheless, at a functional level, the ability to encode material in the form of mental images and the ability to store such representations in long-term memory are clearly essential to the efficacy of imagery instructions (cf. Winograd & Simon, 1980). For instance, Wilson (1981) described a patient with a tumor of the left hemisphere who was unable to learn a list of rhyming peg-words, but who appeared to use mental imagery rather well; and she subsequently (Wilson, 1982) described the patient who had suffered a cerebral vascular accident and who could remember the mnemonic but not the images that he had constructed. It follows that screening for such abilities should be a precursor to any rehabilitative program involving the use of training in imagery mnemonic techniques; the sorts of procedures that have been developed as research tools by Farah, Kosslyn, and their colleagues on the basis of a componential analysis of mental imagery (Farah, 1984; Kosslyn et al., 1985) seem highly suitable for such screening.

Whereas the efficacy of imagery mnemonic instructions is likely to be directly related to the subjects' ability to use mental imagery, it is likely to be inversely related to the subjects' tendency to use mental imagery in a spontaneous manner: such instructions are likely to be ineffective to the extent that they merely confirm the subjects' habitual cognitive strategies. Curiously, there is little information on the spontaneous use of mental imagery on the part of brain-damaged patients. In normal subjects, this is commonly studied by means of postlearning questionnaires in which subjects retrospectively report the particular form of mediating device employed to remember individual stimulus items; although there are considerable individual differences in reports of different categories of mediator, the use of mental imagery is fairly frequent under standard learning instructions and is enhanced under imagery mnemonic instructions (Richardson, 1985a). These findings were in fact originally demonstrated by Hulicka and Grossman (1967), who found in addition that elderly subjects were much less likely to report the use of imaginal mediators than younger subjects under either instructional set.

An alternative approach is to focus upon the relative superiority of the retention of concrete material over that of abstract material. In the case of patients with closed head injuries, Richardson (1979b) found that the effect of stimulus concreteness was reduced to nonsignificance, and he therefore concluded that closed head injury gave rise to an impairment in the use of mental imagery as a form of elaborative encoding in long-term memory. Consistent with the relatively diffuse nature of the neurological damage engendered by closed head injuries, this pattern of performance was largely independent of the site of impact. Nevertheless, Richardson and Barry (1985) subsequently showed that imagery instructions reinstated the effect of concreteness and raised the performance of head-injured subjects to the level achieved by control patients.

It is also likely that premorbid characteristics of brain-damaged patients will influence the efficacy of such programs of remediation. An obvious candidate would be intelligence. Griffith and Actkinson (1978) found that training in the use of a pegword mnemonic produced a significant improvement only in the case of subjects with scores of 110 and above on the U.S. Army's General-Technical Test, who were "thought to approximate most closely the college population with respect to general academic aptitude." Intuitively, this outcome is not surprising: pegword mnemonics are rather complex devices that might well present great difficulty for subjects of lower intelligence (cf. Poon et al., 1980; Robertson-Tchabo, 1980). Indeed, one of the relevant subjects in Griffith and Actkinson's study had to be replaced because he was simply unable to understand the experimental instructions. In this context, the results of Patten (1972) may be recalled. He used a still more difficult version of the pegword mnemonic in which the pegwords did not even rhyme with their associated digits, and it is therefore not surprising that the mnemonic defeated patients with more severe, global impairments. As he himself commented, "Naturally, low intelligence, poor motivation, and poor imagination interfere with the application of the mnemonic system" (p. 31).

However, within the range of intellectual ability demonstrated by college students, exactly the opposite pattern of results was obtained by McDaniel and

Pressley (1984) in an investigation of the efficacy of the keyword mnemonic. For their sample of college students, the effectiveness of imagery instructions was found to be inversely related to the subjects' verbal ability. Moreover, when they considered the results obtained from different studies conducted in a variety of higher education institutions, the efficacy of such instructions was found to be negatively related to the selectivity of the institutions in terms of their admissions policy. McDaniel and Pressley concluded that subjects of high verbal ability were able to use effective learning strategies even in the absence of specific instructions. Moreover, a crucial objection to Griffith and Actkinson's (1978) account is that imagery instructions may be beneficial even in the educable mentally retarded (e.g., Paris, Mahoney, & Buckhalt, 1974; see Chapters 15 by Turnure and Lane and 16 by Mastropieri et al. in this volume).

A second dimension that may influence the efficacy of training or instructions in the use of imagery is educational attainment. According to recent research on student learning, the extent to which an individual learner is able to deploy a range of cognitive strategies according to the demands of the learning situation may be materially influenced by the educational level which that individual has achieved, and especially by participation in courses of study in higher education (Säljö, 1979, 1984). It is interesting in this connection to note a suggestion made by Gasparrini (1978) that training in the use of mnemonic techniques would be useful only in the case of high school graduates. More recently, Levin et al. (1982, pp. 218–219) pointed out that most demonstrations of the value of imagery mnemonic techniques following closed head injury have employed subjects educated to college standard (see also Gianutsos, 1981).

However, this line of thought is contradicted by the extensive research on the usefulness of imagery mnemonics with young children. In particular, children 11 years of age appear to be able to use self-generated imagery as effectively as adults (Denis, 1984; Pressley, 1982). It is true, as Pressley, Levin, and Delaney (1982) acknowledged, that younger children may have difficulty with standard versions of imagery mnemonics and may therefore require greater experimenter structuring and prompting. Nevertheless, Pressley et al. pointed out that, given appropriate procedures, even children as young as 8 years of age can benefit from training in the use of imagery. Analogous points were made by Poon et al. (1980) regarding the usefulness of imagery mnemonic training with the elderly. In general, it can be readily appreciated that adapted procedures may well be needed in training subjects with reduced information-processing capacity.

Task Variables

In his original study, Patten (1972) made no systematic attempt to follow up his patients' use of imagery mnemonics. However, in many cases the patients' subjective and anecdotal reports indicated that they continued to benefit from the use of mental imagery many months after their original training. This raises three questions that are of general relevance to research on mnemonics but that need particular discussion in the case of brain-damaged patients: (a) Do such patients use mental imagery at the time of retrieval in the absence of specific prompting? (b) Do they continue to use mental imagery in similar learning situations? (c) Do they transfer their use of mental imagery to new learning situations?

The general picture concerning the long-term retention of imagery mnemonics on the part of brain-damaged patients is rather gloomy. Some researchers have found that training in the use of mental imagery may facilitate such patients' memory for only a relatively short period of time. For instance, Hellebusch (1976) found that training in the use of the pegword mnemonic enhanced the performance of elderly subjects after a 3-min delay but not after an interval of roughly 2 weeks. Similarly, Lewinsohn et al. (1977) found that head-injured patients who were taught to use mental imagery in order to carry out a paired-associate learning task and a face–name association task showed improved performance both during the original acquisition phase and on retraining after a 30-min delay but showed no sign of any improvement on retraining after 1 week.

A major determinant of the effectiveness of imagery mnemonics with brain-damaged patients seems to be the extent to which the learning task is explicitly structured at the time of both encoding and retrieval. As mentioned earlier in this chapter, one implication of research on alcoholic Korsakoff patients is that the effectiveness of imagery instructions at the time of encoding and storage depends upon cuing and prompting at the time of recall (Cermak, 1980), and a similar conclusion may be in order with regard to the elderly (Robertson-Tchabo et al., 1976). Crovitz (1979) has consistently stressed the importance of using retrieval cues when trying to apply imagery techniques with brain-damaged patients. His chain-type of mnemonic (the "Airplane List") was read to both a Korsakoff patient and a patient with closed head injury. Neither of these individuals was able to recall the list unless provided with retrieval cues. In a similar report, Jaffe and Katz (1975) suggested that by focusing upon both the encoding and retrieval aspects of information processing one could effectively encourage the organization of incoming information and structure the search process at the time of recall: only in this manner might brain-damaged patients demonstrate enhanced memory by utilizing mental imagery. However, explicit structure at the time of recall is obviously unlikely to be encountered outside the psychological laboratory, and so training neurological patients in the use of imagery mnemonics is likely to be of little practical value to them in everyday life unless they can also be trained to generate appropriate internal retrieval cues.

The continued use of mental imagery in other, similar learning situations also appears to be very limited, at least in the case of elderly subjects. DeLeon (1974) found that training in the use of mental imagery led to a much more modest improvement on new materials than on the original, training materials, whereas control subjects using a repetition strategy actually showed a slight increase in performance on the new materials. Questioning after testing suggested that the repetition group had actually adopted an effective mediation strategy on their own. Similarly, Hellebusch (1976) found no improvement on new materials 2

weeks after the original training; fewer than 50% of his elderly subjects transferred the use of learned mnemonic strategies to other materials learned 2 weeks
after the original training. It might of course be argued that the effective transfer
of mnemonic devices would require considerable practice in their use, but it
should be noted that 83% of Hellebusch's younger subjects appeared to transfer
the mnemonic in question to new materials.

Gianutsos (1981) found that the elaboration of word triplets by means of mental
images or simple stories enhanced the free-recall performance of her postencephalitic amnesic, and this modest improvement did appear to be maintained for
2 or 3 weeks after training had been discontinued. However, Crosson and Buenning (1984) obtained less promising results with their single case of closed head
injury. Their patient's performance on prose passages 9 months after training had
fallen almost to its original level, and he reported that he was no longer using the
mnemonic strategies that he had been taught. This patient did show some evidence that the retraining program had enhanced his performance on a variety of
criterion tasks. Although the training had been confined to prose passages, some
modest improvement was also apparent on the Mental Control, Digit Span, and
Paired Associates Subtests of the Wechsler Memory Scale, with the result that he
achieved a memory quotient (MQ) commensurate with his premorbid education
and attainment. Unfortunately, the whole Memory Scale was not administered at
the 9-month followup examination, but his performance on prose passages suggests that there was probably no permanent generalized improvement. Crosson
and Buenning mentioned that they encouraged their patient to practice the original mnemonic strategies in various everyday situations, but it is possible that
the patient had simply rejected these strategies as being inappropriate to his
needs in daily life (cf. Gianutsos & Grynbaum, 1983; Robertson-Tchabo, 1980;
Wilson, 1982).

Unfortunately, one of the problems in evaluating the usefulness of mnemonic
devices following neurological damage is that there have been very few systematic attempts to identify what skills in everyday life brain-damaged patients actually lack. It has therefore been difficult to judge whether formally taught
mnemonic techniques are of any practical benefit to such patients in their day to
day activities (Diller & Gordon, 1981). Nevertheless, the perceived relevance of
imagery mnemonics to these activities is likely to determine the patients' motivation to master such techniques (Wilson & Moffat, 1984). The most common
symptoms reported in a recent survey of brain-damaged patients were concerned
with remembering names, recent events, and spoken messages, and remembering to do things (Kapur & Pearson, 1983). Once again, the small amount of relevant evidence on the value of mental imagery in such tasks concerns the elderly.
The study reported by DeLeon (1974) trained elderly subjects on paired associates but involved additional pre- and posttesting on three practical memory tests:
the recall of a personal narrative, a grocery list, and the names and occupations
of photographed persons. There was no evidence at all that mnemonic training on
paired associates generalized to these tasks. This may be taken to suggest that

mnemonic training is task specific, that paired-associate learning has no analog in everyday remembering and so is inappropriate for use in memory retraining (Poon et al., 1980), or that no such analog is apparent to older subjects.

There are at least three points to be considered in evaluating the general usefulness of training in the use of mental imagery. First, it should be pointed out that virtually all of the research discussed in this chapter has been concerned with the practical utility of mental imagery in trying to remember information about one's past: that is, "retrospective" memory. There has been no attempt to study the role of mental imagery in "prospective" memory, in remembering to do something in the future (Meacham & Leiman, 1982; Harris, 1984). Although it would certainly be premature to conclude with Morris (1977) that the classical mnemonic aids are largely useless in this respect, it is certainly the implication of descriptive studies that mental imagery is rarely used spontaneously in prospective remembering: external reminders, such as diaries and knots in handkerchiefs, are much more readily used by both adults (Harris, 1978) and children (Kreutzer, Leonard, & Flavell, 1975; Meacham & Colombo, 1980), and the same seems to be true of recovering neurological patients (Crosson & Buenning, 1984; Gianutsos & Grynbaum, 1983). Kapur and Pearson (1983) found that brain-damaged patients were much less likely to complain of problems in remembering to do things than control patients, but they ascribed this to impaired retention of instances of failure in this area.

Second, instructions to use mental imagery generally lead to enhanced performance on concrete material, but not on abstract material (Denis, in press; Gupton & Frincke, 1970; Janssen, 1976, pp. 42–43; Morris & Reid, 1974; Paivio & Yuille, 1967; Richardson, 1985a; Yuille & Paivio, 1968). The failure of imagery mnemonics to produce an increase in the retention of abstract material arises not because the relevant instructions fail to enhance the availability of imaginal mediators, but because mental images tend not to be effective mediators in the case of abstract material (Richardson, 1985a). The keyword mnemonic seems to be a specific exception to these generalizations, because it leads to enhanced performance with both concrete and abstract nouns (Miller, Levin, & Pressley, 1980) and is at least as effective with other categories of lexical items (Pressley, Levin, & Miller, 1981). Nevertheless, the pattern of results described above has been replicated in some of the studies of neurological patients mentioned earlier in this chapter (e.g., Jones, 1974; Richardson & Barry, 1985), and the possibility therefore remains that techniques other than those based upon the use of imagery may need to be developed in order to help brain-damaged patients to acquire more abstract information.

Third, it has been suggested that the classical mnemonic techniques are of little value in learning structured, meaningful material (Hunter, 1977; Morris, 1977). It is certainly true that the benefits to be gained from such techniques tend to be greater in associative learning than in the retention of prose (Pressley, 1977), and that at least under certain circumstances imagery instructions may prove to be of little or no value in learning meaningful sentences (Richardson, 1985b). However, this is partly because under control conditions many subjects are spontaneously inclined to use mental imagery to learn such material (Anderson & Kulhavy, 1972). There is now convincing evidence that training and instructions in the use of mental imagery may be helpful in prose learning in both adults (Denis, 1982, in press, and Chapter 9, this volume) and children (Denis, 1984; Pressley, Forrest-Pressley, Elliott-Faust, & Miller, 1985; Mastropieri et al., Chapter 16, this volume).

On the basis of a critical evaluation of this evidence, Denis (1984) concluded that semantic processing was normally of primary importance in the comprehension and retention of text, but that it might be supplemented by the use of mental imagery. Subsequently, Denis (in press) identified an important corollary of this position, that mental imagery would be of crucial importance in the case of subjects with impaired or nonexistent semantic processing. Because the latter may well be a consequence of organic brain damage, this suggests that training and instructions in the use of mental imagery should enhance prose learning among neurological patients. Even this weak interpretation of Denis' proposal has apparently only been explored to date in one single case (Crosson & Buenning, 1984), although the results are moderately encouraging. A much stronger inference is that imagery instructions should have a disproportionate benefit in prose retention only for those categories of patients who demonstrate a selective impairment of semantic processing. The latter may include Korsakoff patients, who seem to be unable to retrieve semantically encoded material in the absence of appropriate cues (McDowall, 1979; Wetzel & Squire, 1980), and the elderly, who appear less able to engage in abstract levels of processing (Erber, Herman, & Botwinick, 1980; Puglisi, 1980).

General Therapeutic Variables

Elaborate encoding of the sort demanded by most imagery mnemonics requires vigilance and planning, which is quite effortful for normal individuals and may be quite beyond the capabilities of brain-damaged patients. If such patients are to be motivated to devote time and effort to acquiring and using these novel means of remembering, they have to recognize their handicaps as involving a memory problem. For instance, in Patten's (1972) original study, the three patients with midline lesions were unaware of their memory impairment and were therefore unmotivated to change their mediational strategies. Similarly, the development of memory retraining programs at the Boston Veterans Administration Medical Center with alcoholic Korsakoff patients has consistently been limited by the fact that most of these patients are simply not aware of their own memory deficits. This results in a lack of motivation to participate in the remedial programs, primarily because of a failure to grasp their necessity. As Robertson-Tchabo (1980) pointed out, the problem of motivation is compounded by the fact that the incidence of memory complaints may not be highly correlated with the level of objective memory deficit (see also Gianutsos & Grynbaum, 1983; Kapur & Pearson, 1983).

Patients with amnesic disorders of an etiology other than Korsakoff's syndrome have also entered extensive individualized programs of memory retraining at the Boston facility. Most notable was a postencephalitic patient with a dense anterograde and retrograde amnesia. Attempts to retrain this patient have been documented elsewhere (Cermak, 1976; Cermak & O'Connor, 1983) but can be summarized quite simply. Basically, after many months of participating in a program focused on the use of mental imagery, verbal mediation, and rote memorization, it was found that the patient could be trained to memorize information but could not incorporate it into his knowledge base in any comprehensible fashion. For instance, he was taught to answer the question "Who broke Babe Ruth's record for lifetime runs?" by replying "Henry Aaron"; but when asked who held the record for the most home run hits in a career he would reply "Babe Ruth." It was concluded that this patient was not able to profit from memory aids including imagery because new learning remained insulated from his comprehension of the information. In short, his memory (consisting of the manipulation, reconstruction, and extension of information) seemed beyond hope of recovery. This patient clearly exemplified a problem that recurrently undermines memory retraining endeavors; namely, that specific information can be taught readily via a mnemonic device, such as mental imagery, but is rarely integrated into a patient's true comprehension of material.

A patient who was somewhat more adept at employing mnemonic strategies came to our attention after suffering a ruptured aneurysm of the anterior communicating artery. Following surgical intervention to clip the aneurysm, he displayed a dense anterograde amnesia with a retrograde amnesia extending back over several years. His memory deficits were manifested in his confusion concerning his whereabouts and his difficulty in learning people's names. Unlike the patient described previously, this patient used mnemonics spontaneously. He had, in fact, learned a series of memory aids including mental imagery prior to his disability. This advantage probably allowed him to rely upon old knowledge in order to gain access to new information. Unfortunately, even the use of these mnemonics did not help the patient's memory in any dramatic way. He, like all others, was never able to incorporate new learning into his semantic memory. Despite adroit utilization of mnemonics, the patient remained amnesic.

Still another patient treated extensively was a head-injury victim whose memory problems were secondary to other neuropsychological disorders. Such "secondary memory problems" seem to afford the greatest potential for therapy, because cognitive functions, such as attention and sequencing, may lend themselves to therapy more readily than pure memory disorders. This patient's memory deficit (MQ = 64) was superimposed upon such difficulties. She was unable to sequence properly and had problems distinguishing a portion of a stimulus from the whole. Obviously these impairments confounded any attempts to measure her intelligence, but we suspected that she was a very bright person because of her former profession and various indices of her previous intellect. She was keenly aware of her disorders and quite determined to learn compensatory techniques.

Most of the compensatory techniques were designed by her occupational therapist, and they provided the patient with ways of overcoming her perceptual and sequencing problems. Instructions that seemed too complicated for the patient to remember (such as which medication to take, when to take it, and the appropriate quantity) were sequenced and organized by placing the appropriate amounts in individual containers on a large spice rack labeled by days of the week and hours. The patient's house keys were color coded with arrows placed above the lock to provide direction. Memory for information that did not have to be sequenced or that was not perceptually confusing (such as people's names) proved to be amenable to remediation. The patient enjoyed these games and proved to be remarkably good at them. Nevertheless, her ability to put these pieces together in a comprehensive way remained poor.

It is important to note that this patient enjoyed limited success in memory retraining because her memory difficulties were secondary to other neuropsychological deficits (sequencing and perception). Her ability to grasp the nature of her difficulties was also essential to her successful outcome. Imagery, however, never proved successful largely because of her overwhelming perceptual difficulties. Furthermore, it must be noted that the patient's deficit was never really overcome but merely bypassed via environmental restructuring.

The implication that can be drawn for the use of imagery by amnesics is similar to the explanation that has been given for their inability to utilize semantic encoding as a mnemonic aid (Cermak, 1982). There has never been any doubt that amnesics can understand verbal information on the basis of its semantic content; what they cannot do is utilize this ability as a means of storing and retaining the verbal information. They can decipher and comprehend what is being presented to them, but they cannot utilize the products of this comprehension to process the material further for later reconstruction during retrieval. Similarly, amnesic patients are able to form images of verbal material while failing to capitalize on this ability. They cannot cognitively manipulate their previously established memory hierarchy in such a way that the products of this analysis can be incorporated permanently. The postencephalitic patient described by Cermak (1976) could not incorporate well-formed novel images into his memory hierarchy. As a consequence, the images remained isolated islands of unincorporated information. They could sometimes be teased out by cuing methods but the patient did not seem to realize that he was retrieving the very material the examiner was requesting. He appeared almost parrot-like in his response, not understanding what he was retrieving or where he might have learned it.

Conclusions

Reference has already been made to the point that if interventions are to be successful, then training procedures need to be developed and tested that are appropriate to the target population. In making this observation with regard to the elderly, Poon et al. (1980) emphasized the importance of insuring that the elaborated task makes only reasonable demands upon information-processing capacity. For instance, the subjects may have to be allowed longer acquisition and retrieval times if they are to benefit from imagery training (see also Levin & Divine-Hawkins, 1974; Pressley & Levin, 1977; Treat & Reese, 1976).

It is also important to insure that subjects retain the relevant techniques during the interval between acquisition and retrieval, that they maintain the use of these techniques in similar learning tasks, and that they transfer their use to other situations. It is clear from the findings reviewed earlier that explicitly prescribing a mnemonic technique does not in itself guarantee this. DeLeon (1974) proposed that it would be more effective to use instructions that increased the subjects' attention to the task at hand and prompted them to develop their own strategies. Poon et al. (1980) also emphasized the importance of encouraging self-monitoring and other metacognitive skills in achieving these goals. This underlines the general point that all individuals need to have the appropriate metastrategic knowledge of how, when, and where to employ imagery mnemonics if they are to use such techniques effectively in their everyday lives (cf. Pressley, Borkowski, & Schneider, in press; and Chapters 8, by Katz, and 13, by Pressley, Borkowski, & Johnson, in this volume).

Acknowledgments. The two senior authors contributed equally to this chapter, although the first-named author was responsible for integrating their respective contributions. Laird Cermak's research was supported by Grant AA-00187 from the National Institute of Alcohol and Alcohol Abuse and by the Medical Research Service of the Veterans Administration.

References

Anderson, R. C., & Kulhavy, R. W. (1972). Imagery and prose learning. *Journal of Educational Psychology, 63,* 242–243.

Baddeley, A. D. (1982). Amnesia: A minimal model and an interpretation. In L. S. Cermak (Ed.), *Human memory and amnesia* (pp. 305–336). Hillsdale, NJ: Erlbaum Associates.

Baddeley, A. D., & Warrington, E. K. (1973). Memory coding and amnesia. *Neuropsychologia, 11,* 159–165.

Caird, W. K., & Hannah, F. (1964). Short-term memory disorder in elderly psychiatric patients. *Diseases of the Nervous System, 25,* 564–568.

Canestrari, R. E., Jr. (1968). Age differences in verbal learning and verbal behavior. *Interdisciplinary Topics in Gerontology, 1,* 2–14.

Cermak, L. S. (1975). Imagery as an aid to retrieval for Korsakoff patients. *Cortex, 11,* 163–169.

Cermak, L. S. (1976). The encoding capacity of a patient with amnesia due to encephalitis. *Neuropsychologia, 14,* 311–326.

Cermak, L. S. (1980). Comments on imagery as a therapeutic mnemonic. In L. W. Poon, J. L. Fozard, L. S. Cermak, D. Arenberg, & L. W. Thompson (Eds.), *New directions in memory and aging* (pp. 507–510). Hillsdale, NJ: Erlbaum Associates.

Cermak, L. S. (1982). The long and the short of it in amnesia. In L. S. Cermak (Ed.), *Human Memory and Amnesia* (pp. 43–59). Hillsdale, NJ: Erlbaum Associates.

Cermak, L. S., & O'Connor, M. (1983). The anterograde and retrograde retrieval ability of a patient with amnesia due to encephalitis. *Neuropsychologia, 21,* 213–234.

Craik, F. I. M. (1977). Age differences in human memory. In J. E. Birren & K. W. Schaie (Eds.), *Handbook of the psychology of aging* (pp. 384–420). New York: Van Nostrand Reinhold.

Crosson, B., & Buenning, W. (1984). An individualized memory retraining program after closed-head injury: A single-case study. *Journal of Clinical Neuropsychology, 6,* 287–301.

Crovitz, H. F. (1979). Memory retraining in brain-damaged patients: The airplane list. *Cortex, 15,* 131–134.

Crovitz, H. F., Harvey, M. T., & Horn, R. W. (1979). Problems in the acquisition of imagery mnemonics: Three brain-damaged cases. *Cortex, 15,* 225–234.

Cutting, J. (1978). A cognitive approach to Korsakoff's syndrome. *Cortex, 14,* 485–495.

DeLeon, J. L. M. (1974). Effects of training in repetition and mediation on paired-associate learning and practical memory in the aged. *Dissertation Abstracts International, 35,* 3011B.

Denis, M. (1982). Imaging while reading text: A study of individual differences. *Memory and Cognition, 10,* 540–545.

Denis, M. (1984). Imagery and prose: A critical review of research on adults and children. *Text, 4,* 381–401.

Denis, M. (in press). Visual imagery: Effects or role in prose processing? In F. Klix & H. Hagendorf (Eds.), *Human Memory and Cognitive Capabilities.* Amsterdam: North-Holland.

Diller, L., & Gordon, W. A. (1981). Interventions for cognitive deficits in brain-injured adults. *Journal of Consulting and Clinical Psychology, 49,* 822–834.

Erber, J., Herman, T. G., & Botwinick, J. (1980). Age differences in memory as a function of depth of processing. *Experimental Aging Research, 6,* 341–348.

Erlichman, H., & Barrett, J. (1983). Right hemisphere specialization for mental imagery: A review of the evidence. *Brain and Cognition, 2,* 55–76.

Farah, M. J. (1984). The neurological basis of mental imagery: A componential analysis. *Cognition, 18,* 241–269.

Farah, M. J. (in press). The laterality of mental image generation: A test with normal subjects. *Neuropsychologia.*

Farah, M. J., Gazzaniga, M. S., Holtzman, J. D., & Kosslyn, S. M. (1985). A left hemisphere basis for visual mental imagery. *Neuropsychologia, 23,* 115–118.

Gasparrini, B., & Satz, P. (1979). A treatment for memory problems in left hemisphere CVA patients. *Journal of Clinical Neuropsychology, 1,* 137–150.

Gasparrini, W. G. (1978). A treatment for memory problems in brain-damaged patients. *Dissertation Abstracts International, 39,* 379B.

Gianutsos, R. (1981). Training the short- and long-term verbal recall of a postencephalitic amnesic. *Journal of Clinical Neurology, 3,* 143–153.

Gianutsos, R., & Grynbaum, B. B. (1983). Helping brain-injured people to contend with hidden deficits. *International Rehabilitation Medicine, 5,* 37–40.

Glasgow, R. E., Zeiss, R. A., Barrera, M., Jr., & Lewinsohn, P. M. (1977). Case studies on remediating memory deficits in brain-damaged individuals. *Journal of Clinical Psychology, 33,* 1049–1054.

Griffith, D., & Actkinson, T. R. (1978). Mental aptitude and mnemonic enhancement. *Bulletin of the Psychonomic Society, 12*, 347–348.

Gupton, T., & Frincke, G. (1970). Imagery, mediational instructions, and noun position in free recall of noun-verb pairs. *Journal of Experimental Psychology, 86*, 461–462.

Harris, J. E. (1978). External memory aids. In M. M. Gruneberg, P. E. Morris, & R. N. Sykes (Eds.), *Practical aspects of memory* (pp. 172–179). London: Academic Press.

Harris, J. E. (1984). Remembering to do things: A forgotten topic. In J. E. Harris & P. E. Morris (Eds.), *Everyday memory, actions, and absent-mindedness* (pp. 71–92). London: Academic Press.

Hellebusch, S. J. (1976). On improving learning and memory in the aged: The effects of mnemonics on strategy transfer and generalization. *Dissertation Abstracts International, 37*, 1459B–1460B.

Hulicka, I. M., & Grossman, J. L. (1967). Age-group comparisons for the use of mediators in paired-associate learning. *Journal of Gerontology, 22*, 46–51.

Hulicka, I. M., Sterns, H., & Grossman, J. L. (1967). Age-group comparisons of paired-associate learning as a function of paced and self-paced association and response times. *Journal of Gerontology, 22*, 274–280.

Hunter, I. M. L. (1977). Imagery, comprehension, and mnemonics. *Journal of Mental Imagery, 1*, 65–72.

Jaffe, P. G., & Katz, A. N. (1975). Attenuating anterograde amnesia in Korsakoff's psychosis. *Journal of Abnormal Psychology, 84*, 559–562.

Janssen, W. (1976). *On the nature of the mental image.* Soesterberg, The Netherlands: Institute for Perception TNO.

Jones, M. K. (1974). Imagery as a mnemonic aid after left temporal lobectomy: Contrast between material-specific and generalized memory disorders. *Neuropsychologia, 12*, 21–30.

Jones-Gotman, M. (1979). Incidental learning of image-mediated or pronounced words after right temporal lobectomy. *Cortex, 15*, 187–197.

Jones-Gotman, M., & Milner, B. (1978). Right temporal-lobe contribution to image-mediated verbal learning. *Neuropsychologia, 16*, 61–71.

Kapur, N. (1978). Visual imagery capacity of alcoholic Korsakoff patients. *Neuropsychologia, 16*, 517–519.

Kapur, N., & Pearson, D. (1983). Memory symptoms and memory performance of neurological patients. *British Journal of Psychology, 74*, 409–415.

Kosslyn, S. M., Holtzman, J. D., Farah, M. J., & Gazzaniga, M. S. (1985). A computational analysis of mental image generation: Evidence from functional dissociations in split-brain patients. *Journal of Experimental Psychology: General, 114*, 311–341.

Kovner, R., Mattis, S., & Goldmeier, E. (1983). A technique for promoting robust free recall in chronic organic amnesia. *Journal of Clinical Neuropsychology, 5*, 65–71.

Kovner, R., Mattis, S., & Pass, R. (1985). Some patients can freely recall large amounts of information in new contexts. *Journal of Clinical and Experimental Neuropsychology, 7*, 395–411.

Kreutzer, M. A., Leonard, C., & Flavell, J. H. (1975). An interview study of children's knowledge about memory. *Monographs of the Society for Research in Child Development, 40*(1, Serial No. 159).

Levin, H. S., Benton, A. L., & Grossman, R. G. (1982). *Neurobehavioral consequences of closed head injury.* New York: Oxford University Press.

Levin, J. R., & Divine-Hawkins, P. (1974). Visual imagery as a prose-learning process. *Journal of Reading Behavior, 6*, 23–30.

Lewinsohn, P. M., Danaher, B. G., & Kikel, S. (1977). Visual imagery as a mnemonic aid for brain-injured persons. *Journal of Consulting and Clinical Psychology, 45*, 717–723.

Mason, S. E., & Smith, A. D. (1977). Imagery in the aged. *Experimental Aging Research, 3*, 17–32.

McDaniel, M. A., & Pressley, M. (1984). Putting the keyword method in context. *Journal of Educational Psychology, 76*, 598–609.

McDowall, J. (1979). Effects of encoding instructions and retrieval cuing on recall in Korsakoff patients. *Memory and Cognition, 7*, 232–239.

Meacham, J., & Colombo, J. A. (1980). External cues facilitate remembering in children. *Journal of Educational Research, 73*, 299–301.

Meacham, J., & Leiman, B. (1982). Remembering to perform future actions. In U. Neisser (Ed.), *Remembering in natural contexts* (pp. 327–335). San Francisco: W. H. Freeman.

Miller, G. E., Levin, J. R., & Pressley, M. (1980). An adaptation of the keyword method to children's learning of foreign verbs. *Journal of Mental Imagery, 4*, 57–61.

Milner, B. (1971). Interhemispheric differences in the localization of psychological processes in man. *British Medical Bulletin, 27*, 272–277.

Milner, B. (1973). Hemispheric specialization: Scope and limits. In F. O. Schmitt & G. F. Worden (Eds.), *The neurosciences: Third study program* (pp. 75–89). Boston, MA: The MIT Press.

Morris, P. E. (1977). Practical strategies for human learning and remembering. In M. J. A. Howe (Ed.), *Adult learning: Psychological research and applications* (pp. 125–144). London: Wiley.

Morris, P. E., & Reid, R. L. (1974). Imagery and recognition. *British Journal of Psychology, 65*, 7–12.

Paivio, A., & Yuille, J. C. (1967). Mediation instructions and word attributes in paired-associate learning. *Psychonomic Science, 8*, 65–66.

Paris, S. G., Mahoney, G. J., & Buckhalt, J. A. (1974). Facilitation of semantic integration in sentence memory of retarded children. *American Journal of Mental Deficiency, 78*, 714–720.

Patten, B. M. (1972). The ancient art of memory: Usefulness in treatment. *Archives of Neurology, 26*, 25–31.

Poon, L. W., Walsh-Sweeney, L., & Fozard, J. L. (1980). Memory skill training for the elderly: Salient issues on the use of imagery mnemonics. In L. W. Poon, J. L. Fozard, L. S. Cermak, D. Arenberg, & L. W. Thompson (Eds.), *New directions in memory and aging* (pp. 461–484). Hillsdale, NJ: Erlbaum Associates.

Pressley, M. (1977). Imagery and children's learning: Putting the picture in developmental perspective. *Review of Educational Research, 47*, 585–622.

Pressley, M. (1982). Elaboration and memory development. *Child Development, 53*, 296–309.

Pressley, M., Borkowski, J. G., & Schneider, W. (in press). Good strategy users coordinate metacognition, strategy use, and knowledge. In R. Vasta & G. Whitehurst (Eds.), *Annals of child development* (Vol. 4). Greenwich, CT: JAI Press.

Pressley, M., Forrest-Pressley, D. L., Elliott-Faust, D., & Miller, G. (1985). Children's use of cognitive strategies, how to teach strategies and what to do if they can't be taught. In M. Pressley & C. J. Brainerd (Eds.), *Cognitive learning and memory in children* (pp. 1–47). New York: Springer-Verlag.

Pressley, M., & Levin, J. R. (1977). Task parameters affecting the efficacy of a visual imagery learning strategy in younger and older children. *Journal of Experimental Child Psychology, 24*, 53–59.

Pressley, M., Levin, J. R., & Delaney, H. D. (1982). The mnemonic keyword method. *Review of Educational Research, 52,* 61–91.

Pressley, M., Levin, J. R., & Miller, G. E. (1981). The keyword method and children's learning of foreign vocabulary with abstract meanings. *Canadian Journal of Psychology, 35,* 283–287.

Puglisi, J. T. (1980). Semantic encoding in older adults as evidenced by release from proactive inhibition. *Journal of Gerontology, 34,* 58–65.

Richardson, J. T. E. (1979a). Correlations between imagery and memory scores across stimuli and across subjects. *Bulletin of the Psychonomic Society, 14,* 368–370.

Richardson, J. T. E. (1979b). Mental imagery, human memory, and the effects of closed head injury. *British Journal of Social and Clinical Psychology, 18,* 319–327.

Richardson, J. T. E. (1980). *Mental imagery and human memory.* London: Macmillan.

Richardson, J. T. E. (1982). Memory disorders. In A. Burton (Ed.), *The pathology and psychology of cognition* (pp. 48–77). London: Methuen.

Richardson, J. T. E. (1985a). Converging operations and reported mediators in the investigation of mental imagery. *British Journal of Psychology, 76,* 205–214.

Richardson, J. T. E. (1985b). Integration and decomposition in the retention of complex ideas. *Memory and Cognition, 13,* 112–127.

Richardson, J. T. E., & Barry, C. (1985). The effects of minor closed head injury upon human memory: Further evidence on the role of mental imagery. *Cognitive Neuropsychology, 2,* 149–168.

Robertson-Tchabo, E. A. (1980). Cognitive-skill training for the elderly: Why should "old dogs" acquire new tricks? In L. W. Poon, J. L. Fozard, L. S. Cermak, D. Arenberg, & L. W. Thompson (Eds.), *New directions in memory and aging* (pp. 511–517). Hillsdale, NJ: Erlbaum Associates.

Robertson-Tchabo, E. A., Hausman, C. P., & Arenberg, D. (1976). A classical mnemonic for older learners: A trip that works! *Educational Gerontology, 1,* 215–226.

Rowe, E. J., & Schnore, M. M. (1971). Item concreteness and reported strategies in paired-associate learning as a function of age. *Journal of Gerontology, 26,* 470–475.

Säljö, R. (1979). Learning about learning. *Higher Education, 8,* 443–451.

Säljö, R. (1984). Learning from reading. In F. Marton, D. Hounsell, & N. Entwistle (Eds.), *The experience of learning* (pp. 71–89). Edinburgh: Scottish Academic Press.

Treat, N. J., & Reese, H. W. (1976). Age, pacing, and imagery in paired-associate learning. *Developmental Psychology, 12,* 119–124.

Treat, N. J., Poon, L. W., & Fozard, J. L. (1978). From clinical and research findings on memory to intervention programs. *Experimental Aging Research, 4,* 235–253.

Wetzel, C. D., & Squire, L. R. (1980). Encoding in anterograde amnesia. *Neuropsychologia, 18,* 177–184.

Wilson, B. (1981). Teaching a patient to remember people's names after removal of a left temporal lobe tumour. *Behavioral Psychotherapy, 9,* 338–344.

Wilson, B. (1982). Success and failure in memory training following a cerebral vascular accident. *Cortex, 18,* 581–594.

Wilson, B., & Moffat, N. (1984). Rehabilitation of memory for everyday life. In J. E. Harris & P. E. Morris (Eds.), *Everyday memory, actions, and absent-mindedness* (pp. 207–233). London: Academic Press.

Winograd, E., & Simon, E. W. (1980). Visual memory and imagery in the aged. In L. W. Poon, J. L. Fozard, L. S. Cermak, D. Arenberg, & L. W. Thompson (Eds.), *New directions in memory and aging* (pp. 485–506). Hillsdale, NJ: Erlbaum Associates.

Yuille, J. C., & Paivio, A. (1968). Imagery and verbal mediation instructions in paired-associate learning. *Journal of Experimental Psychology, 78,* 436–441.

CHAPTER 15

Special Educational Applications of Mnemonics

James E. Turnure and John F. Lane

This chapter is devoted to a review and analysis of the use of mnemonic techniques in special areas of education, particularly with handicapped children and other nonstandard groups. Whereas this statement of purpose is straightforward, it has been our experience that considerable complexities are involved in fully establishing the value of mnemonics, itself a complex topic, in the realm of special education.

For instance, attempts to utilize mnemonics in what we are considering special educational programs may be considered interventions in an intervention. Recent cross-cultural research on the cognitive development of children in diverse societies has been emphasizing the apparently potent impact of "formal education" on the cognitive proclivities, practices, and skills of the youths in these cultures (e.g., Scribner & Cole, 1973; Sharp, Cole, & Lave, 1979). For example, the familiar and "natural" appearing experience of universal education in modern industrialized societies is itself a massive intervention into the lives of children and families. Whereas the complex implications of this rather recent insight for psychological theory and educational practice remain under debate as regards general education [see *Review of Educational Research*, 1984, *54*(4), whole issue; see also Sarason, 1983; Sharp et al., 1979], it is our impression that matters are even more complicated when considering the sort of "special" educational enterprises we have been reviewing. That is, we seem to be analyzing attempts to intervene in interventions developed to expand or remediate inadequacies of the original educational interventions in people's lives.

The emphasis we place on cultural and societal factors in education reflects the inescapable observation that the "special" identities of the populations and programs with which we are concerned are usually established because some particular social need or pressure provokes a political response in the form of legislation mandating the expansion or unique segmentation of the generic educational system. With the imposition of each new set of "marching orders," the educational establishment is required to reorganize for the provision of new services to new, or previously "irregular," recruits. Subsequently, while the general populace remains cognizant only of the political or social issues (the status and rights of handicapped citizens, problems of a multilingual citizenry, lifelong education and occupational change, etc.), responsible educators grapple with such questions as the structure of schooling and the forms classrooms should take (Heintz & Blackman, 1977).

The complexities and controversies regarding the particular circumstances in which special populations are educated, are mentioned to establish the reason why it is so difficult to make generalized statements about the utility of mnemonics in special educational programs. It is entirely an open question whether a child who may be trained in a mnemonic technique in a "resource room," or a "self-contained" special classroom, or during an "English as a second language" (ESL) or other component of a bilingual program, and so on, will transfer that skill to lessons in the regular educational stream of activities, or anywhere else. This is not a problem unique to education or to mnemonics training, of course, for the widely applauded and extensively utilized techniques of behavior modification are generally acknowledged to suffer the same limitations (Meichenbaum, 1985). This state of affairs recently has led to attempts at a rapprochement between some behaviorally inclined and some cognitively oriented researchers, possibly in the hope that the counterbalancing strengths of the two inadequacies will somehow produce a sufficiency in programming generalizable intervention outcomes (e.g., Borkowski & Cavanaugh, 1979; Kendall & Hollon, 1979; Meichenbaum, 1985). In fact, the issue of transfer of training or generalizable learning has clearly emerged as a central issue in general efforts to reorganize curricula (Bender & Turnure, 1980; Chipman & Segal, 1985; Perkins, 1985).

Obviously, there is a need to consider the circumstances and the purposes for which a cognitive skill, such as a mnemonic device, may be pertinent, as Perkins (1985) has been emphasizing recently. Therefore, while some scholars of education endorse the wholehearted use of mnemonics (e.g., Gage & Berliner, 1984), we should be chary about succumbing to illusions that people can be rescued from all their learning, memory, and thinking problems by instilling an array of monolithic information-processing mnemonics in their minds, rather like a mental Maginot Line, designed to subdue the onslaughts of incoming information. Therefore, we have considered the criticisms of mnemonic techniques (e.g., Perkins, 1985) very seriously and judged them to be pertinent when applied to the limited, static, standard view of recall mnemonics, the view reflected in Norman's (1976) traditional definition, "all mnemonic devices try to relate the material to be learned to some previously learned organizational scheme" (p. 135), where the emphasis is on a rigid technique of somewhat narrow applicability. We consider mnemonic techniques to fall within the more general domain of elaboration: not only are previously learned schemes important, but it is also the relational context generated at the time a technique is employed (perhaps in Bellezza's (1981) sense of a cognitive cuing structure) that allows such techniques to have their reported effects (Taylor & Turnure, 1979). Recent conceptualizations of mnemonics as problem-solving techniques (Bransford & Stein, 1984), as components of intelligent, adaptive mental systems (Kail & Siegel, 1977), or, in our emerging view, as all sorts of cognitive accessories to the major mental processes of learning, comprehension and memory, make mnemonic techniques too useful to be quibbled over, or to be ignored theoretically or practically.

Given these cautions and concerns, we have little doubt that it is extremely important to publicize as emphatically as possible the successful demonstrations of effective mnemonics we have found in our review of the literature. This is especially important because there is little evidence that very many special education teachers place any emphasis on training cognitive skills of any sort with their pupils whose cognitive capabilities may be faulty. Most special education programs, for example, still rely predominantly on systems of instruction derived from behavior modification approaches, such as precision teaching, direct instruction, and varieties of programmed instruction (MacMillan & Meyers, 1984; Smith, Forsberg, Herb, & Neisworth, 1978).

Some diversity exists in the kinds of mnemonic strategies that are available for study with special populations. Modalities other than the visual—which is the approach emphasized in this volume—have been used. Lininger (1984) used mime to provide a kinesthetic elaborative content for memory tasks. Williams (1983) has collected many examples of the uses of kinesthetic elaboration in general educational contexts. Verbal elaboration techniques are more common in the literature (e.g., Taylor & Turnure, 1979), and we shall refer to them where appropriate. However, most of the research on mnemonic training has used some kind of imagery-based technique. Therefore, our review focuses on this type of technique.

Imagery-Based Mnemonic Techniques

Imagery

The basic nature of imagery is not the subject of the present review. For our present purposes, we consider images to be any mental representations that appear similar to sensory input, or similar to representations that derive directly from the senses. They may be especially effective for the representation of spatial information (Kosslyn, 1980; Paivio, 1979); in any case, the best discriminandum is that they are not verbal. The most common modality used in mnemonics is the visual, but imagery may involve any modality: visual, auditory, haptic, kinesthetic, olfactory, and so forth. Imagery can be multimodal; Luria's famous subject S used imagery in the broadest sense: synesthetic combinations of vision, hearing, touch, taste, and smell (Luria, 1968). The most significant point for our purposes is that imagery has consistently been found to aid learning: Indeed, Bugelski (1970) described experiments in which subjects who were instructed to image, but not to learn, were nevertheless unable to prevent learning.

Mnemonic Techniques

A mnemonic technique can be defined as any mental strategy that aids the learning of one material by using other, initially extraneous, material as an aid to such learning. Imagery-based mnemonic techniques traditionally have been known as mnemonic "devices"; we shall use the more general term "technique," with the qualification that the ones we are mainly concerned with are imagery based.

Bellezza (1981; also Bellezza, Chapter 2, this volume) considers mnemonic techniques to be "cognitive cuing structures"—mental representations whose purpose is to enhance memory by providing effective cues for recall. In order for a cognitive cuing structure to be of sufficiently high quality, its components or elements should have four properties: constructibility, or ease and reliably of cue generation; discriminability of cues from one another; associativity of elements with one another; and invertibility, the ability of the originally encoded stimulus to be decoded from the cuing structure.

The history of the use of mnemonic techniques is predominantly that of the use of visual images and arrays as pegs or positions on which or in which to mentally "place" material to be learned. Yates (1966) has compiled much of this historical material. Higbee (1979) has reviewed such techniques as they apply in education, especially that of nonspecial populations. Such popular books as those of the mnemonist Harry Lorayne (Lorayne, 1974; Lorayne & Lucas, 1974) also emphasize the use of visual imagery.

The componential approach to human information processing provides a useful framework within which to investigate the efficacy of such imagery-based mnemonics. In this approach, specific processes or components of the information-processing system are isolated. Different sets of components have been proposed by various researchers. Lea (1975) identified three components of the method of loci: "find" activates the representation of a locus; "move" scans from locus to locus, keeping track of the number of loci scanned; "retrieve" decodes the locus–item association and retrieves the name of the item. McCarty (1980) identified three components of the face–name mnemonic that he considered necessary for successful use of the technique: a prominent facial feature; a concrete, high-imagery transformation of the name; and an interactive visual image connecting these two components. Mastropieri, Scruggs, & Levin (1985) suggested that the three components of retrieval, recoding, and relating are especially relevant to mnemonic techniques in general. Sternberg (1985) has proposed a set of components in the context of his theory of intelligence. In a subsequent section, we use Sternberg's componential model in our analysis of mnemonic techniques because of its fuller and more general development compared to other componential models.

The Uses of Mnemonic Techniques

Three benefits accrue from learning any mnemonic technique: (1) such techniques are intrinsically helpful in memorizing specific kinds of material; (2) learning a mnemonic technique gives students a sense that they can control their own memory processes; and (3) mnemonic techniques are easily learned knowledge bases from which, under appropriate internal or external guidance, the ability to use the component processes that they embody may be extended. The first benefit has been well supported by research, some of which we cite below. The second benefit has also been demonstrated, although less fully. It is the third benefit, that which supports interdomain transfer, or the transfer to other domains of skills acquired while learning mnemonic techniques, which we emphasize in this chapter. There has been little research into this aspect of mnemonic techniques. We hope to provide a framework, based upon Sternberg's componential model, that may lead to more specific investigations of it.

The Structures of Three Mnemonic Techniques

In this section, examples are given of three mnemonic techniques – the keyword method, the face–name technique, and the method of loci. The techniques are then described in such a way as to emphasize their structural similarity as sequences of steps. In the examples, references to the appropriate steps are indicated in brackets.

The Keyword Method

The keyword method has been studied intensively in its application to the learning of a second language (e.g., Atkinson, 1975; Atkinson & Raugh, 1975). Mastropieri et al. (1985) have found that groups of students using the keyword method consistently learn vocabulary words significantly better than do groups using other techniques of vocabulary learning, especially direct instruction with rehearsal. The following example is from Hayes (1981, p. 101):

Consider the first Italian word, "agnello". The Italian pronunciation [AN YELL' OH] [Step 1] sounds quite similar to the English words "ANN YELLOW" [Step 2], our chosen keywords for "agnello". Next we will relate the keywords to the English translation: "lamb". To do this we can create an image [Step 5] of a girl, Ann [Step 3], leading a bright yellow [Step 3] lamb [Step 4].

The Face–Name Technique

The face–name technique (Lorayne & Lucas, 1974) is used to connect people's names with salient features of their faces. Lorayne and Lucas (1974, p. 68) give the following example:

Mr. Colletti has very thick lips [Step 4A]. Picture those lips [Step 4B] and see millions of cups of tea or tea bags coming out of them; you're calling one of those cups or bags [Steps 5, 6]. Really try to visualize that silly action , and CALL A TEA [Steps 1, 2] will remind you of Colletti [Step 7].

The Method of Loci

The method of loci is one of the most widely employed mnemonic techniques using visual images and has been found to be very effective with nonspecial populations (e.g., Ross & Lawrence, 1968). In this technique, a physical setting with many parts which are able to be easily discriminated from one another, or a pathway with many objects or places on it, is first memorized by rote. These parts, objects, or places are the loci. A list of items to be remembered is then mentally placed in these loci. The preferred method is to form images that represent an interaction between the locus and the item to be remembered. The following example is based upon the second author's use of the method of loci with a high-school class.

A 40-item list was memorized, whose first three items were DOG, UMBRELLA, and SAND PILE. The pathway that was used to connect the items began at a CULVERT in the driveway of his house, which led to an OAK TREE, from which one could reach the back STAIRWAY of the house. In using the technique, an image was created of a white dog digging at the culvert to create a moat to keep people out, an umbrella keeping the rain from hurting an oak tree, and a stairway that was hard to climb because its steps were excavations in the sand.

All three techniques can be seen as consisting of eight general steps, each step being characterized by a specific process or component. In the descriptions that follow, the capitalized words represent what we consider to be one of the most salient components needed at that step. Readers who have used these techniques will realize that the steps tend not to be followed in a strict serial order. They interact in various ways, and various sequences may iterate in order for the most adequate images to be constructed. One aspect of the sequential structure of these techniques is more strictly ordered, however: the steps forming a "storage phase" are essentially prerequisite to those of the subsequent "retrieval phase" (cf. Bellezza, 1981). Table 15.1 summarizes the similarities among these techniques.

Storage Phase

1. Discriminate. In the keyword method, parts of the foreign word to be learned are discriminated, such that to each part a similar concrete (i.e., high-imagery) English word can be matched. The match is usually phonological, although other physical dimensions can be involved. This English word is the "keyword." In the face–name technique, parts of the name to be learned are discriminated, for which phonologically similar concrete words can be found; one or more salient features of the face are also discriminated (this is step 4A in Table 15.1). In the method of loci, parts of the word to be remembered are discriminated, for the same purpose.
2. Access. In all three techniques, an appropriate concrete English word is accessed from the mental lexicon. For the face–name technique, these are what Lorayne and Lucas (1974) call "substitute words."
3. Generate. An image is generated to represent each of these concrete words.
4A. Generate. In the keyword method, an image, or set of images, is generated to represent the English meaning of the foreign word. In the face–name technique, one or more images are generated embodying the salient features of the face.
4B. Retrieve. In the method of loci, a previously stored image of the appropriate locus is retrieved.

TABLE 15.1. Steps in the use of three mnemonic techniques.

Step	Keyword	Face–name	Method of loci
Storage phase			
1A Discriminate parts of _____ if necessary.	Foreign word	Name	TBR word[a]
1B Discriminate features of _____.		Face	
2 Access _____ similar in sound to _____ or its parts.	Concrete word Foreign word	Concrete word Name	Concrete word TBR word[b]
3 Generate _____ to _____.	Word–image Concrete word	Name–image Concrete word	Word–image Concrete word
4A Generate _____ to _____.	Meaning–image Foreign word	Feature–image Chosen features of face	Locus–image[c] Locus
4B Retrieve _____.			Locus–image
5 Combine _____ and _____ into interactive image.	Word–image Meaning–image	Name–image Feature–image	Word–image Locus–image
Retrieval phase			
6 Cue interactive image with _____.	Word–image	Feature–image	Previous locus–image in sequence
7 Decompose interactive image into _____ and _____.	Word–image Meaning–image	Name–image Feature–image	Word–image Locus–image
8 Respond with _____.	English word	Name	TBR word

[a] TBR, to be remembered.
[b] This step is not necessary if the TBR word does not need to be analyzed in step 1A.
[c] This process was completed as part of the prior memorization of the mental "pathway."

5. Combine. In the keyword method and the face–name technique, an interactive image is constructed to connect the two images, or sets of images, which were generated in steps 3 and 4A. In the method of loci, the interactive image connects the image generated in step 3 with the image of the locus retrieved in step 4B.

Retrieval Phase

6. Cue. In the keyword method, the foreign word is presented as a stimulus for the recall of its English equivalent. The images which were generated in step 3 cue the interactive image generated in step 5, and this image is retrieved. In the face–name technique, when the person whose name is to be recalled is seen again, the salient features of his or her face cue the interactive image generated in step 5. In the method of loci, when it is necessary to recall the

list, contextual cues stored with the first interactive image are used to retrieve this image; this first interactive image then cues the second, and so forth in sequence through the list.

7. Decompose. In the keyword method, the interactive image is decomposed to extract the English word corresponding to the meaning of the foreign word. In the face–name technique, the interactive image is decomposed to extract the substitute words corresponding to the name of the person. In the method of loci, when each interactive image is retrieved, it is decomposed into the image representing the locus and that representing the word to be remembered; the image representing the word to be remembered cues retrieval of the word.

8. Respond. In the keyword method the English word, and in the method of loci the word to be remembered, is produced. In the face–name technique, the name of the person is reconstructed from the substitute words, and this name is produced.

Mnemonic Techniques With Special Populations

We now briefly review studies that have demonstrated the usefulness of these three techniques among the special populations of the mentally handicapped, elderly, blind, deaf, gifted, schizophrenic, and brain-damaged subjects, as well as in vocational and military training. In addition to the studies we cite, a number of dissertations have investigated aspects of the use of the techniques. Although we shall not cite these except in special cases, a list of such dissertations may be obtained from the authors.

Mentally Handicapped Subjects

Lebrato and Ellis (1974) found that the use of a pegword mnemonic reduced intralist intrusion errors for mentally retarded (MR) subjects. The keyword method has also been used extensively and successfully with learning-disabled (LD) subjects, and much of this work is discussed in Mastropieri, Scruggs, and Levin's contribution (Chapter 16) to this volume.

There is evidence of differences between LD and non-LD subjects in the efficiency of various cognitive processes (Dunn, 1973): time to process or scan information in working memory (Cermak, 1983; Hess & Radtke, 1981), time to access semantic content (Cermak, 1983; Elbert, 1984; Torgesen & Houck, 1980), selective attention (Gelzheiser, Solar, Shepherd, & Wozniak, 1983; Torgesen, 1981), digit span (Torgesen & Houck, 1980), strategies for rehearsing and analyzing information (Cermak, 1983), and general control processes (Torgesen & Houck, 1980).

These processing differences have in some cases been ameliorated through the use of various kinds of cues, which presumably focus the subjects' attention on relevant rather than irrelevant aspects of the stimulus. Using movement tasks, Horgan (1983) taught MR children a mnemonic using extent and location cues;

Reid (1980) used the feel of a movement and spatial location as cues. Glidden and Mar (1978) found that subcategory cues enhanced MR subjects' retrieval of information from semantic categories.

The need for extensive training has been pointed out by Gelzheiser et al. (1983). They emphasized that because LD subjects' limited attentional capacity may preclude their focusing on the goal of a task, enough time should be allotted for instruction on lower order components of learning strategies for such processes to become automatic (cf. Fitts & Posner, 1967). This automaticity may in great degree compensate for these subjects' attentional limitations.

There has been a substantial number of studies of mnemonics with mentally handicapped people, including a range of experiments exploring techniques for inducing imaginal processing. This work has been thoroughly analyzed recently in a review by Taylor and Turnure (1979), which emphasized methodological, as well as theoretical and applied, aspects of such attempts to investigate and intervene in cognitive processing. We encourage the interested reader to read that chapter for details, but we cite several conclusions from the Taylor and Turnure (1979) review that support the use of mnemonic instruction with mentally handicapped populations.

First of all, Taylor and Turnure (1979) make it abundantly clear that the mentally retarded can learn and use imagery-based strategies to enhance substantially the learning and memory of a variety of materials. Taylor and Turnure emphasize that the training employed with these populations often must be more extensive or more carefully crafted than with nonhandicapped peers. These special demands have led to some creative techniques. For instance, Ross and Ross (1978) utilized a procedure that involved the modeling of a "pretend television set" in the child's head, that could be turned on and off, adjusted and controlled by the child. Effectively instilling this technique did take several weeks of intensive training, but the impressive recall engendered makes it a noteworthy accomplishment. A major benefit of their training procedures versus some other successful imagery training techniques that have been utilized, such as drawing (Danner & Taylor, 1973), overt activity (Wolff & Levin, 1972), and overt verbalization (Whitely & Taylor, 1973), was identified by Ross and Ross (1978) as inhering in the general and immediate availability of their covert mentally based technique.

Taylor and Turnure (1979) also reviewed research in the area of verbal elaboration, the outcomes of which closely parallel those just mentioned for imagery training. Research on verbal elaboration mnemonics with the mentally retarded has just been extensively reviewed by Turnure (1985), and so will not be recounted here. However, one conclusion regarding the relationship between imagery and verbal elaboration drawn by Taylor and Turnure has applied implications. They note that "conditions under which both pictorial and verbal elaborations are available and acted upon by the learner seem to produce the most facilitation of learning and memory" (1979, p. 691). Specific reports of applied work utilizing principles of imagery and verbal elaboration training may be found in Kramer, Nagle, and Engel (1980); Taylor, Thurlow, and Turnure (1977), and Thurlow and Turnure (1977).

Rote memory is often used with MR students because teachers think that they cannot handle large quantities of elaborative material, such as complex interactive images. However, MR students "show increased learning and memory when the content is presented in meaningful contexts and/or when carefully designed instruction guides the learner to relate actively the information" to be remembered (Taylor & Turnure, 1979, p. 660). It is our belief that emphasis on such meaningful relations will further the efficient use of mnemonic techniques in general, as well as with special populations, such as MR or LD students. We have noted that more imagery research seems to have been done with LD students and more verbal elaboration work with the mentally retarded. There does not seem to be any theoretical reason for this disparity in research emphasis, so this observation simply identifies areas for further research.

Elderly Subjects

Investigators have found the method of loci (Robertson-Tchabo, Hausman, & Arenberg, 1976; Yesavage & Rose, 1984a) and face–name techniques (Yesavage, 1984; Yesavage & Rose, 1984a, 1984b; Yesavage, Rose, & Bower, 1983) to be effective with the elderly. Robertson-Tchabo et al. (1976) interpreted the success of the method of loci with elderly subjects to the presumed fact that it "capitalizes on the familiarity of the stopping places and their natural order; these attributes provide strong retrieval cues that can be applied without adding to the information overload typically experienced by older learners" (p. 215). Such strong retrieval cues may also have been involved in a study of memory for urban locations by Evans, Brennan, Skorpanich, and Held (1984), which is discussed in more detail later.

The use of such mnemonic techniques has been found to be enhanced by the addition of semantic elaboration, such as rating the pleasantness of images (Yesavage et al., 1983; Yesavage & Rose, 1984a), as well as by training in relaxation (Yesavage, 1984) and concentration (Yesavage & Rose, 1983). "Nonredundant forms of stimulus elaboration" can enhance the effectiveness of these techniques (Yesavage & Rose, 1984a, p. 155). The use of familiar locations also reduces the probability that, for older subjects, there is interference among items at the time of recall because of the greater search time in memory required by the elderly.

Programs that include visual mnemonics have been developed to train cognitive skills in the elderly (Treat, Poon, Fozard, & Popkin, 1978), especially in subjects with generally intact memories (Tavon, 1984).

The use of imagery-based techniques with the elderly is connected to the processing deficiencies generally reported for this population, especially those concerning sensory memory, attention, registration, short term memory (STM) capacity, speed of processing, semantic and especially visual encoding, and retrieval (Fleischmann, 1982). For example, Treat and Reese (1976) found that elderly subjects needed a longer anticipation time in order to benefit from imagery instructions. Difficulties in organizing material may also occur. For example, Hess (1982) found that older subjects experienced greater interference in concept acquisition when the new concept "was based on a reorganization of attributes associated with an established conceptual structure" (p. 473); and Waddell and Rogoff (1981) found that elderly subjects had greater difficulty in reconstructing spatial arrays when they had to "invent an organizational structure to facilitate recall" (p. 878).

Effective use of imagery-based techniques with the elderly may be related to these and other characteristics of elderly people. Brigham and Pressley (in preparation), have pointed out that elderly subjects often prefer not to use imagery techniques even if they know the techniques work better than others, perhaps because they require too much effort to learn or to apply. Craik's attentional deficit theory of memory decline (e.g., Rabinowitz, Craik, & Ackerman, 1982) hypothesizes that deficits in recall with advancing age result from reduction in available processing resources. Lane (1980, 1981), although working in the context of athletic performance, found that subjects' ability to focus on critical aspects of a situation—to discriminate important features of their performances and to generate useful images to help mentally practice them—was enhanced by relaxation and concentration. Such techniques might be used to help ameliorate attentional deficits.

The spontaneous use of imagery strategies by the elderly is rare (Camp-Cameron, Markley, & Kramer, 1983), and often, instructions to use imagery are ineffective (Mason & Smith, 1977; Whitbourne & Slavin, 1978). The elderly may use such strategies more frequently with concrete than with abstract material (Rowe & Schnore, 1971); this difference, of course, is not limited to elderly subjects (Paivio, 1979). Generalization or transfer of strategies from a training situation to other situations may occur, if at all, mainly when specific instructions to transfer are given, as well as explicit information concerning the sorts of situations to which the strategy or technique should be generalized (Robertson-Tchabo et al., 1976); this phenomenon is general (cf. Gick & Holyoak, 1983), and the subject is taken up again later on.

Blind Subjects

The general results of research with congenitally blind subjects is that, given tasks, such as mental rotation, which involve visual imagery either explicitly or implicitly, congenitally blind and sighted subjects perform with similar accuracy (Carpenter & Eisenberg, 1978; Craig, 1973; Hall, 1981; Jonides, Kahn, & Rozin, 1975; Kerr, 1983; Marmor & Zaback, 1976; Zimler & Keenan, 1983), although the blind often take longer to complete the tasks. Blind subjects can acquire spatial information while walking through large-scale environments (Herman, Chatman, & Roth, 1983; Landau, Gleitman, & Spelke, 1981), or in small-scale environments (Sasaki, 1981).

Blind subjects may use representations other than visual ones to perform these tasks. They may use spatial representations (Carpenter & Eisenberg, 1978; Marmor & Zaback, 1976), route structure (Hollyfield, 1982), or "knowledge of the

Euclidean properties of a spatial layout and . . . principles for making inferences based on those properties" (Landau et al., 1981, p. 1275). They may be using haptic information (Sasaki, 1981), or "haptic images" (Zimler & Keenan, 1983, p. 269). Their representations may be verbal (Dodds, 1983), as posited by Paivio's dual-coding theory (e.g., Paivio & Okavita, 1971), although the evidence for this dichotomy is not yet conclusive.

Deaf Subjects

Imagery has been found to be effective in paired-associate learning by deaf children (Bugelski, 1970; Cornoldi & Sanavio, 1980; Heinen, Cobb, & Pollard, 1976; Reese & Parkington, 1973). In some cases deaf children have been better able to imaginally code words than hearing children (Cornoldi & Sanavio, 1980). Arnold (1978) found deaf children better able to rotate mental images than hearing children. However, Heinen et al. (1976) found that their deaf group experienced difficulty in learning word pairs that had high auditory, rather than visual, imagery. Reese and Parkington (1973), in their work with the deaf, concluded that interactive imagery (a) facilitates performance by increasing the memorability of stimulus-response associations, and (b) reduces interference by reducing confusion among similar stimuli.

Gifted Students

Scruggs and Mastropieri (1984) have found that gifted students not only benefit from imagery-based techniques but may benefit more than others from such techniques. Carrier, Karbo, Kindem, Legisa, & Newstrom (1983) also reported such benefits with a sample of gifted students. However, contrary to their hypothesis that the elaboration allowed by "the personal meaning of self-generated visual displays would promote more recall than supplied visual elaboration" (p. 236), these investigators found that teacher-generated visual images worked better with gifted students than did self-generated images. The explanation given by Carrier et al. (1983) for this divergence from the expected results supports one of the general points that we are emphasizing in this chapter, that adequate instruction and sufficient practice time are crucially prerequisite to the learning of mnemonic techniques: "Direct training and additional practice on forming (interactive) images might lead to better memory . . . . Perhaps even gifted children need to be taught explicitly to use mental imagery as a memory strategy" (Carrier et al., 1983, pp. 239–240).

Schizophrenics

Imagery-based mnemonics may help in both recognition and recall, at least for reactive, i.e., nonpsychotic, schizophrenics (Traupmann, 1975). This has been attributed to the important roles played in the mnemonic abilities of schizophrenics by the organizing of materials to be remembered (Koh & Kayton, 1974; Traupmann, 1975), and the maintenance of such organization (Larsen & Fromholt, 1976).

Brain-Damaged Patients

Imagery mediators have been used with paired-associate tasks to help restore verbal memory in patients with cerebral vascular accidents (CVA) (Gasparrini & Satz, 1979); temporal lobectomy (Jones, 1974); "unequivocal neurological evidence of brain damage" (Lewinsohn, Danaher, & Kikel, 1977, p. 718); and left-hemisphere damage (Patten, 1972). Results with such mediators have not all been positive. Wilson (1982), for example, found that in learning a shopping list, her subject found a visual peg method ("one is a bun, two is a shoe") "extremely difficult and did worse than in free recall" (Wilson, 1982, p. 584); however, subsequent use of a first-letter technique was successful.

Crosson and Buenning (1984) used an interesting technique as part of an attempt to design "a memory remediation program which would meet the day-to-day needs of a closed-head injury patient" (p. 291), i.e., one that would generalize. They asked the patient to visualize the contents of a paragraph which was read to him. He was allowed, but not required, to use bizarre images, link images with one another, or use other suggested techniques; "in short, the patient was encouraged to experiment to find a technique which worked for him" (p. 295). This mnemonic strategy was more effective than a feedback and concentration strategy, and similar in effectiveness to a questioning strategy. Memory performance at a 9-month followup had dropped; the investigators thought this might have been because "the patient was not actively practicing memory strategies at this time" (p. 298).

Wilson (1982) found that the learning of names by a patient following a cerebral vascular accident was aided with a variant of the face–name technique which used interactive pictures to represent parts of the names. Poorer results with the basic technique (Lorayne & Lucas, 1974) have been reported, however, by Lewinsohn and his co-workers (Glasgow, Zeiss, Barrera, & Lewinsohn, 1977; Lewinsohn et al., 1977). Glasgow et al. (1977) thought that the technique as they employed it might have been relatively ineffective because although "the steps required in the successful linking of two concrete nouns in the paired-associate learning task have been thoroughly explicated in the literature, ... the steps needed in linking complex visual stimuli such as people's faces with their associated names are considerably more tentative" (p. 722). We hope that the model we are presenting in this chapter helps bridge this gap.

Vocational and Military Training

There has been little published research on the use of imagery-based mnemonic techniques in vocational or military training. Sprenger (1971) found a mnemonic technique effective in the learning of shorthand symbols. Griffith (1979), in a review of the use of mnemonics for the U.S. Army, found few studies specifically related to such use. A pictorial mnemonic was effective in teaching Morse code sending (but not receiving) skills to naval personnel (Ainsworth, 1979; Braby, Kincaid, & Aagard, 1978). Braby et al. (1978) developed specific images for each signal flag. For example, the flag for "B" is red and shaped like an angular letter B; subjects are instructed to imagine that it is a bullfighter's cape and that the crowd is yelling "Bravo!" for him. Griffith and Actkinson (1978) reported marginal success of a similar technique for learning the meaning of international road signs.

Chuang (1974) used an imagery-based method with moderate effectiveness to teach English translations for Chinese ideographs. For example, the character for "moon" looks something like a block "A" with two horizontal bars in the middle; the image might be that of a ladder to the moon (the example is from Griffith, 1979). Such techniques, as well as the basic keyword method (e.g., Atkinson & Raugh, 1975), should be effective in language learning for the military, but there seem to be no published studies specifically targeting this population.

The vocational domain is, as Swezey (1977–78) has pointed out, a fruitful educational domain for the application of mnemonics. In both industrial and military settings, the need not only to memorize lists, for which mnemonic techniques are demonstrably useful, but to learn operational models, is widespread. Both of these tasks lend themselves to imagery-based learning. With technological obsolescence leading to the need for retraining of large numbers of workers, it would seem that the paucity of studies in the area of mnemonic techniques is an important oversight.

At this point, we think it appropriate to point out a limitation or boundary condition for the use of mnemonics. In many real life settings, activities are so complicated, and each element is so important, that we are inclined to agree with Perkins (1985) that reliance on even very powerful, but not perfect, mnemonic schemes is inadvisable. For instance, few people would want airline flight personnel to rely on their memory as they go through their checkoff of all the appropriate switches, gauge readings, and other indicators of airworthiness and preparation for flying.

A Componential Analysis of Mnemonic Techniques

Sternberg's Componential Model

Sternberg's (1985) componential model allows us to consider mnemonic techniques in a more systematic way than appears to have been accomplished up to this point. The model is described only briefly here because it has been described in detail in many other sources (e.g., Sternberg, 1977, 1985). Sternberg (1985) defines a component as "an elementary information process that operates upon internal representations of objects or symbols," where "what is considered elementary enough to be labelled a component depends upon the desired level of theorizing" (p. 97). Any component has three parametric properties: probability of execution, duration, and difficulty (the probability that errors will be made during its execution). There are three kinds of components, based upon the processing functions they serve: metacomponents, performance components, and knowledge acquisition components.

Metacomponents are used in planning, monitoring, and decision making during task performance. Sternberg (1985) identifies seven metacomponents. In our discussion, we shall not consider metacomponents further. They are potentially of major importance to a full consideration of the factors, including transfer, that are involved in intellectual functioning (cf. Pressley, Borkowski, & Schneider, in press). In this section, however, it is the performance and knowledge acquisition components involved in processing with which we are concerned primarily, rather than the metacomponential strategies, which are about processing.

Performance components are used in the execution of a task. Although the number of performance components is very large and depends upon the specific task, they "tend to organize themselves into stages of task solution that seem to be fairly general across tasks" (Sternberg, 1985, p. 105): encoding, combination and comparison, and response.

Knowledge acquisition components are used in learning new information. There are three general kinds. Selective encoding components sift out relevant from irrelevant information. Selective combination components combine "selectively encoded information in such a way as to form an integrated, plausible definition" (Sternberg, 1985, p. 225). Selective comparison components relate new information to previously acquired information.

Applying the Componential Model to Mnemonic Techniques

The discussion accompanying Table 15.1 gave a general idea of how a componential analysis of mnemonic techniques might be undertaken. At the present stage of development of the componential model, the purpose of such an analysis is heuristic: it is to develop a sense for what kinds of generalities there may be between mnemonic techniques viewed as cognitive tasks, and other kinds of cognitive tasks which, on the surface, appear not to be at all similar. In this light, it is interesting to see that Sternberg's knowledge-acquisition and performance components map fairly well onto the component processes of our analysis of the three mnemonic techniques. These correspondences are shown in Table 15.2.

"Access" selectively compares words from the subject's lexicon with sound stimuli; "generate" selectively encodes a word or other stimulus in imaginal form; "combine" selectively combines images to form interactive ones; "decompose" is a combination component whose function is to "invert" (Bellezza, 1981) the interactive image; and "respond" is a response component.

The "cue" component compares an input cue with corresponding elements of an image. This component is an essential one in Bellezza's (1981) definition of mnemonic techniques as cognitive cuing structures; in the context of analogical problem solving, Gick (1985) has suggested that emphasis on optimal retrieval cues may be more educationally relevant than emphasis on optimal encoding conditions, because "the relevance of information is not always known at the time of initial learning" (p. 466). In order for such cues to be effective, they must relate to what the learner knows, as has been emphasized by Tulving's encoding specificity principle (Tulving & Thompson, 1973; Turnure & Gudeman, 1984), as well as by the more general notion of transfer-appropriate processing (Morris, Bransford, & Franks, 1977). A cognitive cuing structure is presumably such a knowledge base.

TABLE 15.2. Correspondence of Sternberg's components to steps in the use of mnemonic techniques.

Storage-phase steps	Knowledge-acquisition components
1 Discriminate stimulus parts or features	Selective encoding
2 Access words phonologically similar to stimuli	Selective comparison
3 Generate image to word	Selective encoding
4 Generate image to stimulus[a]	Selective encoding
5 Combine images interactively	Selective combination

Retrieval-phase steps	Performance components
6 Cue interactive image	Comparison
7 Decompose interactive image	Combination
8 Respond	Response

[a] In the method of loci, retrieval, a performance component, also occurs at this step. See Table 15.1.

"Discriminate" may be interpreted as either a knowledge-acquisition component or a performance component. As a knowledge-acquisition component it selectively encodes a stimulus word into concrete or imageable parts to which other concrete words can be associated; the selectivity consists in encoding only those aspects of the word that are, indeed, capable of being associated with other concrete words. When "discriminate" can be performed automatically (Fitts & Posner, 1967; LaBerge & Samuels, 1974), it is a performance component. Prior to such automatization the same process is a knowledge-acquisition component, because it is operating, in Fitts and Posner's (1967) terms, at the cognitive or associative stage rather than at the autonomous stage. This distinction is important when considering, for example, such studies as that by Gelzheiser et al. (1983) in which it is recommended that lower-order components be automatized in order to maximize otherwise limited attentional resources. It is also relevant to research with LD and elderly populations, where attentional deficits, if indeed they are a concern, may be translated for intervention or research purposes into problems of the ability to discriminate (Samuels & Miller, 1985; Turnure, Samuels, & Carlson, 1985).

Sternberg (1985) has collected much evidence for the parametric properties of his components—duration, difficulty, and probability of execution—in the context of problem-solving research. To apply the parameters of Sternberg's model to the components of mnemonic techniques that we have identified would be to suggest possible quantifiable differences among them as a function of their differential employment in various tasks or with various populations. At the present stage of development of the model, this is premature and we do not attempt it. However, a few examples may indicate the potential for such an application: that LD subjects have more trouble than do non-LD subjects in accessing semantic codes for digits (Torgesen & Houck, 1980) may be related to the duration of an "access" component (cf. Hunt, Lunneborg, & Lewis, 1975). The difficulty value of a "combine" component may be higher for the elderly because of the greater probability of their failing to reorganize conceptual structure

(Hess, 1982; Waddell & Rogoff, 1981). For a final example, the probability that the "generate" component will be executed at all may reflect the tendency of LD, MR, and elderly subjects not to generate images without outside prompting (Pressley, 1982; Rohwer, 1973; Taylor & Turnure, 1979).

Transfer and Generalization of Mnemonic Techniques

The Social and Educational Context of Transfer and Generalization

As we noted in the introduction to this review, there have been persistent complaints and reservations regarding the transfer and generalization of cognitive techniques. The mental retardation literature, for instance, has recently been emphasizing that mentally retarded children cannot generalize when the transfer task is markedly different in form from the original training task (e.g., Burger, Blackman, Clark, & Reis, 1982). This failure is generally attributed to some deficit in the retarded individual. However, this interpretation seems unjustified at present, because the literature contains few, if any, conclusive demonstrations of nonretarded preadolescent children engaging in "spontaneous" (i.e., autonomous or uncued) transfer in markedly different (i.e., "far generalization") tasks.

The fact is that until recently there has been little clear and reliable evidence of transfer in school-related tasks by any learners (Bender & Turnure, 1980). Scriven (1976) asserts that "so-called transfer of learning or generalization always turns out to be less than educators had previously supposed" (pp. xiv–xv). Similarly, Murray (1979) refers to "a well known instructional phenomenon in which students' mastery of a principle in one area of the subject fails to transfer to other areas, even those strikingly similar to the mastered area" (p. 38). Numerous studies with bright adults report failure to transfer (Gick & Holyoak, 1983; Hayes, 1985). Therefore, the large number of recent demonstrations of a variety of basic transfer (i.e., "maintenance" and "near generalization") effects in the mental retardation literature could properly be considered a sign of progress (Borkowski & Cavanaugh, 1979; Taylor & Turnure, 1979). Yet there seems to be at best resignation, and at worst pessimism, regarding the benefits of cognitive training (Burger et al., 1982; Campione & Brown, 1977).

The cultural Zeitgeist of the autonomous individual implies that transfer must involve immediate independent functioning in a different situation, or on a radically different task; if there is prompting or cuing of various kinds, the individual is not "really" transferring. On the other hand, a perspective that views individuals as moving along a continuum from other-regulated to self-regulated behavior (e.g., Vygotsky, 1978) produces a model of transfer in which the person is functioning as a transferer even when given prompts through communciation with a knowledgeable social agent, analogous to the "fading" of stimulus support in operant conditioning (Terrace, 1966), and to positive interpretation of a savings score in memory research. This new and, we think, more realistic framework is similar to what Turnure and Zigler (1964) said about the general process of becoming an independent learner (i.e., one who is "inner directed" in their terms):

The shift from outer- to inner-directedness in normal development is a product of both the increasing cognitive ability of the child and the withdrawal of external cues which had previously made the outer-directed style an effective one. (p. 435)

An example of the advantage, and possible developmental necessity, of prolonged external guidance for younger children is illustrated by Pressley and Dennis-Rounds (1980). They trained nonhandicapped children in a keyword strategy to help in associating names of cities with names of their economic products. The children were later given a transfer test consisting of pairs of Latin/English vocabulary words. The use of transfer prompts was varied in three experimental conditions; there was also a control group. One experimental group was given no prompts or instructions to transfer. Another group was given general instructions to learn the word pairs in "the same way" they had learned the city/product pairs. The third group was given the same specific instruction in the keyword method that they had been given while learning the city/product pairs, but adapted to the learning of the Latin/English pairs. Ten to 11-year-old children only generalized when given general or specific instructions; children in the no-instruction condition did no better than the control group on the transfer task. Only the 16- to 17-year-old subjects transferred autonomously in the no-instruction transfer condition.

However, note that the 10- to 11-year-old children were able to use the general (and minimal) instructions to enhance performance on the transfer task, a distinct saving in time and effort. Even more significantly, it is possible that the general guidance or reminder procedure in that study is an exemplar of the general mechanism of the social determination of transfer and generalization. It appears to us that social agents first train and then cue and guide the use of knowledge and skills, including cognitive ones, until the learner is independently or intellectually competent. That is, the process of independence training over time may apply to cognitive skills just as it does to instrumental ones.

Transfer of Skills Learned Through the Practice of Mnemonic Techniques

Much of the work that we have reviewed consists of demonstrations that mnemonic techniques work. As Shepherd and Gelzheiser (in press) point out, however, the important question is not whether they work, but what general value they have for the broader world of education, whether in classroom, clinic, or workplace. Near generalization, or intradomain transfer, certainly occurs: learning the keyword method for one list of vocabulary words, or the method of loci for one list of objects, facilitates the learning of a second list; learning the face/name technique for one person's name facilitates the learning of another. However, most educators hope for transfer of training that is less direct and specific; the desired outcome is the more general transfer known as far generalization or interdomain transfer.

We have reported the dissatisfaction of researchers with most of the transfer that has been obtained through cognitive training. This may have been because what is transferred has not been specified adequately. One way of investigating this aspect of the transfer problem is by way of the paradigm developed by Gick and Holyoak in their extensive studies of transfer in the domain of analogical problem solving (Gick, 1985; Gick & Holyoak, 1980, 1983; Holyoak, 1985). In these studies, subjects were given a "source" problem to solve, followed by a structurally similar "target" problem. Subjects who solved the source problem were most likely also to solve the target problem, i.e., to transfer relevant aspects of the solution of the source problem to the target problem, if (a) they had been given an explicit hint concerning the relevance of the source problem to the target problem, or (b) they had been instructed to compare the two problems in writing, even without a hint as to the applicability of the source to the target. Gick and Holyoak (1983) reasoned that subjects in this second group had abstracted a schema for solving this type of problem in general as a result of making the explicit comparison. In an extension of this study, Gick (1985) found that what she called spontaneous transfer, by which she apparently meant unguided transfer, was aided by including in the target problem a diagram (which we consider a cue; see Turnure, 1985) that had been presented previously as part of the source problem.

Three generalizations can be drawn from these studies: In order for a skill to transfer, either (1) the application must be explicitly indicated, (2) guided discovery of a general problem schema covering both source and target must occur, or (3) at the least, close similarity must exist between salient attributes and relations of source and target.

Application of the Componential Model to Two Target Tasks

In Table 15.3 we have outlined a model for transfer of the skills learned through practice with mnemonic techniques (the source tasks) to two interdomain transfer (i.e., target) tasks. These target tasks have been used by different sets of researchers in studies whose subjects were members of two of the populations we have discussed: elderly subjects and vocational students. Table 15.3 is the result of a sort of rational task analysis. In the first column is a list of the skills or component processes that we have identified as comprising mnemonic techniques (see Table 15.1). The next two columns list skills or component processes that, we presume, are required on the target tasks. We also presume that these components are similar to those in the first column, such similarity being the basis for transfer from the source tasks to the target tasks.

Learning an Urban Route: A Task for the Elderly

This example is based on the study by Evans et al. (1984). In that study, elderly subjects were found to have less accurate verbal recall and location memory than did younger subjects. When they attempted to learn a route through a city, they

TABLE 15.3. Transfer of mnemonic components to two learning tasks.

| | Task | |
Component	Elderly subjects: urban routes	Vocational students: electronic circuits
Storage phase		
Discriminate parts or features of stimuli	Discriminate salient attributes of landmarks	Discriminate symbols
Access words similar to stimuli	Access names of attributes and landmarks	Access meaning of symbols
Generate images to words or stimuli	Generate images of landmarks and neighboring areas	Generate image to meaning of symbols
Combine images interactively	Combine images into a route	Combine images into a functional mental model
Retrieval phase		
Cue interactive image	Cue route with landmarks or attributes	Cue chunks or model
Decompose interactive image	Decompose route into setting-chunks	Decompose model into chunks

relied more upon the most salient attributes of landmarks along the route. These attributes were presumably those with which the elderly subjects were most familiar: high public use, high symbolic significance, naturalness of surroundings, direct access to streets, and unique architectural style.

Because this task consists in learning a route, a "link" variant of the method of loci is an appropriate mnemonic model. The "pathway" variant, which has been referred to in previous sections, requires prior memorization of a "route," and it is precisely this skill that the elderly subjects presumably lack. In the link variant, images representing objects to be remembered are linked directly to one another by interactive images; the "route" underlies the progression from link to link implicitly rather than explicitly. Finding one's way about probably involves use of a "cognitive map," represented in major part by images. Therefore, it may be helpful for subjects to practice generating images of landmarks while accessing names of these imaged objects. If the elderly subjects have learned a mnemonic technique, with its "access" component, their ability to learn names for landmarks should be enhanced.

Learning Electronic Circuitry: A Task for Vocational Students

This task is based on a study by Egan and Schwartz (1979) that replicated the investigations by de Groot (1965) and others (e.g., Chase & Simon, 1973) of expert and novice chess players. Egan and Schwartz observed differences between expert and novice electronics technicians in their ability to reconstruct drawings of circuit diagrams. They found that expert technicians could reconstruct meaningful configurations of electronic symbols, i.e., real circuit diagrams, better than novices; but experts were no better than novices in reconstructing configurations of symbols that had been arranged randomly during the learning task.

The primary difference between this task and the urban routes task is in its emphasis on combining images into mental models of the circuits. Such mental models (Gentner & Stevens, 1983; Holyoak, 1985; Johnson-Laird, 1983) are representations that abstract relational, and especially functional, information from the world and use it as a schema (Gick & Holyoak, 1983; Rumelhart, 1980) to interpret subsequent experience (e.g., Gentner & Gentner, 1983). In training technicians in such domains as electronics, the development of mental models by trainees can be important. The cognitive skill necessary to generate such mental models, i.e., interactive images of electronic functions, may be similar to the "combine" component, which, if learned adequately, quickly, and clearly, forms an interactive image of Ann leading a bright yellow lamb in the keyword technique, of a dog digging at a culvert to change it into a moat in the method of loci, or of a person calling cups of tea to come out of Mr. Colletti's lips in the face–name technique.

In concluding this discussion of transfer we would like to emphasize once again the importance of two crucial elements of any attempt to attain such transfer: (a) adequate time is needed in order for subjects to automatize the processes involved in the mnemonic techniques themselves (Gelzheiser et al., 1983); (b) in order for transfer to occur, the specific applications of the components of the mnemonic techniques must often be explicitly indicated (Gick & Holyoak, 1983).

Conclusions

Ideally, generalization of learning would appear to require new problem recognition, selection of appropriate "strategic" response, monitoring of both the cognitive process and its continuing effectiveness, and other "executive function" or "metacognitive" activity. In the usual course of everyday activities, in or out of school, it is our observation that social agents point out task similarities, suggest ways of thinking about or working on a task, monitor missteps, cue shifts and coordinate cognitive strategies and instrumental skills even for adults in many situations. Holyoak (1985) has recently pointed out how very specific and extensive training, prompting and cuing must be to get even bright college students to generalize knowledge and to see interrelationships in task domains. Realistically, cognitive development is a complex and prolonged process that is incomplete even in college students (Brown, Campione, & Day, 1981), and even throughout adulthood, when new learning is required.

In short, mnemonic techniques must be taught, retaught, demonstrated, and applied in many, many situations where they are expected to be utilized, simply because that is the only way most people master the techniques. Furthermore, most mnemonic systems require some adaptations and modifications when used in various circumstances; for example, rather than just being able to use acronyms, experts learn to name things in such a way that acronyms can be created from the names (Bransford & Stein, 1984). Therefore, it is apparent that simply learning the basic rule or technique, usually by practicing standard examples, is likely to limit the technique initially or stultify it altogether. This is analogous to the problems recently discovered with students learning rules and procedures for solving algebra problems (e.g., Petkovich, 1986; Sweller & Cooper, 1985). Without conclusive evidence regarding realistic expectations for cognitive transfer and for the role of social or other cuing requirements of transfer, critics of mnemonic training as rigid or trivial will continue to find compelling examples for their arguments, and the general efficacy of cognitive training will continue to be relatively unappreciated, and practical applications to be underutilized.

References

Ainsworth, J. S. (1979). *Symbol learning in Navy technical training: An evaluation of strategies and mnemonics* (TAEG Report No. 661). Orlando, FL: U.S. Navy Training Analysis and Evaluation Group.

Arnold, P. (1978). Mental rotation by deaf and hearing children. *Perceptual and Motor Skills, 47,* 977–978.

Atkinson, R. C. (1975). Mnemotechnics in second language learning. *American Psychologist, 30,* 821–828.

Atkinson, R. C., & Raugh, M. R. (1975). An application of the mnemonic keyword method to the acquisition of a Russian vocabulary. *Journal of Experimental Psychology: Human Learning & Memory, 104,* 126–133.

Bellezza, F. S. (1981). Mnemonic devices: Classification, characteristics, and criteria. *Review of Educational Research, 51,* 247–275.

Bender, N., & Turnure, J. E. (1980). *A critique of transfer of training research.* Paper presented at the 88th annual convention of the American Psychological Association, September 1–5, Montreal, Canada.

Borkowski, J. G., & Cavanaugh, J. (1979). Maintenance and generalization of skills and strategies by the retarded. In N. Ellis (Ed.), *Handbook of mental deficiency: Psychological theory and research* (2nd ed.) (pp. 569–617). Hillsdale, NJ: Erlbaum Associates.

Braby, R., Kincaid, J. P., & Aagard, F. A. (1978). *Use of mnemonics in training materials: A guide for technical writers* (TAEG Report No. 60). Orlando, FL: U.S. Navy Training Analysis and Evaluation Group (NTIS No. ADA064218).

Bransford, J. D., & Stein, B. S. (1984). *The ideal problem solver.* San Francisco: W. H. Freeman.

Brigham, S., & Pressley, M. (in preparation). Imagery based mnemonic strategies with the elderly.

Brown, A. L., Campione, J. C., & Day, J. D. (1981). Learning to learn: On training students to learn from texts. *Educational Researcher, 10,* 14–21.

Bugelski, B. R. (1970). Words and things and images. *American Psychologist, 25,* 1002–1012.

Burger, A. L., Blackman, L. S., Clark, H. T., & Reis, E. (1982). Effects of hypothesis testing and variable formal training on generalization of a verbal abstraction strategy by EMR learners. *American Journal of Mental Deficiency, 86,* 405–413.

Camp-Cameron, J., Markley, R. P., & Kramer, J. J. (1983). Spontaneous use of mnemonics by elderly individuals. *Educational Gerontology*, *90*, 57–71.

Campione, J. C., & Brown A. L. (1977). Memory and metamemory development in educable retarded children. In R. V. Kail, Jr., & J. W. Hagen (Eds.), *Perspectives on the development of memory and cognition*. Hillsdale, NJ: Erlbaum Associates.

Carpenter, P. A., & Eisenberg, P. (1978). Mental rotation and the frame of reference in blind and sighted individuals. *Perception and Psychophysics*, *23*, 117–124.

Carrier, C., Karbo, K., Kindem, H., Legisa, G., & Newstrom, L. (1983). Use of self-generated and supplied visuals as mnemonics in gifted children's learning. *Perceptual and Motor Skills*, *57*, 235–240.

Cermak, L. S. (1983). Information processing deficits in children with learning disabilities. *Journal of Learning Disabilities*, *16*, 599–605.

Chase, W. G., & Simon, H. A. (1973). Perception in chess. *Cognitive Psychology*, *14*, 55–81.

Chipman, S. F., & Segal, J. W. (1985). Higher cognitive goals for education: An introduction. In S. F. Chipman, J. W. Segal, & R. Glaser (Eds.), *Thinking and learning skills, Vol. 2: Research and open questions* (pp. 1–18). Hillsdale, NJ: Erlbaum Associates.

Chuang, C. S. (1974). *The effect of elaboration and response made upon acquisition of Chinese ideographs*. Unpublished master's thesis, Brigham Young University, Provo, UT.

Cornoldi, C., & Sanavio, E. (1980). Imagery value and recall in deaf children. *Italian Journal of Psychology*, *7*, 33–39.

Craig, E. M. (1973). Role of mental imagery in free recall of deaf, blind, and normal subjects. *Journal of Experimental Psychology*, *970*, 249–253.

Crosson, B., & Buenning, W. (1984). An individualized memory training program after closed-head injury: A single-case study. *Journal of Clinical Neuropsychology*, *6*, 287–301.

Danner, F. W., & Taylor, A. M. (1973). Integrated pictures and relational imagery training in children's learning. *Journal of Experimental Child Psychology*, *16*, 47–54.

de Groot, A. D. (1965). *Thought and choice in chess*. The Hague: Mouton.

Dodds, A. G. (1983). Mental rotation and visual imagery. *Journal of Visual Impairment and Blindness*, *77*, 16–18.

Dunn, L. M. (Ed.). (1973). *Exceptional children in the schools: Special education in transition* (2nd ed.). New York: Holt, Rinehart & Winston.

Egan, D. E., & Schwartz, B. J. (1979). Chunking in recall of symbolic drawings. *Memory and Cognition*, *7*, 149–158.

Elbert, J. C. (1984). Short-term memory encoding and memory search in the word recognition of learning-disabled children. *Journal of Learning Disabilities*, *17*, 342–345.

Evans, G. W., Brennan, P. L., Skorpanich, M. A., & Held, D. (1984). Cognitive mapping and elderly adults: Verbal and location memory for urban landmarks. *Journal of Gerontology*, *39*, 452–457.

Fitts, P. M., & Posner, M. I. (1967). *Human performance*. Belmont, CA: Brooks Cole.

Fleischmann, U. M. (1982). Gedaechtnistraining im hoheren Lebensalter: Ansatzpunkte und Moeglichkeiten [Memory training in older age: The chance of improvements]. *Zeitschrift für Gerontologie*, *15*, 53–62.

Gage, N. L., & Berliner, D. C. (1984). *Educational Psychology* (3rd ed.). Boston: Houghton Mifflin.

Gasparrini, B., & Satz, P. (1979). A treatment for memory problems in left-hemisphere CVA patients. *Journal of Clinical Neuropsychology, 1*, 137–150.

Gelzheiser, L. M., Solar, R. A., Shepherd, M. J., & Wozniak, R. H. (1983). Teaching learning disabled children to memorize: A rationale for plans and practice. *Journal of Learning Disabilities, 16*, 421–425.

Gentner, D., & Gentner, D. R. (1983). Flowing waters or teeming crowds: Mental models of electricity. In D. Gentner & A. L. Stevens (Eds.), *Mental models* (pp. 99–130). Hillsdale, NJ: Erlbaum Associates.

Gentner, D., & Stevens, A. L., (Eds.) (1983). *Mental models*. Hillsdale, NJ: Erlbaum Associates.

Gick, M. L. (1985). The effect of a diagram retrieval cue on spontaneous analogical transfer. *Canadian Journal of Psychology, 39*, 460–466.

Gick, M. L., & Holyoak, K. J. (1980). Analogical problem solving. *Cognitive Psychology, 12*, 306–355.

Gick, M. L., & Holyoak, K. J. (1983). Schema induction and analogical transfer. *Cognitive Psychology, 15*, 1–38.

Glasgow, R. E., Zeiss, R. A., Barrera, M., & Lewinsohn, P. M. (1977). Case studies on remediating memory deficits in brain-damaged individuals. *Journal of Clinical Psychology, 33*, 1049–1054.

Glidden, L. M., & Mar, H. H. (1978). Availability and accessibility of information in the semantic memory of retarded and nonretarded adolescents. *Journal of Experimental Child Psychology, 25*, 33–40.

Griffith, D. (1979). *A review of the literature on memory enhancement: The potential and relevance of mnemotechnics for military training.* (Tech. Rep. No. 436). Alexandria, VA: U.S. Army Research Institute for the Behavioral and Social Sciences.

Griffith, D., & Actkinson, T. R. (1978). *Mnemonic enhancement and general technical ability.* (Tech. Rep. No. 336). Alexandria, VA: U.S. Army Research Institute for the Behavioral and Social Sciences (NTIS No. AD-A061314).

Hall, A. (1981). A developmental study of cognitive equivalence in the congenitally blind. *Journal of Mental Imagery, 5*, 61–73.

Hayes, J. R. (1981). *The complete problem solver.* Philadelphia: The Franklin Institute Press.

Hayes, J. R. (1985). Three problems in teaching general skills. In S. F. Chipman, J. W. Segal, & R. Glaser (Eds.), *Thinking and learning skills, Vol. 2: Research and open questions* (pp. 391–406). Hillsdale, NJ: Erlbaum Associates.

Heinen, J. R., Cobb, L., & Pollard, J. W. (1976). Word imagery modalities and learning in the deaf and hearing. *Journal of Psychology, 93*, 191–195.

Heintz, P., & Blackman, L. S. (1977). Psychoeducational considerations with the mentally retarded child. In I. Bialer & M. Sternlicht (Eds.), *The psychology of mental retardation: Issues and approaches.* New York: Psychological Dimensions.

Herman, J. F., Chatman, S. P., & Roth, S. F. (1983). Cognitive mapping in blind people: Acquisition of spatial relationships in a large-scale environment. *Journal of Visual Impairment and Blindness, 77*, 161–166.

Hess, T. M. (1982). Visual abstraction processes in young and old adults. *Developmental Psychology, 18*, 473–484.

Hess, T. M., & Radtke, R. C. (1981). Processing and memory factors in children's reading comprehension skill. *Child Development, 52*, 479–488.

Higbee, K. L. (1979). Recent research on visual mnemonics: Historical roots and educational fruits. *Review of Educational Research, 49*, 611–629.

Hollyfield, R. L. (1982). Individual differences in spatial problem solving by the blind. *EDRA: Environmental Design Research Association, 13*, 370–380.

Holyoak, K. J. (1985). The pragmatics of analogical transfer. In G. H. Bower (Ed.), *The psychology of learning and motivation* (Vol. 19, pp. 59–88). Orlando, FL: Academic Press.

Horgan, J. S. (1983). Mnemonic strategy instruction in coding, processing, and recall of movement-strategy cues by mentally retarded children. *Perceptual and Motor Skills, 57*, 547–557.

Hunt, E. B., Lunneborg, C., & Lewis, J. (1975). What does it mean to be high verbal? *Cognitive Psychology, 7*, 194–227.

Johnson-Laird, P. N. (1983). *Mental models: Towards a cognitive science of language, inference, and consciousness.* Cambridge, MA: Harvard University Press.

Jones, M. (1974). Imagery as a mnemonic aid after left temporal lobectomy: Contrast between material specific and general memory disorders. *Neuropsychologia, 12*, 21–30.

Jonides, J., Kahn, R., & Rozin, P. (1975). Imagery instructions improve memory in blind subjects. *Bulletin of the Psychonomic Society, 5*, 424–426.

Kail, R. V., Jr., & Siegel, A. W. (1977). The development of mnemonic encoding in children: From perception to abstraction. In R. V. Kail, Jr., & J. W. Hagen (Eds.), *Perspectives on the development of memory and cognition* (pp. 61–88). Hillsdale, NJ: Erlbaum Associates.

Kendall, P. C., & Hollon, S. D. (1979). *Cognitive-behavioral interventions: Theory, research, and procedures.* New York: Academic Press.

Kerr, N. H. (1983). The role of vision in 'visual imagery' experiments: Evidence from the congenitally blind. *Journal of Experimental Psychology, General, 112*, 265–277.

Koh, S. D., & Kayton, L. (1974). Memorization of 'unrelated' word strings by young nonpsychotic schizophrenics. *Journal of Abnormal Psychology, 83*, 14–22.

Kosslyn, S. M. (1980). *Image and mind.* Cambridge, MA: Harvard University Press.

Kramer, J. J., Nagle, R. J., & Engle, R. W. (1980). Recent advances in mnemonic strategy training with mentally retarded persons: Implications for educational practice. *Journal of Mental Deficiency, 85*, 306–314.

LaBerge, D., & Samuels, S. J. (1974). Toward a theory of automatic information processing in reading. *Cognitive Psychology, 6*, 293–323.

Landau, G., Gleitman, H., & Spelke, E. (1981). Spatial knowledge and geometric representation in a child blind from birth. *Science, 213*, 1275–1278.

Lane, J. F. (1980). Improving athletic performance through visuomotor behavior rehearsal. In R. M. Suinn (Ed.), *Psychology in sports: Methods and applications.* Minneapolis: Burgess.

Lane, J. F. (1981). *The use of imagery for the diagnosis and correction of athletic performance errors.* Paper presented at the third annual meeting of the American Association for the Study of Mental Imagery, June 19–21, Yale University.

Larsen, S. F., & Fromholt, P. (1976). Mnemonic organization and free recall in schizophrenia. *Journal of Abnormal Psychology, 85*, 61–65.

Lea, G. (1975). Chronometric analysis of the method of loci. *Journal of Experimental Psychology: Human Perception and Performance, 104*, 95–104.

Lebrato, M. T., & Ellis, N. R. (1974). Imagery mediation in paired-associate learning by retarded and nonretarded subjects. *American Journal of Mental Deficiency, 78*, 704–713.

Lewinsohn, P. M., Danaher, B. G., & Kikel, S. (1977). Visual imagery as a mnemonic aid for brain-damaged persons. *Journal of Consulting and Clinical Psychology, 45*, 717–723.

Lininger, R. S. (1984). *The use of mime to facilitate learning with mentally retarded students*. Doctoral dissertation, Department of Educational Psychology, University of Minnesota, Minneapolis, MN.

Lorayne, H. (1974). *How to develop a super-power memory.* New York: New American Library.

Lorayne, H., & Lucas, J. (1974). *The memory book.* New York: Ballantine Books.

Luria, A. R. (1968). *The mind of a mnemonist* (L. Solotaroff, Transl.). New York: Basic Books.

MacMillan, D. L., & Meyers, C. E. (1984). Molecular research and molar learning. In P. H. Brooks, R. Sperber, & C. McCauley (Eds.), *Learning and cognition in the mentally retarded* (pp. 433–474). Hillsdale, NJ: Erlbaum Associates.

Marmor, G. S., & Zaback, L. A. (1976). Mental rotation by the blind: Does mental rotation depend upon visual imagery? *Journal of Experimental Psychology: Human Perception & Performance, 2*, 515–521.

Mason, S. E., & Smith, A. D. (1977). Imagery in the aged. *Experimental Aging Research, 3*, 17–32.

Mastropieri, M. A., Scruggs, T. E., & Levin, J. R. (1985). Maximizing what exceptional students can learn: A review of research on the keyword method and related mnemonic techniques. *RASE: Remedial and Special Education, 6*, 39–45.

McCarty, D. L. (1980). Investigation of a visual imagery mnemonic divide for acquiring face-name associations. *Journal of Experimental Psychology: Human Learning and Memory, 6*, 145–155.

Meichenbaum, D. (1985). Teaching thinking: A cognitive-behavioral perspective. In S. F. Chipman, J. W. Segal, & R. Glaser (Eds.), *Thinking and learning skills, Vol. 2: Research and open questions* (pp. 407–426). Hillsdale, NJ: Erlbaum Associates.

Morris, C. D., Bransford, J. D., & Franks, J. J. (1977). Levels of processing versus transfer appropriate processing. *Journal of Verbal Learning and Verbal Behavior, 16*, 519–533.

Murray, F. B. (1979). The generation of educational practice from development theory. *Educational Researcher, 14*, 30–43.

Norman, D. (1976). *Memory and attention* (2nd ed.). New York: Wiley.

Paivio, A. (1979). *Imagery and verbal processes.* Hillsdale, NJ: Erlbaum Associates.

Paivio, A., & Okavita, H. W. (1971). Word imagery modalities and associative learning in blind and sighted subjects. *Journal of Verbal Learning & Verbal Behavior, 10*, 506–510.

Patten, B. M. (1972). The ancient art of memory: Usefulness in treatment. *Archives of Neurology, 26*, 25–31.

Perkins, D. N. (1985). General cognitive skills: Why not? In S. F. Chipman, J. W. Segal, & R. Glaser (Eds.), *Thinking and learning skills* (Vol. 2, pp. 339–364). Hillsdale, NJ: Erlbaum Associates.

Petkovich, M. D. (1986). *Teaching algebra with worked examples: The effects of accompanying text and range of examples on the acquisition and retention of a problem solving skill*. Doctoral dissertation, Department of Curriculum and Instruction, University of Minnesota, Minneapolis, MN.

Pressley, M. (1982). Elaboration and memory development. *Child Development, 53*, 296–309.

Pressley, M., & Dennis-Rounds, J. (1980). Transfer of a mnemonic keyword strategy at two age levels. *Journal of Educational Psychology, 72*, 575–582.

Pressley, M., Borkowski, J. G., & Schneider, W. (in press). Cognitive strategies: Good strategy users coordinate metacognition and knowledge. In R. Vasta & G. Whitehurst (Eds.), *Annals of Child Development* (Vol. 4). New York: JAI Press.

Rabinowitz, J. C., Craik, F. I., & Ackerman, B. P. (1982). A processing resource account of age differences in recall. *Canadian Journal of Psychology, 36*, 325–344.

Reese, H. W., & Parkington, J. J. (1973). Intralist interference and imagery in deaf and hearing children. *Journal of Experimental Child Psychology, 16*, 165–183.

Reid, G. (1980). The effects of memory strategy instruction in the short-term memory of the mentally retarded. *Journal of Motor Behavior, 12*, 221–227.

Robertson-Tchabo, E. A., Hausman, C. P., & Arenberg, D. (1976). A classical mnemonic for older learners: A trip that works. *Educational Gerontology, 1*, 215–226.

Rohwer, W. D., Jr. (1973). Elaboration and learning in childhood and adolescence. In H. W. Reese (Ed.), *Advances in child development and behavior* (Vol. 8, pp. 1–57). New York: Academic Press.

Ross, D. M., & Ross, S. A. (1978). Facilitative effect of mnemonic strategies on multiple-associative learning in EMR children. *American Journal of Mental Deficiency, 82*, 453–459.

Ross, J., & Lawrence, K. A. (1968). Some observations on memory artifice. *Psychonomic Science, 13*, 159–160.

Rowe, E. J., & Schnore, M. M. (1971). Item concreteness and reported strategies in paired-associate learning as a function of age. *Journal of Gerontology, 26*, 470–475.

Rumelhart, D. (1980). Schemata, the building blocks of cognition. In R. J. Spiro, B. C. Bruce, & W. F. Brewer (Eds.), *Theoretical issues in reading comprehension* (pp. 33–58). Hillsdale, NJ: Erlbaum Associates.

Samuels, S. J., & Miller, N. L. (1985). Failure to find attention differences between learning disabled and normal children on classroom and laboratory tasks. *Exceptional Children, 51*, 358–375.

Sarason, S. B. (1983). *Schooling in America*. New York: The Free Press.

Sasaki, M. (1981). The function of visual imagery/map and effect of input modality in spatial transformation task by blind and sighted adults. *Japanese Journal of Psychology, 52*, 281–288.

Scribner, S., & Cole, M. (1973). Cognitive consequences of formal and informal education. *Science, 182*, 553–559.

Scriven, M. (1976). *Reasoning*. New York: McGraw-Hill.

Scruggs, T. E., & Mastropieri, M. A. (1984). How gifted students learn: Implications from recent research. *Roeper Review, 6*, 183–185.

Sharp, D., Cole, M., & Lave, C. (1979). Education and cognitive development: The evidence from experimental research. *Monographs of the Society for Research in Child Development, 44* (1–2, Serial No. 178).

Shepherd, M. J., & Gelzheiser, L. M. (in press). *Strategies and mnemonics go to school.* In H. L. Swanson (Ed.), *Memory and learning disabilities*. Greenwich, CT: JAI Press.

Smith, R. M., Forsberg, S.J., Herb, S. L., & Neisworth, J. T. (1978). Instructional intervention. In J. T. Neisworth & R. M. Smith (Eds.), *Retardation: Issues, assessment, and intervention*. New York: McGraw-Hill.

Sprenger, W. D. (1971). The effects of block size and mnemonic aids upon paired-associate learning of shorthand symbols. *Dissertation Abstracts International, 31*(9-A), 4634–4635.

Sternberg, R. J. (1977). *Intelligence, information processing, and analogical reasoning*. Hillsdale, NJ: Erlbaum Associates.

Sternberg, R. J. (1985). *Beyond IQ: A triarchic theory of human intelligence*. Cambridge: Cambridge University Press.

Sweller, J., & Cooper, G. A. (1985). The use of worked examples as a substitute for problem solving in learning algebra. *Cognition and Instruction, 2*, 59–89.

Swezey, R. W. (1977-78). Future directions in simulation and training. *Journal of Educational Technology Systems*, *6*, 285–292.

Tavon, E. (1984). Tips to trigger memory. *Geriatric Nursing*, *5*, 26–27.

Taylor, A. M., & Turnure, J. E. (1979). Imagery and verbal elaboration with retarded children: Effects on learning and memory. In N. R. Ellis (Ed.), *Handbook of mental deficiency*. Hillsdale, NJ: Erlbaum Associates.

Taylor, A. M., Thurlow, M. L., & Turnure, J. E. (1977). Vocabulary development of educable retarded children. *Exceptional Children*, *43*, 444–450.

Terrace, H. S. (1966). Stimulus control. In W. K. Honig (Ed.), *Operant behavior: Areas of research and application*. New York: Appleton-Century-Crofts.

Thurlow, M. L., & Turnure, J. E. (1977). Children's knowledge of time and money: Effective instruction for the mentally retarded. *Education and Training of the Mentally Retarded*, *12*, 203–212.

Torgesen, J. K. (1981). The relationship between memory and attention in learning disabilities. *Exceptional Education Quarterly*, *2*, 51–59.

Torgesen, J. K., & Houck, D. G. (1980). Processing deficiencies of learning-disabled children who perform poorly on the digit span test. *Journal of Educational Psychology*, *72*, 141–160.

Traupmann, K. L. (1975). Effects of categorization and imagery on recognition and recall by process and reactive schizophrenics. *Journal of Abnormal Psychology*, *84*, 307–314.

Treat, N. J., & Reese, H. W. (1976). Age, pacing, and imagery in paired-associate learning. *Developmental Psychology*, *12*, 119–124.

Treat, N. J., Poon, L. W., Fozard, J. L., & Popkin, S. J. (1978). Toward applying cognitive skill training to memory problems. *Experimental Aging Research*, *4*, 305–319.

Tulving, E., & Thompson, D. M. (1973). Encoding specificity and retrieval processes in episodic memory. *Psychological Review*, *80*, 352–373.

Turnure, J. E. (1985). Communication and cues in the functional cognition of the mentally retarded. In N. R. Ellis & N. W. Bray (Eds.), *International review of research in mental retardation* (Vol. 13, pp. 43–77). New York: Academic Press.

Turnure, J. E., & Gudeman, R. (1984). *Long-term memory and mental retardation: Effects of individual differences and retrieval cues on remembrance of prior discourse*. Final Report: Grant No. 5 RO1 HD 15409-02. Washington, D.C.: National Institute of Child Health and Human Development.

Turnure, J. E., & Zigler, E. (1964). Outer-directedness in the problem solving of normal and retarded children. *Journal of Abnormal and Social Psychology*, *69*, 427–436.

Turnure, J. E., Samuels, S. J., & Carlson, E. (1985). *An investigation of time-on-task for handicapped children in Levels Two, Three, and Four service delivery systems*. Final Report: Grant No. 09-EFF 085. St. Paul, MN: Minnesota State Department of Education, Special Education Effectiveness Project.

Vygotsky, L. S. (1978). *Mind in society: The development of higher psychological processes*. Cambridge, MA: Harvard University Press.

Waddell, K. J., & Rogoff, B. (1981). Effect of contextual organization on spatial memory of middle-aged and older women. *Developmental Psychology*, *17*, 878–885.

Whitbourne, S. K., & Slavin, A. E. (1978). Imagery and sentence retention in elderly and young adults. *Journal of Genetic Psychology*, *133*, 287–298.

Whitely, S. E., & Taylor, A. M. (1973). Overt verbalization and the continued production of effective elaborations by EMR children. *American Journal of Mental Deficiency*, *78*, 193–198.

Williams, L. V. (1983). *Teaching for the two-sided mind*. Englewood Cliffs, NJ: Prentice-Hall.

Wilson, B. (1982). Success and failure in memory training following a cerebral vascular accident. *Cortex*, *18*, 581–594.

Wolff, P., & Levin, J. R. (1972). The role of overt activity in children's imagery production. *Child Development*, *43*, 537–547.

Yates, F. A. (1966). *The art of memory*. Chicago: University of Chicago Press.

Yesavage, J. A. (1984). Relaxation and memory training in 39 elderly patients. *American Journal of Psychiatry*, *141*, 778–781.

Yesavage, J. A., & Rose, T. L. (1983). Concentration and mnemonic training in elderly subjects with memory complaints: A study of combined therapy and order effects. *Psychiatry Research*, *9*, 157–167.

Yesavage, J. A., & Rose, T. L. (1984a). The effects of a face-name mnemonic in young, middle-aged, and elderly adults. *Experimental Aging Research*, *10*, 55–57.

Yesavage, J. A., & Rose, T. L. (1984b). Semantic elaboration and the method of loci. *Experimental Aging Research*, *10*, 155–159.

Yesavage, J. A., Rose, T. L., & Bower, G. H. (1983). Interactive imagery and affective judgments improve face-name learning in the elderly. *Journal of Gerontology*, *38*, 197–203.

Zimler, J., & Keenan, J. M. (1983). Imagery in the congenitally blind: How visual are visual images? *Journal of Experimental Psychology: Learning, Memory, & Cognition*, *9*, 269–282.

CHAPTER 16

Mnemonic Instruction in Special Education

Margo A. Mastropieri, Thomas E. Scruggs, and Joel R. Levin

A decade has now passed since former President Gerald Ford signed into law PL 94-142, the 1975 Education for All Handicapped Children Act, which recognized handicapped children as an integral part of all education. Today, 10% of the entire school population receives special education services, and over 125,000 personnel have entered the field of special education. Commensurate with these changes, funding for special education has tripled overall, while federal support has increased by a factor of 100 (Council for Exceptional Children, 1985).

The past decade has also witnessed an explosion of research directed toward improving both diagnoses of and prescriptions for educationally handicapped populations. As an example, in 1977 five learning disabilities research institutes were funded by the federal government to increase our knowledge about such populations (Kneedler & Hallahan, 1983). This and related research efforts identified serious deficits in learning and memory skills of the mildly handicapped. These deficits form the basis of commonly reported school failures among handicapped learners. Documentation of these deficits has generated a need for further research to identify optimal teaching and learning strategies to remediate the deficits.

In this chapter we describe recent progress in the use of learning and memory strategies by mildly handicapped students. First, deficits in learning and memory skills in learning disabled (LD) and mentally retarded (MR) populations are summarized. Second, some critical distinctions are made between prevailing methods of instruction and pictorial mnemonic strategies. Following this, specific research involving mnemonic strategy instruction with LD and MR students in the areas of language arts, social studies, and science is presented. Finally, suggestions for the future potential of mnemonic instruction are given.

Strategy Instruction for Handicapped Learners

Commonly reported characteristics of LD and MR students are deficits in memory tasks and poor performance in academic learning tasks (Torgesen, 1982; Torgesen & Kail, 1980). Deficits have been reported with respect to short- and long-term memory, rate of memory search, and spontaneous use of mnemonic strategies (Borkowski & Buchel, 1983; Detterman, 1979; Pressley, Heisel,

McCormick, & Nakamura, 1982; Torgesen & Kail, 1980; Worden, 1983). Evidence exists that improved task-related performance results when these students are given instruction in such strategies as item rehearsal (Torgesen & Goldman, 1977), category organization (Bauer, 1979; Dallago & Moely, 1979), and semantic orientation (Torgesen, Murphy, & Ivey, 1979), as well as in strategies designed to improve handicapped learners' reading comprehension (Palincsar & Brown, 1984; Wong & Jones, 1981).

Early Remediation Efforts

Initial research efforts in differential training of LD students involved identification of weaknesses in specific areas of "information processing" and subsequent attempts to train areas thought to be deficient. Kirk and Kirk (1971), for example, developed a test of "psycholinguistic ability" based upon Osgood's (1957) information-processing model. This Illinois Test of Psycholinguistic Ability (ITPA) was used to attempt to identify processing deficits in visual areas such as "visual sequential memory," in which subjects were required to reconstruct a sequence of geometric figures, or auditory areas such as "auditory closure," in which subjects were required to recognize words for which specific sounds had been omitted (e.g., "type__iter"). Test results were intended to identify aspects of deficient psycholinguistic functioning, for which training programs were available (Minskoff, Wisemann, & Minskoff, 1972). The purpose of the training programs was to provide extensive practice in the processes for which the student had exhibited deficiencies. For example, if a student had exhibited a deficiency in "visual figure–ground" orientations, s/he would be given guided practice in visually identifying individual objects embedded within larger pictures (e.g., "How many FISH can you find in this picture?"). Other similar tests and training programs were developed by Frostig and Horne (1964), and were recommended for the training of MR as well as LD students.

Perhaps because of an inadequate early research base, serious problems began to emerge with perceptual or psycholinguistic training. Evaluation of tests such as the ITPA revealed inadequate reliability and validity, as well as norms that were not clearly defined (Arter & Jenkins, 1979; Coles, 1978). The relative merits of such "process" training became a matter of hot debate (Hammill & Larsen, 1974; Minskoff, 1975). Regardless of the effects of such training efforts on handicapped learners' psychometric "process" measures, there was little improvement in the academic skills (e.g., reading) that had constituted the basis of these students' initials referrals. Theoretically, such efforts have been equated with the "faculty psychology" of the previous century (Mann, 1979), including phrenology and previous attempts to "train the brain."

Direct Instruction

Partly in response to failures of "process" models, an instructional model based upon intensive teacher-led instruction of academic subskills began to gain in popularity. This direct instruction model was initially implemented with culturally disadvantaged children in preschool and primary grades, and later became widely used with handicapped learners (Becker, Engelmann, Carnine, & Maggs, 1982). Basically, direct instruction is a behavioral task-analytic approach that includes components of fast instructional pace, cumulative review, specific correction procedures, and teaching to a "general case" or rule to facilitate generalization when possible. In addition, this instructional model has unique features in that the teacher leads each stage of the learning process (as opposed to encouraging student-initiated learning) and employs a direct question and answer format, usually involving small groups of students responding in unison on cue from the teacher (Gersten, 1985). Published direct instruction materials include nine Direct Instruction Systems for Teaching and Remediation (DISTAR) (Becker et al., 1982) programs for teaching reading, arithmetic, and language; six Corrective Reading and Reading Mastery programs for comprehension and decoding; as well as spelling and math programs. These materials are basically concerned with the acquisition of decoding skills, arithmetic facts and algorithms, and language and "comprehension" skills. The dominant instructional strategy employed in these materials is overt teacher-led verbal responding with specific feedback, repetition, and cumulative review.

Although some have claimed that "research" supports the utility of direct instruction for raising the achievement of disadvantaged and handicapped learners, controlled experimental evidence is lacking, and many findings are equivocal. Although Becker (1977) and Becker et al. (1982) cite the Follow Through evaluation as evidence of the superiority of direct instruction methods, House, Glass, McLean, and Walker (1978) and Anderson, St. Pierre, Proper, and Stebbins (1978) maintain that little can be concluded from this evaluation concerning relative program efficacy. The empirical work that has been conducted, however, has provided limited support for direct instruction programs over other published instructional materials in raising achievement of handicapped learners (e.g., Maggs & Morath, 1976; Stein & Goldman, 1980). And although the various findings are far from conclusive, direct instruction is claimed to be among the most effective treatments for handicapped learners (Gersten, 1985); in fact, it has been heralded as "one of the most significant advances in educational technology in modern times" (Karoly & Steffen, 1982, p. 205).

Gersten (1985) has appropriately called for future efforts to evaluate the relative effectiveness of specific components of direct instruction. Although recent research has evaluated the effects of different stimulus presentations in facilitating discriminations, such as "fleep," meaning "a flower with a leaf either to the left or right of the flower stem" (Carnine, 1980, p. 454), and the acquisition of simple vocabulary concepts (Gersten, White, Falco, & Carnine, 1982), surprisingly little research has been conducted on the relative utility of the dominant learning strategy of direct instruction: fast-paced teacher-led rehearsal of skills, facts, and fact systems. Research documenting the lack of spontaneous rehearsal strategies in LD and MR students, however, has suggested that experimenter-directed rehearsal can facilitate learning in these populations, and, in fact, LD students' serial recall has been found to increase with the use of direct rehearsal (Torgesen & Goldman, 1977).

Elaboration and Mnemonic Instruction

Despite selected instances of reported rehearsal strategy successes, however, considerable research evidence suggests that an even more powerful class of strategies exist for improving handicapped students' learning (Martin, 1978; Pressley & Levin, in press; Taylor & Turnure, 1979). That class of strategies may be referred to as "elaboration" strategies (Rohwer, 1973). Elaboration, construction, or "generation" (Wittrock, 1974) involves adding something to what is being learned in order to make it more memorable. Such elaborations typically involve creating semantically meaningful associations between what is being learned and what is already known, thereby transforming the unfamiliar into the familiar. In the context of handicapped learners, the following anecdote by Rohwer (1968) provides an informative historical overview to our discussion of elaborative learning strategies.

A few years ago we set out to investigate some aspect of the process of paired-associate learning . . . and for our purposes at that time a group of mentally retarded adults provided the appropriate population for study. We asked each person to learn a paired-associate list comprised of eight pairs of common objects such as COW-BALL, COMB-GLASS, etc. I was soon shocked by the inefficiency with which these persons learned; some were never able to master a list that could be mastered by normal adults in only one or two trials. Eventually, I stopped one young woman who was having a particularly difficult time. She had been floundering along getting only two or three of the items correct after fourteen trials. I asked her how she was trying to learn the pairs. She replied that she was simply looking at them each time they were shown to her and trying to remember which ones were presented together. I prodded by asking if it had occurred to her to make up little stories about each pair of pictures or to create some kind of image of the two members of each pair. She said no. I suggested that she make up a short sentence about each of the two objects in each pair, which she did. I then tested her, and she was able to recite perfectly the entire list of pairs. Our interest was aroused by this dramatic improvement, and we proceeded to carry out a full study of the effect of this form of mnemonic elaboration. (Rohwer, 1968, p. 218)

Much research on elaboration strategies has indeed been conducted in the last 20 years (e.g., Bower, 1972; Higbee, 1979; Levin, 1976; Paivio, 1971; Pressley, 1982; Rohwer, 1973), including research on *mnemonic techniques* (e.g., Bellezza, 1981; Levin, 1985a; Paivio, 1983; Pressley, Levin, & Delaney, 1982), which—as will be seen—incorporates elaboration as a central component. Moreover, the utility of mnemonic instruction with mildly handicapped [LD and educable mentally retarded (EMR)] learners has also been investigated (see, for example, Mastropieri, Scruggs, & Levin, 1985a; and Pressley & Levin, in press). Although this line of research is still in its infancy, it nevertheless suggests that mnemonic instruction constitutes a viable, versatile, and very powerful strategy for enhancing the learning of handicapped learners.

Mnemonic Instruction Versus Direct Instruction

Mnemonic instruction shares with direct instruction the principles of explicit and direct teaching. However, whereas direct instruction is essentially a *format* for providing carefully supervised instruction in any content domain (i.e., it is content free), mnemonic instruction is designed in specific relation to the material being learned (i.e., it is content bound). Thus, depending on the content to be learned, one may select among a variety of mnemonic techniques, such as the pegword method, the story mnemonic, the link method, the first-letter mnemonic, the phonetic digit method, the face–name mnemonic, the method of loci, the hook method, and the keyword method (see, for example, Bellezza, 1981; Desrochers & Begg, Chapter 3, this volume). Mnemonic instruction and direct instruction also differ in terms of their assumed underlying components. Whereas direct instruction contains what Scruggs, Mastropieri, Levin, and Gaffney (1985a) have called the three "operant Rs" of responding, reinforcement, and repetition, mnemonic instruction relies upon what Levin (1983) has termed the three "mnemonic Rs" of recoding, relating, and retrieving. Recoding refers to a transformation of unfamiliar stimuli into more familiar, memorable representations. Relating involves the elaborative process of creating a semantic context within which the information to be learned can be meaningfully processed (as in Rohwer's, 1968, anecdote). These recoding and relating components both facilitate aspects of the later retrieving component, which refers to the systematic retrieval path provided from the re-presented stimuli back to the associated information. (For a formal description of the processes associated with the mnemonic keyword method, see Desrochers & Begg, Chapter 3, this volume.)

As was noted previously, mnemonic techniques have dramatically improved the learning performance of handicapped learners. In this chapter, we review the initial mnemonic investigations, as well as some more recent ones. Many of these studies include comparisons of mnemonic instruction with alternative procedures taken from direct instruction materials. Upon reviewing the evidence, we conclude the chapter with a few comments about mnemonic techniques as a component of contemporary classroom instruction in special education.

Research on Mnemonic Instruction for Handicapped Learners

Vocabulary Learning

One of the earliest known attempted applications of the mnemonic *keyword method* (Atkinson, 1975) in special education was reported in a dissertation by Taylor (1981). In this investigation, 34 LD boys (mean age = 13.4 years) were randomly assigned to mnemonic and free-study control conditions. Students were then individually presented 14 "difficult" English nouns and their definitions. Students in the mnemonic condition were provided with a "keyword" for each vocabulary item, as well as a verbal description of the keyword interacting with the definition. For example, to teach that "barrister" means "lawyer," subjects were provided with a keyword for "barrister." The keyword in this case, "bear," is a concrete familiar word that resembles a salient part of the vocabulary word "barrister" (recoding). An interaction between the keyword (bear) and the definition (lawyer) was then described as a bear acting like a lawyer (relating).

Students were then told to recall the meaning of "barrister" by thinking of the key-word "bear" and remembering the bear acting like a lawyer (retrieving). All students were given three vocabulary lists to study: the first to assess "baseline" performance, a second to document mnemonic vs. control performance differences (for which 1-week delayed recall was also assessed), and a third in which students in both conditions were provided with mnemonic instruction. This third list was provided to determine whether the presence or absence of previous mnemonic instruction had an influence on later mnemonic instruction. Taylor (1981) reported that on list 2, students instructed mnemonically significantly outscored free-study students by a margin of over three to one, with respective mean percentages of correct definitions of 82% and 24%. On a 1-week delayed-recall test, mnemonic students maintained more than a two to one advantage over controls (35% vs. 14%, respectively). When both groups were later provided with mnemonic instruction for a third vocabulary list, mean scores did not differ (66% vs. 65%, respectively).

Despite the seemingly impressive benefits of mnemonic vocabulary instruction in the Taylor (1981) study, a questionable feature of her design complicates interpretation of those data. In particular, when students were tested for definition recall, students in the mnemonic condition were additionally provided with the previously presented keywords. Such keyword provision eliminates a potentially critical aspect of the retrieval process, namely remembering the recoded vocabulary word. Moreover, it could be argued that by providing keywords during testing, Taylor reduced her task to Rohwer's (1973) simple paired-associate elaboration (i.e., remembering the interaction involving the keyword), rather than mnemonic vocabulary learning. Fortunately, Taylor's results were replicated and extended (to younger LD students) by Berry (1982) in an experiment that did not suffer from the methodological problem just noted. In the Berry experiment, mnemonic subjects were provided with vocabulary items and interactive illustrations to study, whereas control subjects studied the vocabulary items in the company of their illustrated definitions.

In subsequent research with junior high LD students, Mastropieri, Scruggs, Levin, Gaffney, and McLoone (1985b) compared mnemonic instruction with the fast-paced experimenter-directed rehearsal condition used in direct instruction materials for teaching vocabulary word meanings: "The teaching procedure involves first telling students the definition and having them repeat it" (Carnine & Silbert, 1979, p. 149). For example, to teach the meaning of the English vocabulary word "indolent," the following procedure is scripted for teacher presentation: "INDOLENT means LAZY. What does INDOLENT mean . . . [Repeat until firm]" (Englemann, Haddox, Hanner, & Osborne, 1978). In experiment 1 of the Mastropieri et al. (1985b) study, students in the mnemonic condition were given strategy instruction and provided with interactive pictures depicting recoded stimulus and response items. In contrast, students in the direct instruction condition were shown pictures of the vocabulary words and given instruction using the procedures similar to those outlined above, including cumulative review of learned information (as prescribed by direct instruction).

Mnemonically instructed students outscored students given direct instruction by a wide margin (means of 80 vs. 31% correct definitions, respectively). In experiment 2 of the same investigation, direct instruction techniques were compared with a mnemonic condition in which students were provided with keywords but were prompted to generate their own interactive images. Again, mnemonically instructed students statistically outperformed students in a direct instruction condition, with respective means of 69 vs. 47% correct.

In another vocabulary-learning study (Scruggs, Mastropieri, & Levin, 1985b), mnemonic and direct instruction strategies were compared using a population of EMR junior high school students in a crossover design (i.e., students received both instructional treatments in a counterbalanced order). Mnemonic instruction was highly beneficial for the EMR students. When in the mnemonic condition, students learned an average of 72% of the vocabulary words, whereas when they were in the direct instruction condition, they learned only 48% of the words. Seventeen out of 20 students remembered more vocabulary words under mnemonic instruction than under direct instruction, as compared to only one out of 20 students who remembered more under direct instruction. Moreover, it was found that mnemonically instructed students produced significantly fewer intralist intrusions (i.e., confusion with other within-list reponses), when based on either total number of errors (including omissions) or total number of overt errors (excluding omissions).

McLoone, Scruggs, Mastropieri, and Zucker (in press) recently examined the feasibility of training LD adolescents to generate their own keywords and interactive images following practice with provided keywords and interactive illustrations. Sixty seventh graders were assigned randomly to either a mnemonic condition or an experimenter-directed rehearsal condition. Both groups were initially taught vocabulary words and their definitions according to one of the two instructional conditions. Following this, students were tested and given condition-appropriate feedback on strategy use and the efficacy of their strategy for learning new information. On this experimenter-structured training task, mnemonic subjects by far outrecalled directed-rehearsal subjects, the averages being 84 and 28% correct, respectively.

Students were then taught the stages involved in using their learning strategy independently. In the mnemonic condition, for each item students were told first to verbally state an appropriate keyword, and then to generate an interactive image. Students in the directed-rehearsal condition were told first to state verbally each word and definition, and then to employ principles of self-prompting, feedback, and cumulative review. Students in both conditions were given practice and feedback on three examples, followed by the introduction of a new list of vocabulary words. On the subsequent test, the definition recall of mnemonic subjects was again statistically superior to that of directed-rehearsal subjects, 74 vs. 41%. Such results suggest that handicapped learners can be taught to apply an effective mnemonic strategy independently. Although the McLoone et al. approach is only a first step in implementing a systematic program of strategy instruction (see, Pressley, Borkowski, & Schneider, in press), the findings are promising enough to indicate a productive direction for further research.

In sum, the results of the above investigations are remarkably consistent in their support of mnemonic instruction as a powerful vocabulary-learning strategy for use by handicapped learners. In addition, when mnemonic instruction has been compared with the instructional components analogous to those in direct instruction materials, mnemonic instruction has produced a strong advantage. The section that follows describes applications of mnemonic instruction to the learning of content-area factual information.

Content-Area Learning

Several recent experiments have extended pictorial mnemonic strategies to the teaching of content-area information. Mastropieri, Scruggs, and Levin (1985c, Exp. 1) used a combined keyword–pegword strategy for teaching the hardness levels of North American minerals (Bishop, Lewis, & Sutherland, 1976) to ninth-grade LD students who had been classified as either "lower" or "higher" comprehenders on a standardized reading test. The mineral-learning task was chosen because of its immediate application in the school curriculum, and because it permitted an evaluation of the same combined keyword–pegword mnemonic strategy that had been successfully implemented in a nonhandicapped junior high school population (Levin, McCormick, & Dretzke, 1981). In the initial stage of this application, all students were instructed to use the rhyming pegword number system, where "one is a bun, two is a shoe, . . . ten is hen." Next, students were provided with a keyword for each mineral name, along with an illustration depicting the keyword interacting with the corresponding pegword representation. For example, to remember that pyrite is number six on the hardness scale, the student would be taught that the pegword for 6 is "sticks," and the keyword for "pyrite" is "pie" (recoding). An illustration of a piece of pie being supported by some sticks would then be provided (relating). Finally, the student would be told that when asked for the hardness level of pyrite, (s)he should think back to the keyword "pie," remember the picture of the pie on the sticks, and respond with the appropriate pegword equivalent, six (retrieving).

Two comparison conditions were employed in this study. One group of students (direct questioning) was taught the same information under a teacher-directed question and answer format, similar to the Direct Instruction condition previously described, but different in that materials were shown only once for a predetermined amount of time (equal to that allowed in the mnemonic condition), with no cumulative review provided. In a third condition (Free Study), students were provided with a variety of materials and told to study independently. Results of this experiment indicated that mnemonic instruction (75% correct) was statistically superior to both direct questioning (28% correct) and free study (36% correct). The same mnemonic advantage was found among both higher and lower comprehenders (i.e., instructional conditions did not interact with reading ability). In a second experiment, these results were replicated in a population of nonhandicapped seventh graders.

In the study just described, all students were administered instruction individually (i.e., on a one to one basis). Mastropieri, Scruggs, and Levin (in press, Exp. 1) conducted an additional experiment to determine whether the successful mnemonic approach could be adapted to small-group instructional settings — settings thought to resemble more closely the instructional context used in special education settings. This small-group mnemonic instruction was compared with direct instruction also administered in small groups, which is a recommended feature of direct instruction (Carnine & Silbert, 1979; Gersten, 1985). Fifty-six LD high school students were taught the mineral hardness levels in their regularly scheduled instructional groupings, with 12 small groups randomly assigned to mnemonic instruction and 12 to direct instruction. Students in the mnemonic condition were given small-group instruction similar to that used in the Mastropieri et al. (1985c) investigation, whereas direct instruction students were taught using rapidly paced drill and practice with direct experimenter questioning, unison choral responding on cue, corrective feedback, and cumulative review. Mnemonic instruction (80% correct) was statistically superior to direct instruction (50% correct). In a second experiment, this finding was replicated using a small sample of EMR students taught individually.

Several experiments were then conducted to determine whether mnemonic instruction could be adapted to the teaching of multiple attributes simultaneously. Scruggs et al. (1985a) taught three specific attributes of eight North American minerals (e.g., "PYRITE is number SIX on the hardness scale, YELLOW in color, and used in the manufacture of ACID") to 56 LD adolescents using mnemonic, free-study, and two direct instruction conditions. In the mnemonic condition, materials from previous studies on mineral hardness levels were adapted to incorporate representations of color and use. For example, for pyrite, students were shown an illustration of a yellow (color) pie (keyword for "pyrite") supported by sticks (pegword for six), while acid (use) was being poured on it. The free-study condition and one direct instruction condition resembled those used in previous investigations. In the other direct instruction condition, students spent their time learning about only four minerals (half the list). This reduced-list direct instruction condition, with its additional drill and practice on fewer items, represents an interesting baseline against which the effects of full-list mnemonic instruction could be assessed. Students in the mnemonic condition outperformed students in the other two full-list conditions, with all differences being of considerable magnitude (at least two to one) for each of the three attributes. Moreover, mnemonic students were found to have mastered an average of nearly 17 out of 24 attributes in the same amount of time that reduced-list direct instruction students mastered an average of 6 out of 12 attributes.

In a related study, Mastropieri, Scruggs, McLoone, and Levin (1985d) taught dichotomized mineral attributes (HARD vs. SOFT in hardness, PALE vs. DARK in color, and HOME vs. INDUSTRIAL use) to LD adolescents, with results paralleling those reported by Scruggs et al. (1985a). In this experiment, mnemonic illustrations were adapted to represent the dichotomized attributes by coloring the keyword reference either pale or dark in color, depicting it in either a home or factory setting to denote common use, and including either an old man or a baby to represent hard vs. soft minerals, respectively, in the illustration.

Recently, Engelmann and Carnine (1982) have recommended the use of "visual-spatial displays" and a direct instruction format for the teaching of facts and fact systems to handicapped learners. In a visual-spatial display, relationships between facts are represented pictorially and spatially as an aid to recall. Although some research by Mastropieri and Peters (1982) has suggested that spatially arranged pictures (viz., maps) can facilitate the prose recall of LD students, no previous research validating the use of visual-spatial displays in promoting LD students' recall of fact systems could be found. In two experiments, Scruggs, Mastropieri, Levin, McLoone, Gaffney, and Prater (1985c) compared mnemonic instruction of mineral attributes with visual-spatial displays of the same content couched in a direct instruction format. A free-study condition was also included. Whether the information to be remembered was specific (Exp. 1) or dichotomized (Exp. 2), mnemonic students significantly outperformed both their free-study and visual-spatial display counterparts, with the latter two conditions not differing from one another. Although other adaptations of visual-spatial display instruction may ultimately prove successful, the findings of this investigation are in agreement with conclusions of Levin (1981b) and Levin, Anglin, and Carney (in press) that "transformational" mnemonic illustrations promote higher levels of factual memory than do "organizational" visual-spatial displays.

Mnemonic instruction has been found to be similarly effective in an actual prose-learning context (Scruggs, Mastropieri, McLoone, Levin, & Morrison, in press), wherein LD adolescents independently read passages containing the information on multiple attributes of minerals. In this study, mnemonic illustrations were compared with nonmnemonic (representational) illustrations with respect to students learning either dichotomized (experiment 1) or specific (experiment 2) attribute information. In both experiments, mnemonic students learned significantly more than did nonmnemonic students. In experiment 2, this was also true on a surprise 1-week delayed-recall test. Furthermore, in experiment 2, mnemonic students correctly identified more attribute dichotomies than did nonmnemonic students, even though such information had not been explicitly provided in the lesson on specific attribute. This finding suggests that mnemonically encoded information is "meaningful" to LD students, inasmuch as they are able to perform mental elaborations on the information—a finding consistent with one in the later reported study by Veit, Scruggs, and Mastropieri (1986). It was also found that mnemonically trained students reported that their method of study was significantly more "helpful" than did students not so trained. These perceptions are similar to those reported for nonhandicapped learners (Levin, Morrison, McGivern, Mastropieri, & Scruggs, in press).

As a final prose-learning example of the application of mnemonic strategies to the content-area instruction of handicapped students, we consider the recent studies by Peters and Levin (1986) and Goin, Peters, and Levin (1986). Peters and Levin found that the prose learning of poorly comprehending middle school students can be substantially enhanced by mnemonic instruction. In experiment 2 of that investigation, seventh-grade students read several short passages about famous people and their accomplishments. Mnemonic students were given a key-word for each person's name and instructed to generate an image in which the keyword was interacting with the person's major accomplishment that was described in the passage. In comparison to no-strategy control students, mne-monically trained students remembered more names and accomplishments infor-mation on both immediate and 1-week delayed tests. Goin et al. (1986) adapted the Peters and Levin passages for use by LD students and found that the students benefitted from mnemonic instruction in the form of either experimenter-provided illustrations (as in the Scruggs et al., in press, study) or self-generated visual imagery (as in the Peters & Levin, 1986, study). Once again, therefore, we have evidence to support the claim that the learning performance of "non-learners" or "poor comprehenders" can be considerably elevated by the use of task-appropriate instructional strategies (in this case, mnemonic strategies). More on the topic of "task-appropriate" strategies is included in the final section of this chapter.

Extended Mnemonic Instruction

The research on pictorial mnemonic strategies for improving both vocabulary learning and content-area instruction just reviewed offers promising educational applications for handicapped students. Yet, none of these investigations has exa-mined the effects of prolonged, cumulative, mnemonic instruction over several days. In this section, we report the results of an initial study that focuses on just that issue.

Veit et al. (1986) evaluated the effectiveness of extended mnemonic instruction in a sample of LD adolescents. Their investigation was considered to be a first step in assessing the feasibility of implementing mnemonic instruction in "real-world" settings, that is, when instruction is implemented over several days and factual information is cumulated through different mnemonic approaches for different lessons. Although previous findings have suggested that within-lesson interference is low under mnemonic instruction (Scruggs et al., 1985b), it remained to be seen whether several consecutive mnemonic presentations would result in between-lesson interference. Furthermore, it was of interest to examine the adaptability of mnemonic instruction to several different lessons within a sin-gle content domain.

Veit et al. (1986) taught three lessons in the content area of natural science (i.e., prehistoric reptiles) to LD students using procedures adapted from mnemonic instruction and direct instruction paradigms. All students were taught in small groups that had been randomly assigned to treatment conditions. Les-sons were constructed to be nonoverlapping in specific content so that order of lesson presentation could be counterbalanced. Included were a vocabulary les-son, a multiple-attribute lesson, and a lesson requiring the learning of numbered information. In the vocabulary lesson, students were taught meanings of root words referring to prehistoric reptiles (e.g., *ornith* meaning "bird," *poda* meaning "foot"). In both the mnemonic and direct instruction conditions, students were taught the information using procedures similar to those used in the previously cited vocabulary-learning investigations. In the multiple-attributes lesson, students were taught three attributes of prehistoric reptiles (geological period, eating habits, and a specific characteristic of each prehistoric reptile). Mnemonic and direct instruction subjects were taught using either mnemonic or visual-spatial display instructions adapted from previous studies (e.g., Scruggs et al., 1985c). In the numbered-information lesson, students were taught possible reasons for the extinction of prehistoric reptiles in order of plausibility, using mnemonic pegword and direct instruction approaches similar to those of Mastropieri et al. (in press). Students were tested for immediate recall after each lesson. In addition, after the 3 d of instruction, students were given two fourth-day cumulative recall tests, requiring identification and production of all content covered. Results indicated that mnemonically instructed students generally scored significantly higher on the various recall tests including the two "unit" tests, and—consistent with Scruggs et al. (in press) "inference" finding—they performed significantly better on a test of novel application of previously learned vocabulary content (i.e., "What does *ornitho/poda* mean?"). In addition, more intralesson intrusions occurred in the direct instruction condition, whereas inter-lesson intrusions tended not to be produced in either condition. Descriptive analysis of daily lesson results indicated differences between conditions neither increased nor decreased over successive days. This finding suggests that although previous mnemonic learning does not appear to facilitate later mnemonic learning (see, for example, Dretzke & Levin, 1984), neither is any inhibition from between-lesson confusion apparent.

These findings, and those previously reviewed, indicate that school-related content can be adapted to mnemonic instructional units, and that such instruction results in greatly increased levels of learning in mildly handicapped students. Indeed, the composite results of all studies to date suggest that mnemonic strategies are every bit as effective for handicapped learners as they are for nonhandicapped learners and, in fact, may ultimately provide an important role in furthering the school success of these populations. To quote Lebrato and Ellis (1974):

> ...[I]magery mnemonics may be a powerful tool in increasing learning and retention of educational materials, many of which must be learned in a rote fashion. In view of the poverty of truly *special* training and educational methods for retarded persons, this method bears careful and intensive study. (pp. 712–713)

Concluding Remarks, With an Eye to the Future

Throughout this chapter, we have been unconditionally supportive of mnemonic instruction as an effective learning and memory strategy for handicapped learners. The literature clearly bears out our oft-repeated claim that in both handicapped and nonhandicapped populations no other competing instructional strategy that has been scrutinized under controlled conditions compares with the consistent ability of mnemonic strategies to enhance students' learning and retention of factual information (see, for example, Levin & Pressley, 1985; Pressley & Levin, in press). Although we stand by such a claim here, we would be remiss if we did not briefly underscore the conditions on which it is based.

What Mnemonic Strategies Are and What They Are Not

As has been pointed out many times in the past, specific applications of mnemonic strategies must be interpreted from the perspective of "different strategies for different purposes" (e.g., Higbee, 1979; Levin, in press; Levin & Pressley, 1985; Pressley, Levin, & McDaniel, in press). In short, mnemonic strategies do not represent a panacea for facilitating all desired instructional objectives. They are optimally suited to acquiring factual information efficiently. The theoretical mechanisms underlying their effectiveness for that instructional purpose can be well articulated (Bellezza, 1981; Desrochers & Begg, Chapter 3, this volume; Levin, 1981b). It is both naive and incorrect to assume that those who advocate the use of mnemonic strategies in factual learning and memory contexts (the present authors included) are offering a blanket endorsement of such strategies in all instructional contexts. Although there is good reason to expect mnemonic strategies similarly to facilitate students' performance on any task that demands the efficient retrieval of previously acquired factual content (Higbee, 1979; Levin, in press) — as would be required on tests of inference, problem solving, and other forms of knowledge application — research bearing on that expectation has scarcely been initiated (e.g., Pressley, Levin, & Miller, 1981; Scruggs et al., in press; Veit et al., 1986). The same can be said of research on mnemonically instructed skills, such as learning how to perform mathematical operations, how to diagram chemical compounds, or how to identify a prose passage's main idea (Higbee & Kunihira, 1985; Levin, 1985b; Pressley, 1985).

Mnemonic Instruction and the Handicapped Learner

With specific regard to handicapped learners, we have suggested recently that comparisons of mnemonic instruction and direct instruction may be profitably investigated in relation to acquiring skills of the kind just mentioned (see Mastropieri et al., 1985a). In contrast to the repeated failures of direct instruction to enhance students' acquisition of declarative knowledge in our investigations, it might be reasonably posited that the direct instruction format — with its emphasis on the "three R" components of teacher-led responding, reinforcement, and repetition — might be optimally suited to facilitating students' acquisition of procedural knowledge (see, for example, Gaffney, 1984; Graves, 1986). We have also argued (e.g., Mastropieri et al., 1985a) that good mnemonic instruction incorporates some of the desirable format features of direct instruction, such as careful teacher structuring, sequencing, interaction, feedback, and practice. It is doubtful that the successes we have observed (especially with handicapped learners) would have occurred if the students had not received systematic mnemonic instruction, based on sound pedagogical principles. In that sense, then, good mnemonic instruction combines an effective pedagogical format with an effective psychological information-processing strategy. In addition, strategies that have proved effective for improving handicapped students' reading comprehension skills (e.g., selected components of Palincsar & Brown's, 1984, "reciprocal-teaching" model) may be profitably combined with a mnemonic-instructional approach to teaching the same skill (see, for example, Levin, 1982). Future research efforts can address these issues as well as the more complex issue of transfer of mnemonic strategies. Although results of preliminary research have been positive, the final aim of such instruction involves the improvements of the students' knowledge of relevant task demands and selection of task-appropriate strategies. Such a training orientation to special education is described in detail by Pressley, Johnson, and Symons (in press).

Such domains of mnemonic strategy application remain largely unexplored, and yet they represent domains in which mildly handicapped students are in great need of instructional strategies that "work." All the available research evidence suggests that mnemonic instruction is capable of transforming content that is difficult to learn into easily acquired and remembered content. In addition, preliminary research on strategy maintenance and transfer suggests that mnemonic instruction also has the potential of transforming otherwise inefficient learners into confident, independent, efficient learners. It is hoped that future research efforts will enable the field of special education to explore this potential.

References

Anderson, R. B., St. Pierre, R. G., Proper, E. C., & Stebbins, L. B. (1978). Pardon us, but what was the question again? A response to the critique of the Follow Through Evaluation. *Harvard Educational Review, 48*, 161–170.

Arter, J. A., & Jenkins, J. R. (1979). Differential diagnosis—prescriptive teaching: A critical appraisal. *Review of Educational Research, 49*, 517–555.

Atkinson, R. C. (1975). Mnemotechnics in second-language learning. *American Psychologist, 30*, 821–828.

Bauer, R. H. (1979). Memory, acquisition, and category clustering in learning disabled children. *Journal of Experimental Child Psychology, 27*, 365–383.

Becker, W. C. (1977). Teaching reading and language to the disadvantaged: What we have learned from field research. *Harvard Educational Review, 47*, 518–543.

Becker, W. C., Engelmann, S., Carnine, D. W., & Maggs, A. (1982). Direct instruction technology: Making learning happen. In P. Karoly & J. J. Steffen (Eds.), *Improving children's competence: Advances in child behavior analysis and therapy* (Vol. 1, pp. 151–204). Lexington, MA: Heath.

Bellezza, F. S. (1981). Mnemonic devices: Classification, characteristics, and criteria. *Review of Educational Research, 51*, 247–275.

Berry, J. (1982). Unpublished doctoral research. University of Wisconsin, Madison, WI.

Bishop, M. S., Lewis, P. G., & Sutherland, B. (1976). *Focus on early science.* Columbus, OH: Merrill.

Borkowski, J. G., & Buchel, F. P. (1983). Learning and memory strategies in the mentally retarded. In M. Pressley & J. R. Levin (Eds.), *Cognitive strategy research: Psychological foundations* (pp. 103–128). New York: Springer-Verlag.

Bower, G. H. (1972). Mental imagery and associative learning. In L. Gregg (Ed.), *Cognition in learning and memory.* New York: John Wiley & Sons.

Carnine, D. W. (1980). Three procedures for presenting minimally different positive and negative instances. *Journal of Educational Psychology, 72,* 452–456.

Carnine, D., & Silbert, J. (1979). *Direct instruction: Reading.* Columbus, OH: Merrill.

Coles, G. (1978). The learning disabilities test battery: Empirical and social issues. *Harvard Educational Review, 48,* 313–340.

Council for Exceptional Children. (1985). A special birthday for special education. *Exceptional Children, 52,* 99.

Dallago, M. L. L., & Moely, B. E. (1979). Free recall in boys of normal and poor reading levels as a function of task manipulations. *Journal of Experimental Child Psychology, 30,* 62–78.

Detterman, D. K. (1979). Memory in the mentally retarded. In N. R. Ellis (Ed.), *Handbook of mental deficiency, psychological theory and research* (2nd ed.) (pp. 727–760). Hillsdale, NJ: Erlbaum Associates.

Dretzke, B. J., & Levin, J. R. (1984). *Building factual knowledge about the U.S. Presidents through pictorial mnemonic strategies.* Paper presented at the Annual meeting of the American Educational Research Association, New Orleans.

Englemann, S., & Carnine, D. (1982). *Theory of instruction: Principles and applications.* New York: Irvington.

Englemann, S., Haddox, P., Hanner, S., & Osborne, J. (1978). *Thinking basics: Corrective reading comprehension A.* Chicago: Science Research Associates.

Frostig, M., & Horne, D. (1964). *The Frostig program for the development of visual perception: Teacher's guide.* Chicago: Follett.

Gaffney, J. S. (1984). *LD children's prose recall as a function of prior knowledge, instruction, and context relatedness.* Unpublished doctoral dissertation, Arizona State University, Tempe, AZ.

Gersten, R. (1985). Direct instruction with special education students: A review of evaluation research. *Journal of Special Education, 19,* 41–58.

Gersten, R., White, W. A., Falco, R., & Carnine, D. (1982). Teaching basic discriminations to handicapped and nonhandicapped individuals through a dynamic presentation of instructional stimuli. *Analysis and Intervention in Developmental Disabilities, 2,* 305–317.

Goin, M. T., Peters, E. E., & Levin, J. R. (1986). *Effects of pictorial mnemonic strategies on the reading performance of students classified as learning disabled.* Paper presented at the 64th annual meeting of the Council for Exceptional Children, April 1–4, New Orleans.

Graves, A. W. (1986). Effects of direct instruction and metacomprehension training on finding main ideas by learning disabled children. *Learning Disabilities Research, 1,* 90–100.

Hammill, D. D., & Larsen, S. C. (1974). The effectiveness of psycholinguistic training. *Exceptional Children, 41,* 5–14.

Higbee, K. L. (1979). Recent research on visual mnemonics: Historical roots and educational fruits. *Review of Educational Research, 49,* 611–629.

Higbee, K. L., & Kunihira, S. (1985). Cross-cultural applications of Yodai mnemonics in education. *Educational Psychologist, 20*, 57–64.

House, E. R., Glass, G. V., McLean, L. D., & Walker, D. F. (1978). No simple answer: Critique of the Follow Through Evaluation. *Harvard Educational Review, 48*(2), 128–160.

Karoly, P., & Steffen, J. J. (1982). *Improving children's competence: Advances in child behavioral analysis and therapy* (Vol. 1, pp. 202–205). Lexington, MA: Heath.

Kirk, S. A., & Kirk, W. (1971). *Psycholinguistic learning disabilities: Diagnosis and remediation.* Urbana, IL: University of Illinois Press.

Kneedler, R. D., & Hallahan, D. P. (1983). Foreword. *Exceptional Education Quarterly, 4*, viii–ix.

Lebrato, M. T., & Ellis, N. R. (1974). Imagery mediation in paired-associate learning by retarded and nonretarded subjects. *American Journal of Mental Deficiency, 78*, 704–713.

Levin, J. R. (1976). What have we learned about maximizing what children learn? In J. R. Levin & V. L. Allen (Eds.), *Cognitive learning in children: Theories and strategies.* New York: Academic Press.

Levin, J. R. (1981a). On functions of pictures in prose. In F. J. Pirozzolo & M. C. Witrock (Eds.), *Neuropsychological and cognitive processes in reading* (pp. 203–228). New York: Academic Press.

Levin, J. R. (1985b). The mnemonic '80s: Keywords in the classroom. *Educational Psychologist, 16*, 65–82.

Levin, J. R. (1982). Pictures as prose-learning devices. In A. Flammer & W. Kintsch (Eds.), *Discourse processing* (pp. 412–444). Amsterdam: North-Holland.

Levin, J. R. (1983). Pictorial strategies for school learning: Practical illustrations. In M. Pressley & J. R. Levin (Eds.), *Cognitive strategy research: Educational applications* (pp. 213–237). New York: Springer-Verlag.

Levin, J. R. (1985a). Educational applications of mnemonic pictures: Possibilities beyond your wildest imagination. In A. A. Sheikh (Ed.), *Imagery in education: Imagery in the educational process* (pp. 63–87). Farmingdale, NY: Baywood.

Levin, J. R. (1985b). Yōdai features = mnemonic procedures: A commentary on Higbee and Kunihira. *Educational Psychologist, 20*, 73–76.

Levin, J. R. (in press). Four cognitive principles of learning-strategy instruction. *Educational Psychologist.*

Levin, J. R., & Pressley, M. (1985). Mnemonic vocabulary instruction: What's fact, what's fiction. In R. F. Dillon (Ed.), *Individual differences in cognition* (Vol. 2, pp. 145–172). New York: Academic Press.

Levin, J. R., Anglin, G. J., & Carney, R. N. (in press). On empirically validating functions of pictures in prose. In D. M. Willows & H. A. Houghton (Eds.), *Illustrations, graphs and diagrams: Psychological theory and educational practice.* New York: Springer-Verlag.

Levin, J. R., McCormick, C. B., & Dretzke, B. J. (1981). A combined pictorial mnemonic strategy for ordered information. *Educational Communication and Technology Journal, 29*, 219–225.

Levin, J. R., Morrison, C. R., McGivern, J. E., Mastropieri, M. A., & Scruggs, T. E. (1986). Mnemonic facilitation of text-embedded science facts. *American Educational Research Journal, 23*, 489–506.

Maggs, A., & Morath, P. (1976). Effects of direct verbal instruction on intellectual development of institutionalized moderately retarded children: A 2-year study. *Journal of Special Education, 10*, 357–364.

Mann, L. (1979). *On the trail of process.* New York: Grune and Stratton.

Martin, C. J. (1978). Mediational processes in the retarded: Implications for teaching reading. In N. R. Ellis (Ed.), *International review of research in mental retardation* (Vol. 9, pp. 61–84). New York: Academic Press.

Mastropieri, M. A., & Peters, E. E. (1982). *Maps as schema for prose recall.* Logan, UT: Utah State University. (ERIC Documentation Reproduction Service No. ED 266 619).

Mastropieri, M. A., Scruggs, T. E., & Levin, J. R. (1985a). Maximizing what exceptional students can learn: A review of keyword and other mnemonic strategy research. *Remedial and Special Education, 6*(2), 39–45.

Mastropieri, M. A., Scruggs, T. E., & Levin, J. R. (1985c). Memory strategy instruction with learning disabled adolescents. *Journal of Learning Disabilities, 18*, 94–100.

Mastropieri, M. A., Scruggs, T. E., & Levin, J. R. (in press). Direct instruction vs. mnemonic instruction: Relative benefits for exceptional learners. *Journal of Special Education.*

Mastropieri, M. A., Scruggs, T. E., Levin, J. R., Gaffney, J., & McLoone, B. (1985b). Mnemonic vocabulary instruction for learning disabled students. *Learning Disability Quarterly, 8*, 57–63.

Mastropieri, M. A., Scruggs, T. E., McLoone, B., & Levin, J. R. (1985d). Facilitating the acquisition of science classifications in LD students. *Learning Disability Quarterly, 8*, 299–309.

McLoone, B., Scruggs, T. E., Mastropieri, M. A., & Zucker, S. (in press). Mnemonic instruction and training with LD adolescents. *Learning Disabilities Research.*

Minskoff, E. (1975). Research on psycholinguistic training: Critique and guidelines. *Exceptional Children, 42*, 136–144.

Minskoff, E., Wisemann, D. E., & Minskoff, J. G. (1972). *The MWM program for developing language abilities.* Ridgefield, NJ: Educational Performance Associates.

Osgood, C. E. (1957). A behavioristic analysis of perception and languages as cognitive phenomena. In J. S. Bruner (Ed.), *Contemporary approaches to cognition.* Cambridge, MA: Harvard University Press.

Paivio, A. (1971). *Imagery and verbal processes.* New York: Holt.

Paivio, A. (1983). Strategies in language learning. In M. Pressley & J. R. Levin (Eds.), *Cognitive strategy research: Educational applications* (pp. 189–210). New York: Springer-Verlag.

Palincsar, A. S., & Brown, A. L. (1984). Reciprocal teaching of comprehension-fostering and monitoring activities. *Cognition and Instruction, 1*, 117–175.

Peters, E. E., & Levin, J. R. (1986). Effects of a mnemonic imagery strategy on good and poor readers' prose recall. *Reading Research Quarterly, 21*, 179–192.

Pressley, M. (1982). Elaboration and memory development. *Child Development, 53*, 296–309.

Pressley, M. (1985). More about Yōdai mnemonics: A commentary on Higbee and Kunihira. *Educational Psychologist, 20*, 69–72.

Pressley, M., & Levin, J. R. (in press). Elaborative learning strategies for the inefficient learner. In S. J. Ceci (Ed.), *Handbook of cognitive, social, and neurological aspects of learning disabilities.* Hillsdale, NJ: Erlbaum Associates.

Pressley, M., Borkowski, J. G., & Schneider, W. (in press). Good strategy users coordinate metacognition, strategy use, and knowledge. In R. Vasta & G. Whitehurst (Eds.), *Annals of child development* (Vol. 4). Greenwich, CT: JAI Press.

Pressley, M., Heisel, B. E., McCormick, C. B., & Nakamura, G. V. (1982). Memory strategy instruction with children. In C. J. Brainerd & M. Pressley (Eds.), *Progress in*

Cognitive development research: Verbal processes in children (Vol. 2, pp. 125–160). New York: Springer-Verlag.

Pressley, M., Johnson, C. J., & Symons, S. (in press). Elaborating to learn and learning to elaborate. *Journal of Learning Disabilities.*

Pressley, M., Levin, J. R., & Delaney, H. D. (1982). The mnemonic keyword method. *Review of Educational Research, 52,* 61–91.

Pressley, M., Levin, J. R., & McDaniel, M. A. (in press). Remembering versus inferring what a word means: Mnemonic and contextual approaches. In M. G. Mckeown & M. E. Curtis (Eds.), *The nature of vocabulary acquisition.* Hillsdale, NJ: Erlbaum Associates.

Pressley, M., Levin, J. R., & Miller, G. E. (1981). How does the keyword affect vocabulary comprehension and usage? *Reading Research Quarterly, 16,* 213–226.

Rohwer, W. D., Jr. (1968). Mental mnemonics in early learning. *Teachers College Record, 70,* 213–226.

Rohwer, W. D., Jr. (1973). Elaboration and learning in childhood and adolescence. In H. W. Reese (Ed.), *Advances in child development and behavior* (Vol. 8, pp, 1–57). New York: Academic Press.

Scruggs, T. E., Mastropieri, M. A., & Levin, J. R. (1985b). Vocabulary acquisition of retarded students under direct and mnemonic instruction. *American Journal of Mental Deficiency, 89,* 546–551.

Scruggs, T. E., Mastropieri, M. A., Levin, J. R., & Gaffney, J. S. (1985a). Facilitating the acquisition of science facts in learning disabled students. *American Educational Research Journal, 22,* 575–586.

Scruggs, T. E., Mastropieri, M. A., Levin, J. R., McLoone, B. B., Gaffney, J. S., & Prater, M. (1985c). Increasing content area learning: A comparison of mnemonic and visual-spatial direct instruction. *Learning Disabilities Research, 1,* 18–31.

Scruggs, T. E., Mastropieri, M. A., McLoone, B., Levin, J. R., & Morrison, C. R. (in press). Mnemonic facilitation of text-embedded science facts with LD students. *Journal of Educational Psychology.*

Stein, C. L'E., & Goldman, J. (1980). Beginning reading instruction for children with minimal brain dysfunction. *Journal of Learning Disabilities, 13,* 52–55.

Taylor, S. C. (1981). *The keyword mnemonic method for teaching vocabulary: Its use by learning disabled children with memory difficulties.* Unpublished doctoral dissertation, Oklahoma State University, Stillwater, OK.

Taylor, A. M., & Turnure, J. E. (1979). Imagery and verbal elaboration with retarded children: Effects on learning and memory. In N. R. Ellis (Ed.), *Handbook of mental deficiency, psychological theory, and research* (pp. 659–697). Hillsdale, NJ: Erlbaum Associates.

Torgesen, J. (1982). The learning disabled child as an inactive learner: Educational implications. *Topics in Learning and Learning Disabilities, 2*(1), 45–52.

Torgesen, J. K., & Goldman, T. (1977). Verbal rehearsal and short-term memory in reading-disabled children. *Child Development, 48,* 56–60.

Torgesen, J., & Kail, R. V., Jr. (1980). Memory processes in exceptional children. In B. K. Keogh (Ed.), *Advances in special education* (Vol. 1, pp. 59–99). Greenwich, CT: JAI Press.

Torgesen, J. K., Murphy, H., & Ivey, C. (1979). The effects of an orienting task on the memory performance of reading disabled children. *Journal of Learning Disabilities, 12,* 396–401.

Mastropieri, Thomas E. Scruggs, and Joel R. Levin

_. E., & Mastropieri, M. A. (1986). Extended mnemonic instruction
isabled students. *Journal of Educational Psychology, 78,* 300–308.
(1974). Learning as a generative process. *Educational Psychologist, 11,*

& Jones, W. (1981). Increasing meta comprehension in learning disabled and
achieving students through self-questioning training. *Learning Disability*
ly, 5, 228–240.

Word, P. E. (1983). Memory strategy instruction with the learning disabled. In M.
Pressley & J. R. Levin (Eds.), *Cognitive strategy research: Psychological foundations*
(pp. 129–153). New York: Springer-Verlag.

CHAPTER 17

Explorations in Mnemonic Training

Jack Snowman

The use of mental imagery and mnemonic devices as aids to information encoding and retrieval has been promoted by orators, teachers, and mnemonists for at least the past 2000 years (a comprehensive account of the history of mnemonic devices is given by Yates, 1966; a discussion of the nature of mnemonic devices is offered by Bellezza elsewhere in this volume; examples of mnemonic use in everyday contemporary life can be found in Furst, 1972 and Baddeley, 1976). Until recently, these claims were not widely accepted by the scientific community because the evidence on which they were based was largely anecdotal. That is no longer the case. As the other chapters in this volume make clear, controlled experimental studies conducted over the past 20 years have substantiated the general claim that imagery and mnemonics facilitate the learning and recall of specific items of information and that these techniques can be taught to many types of people.

While the ability to store facts and details in memory and accurately retrieve them at some later date is a necessary academic skill (e.g., for memorizing and recalling names, dates, accomplishments, formulas, the meaning of foreign language vocabulary), it does have its limits. As students move from the early elementary grades to the junior high and high school grades, more of the material to be learned takes the form of increasingly complex prose and more of the teacher's objectives stress the comprehension, analysis, and synthesis of main or general ideas. Thus, students need to employ learning strategies that make it easier to identify and learn both the factual details (often called micropropositions or lower order ideas in the prose-learning literature) and main ideas (also called macropropositions or higher order ideas) that are embedded in prose materials.

On the surface, the solution to this problem may seem obvious and straightforward: teach students to use mnemonic devices that will aid in the learning and recall of both types of ideas. Although such an approach may work for relatively concrete and simply structured passages (see Levin, McCormick, & Dretzke, 1981; McCormick & Levin, Chapter 18, this volume; Shriberg, Levin, McCormick, & Pressley, 1982), it is not likely to generalize to more complex and abstract passages. Levin (1982) has argued that most prose passages differ from those used in the Levin et al. (1981) and Shriberg et al. (1982) studies in at least three ways. First, relevant prior knowledge is more likely to be used to understand the new information. Second, in comparison to micropropositions, macropropositions are usually stated at a higher level of abstraction. Third, in comparison to micropropositions, macropropositions are likely to be associated with a greater number of interpropositional connections. The third issue is seen by Levin (1982) as particularly troublesome. He doubts that one or more mnemonic systems can be combined to represent both passage content and structure. On the other hand, nonmnemonic systems that identify the various types of ideas in a passage (e.g., general topic, topic areas, facts, details) and the ways in which those ideas relate to one another (e.g., A causes B, A occurs before B, A is an example of B), may be more effective in aiding comprehension of passage content and structure (e.g., Dansereau, 1978; Meyer, 1975). A more effective strategy, then, for learning both the micro- and the macrocomponents of prose may be to combine mnemonic and nonmnemonic systems. In the first two sections of this chapter I describe some preliminary steps that my associates and I have taken to evaluate the effectiveness of a mnemonic–nonmnemonic prose-learning strategy. The last section discusses research on mnemonic transfer.

A Preliminary Study of Mnemonic–Nonmnemonic Strategy Use

Our initial attempt at training undergraduates to use a mnemonic–nonmnemonic prose-learning strategy (Krebs, Snowman, & Smith, 1978) grew out of several concerns. Despite the impressive results of mnemonic studies that appeared in the literature during the late 1960s and the 1970s, the modal task involved the learning and recall of lists of discrete items of information (e.g., Bower & Clark, 1969; Cunningham & Snowman, 1975; Levin, Davidson, Wolff, & Citron, 1973). A reason frequently given for using lists of words or nonsense syllables is that learning processes can be studied more clearly with simply structured and easily controlled stimuli (Meyer, 1975). Whereas this argument does have some validity, it also has several drawbacks when prose learning is the task of interest. For one, learning principles found with word lists (e.g., serial position effect) are not always found with prose. Second, prose contains an organizational structure designed to deliver a message. Such is not the case with word lists. Third, prose is the primary medium through which information is transmitted in classroom settings. Therefore, much of the mnemonics research has lacked what is termed "ecological validity" (Bracht & Glass, 1968; Neisser, 1976).

Given that mnemonic use enhances the learning and recall of information, that mnemonic use can be taught, and that much of what is learned in school is gleaned from the reading of or listening to prose, it appeared to us that the time was right to try to train students in the application of a mnemonic–nonmnemonic prose-learning strategy. The strategy we decided upon was a combination of the method of loci mnemonic and a simple scheme for parsing prose into main ideas and supporting details. The method of loci (also called the "place method" because "loci" means "places") was chosen for three reasons. First, it is an old and widely used memory device that has been used to learn and recall complex forms of information. Although the story may be apocryphal, the Greek poet Simonides (556–468 B.C.) was reported to have been the first to use the method of loci to identify the bodies of victims of a disaster that occurred during a feast. Regardless of its origin, there are written accounts of how the device was used by the ancient Greeks to learn and remember lengthy speeches (Yates, 1966). We felt that a mnemonic that could be used to remember a speech (which is oral prose) could just as easily be used to remember written prose. Second, recent research has corroborated early claims of the mnemonic's effectiveness (e.g., Cubberly, Weinstein, & Wicker, 1977; Groninger, 1971; Montague & Carter, 1974; Ross & Lawrence, 1968). Third, the method of loci contains all of the basic elements that make for an effective mnemonic. Bellezza (1981) has defined a mnemonic device as a strategy that creates and uses a cognitive cuing structure in order to organize and/or encode information for the sole purpose of making it more memorable. The loci technique, through the use of mental imagery and memory locations, aids the encoding and organization of information.

The basic rules for using the method of loci are straightforward and, with some practice, easy to implement. The first step is to visualize and commit to memory a series of places or loci that are well known to the learner (for example, the rooms of one's house or buildings on campus). The loci should be arranged in a particular sequence so that recall can proceed in either a forward or a backward direction. The next step is to generate visual images of the things to be remembered. Third, place these images at particular points within each locus (the first item is placed on the piano in the living room, for example). Finally, at the time of recall mentally walk from one location to the next, retrieving and decoding the information that was deposited there previously. Additional rules specify the choice of loci and the conditions that make for effective loci. Because the loci technique requires the incoming information to be organized in a list format, we had to find a method by which students could identify the various ideas mentioned in prose passages. Work that had recently been done by Bonnie Meyer (1975) in text organization suggested a possibility.

Meyer (1975) devised a method of prose analysis that requires the user first to identify the main idea in a paragraph and then note other ideas that provide additional, more specific information. These ideas are arranged in outline form from top to bottom and left to right. General or superordinate ideas are located toward the top and left of the outline, and the specific or subordinate ideas are placed toward the right and bottom. The result is a hierarchical structure of the ideas in the passage. In addition, a total of 27 labels, divided between role relationships and rhetorical predicates, are provided in order to classify the relationships among the ideas.

Although the technique transforms prose into a structure amenable to mnemonic encoding, and provides a basis for calculating the quantity and type of information recalled, it would require an extensive amount of time for students to organize prose materials in this manner and would probably not be very practical. Instead, some sort of simplified system seemed to be called for. Meyer (1977), herself, has suggested that "a simplification of the structure of prose may be a valuable pedagogical tool in helping a child visually comprehend the relationships among ideas in prose . . . ."

We decided upon a four-level hierarchical outline comprised of topic, area, characteristic, and example. These ideas would be arrayed from top to bottom and left to right. The combination of prose analysis and method of loci would then provide a systematic and integrated means of identifying, encoding, storing, and retrieving information from prose.

The topic was defined as the subject or main idea of the section of prose being analyzed. It can be a chapter heading, subheading, or lead sentence in a paragraph and relates to who or what is being discussed. The area represents the scope, range, or extent of coverage of the topic. It can be thought of as a major or key point of a topic. The characteristic is a distinguishing feature, quality, or trait of an area. An example illustrates a characteristic with a typical instance and is the most concrete and specific idea to be found in a passage. Figure 17.1 presents a typical reading sample and analysis.

Our first study of the mnemonic/nonmnemonic system described above was conducted with seven undergraduates as part of a study skills course and was basically a pilot study (Krebs et al., 1978). We met with the students once a week for 2 h each time. During the first session they were given a 1500-word passage taken from a psychology text and told to study the material in their usual manner. This meant they were free to underline, take notes, or do anything else they normally do while studying. After a filled retention interval of several minutes they were asked to write down as much as they could recall of the material they had just read. After 2 and 4 weeks had elapsed, the students were again asked, with no forewarning, to recall as much information as they could from this passage.

During the first training session (week 2), the students were given a short lecture on the organization of textbook material and practice in scanning passages for the central topic and accompanying information units. Short passages were outlined by the students, and each student was given immediate corrective feedback and additional practice paragraphs. In the second hour of the session the students were introduced to the method of loci by a lecture that explained its use and summarized supporting research. This was followed by a demonstration of the technique and practice with the outlines generated during the first hour. Students were required to construct their own lists of loci. The next two training sessions followed the same format. A new passage and recall test were administered during the fourth week. As with the initial passage, this was followed by 2-week and 4-week delayed-recall tests. Students were instructed to use the prose analysis method.

Although we expected the students to improve from their baseline performance of the first week, the magnitude of the change took us quite by surprise. Using their typical study methods, the students correctly recalled an average of 23% of the information units from the initial passage on the immediate free-recall test. Scores ranged from a low of 15 to a high of 35%. The 2-week delayed

The Ice Sheet

Glaciers are important in some areas, but hold only a small portion of the world's water and only a small part of the total volume of the world's ice.

The Greenland icecap, is a very different matter. It is thousands of square miles in area and nearly 5000 feet thick. If melted it would yield enough water to keep the Mississippi River flowing for thousands of years. The greatest single item in the water budget of the world, aside from the ocean itself, is the Antarctic ice sheet.

Since the advent of the International Geophysical Year 1957, much information has been gathered about Antarctica. Data on the thickness of the ice sheet is hard to find, but there is enough data to allow an estimate. The area of the ice sheet is about six million square miles.

Topic	Area	Characteristic	Example
The Ice Sheet	Glaciers	Important but = small % of world's H_1O and ice	
	Greenland Ice Cap	Larger than glaciers	Thousands of sq. miles 5000 ft. thick Holds enough H_1O to keep Mississippi River flowing for thousands of years 10% of all icecaps & glaciers
	Antarctic Ice Sheet	Data gathered on Antarctica since IGY 1957	
		Largest single item in the H_1O budget except for the oceans	About 6 million square miles

FIGURE 17.1. Sample passage and prose analysis.

recall yielded a mean of 13%, with scores ranging from 6 to 27%. The 4-week delayed recall yielded a mean of 10%, with scores ranging form 6 to 16%. By contrast, recall scores from the final reading passage after 3 weeks of training for immediate, 2-week delayed, and 4-week delayed recall were 75, 83, and 84%, respectively.

These data were also subjected to a 2 × 3 within-subjects analysis of variance. The finding of most interest was a significant Strategy × Test interaction. A simple main effects analysis of this interaction showed a significant ($p < .05$) decrease in recall over 2 and 4 weeks when subjects used their typical study methods and a nonsignificant increase in recall over the same time periods when the prose analysis–method of loci technique was used. In addition, the differences between typical study methods and the prose analysis–loci strategy for immediate, 2-week delayed, and 4-week delayed recall were all highly significant.

Given the magnitude of the results, we decided to conduct another study with a larger and more representative sample of students. Besides wanting to see whether we could obtain similar results, we also wanted to evaluate the independent and combined effects of the method of loci mnemonic and the prose analysis techniques.

A Second Mnemonic–Nonmnemonic Training Study

To recruit subjects for this study (Snowman, Krebs, & Kelly, 1980) a 15-week, 2 credit-hour course in memory improvement skills was offered. Ninety-six undergraduates, 55 females and 41 males, enrolled in the course. In terms of major area of study, year in school, and achievement level, it was a very diverse group. Grade-point averages, for example, ranged from almost nonexistent (.50) to perfect (4.0).

Prior to training, all subjects were given a group-mental ability test. Following this, each subject was given a reading passage of about 1600 words and told to read it using whatever reading behaviors were typical. After a rehearsal-preventing task, the subjects were asked to write down as much of the passage as they could recall.

Subjects were then randomly assigned to and trained in one of the following techniques: method of loci (L), prose analysis (PA), prose analysis and loci (PA+L), or loci and prose analysis (L+PA). During the third and fifth weeks, all subjects were unexpectedly asked to freely recall the initial reading passage. During the sixth week, a second test passage was given with instructions to use the strategy being taught. As before, 2- and 4-week unannounced delayed recalls were conducted. During the eleventh week a third and final test passage was given, with recall taken immediately, 2 weeks later, and 4 weeks later. Altogether, there were nine training sessions, each 50 min long.

For the loci group, weeks 2 and 3 were devoted to visual imagery training. Subjects were first given a brief lecture about the history and effectiveness of visual imagery in learning. The instructor then demonstrated how images could be formulated for a brief list of concrete nouns. Subjects were provided with lists of concrete nouns of varying length, studied them for several minutes, and practiced recall. During the latter part of week 3 and for all of week 4, subjects practiced the method of loci on the remaining word lists. For weeks 5–10, the method of loci was practiced on various reading passages.

The prose analysis group began with a brief lecture on recent prose analysis research and an explanation of superordinate–subordinate relationships. Rules for conducting a prose analysis were discussed and several demonstrations were provided. Weeks 4–10 were devoted to practice and corrective feedback.

The prose analysis+loci group received imagery training for weeks 2 and 3 using the materials and procedures described above. Prose analysis was introduced during week 4 and practiced through week 7 in combination with visual imagery. In other words, subjects were given practice passages, conducted a prose analysis, and attempted to encode each set of prose idea units (i.e., topic, area, characteristic, example) as an integrated image. During weeks 8–10, the method of loci was introduced and added on to the above, providing subjects with a systematic means of storing and retrieving their images.

The loci+prose analysis group received essentially the same training as the PA+L group except for the obvious order difference.

A strategy (L, PA, PA+L, L+PA) × Ability (high, low) × Passage (first, second, third) × Recall (immediate, 2-week delayed, 4-week delayed) analysis of variance was conducted on the percentage of idea units correctly recalled. The two most interesting results were the Strategy × Passage interaction and the Strategy × Recall interaction.

The Strategy × Passage interaction (see Figure 17.2) revealed no differences between the groups for recall of passage 1 material. On passage 2, however, the PA and PA+L groups recalled more information than the L or L+PA groups. Finally, on passage 3, the PA+L group outscored the other three groups. The PA and L+PA groups did not differ from each other, although both exceeded the L group. In addition, the PA and L groups improved their recall only from passage 1 to passage 2, whereas the PA+L and L+PA groups improved across all three passages.

The Strategy × Recall interaction showed that the PA, PA+L, and L+PA groups all outperformed the L group on immediate recall while not differing

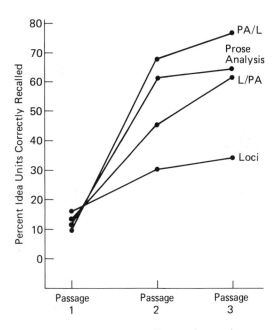

FIGURE 17.2. Strategy × Passage interaction.

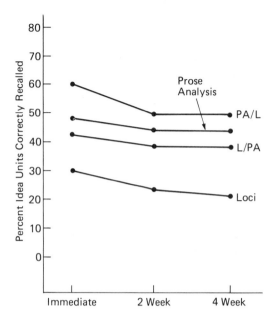

FIGURE 17.3. Strategy × Recall interaction.

among themselves (see Figure 17.3). For 2- and 4-week delayed recall the pattern was similar except that the PA+L group recalled significantly more than the L+PA group.

Discussion

The results of the previous two studies appear to support the contention that training students in the use of a mnemonic–nonmnemonic strategy leads to better retention of prose information than training students in either strategy alone. The results also indicated that the single most important component was the prose analysis training. For the PA and PA+L groups the bulk of the improvement occurred from passage 1 to passage 2. At this point the PA+L group was trained in the method of loci and how to combine that with the prose analysis technique. The PA group continued to receive practice and feedback in prose analysis. As Figure 17.2 shows, the PA+L group showed an additional increase in performance from passage 2 to passage 3 but not nearly of the same magnitude as occurred between passages one and two. In addition, the L+PA group showed almost as much of an improvement from passages 2 to 3 as from passage 1 to 2.

The relative weakness of the loci-only group might seem surprising given the favorable results reported in other studies (e.g., Groninger, 1971; Montague & Carter, 1974). These results, however, typically were obtained with lists of concrete words. The prose passages used in our studies contained some abstract terms as well as complex internal structures. The superiority of the PA+L group over the L group with these materials was probably because the prose analysis scheme transformed the passages into a listlike structure, a form tailor made for the loci mnemonic.

Lastly, the training had beneficial effects on delayed recall. In particular, the PA and PA+L groups experienced very little forgetting in comparison to their initial levels of recall.

In summary, these results seem to suggest that college students (and possibly high school students) can be taught to use a mnemonic–nonmnemonic strategy to remember more information from prose passages than would be likely with either a purely mnemonic system or a purely nonmnemonic system. We think that training of this sort should begin with simple, easily learned tasks and gradually progress to more complex tasks involving larger amounts of information over a period of several months.

Notice, however, that we have offered a qualified conclusion. As stated earlier, this research was seen as being little more than a preliminary step in the investigation of mnemonic–nonmnemonic strategies. There are many questions that remain to be answered. For example, would the same result be obtained with other types of criterion measures? Cued recall, recognition, and comprehension are three that deserve a look. Would a placebo control group do as well as any of the treatment groups? It is quite possible that some portion of the improvement noted in each of the four groups arose from the enthusiasm of the instructor for the treatments. Would the same results be obtained with a more representative sample of subjects? There is little doubt that our subjects were different, at least in terms of motivation, from the student population in general. They did, after all, sign up for and participate in a voluntary course on memory improvement. Perhaps the success of cognitive skill training depends on the presence of a higher than average level of motivation. Finally, and perhaps most importantly, will students spontaneously and appropriately use these skills in the future when they are confronted with prose-learning tasks? Given the obvious improvement in prose recall that occurred, one would think so. The issue of transfer, however, is sufficiently complex that more than just skill training is required. To conclude this chapter, then, I shall discuss a recent study I participated in (White & Snowman, 1985) that attempted to enhance strategy transfer.

Enhancing Memory Strategy Transfer

Despite the dramatic effect of mnemonics on retention, only a modest number of mnemonic training studies have produced transfer. Recent research suggests that strategy training is unlikely to produce maintenance (i.e., subsequent, unprompted strategy use on a task similar to the training task) or generalization (i.e., subsequent, unprompted strategy use on a task different from the training task), particularly among school-age children, unless it includes relevant metacognitive knowledge (such as pointing out a mnemonic's diverse applications and benefits). When learners are given feedback regarding a strategy's effectiveness, for example, they are more likely to maintain the strategy than if no such feedback has been given (e.g., Kennedy & Miller, 1976; Paris, Newman, & McVey, 1982; Ringel & Springer, 1980). The effect of effectiveness feedback on generalization, however, has been generally disappointing (e.g., Borkowski, Levers, & Gruenenfelder, 1976; O'Sullivan & Pressley, 1984).

One possible reason that effectiveness feedback enhances maintenance but not generalization is because the feedback answers the metacognitive question, "Why use this strategy?" but neglects the equally important question, "When should this strategy be used?" That is, effectiveness feedback teaches the value of a mnemonic but it does not help subjects identify the contexts in which the strategy may subsequently be used. To enhance generalization, we conducted a training program that focused on teaching students when to use a mnemonic strategy as well as why it should be used.

Subjects

Fifty-six sixth-grade students attending a midwestern elementary school served as subjects. Data from eight subjects were eliminated from the final analyses for the following reasons: two subjects were dropped midway through the training program because of noncompliance with directions; three subjects were absent when the criterion data were collected; three randomly selected subjects were deleted in order to equate cell sizes. The final analysis involved 48 subjects, 28 males and 20 females, all of whom were enrolled in the school's regular academic program. All subjects were randomly assigned to one of four mnemonic training programs.

Materials

For this study, two mnemonics were taught. Providing subjects with a choice between two mnemonics was considered one way to assess their ability to know when to use each device appropriately. The keyword and pegword mnemonics were chosen because they are considered to aid the retention of different types of material (Bellezza, 1981).

Keyword materials for training and maintenance consisted of people's names and associated bits of biographical information (name–fact). Keyword materials for the generalization task were medical terms and their definitions. Pegword materials for training and maintenance were lists of person's names (name list), and generalization materials were recipe ingredients. The maintenance and generalization tasks were given 1 and 5 weeks after the final training session.

Procedure

The training procedures used in this study were carried out over a period of 13 consecutive days. On the first day the students were told that they would be taught some methods of remembering called mnemonics and that they would be given a memory test. All subjects were then given a modified version of the Kreutzer,

Leonard, and Flavell (1975) metamemory questionnaire. On the following day, a 15-item name–fact test (keyword pretest) and a 15-item name list test (pegword pretest) were administered. On day 3 the students were given a brief lecture about the history and effectiveness of mnemonics. The experimenter then demonstrated how the name–fact and name list materials could have been remembered using the keyword and pegword mnemonics.

For the next 11 days, subjects practiced the keyword and pegword mnemonics according to the conditions established for each condition. The general, daily training procedures consisted of: (1) the experimenter returning and discussing the previous day's quiz and supplying new directions; (2) the students performing a mnemonic activity (e.g., working from name–fact and name list material, the students try to think of a keyword or pegword that matches the one selected by the experimenter); (3) the experimenter circulating to help individual students; (4) the experimenter asking certain students to share their mnemonic with the class; and (5) quiz administration. The main reason for including so many sessions and opportunities for practice was to insure that both types of mnemonics were well learned.

For the mnemonic control group (group 1), training sessions were devoted exclusively to keyword training on name–fact material and pegword training on name list material.

Subjects in the feedback condition (group 2), in addition to mnemonic training, received feedback regarding their improved recall performance using the mnemonics. At the end of each training session a name–fact or name list test was given. On these tests subjects were encouraged to use the appropriate mnemonic to remember the material. Beginning on day 8, and continuing through day 11, feedback subjects were given their test scores. It was pointed out how much their recall performance had improved from day 2 when they had used their usual tactics. In only a few instances was a mnemonic test score equal to or lower than the pretest scores. In these cases the student was told, "You went down on this one but keep trying to use the mnemonic and your scores will get higher."

In addition to the standard mnemonic training, subjects in the generalization condition (group 3) received training on the appropriateness of the two mnemonics for material besides name–fact and name list. This training occurred on the final two days of the training program. Subjects discussed the similarity of pegword-appropriate tasks and keyword-appropriate tasks and formulated rules for the appropriate use of each type (e.g., the pegword is good for tying together a list of items; the keyword is good for tying something that we do not know, such as a name or a word, to something about it, such as what that person did or what the word means). Generalization subjects also completed exercises requiring them to classify learning situations as mnemonic appropriate or mnemonic inappropriate. For example, "Andrea's class is going on a field trip to the zoo. Her teacher says they will get extra points if they remember the names of the animals that they see" (pegword appropriate).

Group 4 received the standard mnemonic training provided to groups 1, 2, and 3; the feedback on mnemonic effectiveness provided to group 2; and the generalization training provided to group 3.

Transfer Tasks

The transfer tasks occurred 1 and 5 weeks after the final training sessions. Each transfer session ran for 2 d and involved four transfer tasks (keyword maintenance and generalization, pegword maintenance and generalization). Subjects were not forewarned of the transfer sessions, and during these sessions no mention was made of the previous training program or the two mnemonics. Mnemonic use was inferred by requiring students to write next to each item recalled a description of the technique that was used to recall that item. If a student simply indicated that the pegword mnemonic was used, he or she was asked to furnish the pegword as well as the image that was used. If the information could not be provided, the student's response was not credited. Strategy descriptions were scored by two judges blind to group membership. Interrater reliability was quite high ($r = .93$).

Results

A Group $\times$ Mnemonic $\times$ Transfer task $\times$ Test time analysis of covariance was conducted on the number of mnemonics used and the probability of correctly recalling material with a mnemonic. Metamemory knowledge and mnemonic proficiency were used as covariates. There were two noteworthy findings.

First, there was little evidence that degree of mnemonic use increased as a function of training. This finding was consistent across mnemonic task (pegword vs. keyword), transfer task (maintenance vs. generalization), and test time (1 week vs. 5 weeks). A significant interaction involving training group, transfer task, and test time, however, indicated that mnemonic use on maintenance tasks remained stable through week 5 for subjects receiving effectiveness feedback, whereas mnemonic use on generalization tasks remained stable through week 5 for subjects receiving generalization feedback.

The lack of a more positive effect for effectiveness feedback may seem surprising given the results reported in other studies (e.g., Kennedy & Miller, 1976; Paris et al., 1982; Pressley, Levin, & Ghatala, 1984). However, those results typically were obtained over maintenance periods ranging from a few minutes to a few days. When effectiveness feedback has been shown to enhance longer term mnemonic maintenance (e.g., Borkowski et al., 1976), the strategy was simple rehearsal. The results of this study therefore raise some doubt about the potency of effectiveness feedback over extended maintenance periods, particularly when complex and multiple mnemonics are used.

Despite the fact that increases in mnemonic use were not observed, positive findings on recall probability were noted. Subjects in the feedback plus generalization group were more likely to correctly recall mateial when they used a mnemonic than were subjects in the other three groups (see Figure 17.4). Also, effectiveness feedback plus generalization training produced more effective use of mnemonics (i.e., fewer recall failures with mnemonic use) despite the fact that it did not affect the overall number of mnemonics used. It may have been the case that, whereas children in all four groups realized the utility and appropriateness

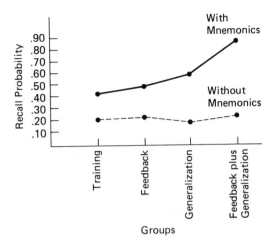

FIGURE 17.4. Mean conditional recall probabilities with and without mnemonics.

of mnemonic use, specific training in these areas allowed feedback plus generalization subjects to focus more of their attention on developing effective mnemonics and spend less time trying to determine whether a mnemonic should be used and, if so, which one. Finally, there was less variability among the groups when mnemonics were not used. This pattern was consistent across mnemonic task, transfer task, and test time.

Conclusion

The findings from the three studies discussed in this chapter suggest at least two things. First, it may be possible to teach subjects who are at least of high school age a combined mnemonic–nonmnemonic strategy for recalling both the micropropositions and macropropositions of prose passages. Second, when mnemonic training is combined with feedback about mnemonic effectiveness and appropriateness, subjects, particularly elementary school-age children, are more likely to maintain mnemonic use on transfer tasks over several weeks time and exhibit more accurate recall when mnemonics are used than when such feedback is not provided.

To be sure, these results and those of other researchers working in the same areas have both theoretical and practical significance. They should, however, be viewed against some larger backdrop in order to gain a perspective on them. Thus, I would argue that this research represents significant but small and somewhat fragmented increments in our knowledge of how to enhance mnemonic use. Following the tetrahedral model of learning proposed by Jenkins (1979) and elaborated by Bransford (1979), considerable additional research needs to be done to delineate the independent and combined effects of learner characteristics (e.g., motives, metacognitive knowledge, learning styles), task characteristics (e.g., amount and type of material to be learned), and learner activities (e.g., mnemonics, imagery, prose analysis) on various measures of cognitive performance (e.g., verbatim recall, comprehension, discrimination, concept formation). When viewed from this perspective, it is, I believe, fair to state that research on mnemonic training and use has only just begun.

References

Baddeley, A. D. (1976). *The psychology of memory.* New York: Basic Books.

Bellezza, F. S. (1981). Mnemonic devices: Classification, characteristics, and criteria. *Review of Educational Research, 51,* 247-275.

Borkowski, J., Levers, S., & Gruenenfelder, T. (1976). Transfer of mediational strategies in children: The role of activity and awareness during strategy acquisition. *Child Development, 47,* 779-786.

Bower, G. H., & Clark, M. C. (1969). Narrative stories as mediators for serial learning. *Psychomomic Science, 14,* 181-182.

Bracht, G. H., & Glass, G. V. (1968). The external validity of experiments. *American Educational Research Journal, 5,* 437-474.

Bransford, J. D. (1979). *Human cognition: Learning, understanding, and remembering.* Belmont, CA: Wadsworth.

Cubberly, W. E., Weinstein, C. E., & Wicker, F. (1977). *Training versus instructions in elaborated and non-elaborated versions of the method of loci.* Paper presented at the annual meeting of the American Educational Research Association, April 4-8, New York.

Cunningham, D. J., & Snowman, J. (1975). *Imagery and narrative stories as mediators for one trial serial and free recall list learning.* Paper presented at the annual meeting of the American Educational Research Association, March 30-April 3, Washington, DC.

Dansereau, D. F. (1978). The development of a learning strategies curriculum. In H. H. O'Neill (Ed.), *Learning strategies.* New York: Academic Press.

Furst, B. (1972). *Stop forgetting.* Garden City, NY: Doubleday.

Groninger, K. D. (1971). Mnemonic imagery and forgetting. *Psychonomic Science, 23,* 161-163.

Jenkins, J. J. (1979). Four points to remember: A tetrahedral model of memory experiments. In L. S. Cermak & F. I. M. Craik (Eds.), *Levels of processing in human memory.* Hillsdale, NJ: Erlbaum Associates.

Kennedy, B., & Miller, D. (1976). Persistent use of verbal rehearsal as a function of information about its value. *Child Development, 47,* 566-569.

Krebs, E. W., Snowman, J., & Smith, S. H. (1978). Teaching new dogs old tricks: Facilitating prose learning through mnemonic training. *Journal of Instructional Psychology, 5,* 33-39.

Kreutzer, M., Leonard, C., & Flavell, J. (1975). An interview study of children's knowledge about memory. *Monographs of The Society for Research in Child Development, 40*(1, Serial No. 159).

Levin, J. R. (1982). Pictures as prose learning devices. In A. Flammer & W. Kintsch (Eds.), *Advances in psychology: Vol. 8. Discourse processing.* Amsterdam: North-Holland Publishing Co.

Levin, J. R., Davidson, R. E., Wolff, P., & Citron, M. (1973). A comparison of induced imagery and sentence strategies in children's paired-associate learning. *Journal of Educational Psychology, 64*, 306–309.

Levin, J. R., McCormick, C. B., & Dretzke, B. J. (1981). A combined pictorial mnemonic strategy for ordered information. *Educational Communications and Technology Journal, 29*, 219–226.

Meyer, B. J. F. (1975). *The organization of prose and its effects on memory.* Amsterdam: North-Holland Publishing Co.

Meyer, B. J. F. (1977). The structure of prose: Effects of learning and memory and implications for educational practice. In R. C. Anderson, R. J. Spiro, & W. E. Montague (Eds.), *Schooling and the acquisition of knowledge.* Hillsdale, NJ: Erlbaum Associates.

Montague, W. E., & Carter, J. (1974). *The loci mnemonic technique in learning and memory.* Paper presented at the annual meeting of the American Educational Research Association, April 15–19, Chicago.

Neisser, U. (1976). *Cognition and reality.* San Francisco: W. H. Freeman.

O'Sullivan, J. T., & Pressley, M. (1984). Completeness of instruction and strategy transfer. *Journal of Experimental Child Psychology, 38*, 275–288.

Paris, S., Newman, R., & McVey, K. (1982). Learning the functional significance of mnemonic actions: A microgenetic study of strategy acquisition. *Journal of Experimental Child Psychology, 34*, 490–509.

Pressley, M., Levin, J. R., & Ghatala, E. (1984). Memory strategy monitoring in adults and children. *Journal of Verbal Learning and Verbal Behavior, 23*, 270–288.

Ringel, B. A., & Springer, C. J. (1980). On knowing how well one is remembering: The persistence of strategy use during transfer. *Journal of Experimental Child Psychology, 29*, 322–333.

Ross, J., & Lawrence, K. A. (1968). Some observations on memory artifice. *Psychonomic Society, 13*, 107–108.

Shriberg, L. K., Levin, J. R., McCormick, C. B., & Pressley, M. (1982). Learning about "famous" people via the keyword method. *Journal of Educational Psychology, 74*, 238–247.

Snowman, J., Krebs, E. W., & Kelly, F. J. (1980). *Enhancing memory for prose through learning strategy training.* Paper presented at the annual meeting of the American Educational Research Association, April 7–11, Boston.

White, M., & Snowman, J. (1985). *Learning to remember: A memory-directed strategy that transfers.* Paper presented at the annual meeting of the American Educational Research Association, March 31–April 4, Chicago.

Yates, F. A. (1966). *The art of memory.* London: Routledge & Kegan Paul.

CHAPTER 18

Mnemonic Prose-Learning Strategies

Christine B. McCormick and Joel R. Levin

The impressive number and quality of chapters represented by this volume testifies both to the usefulness of mnemonic techniques and to the importance of conducting controlled research that continues to probe their "workings." From a theoretical standpoint, one can strive to account for the mechanisms associated with the operation of mnemonic strategies, which in turn will permit precise specifications of the conditions related to their effectiveness (see, for example, Bellezza, Chapter 2, this volume; Desrochers & Begg, Chapter 3, this volume). From an applied educational standpoint, one can strive to design and prescribe different varieties of mnemonic strategies for different varieties of classroom curricula and students (e.g., Levin, 1985; Mastropieri, Scruggs, & Levin, Chapter 16, this volume).

One thing about which we can be very certain from the 20-year accumulation of literature on mnemonic techniques (e.g., Bower, 1972; Paivio, 1971; Pressley, Levin, & Delaney, 1982; Rohwer, 1973) is that such techniques greatly enhance people's memory for discrete pieces of factual information. This conclusion follows from literally dozens of studies in which it has been found that lists of items or item sets (typically, although not always, common nouns) are much better remembered under mnemonic than under no-strategy control instructions. Thus, those who argue that mnemonic techniques are not beneficial appear to be disregarding a vast amount of empirical evidence to the contrary.

Although the documented benefits of mnemonic techniques are impressive, the educational significance of them is not immediately apparent. People are not generally asked to process and remember word lists per se. Perhaps the most frequently employed method of obtaining factual information is through the reading and studying of prose materials. The prose-learning situations differs from the list-learning situation in at least three important ways. First, the information to be acquired is embedded (and often must be discovered) within a broader prose context. Second, these pieces of information usually are presented not as discrete units, but in relation to one another. Third, in some prose passages the factual information is frequently organized around—and presented to support—some central theme. The purpose of this chapter is to review studies investigating the effectiveness of mnemonic strategies in a prose-learning context. The strengths and limitations of selected mnemonic strategies, along with directions for future research, will also be considered.

Mnemonic Prose-Learning Effects

In this section we review a number of empirical studies in which mnemonic strategies have been devised for remembering the contents of prose passages (for an earlier review, see Levin, 1982). We restrict our attention here to strategies that are truly "mnemonic" in that they incorporate the stimulus transformations and elaborations of popular mnemonic devices, such as the method of loci, the pegword method, the keyword method, etc. (see Bellezza, 1981; Levin, 1983; as well as the mnemonic examples and descriptions that we provide throughout this chapter). We do not consider a number of prose-learning strategies that are occasionally referred to as "mnemonic" in a generic "memory-enhancing" sense, including a wide variety of semantic-organizational processing activities (e.g., notetaking, question asking, paraphrasing, and summarizing) — activities that do not demand true mnemonic transformations and elaborations (see, for example, Snowman, in press; Weinstein & Mayer, 1985).

Preliminary Research "Demonstrations"

The suggestion that students apply mnemonic techniques to the study of connected discourse comes from a retrospective study by Gruneberg (1973). Graduates of a British university were asked (via a mail survey) to indicate the kinds of study strategies that they had routinely employed when reviewing material for course examinations. Over 30% of the respondents reported using mnemonic techniques at least "sometimes" (principally the "first-letter" mnemonic). In a subsequent study by Gruneberg and Monks (1974), over 50% of the graduates from a Scottish medical school similarly reported the use of mnemonic techniques.

More recently, Snowman and his colleagues (Krebs, Snowman, & Smith, 1978; Snowman, Krebs, & Kelly, 1980a; Snowman, Krebs, & Lockhart, 1980b; also see Snowman, Chapter 17, this volume) investigated the possibility of teaching mnemonic prose-learning strategies to college students. These studies are regarded as "demonstrations" here, owing to restrictions in randomization and experimental control that resulted from administering treatments within the context of an ongoing college course. In the Krebs et al. (1978) study, undergraduates who were enrolled in a 9-week course in study skills were taught how to analyze prose passages in terms of their superordinate "central ideas" and subordinate "information units." They were additionally instructed to generate corresponding visual images from both types of information, and to incorporate these images into mnemonic loci. Both immediate and 4-week delayed recall of passages read after mnemonic training increased substantially (more than 200 and 700%, respectively) over the recall exhibited on a similar passage studied using "typical study methods" prior to mnemonic training. Unfortunately it is difficult to draw meaningful conclusions from these results inasmuch as an independent control group was not included in the study. Moreover, a very small sample was employed—seven students in an intact classroom group.

The studies by Snowman et al. (1980a, 1980b) utilized more substantial sample sizes of 72 and 96 students, respectively. In the first study, the subjects were "high-risk" freshmen enrolled in a 14-week course designed to improve the students' reading comprehension. Experimental subjects were taught how to combine the mnemonic method of loci with an organizational text analysis strategy (e.g., Bartlett, 1978). Control subjects practiced using traditional reading comprehension strategies, including note taking and main idea identification. After 10 weeks of instruction, experimental subjects recalled more than twice as much posttest passage information than did controls (respective averages of 88 and 42%). Two factors that preclude unambiguous interpretation of the effect of mnemonic instruction, however, include possible reading-time differences between conditions (students were allowed to read at their own paces) and the fact that experimental subjects received their mnemonic instruction in the company of a text analysis strategy.

In an attempt to separate mnemonic and test analysis strategy effects, Snowman et al. (1980a) compared the two types of strategy instruction in the context of another study-skills course. They also included the combined mnemonic/text analysis strategy that was devised for the earlier Snowman et al. (1980b) study, although, as in the Krebs et al. (1980) study, a traditional-strategy control group was not included. Relative to their pretreatment performance, students displayed substantial prose recall gains following combined mnemonic/text analysis instruction. Interestingly, however, the benefits of mnemonic instruction alone were minimal, suggesting that the loci mnemonic as applied to students' free recall of text may not be a very effective strategy. At the same time and as will be seen in the following section, alternative mnemonic approaches have proved to be very substantial prose-learning facilitators.

Controlled Research Studies

Over the last 5 years, we and our colleagues have conducted a number of controlled investigations of mnemonic prose-learning strategies. The focal mnemonic technique of these investigations has consisted of adaptations and extensions of Atkinson's (1975) "keyword method" of foreign vocabulary learning (see also Desrochers & Begg, Chapter 3, this volume). To employ the keyword method in a vocabulary-learning context, one first transforms the unfamiliar vocabulary word (such as the Spanish *carta*, meaning "letter") into a more concrete, familiar, "keyword" (such as the English "cart"). Then the recorded word is connected to the definition via a meaningful pictorial or verbal elaboration (such as a shopping cart carrying a letter). When the foreign word (*carta*) is re-presented, the keyword proxy (cart) reevokes the previous elaboration (the shopping cart carrying the letter), which yields the desired definition (letter).

In our first mnemonic prose-learning study (Shriberg, Levin, McCormick, & Pressley, 1982), eighth graders were read a series of short (three-sentence) passages that described the purported accomplishments of fictitious people. Our keyword adaptation—described here in terms of Levin's (1983) "three R" terminology—consisted of recoding the "famous" person's name into a concrete keyword, relating the keyword to the person's accomplishment, and then subsequently retrieving the appropriate information from the direct path leading from the name to the keyword to the related accomplishment. Thus, to remember that Charlene McKune was famous for owning a counting cat, "McKune" could be "keyworded" as "raccoon," and then pictured in the context of a cat counting raccoons jumping over a fence (see Figure 18.1). When subsequently tested for name–accomplishment recall, the learner now has a systematic retrieval path leading from the person's name to his/her accomplishment: In this case, "McKune" leads directly to "raccoon," which leads to the picture of the cat counting raccoons, which produces the desired response, a counting cat. In each of the three experiments reported by Shriberg et al. (1982), students who applied this mnemonic strategy correctly remembered far more name–accomplishment information than did their non-strategy control counterparts.

There are now available several controlled investigations (representing more than two dozen individual experiments) of different mnemonic prose-learning variations and combinations. The majority of this research was conducted with secondary-school students (Goin, Peters, & Levin, 1986; Levin, Morrison, McGivern, Mastropieri, & Scruggs, 1986; Levin, Shriberg, & Berry, 1983; Morrison & Levin, 1986; Peters & Levin, 1986; Peters, Levin, McGivern, &

FIGURE 18.1. Example of a mnemonic prose-learning illustration. From "Learning about 'famous' people via the keyword method," by L. K. Shriberg, J. R. Levin, C. B. McCormick, and M. Pressley, 1982, *Journal of Educational Psychology, 74*, 238–247. Copyright 1982 by the American Psychological Association. Reprinted by permission of the author.

Pressley, 1985; Scruggs, Mastropieri, McLoone, Levin, & Morrison, 1985; Shriberg, 1982; Shriberg et al., 1982; Tolfa-Veit, Scruggs, & Mastropieri, 1986), with two studies conducted in a college student population (McCormick & Levin, 1984; McCormick, Levin, Cykowski, & Danilovics, 1984; McCormick, Levin, & Valkenaar, 1986). In most of the individual experiments, the learning advantages associated with mnemonic instruction have been impressive. In fact, in a recent metaanalytic review of the literature on prose-learning pictures, Levin, Anglin, and Carney (1987) noted that the average facilitation associated with mnemonic pictures (relative to no-strategy control conditions) amounted to more than 1.33 within-group standard deviation units. In the remainder of this chapter, we do not focus on positive mnemonic effects per se but instead consider a number of issues raised by the studies just cited.

Mnemonic Prose-Learning Issues

Variations in Instructional Procedures

Illustrations Versus Images

The study by Shriberg et al. (1982) is noteworthy not just because it was the first to adapt the mnemonic keyword method to a prose-learning situation, but also because it directly compared two different mnemonic-instructional variations. In experiment 2 of that investigation, mnemonic students were either provided with interactive mnemonic illustrations (as in Figure 18.1) or instructed to generate their own interactive mnemonic images. Although students in both mnemonic conditions recalled more critical name–accomplishment information that did no-strategy control students, mnemonic students who were provided with actual illustrations benefitted more (by about 40%) than did those who generated their own images.

The facilitative effect of mnemonic prose-learning illustrations has been documented in other content domains as well, including those in which students were asked to remember sets of relatively abstract attributes associated with fictitious towns (Levin et al., 1983; Shriberg, 1982) and several characteristics of North American minerals (Levin et al., 1986; Morrison & Levin, 1986; Scruggs et al., 1985). From a cost/efficiency perspective, however, it may not always be feasible to produce mnemonic illustrations for students' use. It therefore bears repeating that students who are taught how to generate their own mnemonic images also exhibit substantial prose-recall gains relative to control subjects (Shriberg et al., 1982). Moreover, the results of a recent study by Peters and Levin (1986) suggest that mnemonic-imagery instruction can improve the prose learning of junior high school students representing both above- and below-average levels of reading ability. (It should be noted, however, that in the Morrison and Levin, 1986, study, where eighth-grade students read a relatively complex science lesson on their own, experimenter-provided mnemonic illustrations were facilitative—relative to a no-strategy control condition—whereas subject-generated mnemonic imagery instructions were not.)

In a related vein, in their review of mnemonic vocabulary-learning research, Pressley et al. (1982) argue that subject-generated visual images are not as consistently facilitative of young children's performance as are experimenter-provided illustrations. In contrast, older children and adults have been found to benefit consistently from both experimenter-provided and self-generated mnemonic-imagery vocabulary-learning strategies. Although analogous mnemonic prose-learning studies have not been conducted with students younger than middle-school age, it is reasonable to assume that the same kind of developmental trend exists in the prose-learning situation as well. It should therefore be mentioned that we have devised a "compromise" pictorial mnemonic variation that has proved quite effective in facilitating secondary school students' prose recall (McCormick & Levin, 1984; McCormick et al., 1984, 1986). With this variation, students are instructed to generate their own mnemonic images in response to a scene described by the experimenter. In the case of Charlene McKune, for example, instead of either being provided with Figure 18.1 or being asked to create their own imaginal elaboration, students may be told to "imagine a cat counting raccoons that are jumping over a fence."

This "structured mnemonic imagery" variation benefits students' prose learning without the concomitant cost of having to produce actual illustrations. Moreover, because descriptions of the images to be generated are provided by the experimenter, greater experimenter control over the nature and quality of the mnemonic elaborations can be achieved. (Note that structured mnemonic imagery may be alternatively construed as a "sentence" or "verbal" mnemonic strategy, to the extent that students do not—or cannot—generate the described images.) It remains to be seen whether younger students, who may not benefit from a *completely* self-generated mnemonic prose-learning strategy, can effectively employ the structured mnemonic imagery variation.

Group Versus Individual Treatment Administration

Another important consideration for research on mnemonic prose-learning strategies is whether or not they can be adapted effectively to group-administered instruction. Given the inconsistency of results reported in studies of group-administered mnemonic vocabulary instruction (Levin & Pressley, 1985), it is encouraging to report that several studies have yielded positive effects of group-administered mnemonic prose-learning instruction by both secondary school and college students (Levin et al., 1983, 1986; McCormick & Levin, 1984; McCormick et al., 1984, 1986; Morrison & Levin, 1986; Peters & Levin, 1986; Shriberg, 1982; Tolfa-Veit et al., 1986). These positive effects occurred whether students were paced through the material by the experimenter or whether the students were allowed to read at their own pace until a fixed amount of time had elapsed.

Other questions related to the issue of group vs. individually administered mnemonic prose-learning strategies include: can young students benefit from either form of strategy administration? Will the form of strategy administration interact with the previously discussed mnemonic strategy variations (illustrations vs. imagery vs. structured imagery)? Will mnemonic prose-learning instruction prove successful when it is applied by a teacher to a curriculum unit in an actual classroom setting? (For preliminary encouraging evidence, see Tolfa-Veit et al., 1986.) These and other questions require additional research attention.

Listening Versus Reading

In the initial mnemonic prose-learning studies, the prose passages were presented orally by an experimenter while students followed along on their own copies (Levin et al., 1983; McCormick et al., 1984; Shriberg et al., 1982). An issue of some practical importance is whether the mnemonic facilitation obtained in those studies extends to a pure reading situation. Fortunately, recent research indicates that students can employ mnemonic strategies effectively while independently reading a prose passage (Goin et al., 1986; Levin et al., 1986; McCormick et al., 1984, 1986; Morrison & Levin, 1986; Peters & Levin, 1986; Scruggs et al., 1985). The results of these studies have been consistent despite differences in the students' ages (junior high vs. college) and reading abilities (including students with diagnosed learning disabilities), mnemonic strategy variations (illustrations vs. imagery vs. structured imagery), and presentation formats (paced vs. unpaced).

Summary

Generally speaking, the research just cited indicates that certain procedural variations crucial to prose-learning generalizability issues do not vitiate the effectiveness of mnemonic instruction. That is, mnemonic images, as well as mnemonic illustrations, can be facilitative. Facilitation occurs under group, as well as individual, mnemonic strategy administration. Moreover, mnemonic facilitation is present when prose passages are read independently, as well as when they are orally presented.

Variations in Prose Characteristics

In the preceding section we provided evidence that mnemonic prose-learning facilitation is robust with respect to a number of procedural variations. Here we consider the question of mnemonic facilitation in relation to variations in prose characteristics.

Content Domains

The studies cited earlier suggest that mnemonic strategy instruction can improve students' memory for text-embedded facts in a variety of content domains, including: concrete biographical information (Goin et al., 1986; McCormick & Levin, 1984; McCormick et al., 1984, 1986; Peters & Levin, 1986, Exp. 1;

Peters et al., 1985; Shriberg et al., 1982); relatively abstract town–attribute information (Levin et al., 1983; Shriberg, 1982); and relatively complex scientific concepts and explanations (Levin et al., 1986; Morrison & Levin, 1986; Scruggs et al., 1985). Moreover, in Peters' and Levin's (1986) second experiment, the prose passages were not specially developed to lend themselves to mnemonic facilitation, coming instead from school-based passages designed to improve students' reading comprehension skills (Liddle, 1977). These nonfictional biographical passages were longer, more complex in structure, and less obvious with respect to the identification of critical information to be remembered than were the passages constructed for the other mnemonic prose-learning studies.

Critical Information Signaling

In the Peters and Levin experiment just mentioned the central biographical information to be remembered typically was not located in the passage's topic sentence because those investigators wished to determine whether mnemonic imagery instruction was effective when the important factual information was not saliently positioned within the passage. Peters and Levin experimentally manipulated the "signaling" (e.g., Meyer, 1981) of that information by underlining it for half of the students. It was found that good readers benefitted from the mnemonic imagery strategy whether or not the critical information was underlined. In contrast, poor readers benefitted considerably more from the mnemonic strategy when the critical information was underlined than when it was not underlined, which strongly suggested that less skilled readers needed to know specifically which elements of a passage were important in order for them to take mnemonic advantage of them. When the critical passage information was signaled via underlining, the poorer readers benefitted from the mnemonic imagery strategy to the same degree as did the better readers.

Additional investigations of critical information signaling for students of lower reading ability are to be encouraged. Of potential theoretical interest are the processing differences that underlie the interaction between mnemonic instruction and signaling among such students. Do poorer readers simply find it difficult to identify the critical text information when it is not signaled, or is their performance interfered with by a limited working-memory capacity? From an educational standpoint, the issue of highlighting important text information appears to be particularly crucial when students are reading actual curricular materials, as opposed to specially constructed experimental materials.

Thematic Passages

A legitimate criticism of the previously described research is that most of the materials constructed for those studies may be characterized as essentially a set of unconnected facts embedded in a prose passage. In particular, several names or labels must be associated with one or more facts or attributes in passages that are only loosely integrated to provide little more than an elaborated listing of the various items to be remembered. Even the factual scientific materials used in the Levin et al. (1986), Morrison and Levin (1986), and Scruggs et al. (1985) studies were simply collections of facts about different minerals that were presented in a prose format. Moreover, the more ecologically valid curricular materials included in Peters and Levin's (1986) second experiment required students' processing of a set of discrete (unconnected) name–accomplishment associations.

Incorporating previous terminology, we assume that mnemonic strategies facilitate students' recall of unfamiliar, loosely connected, text because: (1) unfamiliar items within the prose passage are first *recoded* into a more concrete, meaningful, form; (2) the recoded items are then semantically *related* to the associated text information in order to provide a coherent organizational structure within which (3) the text information can be systematically *retrieved* (Levin, 1982, 1983). Thus, mnemonic facilitation produced for such passages derives primarily from the enhanced meaningfulness and organization bestowed on them. Whether or not mnemonic strategy instruction would similarly facilitate students' recall of thematically connected prose information was investigated in a recent study by McCormick et al. (1986).

In that study, college students were randomly assigned to one of four experimental conditions and were asked to read six fictitious biographical passages. The conditions were as follows: Control, where the biographies were loosely connected as in the previously cited prose-learning studies, and students were left to their own devices to remember the passage content; Mnemonic, where the loosely connected passages were accompanied by a provided mnemonic strategy to integrate the characters' names and biographical information; Thematic, where the coherence of the passage was enhanced by providing an explicit theme and associated text signals; and Mnemonic + Thematic, where the two constituent strategies were combined.

To illustrate the differences among conditions, consider the passage about Charlene McKune. The first few sentences of the control version of that passage were:

Born and raised on a dairy *farm* where she helped take care of the cows, *Charlene McKune* has always been used to hard work. When she was a child, McKune enjoyed creating homes for her pets out of her toy *building blocks*. To earn extra money and because of her hatred for dirt of any kind, McKune began *washing cars* for her parents' friends . . . ."

In contrast, the thematic version of the passage began with a "country" theme, which was elaborated in subsequent sentences, as:

Charlene McKune spent much of her life living in the serenity of the remote countryside. Born and raised on a *farm*, McKune grew to love the peace and quiet of rural living. When she was a child, her father made her *building blocks* out of bits of wood on the farm, and McKune spent hours building "barns" and "silos" with these blocks. To earn extra money, McKune began *washing cars* – and sometimes tractors – for the neighboring farmers . . . .

Subjects in the mnemonic conditions were provided with an integrated scene to imagine while studying the passage. For the above passage, for example, the subjects were told to imagine a pet RACCOON (the recoded concrete word for "McKune") outside a FARMHOUSE jumping over a long row of BUILDING BLOCKS . . . where some kids are WASHING CARS nearby . . . (etc., incorporating all the biographical information into an integrated mnemonic image).

It was expected that the mnemonic strategy would provide students with both effective name–information links and within-passage information links. Consequently, both the total amount of information recalled and the structuring of that information should be facilitated. In contrast, the use of thematic passages would be expected to facilitate students' processing of within-passage information only, inasmuch as such passages do not provide direct name–information links. That is, students in the thematic condition might recall that the person who lived on a farm loved building blocks and washed cars, but would not necessarily make the correct association that this person's name was Charlene McKune. This prediction follows directly from results reported by Levin et al. (1983) for their town–attribute passages, where students who were presented with thematically organized illustrations recalled more passage attributes than did control students but were no better than controls with respect to associating those attributes with the appropriate town names. In contrast, students who were presented mnemonic illustrations not only remembered more attributes than did controls but were also able to make more correct town–attribute associations.

Contrary to McCormick's et al. predictions, students in the mnemonic, thematic, and mnemonic + thematic conditions were *all* able to recall and correctly associate more biographical information than were control subjects. Thus, students who read the thematic passages were somehow able to associate biographical information with the correct names even without benefit of mnemonic strategy instruction. There are a couple of plausible explanations for this unexpected result. In the first place, students read only six biographies and therefore had relatively few name–information associations to keep straight. Moreover, the performance measure used in the McCormick et al. (1986) study—filling in a name by topic-information grid—would be expected to diminish name–information confusions relative to alternative measures (e.g., randomly ordered cued-recall questions). At the same time, it is worth mentioning that the "thematic" materials constructed by McCormick et al. did not permit as complete an exploitation of students' existing schemata and background knowledge as would have occurred had the text contained specific content and themes with which the students were thoroughly familiar. These and other issues are currently being considered in followup research. Indeed, this line of research appears promising. McCormick and Levin (1986) have recently completed a study in which 12 biographies were presented and memory was tested in either two groups of six (short list conditions), or in a single group of 12 (long list conditions). Preliminary analysis of the data revealed that the pattern of results in the short list conditions replicated the results reported by McCormick et al. (1986).

In the long list conditions, in accordance with the predictions outlined above, students in the mnemonic condition outperformed students in all other conditions on a cued recall measure.

Amount of Information to Be Remembered

Besides the thematic coherence of the passage, another important passage variable to be considered is the amount of passage information to be remembered. In all but the Snowman studies, the mnemonic strategies devised have been targeted at the central passage information (e.g., people's major accomplishments or biographical facts, town or mineral attributes). And, as long as all of the information to be remembered is incorporated into the mnemonic strategy, it appears to make little difference whether only one piece or several pieces of information per passage must be remembered. For example, in the McCormick and Levin (1984) study, college students effectively applied a mnemonic strategy to five biographical facts about six different individuals; and in the Levin et al. (1983) study, junior high school students did the same to remember four attributes of five different towns. In contrast, passage information that is not incorporated into the mnemonic strategy does not exhibit the same kind of facilitation (e.g., Peters & Levin, 1986; Peters et al., 1985; Scruggs et al., 1985; Shriberg et al., 1982). It should be noted that nonmnemonically represented passage information is typically less "important" than mnemonically represented information, and so an interesting, yet to be investigated question is whether this less important passage information could also be facilitated through mnemonic instruction, if desired.

Variations in Performance Measures

A final issue for the evaluation of mnemonic prose-learning research concerns the kind of performance measures used. A variety of performance outcomes have been assessed in the studies conducted to date. Mnemonic strategy instruction has proved to be facilitative when students were asked to respond to short-answer questions (McCormick & Levin, 1984, Exp. 1; McCormick et al., 1984; Peters & Levin, 1986, Exp. 1; Peters et al., 1985; Shriberg et al., 1982), to match associated factual information (Peters & Levin, 1986, Exp. 2), to fill in an informational matrix or grid (Levin et al., 1986; McCormick & Levin, 1984, Exp. 2; McCormick et al., 1986; Scruggs et al., 1985), or to freely recall passage information (Morrison & Levin, 1986; but see the previously noted Snowman studies based on the loci mnemonic).

Long-Term Retention

From an educational standpoint, a critical question that must be answered is: Does students' improved memory for passage content resulting from mnemonic instruction withstand the test of time? Affirmatively, positive long-term mnemonic effects have been demonstrated for retention intervals ranging from 2 to 8 days (Levin et al., 1986; McCormick & Levin, 1984; Morrison & Levin, 1986; Peters & Levin, 1986; Scruggs et al., 1985). Such results are encouraging and indicate that even longer retention intervals could profitably be investigated.

Memory Versus Comprehension

One criticism leveled against mnemonic techniques in general is that they encourage memorization of facts at the expense of "deeper" processing of concepts (Higbee, 1978; Levin & Pressley, 1985). In the prose-learning domain, this criticism can be addressed in a number of ways. First, it must be remembered that even though comprehension of ideas is a valued educational objective, it is nevertheless the case that a good deal of school learning centers on students' recall of factual information.

Moreover, a few mnemonic prose-learning investigations already conducted have included performance measures that tap students' prose "understanding," and there is certainly no evidence to suggest that mnemonically instructed students are at any disadvantage (e.g., Peters & Levin, 1986, Exp. 2; Scruggs et al., 1985). As a matter of fact, Scruggs et al. found that learning-disabled adolescents who were given mnemonic instruction were better able than control subjects to "infer" appropriate attribute categories that were not explicitly presented in the passage. They were able to do so on the basis of specific-attribute knowledge that they had extracted from the passage. This extraction process certainly does not require high-level inferential reasoning in the normal sense, but given that mnemonically instructed learning-disabled students were able to accomplish even that degree of transfer is a comprehension clue worth pursuing. The Scruggs et al. finding is also consistent with Levin and Pressley's (1985) claim that because mnemonic strategies elevate the level of students' factual recall, more factual information will be accessible for transfer tasks in which such information is relevant (e.g., application tasks requiring comprehension, inference making, and problem solving) – see also Levin (1986). Future mnemonic prose-learning research should routinely incorporate a variety of performance measures (including those that demand comprehension).

Concluding Comments

This review has documented the effectiveness of mnemonic prose-learning strategies for secondary-school and college students under various instructional and text manipulations, as well as on a number of different performance measures. Moreover, preliminary research has indicated that even handicapped learners can benefit from instruction in mnemonic prose-learning strategies (Goin et al., 1986; Peters & Levin, 1986; Scruggs et al., 1985), and this would seem to be an area of mnemonic strategy application with important educational consequences (see also Mastropieri et al., Chapter 16, this volume). A related issue concerns acquiring a better understanding of both nonhandicapped and handicapped students' metacognitive understanding of the use and utility of mnemonic strategies (see, for example, Pressley, Borkowski, & Schneider, in press-a). Research paradigms that have been applied to metacognitive issues in other domains of strategy application (e.g., Ghatala, Levin, Pressley, & Goodwin, 1986; Pressley, Levin, & Ghatala, 1984a; Pressley, Ross, Levin, & Ghatala, 1984b) should be extended to the mnemonic prose-learning domain. From a theoretical standpoint, component analyses of mnemonic strategies (Levin, 1986; Pressley, Forrest-Pressley, & Elliott-Faust, in press-b) should be conducted in relation to various semantic prose-learning strategies. Potential benefits derived from combining these two different approaches could then be considered (see Levin, 1982).

Finally, now that it has been documented empirically that mnemonic strategy instruction can facilitate students' recall of certain types of prose passages and prose information, more research needs to be conducted to explore both the limits and limitations of such instruction. This research should focus on delineating the specific characteristics of prose materials that lend themselves to mnemonic instruction. As one salient example, mnemonic strategy effectiveness needs to be assessed for more "ecologically valid" prose materials and, in particular, for materials that are actually used in school settings. Other more ecologically valid materials include prose passages that are meaningfully organized to support a coherent theme—something that is not necessarily true of all school materials.

Acknowledgments. The second author's contribution was supported in part by a grant from the National Institute of Education through the Wisconsin Center for Education Research, and by a Romnes Faculty Fellowship from the Graduate School of the University of Wisconsin, Madison.

References

Atkinson, R. C. (1975). Mnemotechnics in second-language learning. *American Psychologist, 30,* 821–828.

Bartlett, B. J. (1978). *Top-level structure as an organizational strategy for recall of classroom text.* Unpublished doctoral dissertation, Arizona State University, Tempe, AZ.

Bellezza, F. S. (1981). Mnemonic devices: Classification, characteristics and criteria. *Review of Educational Research, 51,* 247–275.

Bower, G. H. (1972). Mental imagery and associative learning. In L. Gregg (Ed.), *Cognition in learning and memory.* New York: John Wiley & Sons.

Ghatala, E. S., Levin, J. R., Pressley, M., & Goodwin, D. (1986). A componential analysis of the effects of derived and supplied strategy-utility information on children's strategy selections. *Journal of Experimental Child Psychology, 41,* 76–92.

Goin, M. T., Peters, E. E., & Levin, J. R. (1986). *Effects of pictorial mnemonic strategies on the reading performance of students classified as learning disabled.* Paper presented at the 64th annual meeting of the Council for Exceptional Children, March 31-April 4, New Orleans.

Gruneberg, M. M. (1973). The role of memorization techniques in finals examination preparation: A study of psychology students. *Educational Research*, *15*, 134–139.

Gruneberg, M. M., & Monks, J. (1974). *Medical students' use of mnemonic aids*. Unpublished manuscript, University College of Swansea, Great Britain.

Higbee, K. L. (1978). Some pseudo-limitations of mnemonics. In M. M. Gruneberg, P. E. Morris, & R. N. Sykes (Eds.), *Practical aspects of memory* (pp. 147–154). New York: Academic Press.

Krebs, E. W., Snowman, J., & Smith, S. H. (1978). Teaching new dogs old tricks: Facilitating prose learning through mnemonic training. *Journal of Instructional Psychology*, *5*, 33–39.

Levin, J. R. (1982). Pictures as prose-learning devices. In A. Flammer & W. Kintsch (Eds.), *Discourse processing* (pp. 412–444). Amsterdam: North-Holland.

Levin, J. R. (1983). Pictorial strategies for school learning: Practical illustrations. In M. Pressley & J. R. Levin (Eds.), *Cognitive strategy research: Educational applications* (pp. 213–237). New York: Springer-Verlag.

Levin, J. R. (1985). Educational applications of mnemonic pictures: Possibilities beyond your wildest imagination. In A. A. Sheikh (Ed.), *Imagery in education: Imagery in the educational process* (pp. 63–87). Farmingdale, NY: Baywood.

Levin, J. R. (1986). Four cognitive principles of learning-strategy instruction. *Educational Psychologist*, *21*, 3–17.

Levin, J. R., & Pressley, M. (1985). Mnemonic vocabulary instruction: What's fact what's fiction. In R. F. Dillon (Ed.), *Individual differences in cognition* (Vol. 2, pp. 145–172). New York: Academic Press.

Levin, J. R., Anglin, G. J., & Carney, R. N. (1987). On empirically validating functions of pictures in prose. In D. M. Willows & H. A. Houghton (Eds.), *Psychology of illustrations: Basic research* (Vol. 1, pp. 51–85). New York: Springer-Verlag.

Levin, J. R., Morrison, C. R., McGivern, J. E., Mastropieri, M. A., & Scruggs, T. E. (1986). Mnemonic facilitation of text-embedded science facts. *American Educational Research Journal*, *23*, 489–506.

Levin, J. R., Shriberg, L. K., & Berry, J. K. (1983). A concrete strategy for remembering abstract prose. *American Educational Research Journal*, *20*, 277–290.

Liddle, W. (1977). *Reading for concepts (Levels E and F)*. New York: McGraw-Hill.

McCormick, C. B., & Levin, J. R. (1984). A comparison of different prose-learning variations of the mnemonic keyword method. *American Educational Research Journal*, *21*, 379–398.

McCormick, C. B., & Levin, J. R. (1986). Unpublished data. University of South Carolina.

McCormick, C. B., Levin, J. R., Cykowski, F., & Danilovics, P. (1984). Mnemonic-strategy reduction of prose-learning interference. *Educational Communication and Technology Journal*, *32*, 145–152.

McCormick, C. B., Levin, J. R., & Valkenaar, D. (1986). *A comparison of thematic and mnemonic prose-learning strategies*. Paper presented at the 94th annual meeting of the American Psychological Association, August 22–26, Washington, D.C.

Meyer, B. J. F. (1981). Basic research on prose comprehension: A critical review. In D. F. Fisher & C. W. Peters (Eds.), *Comprehension and the competent reader: Interspecialty perspectives*. New York: Praeger.

Morrison, C. R., & Levin, J. R. (1986). *Degree of mnemonic support and students' acquisition of science facts*. Paper presented at the annual meeting of the American Educational Research Association, April 16–20, San Francisco.

Paivio, A. (1971). *Imagery and verbal processes*. New York: Holt.

Peters, E. E., & Levin, J. R. (1986). Effects of a mnemonic imagery strategy on good and poor readers' prose recall. *Reading Research Quarterly, 21*, 179–192.

Peters, E. E., Levin, J. R., McGivern, J. E., & Pressley, M. (1985). Further comparison of representational and transformational prose-learning imagery. *Journal of Educational Psychology, 77*, 129–136.

Pressley, M., Borkowski, J. G., & Schneider, W. (in press-a). Good strategy users coordinate metacognition, strategy use, and knowledge. In R. Vasta & G. Whitehurst (Eds.), *Annals of child development* (Vol. 4). Greenwich, CT: JAI Press.

Pressley, M., Forrest-Pressley, D., & Elliott-Faust, D. J. (in press-b). What is strategy instructional enrichment and how to study it: Illustrations from research on children's prose memory and comprehension. In F. Weinert & M. Perlmutter (Eds.), *Memory development: Universal changes and individual development*. Hillsdale, NJ: Erlbaum Associates.

Pressley, M., Levin, J. R., & Delaney, H. D. (1982). The mnemonic keyword method. *Review of Educational Research, 52*, 61–91.

Pressley, M., Levin, J. R., & Ghatala, E. S. (1984a). Memory strategy monitoring in adults and children. *Journal of Verbal Learning and Verbal Behavior, 23*, 270–288.

Pressley, M., Ross, K. A., Levin, J. R., & Ghatala, E. S. (1984b). The role of strategy utility knowledge in children's decision making. *Journal of Experimental Child Psychology, 38*, 491–504.

Rohwer, W. D., Jr. (1973). Elaboration and learning in childhood and adolescence. In H. W. Reese (Ed.), *Advances in child development and behavior* (Vol. 8, pp. 1–57). New York: Academic Press.

Scruggs, T. E., Mastropieri, M. A., McLoone, B., Levin, J. R., & Morrison, C. R. (1985). *Mnemonic facilitation of learning-disabled students' memory for expository prose*. Unpublished manuscript, Utah State University, Logan, UT.

Shriberg, L. (1982). *Comparison of two mnemonic encoding strategies on children's recognition and recall of abstract prose information*. Unpublished doctoral dissertation, University of Wisconsin, Madison, WI.

Shriberg, L. K., Levin, J. R., McCormick, C. B., & Pressley, M. (1982). Learning about "famous" people via the keyword method. *Journal of Educational Psychology, 74*, 238–247.

Snowman, J. (in press). Learning tactics and strategies. In G. D. Phye & T. Andre (Eds.), *Cognitive instructional psychology: Components of classroom learning*. New York: Academic Press.

Snowman, J., Krebs, E. W., & Kelly, F. J. (1980a). *Enhancing memory for prose through learning strategy training*. Paper presented at the annual meeting of the American Educational Research Association, April 7–11, Boston.

Snowman, J., Krebs, E. W., & Lockhart, L. (1980b). Improving recall of information from prose in high-risk students through learning strategy training. *Journal of Instructional Psychology, 7*, 35–40.

Tolfa-Veit, D., Scruggs, T. E., & Mastropieri, M. A. (1986). Extended mnemonic instruction with learning disabled students. *Journal of Educational Psychology, 78*, 300–308.

Weinstein, C. E., & Mayer, R. E. (1985). The teaching of learning strategies. In M. C. Wittrock (Ed.), *Handbook of research on teaching* (3rd ed.). New York: MacMillan.

CHAPTER 19

Process Mnemonics: Principles, Prospects, and Problems

Kenneth L. Higbee

Research interest in mnemonics has been continually increasing since the 1960s. Until about the mid-1970s, most research focused on whether mnemonics really worked and how well they worked. Recent research has focused more on how and why mnemonics work, and on ways they can be applied. Some of the large amount of mnemonics research has been summarized elsewhere in this volume, as well as in a number of recent reviews (e.g., Bellezza, 1981, 1984; Higbee, 1979; Levin, 1985a; Pressley, Levin, & Delaney, 1982). The research has typically investigated what might be called "fact" mnemonics, mnemonics that are used on a one to one basis to remember facts—one mnemonic association for each item to be remembered. For example, the rhyme, "In fourteen hundred and ninety two, Columbus sailed the ocean blue," can help us remember when Columbus discovered America; the acronym, "HOMES," can help us remember the names of the five Great Lakes; and the association "pato-pot-duck" can help us remember the Spanish word for "duck." These mnemonics, however, are not useful for remembering information other than these specific facts.

In contrast to "fact" mnemonics, this chapter deals with another kind of mnemonics that has been called *process mnemonics* (Kunihira, 1981), because they are helpful in remembering rules, principles, and procedures—the processes underlying problem solving. This chapter describes some Japanese process mnemonics and an attempt to adapt them to the United States, relates the mnemonics to some known principles of learning and memory, explores the problem of defining process mnemonics, and suggests some other problems and some prospects for research and application of process mnemonics. My objective is to make mnemonics researchers and educators aware of an approach that might help expand the traditional concept of mnemonics to more sophisticated and more generally applicable mnemonics, and so stimulate our interest in developing, studying, and applying more complex mnemonics in the future. Much of this chapter is adapted from, and builds on, discussions by Higbee and Kunihira (1985a, 1985b), Higbee and Oaks (1985), and Oaks and Higbee (1985).

Nakane's Yōdai Mnemonics

Masachika Nakane, a Japanese educator who was 95 years old at the time of his death in 1984, developed a wide range of mnemonics for instruction. His work extended over a 70-year period, and he was still active as principal and teacher at his school, the Ryoyo Institute in Kyoto, until shortly before his death. Nakane believed that everything is based on rules, so that the important secret to a subject matter is to crystallize its basic underlying rules or theory. For example, in the spelling of English words the basic idea can be attained better by studying spelling rules than by memorizing the spelling of each word. Similarly, for molecular formulas in chemistry and for mathematical formulas, the language, symbols, or letters can be condensed and simplified to be used as action media (Nakane, 1968).

Nakane named his mnemonics "Yōdai," which means "the essence of structure," because they summarize the organization and the process of problem solving into short phrases. According to Nakane, the essence of a subject of study is like a textbook with the least number of pages compressed by the greatest force. Thus, Yōdai is the essence, summary, or structure of the whole subject. For example, Nakane claimed that he had compressed the essence of trigonometry into a few rhymes that can be read within 60 seconds (Nakane, 1981).

The Yōdai system consists of verbal mediators (phrases, sentences, rhymes, songs, etc.) that have been used to teach mathematics (arithmetic, algebra, geometry, trigonometry, and calculus), science (inorganic and organic chemistry, physics, and biology), spelling and grammar, and the English language (Nakane, 1979, 1981). There are Yōdai mnemonics for formulas and numerals, for definitions, principles, and concepts, and for the process of solving problems. The mnemonics are intended to serve as readily retrievable mediators for learning and recalling the orderly cognitive processes required in problem solving — therefore the term "process mnemonics" (Kunihira, 1981). Symbols and words found in the problem to be solved are used as cues for solving it. They act as cues to extract the essence of the problem, which helps the students recognize the process for the solution (examples of this, and other features of Yōdai, are given in the next section).

Nakane contended that it was not necessary to introduce children to an entirely new language of mathematics with new symbols, vocabulary, and concepts, in order to develop understanding of mathematical rules and computational skills. Yōdai mnemonics consist of meaningful verbal chains in language that is familiar and simple, some of which are rhymes sung with familiar tunes (see Kunihira, 1979, 1982; Machida, 1982).

Some of the mnemonics are verbal commands for motor activities involving chalk and chalkboard, colored pens and sheets of paper, or gestures. Yōdai mnemonics are called "action words," because they typically depict sequential actions to be taken in the process of problem solving. Contrary to the common approach in Japanese (and Western) education that understanding should precede doing, Yōdai mnemonics involve doing before understanding (as do most mnemonics). This is also the approach of the Suzuki School of Music in Japan, where young children learn to play a violin guided by auditory memory and verbal cues provided by the instructor long before music sheets are introduced. Similarly, Kunihira and Asher (1965) demonstrated that doing might lead to learning a foreign language (Japanese) without the mediation of the first language; and a recent set of mathematics textbooks that emphasize doing more than conceptual understanding seems to be quite successful (Armbrister, 1985; J. Saxon, personal communication, October 14, 1985).

Yōdai Examples and Evidence

Examples of selected aspects of Yōdai mnemonics may help clarify the nature of Yōdai. Even in Japanese, Yōdai is not easy to understand. A Japanese psychologist, Takehisa Takizawa, told about his first exposure to Yōdai — after several days at the Ryoyo Institute, he said he still had a difficult time fully comprehending Yōdai because of the way Nakane's creative ideas are maximally used in Yōdai to suggest not only the laws and theorems but also the steps to solving problems using compressed phrases with many meanings (Takizawa, 1982). The following examples are all based on my analysis of printed materials translated from Japanese, and of videotapes of five-year-old kindergarten children at Nakane's school. The tapes show the kindergarten children using the Yōdai mnemonics to solve various mathematics problems (arithmetic, algebra, and calculus), including the following:

$$2/5 + 1/3, 3/5 \times 1/2, 2/5 \div 1/3, 3a_2b^3 \times 2a^3b^5\#,$$

$$2X^2 + 3X + 1 = 0, d/dx\,(5X^3 + 3X^2), \int 5X^3\,dx, \log_2 8$$

and simplifying expressions including the following:

$$(5X - 2) - (\tfrac{2}{3}8X + 3), 4a^2 = 9b^2 - 12ab,$$

$$3a - 4b + 2a - 3b, 3X^2(X + 1)(X - 1)$$

The tapes also show the 5-year-old children generating formulas for chemical compounds and diagramming their molecular structure, and translating Japanese words into English. The whole class recites the mnemonics aloud while one student does the work on the chalkboard.

To teach children mathematical operations with fractions, Yōdai mnemonics use familiar metaphors about bugs (beetles) expressed in familiar words. Thus, a fraction is called a "bug" with a "head" and a "wing" (Japanese children like to play with bugs). The head is the numerator and the wing is the denominator (such words as "fraction," "numerator," and "denominator" are not used at first). To add fractions with equal denominators, for example, the child is instructed to "count the heads when the wings are the same." The multiplication sign ($\times$) represents the bug's crossed "horns," or feelers, and cues the child to put the heads together and put the wings together. Dividing fractions requires turning one of the bugs upside down, then multiplying.

Multiplying binomials of the form $(a + b)(c + d)$ is expressed in terms of sumo wrestling, with each term in parentheses being a wrestler of either the West team or the East team. Each wrestler on the West team wrestles each wrestler on the East team, so that $(a + b)(c + d) = ac + ad + bc + bd$. Multiplying binomials of the form $(a + b)$fi or $(a + b)(a - b)$ is described in terms of passengers and luggage on a train.

Multiplying a monomial times a polynomial of the form $a(b + c + d)$ involves a popular Japanese folktale of a boy named Momotaro (see Uchida, 1949). On a journey, Momotaro (a) meets a dog (b), a pheasant (c), and a monkey (d), and takes each of them with him. Thus, $a(b + c + d) = ab + ac + ad$.

Parentheses are "baskets," and $+$ and $-$ represent "male" and "female" respectively. Thus, for example, $(a - b)$ could be a male bug and a female bug in a basket.

In organic chemistry the various molecules from the elements C, H, and O are family members including mother, father, brother, sister, grandmother, grandfather, aunt, uncle, etc. The children use the mnemonics to recognize and name various compounds, and to combine them and identify the results. Diagramming the ring compounds involves drawing "kites" ($\bigcirc$).

Some of these examples of Yōdai are not as meaningful in the English language as in Japanese, because many of them involve Japanese syllables or words with double meanings—one related to the problem and one related to the metaphor. For example, in the *Būn Būn* song used for fractions, *būn* represents the sound the bug makes, and *būn* also means "parts" or "fractions" This characteristic of Yōdai is also illustrated by the use of the quadratic formula

$$X = \frac{-b \, fi \, \sqrt{b fi - 4ac}}{2a}$$

to solve equations of the form $aX^2 + bX + c = 0$. Figure 19.1a shows the children singing the "flute song" which is used for this problem. (I must accept responsibility for the quality of the pictures in Figure 19.1, which are my own snapshots taken from a fair quality videotape on my TV.) In Figure 19.1a the children are playing the flute, and the flute song is written as the bottom line on the chalkboard behind them (in a mixture of hiragana and katakana, the two Japanese writing systems).

Each symbol in the flute song is a syllable (e.g., $\diagup$ = fu, I = e, $\exists$ = yo, $\diagup/$ = shi). The song says: *fu-e-no* ("flute's"), *hi-bi-ki* ("sound"), *wa* (topic marker meaning "as for the previous"), *mi-mi* ("ear"), $-$ (means to hold the previous sound when singing), *yo-a-shi* ("good"). Literally, the sentence says, "As for the flute's sound, it is good to the ear," or "The flute sounds good to the ear."

In Figure 19.1b, a kindergarten girl has started solving the problem, $2X^2 + 3X + 1 = 0$, on the chalkboard. She first circled each of the three coefficients (a, b, and c), and wrote a syllable under each one: e (pronounced $\breve{e}$) under 2, bi (pronounced "bee") under 3, and su (pronounced "sue") under 1. Then she wrote the quadratic formula using the syllables from the flute song:

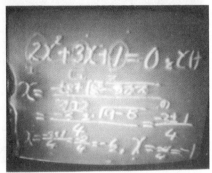

FIGURE 19.1. Yōdai method for solving a
quadratic equation.

$$X = \frac{-b \pm \sqrt{b^2 - 4ac}}{2a} = \frac{-bi\ ki\ \sqrt{mi\ mi\ -\ yo\ a\ su}}{fu\ e}$$

Every syllable in the formula is taken from the song except for *su*, which
replaces *shi*. Each syllable has a meaning in the formula in addition to its meaning
in the song. For example, the denominator says "flute" (*fu-e*); "fu" (pronounced
somewhat like "who") is also the first syllable of a Japanese word for the number
2 (*futatsu*), and "e" sounds like the letter *a*. Figure 19.1c shows the completed
problem; the girl has circled each syllable and written the corresponding number
by it, and has calculated the answers ($X = -1/2$ and $X = -1$).

In the United States Shirou Kunihira has developed some mnemonics that are
patterned after Nakane's mnemonics for mathematical operations with fractions
(Kunihira, Kuzma, Meadows, & Lotz, 1981). Because children in the United
States are not as interested in bugs as Japanese children are, Kunihira's mnemonics are based on activities that children in the United States (particularly
Kunihira's area, southern California) are more interested in and familiar with—
swimming pools and jogging. The mnemonics are short rhymes and are taught
with visual aids (pictures illustrating some of these visual aids can be found in
Higbee and Kunihira, 1985a).

In Kunihira's "Pool mnemonics" a fraction is represented by a jogger, with a number on his jersey representing the numerator, and the number of patches on his pants representing the denominator. Multiplication of fractions is represented by two joggers. The "X" between them reminds the child of an X-shaped swimming pool, and cues him that this is the "Multi-POOL" game. To play the game, the rhyme, "Pool shirts to shirts, patches to patches," tells the child to multiply the numerators together and the denominators together.

A "÷" between the two joggers represents a diving board with a small beach ball above it and one below it. This cues the child to play the "DIVE-ide" game. Whenever the diving board is present, the jogger on the right is always fooling around and standing on his head. Thus, the rhyme, "Flip the fool into the pool," tells the child to flip the jogger on the right so he is right side up ("Flip the fool"), and the game now becomes the "Multi-POOL" game ("into the pool").

To add or subtract fractions, the children play the "MATCH-PATCH" game. The letter "T" in each of the two words is printed to resemble a + sign, and the hyphen between the two words represents a − sign; these three symbols are printed in a different color from the other letters in the words "MATCH-PATCH" to cue the child when to play this game. For fractions with equal denominators (same number of patches on pants) the rhyme is: "Match the patches, don't take a chance; count the shirts and leave the pants." This rhyme tells the child to add the numerators and leave the denominator the same. For unequal denominators (different number of patches) the rhyme is: "If the patches do not match, pool the other person's patch." This rhyme tells the child that when the denominators are unequal he plays the "Multi-POOL" game with each jogger, using the number of patches on the other jogger's shorts. For example, for the problem $4/5 + 2/3$, the first step would be to pool the other person's patch ($3/3 \times 4/5 = 12/15$, and $5/5 \times 2/3 = 10/15$). The child now has two fractions with equal denominators ($12/15$ and $10/15$) so, using the first rhyme, he counts the shirts and leaves the pants.

There is some evidence of the value of Yōdai in the performance of Nakane's graduates. A high percentage of them have gone into various professions, such as medicine and engineering, and many of them have attributed their interest in science and math to their initial exposure at the Ryoyo Institute. The power of Yōdai is also shown in impressive demonstrations by young students, as illustrated by the videotapes of Japanese kindergarten children generating formulas for chemical compounds and solving mathematical problems (discussed above).

Empirical evidence on the value of Yōdai mnemonics is not limited to anecdotal reports and demonstrations, however. Research studies have found that the Yōdai "bug" mnemonics significantly helped third to sixth-grade Japanese children learn to add, subtract, multiply, and divide fractions (Takizawa, Hatori, Kunihira, & Machida, 1980). Yōdai mnemonics significantly improved performance of high school students in solving complex computational problems in algebra, geometry, trigonometry, and calculus (Hatori & Takizawa, 1959; Hatori, Takizawa, Kunihira, & Machida, 1980; Takizawa, 1982). Yōdai also helped Japanese junior high school students learn to construct trigonometric ratios and functions and compute with them (Kunihira & Machida, 1981), and to construct and use appropriate equations to solve algebra sentence problems using monomials and polynomials (Machida & Carlson, 1984). In the United States, children in the third grade (age 8) who had not started studying fractions were taught to add, subtract, multiply, and divide fractions using Kunihira's Pool mnemonics. This instruction, done in three 1-hour class sessions, enabled the third graders to perform calculations as well as sixth graders who had been taught for 3 years the traditional way, and better than fourth and fifth graders (Kunihira et al., 1981).

Unfortunately, only one of the above research studies on Yōdai math mnemonics has been published (Machida & Carlson, 1984), but all of them are described in more detail by Higbee and Kunihira (1985a). One study (described by Takizawa, 1982) has also been conducted on Nakane's methods for English, finding that Nakane's high school students were generally superior to a comparable group of students in speaking ability (e.g., pronunciation and listening comprehension), but not necessarily in writing ability (e.g., vocabulary and reading comprehension). In addition, a Japanese student is currently doing a Master's thesis on the application of Yōdai in chemistry (S. Kunihira, personal communication, January, 1986).

Process Mnemonics and Principles of Memory

Mnemonics are often viewed as "artificial" memory aids to distinguish them from natural memory processes. However, during the 1970s several memory researchers observed that the artificial–natural distinction might be an artificial distinction (see Higbee, 1978). More recently, Bellezza (1981) argued that the distinction between what is "natural" memory and what is "artificial" memory is often not clear, and there may be more similarities than there are differences; and in this volume, Bellezza (Chapter 2, this volume) and Begg and Desrochers (Chapter 3, this volume) have analyzed several mnemonics in terms of basic theories of memory. It seems to me that the natural–artificial issue stems in part from equating "unaided" with "natural," but that unaided rote rehearsal feels no more natural to many people than do their attempts to impose meaning on material.

Elsewhere I have suggested that mnemonics do not replace the basic psychological principles of learning and memory, but instead they use these principles (Higbee, 1977, 1978). I described some ways mnemonic systems incorporate specific principles, such as association, organization, meaningfulness, attention, and visual imagery. Some of these same basic principles also appear to be incorporated in the Yōdai and Pool process mnemonics, as illustrated by the following selected brief examples.

Meaningfulness

Rather than learn a whole new language of mathematics, children are initially taught math in familiar language that is already meaningful to them. Thus, a "fraction" with "numerator" and "denominator" is a "bug" with "head" and "wing" in Japan, or a "jogger" with a number on his jersey and patches on his shorts in southern California. (However, the language of Yōdai also includes some coined "words" that have no meaning outside of the Yōdai system.) In addition to familiarity, another technique that helps make material meaningful is rhyme. For example, "flip the fool into the pool" is a more meaningful way to remember how to divide fractions than are the following examples from two textbooks: "To divide fractions, multiply by a reciprocal" (fifth grade); and, "A quotient can be expressed as the product of the dividend and the reciprocal of the divisor" (eighth grade).

Organization

The organization (structure and sequence) of rhymes aids memory because the number of alternatives that will fit is limited, and if a person forgets part of the rhyme or gets a part wrong, the meter or rhythm is lost, cuing the error. The organization of rhymes also indicates the proper order in which to perform the steps in solving a problem. It should be noted that "rhyme" in Nakane's mnemonics does not always refer to words that sound alike, but often consists merely of stringing words or syllables together rhythmically or setting them to a tune so they can be sung. Categorization is illustrated by grouping bugs as boy bugs (preceded by a plus sign, +) and girl bugs (preceded by a minus sign, −). Chunking is incorporated in using one rhyme to generate hundreds of chemical formulas, or one basic set of mnemonics to solve a wide variety of math problems. In chemistry, a family structure is used to organize the elements into different molecules.

Association

Abstract symbols and terms are made more concrete by associating them with concrete items. Thus, parentheses in math are associated with baskets, the + and − signs are associated with male and female bugs, and the division sign in the Pool mnemonics is related to a diving board with small beach balls above and below it.

Attention

Attention is encouraged by active group involvement where the whole group of children recites a rhyme while one child works the problem on the board, by having the children engage in gestures and motor activities, and by incorporating metaphors that the children are interested in (such as bugs for Japanese children, and swimming pools for children in southern California).

Visualization

Although Nakane and Kunihira characterize their mnemonics as verbal or linguistic mnemonics, many of the verbal rhymes and phrases are concrete ones that foster visual imagery. The reference to concrete objects (such as bugs, runners, and pools) and activities (such as wrestling, swimming, and running) also fosters visualization. The Pool mnemonics even supplement the rhymes with visual aids. When one is shown a visual aid of a "fool" standing on his head near a swimming pool, it is hard to think of the rhyme "flip the fool into the pool" without some kind of accompanying visual image.

What Are Process Mnemonics?

Probably the most fundamental issue in evaluating Yōdai and other process mnemonics is their definitions—what they are, and how they differ from fact mnemonics. One reason this issue is important is that, as Pressley (1985) has observed, vagueness of conceptual specification can result in research efforts that are ill-conceived and conclusions that are diametrically opposed. He suggested that more exacting criteria for Yōdai construction, and more completely developed examples, would help avoid this problem in the area of Yōdai mnemonics. Levin (1985b) has also noted that examples of Yōdai mnemonics such as those given in this chapter provide only a general sense of what Yōdai mnemonics are, and it is still difficult to define exactly what the Yōdai system encompasses and what it does not.

At the beginning of this chapter I gave a working definition of fact mnemonics as mnemonics that are used on a one to one basis to remember facts—one mnemonic association for each item to be remembered. Process mnemonics were defined as mnemonics that are used to remember rules, principles, and procedures—the processes underlying problem solving—rather than specific facts. Unfortunately, the distinction between these two types of mnemonics may not be quite so simple or straightforward. Let us consider some dimensions that may be relevant in attempting to define process mnemonics: what is remembered vs. how it is remembered, general techniques vs. specific devices, and declarative vs. procedural knowledge.

What Is Remembered Versus How It is Remembered

A simple definition for a mnemonic is "an aid for remembering information." Based on this definition, it may be worthwhile to consider whether the fact–process distinction lies in the "aid" or in the "information." That is, which dimension should be used to distinguish between fact mnemonics and process mnemonics—the nature of the mnemonic itself (how the information is remembered), or what the mnemonic is used for (what information is remembered)?

If process mnemonics were defined on the dimension of what is remembered, then a "fact" mnemonic would be used to remember facts and a "process" mnemonic would be used to remember processes. For example, the rhyme, "In fourteen hundred and ninety-two, Columbus sailed the ocean blue," would be a fact mnemonic because it helps remember the factual information of when Columbus discovered America. On the other hand, the rhyme, "Flip the fool into the pool," would be considered a process mnemonic because it helps remember the process for dividing fractions.

If process mnemonics were defined on the dimension of how the information is remembered, then a "fact" mnemonic would give us the information directly, and a "process" mnemonic would give us the process for getting the information. We might say that a fact mnemonic would be duplicative (duplicating the information from the mnemonic itself), and a process mnemonic would be generative (allowing us to generate the information from the mnemonic). For example, the rhyme, "Thirty days has September, April, June, and November . . ." would be a fact mnemonic because all the information to be retrieved is contained in the rhyme itself. (Someone has suggested that a more appropriate version of this rhyme may be, "Thirty days has September, all the rest I can't remember".) The "1492" rhyme above would also be a fact mnemonic on this dimension. On the other hand, the rhyme, "*I* before *e* except after *c*, or when sounded like *a* as in *neighbor* and *weigh*," would be a process mnemonic; it helps us remember the factual information of how to spell words with *ie* or *ei* in them, but all the words are not contained in the rhyme itself. Similarly, Yōdai rhymes such as "Flip the fool into the pool" do not give us direct retrieval of the desired information (the quotient obtained when dividing fractions) but allow us to generate the information from the mnemonic.

A process mnemonic may thus be defined either as a mnemonic that is used to remember a process or as one that gives a process for remembering many different facts. The first definition is the one that has been used so far in this chapter and appears to be the primary emphasis that Nakane had in mind. However, the second definition may also be relevant to Yōdai. The math mnemonics, for example, seem to be based on a structural understanding of several levels of math, so that the same basic set of mnemonics is applied to algebra, trigonometry, and calculus. Similarly, a few rhymes can be used to generate hundreds of chemical formulas. Both definitions broaden the scope of mnemonics beyond traditional fact mnemonics, provide reasonable justification to call a mnemonic a "process" mnemonic, and are relevant to Yōdai mnemonics.

It should be noted that "Yōdai" and "process" are not synonymous terms. While examples from Yōdai mnemonics have been used to illustrate process mnemonics, there can be process mnemonics that are not part of Yōdai and there are Yōdai mnemonics that are not process mnemonics. Yōdai is a comprehensive program, an extensive system of mnemonics that also includes traditional encoding and organizational mnemonics (cf. Bellezza, 1981). For example, the use of baskets for parentheses illustrates encoding mnemonics, and the Momotaro story illustrates organizational mnemonics.

General Techniques Versus Specific Devices

The word "mnemonic" can be defined at several levels of specificity. For sake of discussion, I will refer to the most specific level as a mnemonic *device* and the next level as a mnemonic *technique*. For example, the "1492" rhyme and the "30 days" rhyme are specific mnemonic devices illustrating the more general mnemonic technique of rhymes. Similarly, HOMES and ROY G. BIV (for the colors of the visible spectrum) are specific devices illustrating the general technique of acronyms.

At which level of specificity should we attempt to distinguish between fact and process mnemonics—the specific mnemonic device or the general mnemonic technique? It seems to me that the distinction must be made at the specific device level. Thus, for example, the technique of rhymes would not be viewed as either fact or process. Instead, as illustrated previously, a specific rhyming device would be viewed as either fact (e.g., "In 1492 ...," "30 days ...") or process (e.g., "Flip the fool ...," "*I* before *e* ..."). Although this criterion for categorizing is generally adequate, it is complicated by the possibility that the same specific mnemonic device can even be used to retrieve either a process or a fact. For example, the acronym FOIL is used to remember the process for multiplying binomials (First, Outer, Inner, Last; Kilpatrick, 1985); but it could also be used to remember items on a shopping list (e.g., Fish, Oranges, Ice cream, Lettuce). Thus, not only do we need to make the fact-process distinction at the level of specific devices, but in some cases we may need to be even more specific and base the distinction on the application of that device to specific information.

This issue of different levels of specificity can cause difficulty not only in attempting to distinguish between process mnemonics and fact mnemonics, but also in attempting to distinguish among different fact mnemonics. For example, Bellezza (1981) categorized organizational mnemonics as either "multiple use" or "single use" (see Table 19.1, from Bellezza, 1981). All four of Bellezza's multiple-use mnemonics are what I have called general mnemonic techniques. His two single-use mnemonics—acronyms ("first-letter recoding") and rhymes— are also general techniques, each illustrated by a specific device ("HOMES" and "30 days ...").

The categorizing in Table 19.1 seems to suffer from failure to differentiate between general techniques and specific devices. Consider the so-called single-use mnemonics. Whereas it is true that the specific device HOMES may be used only to remember the Great Lakes, the general technique of acronyms can be used to remember many other kinds of information by making up different specific acronyms; and whereas the specific 30-days device may be used only to remember the short months, the general technique of rhyme can be used many times by making up different specific rhymes (just as the "multiple-use" link mnemonic, for example, can be used many times by making up different specific links). Now consider the so-called multiple-use mnemonics in

TABLE 19.1. Organizational mnemonics.

	Multiple use	Single use
Peg type	Method of loci	First-letter recoding
(extrinsic cuing)	Pegword mnemonic	("HOMES")
Chain type	Story mnemonic	Rhymes ("Thirty days hath
(intrinsic cuing)	Link mnemonic	September ...")

From "Mnemonic devices: Classification, characteristics, and criteria," by F. S. Bellezza. 1981. *Review of Educational Research, 51,* 247–275. Copyright 1981 by the American Educational Research Association. Adapted by permission.

Table 19.1. The pegword and story techniques, for example, can be used to remember many different kinds of lists, but a specific set of pegword associations that is used to remember, say, the Ten Commandments, only has one use (like a specific acronym); and a specific story, such as the one used for remembering the names of the 13 original states (Higbee, 1977), does not have multiple uses either. It seems feasible, then, to view all six of the general techniques in Table 19.1 as multiple-use mnemonics, and both of the specific devices as single-use mnemonics.

Bellezza (1981) also distinguished between extrinsic cuing and intrinsic cuing, with the acronym technique illustrating extrinsic and the link technique illustrating intrinsic (see Table 19.1). However, it seems to me that linking the letters H–O–M–E–S into a meaningful acronym is equivalent to linking the words Huron –Ontario–Michigan–Erie–Superior into a meaningful link (or story). The only difference is that the acronym uses the first letter of each word rather than the whole word; but the first letter of a word is just as much an intrinsic part of the word as are the rest of the letters, not something imposed on it from outside. This brief diversion on intrinsic and extrinsic cuing is not directly relevant to the issue of general techniques vs. specific devices, but is just another illustration of the fact that it is not easy to make clearcut distinctions among different kinds of traditional fact mnemonics, let alone distinctions between fact mnemonics and process mnemonics.

Declarative Versus Procedural Knowledge

Contemporary cognitive psychology distinguishes between two kinds of knowledge that seem to be closely related to the fact–process distinction: (a) declarative knowledge—knowing *that*, or recalling factual information; and (b) procedural knowledge—knowing *how*, or using the information to perform tasks (see recent explanations by Anderson, 1982; Gagné, 1985, pp. 48–56). Fact mnemonics may appear to correspond with declarative knowledge, and process mnemonics with procedural knowledge. In fact, Levin (1985b) suggested that the procedural–declarative distinction is what truly sets Yōdai mnemonics apart from the rest, because Yōdai are aimed at teaching how rather than teaching that. Should we then just refer to declarative vs. procedural mnemonics rather than fact vs. process mnemonics? Why create more terms?

While there are similarities, there are also some aspects of the declarative–procedural distinction that do not apply directly to the fact–process distinction. First, declarative knowledge requires verbal rehearsal or mediation in working memory and so is slow and deliberate. Also, as the term suggests, declarative knowedge tends to be information that can be expressed easily and communicated verbally. Procedural knowledge is more automatic and less conscious and so is faster and more difficult to communicate verbally. Knowing a phone number, the locations of the keys on a typewriter, or the rules of grammar illustrate declarative knowledge. Such declarative knowledge becomes procedural knowledge when one can dial phone numbers without recalling the numbers verbally, type without thinking of where the letters are on the typewriter, or speak a language fluently without remembering the rules of grammar. Thus, declarative knowledge becomes procedural when our use of the knowledge becomes automatic so that we no longer need to be consciously aware of it enough to be able to express it verbally; Neves and Anderson (1981) explain how this may occur. (This does not necessarily mean that we cannot express some procedural knowledge verbally if the need arises; inability to verbalize is not a necessary condition of procedural knowledge.)

However, users of process mnemonics such as Yōdai not only are able to express their knowledge verbally, but may even be required to do so (children typically say or sing Yōdai rhymes out loud while performing the procedures). Verbal mediation requiring the use of working memory is a key element of Yōdai, and it results in slow, deliberate operations. Thus, process mnemonics such as Yōdai seem to fit the category of declarative knowledge better than procedural knowledge. In fact, it may be questionable whether a true "procedural" mnemonic can even exist, because a person must be consciously aware of a mnemonic in order to use it (although information that is initially learned with a mnemonic may later become automatized through frequent use, so that the mnemonic is no longer needed).

Another aspect of the declarative–procedural distinction is that there is no significant difference between remembering facts and remembering rules; they are equivalent as long as the person is consciously aware of them. For example, when we follow the rules of a language in speaking it, our knowledge of the language is still declarative as long as we are consciously aware of those rules. On the other hand, a key element of process mnemonics, such as Yōdai, is the learning of rules rather than facts.

Thus, the essence of the declarative–procedural distinction seems to lie more in the conscious awareness vs. automatic application of rules than in the difference between facts and rules, whereas the essence of the fact–process distinction lies more in the difference between facts and rules and requires conscious awareness of the rules. This is why it may be more approprite to call mnemonics such as Yōdai "process mnemonics" than "procedural mnemonics."

Prospects and Problems

The earlier description and discussion of process mnemonics such as the Yōdai and Pool mnemonics raises a number of questions that may be worthy prospects for future research and for application. It may be fruitful to analyze Yōdai critically in light of current theoretical and empirical knowledge of mnemonics, and also to analyze the current knowledge of mnemonics in light of such process mnemonics as Yōdai. In addition to its theoretical value, research on such process mnemonics may have applied value as well, particularly in education.

One possible question for investigation—What are process mnemonics?—has been discussed in the previous section. Some additional questions for investigation are suggested below. The first four focus on Yōdai mnemonics (which include the Pool mnemonics), while the other five broaden to more general process mnemonics (which include Yōdai mnemonics).

How Well Do Yōdai Mnemonics Work?

Several studies cited in this chapter indicate that Yōdai mnemonics are very powerful. However, some of these studies may be perceived more as demonstrations and quasi-experimental studies than as true experiments, so that Yōdai might need to be more adequately tested (Levin, 1985b; Pressley, 1985). In addition, as noted previously, only one of these studies has been published. Researchers and educators may be more confident in the value of Yōdai mnemonics if the mnemonics are tested in more well-controlled experiments, which are made more accessible.

Why Do Yōdai Mnemonics Work?

I noted earlier that mnemonics are not completely artificial but seem to operate on the same principles as other memory processes. The earlier section relating Yōdai mnemonics to some of these general principles is a small step in the direction of investigating why such mnemonics work. Other principles and theoretical mechanisms of memory that have been suggested as being relevant to Yōdai mnemonics are analogies, concreteness, and proxies (Pressley, 1985). Additional principles that researchers have suggested are related to fact mnemonics include: depth of encoding (Morris, 1977); recoding (Dickel, 1983); cognitive cuing (Bellezza, 1981; Morris, 1977); and constructibility, discriminability, associability, and invertibility (Bellezza, 1981; Chapter 2, this volume). Do process mnemonics use some of these same principles? Do they use them in the same way as do fact mnemonics? Are there other mechanisms and principles that are unique to process mnemonics?

Other than what has been attempted in this chapter, there has been very little theoretical analysis of Yōdai (see Kunihira, 1981, 1982). However, in his doctoral dissertation, Kenichi Machida is working on the theoretical analysis of verbal mediators, such as those in Yōdai (personal communication, May 3, 1985). In this connection, it is interesting to note that even after 20 years of considerable research and theoretical analysis on traditional fact mnemonics, there is still much to be learned about the basic mechanisms by which they operate; in fact, exactly what cognitive factors are involved in the formation of any memory process is a complex question (Bellezza, 1981).

What Role Does Visual Imagery Play in Yōdai Mnemonics?

Nakane and Kunihira both called their mnemonics "verbal" or "linguistic" mnemonics. However, as was noted in the discussion of principles, visual imagery appears to be involved in these Yōdai mnemonics. Some of the verbal phrases and rhymes seem to be very concrete ones that may also involve visual imagery (e.g., bugs' heads and wings). In fact, in the Pool mnemonics pictures are used along with the rhymes. Are visual images and/or pictures helpful in Yōdai? Are they necessary? Most mnemonics research in Western cultures has focused on visual-imagery mnemonics and so is relevant to Yōdai to the extent that Nakane's and Kunihira's "verbal" mediators are high in imagery value.

How Adaptable Are Yōdai Mnemonics to Other Cultures?

The question of cross-cultural application can be viewed in two parts. First, how adaptable are the specific Yōdai mnemonics, such as those described in this chapter? Language differences (such as those illustrated in the *būn būn* and quadratic formula examples) and cultural differences (such as interest in bugs and emphasis on computational skills) would create limitations on direct cross-cultural applications (cf. Kilpatrick, 1985). The second (perhaps more significant) part of the question on cross-cultural application is, how adaptable is the Yōdai philosophy and approach? The answer to this second part may be a little more optimistic. For example, children in the United States do not play with bugs as Japanese children do, so the "bug" mnemonics for fractions are not directly transferable, but the basic approach underlying the bug mnemonics appears to have been adapted successfully by Kunihira for his Pool mnemonics.

There may be some value in studying Nakane's methods regardless of how adaptable Yōdai mnemonics are across cultures. Virtually all mnemonics research has been conducted in the United States, Canada, and Great Britain, although there has been some recent mnemonics research in other countries (e.g., Cornoldi & DeBeni, 1983; Cornoldi & Paivio, 1982), and there is a rich history of the use of mnemonics in other countries (cf. Yates, 1966). Similarities and differences between the Japanese children's use of Yōdai and the research on mnemonics in Western cultures could give us insight into developmental differences in children's cognition from a cross-cultural perspective. This is an area in which research has been lacking, as cross-cultural research has not been very successful in increasing the generality of psychological laws (Laboratory of Comparative Human Cognition, 1979). Thus, Nakane's methods might be of value not only to psychologists interested in cognitive processes and to educators interested in instructional techniques, but also to other researchers interested in cross-cultural comparisons or in child development.

How Adaptable Are Process Mnemonics to Other Topics?

Recent research on educational applications of traditional fact mnemonics has found profitable applications for a wide range of topics, such as vocabulary, states and capitals, names of presidents, languages, prose learning, and history dates (cf. Higbee, 1979; Levin, 1981, 1985a; Pressley et al., 1982; Mastropieri, Scruggs, & Levin, 1985; Mastropieri et al., Chapter 16, this volume). Obviously, the broader the range of applications, the more applied value process mnemonics would have. This chapter has focused primarily on mathematics, an area in which Yōdai mnemonics appear to have a wide range of applications in Japan. However, as noted previously, the Yōdai approach also appears to have been applied successfully in chemistry, physics, biology, spelling and grammar, and English, although there is no research evidence yet in these areas. Can the process approach be used to develop mnemonics for mathematics other than fractions in Western cultures? Can process mnemonics be profitably developed for topics other than mathematics? What other topics have enough "processes" vs. facts to be amenable to process mnemonics?

Do Process Mnemonics Affect Conceptual Understanding?

The purpose of mnemonics is to increase memorability, not necessarily conceptual understanding; in fact, most traditional fact mnemonics are not even conceptually related to the material to be remembered (Bellezza, 1981). Thus, there has been some controversy regarding the effects of mnemonics on conceptual understanding: Do they hinder understanding, help understanding, or neither (cf. Higbee, 1978)? This issue of the relationship between conceptual understanding and the use of mnemonics has also been raised with respect to Yōdai, and is discussed elsewhere (Higbee & Kunihira, 1985b; Kilpatrick, 1985). Anecdotal reports by Nakane's graduates, including top Japanese inventors and scientists, suggest that Yōdai mnemonics do not hinder creativity or conceptual understanding. However, there is no actual research evidence yet to answer this question.

It may be that process mnemonics do not have to be used at the expense of understanding the principles or procedures involved but may be used in connection with such understanding—process mnemonics may precede, accompany, or follow understanding rather than replace understanding. Machida reported that he teaches Yōdai mnemonics in conjunction with understanding (personal communication, May 3, 1985). Kunihira has helped develop a Japanese mathematics course that combines Yōdai mnemonics with traditional approaches including understanding (a combination that Mr. Nakane, incidentally, did not like).

Are Process Mnemonics Relevant to Problem Solving?

Nakane and Kunihira claimed that their mnemonics are used to solve problems. However, Kilpatrick (1985) claimed that Yōdai helps only with mechanical procedures for getting answers, not with realistic "problems" such as word problems. He would not call this problem solving, because procedures are different from problems. The issue seems to be the relationship among the terms "process," "procedure," and "problem." This issue is discussed briefly by Higbee and Kunihira (1985b) and may warrant further study. Are procedures, processes, and problems significantly different? Does it matter what label one gives to what Yōdai mnemonics do? To be useful, must process mnemonics aid in the process of converting words to mathematical symbols as well as in the process of operating on the symbols? If so, can process mnemonics be developed for the process of converting words to symbols?

How Spontaneous Is the Use of Process Mnemonics?

Research indicates that even though very young children can be taught to use verbal and visual mnemonics effectively, children rarely use them spontaneously on their own (cf. Pressley, 1982). However, children's transfer of a mnemonic to new tasks can be increased by comprehensive instructions on how, when, why, and where to use the mnemonic, and additional practice with the mnemonic during instruction (O'Sullivan & Pressley, 1984), and by prompting (Pressley & Dennis-Rounds, 1980). Do young children need to be reminded to use process mnemonics such as Yōdai each time they encounter a new application situation? Do aspects of the Yōdai mnemonics that cue the user to key elements of the problem help alleviate this limitation of fact mnemonics?

Levin (1985b) observed that researchers have attempted to identify factors underlying students' independent application of effective learning strategies, and that process mnemonics may be one key to help unlock the door to a student's efficient independent learning. He suggested that systematic instruction in the use of procedural mnemonic "control" strategies may help to facilitate students' remembering when and why to apply a particular fact mnemonic, and how to do so effectively. In addition, independent use of process mnemonics might be facilitated if elements of the mnemonic are keyed to symbols and words in the problem (such as a + or ÷ sign), so the child is reminded of the mnemonic by looking at the problem (as is done in some Yōdai mnemonics).

Can Process Mnemonics Reduce Math Anxiety?

Nakane and Kunihira claimed that Yōdai mnemonics can reduce the anxiety that can be associated with learning mathematics. In fact, one of Nakane's intentions in developing his methods was to ease the pain of learning mathematics and science; he assumed that the learning of the new language of math and science is a major source of pain and difficulty. The problem of learning a new language in math, and the anxiety to which it may contribute, is especially relevant to children who have not yet mastered their regular language. This would include children (such as minority group children) who are culturally and/or linguistically disadvantaged, and mentally retarded and learning-disabled children. If they already have a burden of learning one language, the introduction of another language developed by mathematicians might overburden them. Process mnemonics may offer some hope for them. There is considerable research evidence that disadvantaged people, such as the learning disabled, mentally retarded, and even brain damaged, can benefit by using traditional mnemonics (cf. Mastropieri et al., 1985, Chapter 16, this volume; Pressley & Levin, 1986; Richardson, Cermak, Blacford, and O'Connor, Chapter 14, this volume; Wilson & Moffat, 1984).

Gagné (1983) suggested that students enjoy mathematics more if they can apply the procedural rules easily, and that the key to developing future interest in math may be in giving successful, pleasurable experiences. Can process mnemonics such as Yōdai give more successful, pleasurable experiences? Do they make math more fun? If process mnemonics can foster the development of efficient procedural skills in an enjoyable, non-anxiety-producing context, one possible result may be to diminish reported gender differences (in favor of males) in math abilities (Levin, 1985b).

Summary

Considerable research has been done on "fact" mnemonics, mnemonics that are used on a one to one basis to remember facts. This chapter discusses some mnemonics that have been called "process" mnemonics, because they help in remembering principles and rules. These process mnemonics were developed and used by Masachika Nakane in Japan for teaching mathematics, science, spelling, grammar, and English. Nakane named his mnemonics "Yōdai," which means "the essence of structure," because they summarize the essence of the structure of subjects, and of the processes of problem solving, into short phases. Shirou Kunihira has adapted Nakane's mnemonics for mathematical operations with fractions for use in the United States. The reported accomplishments of Nakane's students are striking, and there have been several research studies verifying the effectiveness of Nakane's and Kunihira's mnemonics. Yōdai mnemonics are based on basic principles of learning and memory, such as organization and association. Some factors involved in the problem of defining process mnemonics are suggested, such as the distinction between what is remembered and how it is remembered, and the relationship to procedural knowledge. Other possible research questions suggest some additional prospects and problems for understanding and applying process mnemonics such as Yōdai. These include such questions as: Why do Yōdai mnemonics work? How adaptable are Yōdai mnemonics to other cultures? Do process mnemonics affect conceptual understanding?

Acknowledgments. I am grateful to Shirou Kunihira, Mark McDaniel, John Oaks, James Pratt, Michael Pressley, Jan Semple, Nancy Stevenson, and Larry Wood for their comments on earlier drafts of this chapter, and to Seiko Higgins for her help in translating material from Japanese (and for trying to help me understand what it meant).

References

Anderson, J. R. (1982). Acquisition of cognitive skill. *Psychological Review, 89,* 369–406.

Armbrister, T. (1985). The teacher who took on the establishment. *Reader's Digest,* March, pp. 23–28.

Bellezza, F. S. (1981). Mnemonic devices: Classification, characteristics, and criteria. *Review of Educational Research, 51,* 247–275.

Bellezza, F. S. (1984). Mnemonic-device instruction with adults. In M. Pressley & J. R. Levin (Eds.), *Cognitive strategy research: Psychological foundations* (pp. 51-73). New York: Springer-Verlag.

Cornoldi, C., & DeBeni, R. (1983). Effetti a breve e lungo termine di una mnemotecnia a carattere immaginativo. *Psicologia Italiana, 5*, 4-7.

Cornoldi, C., & Paivio, A. (1982). Imagery value and its effects on verbal memory: A review. *Archivio di Psicologia, Neurologia e Psichiatria, 43*, 171-192.

Dickel, M. J. (1983). Principles of encoding mnemonics. *Perceptual and Motor Skills, 57*, 111-118.

Gagné, E. D. (1985). *The cognitive psychology of school learning.* Boston: Little, Brown.

Gagné, R. M. (1983). A reply to critiques of some issues in the psychology of mathematics instruction. *Journal for Research in Mathematics Education, 14*, 214-216.

Hatori, H., & Takizawa, T. (1959). Psychological study of the Nakane method in teaching mathematics. *Abstracts of the papers presented at 26th annual convention of the Japan Association of Applied Psychology, Tokyo*, pp. 40-41.

Hatori, H., Takizawa, T., Kunihira, S., & Machida, K. (1980). *Effects of verbal mediation in arithmetic and mathematics education: (1) Verbally mediated learning in Yōdai instructional method.* Paper presented at the 22nd meeting of the Japanese Association of Educational Psychology, October 31, Tokyo.

Higbee, K. L. (1977). *Your memory: How it works and how to improve it.* Englewood Cliffs, NJ: Prentice-Hall.

Higbee, K. L. (1978). Some pseudo-limitations of mnemonics. In M. M. Gruneberg, P. E. Morris, & R. S. Sykes (Eds.), *Practical aspects of memory* (pp. 147-154). London: Academic Press. [Condensed from paper presented at the International Conference on Practical Aspects of Memory, Cardiff, Wales, September 1978; complete paper available in *JSAS Catalog of Selected Documents in Psychology, 9*, 19-20.]

Higbee, K. L. (1979). Recent research on visual mnemonics: Historical roots and educational fruits. *Review of Educational Research, 49*, 611-629.

Higbee, K. L., & Kunihira, S. (1985a). Cross-cultural applications of Yōdai mnemonics in education. *Educational Psychologist, 20*, 57-64.

Higbee, K. L., & Kunihira, S. (1985b). Some questions (and a few answers) about Yōdai mnemonics: A reply to Kilpatrick, Pressley, & Levin. *Educational Psychologist, 20*, 77-81.

Higbee, K., Oaks, J. L. (1985). *Process mnemonics: Prospects and problems.* Paper presented at the 26th annual meeting of the Psychonomic Society, November 22-24, Boston, MA.

Kilpatrick, J. (1985). Doing mathematics without understanding it. *Educational Psychologist, 20*, 65-68.

Kunihira, S. (1979). *Beyond a century of research on mnemonics.* Paper presented at the 59th annual meeting of the Western Psychological Association, April 5-8, San Diego, CA.

Kunihira, S. (1981). *A theory of "process" mnemonics.* Paper presented at the 61st annual meeting of the Western Psychological Association, April 9-12, Los Angeles, CA.

Kunihira, S. (1982). *Theory and application of verbal mnemonics in learning mathematics.* Paper presented at the 20th International Congress of Applied Psychology, July, Edinburgh, Scotland.

Kunihira, S., & Asher, J. J. (1965). The strategy of the total physical response: An application for learning Japanese. *International Review of Applied Linguistics, 3*, 277-289.

Kunihira, S., & Machida, K. (1981). *Effects of verbal mnemonics in developing concepts and computational skills for trigonometric ratios and functions.* Paper presented at the 61st annual meeting of the Western Psychological Association, April 9–12, Los Angeles, CA.

Kunihira, S., Kuzma, R., Meadows, G., & Lotz, T. (1981). *Effects of visually-aided verbal mnemonics in developing computational skills with fractional numbers.* Paper presented at the 61st annual meeting of the Western Psychological Association, April 9–12, Los Angeles, CA.

Laboratory of Comparative Human Cognition. (1979). Cross-cultural psychology's challenges to our ideas of children and development. *American Psychologist, 34,* 827–833.

Levin, J. R. (1981). The mnemonic '80s: Keywords in the classroom. *Educational Psychologist, 16,* 65–82.

Levin, J. R. (1985a). Educational applications of mnemonic pictures: Possibilities beyond your wildest imagination. In A. A. Sheikh (Ed.), *Imagery in the educational process.* Farmingdale, NY: Baywood.

Levin, J. R. (1985b). Yōdai features = mnemonic procedures. *Educational Psychologist, 20,* 73–76.

Machida, K. (1982). The application and effects of verbal mediators in arithmetic and mathematics education: An overview of Yōdai mathematics. *The Journal of the International Learning Science Association, 1,* 14–18.

Machida, K., & Carlson, J. (1984). The effects of a verbal mediation strategy on cognitive processes in mathematics learning. *Journal of Educational Psychology, 76,* 1382–1385.

Mastropieri, M. A., Scruggs, T. E., & Levin, J. R. (1985). Maximizing what exceptional students can learn: A review of research on mnemonic techniques. *Remedial and Special Education, 6,* 39–45.

Morris, P. (1977). Practical strategies for human learning and remembering. In M. Howe (Ed.), *Adult learning: Psychological research and applications* (pp. 125–144). London: Wiley.

Nakane, M. (1968). *Yōdai education is the right way.* Unpublished manuscript.

Nakane, M. (1979). *Birth of the English alphabet for kindergartners.* Kyoto, Japan: New Teaching Method Research Center, Ryoyo Schools.

Nakane, M. (1981). *Yōdai.* Kyoto, Japan: New Teaching Method Research Center, Ryoyo Schools.

Neves, D. M., & Anderson, J. R. (1981). Knowledge compilation: Mechanisms for the automatization of cognitive skills. In J. R. Anderson (Ed.), *Cognitive skills and their acquisition* (pp. 57–84). Hillsdale, NJ: Erlbaum Associates.

Oaks, J. L., & Higbee, K. L. (1985). *Process mnemonics and principles of memory.* Paper presented at the 65th annual meeting of the Western Psychological Association, April 18–21, San Jose, CA.

O'Sullivan, J. T., & Pressley, M. (1984). Completeness of instruction and strategy transfer. *Journal of Experimental Child Psychology, 38,* 275–288.

Pressley, M. (1982). Elaboration and memory development. *Child Development, 53,* 296–309.

Pressley, M. (1985). More about Yōdai mnemonics: A commentary on Higbee & Kunihira (1985). *Educational Psychologist, 20,* 69–72.

Pressley, M., & Dennis-Rounds, J. (1980). Transfer of a mnemonic keyword strategy at two age levels. *Journal of Educational Psychology, 72,* 575–582.

Pressley, M., & Levin, J. R. (1986). Elaborative learning strategies for the inefficient learner. In S. J. Ceci (Ed.), *Handbook of cognitive, social, and neuropsychological aspects of learning disabilities* (pp. 175–212). Hillsdale, NJ: Erlbaum Associates.

Pressley, M., Levin, J. R., & Delaney, H. D. (1982). The mnemonic keyword method. *Review of Educational Research, 52,* 61–92.

Takizawa, T. (1982). My research experience with Yōdai education. *Journal of the International Learning Science Association, 1,* 3–5.

Takizawa, T., Hatori, H., Kunihira, S., & Machida, K. (1980). *Effects of verbal mediation in arithmetic and mathematics education: (2) Development of computational skills with fractions.* Paper presented at the 22nd meeting of the Japanese Association of Educational Psychology, October 31, Tokyo.

Uchida, Y. (1949). *The dancing kettle, and other Japanese folk tales.* New York: Harcourt, Brace and World.

Wilson, B. A., & Moffat, N. (Eds.). (1984). *Clinical management of memory problems.* London: Croom Helm.

Yates, F. A. (1966). *The art of memory.* London: Routledge & Kegan Paul.

CHAPTER 20

The Role of Mnemonic Strategies in Study Effectiveness

William D. Rohwer, Jr., and John W. Thomas

To achieve academic success, students must be adept in a variety of kinds of remembering. They must remember in order to recite or to make presentations in class. They must remember in a different way in order to compose coherent and convincing papers. They must remember in yet another way in order to excel in taking tests. Furthermore, variety characterizes not only the purposes of remembering but also the content to be remembered. Students must remember information, in the form of facts, concepts, or principles. In addition, they must remember procedures of the kinds involved in constructing proofs or solving problems.

To simplify matters a bit, consider what adeptness entails for only one of these varieties, that of remembering information in the course of taking instructor-made tests. Even for this apparently single variety, the ingredients of adeptness are hardly simple in any absolute sense, for the circumstances surrounding test taking also exhibit impressive variation. Nevertheless, across such variations, adeptness involves a core: remembering, converting remembrances into performances, and, by no means least, preparing to remember. These components of adeptness, especially the last, preparation, fall squarely within any reasonable conception of the activities called studying.

Now add to this line of argument the results of an extensive body of research demonstrating (most clearly in the case of laboratory research) that mnemonic strategies can markedly increase the adeptness of student remembering. The result is an apparently undeniable truism: If academic success requires adept remembering, and if the components of adeptness constitute a substantial aspect of studying, and if mnemonic strategies foster adeptness, then such strategies should play a critical role in study effectiveness.

Even though the truth of this claim appears to be self-evident, a central purpose of this chapter is to subject it to critical examination. We begin with a description of the characteristics that distinguish the process of studying in academic contexts, characteristics that provide the foundation for three principles of learner adeptness at studying. We then describe two additional characteristics associated with the context of academic studying and a model of studying designed to capture these distinctive features. Context considerations yield an additional principle of study effectiveness, which is then used along with a framework for categorizing study outcomes to examine the role of mnemonic strategies in study effectiveness. As this analysis leaves a number of questions unanswered, a final section lists issues and questions for further research.

The Process of Academic Studying

Process characteristics of studying in academic contexts distinguish it from a number of other activities in these contexts. Three of these distinctive characteristics are effortfulness, isolation, and affective significance (cf. Brown, Bransford, Ferrara, & Campione, 1983).

Studying is effortful in two important ways. One is that it must be self-instigated and sustained in the absence of feedback and rewards. In addition, successful studying requires not only time on task, but also deliberate and elaborative cognitive effort in the form of learner-generated constructions, both covert and overt, e.g., notes, outlines, charts.

A second feature of studying is its isolated and individual character. Whereas academic cognition in the classroom takes place in a social setting, often being induced, guided, and directed by others, in study activities it typically takes place in isolation. Studying, therefore, requires students themselves to process information, and to provide their own instruction, including the steps of locating information, maintaining their own attention, making provision for practice, and gaining feedback (Anderson, 1980).

Third, studying is laden with affective significance. To be sure, studying in some respects resembles other forms of academic cognition, in that it involves "cold" content and competencies and an emphasis on efficiency, as Brown et al. (1983) correctly note. However, when examined in its natural state from the viewpoint of an individual student, studying is decidedly "hot" in emotional consequences. Effective studying demands a mixture of "skill and will" (Paris, Lipson, & Wixson, 1983). It requires the application of methods for mastering bodies of knowledge, but it also requires volition: the disposition to exert effort, to persist, to seek out and often transform information. Although incomplete and indirect, the available evidence suggests that the quantity and quality of student study activities depend as much on factors such as a sense of personal efficacy and expectations of success as on knowledge and skill in cognitive processing (Diener & Dweck, 1978, 1980; Kuhl, 1985; Pearl, Bryan, & Herzog, 1983; Schunk, 1984).

The preceding three characteristics have potentially critical implications for the possible role of mnemonic strategies in academic studying. Research on mnemonic strategies has shown that special provisions must be made if students are to continue to use and generalize such strategies beyond the specific context in which they were acquired (e.g., Armbruster, Echols, & Brown, 1982; Palincsar & Brown, 1984; Pressley, Borkowski, & O'Sullivan, 1985; Pressley, Borkowski, & Schneider, in press-a). These provisions, which include giving students direct experience of the effectiveness of a given strategy for a given performance criterion, instructing students when and why to use particular strategies, and promoting self-management behaviors and self-worth attributions during training can be seen as direct consequences of the peculiar demands of academic studying.

If these provisions are necessary when instructors carefully and intentionally induce students to adopt strategies, they must be at least equally important in naturalistic settings, where such care and intent is atypical. The issue is whether students encounter the necessary provisions in the course of their ordinary academic experience. Available evidence suggests that they may not. Glover, Plake, Roberts, Zimmer, and Palmere (1981), for example, found that fewer than half of a sample of college students complied with instructions to adopt a paraphrase strategy in order to remember the ideas in an essay. Moreover, using idea unit recall as an indicator, even fewer students exhibited this or any other effective strategy spontaneously.

The results of our own pilot surveys at the junior high school, senior high school, and college levels reveal somewhat compatible results. More than half of the average to high ability students we surveyed reported "often" or "always" knowing what steps to take to make something more memorable when studying for a test (as opposed to "never," "rarely," or "sometimes"). Moreover, across the grade levels surveyed, there is a decrease in reliance on unaided memory and an increase in use of notetaking when "something seems hard to remember." Despite this growing awareness of memory demands, the percentages of students who "often" or "always" use mnemonic devices ("a story, rhyme, or some other trick") are only 29.3, 29.7, and 11.0 for the three grade levels, respectively, and the percentages using representational techniques ("charts, graphs, or other pictures") are only 8.1, 9.0, and 9.2.

These frequencies of reported strategy use are strikingly low and are especially surprising for the sample of college students in that it was drawn from an elite university. Because research has shown such students to be eminently capable of deploying mnemonic strategies, the sources of their failure to do so must be found elsewhere. One possibility is that the particular course surveyed did not impose memory demands severe enough to require the use of high-effort mnemonic strategies. Another possibility is that the academic experiences of the majority of the students had provided them with insufficient training in or even exposure to such strategies (O'Sullivan & Pressley, 1984; Pressley & Ahmad, 1986).

Principles of Adept Studying

The effortful, isolated, and volitional nature of academic studying leads to considerable variation among students in the probability and quality of strategy use. The sources of such variation can be summarized in the form of three general principles governing strategy use: generativity, executive monitoring, and personal efficacy.

Generativity

For any given memory task, some mnemonic strategies are effective in that they enhance criterion performance relative to a specified baseline, whereas others are ineffective in that they either do not affect performance or may even degrade it. Within the class of strategies that are effective for a given task, according to the generativity principle, the more a mnemonic strategy involves the reformulation of given information or the generation of information beyond that which is explicitly given, the more it will enhance performance. Given the task of recognizing or producing the gist of a text, for example, summarization should be more effective than rote repetition.

Acts of generating or reformulating information during learning appear to have different purposes and different effects across tasks. For example, strategies for selection can be more or less generative in nature as can strategies for comprehension, memory, and integration. The use of these strategies can lead to such diverse capabilities as, respectively, identifying main ideas, describing the "deep structure" of a passage, retaining information over long periods of time, and generalizing learned information to solve problems. In our conception, then, the generativity principle encompasses certain other processing principles, such as levels of processing (Craik & Lockhart, 1972), distinctiveness of encoding (Craik & Tulving, 1975; Glover, Plake, & Zimmer, 1982), and transfer-appropriate processing (Morris, Bransford, & Franks, 1977).

Executive Monitoring

For present purposes, the second principle, that of executive monitoring, refers to three functions. The first function is appraising the need imposed by a given task for the deployment of mnemonic strategies (Flavell & Wellman, 1977). The second function is selecting the strategies to be deployed, given a determination of need (Pressley et al., 1985). When strategies are deployed, the third function is assessing periodically the quality of strategy execution for the purpose of regulating effectiveness (Brown, Campione, & Barclay, 1979; Brown, Campione, & Day, 1981). The principle of executive monitoring, then, is that productive strategy deployment depends on accurate need appraisal, wise strategy selection, and regulatory assessment of the quality of strategy execution.

Personal Efficacy

Research and theory suggest that students differ in the extent to which they believe they can control the outcomes of their own learning, that is, in their own sense of efficacy. At one end of this efficacy dimension are students convinced that they have little power to influence their academic achievement, for they believe their academic ability to be inadequate to meet the demands of their courses. At the other end of this continuum are students confident of their own ability who believe they can control their level of achievement by the effort they expend in meeting course demands (Covington, 1984; Schunk, 1984).

Although the requisite research linking personal efficacy to academic studying has not yet been conducted, by extrapolating from existing research on laboratory learning tasks five kinds of potential linkages can be described. First, persons having a low sense of personal efficacy may avoid studying in general and intellectually challenging tasks in particular (Bandura, 1982; Weiner, 1976). Second, personal efficacy could mediate the amount, intensity, and persistence of effort expenditure on learning tasks (Bandura, 1982; Butkowsky & Willows, 1980; Weiner, 1976). Third, personal efficacy may relate to the quality of learning strategies constructed or generated spontaneously in study situations (Kurtz & Borkowski, 1984), especially following a failure experience (Diener & Dweck, 1978, 1980). Fourth, learners with a strong sense of personal efficacy appear to produce more self-monitoring and self-instructional verbalization and fewer self-deprecating comments during learning tasks than do learners with a low sense of personal efficacy (Diener & Dweck, 1978; Kuhl, 1985; Pearl et al., 1983). Finally, efficacy may affect the extent to which the outcomes of studying are transferred to new situations (Krause & Borkowski, 1984).

Taken as a whole, the personal efficacy principle serves to mediate or set boundaries on the operation of other principles, a common feature of all the principles governing academic studying. These three principles, considered together, may be summarized in a set of assertions. With respect to a particular study task, given that the strategy employed is congruent with the criterion, the more generative the mnemonic strategies that govern such processing, the more effective the studying. In order for students to deploy appropriate mnemonic strategies, they must appraise strategy needs accurately, select strategies wisely, and regulate the quality of strategy execution. Finally, students must believe in the efficacy of investing effort in the selection, deployment, and regulation of criterion-congruent mnemonic strategies.

The Context of Academic Studying

Two additional characteristics of academic studying relate more directly to the context than to the act of studying. The first such characteristic is the dependency of studying on contextual factors. The second characteristic is ambiguity in the purposes of academic studying.

Research has documented the context dependency of study effectiveness. For example, with respect to the goal of successful remembering, notetaking has been found to be more effective, equivalently effective, and less effective than other methods, depending on such factors as the material to be studied, task conditions, and the nature of the criterion (Anderson & Armbruster, 1984; Kiewra, 1985). Furthermore, study effectiveness in academic settings may depend on additional contextual features that have not yet received research attention. The effectiveness of notetaking, for example, may depend on a host of factors in addition to those already mentioned. A few such factors are time of year, the perceived importance of a particular information source for obtaining a good grade in the course, and whether or not the instructor calls on students in class to discuss the assigned reading.

A final characteristic of studying is ambiguity of purpose. In many instances, to be sure, studying is characterized by clarity of purpose on the part of the studier. In these instances, while they are studying, the studiers know, at least approximately, and sometimes precisely, what they are enabling themselves to do. The majority of such instances, however, fall outside the academic arena. Within this arena, especially at the high-school and college levels, students rarely know with any precision what it is that they are preparing themselves to do. Often they may know that they are preparing themselves to answer an instructor's questions in class or on an examination, and they may even know whether their answers must take the form of an essay or a multiple-choice response. Only infrequently, however, do they know just what information they will need, how it must be organized, or the specific form in which it must be exhibited in order to satisfy the instructor's criteria. (Sometimes, not even the instructor knows in advance.) Moreover, this uncertainty increases as students move from elementary school through junior and senior high school and into college, for they must deal, progressively, with increasing numbers of instructors, correspondingly greater fluctuations in associated performance criteria, and decreasing numbers of opportunities to meet the criteria of any one instructor, as in the case of college courses for which the only criterion is performance on a single final examination.

If, in the academic arena, ambiguity of purpose is more often the rule than the exception, this arena contrasts sharply with the conditions that typify research on mnemonic strategies. Most laboratory research, and even most research in school-like but controlled settings (e.g., Palincsar & Brown, 1984), is characterized by clarity of purpose. Either students are fully informed about and have direct experience with performance criteria, or the criteria imposed are fully congruent with the strategies they are induced to adopt. As shown by a plethora of research on incidental learning and memory (McDaniel, Friedman, & Bourne, 1978; Postman, 1964), and on transfer-appropriate processing (Morris et al., 1977), induced processing enhances learning and performance only when that processing is tailored to the criterion task. Because such beneficial tailoring cannot be assumed to characterize the academic arena, great caution must be exercised in extrapolating propositions directly from the arena of laboratory-like research to academic contexts.

A Model of Academic Studying

The implications of these latter two characteristics, context dependency and ambiguity of purpose, can perhaps be understood better with reference to a general model of academic studying. This model, the Autonomous Learning Model, is being used to guide our current project, a developmental investigation of the antecedents and consequences of student study activities.

The Autonomous Learning Model includes components similar to those described in the tetrahedral model of Brown et al. (1983), and the heuristic model of Entwistle (1985): (a) outcomes, (b) study activities, (c) course characteristics, and (d) student characteristics. These components and their interrelationships are shown in Figure 20.1. (See Thomas & Rohwer, 1986, for a more detailed description of the model.)

Outcomes

Studying can result in specific outcomes so numerous that a classification scheme is needed to render them manageable. Three separate but relatable (if not already related) lines of research and theorizing suggest the dimensions of such a scheme. For heuristic purposes, then, we assume that study outcomes can be classified with reference to three intersecting dimensions.

In character, the first of these dimensions is categorical. This dimension, suggested by work on transfer-appropriate processing (McDaniel et al., 1978; Morris et al., 1977), consists of three categories of informational products. Such

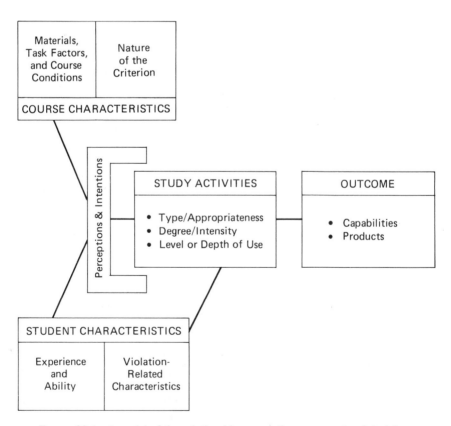

FIGURE 20.1. A model of the relationship among the components of studying.

products differ in terms of the forms of information that can be dealt with effectively, (a) verbatim, (b) interpreted, and (c) constructed.

The second of the dimensions also seems to be categorical in nature. Related to work such as that of Jacoby (1983) on processing-related differences between the performances of perceptually identifying and recognizing words, this second dimension consists of two categories of performance capabilities. These categories differ in terms of what students can do in dealing with each of the forms of informational products; that is, they can (a) recognize them, or (b) produce (or recall) them.

The third dimension, cue similarity, suggested by Tulving's Synergistic Ecphory Model (1982), is probably more continuous than categorical in character, for it represents the relationship between the information available in the performance (retrieval) environment and the information available in any of the preceding study (encoding or recoding) environments. Nevertheless, for expository purposes, it is convenient to identify four points on this dimension and treat them as if they were categories. In the category at one extreme, identity, performance and study information are virtually identical in that both cue and target information available during study are available again at test (although distractors may be present as well). This extreme is approximated in the case of a high school course we have examined in our current research. A few days before administering a multiple-choice examination, the instructor read to the students every item, including stems and alternatives, and also explicitly identified the correct alternatives. In the next category along the dimension, partial identity, either cue or target information available at study is available again at test. This category encompasses a variety of examination-item types, including simple recognition and short answer. The next category, related, includes cases in which the cue information available in the performance environment is compatible but not identical with the cue information available in the study environment. Thus, performance conditions in this category require varying degrees of transfer or generalization of informational products. Still further along the dimension, near the other extreme, lies the fourth category, minimal, in which little or none of the cue or target information available in the study environment is present in the performance environment. An examination item might approximate free recall by directing students, for example, simply to list and discuss the major themes in the course.

Study Activities

Study activities consist of the universe of processes and behaviors, both covert and overt, that come into play during a study episode. These activities can be divided into two general classes: (a) cognitive activities, those that serve to facilitate information processing and to improve criterion performance; and (b) self-management activities, those that serve to maintain and enhance the attention, effort, and time students devote to learning. Further, these classes can be divided into five cognitive functions – selection, comprehension, memorability, integration, and cognitive monitoring—and three self-management functions—effort management, time management, and volitional monitoring. Each of these functions, in principle, can be enhanced by the deployment of strategies. A pertinent example, given the topic of the present chapter, is the potentially facilitating effect of mnemonic strategies on the memory function.

The functions within these general classes define accomplishments that are differentially required depending on the demands posed by course characteristics. For example, particular courses may or may not require selection. Furthermore, any single activity or strategy may serve more than one function. Summarizing, for example, may foster comprehension, memory, and integration as well as selection (Brown & Palincsar, 1982).

Course Characteristics

Course characteristics consist of those in-class and out-of-class features of course that can influence studying. Among the in-class factors are, for example, lecture characteristics, grading practices, review and instructional support practices, and features of the criterion, including whether or not and how much students know about its nature. Examples of out-of-class factors include characteristics of the readings assigned and of all other extra class assignments, such as exercises, projects, and review activities. The effects of these different categories of course characteristics on the probability of students engaging in particular activities are, to a large extent, specific to the several different functions.

Course characteristics can affect the incidence of study activities in each of three general ways: (a) they can create *demands* for particular activities; (b) they can serve to foster and *support* particular activities; or (c) they can obviate the need or *compensate* for particular study activities. Other considerations add further complexity to this picture. Course characteristics can not only support particular study activities, they can also discourage them. Furthermore, course characteristics can affect study activities not only singly, but also in combination, with the effect of a particular factor differing depending on its interactions with other factors. In addition, the effects of a course characteristic on study activities may depend on student perceptions and interpretations of that characteristic.

The nature of performance criteria, mediated by student perceptions of them, are especially important course characteristics, for they can determine both the kinds of study activities students elect to engage in and the effectiveness of those activities in terms of subsequent performance tests (Anderson & Armbruster, 1984; Rohwer, 1984). Thus, these criterion characteristics can influence not only (a) what students learn in a course, and (b) what students achieve in a course, but also (c) what instructors conclude about what students have learned. Accordingly, performance criteria are given a distinct place in the Autonomous Learning Model (see Figure 20.1).

Student Characteristics

As indicated in Figure 20.1, study activities are also influenced by characteristics of students. Indeed, because of the number of sources of individual differences that can affect studying, the variance in study activities within particular courses may be almost as large as the variance between courses.

The importance of student characteristics stems from the wide range of decisions and capabilities required for effective studying. Students themselves must (a) appreciate the need for studying, (b) determine what they will be called on to do as a result of studying, (c) know what to study, (d) be able to select from their repertoire those activities that will be effective under the given conditions, (e) know when best to carry out the activities, and (f) have the skills to carry out their plan and know how to use them. Because studying is also replete with emotional and volitional demands, students must be (g) willing to study, (h) willing to continue with intensity, and (i) willing to persevere, in the face of difficulties, until they are adequately prepared.

Student characteristics that might influence the type, intensity, and quality of student study activities are of two general kinds, cognitive and volitional. Cognitive characteristics include developmental level (e.g., Rohwer, 1973, 1980), academic ability (e.g., Bransford, Stein, Shelton, & Owings, 1981), prior experience (e.g., Brown, Smiley, & Lawton, 1978), subject matter knowledge (e.g., Brooks & Dansereau, 1983), and metacognitive knowledge (e.g., Pressley et al., in press-a). The two principal volitional characteristics are those of study orientation (e.g., the combination of an intent to learn course content, a preference for autonomous learning, and a reported use of study strategies that represent a "deep approach" to learning, Entwistle & Ramsden, 1983), and perceived self-efficacy (e.g., Covington, 1984).

These, then, are the major components of the model that guides our current thinking and research on studying in academic contexts. Central to the model are the relationships that are depicted by the lines between the boxes in Figure 20.1 – relationships that arise from the context dependency and the ambiguity of purpose that characterize studying in academic settings. These relationships can be summarized in yet another principle of academic studying: specificity.

The Specificity Principle of Study Effectiveness

According to the specificity principle, the effectiveness of mnemonic strategies varies as a function of their congruence with course characteristics on the one hand and student characteristics on the other. The relevant course characteristics consist principally of the kinds of processing presupposed by performance criteria. For example, the induction of one kind of elaborative processing (by instructing students to invent new applications, examples, implications, and analogies for presented information) has been found to diminish performance on a test requiring the production of factual information (Barnett, DiVesta, & Rogozinski, 1981). Mnemonic strategy effectiveness can also vary with student characteristics. The keyword method, for example, has been shown to enhance the performance of average-ability but not of high-ability college students (McDaniel & Pressley, 1984).

The specificity principle appears to be at odds with the contention that the strategies of experts are comparatively context-free (Brown et al., 1983). This contention may indeed be valid, but only for the special case of experts. One of the distinguishing features of experts in a field is their consensus about the nature of criterion performances that signify proficiency on the part of their peers. In contrast to the high level of agreement among experts about performance criteria for themselves, their consensus dissolved when, in the role of instructor, they attempt to specify performance criteria for novices in their field.

To verify this claim, in our current project we have appraised the examinations designed by different instructors in charge of (a) two versions of the introductory psychology course at a single university, and (b) several versions of the junior high and senior high school American history courses within and across several public schools. Even when we restricted our comparisons to those within common grade levels and subject matters, the differences in performance criteria were striking. Thus, if experts, as instructors of novices, disagree about performance criteria, it is small wonder that student conceptions of the specific purposes of their learning are frequently ambiguous.

Mnemonic Strategies and Study Effectiveness

According to the specificity principle, both course and student characteristics determine whether mnemonic strategies will enhance study effectiveness. Of these two classes of determinants, the main emphasis in the present section is on course characteristics, and within this class the focus is primarily on the characteristic of performance criteria. The reason for this focus is that in academic settings performance criteria are the measure of study effectiveness.

To be examined here are two sets of propositions. One set concerns the degree of congruence between the study outcomes produced by mnemonic strategies and the performance criteria that must be met. Within this set, the first proposition is that performance criteria vary in their sensitivity to different study outcomes. The second is that mnemonic strategies vary in terms of the kinds of study outcomes they promote. The third proposition, therefore, is that the value of any given mnemonic strategy for remembering in an academic context depends on the degree of congruence between the study outcomes it promotes and the performance criterion to be attained.

Readily apparent is the kinship between the preceding congruence propositions and the principles that form the notion of transfer-appropriate processing. Indeed, the latter propositions are incorporated in the previously proposed conception of study outcomes, principally in the form of the dimension referred to as that of informational products (verbatim, interpreted, constructed). As Table 20.1 shows, when this dimension is crossed with those of performance capability (recognition, production) and cue similarity (identical, partial, related, minimal), 24 varieties of study outcomes can be distinguished. The present conception of outcome–criterion congruence, then, includes the principles of transfer-appropriate processing, but arguments these principles by the addition of the two remaining dimensions. The potential utility of this augmentation is illustrated in the next section.

TABLE 20.1. Matrix of study outcomes.

Informational product	Performance capability	Cue similarity			
		Identity	Partial	Related	Minimal
Verbatim	Recognition				
	Production				
Interpreted	Recognition				
	Production				
Constructed	Recognition				
	Production				

On the assumption that outcome–criterion congruence is critical, also critical is a second set of proposition concerning factors that determine what strategies students elect to deploy. According to these propositions, four such factors are (a) student expectations of the criteria to be met, (b) student knowledge of the memory demands imposed by different performance criteria and of the outcomes promoted by different strategies, (c) student monitoring of the degree of congruence between strategies and criteria, and (d) student willingness to deploy strategies appropriate to the criteria.

Strategy–Criterion Congruence

Variations in study outcomes are at the core of the set of propositions concerning the value of mnemonic strategies. Accordingly, in this section, the congruence propositions are evaluated with reference to mnemonic-strategy research that has included performance criteria related to multiple cells of the study–outcomes matrix displayed in Table 20.1. Although the set of mnemonic strategies considered is by no means exhaustive, each of the strategies selected has figured prominently in published research and discussion. The results of this research illustrate not only the application of the specificity principle but of the generativity principle as well.

Recognition and Production of Verbatim Information

Laboratory research has shown that mnemonic strategies have widely varied effects on the recognition and production of verbatim informational products. These variations, however, cannot be accounted for solely by the distinction between recognition and production. Needed in addition are distinction in the character of the strategies themselves and in conditions of cue similarity.

Dempster and Rohwer (1974), for example, compared the effects of three mnemonic strategies on the learning of noun paired associates by sixth-grade children. During the study phase of the task, students were asked to proceed by (a) repetitiously rehearsing each pair, (b) constructing an interactive mental image of the two referents in each pair, or (c) constructing an interactive description of the two referents in each pair. The strategies induced by the latter two conditions, referred to as *mnemonic elaboration*, are presumably more generative than that induced by the repetition condition. Note that even though the product to be dealt with in this case is verbatim information, the underlying processing can nevertheless vary in generativity.

Cue similarity was also manipulated by administering three different criterion tests. These tests and the categories of cue similarity they represent were free recall (minimal), cued recall (partial), and multiple choice (identical).

Across three experiments, the results were quite clearcut and, in conformance with the specificity principle, distinctly different for the various criterion tests. For free recall, the performance levels were generally quite low (no more than 16% correct), and those produced by the mnemonic elaboration strategies were no higher than that produced by the repetition strategy. In contrast, for multiple-choice and cued-recall tests, for which cue similarity was greater, the elaboration strategies produced markedly higher performance levels (as high as 75% correct) than the repetition strategy (as low as 9% correct). Similarly, McDaniel and Tillman (reported in Pressley, Levin, & McDaniel, in press-b) have found that the keyword strategy facilitates performance as indexed by a cued-recall but not by a free-recall test.

The preceding results illustrate an implication of the specificity principle for a mnemonic-strategy analysis of studying in academic contexts on the presumption that such contexts are characterized by ambiguity of purpose. Suppose students had executed a mnemonic elaboration or a keyword strategy in preparation for a test in a course. If the test they actually received was analogous to the experimental cued-recall test, their performance would have earned them considerably higher grades than if they had executed a repetition strategy. If the test were instead analogous to the free-recall test, however, they would have been as well off to have adopted the less generative repetition strategy.

Production of Interpreted and Constructed Information

Although generative processing enhances the capabilities of recognizing and producing verbatim information under favorable cue-similarity conditions, such information could, in principle, be dealt with effectively without achieving understanding. In contrast, comprehension is prerequisite to dealing effectively with interpreted information. Indeed, success in dealing with paraphrased forms of previously studied information is often taken as primary evidence of comprehension (Anderson, 1972). In the case of both intepreted and constructed information, the bulk of laboratory research has focused on the outcome capability of production, although cue-similarity conditions have varied substantially both within and across studies.

Glover et al. (1981), for example, investigated the production of idea units and logical extensions from an essay that college students studied in each of several different instructional conditions. These conditions included a baseline control ("read carefully"), instructions to list the significant terms in each paragraph, to write a paraphrase of each paragraph, and to write logical extensions of the information in each paragraph. On a free-recall test, one of the major dependent variables was the number of idea units (verbatim or paraphrased) produced from the original passage, whereas the other was the number of logical extensions produced.

Four aspects of the results are especially noteworthy. First, more than half of the students in the three treatment conditions did not comply with the instructions given, as judged by the contents of the notes they wrote. Apparently, generative processing of the kinds called for by these instructions is not readily forthcoming in college students of the kinds sampled in this experiment. Second, among students who complied with study instructions, those in the paraphrase and logical extension conditions produced more than twice as many idea units from the essay as did students in the significant terms and control conditions (which did not differ). Third, the number of idea units produced by students in the logical extension condition was not significantly greater than that of students in the paraphrase condition. Fourth, however, students given instructions to study by means of the logical extension activity produced appropriate logical intrusions more frequently than students in all other conditions, including that of paraphrase instructions. This result is especially impressive in that the use of the generative strategy that presumably underlies this logical extension activity did not impede the performance of students on the interpreted information criterion (i.e., idea unit recall). Thus, if a criterion test demanding constructed information had been administered, performance should have been enhanced in this condition.

Other investigators have obtained evidence that generative strategies can facilitate the production of interpreted and constructed information not only when cue-similarity conditions fall in the minimal category (as in free recall), but also when they fall in the related category and so reflect the generalization or transfer of these informational products. Loman and Mayer (1983), for example, examined the effects of a conceptual model-building reading strategy on varieties of memory for information from passages. This strategy was induced, presumably, by incorporating signals (preview sentences, underlined headings, and logical connective phrases) of top-level text structures directly within reading passages administered to tenth-grade, high school students. The performance of those who received the signaled version of the passage was compared with that of those who received a nonsignaled version on four criterion tests: multiple-choice fact retention (identity), forced-choice verbatim retention (identity), free recall (minimal), and problem solving (related).

Unfortunately, on the first two of these tests, the performance of students in both conditions was at ceiling and the results they yielded were therefore uninterpretable. Free-recall performance was indexed by three categories of the number of idea units recalled. These categories, conceptual idea units (i.e., cause and effect elements), facts and definitions, and primacy–recency (idea units from initial and concluding passage statements) appear to fit, respectively, the present definitions of constructed or interpreted information, interpreted or verbatim information, and verbatim information, although the published report is not entirely clear on these points. Production of both conceptual idea units and fact and definition units was higher in the signaled than in the nonsignaled condition, whereas primacy–recency performance was equivalent. Problem-solving performance was scored for solution quality. Students in the signaled condition produced more high-quality solutions than did students in the nonsignaled condition. As the problem-solving questions had not appeared in the passage, they qualified as related cues requiring generalization. Moreover, as solutions designated as high-quality were not contained in the passage, constructed informational products were presumably involved. Thus, it seems warranted to conclude that the strategy induced by signaling fosters the generalization of construction information.

The results of a subsequent study (Mayer, Dyck, & Cook, 1984, Exp. 2) corroborate this conclusion. Either signaled or nonsignaled versions of a reading passage were administered to college students who then received four criterion tests: forced-choice verbatim retention (identity), free recall (minimal), linking questions (partial), and problem-solving questions (related). Performance on the verbatim recognition test did not differ across conditions, but the numbers of correct choices on this task (one that required discrimination of surface features) appears to be at chance levels in both groups. As in the preceding study, students in the signaled condition produced more idea units than those in the nonsignaled condition for all categories but that of primacy–recency, indicating that the induced strategy facilitates memory for verbatim or interpreted information. Similarly, the signaled condition facilitated cued recall of the intepreted information required by the linking test (consisting of questions about the relationships among steps in the nitrogen cycle). Moreover, the signaling treatment enhanced the production of constructed information in response to the generalization cues represented by the problem-solving questions. Thus, the effects of the mnemonic strategy induced by signaling, like elaboration strategies, are specific to the particular study outcomes required by different performance criteria. The strategy evidently does not improve memory for verbatim information under minimal or identity cue conditions. It does, however, facilitate the production of interpreted information under minimal or partial identity conditions, and of constructed information given related cues that require generalization.

The latter claim, that mnemonic strategies can enhance generalization, is subject to dispute, as is evident in other chapters of the present volume. In clarifying the issues involved in this dispute, the terms of reference provided by the study outcomes matrix may be useful. If the appellation *mnemonic strategy* is reserved for mental procedures that affect the recognition or production of verbatim and constructed information given identical, partial, or minimal conditions of cue similarity, then the generalization claim is ruled out by definition. In contrast, if the appellation can, in principle, apply to cases of related cue conditions, especially when constructed informational products are to be dealt with, then the claim is subject to empirical verification. We prefer this more lenient definition, for it does not prejudge the question of whether or not strategies differ in how effectively they promote generalization. Moreover, the more lenient version is also consonant with the general notion that memory can be constructive as well as reproductive in character. In Vygotsky's (1978, p. 51) terms, "For the young child, to think means to recall; but for the adolescent, to recall means to think."

The results of the sample of research investigations reviewed in this section illustrate the utility of the three-dimensional study outcomes framework. The effectiveness of mnemonic strategies varies not only with the character of informational products, but also with the kinds of performance capabilities required coupled with the conditions of cue similarity that obtain. For example, the heightened effectiveness associated with more generative strategies is specific to the particular study outcomes presupposed by performance criteria.

Strategy Selection and Deployment

In all of the investigations cited in the preceding section, conditions were favorable for the selection and deployment of generative, criterion-congruent mnemonic strategies. The second major issue that arises, then, is whether students are likely to engage spontaneously in such selection and deployment in naturally occurring academic settings. The available evidence suggests that this likelihood varies with the strategies in question, and with course characteristics as well.

On the positive side, McDaniel and Kearney (1984) administered to college students three different memory tasks: vocabulary (unfamiliar words and their definitions), free recall of a categorized word list, and a list of paired concrete nouns. Both observed levels of memory performance and posttask self-reports indicated that these students spontaneously deployed mnemonic strategies and, to some extent, varied the strategies they used depending on the nature of the different tasks. In contrast, as previously mentioned, the Glover et al. (1981) investigation revealed a comparatively low normative level of generative study activities, even when carefully designed steps were taken to induce the use of such strategies.

Additional evidence pointing in this same direction comes from the voluminous literature of research on notetaking activities. In an investigation reported by Kiewra (1985), for example, students were left to engage in their own processing activities. College students either were or were not afforded opportunities to review instructors' lecture notes prior to a criterion test composed of items regarded as tapping factual or higher order information. Whereas the opportunity for note review significantly enhanced performance on the factual items, it had no discernible effect on the higher order items. Apparently, when left to their own devices, college students do not pervasively deploy mnemonic strategies that support the performance of producing constructed information.

Notetaking, even when analyzed into specific varieties as, for example, in the Glover et al. (1981) investigation, is a study activity rather than a mnemonic strategy per se. Some of the component strategies that can underlie notetaking activities have been subjected to examination by Brown and her colleagues in their research on summarization. Brown and Day (1983) have identified five such strategies: (a) deletion of trivial or redundant information, (b) substitution of superordinates for lists of informational instances, (c) selection of a topic sentence to stand as a paragraph summary, (d) invention of a topic sentence to serve this paragraph summary function, and (e) invention of a topic sentence to serve as a combined summary of two or more related paragraphs. Note that these strategies appear to form a continuum of increasing generativity. The incidence of use of these strategies was examined in the summaries of fifth-grade, seventh-grade, tenth-grade, junior-college, and four-year college students, as well as of experts (advanced graduate students in English).

The selection strategy was not used with great frequency (i.e., in more than 50% of the opportunities) except in the four-year college sample. Moreover, even these presumably seasoned studiers only infrequently employed the more generative strategies of inventing topic sentences and combining them across paragraphs (less than 50% of the opportunities). These more generative strategies, presumably needed for the capabilities of dealing with constructed information performance criteria, were used frequently only in the expert sample (advanced graduate students in English).

Thus, even though generative mnemonic strategies are well within the abilities of students, the frequency with which they actually deploy them evidently varies substantially from situation to situation. Moreover, the picture is further complicated by the fact that students' criterion expectations and their experience with particular performance criteria can also influence strategy selection and deployment.

The effect of knowledge of the criterion on study behavior and performance has been summarized in recent reviews (Anderson & Armbruster, 1984; Rohwer, 1984). To paraphrase the conclusions of these reviewers, the effectiveness of studying generally improves with the specificity of criterion knowledge on the part of students. This generalization holds, however, only with the provisos that (a) this foreknowledge includes awareness of the particular informational product required by the criterion task as well as the performance capability involved, and (b) this knowledge elicits the selection and use of study strategies that are congruent with the performance criterion.

Limited evidence in support of the preceding conclusions can be gained by examining selected conditions within more complex investigations where expectations and processing strategies are congruent with the informational product required by the criterion measure (Kulhavy, Dyer, & Silver, 1975), by ignoring overall performance levels and looking instead at what students have stored as a result of their expectations (Bretzing & Kulhavy, 1981; Rickards & Friedman, 1978), and by examining performance differences between students in terms of both their reported criterion expectations and study strategies (Van Rossum & Schenk, 1984). Unfortunately, however, much of the evidence relevant to these conclusions is indirect in that it must be extrapolated from studies that have been designed to answer different questions and are, therefore, incomplete with respect to one key factor or another. When students have been given capability information but not product information about the criterion, for example, such foreknowledge does not typically facilitate performance (Carrier & Titus, 1981; Hakstian, 1971).

On a more promising note, d'Ydewalle, Swerts, and DeCorte (1983) have introduced a procedure that may allow for separating the effects of capability (format) and product (substance) expectations. Students were instructed to study a history text given the expectation of either a multiple-choice or an open-question test. After a study–test trial, they were asked to estimate how much time they would need to study for a second test of the same type. This test experience presumably afforded the students information not only about the capability demanded but also about the character of the product information with which they would have to deal. As in the first trial, they were than allowed as much study time as they wanted. Students expecting open questions did significantly better on both types of tests. More important for the present analysis, however, are two other facets of the results. During the first study opportunity, when students knew the format but not the nature of the product required by the criterion test, the amount of time allocated to studying was equivalent across the two conditions. In contrast, after experience of the first test trial, students expecting open questions planned and used more study time than students expecting multiple-choice questions.

An additional finding from this study has bearing on the role of expectations in naturalistic settings. The correlation between performance on the first test and subsequent time investment in studying was $-.40$ for students who received and expected a second open-question test. However, that correlation was near zero for students who received and expected a multiple-choice test. Thus, the effect of criterion knowledge appears not only to depend on the nature of the expected criterion task but also to be mediated by student beliefs that altering their study behavior will result in a performance benefit.

Unresolved Issues

The preceding inference raises one of a number of issues that research has yet to resolve. This issue, that posed by the potential effects of intervening beliefs, presents an almost intimidating research challenge. Nevertheless, it may be one of the most important because of the ambiguity of purpose and the latitude for student selection of study strategies and apportionment of study time that characterize academic studying. In academic performance situations, criterion knowledge is apt to be only partial, and the effectiveness of strategy deployment will depend not only on the fit between expectations and actual performance requirements, but also on student beliefs about (a) the benefits that will accrue from strategy deployment given the expected criterion; (b) their chances of success or failure on the particular criterion measure in comparison to their classmates; (c) whether they have deployed a strategy sufficiently to attain an adequate state of preparation; and (d) the relative importance, in subjective terms, of a particular test event. Although some components of the theory and research necessary to link these kinds of beliefs and perceptions to the quality of students' study strategies have begun to be conceptualized (Borkowski, Carr, & Pressley, 1986;

Pressley, Borkowski, & O'Sullivan, 1984), the task of interrelating beliefs with strategic behavior under different task, outcome, and expectation conditions remains to be undertaken. In short, the principle of personal efficacy has yet to be integrated into and systematically verified with reference to the role of mnemonic strategies in studying as a function of context and purpose.

Similarly, verification of the specificity and generativity principles awaits further research on at least two fronts. First, the relationship between the generativity of mnemonic strategies and their effectiveness needs to be assessed systematically for each of the varieties of study outcome displayed in Table 20.1. Only selected strategies in combination with selected outcomes have been investigated previously, and the comparisons that have been made were fortuitous rather than being guided by the matrix framework. Furthermore, the assessments needed should include, in addition to an exact specification of the product, capability, and cue-similarity outcomes, provisions for manipulating student criterion expectations and for indexing degree and quality of strategy use. On a related front, further analysis is needed of variations within criterion tasks with reference to the study outcomes they presuppose; that is, such analyses must be made at the item level of teacher-made tests. They must, moreover, take account of the dimension of cue similarity, that is, the degree of congruence between the presentation of information during instruction and the availability of this information in actual test items. Progress on both of these fronts, then, would test the specificity principle as well as that of generativity.

A final set of issues that command attention concerns the principle of executive monitoring. This principle has received substantial support from investigations concerned with inducing strategy maintenance and generalization in comparatively controlled settings (e.g., Brown & Palincsar, 1982; Pressley et al., 1984, in press-a). While such investigations proceed, allied research should be conducted in more naturally occurring academic settings. Three kinds of such research are needed.

One kind would be designed to identify the conditions under which the spontaneous deployment of generative mnemonic strategies was infrequent, and to identify the sources of these phenomena. Do these sources include failures of executive monitoring, a paucity of opportunities to experience the utility of generative strategies, or incongruence between them and the performance criteria sometimes encountered in academic settings?

A second kind of research would be designed to identify the sources of individual differences among students in the probability and quality of strategy deployment. Do such differences arise from corresponding differences in strategy knowledge, in monitoring skill, or in willingness to invest the effort required?

A third kind of research would be designed to identify those naturally occurring conditions that promote and impede the acquisition and modification of strategies. Such research may well begin with systematic comparisons of the conditions that characterize naturalistic settings with those laboratory conditions that have been shown to promote strategy acquisition and generalization.

The unresolved items highlighted here have a common theme, the same theme that has threaded its way through this entire chapter: studying in academic settings has a number of distinctive features that deserve acknowledgment and analysis. Such analysis is needed in order that the results of research on mnemonic strategies can be assessed as a function of differences in student characteristics—beliefs, knowledge, skill, motivation, and experience. These assessments, we contend, are prerequisite for enhancing the role of mnemonic strategies in study effectiveness.

Acknowledgments. Preparation of this paper was supported by a grant from the National Institute of Child Health and Human Development (HD17984-02).

References

Anderson, R. C. (1972). How to construct achievement tests to assess comprehension. *Review of Educational Research, 42*, 145–170.

Anderson, T. H. (1980). Study strategies and adjunct aids. In R. J. Spiro, B. C. Bruce, & W. F. Brewer (Eds.), *Theoretical issues in reading comprehension* (pp. 483–502). Hillsdale, NJ: Erlbaum Associates.

Anderson, T. H., & Armbruster, B. B. (1984). Studying. In P. D. Pearson (Ed.), *Handbook of reading research* (pp. 657–680). New York: Longman.

Armbruster, B. B., Echols, C. H., & Brown, A. L. (1982). The role of metacognition in reading to learn: A developmental perspective. *Volta Review, 84*(5), 45–56.

Bandura, A. (1982). Self-efficacy mechanism in human agency. *American Psychologist, 37*, 122–147.

Barnett, J. E., DiVesta, F. J., & Rogozinski, J. T. (1981). What is learned in note taking? *Journal of Educational Psychology, 73*, 181–192.

Borkowski, J. G., Carr, M., & Pressley, M. (1986). *"Spontaneous" strategy use: Perspectives for metacognitive theory.* Unpublished manuscript. University of Notre Dame, Notre Dame, IN.

Bransford, J. D., Stein, B. S., Shelton, T. S., & Owings, R. A. (1981). Cognition and adaptation: The importance of learning to learn. In J. H. Harvey (Ed.), *Cognition, social behavior and the environment* (pp. 93–110). Hillsdale, NJ: Erlbaum Associates.

Bretzing, B. H., & Kulhavy, R. W. (1981). Notetaking and passage style. *Journal of Educational Psychology, 73*, 242–250.

Brooks, L. W., & Dansereau, D. F. (1983). Effects of structural schema training and text organization on expository prose processing. *Journal of Educational Psychology, 75*, 811–820.

Brown, A. L., & Day, J. D. (1983). Macrorules for summarizing texts: The development of expertise. *Journal of Verbal Learning and Verbal Behavior, 22*, 1–14.

Brown, A. L., & Palincsar, A. S. (1982). Inducing strategic learning from texts by means of informed, self-control training. *Topics in Learning and Learning Disabilities, 2*, 1–17.

Brown, A. L., Bransford, J. D., Ferrara, R. A., & Campione, J. C. (1983). Learning, remembering, and understanding. In J. H. Flavell & E. H. Markman (Eds.), *Handbook of child psychology: Cognitive development* (Vol. 3, pp. 77–176). New York: Wiley.

Brown, A. L., Campione, J., & Barclay, C. R. (1979). Training self checking routines for estimating test readiness: Generalization from list learning to prose recall. *Child Development, 50*, 501–512.

Brown, A. L., Campione, J., & Day, J. D. (1981). Learning to learn: On training students to learn from texts. *Educational Researcher, 10*(2), 14–21.

Brown, A. L., Smiley, S. S., & Lawton, S. W. C. (1978). The effects of experience on the selection of suitable retrieval cues for studying texts. *Child Development, 49*, 829–835.

Butkowsky, I. S., & Willows, D. M. (1980). Cognitive-motivational characteristics of children varying in reading ability: Evidence for learned helplessness in poor readers. *Journal of Educational Psychology, 72*, 408–422.

Carrier, C. A., & Titus, A. (1981). Effects of notetaking pretraining and test mode expectations on learning from lectures. *American Educational Research Journal, 18*, 385–397.

Covington, M. V. (1984). The motive for self worth. In R. E. Ames & C. Ames (Eds.), *Motivation in education* (pp. 78–113). New York: Academic Press.

Craik, F. I. M., & Lockhart, R. S. (1972). Levels of processing: A framework for memory research. *Journal of Verbal Learning and Verbal Behavior, 11*, 671–684.

Craik, F. I. M., & Tulving, E. (1975). Depth of processing and the retention of words in episodic memory. *Journal of Experimental Psychology: General, 104*, 268–294.

Dempster, F. N., & Rohwer, W. D., Jr. (1974). Component analysis of the elaborative encoding effect in paired-associate learning. *Journal of Experimental Psychology, 103*, 400–408.

Diener, C. I., & Dweck, C. S. (1978). An analysis of learned helplessness: Continuous changes in performance strategy and achievement cognitions following failure. *Journal of Personality and Social Psychology, 36*, 451–462.

Diener, C. I., & Dweck, C. S. (1980). An analysis of learned helplessness: II. The processing of success. *Journal of Personality and Social Psychology, 39*, 940–952.

d'Ydewalle, G., Swerts, A., & De Corte, E. (1983). Study time and test performance as a function of test expectations. *Contemporary Educational Psychology, 8*, 55–67.

Entwistle, N. J. (1985). *A model of the teaching-learning process derived from research on student learning.* Paper presented at the International Conference on Cognitive Processes in Student Learning, July, University of Lancaster, Lancaster, England.

Entwistle, N. J., & Ramsden, P. (1983). *Understanding student learning.* New York: Nichols Publishing Co.

Flavell, J. H., & Wellman, H. M. (1977). Metamemory. In R. Kail, Jr. & J. Hagen (Eds.), *Perspectives on the development of memory and cognition* (pp. 3–33). Hillsdale, NJ: Erlbaum Associates.

Glover, J. A., Plake, B. S., Roberts, B., Zimmer, J. W., & Palmere, M. (1981). Distinctiveness of encoding: The effects of paraphrasing and drawing inferences on memory from prose. *Journal of Educational Psychology, 73*, 736–744.

Glover, J. A., Plake, B. S., & Zimmer, J. W. (1982). Distinctiveness of encoding and memory for learning tasks. *Journal of Educational Psychology, 74*, 189–198.

Hakstian, A. R. (1971). The effects of type of examination anticipated on test preparation and performance. *Journal of Educational Research, 64*, 319–324.

Jacoby, L. L. (1983). Remembering the data: Analyzing interactive processes in reading. *Journal of Verbal Learning & Verbal Behavior , 22*, 485–508.

Kiewra, K. A. (1985). Investigating notetaking and review: A depth of processing alternative. *Educational Psychologist, 20*, 23–32.

Krause, A. J., & Borkowski, J. G. (1984). *Attributions, intrinsic motivation, and metamemory: Determinants of strategic behavior.* Unpublished manuscript, University of Notre Dame, Notre Dame, IN.

Kuhl, J. (1985). Volitional mediators of cognition-behavior consistency: Self-regulatory processes and action versus state orientation. In J. Kuhl & J. Beckman (Eds.), *Action control.* New York: Springer-Verlag.

Kulhavy, R. W., Dyer, J. W., & Silver, L. (1975). The effects of notetaking and test expectancy on the learning of text material. *Journal of Educational Research, 68,* 363-365.

Kurtz, B. E., & Borkowski, J. G. (1984). Children's metacognition: Exploring relations among knowledge process and motivational variables. *Journal of Experimental Child Psychology, 37,* 335-354.

Loman, N. L., & Mayer, R. E. (1983). Signaling techniques that increase the understandability of expository prose. *Journal of Educational Psychology, 75,* 402-412.

Mayer, R. E., Dyck, J. L., & Cook, L. K. (1984). Techniques that help readers build mental models from scientific text: Definitions pretraining and signaling. *Journal of Educational Psychology, 76,* 1089-1105.

McDaniel, M. A., & Kearny, E. M. (1984). Optimal learning strategies and their spontaneous use: The importance of task-appropriate processing. *Memory and Cognition, 12,* 361-373.

McDaniel, M. A., Friedman, A., Bourne, L. E., Jr. (1978). Remembering the levels of information in words. *Memory and Cognition, 6,* 156-164.

McDaniel, M. A., & Pressley, M. (1984). Putting the keyword method in context. *Journal of Educational Psychology, 76,* 598-609.

Morris, C. D., Bransford, J. D., & Franks, J. J. (1977). Levels of processing versus transfer appropriate processing. *Journal of Verbal Learning and Verbal Behavior, 16,* 519-533.

O'Sullivan, J. T., & Pressley, M. (1984). Completeness of instruction and strategy transfer. *Journal of Experimental Child Psychology, 38,* 275-288.

Palincsar, A. S., & Brown, A. L. (1984). Reciprocal teaching of comprehension fostering and monitoring activities. *Cognition and Instruction, 1,* 117-175.

Paris, S. G., Lipson, M. Y., & Wixson, K. K. (1983). Becoming a strategic reader. *Contemporary Educational Psychology, 8,* 293-316.

Pearl, R., Bryan, T., & Herzog, A. (1983). Learning disabled and nondisabled children's strategy analyses under high and low success conditions. *Learning Disability Quarterly, 6,* 67-74.

Postman, L. (1964). Short-term memory and incidental learning. In A. W. Melton (Ed.), *Categories of human learning.* New York: Academic Press.

Pressley, M., & Ahmad, M. (1986). Transfer of imagery-based mnemonics by adult learners. *Contemporary Educational Psychology, 11,* 50-60.

Pressley, M., Borkowski, J. G., & O'Sullivan, J. T. (1984). Memory strategy instruction is made of this: Metamemory and durable strategy use. *Educational Psychologist, 19,* 94-107.

Pressley, M., Borkowski, J. G., & O'Sullivan, J. T. (1985). Children's metamemory and the teaching of memory strategies. In D. L. Forrest-Pressley, G. E. MacKinnon, & T. G. Waller (Eds.), *Metacognition, cognition & human performance: Vol. 1. Theoretical perspectives* (pp. 111-153). New York: Academic Press.

Pressley, M., Borkowski, J. G., & Schneider, W. (in press-a). Good strategy users coordinate metacognition, strategy use and knowledge. In R. Vasta & G. Whitehurst (Eds.), *Annals of child development* (Vol. 4). Greenwich, CT: JAI Press.

Pressley, M., Levin, J. R., & Delaney, H. D. (1982). The mnemonic keyword method. *Review of Educational Research, 52*, 61–91.

Pressley, M., Levin, J., & McDaniel, M. (in press-b). Remembering versus inferring what a word means: Mnemonic and contextual approaches. In M. G. McKeown & M. E. Curtis (Eds.), *The nature of vocabulary acquisition*. Hillsdale, NJ: Erlbaum Associates.

Rickards, J. P., & Friedman, F. (1978). The encoding versus the external storage hypothesis in note-taking. *Journal of Educational Psychology, 3*, 136–143.

Rohwer, W. D., Jr. (1973). Elaboration and learning in childhood and adolescence. In H. W. Reese (Ed.), *Advances in child development and behavior* (Vol. 8). New York: Academic Press.

Rohwer, W. D., Jr. (1980). An elaborative conception of learner differences. In R. E. Snow, P-A. Federico, & W. E. Montague (Eds.), *Aptitude, Learning and Instruction* (Vol. 2, pp. 23–46). Hillsdale, NJ: Erlbaum Associates.

Rohwer, W. D., Jr. (1984). An invitation to a developmental psychology of studying. In F. J. Morrison, C. A. Lord, & D. P. Keating (Eds.), *Advances in applied developmental psychology* (Vol. 1, pp. 75–114). New York: Academic Press.

Schunk, D. H. (1984). Self-efficacy perspective on achievement behavior. *Educational Psychologist, 19*, 48–58.

Thomas, J. W., & Rohwer, W. D., Jr. (1986). Academic studying: The role of learning strategies. *Educational Psychologist, 21*, 19–41.

Tulving, E. (1982). Synergistic ecphory in recall and recognition. *Canadian Journal of Psychology, 36*, 130–147.

Van Rossum, E. J., & Schenk, S. M. (1984). The relationship between learning conception, study strategy and learning outcome. *British Journal of Educational Psychology, 54*, 73–83.

Vygotsky, L. S. (1978). *Mind in society*. Cambridge, MA: Harvard University Press.

Weiner, B. (1976). An attributional approach for educational psychology. In L. S. Shulman (Ed.), *Review of educational research 4*. Itasca, IL: F. E. Peacock.

Author Index

Subject Index